Twentieth-Century Dictionary of Christian Biography

Twentieth-Century
Dictionary
of Christian
Biography

edited by **J. D. Douglas**

PATERNOSTER
PRESS
CARLISLE, UNITED KINGDOM

BakerBooks
A Division of Baker Book House Co
Grand Rapids, Michigan 49516

Published by Baker Books
a division of Baker Book House Company
P.O. Box 6287, Grand Rapids, MI 49516-6287

and

Paternoster Press
P.O. Box 300
Kingston Broadway
Carlisle, Cumbria CA3 0Q5
England

Printed in the United States of America

Library of Congress Cataloging-in-Publication Data

Twentieth-century dictionary of Christian biography / edited by J. D. Douglas
    p. cm.
    Includes bibliographical references (p.).
    ISBN 0-8010-3031-5 (cloth)
    I. Douglas, J. D. (James Dixon) II. Title: 20th-century dictionary of Christian biography.
BR1700.2.T9   1995
270.8'2'0922—dc20
    [B]   95-91

Contributors

Akers, John N., special assistant, Billy Graham Evangelistic Association, Montreat, North Carolina

Allen, Frank, pastor, Missions/Outreach, Highland Park Baptist Church, Southfield, Michigan

Anderson, Donald G., rector of Sylvania, New South Wales, Australia

Babbage, S. Barton, former dean of Melbourne and master of New College, Sydney, Australia

Barclay, Oliver R., editor, *Science and Christian Belief,* Leicester, England

Barnaba, Atef, researcher and writer, Cairo, Egypt

Beougher, Timothy K., assistant professor of evangelism, Wheaton Graduate School, Wheaton, Illinois

Blycker, Philip, music missionary, CAM International

Bray, Gerald, professor of theology, Beeson Divinity School, Samford University, Alabama

Breward, Ian, professor of ecclesiastical history, Ormond College, Melbourne, Australia

Buckwalter, H. Douglas, assistant professor of New Testament, Evangelical School of Theology, Myerstown, Pennsylvania

Burch, Maxie, minister to college students, Calvary Baptist Church, Waco, Texas

Calvert, Nancy, assistant professor of New Testament studies, Wheaton College, Wheaton, Illinois

Camera, David P., candidate, Wheaton College, Wheaton, Illinois

Canclini, Arnoldo, Baptist pastor in Argentina

Carroll, Daniel R., professor of Old Testament, Central American Theological Seminary, Guatemala City

Clouse, Robert G., professor of history, Indiana State University, Terre Haute, Indiana

Comfort, Philip W., visiting associate professor of New Testament, Wheaton College, Wheaton, Illinois

Cornett, Norman F., Faculty of Religious Studies, McGill University, Montreal, Quebec, Canada

Dawes, Peter S., bishop of Derby, England

5

Deyo, Arthur W., international liaison director, Youth for Christ, Denver, Colorado

Dorsett, Lyle W., professor of evangelism and urban studies, Wheaton College, Wheaton, Illinois

Douglas, J. D., lecturer in Singapore Bible College

Elwell, Walter A., professor of Bible and theology, Wheaton College, Wheaton, Illinois

Ericksen, Paul A., associate director of Billy Graham Center archives, Wheaton, Illinois

Ericson, Norman R., professor of New Testament studies, Wheaton College, Illinois

Estep, W. R., former distinguished professor of church history, Southwest Baptist Theological Seminary, Fort Worth, Texas

Fawcett, John, head of public services, Buswell Memorial Library, Wheaton College, Wheaton, Illinois

Fergie, R. D., principal, Christian Leaders Training College, Port Moresby, Papua New Guinea

Fernando, Ajith, national director, Youth for Christ, Colombo, Sri Lanka

Freundt, Albert H., professor of church history, Reformed Theological Seminary, Jackson, Mississippi

Furcha, Edward J., professor of church history, McGill University, Montreal, Quebec, Canada

Garrett, J. Leo, Jr., professor of theology, Southwest Baptist Theological Seminary, Fort Worth, Texas

Grant, Myrna R., associate professor, graduate communications, Wheaton College, Wheaton, Illinois

Gration, John A., professor of missions, Wheaton College, Wheaton, Illinois

Griffin, Bruce, Ph.D. student, Oxford University, Oxford, England

Griffith, Richard, lecturer in Singapore Bible College

Grimley, L. K., professor of education and school psychology, Indiana State University, Terre Haute, Indiana

Hammond, C. K., former rector, Anglican Church in Australia

Hamstra, Sam, Jr., chaplain, Trinity Christian College, Palos Heights, Illinois

Harakas, Stanley S., professor of Orthodox theology, Holy Cross Greek Orthodox School of Theology, Brookline, Massachusetts

Hay, Ian M., general director emeritus, Society for International Ministries

Henry, Carl F. H., founding editor, *Christianity Today*

Henry, Helga Bender, writer and editor, Watertown, Wisconsin

Hillyer, Philip, freelance theological editor and author, Edinburgh, Scotland

Horrell, J. Scott, professor of systematic theology, Faculdade Teologica Batista de São Paulo, São Paulo, Brazil

Hufstetler, Charles A., former missionary consultant for church planting, SEND International

Hull, Gretchen Gaebelein, writer, New York City

Hywel-Davies, Jack, broadcaster and writer, Surrey, England.

James, B. Violet, lecturer in Singapore Bible College

James, Frank A., III, associate professor, Reformed Theological Seminary, Maitland, Florida

Jeeves, Malcolm A., former professor of psychology, St. Andrews University, Scotland

Jennings, J. Nelson, researcher, Tokyo, Japan

Jensen, Peter F., principal, Moore College, Sydney, Australia

Judd, Bernard G., former rector, Anglican Church in Australia

Kemp, Roger, lecturer in church history and missiology, Morling College, Australia

Keylock, Leslie R., professor of Bible and theology, Moody Bible Institute, Chicago, Illinois

Kombo, James, teaching fellow, Nairobi International School of Theology, Nairobi, Kenya

Kregness, Curtis Alan, missionary, CB International, São Paulo, Brazil

Krischner, Estevan F., professor of New Testament, Centro de Ensino Theologico (CETEOL), Santa Catarina, Brazil

Kuhn, Eileen J., former missionary in Thailand and head of English department, Singapore Bible College

Kyomya, Michael, academic dean, Nairobi International School of Theology, Nairobi, Kenya

Larson, Wendy S., research assistant, Wheaton Graduate School, Wheaton, Illinois

Lee, Christopher, dean of Chinese department, Singapore Bible College

Lewis, Jonathan, associate director of Latin America, World Evangelical Fellowship

Lima, Daniel Fernandes, pastor, Morumbi Baptist Church, São Paulo, Brazil

Linder, Robert D., professor of history, Kansas State University, Manhattan, Kansas

Ling, Samuel, senior pastor, Chinese Christian Union Church, Chicago, Illinois

Loane, (Sir) Marcus L., former archbishop of Sydney, Australia

Lowe, Charles, lecturer in Singapore Bible College

Magnusson, Sally, writer and broadcaster, London

Marsh, John, surgeon; former editor, Christian Graduate, London

Maust, John, editor, *Latin America Evangelist,* Miami, Florida

McGraw, Gerald F., director, School of Bible and Theology, Toccoa Falls College, Toccoa Falls, Georgia

Mendez, Guillermo, professor of theology, Central American Theological Seminary, Guatemala City

Mitchell, Jack, teaching elder, Sunset Presbyterian Church, Portland, Oregon

Moffett, Samuel H., professor of ecumenics and mission emeritus, Princeton Theological Seminary

Molyneux, Gordon, missionary-educator, Eastbourne, England

Moreau, A. Scott, assistant professor, missions/intercultural studies, Wheaton College Graduate School, Illinois

Morrison, Robert L., writer and researcher, Arlington, Massachusetts

Muether, John R., librarian and associate professor of theology and Bible, Reformed Theological Seminary, Jackson, Mississippi

Murray, Joycelyn, writer and lecturer, London, England

Musyoka, Benjamin, E.D.D. student, Biola University, La Mirada, California

Nunez, Emilio, professor of theology, Central American Theological Seminary, Guatemala City

Olson, W. H., managing director, Pilgrim International, Australia

Phemister, William, professor of music, Wheaton College, Wheaton, Illinois

Phillips, Timothy R., assistant professor of theological studies, Wheaton College, Wheaton, Illinois

Pierard, Richard V., professor of history, Indiana State University, Terre Haute, Indiana

Pollard, Noel S., former vice-principal, Ridley Hall, Cambridge, England

Rankin, W. Duncan, assistant professor, Reformed Theological Seminary, Jackson, Mississippi

Reid, Thomas G., Jr., minister, Reformed Prebytery Church, Edmonton, Alberta, Canada

Roberg, O. Theodore, North Park Theological Seminary, Chicago, Illinois

Robinson, Donald W. B., former archbishop of Sydney, Australia

Rogers, E. R., former principal of the Baptist College, Sydney, Australia

Saint Berberian, Martha, cofounder and director, Frederick Crowe Institute

Schuster, Robert, director of archives, Billy Graham Center, Wheaton, Illinois

Scorgie, Glen G., academic dean, North American Baptist College, Edmonton, Alberta, Canada

Scott, Florence, writer and homemaker, Wheaton, Illinois

Seaman, Alan, visiting assistant professor of missions/intercultural studies, Wheaton Graduate School, Wheaton, Illinois

Sefton, Henry R., former master of Christ's College, Aberdeen, Scotland

Seruyange, Lazarus, principal, Nairobi International School of Theology, Nairobi, Kenya

Shaw, Mark R., lecturer in church history and theology, Scottish Theological College, Machakos, Kenya

Shen, Michael, principal, Singapore Bible College

Smith, Clyde Curry, professor of ancient history and religion, University of Wisconsin, River Falls, Wisconsin

Soderberg, Julie, World Relief, Wheaton, Illinois

Sookhdeo, Patrick, director, International Institute for the Study of Islam and Christianity

Stackhouse, John G., religion department, University of Manitoba, Winnipeg, Manitoba, Canada

Stamoolis, James J., graduate dean, Wheaton College Graduate School, Wheaton, Illinois

Steigenga, John P., pastor, La Grave Avenue Christian Reformed Church, Grand Rapids, Michigan

Sturz, Richard J., professor of systematic theology, Faculdade Teological Batista de São Paulo, São Paulo, Brazil

Suazo, David J., professor of church history and theology, Central American Theological Seminary, Guatemala City, Guatemala

Suggs, Robert C., academic dean, Cornerstone College and Seminary, Grand Rapids, Michigan

Sunderaraj, Francis, general secretary, Evangelical Fellowship of India, Hyderabad, India

Sywulka, Stephen R., director, radio station TGNA, Guatemala City, Guatemala

Taylor, James, minister, Stirling Baptist Church, Scotland

Taylor, John B., bishop of St. Albans, England

Taylor, William D., director of missions commission, World Evangelical Fellowship

Tulluan, Ola, dean of English department, Singapore Bible College

Velásquez, Javier, missionary, South America Mission

Veronis, Luke, Orthodox missionary in Albania under the Albanian Orthodox Church

Waterman, Carla C., assistant professor of educational ministries, Wheaton College Graduate School, Wheaton, Illinois

Whitlock, Luder G., Jr., president, Reformed Theological Seminary, Jackson, Mississippi

Wiarda, Timothy, former missionary in North Africa, and lecturer in Singapore Bible College

Williams, David J., vice-principal, Ridley College, Melbourne, Australia

Wilson, Fred P., associate professor of educational ministries, Wheaton College, Wheaton, Illinois

Wilson, John W., bishop in the diocese of Melbourne, Australia

Wirt, Sherwood E., founding editor, *Decision* magazine

Wong, Chan Kok, lecturer in Singapore Bible College

Wright, David F., senior lecturer in church history, Edinburgh University, Scotland

Preface

Ralph Waldo Emerson once declared, "There is properly no history; only biography." For those of us charged with teaching church history in the non-Western world, here is the antidote for glazed eyes and flagging feet. Hit students with people (do they not matter more than things?) and they can be lured into discussion. Tell them that Origen was never canonized, was a universalist who had some profound comments on prayer and textual criticism, was fired by a jealous bishop, and took Scripture literally to the point of self-mutilation. Add that he would have rushed out to be martyred with his father had not his mother hidden his clothes—and ask innocently why clothes should be considered an essential qualification for martyrdom. In the process a chunk of church history, and even a little theology, are taken painlessly into the system. One can imagine that Emerson (himself uncanonized and with a low view of consistency) would have approved.

The present volume was conceived because of the difficulty of gathering information about twentieth-century Christians. Most of them are not listed in reference books that profess to tell who's who; when they are so highlighted, they are presented with as much emotion as the multiplication table. There is a marked tendency, moreover, to people such books with professionals of one sort or another, notably scholars (not invariably great men), to the exclusion of the nonscholarly great.

Our quest to make amends for this led to another horizon-expander—and to a redefinition of greatness. With the help of friends in many lands we identified toilers for the kingdom who deserved to be better known outside their own vineyard. Our grasp of geography became firmer; we ruefully acknowledged that we who sing "This is my Father's world" might know very little about our Father's world.

Nor was it helpful to devise criteria for who should be included, except in the most general terms. All this goalpost moving brought on an editorial nightmare. False priorities had to be discarded. Was membership of a minority or special-interest group sufficient claim in itself for entry (a beguiling one, that)? What about the occasional mandatory or notional this or that? Should we make life simpler by sticking to evangelicals? Should we exclude the still living? (No, in all four cases.)

11

G. K. Chesterton held that the acid test of all religions is, What does it deny? Reviewers of this volume are sure to react indignantly over who has been left out. What the editor will deny is any claim to comprehensiveness. If he has any sense he will state that here is a modestly sized book that gives some eight hundred brief entries on a cross-section of Christians who lived during, or whose lives extended into, the present century.

We have sought to offer not just the bare biographical bones in each case, but wherever possible a brief assessment of the subject's impact on his or her generation. Where we know of a biography we have given author and year of publication to aid further reading. Because we are dealing with a wide variety of people, places, and ministries, uniformity of presentation has sometimes been sacrificed in order to retain the local flavor of some entries. No subject was invited to write his own entry (that way madness lies), but a few have been consulted in order to confirm factual details not readily obtainable any other way.

To bring all these data together has called for the cooperation of busy men and women—writers, consultants, secretaries—and we are grateful for their expertise and willingness to participate; Steven Sywulka and Walter Elwell repeatedly pitched in with supererogatory labors; Ruj Vanavisut saw that manuscripts reached an editor commuting between two continents; and Jim Weaver and Maria denBoer of Baker Book House were patient and encouraging over the flintier furlongs.

Associate editor A. Scott Moreau brought an invaluable missionary emphasis to the proceedings, recruited knowledgeable contributors from improbable places, and his computer, tireless industry, and unfailing good humor gladdened the hearts of publisher and editor.

A

Abbott, Lyman (1835–1922)

Journalist, author, and preacher. After graduating from New York University (1853) he practiced law in New York City with his brothers. During the 1858 revival he received a call to the ministry, and was ordained as a Congregationalist pastor (1860). During his first pastorate in Indiana (1860–1865) he concluded that the nation's social and political challenges were of foremost importance. His subsequent appointments include the editorship of *The Illustrated Christian Weekly* (1871), associate editor (1876) and editor-in-chief (1881) of the *Christian Union*, and pastor of Plymouth Church, Brooklyn (1887–1899). Abbott belonged to the "prologue" (Ahlstrom) of the social gospel, for he placed "the reconstruction of the individual" as the only "means to social reconstruction." Moreover, he was a moderate reformer, resisting women's suffrage and supporting the separate institutions of education in the South. Abbott maintained that Jesus was not God's unique action in history, that sin was a moral disease that could be cured, that Scripture was the experiences of "men who had some perception of the Infinite" and was authoritative to the degree it coincides with conscience. The Christian faith, Abbott concluded, can be "expressed in the lives and character of agnostic, Jew and pagan." His published works include *Christianity and Social Problems* (1896), *Theology of an Evolutionist* (1897), *Life and Literature of the Ancient Hebrews* (1901), and *Reminiscences* (1915).

TIMOTHY R. PHILLIPS

Abdul Noor, Menis (1930–)

Egyptian pastor, writer, radio evangelist, and Christian apologist. Born in Upper Egypt, son of a godly Presbyterian pastor, he graduated from seminary in Cairo and began his ministry at the age of twenty. He has written, translated, or edited over fifty books and numerous articles, and conducted years of effective Trans-World Radio programs for which he has also produced follow-up materials, all in Arabic. With an outstanding gift of communication he has a wide ministry in teaching Christian apologetics in the Middle Eastern context. For twenty-five years he taught at Cairo Evangelical Seminary, affecting the lives of scores of pastors all over the Arab world. Abdul Noor is the pastor of the largest evangelical church in the Middle East, ministering to the center of Cairo, a city of 15 million people.

This church has doubled three times under his leadership, pioneering in several crucial fields of ministry.

ATEF BARNABA

Abel, Charles William (1862–1930)

Missionary to Papua New Guinea. Born in London, he emigrated as a young man to New Zealand, where he worked as a farm laborer. Returning to England, he was appointed as missionary to Papua New Guinea by the London Missionary Society (LMS). In 1891 he helped establish a mission station on Kwato Island in China Strait. He developed a distinctive settlement system in which native children were segregated as infants from their parents and village life, and then later received technical education and employment. Abel's system was well received in England as a result of his popular lectures during his furlough in 1900 and a children's gift book published by the LMS in 1901. On his return, as New Guinea came under Australian administration he became embroiled in several political squabbles in championing the rights of Papuans against Europeans. Abel's relationship with the LMS became strained over his scheme to develop a coconut plantation, and this eventually led him to visit America, where his supporters organized themselves into the New Guinea Evangelization Society. He returned to the field in 1924, but died in a car accident on a later trip to England.

Biographies by R. W. Abel (1934) and M. K. Abel (1957).

DAVID A. CURRIE

Aberhart, William (1878–1943)

Fundamentalist premier of Alberta. Born in Ontario and trained as a schoolteacher, "Bible Bill" moved west in 1910 to Calgary, where his popular though controversial activities as Bible teacher and "apostle" at Westbourne Baptist Church expanded by 1925 into the new field of religious radio broadcasting. He also founded the Calgary Prophetic Bible Institute in 1927. His theology was dispensational and eclectic, his ecclesiology highly separatistic. Alien to any cooperative style of leadership, he eventually formed his own small denomination. During the desperate provincial conditions of the Depression, Aberhart ran for political office as an advocate of radical economic theories rooted in the thought of British Major C. H. Douglas. Capitalizing on his province-wide credibility as a radio preacher, Aberhart led his new Social Credit party to a sweeping victory in the 1935 provincial election. He struggled to implement Social Credit theory once in office. He was succeeded as premier by Ernest C. Manning, the first graduate of the Prophetic Bible Institute, and the Socreds remained in uninterrupted power in Alberta until 1971. The dissonance between Aberhart's political engagement and radically sectarian ecclesiology was never resolved. Nonetheless his media and political careers highlighted and legitimized conservative Protestantism to a degree uncommon elsewhere in Canada.

Biography by D. R. Elliot and I. Miller (1987).

GLEN G. SCORGIE

Abraham, K. E. (1899–1974)

Indian Pentecostal church planter and apologist. Born in Kerala State, he grew up in a family with Syrian Christian origins. He received Christ at age seven, and while attending a revival meeting eight years later experienced God's presence and call to ministry, and he responded positively. On returning to his home he began to evangelize among fellow teenagers, several of whom came to Christ. After completing secondary school education he was accepted as a teacher in a school managed by the Jacobite church. Two months later he was appointed headmaster, and three months after that he obtained a coveted teaching post with the government. During this time he was involved in street evangelism and leading evening Bible studies in the community. He entered private studies under K. V. Simon, whose influence resulted in Abraham's baptism in 1916. Shortly afterwards, in obedience to God's call, he quit his teaching job and devoted himself full-time to the ministry. In 1924 he found renewed energy in his own Pentecostal experience, and for the rest of his life he was the key Indian apologist for Pentecostal doctrines. He is now remembered as the founder of the Indian Pentecostal Church, and toured internationally to proclaim the Pentecostal message at least eight times. He authored over a dozen books and pamphlets, including *Baptism in the Holy Spirit, Christian Baptism, Tongues, Babylon the Great*, and *An Exposition of False Teachings*.

Biography by H. Verghese (1974).

A. SCOTT MOREAU

Abraham, Mar Thoma (1880–1947)

Indian church leader and bishop in the Mar Thoma Church. Born Marettu Ninan Abraham in Kallooppara, Central Travancore, India, he became a committed Christian at age thirteen, and was educated at Madras Christian College and Trichy College. As a student he was attracted to ministry among the masses by Sherwood Eddy of the Student Volunteer Movement. He was ordained in 1911 to the ministry of the Mar Thoma Christian Church, and for the next three years studied at Wycliffe College, Toronto. After a brief period in parish ministry he was consecrated assistant bishop in 1917, and adopted the title by which he is usually known. Although he was assistant to Metropolitan Titus II for twenty-six years and metropolitan himself for only the last three years of his life, his influence over the development of the

15

Mar Thoma Church was important and creative. For him the twin emphases of lay leadership and evangelism were supreme. He fostered the Mar Thoma ashrams and the Maramon conventions as means of outreach. Through his own example he attracted educated young men as evangelists and ministers, and so revolutionized the leadership of his church.

NOEL S. POLLARD

Adams, Theodore Floyd (1898–1980)

Baptist minister and statesman. Born in Palmyra, New York, son of a Baptist pastor, he was converted to Christ at age six, and called to the ministry while in high school. He graduated from Denison University and Colgate Rochester Divinity School, was ordained in 1924, and served Baptist churches in Cleveland (1924–1927) and Toledo (1927–1936). He then became minister of the historic First Baptist Church of Richmond, Virginia, where he remained as pastor (1936–1968) and pastor emeritus until his death.

Adams served on numerous Southern Baptist Convention boards and commissions, was a member of the SBC executive committee (1934–1978), and was SBC president (1955–1960). In 1955 he and three Baptist companions visited the Soviet Union, and while there he became the first Protestant minister since the 1917 Revolution to celebrate the Lord's Supper for a Soviet congregation. A winsome diplomat, he did much to draw more closely together Baptists of different kinds in the United States, and to encourage Baptists throughout the world to work more closely with each other. Some of his ecumenical activism led to charges of liberal theological tendencies; others criticized his excessive biblicism, but he died a much esteemed Baptist statesman, admired by most of the Christian world. Among his publications were *Tell Me How?* (1964) and *Baptists Around the World* (1967).

ROBERT D. LINDER

Addams, Jane (1860–1935)

Social reformer. Born in Cedarville, Illinois, she graduated from Rockford Female Seminary, Illinois, in 1882, briefly studied medicine, then spent much of 1883–1889 in Europe. Toynbee Hall, London, was her model when in 1889 with Ellen Gates Starr she founded Hull House, a Chicago social settlement, chiefly to meet the needs of the immigrant poor. Originally from a Quaker background, she became a Presbyterian, but the maintenance of religious orthodoxy was never one of her chief aims. She held high posts in the peace and suffrage movements, was a cofounder of the American Civil Liberties Union, and shared the Nobel Peace Prize in 1931. Her published works included *Democracy and Social Ethics* (1902), *The Spirit of Youth and the City Streets* (1909), and *The Long Road of Women's Memory* (1916).

Biographies by J. W. Linn (1935) and W. E. Wise (1935).

J. D. DOUGLAS

Adeyemo, Tokunboh (1944–)

General secretary of the Association of Evangelicals of Africa and Madagascar from 1978, and chairman of the executive council, World Evangelical Fellowship from 1981. Born into a Muslim Yoruba family in Ibadan, Nigeria, he was converted in 1966. He graduated from ECWA Theological Seminary, Igbaja, Nigeria, in 1973, followed by graduate studies at Talbot Theological Seminary and Dallas Theological Seminary (Th.D., 1978). Aberdeen University awarded him a Ph.D. in 1979. Adeyemo's major contribution has been to strengthen and help unify the large evangelical movement on the continent of Africa. He has challenged African Christians to express their theology in its African context while maintaining a strong evangelical and biblical base. Among his published works are *Salvation in African Tradition* (1979), *Selfhood of the Church in Africa* (1993), and *The Making of a Servant of God* (1993).

IAN M. HAY

Aggrey, James Emman Kwegyir (1875–1927)

African educator. Born in Anamabu in the British colony of Gold Coast (now Ghana), he received a Christian education at a Methodist school in Cape Coast. He began teaching at age fifteen, and by twenty-one he was a headmaster. In 1898 he went to study at Livingstone College, Salisbury, North Carolina. On graduation he was invited to join the teaching staff, and he taught also in Hood Theological Seminary. In 1920 he became a leading advisory member of the International Commission on Education in Africa, financed by the Phelps-Stokes fund, and supported by missionary societies in America and Europe with encouragement from the British Colonial Office. In 1942 Aggrey became assistant vice principal of the new Achimota College in his homeland. With a staff that included Europeans, Africans, West Indians, and Indians, this college embodied his ideals of African educational advancement and racial harmony in the name of Christ. Prophet of better race relationships, he excelled as an extemporaneous orator and preacher. Proud of being black African, he married a white American. He saw education as a means whereby his people might take their proper place in the world in cooperation with the white colonials.

Biography by E. W. Smith (1929).

HENRY R. SEFTON

Ahlstrom, Sydney E. (1919–1984)

Historian of American religious history. Born in Cokato, Minnesota, he received his B.A. in 1941 from Gustavus Adolphus College and then enlisted in the U.S. army in 1942. After leaving the service he completed his M.A. at the University of Minnesota in 1946. He studied further in Strasbourg,

17

France, and eventually received his Ph.D. from Harvard University in 1952. Ahlstrom joined the Yale history faculty in 1954 and was appointed the first holder of the Samuel Knight Chair in 1979. During his notable career he served as president of the American Society of Church History and chairman of the Consulting Committee on the Bicentenary of the Lutheran Church in America.

His magnum opus was *A Religious History of the American People* (1972), which received the National Book Award in the category of philosophy and religion in 1973, the Brotherhood Award of the National Conference of Christians and Jews in 1974, and was honored in a *Time* magazine poll of book reviewers as the outstanding book on religion published in the 1970s. Through his teaching and numerous books and articles, he distinguished himself as a leading scholar in the field of American religious and intellectual history.

TIMOTHY K. BEOUGHER

Albright, William Foxwell (1891–1971)

Archaeologist and biblical scholar. He was born of Methodist missionary parents in Coquimbo, Chile, where he grew up. After graduating from Upper Iowa University (1912) and Johns Hopkins University (Ph.D., 1916) he studied at the American Schools of Oriental Research in Jerusalem, of which he later became director (1921–1929). He was appointed professor of Semitic languages at Johns Hopkins University in 1929 where he remained until retirement in 1958. In spite of lifelong physical handicaps he continued his vigorous activity until his death. He was honored by his students with a festschrift, *The Bible and the Ancient Near East* (1961).

Albright's scholarship and range of knowledge were prodigious; he produced over a thousand books and articles. His expertise covered all aspects of biblical archaeology, including linguistics, pottery chronology, and fieldwork. His studies over the years steadily increased his conviction of the historical reliability of the Scriptures. His own fundamentally orthodox theology was strengthened rather than weakened by his intimate knowledge of the factual elements of the past, and more than anyone else he was responsible for the discrediting of the highly speculative Graf–Wellhausen theory of pentateuchal origins. He was editor of the *Bulletin of the American Schools of Oriental Research* for thirty-eight years, and his *The Archaeology of Palestine* (1949), *Archaeology and the Religion of Israel* (1942), and *From the Stone Age to Christianity* (1940) are still used today.

Biography by L. G. Running and D. N. Freedman (1975).

WALTER A. ELWELL

Alexander, Charles McCallon (1867–1920)

Evangelistic songleader. He was born on a Tennessee farm of devout parents whose community-wide impact through music left a lasting impression on their son. As a boy he was further influenced by Ira Sankey. While attending Moody Bible Institute he began to lead large groups of people in singing gospel songs. This background, coupled with the warmth of his character and his passion for personal work, made him perfectly suited for evangelistic work. He joined with an evangelist and held meetings across America for eight years. It was, however, his teaming with R. A. Torrey that ultimately enabled him to exercise his greatest influence. Together they conducted a four-year evangelistic tour (1902–1906) that covered Australia, Asia, and Great Britain. The results of that tour were remarkable, and "Charlie's" humor and lively singing made him the foremost singing evangelist in the world. His style was copied by others, and continues to influence evangelical outreach in America. After a second world tour accompanied by his wife (1906–1907) he settled in New York where he continued in evangelistic work until 1918. With his wife's assistance he also organized the Pocket Testament League and compiled several volumes of hymns. Alexander wrote *Soul Winning Around the World* (1907).

Biographies by H. C. A. Dixon (1920) and P. I. Roberts (1920).

JACK MITCHELL

Alexander, Samuel (1859–1938)

British philosopher. Born in Sydney, Australia, he studied at the University of Melbourne and then completed his degree at Oxford (1881). He taught philosophy at Oxford for the next eleven years, except for a brief leave to study psychology in Germany. In 1887 he was awarded the Green Moral Philosophy Prize for a dissertation in ethics, later published as *Moral Order and Progress* (1889). He taught from 1893 to 1924 at Owens College (now the University of Manchester). In 1930 he was awarded the Order of Merit, the highest honor in British intellectual life.

Alexander is best remembered for his *Space, Time and Deity* (1920), in which he developed the theory of "emergent evolution." He argued that there are various levels in the unfolding of reality (space-time, matter, life, mind, and deity), each of which is rooted in the one preceding it and emerges from it. According to Alexander, God exists wholly within the world, which is his "body," but he does not yet exist as deity. Deity (a state of infinite perfection) is a goal for which the world (or God considered as the world) continually strives. Alexander could thus be characterized as an early thinker in the field of "process theology."

Books on his philosophy have been published by M. Konvitz (*On the Nature of Value* [1946]) and J. W. McCarthy (*The Naturalism of Samuel Alexander* [1948]).

Timothy K. Beougher

Allen, Asa A. (1911–1970)

Healing revivalist. Born in Sulphur Rock, Arkansas, he grew up in extreme poverty. Converted in 1934, he was licensed as an Assemblies of God minister some two years later and began pastoring a church in Colorado. In 1943 he set out in full-time revival ministry. Finding it difficult to support his wife and four children, in 1947 he accepted the call to pastor in Corpus Christi, Texas. While attending an Oral Roberts campaign in Dallas in 1949, he felt led to pursue a healing ministry. He resigned his pastorate and again set out in itinerant ministry. By 1953 the "Allen Revival Hour" was being heard on radio across America.

His ministry was characterized by an appeal to the poor and sensational claims about unusual miracles. He lost his ordination with the Assemblies of God in 1955 following his arrest for drunken driving. He retained a group of devoted followers and launched *Miracle Magazine* and the Miracle Revival Fellowship. In 1958 he built the Miracle Valley Training Center near Bisbee, Arizona. Wherever he went, he was hounded by questions concerning his life and ministry. Allen's ministry foreshadowed the health and wealth emphasis of many later revivalists.

Timothy K. Beougher

Allen, Roland (1868–1947)

English missionary strategist. Educated at Oxford, he was ordained in 1893 and was a curate in Darlington. In 1895 he went to China with the Society for the Propagation of the Gospel. By 1897 he was running a training school for native ministry. This work was disrupted by the Boxer Rebellion. After home leave and marriage he began writing on indigenous ministry. In 1903 he withdrew from China for health reasons, and became vicar of a Buckinghamshire parish. In 1907 he resigned over the question of baptismal discipline, and never held any further official post.

In 1912 his *Missionary Methods: St. Paul's or Ours?* summed up his ideas. In 1927 came his *The Spontaneous Expansion of the Church*. His ideas were propagated by the World Dominion Press, but were little appreciated in his lifetime. In 1932 he settled in Nairobi, Kenya. His theme that the local church needs local, nonprofessional leaders has been commended since his death. His books have been republished and have been influential in missionary thinking.

In 1968 D. M. Paton edited *Reform of the Ministry: A Study in the Work of Roland Allen*.

Noel S. Pollard

Allis, Oswald Thompson (1880–1973)

Old Testament scholar. Born in Wallingford, Pennsylvania, son of a Presbyterian physician, he graduated from the University of Pennsylvania and Princeton Theological Seminary before taking his Ph.D. degree under Friedrich Delitzsch at the University of Berlin (1913). He had earlier joined the faculty at Princeton Seminary (1910–1929), then becoming professor of Semitic studies and also editing the *Princeton Theological Review* (1918–1929). With the spread of liberal tendencies within the Presbyterian Church, USA, reflected notably in the case of H. E. Fosdick, Allis was among those who left Princeton Seminary for the new Westminster Theological Seminary (1929–1936). When the PCUSA's disciplinary action against J. G. Machen led to the founding of what was to become the Orthodox Presbyterian Church, Allis declined to leave the main Presbyterian body, resigned from Westminster, and spent the rest of his life on literary work. His books included *The Five Books of Moses* (1943), *Prophecy and the Church* (1945), *The Unity of Isaiah* (1950), *God Spake by Moses* (1951), and *The Old Testament: Its Claims and Its Critics* (1972).

J. D. DOUGLAS

Althaus, (August Wilhelm Hermann) Paul (1888–1966)

German Lutheran theologian. Born in Hanover, he studied at the universities of Tübingen and Göttingen (D.Theol.) and at the theological seminary at Erichsburg, Hanover. After serving as medical corpsman and then chaplain in World War I (1915–1918), he taught at the University of Rostock (1919–1925) before becoming professor of systematic theology at the University of Erlangen (1925–1966). In 1926 he succeeded Karl Holl as president of the Luther Society, and served in that position for thirty years. Although a popular preacher, Althaus's chief claim to fame is as a Luther scholar who rejected theological liberalism, published prolifically, and directed German Christians back to Luther himself as an appropriate source of modern theology. Focusing mostly on dogmatics and ethics, he criticized Karl Barth's dialectical theology and Rudolf Bultmann's denial of the essential link between faith and history in the kerygma.

Driven by patriotism, a romantic view of the world, and fear of political instability and the encroachments of modern secularism, he embraced conservative politics and joined the German National Party during the 1920s. He dreamed of the rebirth of community through discipline, obedience to those in authority, national pride and unity, and belief in a mysterious, organic *Volk*. From 1933 to 1937, when he became disillusioned with Nazi policies, Althaus supported National Socialism. A fear of modernity combined with conservative theology led him to erect a political-intellectual position that allowed him to support Nazism during its first years in power. This in turn tarnished the image of an otherwise intelligent and intellectually honest church leader, and reduced his influence in the post-war Christian community.

His main publications (all in German) include *Grundriss der Dogmatik* (2 vols., 1929), *Die Christliche Wahrheit* (1948), and *Die Theologie M. Luthers* (1962).

ROBERT D. LINDER

Altizer, Thomas J(onathan) J(ackson) (1927–)

Theologian. Born in Cambridge, Massachusetts, he graduated from the University of Chicago, and in 1955 earned a Ph.D. degree there. He taught at Wabash College, Indiana (1954–1956), and at Emory University (1956–1968) before appointment as professor of English and religious studies at the University of New York, Stony Brook. Altizer is best known for his "death of God" theology, which received public attention in the late 1960s in connection with publications such as *Radical Theology and the Death of God* (1966) and *The Gospel of Christian Atheism* (1966). His theology was based on the problem of divine transcendence which, he concluded, made God irrelevant to the human situation. He has continued to publish titles such as *Total Presence: The Language of Jesus and the Language of Today* (1980) and *Deconstruction and Theology* (1982).

NORMAN R. ERICSON

Alves, Rubem Azevedo (1933–)

Brazilian theologian; an initiator of the liberation theology movement that burst on the Latin American scene in the late 1960s. Alves graduated from the Presbyterian Seminary in Campinas (SP) and was ordained by the Presbyterian Church of Brazil (IPB). In the mid-1960s he was marginalized from this ministry when his move toward the left clashed with the church's move toward the right. By the early 1970s Alves was a director of Church and Society in Latin America (ISAL), a member of the Commission on Faith and Order (WCC), and professor of social science at the University of Campinas (UNICAMPS). *Theology of Human Hope* (1969) is based on Alves' doctoral dissertation at Princeton Seminary and *Tomorrow's Child* (1972) was written while he was Luce Visiting Professor at Union Theological Seminary (New York). By the end of the 1970s Alves' experience with the Presbyterian Church led him to write *Protestantism and Repression* (1985). Having abandoned liberation theology, Alves continues to teach at UNICAMPS and practices as a psychoanalyst. Writing on a diversity of subjects, Alves' interests in the 1980s and 1990s have tended much more toward the subjective—art, poetry, and music.

RICHARD J. STURZ

Ames, Edward Scribner (1870–1958)

Philosopher, Disciples of Christ minister, and theologian. Born in Eau Claire, Wisconsin, he grew to love education in spite of the anti-intellectual bias in much of his church's life. He graduated from Drake University and Yale Divinity School, and received the first Ph.D. in philosophy granted by the University of Chicago in 1895. After a three-year teaching appointment at Butler College, Ames returned to the University of Chicago, where he remained until retiring in 1935. He accepted the position of dean of Disciples of Divinity House from 1935 until his second retirement in 1948. From 1900 to 1940 Ames pastored the University Church of the Disciples of Christ, where he became a leading pulpit expositor of liberal Protestantism. He played a significant role in bringing his denomination into the modernist camp during the fundamentalist controversy.

Ames generally followed a pragmatic approach to religion, built on the psychological framework that emphasized the experience of living as the primary source of our view of reality. He viewed religion as a natural phenomenon that rose out of human experience and followed a clear evolutionary pattern. As was common among the early proponents of evolutionary religion, he held that Christianity was the highest expression of religious faith. He taught that heaven was the participation in the ethical process of salvation; hell was failure to realize the soul's natural powers. His two most important works were *The Psychology of Religion* (1910) and *Religion* (1929). Books he authored that presented his theological reflections included *The Divinity of Christ* (1911), *The Higher Individualism* (1915), *The New Orthodoxy* (1918), and *Letters to God and the Devil* (1933). His *Autobiography* was published in 1959.

A. SCOTT MOREAU

Ames, Jessie Daniel (1883–1972)

American Methodist antilynching reformer. Born in Texas, she graduated from Southwestern University in 1902. In 1905 she married Roger Ames, an army surgeon who died in 1914, leaving her with three children. She soon became one of the most politically active women in Texas. In 1922 she helped organize the Texas women's branch of the Commission on Interracial Cooperation (CIC), and came to be one of the three dominant white women in the organization, of which she accepted the directorship of the Women's Committee in 1929. In 1930 she founded the Association of Southern Women for the Prevention of Lynching (ASWPL), leading it until disbandment in 1942 because of a decrease in the number of lynchings. During its existence 43,000 women signed the ASWPL pledge to seek to abolish lynchings. Ames continued working for the CIC, developing in 1942 a new periodical, *The Southern Frontier*, calling for more rights for African Americans. When the CIC was replaced by the Southern Regional

Council in 1944, Ames was forced to resign. She retired to Tyron, North Carolina, where she was active in Methodist conference affairs. She wrote *Revolt Against Chivalry: . . . the Women's Campaign Against Lynching* (1979).

DAVID A. CURRIE

Anderson, (James) Norman (Dalrymple) (1908–1994)

English lawyer, Orientalist, and leading Anglican layman. Born in Suffolk, he performed brilliantly in legal studies at Cambridge, and in 1932 joined the Egypt General Mission in Cairo. His knowledge of the Arab world proved useful in World War II when as an Intelligence Corps colonel he served in Cairo as chief secretary for Arab affairs. The same swift progress marked his postwar course. By 1954 he was professor of Oriental laws in London, to which was added in 1958 the directorship of the Institute of Legal Studies. When the Church of England adopted synodical government in 1970, Anderson's strong evangelicalism was no bar to appointment as chairman of the House of Laity. He was knighted by Queen Elizabeth in 1974. A humble and friendly man highly acclaimed in his professional field, he was a regular supporter of evangelical causes (especially InterVarsity). His religious works include *A Lawyer among the Theologians* (1973), *God's Word for God's World* (1981), and the fascinating and refreshing autobiography, *An Adopted Son* (1986).

J. D. DOUGLAS

Anderson, Robert (1841–1918)

Irish-born Bible teacher and police chief. Born in Dublin where he was educated at Trinity College, he embarked on a career in law in 1863. He became political crimes adviser to the British Home Office in 1868, and later headed Scotland Yard's criminal investigation department (1888–1901). After his conversion at age nineteen, Anderson was active in the religious field. Although Presbyterian and dispensationalist, his addresses and writings were widely known and highly respected both inside and outside evangelical circles. His activities continued after his retirement in 1901. In that year the professionalism he had displayed in his secular vocation was rewarded by knighthood. Anderson was a prolific writer. His many works include *The Coming Prince* (1882), *The Silence of God* (1897), *The Bible and Modern Criticism* (1902), and *Misunderstood Texts of the New Testament* (1916).

J. D. DOUGLAS

Andrews, Charles Freer (1871–1940)

Anglican missionary to India. Born in Newcastle upon Tyne, England, the son of a minister of the Catholic Apostolic Church, he graduated from

Cambridge and went to India in 1904. Going to South Africa in 1914 to help the oppressed Indian laborers there, he began a lifelong friendship with Gandhi. On his return to India he resigned his teaching post at St. Stephen's College, Delhi, and renounced—at least as far as he was concerned—his Church of England priesthood, transferring to Tagore's Santiniketan settlement in order to fully identify himself with Indian aspirations. As the "friend of India" and "friend of the poor," Andrews devoted himself to promoting discussion of topical issues in India through frequent contributions to the *Modern Review*, sought to explain Gandhi and Tagore to the West by editing their books, and wrote studies on social and political reform. He traveled widely outside India in support of the interests of Indian migrant laborers. His religious writings include a biography of his friend Sadhu Sundar Singh (1934), a spiritual autobiography, *What I Owe to Christ* (1932), and a number of devotional books, among them *Christ in the Silence* (1933).

Biographies by D. O'Conner (1944) and B. Chaturvedi and M. Sykes (1949).

PHILIP HILLYER

Annacondia, Carlos (1944–)

Argentine evangelist. Born in Argentina, he worked for some years in the metallurgical field. Through the ministry of a Panamanian evangelist he, along with some of his employees, accepted the gospel in 1979. They formed the "Christian Evangelical Church." After discovering there were other entities already using that name, they changed their movement's name to the "Church of the Salvation Message," with headquarters in Quilmes, near Buenos Aires. Subsequently they became identified with Pentecostalism. Annacondia began preaching as an evangelist, although he has never been ordained to the ministry. His first campaign was in the Itari section of Buenos Aires, and since then he has conducted up to twenty crusades each year, reaching the suburbs of Buenos Aires, then the rest of Argentina, and later extending to other countries such as Finland, the former Soviet Union, Denmark, Spain, Italy, Germany, Singapore, and Japan. He also has a radio ministry.

Annacondia's campaigns are long, often going from twenty to as many as sixty days. Normally they are held in open fields, and have a spontaneous style that has had great impact on all the evangelical churches of Argentina. He points to the signs promised in Mark 16 as his doctrinal basis; liberation from satanic powers has had a primary place in his meetings. He is considered to be the evangelical preacher who has been heard by the most people in open air meetings.

ARNOLDO CANCLINI

Anthony, Susan B. (1820–1906)

Social reformer. Born in Adams, Massachusetts, she had a Quaker upbringing, including the belief in the equality of women before God. She taught school from 1835 to 1850, and then actively took up the cause of temperance reform. When denied permission to speak at a Sons of Temperance rally, she responded by organizing the Woman's New York State Temperance Society in 1852. She was a fierce abolitionist, and worked with the American Anti-Slavery Society from 1856 to 1861. Following the Civil War she devoted her life to the cause of women's suffrage, making hundreds of speeches, writing countless letters, and testifying before numerous congressional committees.

In 1868 she teamed with Elizabeth Cady Stanton to publish *The Revolution*, a weekly newspaper devoted to women's rights. In 1869 they organized the National Woman Suffrage Association, which merged with another organization to form the National American Woman Suffrage Association in 1890. From 1892 to 1900 Anthony served as president. Anthony also helped organize the International Council of Women in 1888 and the International Woman Suffrage Alliance in 1904. She helped complete the four-volume *The History of Woman Suffrage* (1881–1902). Through her many efforts, she helped reshape the role of women in America and around the world.

Biographies by K. Anthony (1954) and A. Lutz (1959).

TIMOTHY K. BEOUGHER

Arana Quiróz, Pedro (1938–)

Latin American church leader. Born in Lima, Peru, he professed personal faith in Christ during high school, and actively shared his faith while earning his degree in chemical engineering at Lima's historic University of San Marcos. After graduation, Arana went into full-time student ministry. He helped found Peru's counterpart to InterVarsity Christian Fellowship and later became Latin America general secretary for the parent movement, the International Fellowship of Evangelical Students. Always concerned about applying the Christian faith to Latin America's crushing social and political crises, Arana in 1978 ran on the APRA party ticket for election to Peru's constitutional assembly. Backed by evangelical Protestant voters, Arana surprised the nation by getting the fourth highest number of votes out of one thousand candidates on the ballot. He won fellow delegates' respect for his integrity and work in the year-long constitution-drafting process. A Presbyterian pastor and educator, he became a leader in Peru's National Evangelical Council. In 1984 he led in founding the council's Peace and Hope Commission, which gave relief aid and relocated evangelical Christian refugees suffering from terrorist violence in Peru's Andean region. Because of his unique experience in politics and holistic ministry, Arana became recognized across Latin

America and in international evangelical circles as a thoughtful spokesman and writer on biblical and social issues. Later he served with World Vision–Peru and founded MISIUR (wholistic Urban/Rural Mission). In 1991 Arama became general secretary of the Peruvian Bible Society.

JOHN MAUST

Archilla, Rogelio (1906–)

Pastor, evangelist, and educator. Born in Ciales, Puerto Rico, he studied at the Evangelical Seminary of Puerto Rico and Hardwick Theological Seminary in Brooklyn (Th.B., 1933) before beginning a seventeen-year career as professor at the Latin American Biblical Seminary in San Jose, Costa Rica. During this time he made evangelistic tours throughout Latin America, and carried out pastoral and radio ministries, including helping to found Radio TIFC, the first evangelical station in Central America. In 1950 he moved to New York City, where he pastored several Hispanic congregations. He has also taught since 1979 at the Seminario Biblico Alianza (CMA), and since 1990 has been minister-at-large with the Christian and Missionary Alliance. He has been interpreter for Billy Graham during crusades in New York, the Caribbean, and Central America, has written six books, and has translated several others.

STEPHEN R. SYWULKA

Argue, Andrew Harvey (1868–1959)

Canadian Pentecostal pioneer. Born into a strong Methodist family in Ontario, he obtained only a sixth-grade education before moving west to Winnipeg where he established himself as a very successful realtor and lay preacher with the Holiness Movement Church. In 1907 he traveled to Chicago to investigate the new Pentecostal phenomena, and there under the ministry of William Durham personally spoke in tongues. He returned to establish "tarrying meetings" in his large Winnipeg home, and to become the leading Pentecostal in that city. Financially independent, he left his business career for full-time ministries. He founded Winnipeg's Calvary Temple, for many years Canada's largest Pentecostal church; was instrumental in the formation of many Pentecostal congregations in other Canadian urban centers; and was a key figure in the emergence of the Pentecostal Assemblies of Canada denomination (1910–1920). He published several magazines, including the *Apostolic Messenger*, conducted numerous revival meetings in both Canada and the United States, and was involved in native evangelism. Through his preaching, publishing, church-planting, and organizational efforts, he vigorously promoted and helped establish the Pentecostal movement in Canada.

Biography by Zelma Argue (1928).

GLEN G. SCORGIE

27

Armstrong, Annie Walker (1850–1938)

Cofounder and first corresponding secretary of the Woman's Mission Union (WMU). Born into a wealthy Baltimore family and reared by her mother, a committed church attender, she did not become a Christian until she was twenty. Later, when confronted by the needs of American Indian schools, she was roused to action on their behalf. As her interest and commitment to missions within the United States increased, so did the demand for her abilities. In 1887 she became the WMU's corresponding secretary. Her Baltimore office served as the headquarters out of which she worked faithfully and tirelessly for eighteen years without salary. Largely responsible for the organized promotion of home missions, she spearheaded ministries among the Indians, the disabled, and African-Americans, as well as organizing fund-raising for missions, corresponding extensively with missionaries at home and abroad, and writing for various publications. Pioneer, visionary for mission, lover of souls, and a fervent follower of Christ, she is remembered as one who did more than any other for Baptist home missions.

Biographies by E. M. Evans (1963) and Bobbie Sorrill (1984).

WENDY S. LARSON

Armstrong, Laura Dell "Malotte" (1886–1945)

Southern Baptist mission leader. Born in Graham, Missouri, to the family of a Baptist minister, she graduated from Northwest Missouri State Teacher's College, after which she taught in the public school system. Armstrong distinguished herself through her various leadership roles within the Southern Baptist Convention. She served on the executive board of the Missouri Baptist General Association from 1919 to 1936 and the executive committee of the Southern Baptist Convention from 1927 to 1945. She was president of the Woman's Missionary Union from 1933 to 1945, which came with the additional responsibilities of chair of the board of trustees of the Woman's Missionary Union Training School (now Carver School of Missions and Social Work) and provided leadership for the development of the new facility adjacent to the Southern Baptist Theological Seminary in Louisville. She was also instrumental in designating funds from the Golden Jubilee Offering to facilitate training for African-American women and cooperation between white and African-American women in missionary endeavors. After her death several memorials were established to recognize her life of service, including the Armstrong Terrace at Carver School, the Armstrong Memorial Training School in Rome, Italy, and the Baptist Seminary in Havana, Cuba.

A. SCOTT MOREAU

Arndt, William Frederick (1880–1957)

Lutheran minister and New Testament scholar. Born in Mayville, Wisconsin, he studied at Concordia College, Concordia Seminary, the University of Chicago, and Washington University, St. Louis (Ph.D., 1935). In 1903 he was ordained in the Lutheran Church–Missouri Synod, and ministered in Tennessee, Missouri, and Brooklyn (1902–1912). Even after turning to a career in education he remained active in parish work. He was professor of ancient languages at St. Paul's College, Concordia (1912–1921), and professor of New Testament exegesis and literature at Concordia Seminary (1921–1951). Deeply concerned for the unity of the Lutheran Church he chaired his denomination's committee that reached doctrinal agreement with the American Lutheran Church. In 1956 he traveled to England to help set up a program for training ministers in the Evangelical Lutheran Church of England. Arndt authored numerous books, including *Does the Bible Contradict Itself?* (1926), a life of Paul (1944), and a commentary on Luke's Gospel (1956). His most enduring contribution to New Testament studies is the renowned *Greek-English Lexicon of the New Testament* (1957), done in collaboration with F. W. Gingrich.

H. DOUGLAS BUCKWALTER

Arnold, Eberhard (1883–1935)

Founder of the Bruderhof movement in Nazi Germany. Born in Breslau, he studied theology at Halle University, but through his insistence on believer's baptism he disqualified himself from graduating (he later obtained a doctorate with a thesis on Nietzsche). The Bruderhof economic and residential community had its beginnings at Sannerz in 1920. Even before that, Arnold had become well known and respected on the German lecture circuit, especially in Student Christian movement circles. A convinced pacifist, he linked spiritual authenticity with an awareness of economic injustice. He early incurred the hostility of the Gestapo, which felt threatened by religious groups professing a higher allegiance than that due to the state. "The most sinister powers of our civilization," he wrote in 1934, "are . . . the State, the military and the capitalist structure." He prophesied imminent death for "the tremendous edifice built up by a fallen creation." In 1930 he went to western Canada and established links with the Hutterian Brethren whose forebears had emigrated there from Russia in the 1870s. Arnold, whose movement spread from mainland Europe to England, Paraguay, and the United States, died of complications following a leg injury. In 1984 the Hutterian Society and J. H. Yoder published *God's Revolution*, a selection of his writings and addresses.

J. D. DOUGLAS

Arnot, Frederick Stanley (1858–1914)

Missionary to Africa. Born in Glasgow, Scotland, of Brethren parents, he was in early childhood a frequent visitor to David Livingstone's home, which instilled into the young Frederick a passion to serve God in Africa. Everything he did from that time was focused toward this divine call. He first went to Africa in 1881 as a Brethren missionary. His dealings with King Lewanika of the Barotse tribe are legendary. The experiences he had during his treks are just as numerous and memorable as were those of Livingstone. After his time in Barotse territory he trekked across to Benguella on the west coast. After furlough in Britain in 1888 he worked in Garenganze (in Zaire, near the border of Zambia and Angola). Apart from preaching Christ, he and his wife Harriet began schools and medical clinics in order to meet the complete needs of the national people. He returned to Britain several times, mainly due to ill health, but his influence did not diminish.

Perhaps even greater than his own tireless work is Arnot's influence on others. Apart from the many Brethren missionaries whom God called through Arnot, two missionary societies (the South African General Mission, now Africa Evangelical Fellowship; and the South African Baptist Missionary Society) owe the motivation for their work in Central Africa to his direct influence. Today's vibrant and growing evangelical church throughout Central Africa—particularly Zambia—is a living monument to Arnot.

ROGER KEMP

Arns, Paulo Evaristo (1921–)

Roman Catholic cardinal in São Paulo, Brazil, and spokesman for practical liberation theology. Born in southern Brazil, Arns concluded his theological training with a D.Litt. from the Sorbonne in 1952. After serving as professor in several Brazilian seminaries, he became auxiliary bishop (1966), archbishop (1970), and cardinal (1973) of São Paulo, which was to become the largest diocese in the world. Together with Helder Camara, Arns helped to sway CELAM III in Puebla (Mexico, 1979) to reconfirm in part the earlier perspective of CELAM II in Medillín (Colombia, 1968) concerning the church's struggle for justice and its preferential option for the poor. For twenty years Arns wielded strong influence in the liberation-oriented National Conference of Brazilian Bishops. Concern for pastoral and practical matters has been expressed by the cardinal in his campaign for free elections against the reigning military regime, and again in his programs for the poor in the socially plagued megalopolis of São Paulo. Because of his sympathy for liberation theology, Arns' diocese was divided into five dioceses by the Vatican in the early 1990s, thus substantially diminishing his jurisdiction. A candidate for the Nobel Peace Prize, Arns continues as an active agent of interfaith cooperation and human rights.

ESTEVAN F. KIRSCHNER

Arrastia, Cecilio (1922–)

Cuban evangelist and pastor. Born in Guanajay, Pinar del Rio, Cuba, he studied at the University of Havana and received his theological training at the Evangelical Seminary of Puerto Rico at Rio Piedras, McCormick Seminary, and Princeton Seminary (D.Min.), followed by postgraduate work at Union Theological Seminary in New York. He served as a Presbyterian pastor and radio and television speaker in Cuba, founded the San Andres Church in the Bronx, New York, and was the first Hispanic moderator of the New York City Presbytery (UPCUSA). An eloquent orator, he was for twelve years an evangelist for Latin America under the National Council of Churches, and has preached throughout the continent. He taught at three seminaries, worked with the Association of Theological Schools in the United States, and held various posts with the International Missionary Council, the World Council of Churches, and the UPCUSA. He has written several books in Spanish.

STEPHEN R. SYWULKA

Arrupe, Pedro (1907–1991)

Superior general of the Order of Jesus (Jesuits). Born in Bilbao, Spain, he joined the Jesuits in 1927, but when the order was dissolved in his homeland (1931) he continued his studies in Belgium, the Netherlands, and the United States, where he was ordained in 1936. He taught in Japan (1938–1943) and after taking final vows as a Jesuit continued to serve there. He witnessed the "blinding flash" when the atomic bomb was dropped on nearby Hiroshima (1945). His was a leading reformist voice in post-Vatican II years. His concern that the poor and underprivileged should have social and economic justice made him in the 1970s a prominent advocate of liberation theology, and brought him into controversy with the Roman hierarchy and influential members of his own order. After a stroke that partially incapacitated him he resigned his post as "black pope" in 1981, the first Jesuit superior general ever to have done so. Arrupe published works in Japanese, Spanish, Italian, French, and English. Among the latter were *Challenge to Religious Life Today* (1979) and *Justice with Faith Today* (1980).

J. D. DOUGLAS

Assmann, Hugo (1933–)

One of the Roman Catholic fathers of liberation theology in the late 1960s and early 1970s. His importance in the liberation theology movement is

31

greater than the quantity of published material would indicate. After studying philosophy in Brazil, Assmann received his D.Theol. from the Gregorian University (Rome) and later earned a special diploma in mass communications from the Catholic University in Santiago (Chile). From 1962 to 1965 Assmann taught theology and ethics at the Jesuit seminary in São Leopoldo and at the same time, sociology at the Pontifical Catholic University in Pôrto Alegre in the far south of Brazil. From 1966–1968 he coordinated studies at São Paulo Institute of Philosophy and Theology. Due to his active participation in the struggle for socioeconomic liberation from military governments, Assmann was forced out of Brazil (1968), Bolivia (1971), and Chile (1974). In 1969 he was visiting professor at the theological faculty of the University of Münster (Germany). In Chile, he was a part of Allende's government. With Gustavo Gutiérrez he helped draft the documents for the Christians for Socialism movement. Driven out of Chile by the military coup, Assmann became professor of communications at the University in San José, Costa Rica (1974). During the years that Assmann was in Costa Rica he made at least fourteen trips to Nicaragua. By the mid-1980s Assmann had left the priesthood and married. Returning to Brazil in 1981, he has since taught in the field of communications at the Methodist University in Piracicaba (São Paulo). An articulate thinker and debater, in the 1980s Assmann was one of the first liberationists to question certain socialist ideals. Among his books translated into English is *Practical Theology of Liberation* (1975).

RICHARD J. STURZ

Athyal, Saphir (1931–)

Indian churchman, theologian, and educator. Born in Kerala, he graduated from the University of Allahabad, Asbury Theological Seminary, Rutgers State University, and Princeton Theological Seminary (Ph.D.). An outstanding ecumenical churchman with a passion for educating people for effective service, he has had an extensive ministry in both the Indian and the world church. He served as president of Union Biblical Seminary in Pune, India, as founder-chairman of the Asia Theological Association, and as guest professor in over fifteen universities worldwide. Currently he is director of mission and evangelism for World Vision International, and is editing the *India Christian Handbook* and *The Church in Asia: Challenges for the 90s*. Athyal's long-term focus has been on the need for the church to squarely face the issues of modern culture, and the need for the various parts of the church universal to face this task together. His published works include *The Bible and Asia Today* and *Towards an Asian Christian Theology*.

A. SCOTT MOREAU

Atkinson, David John (1943–)

Theologian, student counselor, and organic chemist. Educated in science at King's College, London (Ph.D., 1969), he earned further degrees in theology at Bristol and Oxford, and was ordained in the Church of England in 1972. He served curacies in Bolton and Birmingham (1972–1977), and was librarian of Latimer House (Anglican Evangelical research center), Oxford (1977–1980), and visiting chaplain at Corpus Christi College, London (1977–1989). He has been visiting lecturer in Christian ethics at various institutions, including Fuller Theological Seminary, Pasadena; Hope College, Michigan; and London Bible College. Since 1983 he has been visiting lecturer in pastoral theology at Wycliffe Hall, Oxford. Atkinson has made a special study of student counseling, and his services have been much in demand, especially in evangelical circles. Among his written works are *The Values of Science* (1980), *Life and Death* (1985), and *Ethics* (1987).

J. D. DOUGLAS

Aulen, Gustaf Emanuel Hildebrand (1879–1977)

Swedish theologian and bishop. Born in Ljungby, Sweden, he studied theology under Soderblom and church history with Harnack, began his teaching career at Uppsala, and continued at Lund as professor of dogmatic theology (1913–1933). He was bishop of Strangnas (1932–1952), working against nationalist domination in Scandinavia and contributing significantly toward liturgical renewal within the Swedish Lutheran Church. His theological position was informed by the atonement theory of Irenaeus, according to which God's action in Jesus the Christ sets human beings free from all destructive powers. In Martin Luther's reform work he saw a high point of conformity to the ideals of early Christianity and to the teachings of the church fathers. Seeking to evolve a scientific method for doing systematic theology, Aulen opposed Lutheran Orthodoxy, broke with Harnack's reading of Luther, and became an exponent, along with N. Soderblom and A. Nygren, of the Lundensian School. Along with Nygren and Soderblom he participated actively in the emerging modern ecumenical movement. Aulen also wrote choral music and helped revise the hymnbooks and service books of his church. In 1952 he became professor emeritus at Lund. His mature theological works were translated into German and English. The most prominent were *Christus Victor* (1931), *The Faith of the Christian Church* (1948), and *Jesus in Contemporary Historical Research* (1976).

EDWARD J. FURCHA

33

Aylward, Gladys (1902–1970)

Missionary to China. Born near London, daughter of a mailman, she had a rudimentary education. She then worked as a shop girl, a nanny, and a housemaid. She was converted at age eighteen while employed as a parlor maid. She set her heart on going as a missionary to China but was rejected by the China Inland Mission because of her poor educational qualifications. Later, in a Primitive Methodist meeting she heard of a small, independent mission in North China that needed a worker. Little by little from her meager salary she saved up enough money for the fare on the Trans-Siberian Railway. In 1932 she traveled east to Shanghai Province at a time when Russia and China were at war. Despite all hindrances she finally made it through Japan to China, joining missionary Jeannie Lawson—a mercurial Scot who died a year after Aylward arrived—in remote Yangcheng. She learned Chinese by listening to it. After Lawson's death, she continued the inn that they had opened for muleteers. Listeners were attracted to the inn through the telling of Bible stories. She was supported by a local official who appointed her Inspector of Feet in his campaign against the foot-binding of girls. She served in this capacity until an official edict set the girls free. So fully did Aylward identify with the people that she became a naturalized Chinese citizen in 1936. When the Japanese invasion reached Shanghai province in 1940, she led one hundred children on a long journey to safety, an epic undertaking that was made into a film entitled *Inn of the Sixth Happiness*. A serious illness forced her to return to England in 1949. Her heart was in the Orient, however, and she went back in 1955. She opened an orphanage in Formosa and worked there until her death. This diminutive woman (only five feet tall) was an effective missionary because of her lack of prejudice and her skill as a storyteller of simple Christianity.

Biographies by Alan Burgess (1957) and Phyllis Thompson (1971).

EILEEN J. KUHN
NOEL S. POLLARD

Azariah, Vedanayakam Samuel (1874–1945)

First Indian Anglican bishop. Born in Vellalanvillai, Madras State, son of a village pastor, he became a YMCA secretary in 1895. A firm believer in cooperation between foreign and Indian church workers (on which topic he addressed the 1910 Edinburgh World Missionary Conference, asking for more equal treatment, including love and friendship, from expatriate missionaries), he supported the development of an indigenous leadership in a united Indian church. In 1902 he helped found the Indian Missionary Society (India's first). In 1912 he became bishop of Dornakal despite strong opposition from Indians (because of his humble origins) and Britons (who thought it a premature step). Happily, he had a series of gifted European archdeacons who did the administrative work and freed him to travel and to teach, inspire, and lead a great mass movement. In his thirty-year episcopate, one hundred thousand people were added to the church. He ordained to the priesthood village workers who had proved themselves as catechists. On the national scene, he took a leading role in the Tranquebar (1919) and Nagpur (1931) conferences for church union, and was chairman of the National Christian Council of India from 1929. Azariah repudiated syncretism, but encouraged the use of Indian cultural forms by the church. He played a major role in what became the united Church of South India. His writings included *South India Union* (1936) and *Christian Giving* (repr. 1965).

Biographies by C. Graham (1946) and K. Heiburg (1950).

PHILIP HILLYER
AJITH FERNANDO

B

Baba, Panya (1932–)

Nigerian church leader and missiologist. Born into a Christian family from the Gbagyi tribe in Karu, Central Nigeria, he became a committed Christian in 1945. He graduated from the ECWA Bible Training School, Karu (1947), and ECWA Bible College, Kagoro (1962), and pursued further studies in England and the United States. He served as a missionary, pastor, and church leader for twenty years before assuming the leadership of the Evangelical Missionary Society, the mission arm of the Evangelical Churches of West Africa in Nigeria. He directed this mission for eighteen years from 1970 and saw it expand from 194 to more than 750 missionaries. In 1988 he became president of the Evangelical Churches of West Africa, a denomination with more than three thousand churches and that now has a missionary force of more than nine hundred. Baba's major contribution is to world missions. He is a leading theologian and missiologist in the field of indigenous cross-cultural missions, and is a major motivating force in the worldwide missionary enterprise. He serves on the boards of six international fellowships, and is the author of more than thirty-five major papers and addresses dealing with Third World missions.

IAN M. HAY

Babbage, Stuart Barton (1916–)

New Zealand Anglican scholar. Born in Auckland, son of a famous mathematician, he was educated at the city's University College and at the Bible Churchmen's Society College (now Trinity College), Bristol, England. Ordained in 1939, he combined a curacy with a lectureship at Oak Hill Theological College, London. After earning a Ph.D. at London University in 1942, he became a Royal Air Force chaplain and served in Iraq and Iran. After the war he was dean of Sydney (1947–1953) and of Melbourne (1953–1963), where he was also principal of Ridley College. He then left for the United States where he lectured and ministered until his 1969 appointment as president of the Conwell School of Theology in Philadelphia (later united with Gordon Divinity School to form the Gordon-Conwell Seminary). In 1974 Babbage returned to Australia to become master of New College in the University of Sydney and (in 1977) also registrar of the Australian School of Theology. He relinquished these posts in 1982 and 1991, respectively, but continued to maintain a very active ministry.

Babbage brought to all his work a dynamic energy. Unafraid of innovation, he was always ready to embark on a fresh enterprise.

MARCUS L. LOANE

Bader, Jesse Moren (1886–1963)

Evangelist and ecumenical leader. He was born in Bader, Illinois, a small town named for his settler-grandfather. He was baptized at age fourteen, and preached his first sermon while still in high school. In 1905 he entered the University of Kansas to study medicine, and preached on Sundays to a small congregation in nearby Perry. His experiences there convinced him of God's call to the ministry; he transferred to Drake University in Des Moines, Iowa, to study at its College of the Bible, and graduated in 1911. During a seven-year pastorate at Atchison, Kansas, the church grew from 300 to 1,400 members. Using the slogan "Each one win one," Bader equipped laypersons to be involved in outreach, and his ministry approach of "visitation evangelism" became a model for churches across the country. Soon after returning from working as YMCA secretary with American troops overseas (1917–1919) he became the first superintendent of evangelism in the United Christian Missionary Society. In 1932 he joined the Federal Council of Churches staff. Succeeding as executive secretary of the department of evangelism, he provided evangelistic leadership in the FCC and its successor, the National Council of Churches in the USA. He developed and oversaw many national thrusts in evangelism, such as the national Preaching Mission (1936–1937). In 1954 Bader returned to his own communion, the Christian Churches (Disciples), in a full-time assignment as general secretary of the World Convention. In 1957 his *Evangelism in a Changing America* was published. For Bader, evangelism was the most important business of every Christian and every church. His watchword: "What our Lord made primary we have no right to make secondary."

TIMOTHY K. BEOUGHER

Baez-Camargo, Gonzalo (1899–1983)

Mexican biblical scholar, translator, and writer. Born in Oaxaca, Mexico, he fought in the Mexican Revolution with General Venustiano Carranza, later studied at the United Evangelical Seminary in Mexico City and the National University, and served as a Methodist pastor. In 1929, at age thirty, he served as president of the Second Latin American Evangelical Congress in Havana. Largely self-taught, he became one of Latin America's leading intellectuals—an expert on biblical languages and Near Eastern archaeology, geography, and history, as well as Spanish language and literature, teaching and lecturing on these subjects in Mexico and elsewhere. Baez-Camargo wrote over twenty books on biblical science, languages, archaeology, Christian education, and devotional topics, and translated numerous works into Spanish. He also wrote three articles weekly for the Mexican newspaper *Excelsior* for fifty-three years, under the pseudonym "Pedro Gringoire." But perhaps his greatest contribution was his work on the 1960 revision of the Reina Valera Spanish Bible and the popular-language version *Dios Habla Hoy* (equivalent to *Today's English Version*) of the Bible.

STEPHEN R. SYWULKA

Baillie, Donald Macpherson (1887–1954)

Scottish theologian, pastor, and ecumenist. Born into a manse in Gairloch, he studied at Edinburgh, Marburg, and Heidelberg and was ordained in 1923. After three pastorates he was appointed professor of systematic theology at St. Andrews (1934–1954). His major work, *God Was in Christ* (1948), is one of the classics of the twentieth-century theology. The posthumously published *Theology of the Sacraments* (1957) reflects his ecumenical concern and his desire to reconcile the best in differing sacramental traditions. His first work, *Faith in God* (1927), makes clear his conviction that at every vital point the theologian is compelled to use paradoxical expressions since theology is an attempt to comprehend in human terms a mystery that eludes the human mind. For Baillie the incarnation was the supreme paradox. He believed that we can never eliminate from it the element of paradox without losing the incarnation itself.

Although a shy man, Baillie was revered by his students, and through his support of the Student Christian movement his influence extended well beyond the divinity faculty. He attracted to St. Andrews postgraduate students from many countries. He excelled also as a preacher. His two volumes on sermons, *To Whom Shall We Go?* (1955) and *Out of Nazareth* (1958), exhibit an elegant but simple and direct style.

HENRY R. SEFTON

Baillie, John (1886–1960)

Scottish theologian and writer. Born into a remote Highland manse, he, like his brother Donald, had a strict Calvinist upbringing. After studies at Edinburgh, Jena, and Marburg and service with the YMCA in France (1915–1919), he taught in the United States and Canada (1919–1934) until appointed professor of divinity at Edinburgh University (1934–1956). He achieved worldwide reputation as a liberal orthodox, mediating theologian who wielded an immense influence in church affairs. Baillie's theology was much influenced by Kantian philosophy as mediated by A. S. Pringle-Pattison and Wilhelm Hermann. This is reflected in *The Roots of Religion in the Human Soul* (1926) and *The Interpretation of Religion* (1929). His best-known theological work, *Our Knowledge of God* (1939), owes more to W. E. Hocking and Martin Heidegger. *The Idea of Revelation in Modern Thought* (1956) is in part a reply to Karl Barth's view of revelation. Baillie's best-loved work is *A Diary of Private Prayer* (1936), which has sold 125,000 copies in Britain alone and has been translated into several languages. Baillie was associated (1938–1947) with J. H. Oldham in "The Moot" of Christian intellectuals whose discussions probably influenced his chairmanship of the Church of Scotland Commission on the Interpretation of God's Will in the Present Crisis (1940–1945). Baillie was appointed a president of the World Council of Churches in 1954.

In 1993 David Fergusson edited *Christ, Church and Society: Essays on John Baillie and Donald Baillie.*

HENRY R. SEFTON

Bainton, Roland Herbert (1894–1984)

Church historian. Born in Derbyshire, England, he was the son of a Congregational minister who immigrated to Vancouver with his family in 1896. He graduated from Whitman College and Yale Divinity School, then served with the Red Cross in France during World War I (1917–1918). He took his Ph.D. from Yale University (1921), and served on the faculty, notably as professor of ecclesiastical history (1936–1962; emeritus from 1962). Bainton was both a Congregational minister and an affiliated member of the Society of Friends, with whose Service Committee he worked to relocate refugees from Europe during the Hitler regime. His greatest contributions, however, were in the fields of teaching, research, and writing. His classes were always packed with students and visitors. He maintained unfailing good humor, and rode a ten-speed bicycle between home and office until he was eighty-nine.

His books made a marked impact; sound scholarship combined with readable clarity made him perhaps the most influential church historian of his day. Two books sold more than a million copies: *The Church of Our Fathers* (1941) and *Here I Stand: A Life of Martin Luther* (1950). Other important works included *The Travail of Religious Liberty* (1951), *The Reformation of the Sixteenth Century* (1952), three volumes on *Women of the Reformation* (1971–1977), and the semiautobiographical *Yesterday, Today, and What Next?* (1978).

ROBERT D. LINDER

Balfour, Arthur James (1848–1930)

British prime minister and philosopher. Born in Whittinghame, Scotland, he was educated at Cambridge, and in 1874 entered the House of Commons as a Conservative. He occupied most of the major government offices, culminating in appointment to succeed his uncle, Lord Salisbury, as prime minister (1902–1905). He never shrank from controversy. The vexing questions with which he had to deal included the perennial problem of Ireland and the position of the Jews in Palestine. In 1907 he was responsible for the "Balfour Declaration" in which Britain promised to secure a national home for the Jewish people. Balfour's honors included the prestigious Order of Merit bestowed by King George V, the chancellorship of Cambridge University, the presidency of the British Academy, and an earldom in 1922. When he retired as leader of the Opposition in the House of Commons he was described as being "by universal consent, the most distinguished member of the greatest deliberative assembly in the world." In 1879 Balfour published *A Defence of Philosophic Doubt,* in which he declared that basic convictions rest on the nonrational ground of religious faith. Among his other publications were *The Foundations of Belief* (1895), *Theism and Humanism* (1915), and *Theism and Thought* (1923).

B. E. C. Dugdale, who edited Balfour's *Chapters of Autobiography* (1930), later produced a two-volume biography (1936).

JAMES TAYLOR

Ball, H(enry) C(leophas) (1896–1989)

American publisher of *La Luz Apostólica,* Spanish hymnals, and Spanish Sunday school literature. A native of Brooklyn, Iowa, Ball moved south with his mother and grandfather when he was still a youngster, his Quaker father having died when he was only eight. Intending to move to Mexico, they settled instead in Ricardo, Texas. At the age of fourteen he was saved under the ministry of a Baptist preacher, but, following his mother, joined the Methodist Church. He learned Spanish and immediately began preaching in his hometown, joining the Assemblies of God in 1915. The following year, he began the publication of *La Luz Apostólica,* which continued for fifty years. Ball's mother insisted that her son take piano lessons; although he did not enjoy them, God used that talent in a special way. Seeing the great ministry of the printed word, he began printing song books; in 1917 he published his first, *Himnos de Gloria* (Hymns of Glory), in a words-only edition. Financed with money from his father's estate, he published a new edition with musical notation in 1921. Almost eighty years later, ten thousand copies are still being published every year; it presently contains 329 hymns, of which 66 are from his pen. Other hymnals he published are *Cantos de Triunfo, El Cantor Evangelista,* and *Arpa y Voz de Salmodia.* Ball also published large amounts of Spanish Sunday school literature, and founded the *Casa Evangélica de Publicaciones.* In 1918 he married Sunshine Marshall (who had done missionary work in Mexico with Alice E. Luce). That same year he became the pastor of Templo Cristiano in San Antonio and was also elected the first superintendent of the Latin American District, a post he held until 1939. In 1926 he founded the Latin American Bible Institute. From 1941 to 1943 he served as a missionary to Chile, and for the next ten years he was field secretary for Latin America and the West Indies. From 1943 through 1961 he oversaw the publishing of Spanish literature through *Editorial Vida* until his retirement. He and his wife pioneered the "El Salvador" church in San Antonio.

PHILIP BLYCKER

Barclay, Oliver Rainsford (1919–)

Former general secretary of InterVarsity (UK), scientist, and Anglican lay leader. After an initial science degree at Cambridge University, he went on to a Ph.D. in zoology (1945) and to teaching and further research in that department. Meanwhile, however, he had become closely involved in the work of the InterVarsity Fellowship. He finally forsook a scientific career and gave himself full-time to student work. There was much to do in building up and consolidating IVF chapters in the immediate postwar years and Barclay worked tirelessly, first as universities' secretary, then as deputy secretary, and later on as successor to Douglas Johnson in the top IVF post. Thousands of students have reason to be grateful for Barclay's encouragement and unobtrusive kindness. During those years IVF (now Universities and Colleges Christian Fellowship) grew in numbers and influence, as did its role in the nurture of scholarship, seen in the establishment of Tyndale House, Cambridge, as an evangelical research center. In all of these developments Barclay made a substantial contribution, not least in his own writings, which include *Reasons for Faith* (1974) and *Developing a Christian Mind* (1984), published in the United States as *The Intellect and Beyond* (1985). In retirement he has been editor of *Christians in Science* since 1989.

J. D. DOUGLAS

Barclay, William (1907–1978)

New Testament scholar. Born in Wick, Scotland, he studied at Glasgow and Marburg universities, was ordained in the Church of Scotland, and ministered in industrial Renfrew (1933–1946) before appointment as lecturer (1947) and professor (1964) at Glasgow University. Barclay combined sound classical scholarship with an ability to communicate with ordinary people. His *Daily Study Bible* (New Testament) series sold some 1.5 million copies and was translated into many languages. Like C. S. Lewis, he sought to "make righteousness readable." His ministry extended beyond preaching to a successful religious television series, a worldwide correspondence, conducting the college choir, a long-running column in the *British Weekly*, a pastoral concern for his students, and the authorship of more than fifty books.

His *Testament of Faith* (American title *A Spiritual Autobiography*) (1975) rejected substitutionary atonement and regarded miracles mainly as symbols of what God can still do. Barclay was reticent about the inspiration of

Scripture and expressed serious doubts about the Virgin Birth. Yet the man described by a close friend as "an incorrigible coat-trailer" and by himself as "a liberal evangelical" believed that Matthew, Luke, and John wrote the Gospels attributed to them, and put Bultmann in the forefront of evangelical preachers because he confronted the individual with the living Christ. Barclay advised male ministers to marry, but their women colleagues to remain single, urged the clergy to have nonreligious interests, and encouraged all believers to have "a time set aside in daily life when you look and speak (even in slender faith) to Him." Barclay retired officially in 1974, but became visiting professor at Strathclyde University where he lectured on professional ethics. In 1969 Queen Elizabeth II made him Commander of the Order of the British Empire (CBE).

Biographies by R. D. Kernohan (ed.) (1980), James Martin (1984), and C. L. Rawlins (1984).

J. D. Douglas

Baring-Gould, Sabine (1834–1924)

Anglican clergyman and writer. Born in Exeter and educated at Cambridge, he taught school until ordination in 1964. A High Churchman, he served parishes in Yorkshire and Essex, during which time he inherited considerable family estates, enabling him to indulge his love of travel and literature. His output was immense and wide-ranging, including works on werewolves, medieval myths, and Iceland and other regions. While not generally regarded as a weighty writer, he had a lively and refreshing style. His more religious works included several volumes on the lives of the saints (which the Roman Catholic Church banned), *Origin and Development of Religious Belief* (1871), *The Evangelical Revival* (1920), and *Early Reminiscences, 1834–64* (1923). Baring-Gould, who spent his last years in charge of the parish of Lew Trenchard, Devon, is best remembered for two hymns: "Onward, Christian Soldiers" and "Now the Day Is Over."

J. D. Douglas

Barnardo, Thomas John (1845–1905)

Evangelist and philanthropist. Born in Dublin, he was converted in 1862, was turned down by the China Inland Mission, and dropped his medical studies for work with destitute children. He founded the East End Juvenile Mission in 1868, and opened his first homes for boys (1870) and girls (1876) on the principle of "no destitute child ever refused admission." Besides basic schooling, boys learned industrial trades and girls domestic skills. Nearly 60,000 children were housed during his lifetime, and over 16,000 were helped to emigrate, chiefly to Canada. He also ran schemes for boarding out orphans and the children of unmarried mothers. Convinced that parental alcoholism was the root cause of most of his charges' troubles, he became a total abstainer, and in 1872 turned the Edinburgh Castle, a notorious London gin palace, into an attractive adult recreation center, coffee house, library, and mission church. Barnardo was a man of strong beliefs who excited strong reactions. Neither contemporary controversy nor later legend can mask the void in public child care provision that his work filled until legislation was enacted over forty years after his death.

Memoirs of the Late Dr. Barnardo were produced by Mrs. Barnardo and J. Marchant (1907). Biographies by J. W. Bready (1930) and G. Wagner (1979).

PHILIP HILLYER

Barnes, Ernest William (1874–1953)

Anglican bishop and controversialist. Born into a Baptist family in Birmingham, he did brilliantly at Cambridge where he lectured in mathematics until 1915. In 1902 he was ordained in the Church of England without any theological training. He ministered in the Temple Church, London, and was then canon of Westminster before appointment to Birmingham in 1924. He fiercely preached pacifism during World War I, but ended up "going to war" with his Anglo-Catholic clergy, and was a thorn in the flesh to four successive archbishops of Canterbury. He caused uproar after uproar, culminating in *The Rise of Christianity* (1947), which denied Gospel miracles and generally questioned historic Christian doctrine. Barnes distrusted Roman Catholicism for its "sheltering a host of pagan corruptions and moral evasions." In 1933 he publicly protested against Nazi treatment of the Jews, yet he tentatively advocated euthanasia and sterilization of the feeble-minded. He championed women's causes, including the right of ordination, and wanted the Anglican communion service open to all Christians. He condemned abortion, bad housing, and inadequate film censorship. He strongly upheld sexual purity and Sunday observance, and was a supporter of missionary work in China. His saints were of the activist type: St. Paul, David Livingstone, Elizabeth Fry, General Booth.

John Barnes called the biography of his radical yet oddly conservative father *Ahead of His Time* (1979).

J. D. DOUGLAS

Barnhouse, Donald Grey (1895–1960)

American Presbyterian pastor, preacher, and writer. Born in Watsonville, California, he earned a Th.D. from Aix-en-Provence, France, after attending Biola, Princeton Seminary, the University of Chicago, and the University of Pennsylvania. Having served in World War I, he was ordained in 1918. Under the Belgian Gospel Mission (1919–1921) he directed a Bible school in Brussels and pastored two French Reformed churches in southern France. He early and strongly disagreed with what he saw as encroaching liberalism within the church. As minister of the Tenth Presbyterian Church, Philadelphia, from 1927 he became a leading figure in the fundamentalist-modernist controversy within the Presbyterian Church, USA. His fiery defense of fundamentalist doctrine led to a reprimand by the Philadelphia presbytery in 1932. Barnhouse brought the nearly dissolved Tenth Presbyterian Church to an international ministry. His multifaceted career included Monday night classes in New York's theater district, national radio Bible preaching from 1928 until his death, the founding and editing of two monthly magazines (*Revelation*, 1931–1949 and *Eternity*, 1950–1960), authorship of numerous books, and the writing and narrating of television films. Later in life his attitude mellowed and he sought to heal the breach with the presbytery, the World Council of Churches, and liberal Christianity.

Biography by M. N. Barnhouse (1983).

JACK MITCHELL

Barrows, Cliff (1923–)

Music and program director. Born in Ceres, California, he was ordained as a Baptist minister in 1944. His association with Billy Graham began the following year at a Youth for Christ rally in Asheville, North Carolina, and he has been responsible for the music programming in Billy Graham crusades since they started in 1949. "The Christian faith is a singing faith," he says, "and a good way to express it and share it with others is in community singing." His warm and encouraging presence has brought out the best in crusade choirs throughout the world. Barrows has also been heard on the "Hour of Decision" for four decades. His significant contributions to gospel music were recognized in 1988 when he was inducted into the Nashville Gospel Music Association Hall of Fame.

J. D. DOUGLAS

Barth, Karl (1886–1968)

Probably the most influential theologian of the twentieth century. Born in Basel, Barth's earliest theological orientation was the conservative Swiss Calvinism of his father, Fritz Barth. However, his student years at the universities of Berlin and Marburg saw Barth embrace the Protestant liberalism of Harnack and Hermann, only to reject its "relgious individualism" and its emphasis on "historical relativism" a few years later. Having taken on a pastorate in Safenwil in 1911, Barth found that liberalism was inadequate to the pastor's task. Further, Barth's faith in liberalism was decisively shaken by the capitulation of his liberal mentors to the German war policy in World War I, thus forcing him to reappraise his theological commitments. The result of his reorientation was the epoch-making commentary on Romans in 1919, which established what was designated dialectical theology or the theology of crisis.

New influences continued to assert themselves. Kierkegaardian existentialism came within the Barthian orbit, but above all, the young Barth carefully read Luther and Calvin. A greatly revised second edition of Barth's commentary that was published in 1922 reflected a deeper acquaintance with the sixteenth-century Reformers. The success of his *Romans* led to a succession of academic appointments, beginning in Göttingen in 1922, and then subsequently at Münster, Bonn, and finally Basel until his retirement in 1962. While at Bonn, Barth's opposition to the Nazis led to his expulsion from Germany in 1935. He returned to Basel where he continued to develop his theological vision that was articulated in his magnum opus, the *Church Dogmatics* (1936–1977). It was also during the 1930s that Barth broke with Emil Brunner over the question of natural theology.

The significance of Barth rests principally on his devastating critique of nineteenth-century Protestant liberalism, which inaugurated a theological revolution. Barth's importance is not merely negative. He sought to construct a positive theology that gave central importance to Christ as the Word of God. As critic and theologian, he returned the center of theological attention to historic questions such as the absolute sovereignty of God, the authority of biblical revelation, and the role of Christ in reconciliation. His *Church Dogmatics* will remain a monument to his genius and ingenuity. Modern judgments of Barth's enduring significance, however, differ greatly. Those who count themselves as followers judge him to have established the basis for all future theology, while others confine his theological importance to his eloquent criticism of nineteenth-century Protestant liberalism. Indeed, the latter argue that Barth himself did not escape fully the bounds of Protestant liberalism.

Among Barth's publications are *The Word of God and the Word of Man* (1928), *Letters* (1960–1968), *Prayer and Preaching* (1964), *Evangelical Theology* (1968), *Ethics* (1981), and *Witness to the Word* (1986).

In addition to the biography by Eberhard Busch (1976), numerous studies on Barth's theology have been published, including those by G. C. Berkouwer (1956), F. H. Klooster (1961), K. Runia (1962), T. F. Torrance (1962), C. Van Til (1962), H. Kung (1966), Colin Brown (1967), J. Bowden (1971), S. W. Sykes (1979), G. C. Bolich (1980), and D. K. McKim, ed. (1986).

FRANK A. JAMES III

Bashir, Anthony (1898–1966)

Antiochean Orthodox archbishop of New York. Born in Douma, Lebanon, to a devout Orthodox family, he studied at the American University in Beirut and the School of Law in Baabda. He joined the teaching staff at American University. He oversaw a new Arabic translation of the New Testament. He was sent to the United States by the patriarch of Antioch in 1922, and served as a special representative of the church to the general convention of the Episcopal Church. He made good use of his bilingual skills, translating works from Arabic to English, including many of Khalil Gibran's writings. Additionally, he instituted the use of English in the liturgy and encouraged translation of *The Word*, a periodical of the archdiocese, into English. In 1935 he was elected to fill the post of archbishop for the North American Church. He worked tirelessly for the uniting of American branches of the Orthodox Church. As part of that work, he established ties with St. Vladimir's Orthodox Seminary (of the Russian Orthodox Church) when his own church was unable to support its own seminary. He also played a significant role in the founding of the Orthodox Federation (now the Standing Conference of Orthodox Bishops), holding the office of vice president from its inception in 1960 until his death.

A. SCOTT MOREAU

Battles, Ford Lewis (1915–1979)

Church historian. Born in Erie, Pennsylvania, he graduated in classics from West Virginia University (1936) and in English from Tufts University (1938). His time as Rhodes scholar at Exeter College, Oxford, under the tutelage of C. S. Lewis was disrupted by World War II. During the war Battles served in intelligence with the U.S. Air Force, but remained an active member of the Association of American Rhodes Scholars. He earned his Ph.D. in church history at the Hartford Seminary Foundation with a translation and critical analysis of the *First Book of the Homilies of Gregory the Great*. He taught there with distinction (1950–1967), at the Pittsburgh Seminary (1967–1978), and at Calvin Theological Seminary (1978–1979).

Battles earned the respect of his numerous graduate students in whom he inspired a lasting love of learning, and he established a reputation among historians for his analytic skills that were balanced by a profound spirituality. In addition to writing hymns, he served on the hymnal committee of the United Church of Christ, USA. He combined dedicated churchmanship with the highest scholarship, exemplifying characteristics of the ideal Christian humanist. In his extensive literary legacy are carefully annotated translations of selected texts from the writings of Gregory the Great, John Wycliffe, Thomas à Kempis, and Erasmus of Rotterdam. Particularly noteworthy are his translations of *Calvin's Commentary on Seneca's De Clementia*, and of Calvin's 1536 and 1559 editions of *The Institutes of the Christian Religion*.

EDWARD J. FURCHA

Bavinck, Herman (1854–1921)

Dutch Reformed theologian. Born in Hogeveen, he was educated at the University of Leiden and the Theological Seminary at Kampen. After serving a church at Franeker (1881–1882) he became professor of systematic theology at Kampen (1882–1902) and then succeeded Abraham Kuyper at the Free University of Amsterdam (1902–1921). He attempted to reconcile opposing viewpoints in the Dutch Reformed Church, and related education and social science to theology. His major contribution was his four-volume *Reformed Dogmatics* (*Gereformeerde Dogmatiek*) published between 1895 and 1901, the second volume of which, translated into English as *The Doctrine of God* in 1955, demonstrates the biblical basis of his thought as well as his firm grasp of historical theology. Among his other works are *Our Reasonable Faith,* a popularized version of *Gereformeerde Dogmatiek* (1956), and *The Philosophy of Revelation* (1953).

ROBERT G. CLOUSE

Bavinck, Johan Herman (1895–1964)

Dutch missiologist. Born in Rotterdam, nephew of the famous theologian Herman Bavinck, he was reared in the pietistic wing of the Gereformeerde Kerken. He showed an early predilection for psychology, the subject of his Erlangen doctoral thesis (1919). However, Bavinck also studied theology at the Free University of Amsterdam, and served as a pastor of Dutch churches in Sumatra and Java (1919–1926), pastor in Heemstede, the Netherlands (1926–1929), missionary to central Java (1929–1939), and first professor of missions at the Theological Seminary in Kampen, the Netherlands (1939–1955). He also taught at the Free University of Amsterdam, and eventually became professor of practical theology there (1955–1964).

In the early 1940s Bavinck attempted unsuccessfully to mediate in the doctrinal crisis in the Gereformeerde Kerken. After World War II ended he helped both to bring to a halt the paternalism of his church's foreign missionary enterprises and to set up the Missionary Center in Baarn and the Missionary Seminary (later part of the Hendrik Kraemer Institute). He became an expert on Javanese religion, especially its mysticism, and a popular teacher. A prolific and fluent author, he arranged for his major works to be translated into English: *The Impact of Christianity on the Non-Christian World* (1948), *Introduction to the Science of Missions* (1960), and *The Church between Temple and Mosque* (1966).

THOMAS G. REID, JR.

Bayne, Stephen Fielding (1908–1974)

Anglican bishop and educator. Born in New York City, he earned degrees at Amherst College (1929) and General Theological Seminary (1933). He was ordained to the priesthood of the Episcopal Church (also known as the Protestant Espiscopal Church in the USA) in 1933. He pastored churches in St. Louis and Northampton, Massachusetts (1934–1942), and then was chaplain of Columbia University (1942–1947), during which time he took a two-year leave to serve as chaplain to the U.S. Navy during World War II. In 1947 he was elected bishop of Olympia, Washington, the membership of which doubled by the time he retired in 1959. He was executive officer of the 40 million-member Anglican communion from 1960 to 1964, and was first vice president of the executive council of the Episcopal Church (1964–1970). As an educator he chaired the Religions Department at Columbia University from 1942 to 1947. In 1970 he became professor of Christian mission and ascetical theology at General Theological Seminary for three years. He authored numerous books, among them *The Optional God* (1953), *Christian Living* (1957), *Enter with Joy* (1961), and *An Anglican Turning Point* (1964).

H. DOUGLAS BUCKWALTER

Bea, Augustin (1881–1968)

Cardinal and ecumenist. Born in Riedbohringen, Germany, he entered the Society of Jesus (Jesuits) in 1902 and was ordained a priest in 1912. In 1921 he was appointed provincial of the Jesuits in Germany and six years later became a professor at the Gregorian University in Rome. In 1928 he was appointed as professor of Old Testament at the Pontifical Biblical Institute in Rome, where he also served as rector of the university (1930–1949). From 1931 to 1951 he served as editor of the scholarly journal, *Biblica.* In 1945 Pope Pius XII appointed him as his personal confessor. In 1959 he was made a cardinal by Pope John XXIII and one year later was appointed president of the newly created Secretariat for Promoting Christian Unity. During the Second Vatican Council both Bea and the Secretariat played a prominent role both in guiding the deliberations of the Council and in maintaining contact with the non-Roman Catholic observer-delegates whose presence at the Council was unprecedented in history. Many of his writings deal with ecumenism including *The Unity of Christians* (1963), *Unity in Freedom* (1964), *The Study of the Synoptic Gospels* (1965), *Church and the Jewish People* (1966), *Word of God and Mankind* (1967), *Peace among Christians* (1967), *We Who Serve* (1969), and *Ecumenism in Focus* (1969).

L. K. GRIMLEY

Beach, Harlan Page (1845–1933)

Congregationalist minister and missiologist. Born in South Orange, New Jersey, he graduated from Yale (1878) and Andover Theological Seminary (1883), and after ordination was a missionary in China where he displayed extraordinary ability in mastering the language. By 1890 he had returned because of his wife's health, and in 1892 took a teaching position at the School for Christian Workers in Springfield, Massachusetts. As educational secretary of the Student Volunteer movement (1895–1906) he exerted a wide influence in missionary education as one of the originators of the annual study books on missionary countries, and as head of the preparation of the first-ever compendium of *The Geography and Atlas of Protestant Missions* (2 vols., 1901–1903). In 1906 he became professor of theory and practice of missions at Yale Divinity School, where he initiated the first department of Christian missions at any seat of learning in the world. During 1920–1928 he was lecturer on missions at Drew Theological Seminary. As a Fellow of the Royal Geographical Society he rendered great service to the cause of Christian missions by his sane, well-informed lectures and writings on many phases of the church's work. His publications include *New Testament Studies in Missions* (1898), *India and Christian Opportunity* (1904), *Missions as a Cultural Factor in the Pacific* (1927), and (as co-author) *World Missionary Atlas* (1925).

JACK MITCHELL

Bell, George Kennedy Allen (1883–1958)

Anglican bishop and ecumenist. Born in Hayling Island, Hampshire, he was educated at Oxford, and after ordination in 1907 served a parish in Leeds. In 1910 he returned to Oxford as tutor, and then became chaplain to Archbishop Davidson (1914–1922), whose biography he would later write (1935). Bell became dean of Canterbury (1924–1929) before consecration as bishop of Chichester (1929–1958). He was secretary of the 1930 Lambeth Conference, and was a strong ecumenist, especially in the promotion of relations with the Lutheran churches.

In World War II he courted unpopularity when, a lone voice in the House of Lords, he condemned the saturation bombing of German cities and criticized Winston Churchill's policy of unconditional surrender as the only way of ending the conflict. Bell had earlier made friends with Martin Niemoeller and Dietrich Bonhoeffer, having met the latter in neutral Sweden in 1942. Bell's stance may have disqualified him for the primacy when Archbishop Temple died suddenly in 1944.

Bell played a key part in the establishment of the World Council of Churches, of which he was the first chairman of the central committee (1948–1958) and an honorary president (1954). Apart from four series of *Documents on Christian Unity* (1924–1958), his published works included *The Church and Humanity* (1946), *Christian Unity: The Anglican Position* (1948), and *The Kingship of Christ* (1954).

Biography by R. C. D. Jasper (1967).

J. D. DOUGLAS

Bell, L(emuel) Nelson (1894–1973)

Medical missionary, author, and church leader. Born in Virginia of devout Presbyterian parents, he committed himself to medical missions while pursuing a law degree at Washington and Lee University. Following graduation from the Medical College of Virginia (1916) he accepted an appointment to a Presbyterian hospital in Kiangsu (now Jiangsu) Province, China. Under his supervision it became the largest Presbyterian mission hospital in the world, despite difficult social and political conditions. Deeply

49

committed to meeting both physical and spiritual needs, Bell made it a center for advanced medical care, medical training, and evangelism. He was made a Fellow of the American College of Surgeons for his pioneering work on kala-azar (black fever).

Forced to leave China in 1941 because of the Japanese invasion, Nelson and Virginia Bell and their four children moved to Montreat, North Carolina. Although busy as a surgeon, Bell soon became active in his denomination (Presbyterian Church in the USA), helping establish the *Presbyterian Journal* to combat growing liberal trends. More influential was his role as founder (with son-in-law Billy Graham and Carl Henry) and executive editor of *Christianity Today* magazine. In 1972 he was elected moderator of the Presbyterian Church in the USA. He was the subject of J. C. Pollock's *A Foreign Devil in China* (1971).

JOHN N. AKERS

Bellavin, Tikhon B. (1865–1925)

Russian Orthodox archbishop. Born near Pskov, Russia, he attended seminary there and at the theological academy at St. Petersburg. In the years after his graduation, he accepted posts at the seminaries in Pskov, Kholm, and Kazan. In 1897 he was consecrated bishop of Lublin. He was elected bishop of the Aleutians and Alaska in 1898, giving him responsibility over the North American work of the Orthodox Church. In 1905, to meet the needs of the Ukrainian immigrants in New York, he arranged for the transfer of the diocesan center from San Francisco to New York. In the same year he was given the title of archbishop. Before his return to Russia in 1907, he was a strong proponent of Orthodox unity in the Americas and the use of English in liturgical services. After his return to Russia, he was elected metropolitan of Moscow (1917). The office of patriarch, which had been banned in 1700 by Peter the Great, was reestablished in 1917, and Bellavin was elected to the office. Though he tried to take a politically neutral stand during and after the Bolshevik revolution and the Russian civil war, he was incarcerated for one year (1922–1923). He died under unknown circumstances.

A. SCOTT MOREAU

Bender, Carl Jacob (1869–1935)

Pioneer missionary to German Kamerun (West Africa). Born in Baden, Germany, he emigrated at age twelve to Buffalo, New York. Following studies (1893–1899) at German Baptist Seminary in Rochester, New York, he was sent to West Africa by the Berlin-based German Baptist Missionary Society. After ten years in the Douala and Abo regions he transferred to Soppo, in the Mount Cameroon foothills, to develop training facilities for nationals and a convalescent center for missionaries. He worked also in Victoria (Linhe) with some of Alfred Saker's successors and converts.

By early 1914 all Protestant ventures in Cameroon were thriving; representatives met in unprecedented cooperation to plan the future. But in July—contrary to Allied assurances of nonbelligerence in the colonies—World War I expanded to Africa. Berlin-related missionaries were imprisoned and shipped to holding camps. Neutral country workers were deported; the Baselers (Swiss) suffered the worst treatment and greatest property loss. After a short imprisonment in Douala, the Benders adamantly resisted expulsion on grounds of American citizenship. They finally were allowed to return to Soppo, but under stringent conditions: no salary, no communication with children in Europe, no food but what they could raise, no imported supplies, no extended travel. Nonetheless, by 1919 a network of thirty Soppo outstations had been founded for which Bender trained Cameroonians as pastors, evangelists, and teachers. He ordained several special leaders as the first overseers of what he foresaw as an indigenous enterprise. From America he later sent them funds, supplies, and numerous encouraging letters. Other men he sent to Douala to assist Paris Mission workers who in 1917 had come to preserve all orphaned Protestant work. Bender pastored and promoted missions in America (1920–1929), but in late 1929 returned to Soppo to supervise postwar reconstruction of the coastal and inland Baptist work. He died there and was buried alongside the church he had designed and built.

HELGA BENDER HENRY

Bender, Harold Stauffer (1897–1962)

Mennonite historian, theologian, and churchman. Born in Elkhart, Indiana, he graduated from Goshen College, Garrett Biblical Institute, Princeton University, Princeton Theological Seminary, and Heidelberg University (D.Theol., 1935). He joined the faculty of Goshen College to teach Bible and church history in 1924, left to study in Heidelberg in 1930, but became so involved in relief work for Russian Mennonites in North Germany that he was unable to complete his dissertation until he returned to the United States. The Mennonite Central Committee was so pleased with his work that he was asked to become assistant secretary in 1931. He became dean of Goshen College in 1933, and dean of Goshen Seminary in 1944, a position he held until his death. An active churchman, he served on many committees and organizations, and presided over the Mennonite World Conference (1952–1962). His written works include *Two Centuries of American Mennonite Literature* (1929) and *The Anabaptist Vision* (1943). He founded what became the *Mennonite Quarterly Review* and edited it until 1962. He also edited *The Mennonite Encyclopedia* (4 vols., 1955–1959).

Biography by J. C. Wenger et al. (1964).

A. SCOTT MOREAU

Benedict XV (1854–1922)

Pope from 1914. Born Giacomo della Chiesa into an aristocratic family in Genoa, he graduated from the university there, studied theology in Rome, and was ordained in 1878. He entered the papal diplomatic service and served in Spain (1883–1887) before returning to the Vatican where his work involved him in much travel. He was appointed archbishop of Bologna in 1907 and cardinal in 1914. In that same year he became pontiff. Much of his attention was taken up by problems arising from World War I (1914–1918). He sought to maintain a neutral stance and unsuccessfully tried to be a mediator between the warring powers. He did, however, negotiate the exchange of prisoners of war and promoted relief work in war-torn countries. Also a supporter of missions, in the postwar years Benedict endeavored to normalize relations with the secular powers. He mended the breach with France, and arranged for a British representative to be appointed to the Vatican for the first time since the seventeenth century.

Biography by W. H. Peters (1959).

J. D. Douglas

Bennett, John Coleman (1902–)

Theologian, educator, and ecumenical leader. Born in Kingston, Ontario, into the home of a Presbyterian minister, he grew up in Morristown, New Jersey, and graduated from Williams College, Oxford University, and Union Theological Seminary. In 1930 he became assistant professor of Christian theology at Auburn Theological Seminary in New York (1931–1938). Bennett identified himself with the liberal Protestant theological movement, and pursued as his primary interest the relation of the church and its immediate social context (*Social Salvation: A Religious Approach to the Problems of Social Change* [1935] and *Christianity—And Our World* [1936]). After teaching at the Pacific School of Religion (1938–1943) and serving as a minister in the Congregational and Christian Churches, Bennett in 1943 joined the faculty at Union Theological Seminary as the Reinhold Niebuhr professor of social ethics. He remained at Union until his retirement in 1970. From 1955 until 1963 he served as dean, and from 1963 until 1970 as president. While at Union he became a leader in the ecumenical movement, attending the first assembly of the World Council of Churches in 1948 as a delegate. His works include *Christian Realism* (1941), *The Radical Imperative* (1975), and *U.S. Foreign Policy and Christian Ethics* (1977).

A. Scott Moreau

Benson, Clarence Herbert (1879–1954)

Presbyterian pastor, educator, and author. Coming from a family line peopled by Moravian missionaries, public school teachers, and school superintendents, he studied at the University of Minnesota, Macalester College, and Princeton Seminary. After serving pastorates in New York and Pennsylvania (1908–1919) he was called to the Union Church of Kobe, Japan, but returned to the United States in 1922 and taught at Moody Bible Institute, where in 1924 he became director of the Christian education department. Convinced that teachers needed to be trained to teach others the Word of God, he wrote a number of textbooks on Christian education, and produced the *All-Bible Graded Series* of Sunday school lessons. In order to publish his works, he co-founded Scripture Press (1924), and then further implemented his vision by founding both the Evangelical Teacher Training Association and the National Sunday School Association. Through a steady stream of student-disciples, the effect of his books, and the worldwide impact of the organizations he started, his ministry has influenced literally millions of people throughout the world.

JACK MITCHELL

Berdyaev, Nicolai Alexandrovich (1874–1948)

Eastern Orthodox philosopher and writer. Born in Kiev, Russia, he was educated at the universities of Kiev and Heidelberg. His strong advocacy of Marxism during student days led to a three-year exile in northern Russia. In 1907 he joined the Russian Orthodox Church, which in 1914 initiated proceedings against him for nonconformity, and would have led eventually to sentencing had not the Russian Revolution thrown the country into turmoil. He became professor of philosophy at Moscow University (1920–1922) but his lifelong nonconformity again proved to be his undoing. He was dismissed from his post and banished from the Soviet Union for his steady opposition to the country's new rulers. He spent the rest of his life in Berlin and Paris. A prolific writer influenced by Immanuel Kant and the mystic Jakob Boehme, Berdyaev is often identified as a "Christian existentialist." He seemed to be obsessed by the problem of man's freedom, and held that truth originated in "a light which breaks through from the transcendent world of the spirit" into our confused world. Among his books available in English translation are *Freedom and the Spirit* (1935), *The Destiny of Man* (1937), *The Origin of Russian Communism* (1937), *Dream and Reality: An Essay in Autobiography* (1950), and *The Beginning and the End* (1952).

Biography by Matthew Spinka (1950).

J. D. DOUGLAS

Berggrav, Eivind (1884–1959)

Norwegian bishop and ecumenist. Born in Stavanger, he studied at the universities of Oslo, Copenhagen, Marburg, Oxford, and Cambridge. He served as teacher, pastor, and prison chaplain before becoming bishop of Tromso (1928–1937) and Oslo (1937–1950). During World War II he became a leader in the church's resistance to the German occupation. He was the driving force behind strong declarations and pastoral letters that gave clear guidance in an hour of peril. During 1942–1945 he was under heavily guarded house arrest, but still managed to lead the church's struggle. Having been impressed as a young man by meeting John Mott, Berggrav developed into what W. A. Visser 't Hooft called "one of the shepherds of the ecumenical movement"; he later served as a WCC president (1950–1954). He was never, however, a spokesman for unity based on external institutional fusions. His main interests were the "practical" aspects of ecumenism: a common experience of Christian fellowship and common actions of social responsibility. He saw no contradiction between a confessional basis and an ecumenical attitude. Lay Christians of the pietist tradition were sometimes uneasy because he wanted to establish a fruitful relation between the church and contemporary cultural life. Generally, however, he chose to remain outside theological conflicts. He published about thirty books. Among English translations of his works are *War and Religion* (1920), *The Norwegian Church in Its International Setting* (1946), and *Man and State* (1951).

Biographies by Alex Johnson (1949) and Odd Godal (1960).

OLLA TULLUAN

Berkhof, Louis (1873–1957)

Reformed theologian. Born in Emmen, Holland, he came to the United States in 1882, settling in Grand Rapids, Michigan, where he basically lived the rest of his life. He graduated from the Theological School of the Christian Reformed Church (later Calvin College and Seminary) and Princeton Theological Seminary. In 1906 Berkhof was appointed to Calvin Seminary, teaching in the biblical department from 1906 to 1926 and systematic theology from 1926 to 1944, when he retired. He was also Calvin Seminary's president from 1931 to 1944.

Berkhof steered the Christian Reformed Church through turbulent days that included the Bultema controversy (premillennialism), the Janssen controversy (higher criticism), and the common grace controversy surrounding Herman Hoeksema and Henry Danhof.

In his later years Berkhof became increasingly vigorous in his rejection of liberalism and in a call for conservative theologians to work more closely together. Berkhof's life has been summarized as "a fusion of simple piety, a high theology, and an unswerving devotion to the Reformed faith."

Berkhof was author of numerous works (a bibliography covers 52 pages), including *New Testament Introduction* (1915), *The History of Christian Doctrine* (1949), *The Kingdom of God* (1951), *Aspects of Liberalism* (1951), and his magnum opus, *Systematic Theology* (rev. 1941), which has been through twenty-three printings to date. In it he carefully sets out a classic Calvinistic formulation of theology, in the tradition of G. Vos, A. Kuyper, C. Hodge, and, especially, H. Bavinck, whose work he follows very closely.

WALTER A. ELWELL

Berkouwer, Gerrit Cornelis (1903–)

Reformed theologian. Born in Amsterdam, he received his theological training at the Free University there (Ph.D., 1932). He began teaching there in 1940, and was appointed to the chair of dogmatics in 1945, succeeding both Abraham Kuyper and Herman Bavinck who had strongly influenced his theological life. He retired in 1973. Berkouwer was strongly committed to the Reformation principles of *sola scripture* and *sola fide*, and thus found himself staunchly lined up against liberalism for its denial of normative revelation, neo-orthodoxy for its denial of theological objectivity, and Roman Catholicism for its denial of Faith Alone. In *Conflict with Rome* (ET, 1958) and *The Second Vatican Council and the New Theology* (1965), Berkouwer's trenchant analyses of Roman Catholic thought are developed. In *The Triumph of Grace in the Theology of Karl Barth* (ET, 1956) a more mellow approach to Barth prevails over an earlier, harsher polemic. Berkouwer is best remembered for his fourteen volumes (in English), *Studies in Dogmatics* (1952–1975), in which he covers the basic topics of theology from revelation to the age to come. Throughout the series Berkouwer remains true to his Reformation position by arguing biblically (not dogmatically), stressing that faith is always receptive and not a correlative of grace, and downplaying the place of fallen human rationality.

WALTER A. ELWELL

Bertuzzi, Federico (1948–)

Baptist pastor and missiologist. Born in Santa Fe, Argentina, where he was reared by his widowed German mother, he experienced rebirth at the age of eighteen while studying in Berlin, and was baptized in the Danube. He then participated in three summer crusades (1967–1969) with Operation Mobilization. A semester at Bibel und Missiosschule Brake in Germany was followed by a four-year pastoral program in the Buenos Aires Bible Institute in 1974, in which year Bertuzzi was ordained as a Baptist pastor. He is the founder and director of Misiones Mundiales, a national catalyst for world missions. He helped initiate the first Latin agency to Muslims, (PM International) and is their current vice president. He is executive secretary of COMIBAM, a Latin agency dedicated to missions promotion throughout the continent, and edits its bulletin, *Luz Para las Naciones.* He serves on various national and international committees, and has edited some twenty books and missions articles.

JONATHAN LEWIS

Bethune, Mary McLeod (1875–1955)

Educator and advocate. Born to former slaves in Mayesville, South Carolina, she was the only one of the seventeen children in her family who was able to attend the local school (Mayesville Presbyterian Mission for

Negroes). She also studied at Scotia Seminary (Concord, North Carolina) and graduated from Moody Bible Institute in 1895. She applied and was rejected twice for missionary work in Africa, and then turned her focus to the education of African-Americans in the United States. After teaching for several years, she founded her own school, Daytona Normal and Industrial School for Girls (in Daytona Beach) in 1904. The school started with five students but grew steadily. In 1923 it merged with Cookman Institute to become Bethune–Cookman College, and achieved full accreditation as a liberal arts college in 1941. Bethune served as the college president until 1942. She was also active in the National Association for Colored Women, being elected to the presidency in 1927. In 1935 she founded the National Council of Negro Women, which presented a comprehensive agenda for women to the U.S. government. She also accepted the position of Director for Negro Affairs and thus joined Roosevelt's "Black Cabinet" from 1935 to 1943. She dedicated her life to the restoration of dignity to African-American women in the United States.

Biography by C. O. Peare (1951).

A. SCOTT MOREAU

Beyerhaus, Peter (1929–)

German missiologist. Following missionary service in South Africa and doctoral studies at Uppsala, Beyerhaus has taught at the University of Tübingen for many years. He has been particularly interested in demonstrating the relationship between a high view of the authority of the Bible and a strong commitment to missionary work. Thus Beyerhaus has become one of the most trenchant critics of the approach of the World Council of Churches to missionary and theological questions in recent decades. He was one of the prime movers in the Theological Convention in Frankfurt in 1970, which produced the Frankfurt Declaration. A number of Beyerhaus's major works are available in English: *The Responsible Church and the Foreign Mission* (1964), *Missions: Which Way?* (1971), *Shaken Foundations: Theological Foundations for Mission* (1972), and *Bangkok '73: The Beginning or the End of World Mission?* (1974).

THOMAS G. REID, JR.

Biederwolf, William Edward (1867–1939)

Presbyterian evangelist. Born in Monticello, Indiana, he was converted after overhearing a sermon while waiting for his parents outside the local Presbyterian church. He graduated from Princeton University (1892) and Theological Seminary (1895), studied further at the universities of Erlangen and Berlin, and was ordained in 1897. He pastored for three years in Logansport, Indiana, served briefly as a chaplain in the Spanish American War, then assisted J. Wilbur Chapman before launching his own ministry in 1906. Over the next three decades he held scores of evangelistic meetings in small and medium-sized cities. He also wrote numerous works against the cults, was a strong advocate of premillennialism, and promoted integrity among evangelists. In 1909 he organized the Family Altar League to encourage family Bible study. In 1922 he became director of the Winona Lake Bible Conference, and the following year assumed the directorship of the Winona Lake School of Theology. From 1929 until his death he ministered in a unique church in Palm Beach, Florida, which held services only during the winter tourist season. Biederwolf wrote *The Millennium Bible* (1924).

Biography by R. E. Garrett (1948).

TIMOTHY K. BEOUGHER

Billing, Einar Magnus (1871–1939)

Lutheran bishop and theologian. Born a bishop's son in Lund, Sweden, he was educated at the University of Uppsala where he was lecturer (1900) and professor of systematic theology (1909) before becoming bishop of Vasteras (1920–1939). His first major writing, on Luther's attitude toward the state, published in 1900, signaled a revival of Luther studies in Sweden. Billings' approach was historical and systematic. He also wrote on revelation and the Bible, and in doing so facilitated an acceptance of liberal critical studies in Swedish theology. After his appointment as bishop he wrote a major study of the national church, which emphasized the authority of the church over against the state. His theology had two themes: the exodus stemming from the Old Testament and the forgiveness of sins based on the Gospels. While emphasizing the national church and its parishes, he argued for the right of free churchmen to opt out of the state church. G. Wingren wrote *An Exodus Theology: Einar Billing and the Development of Modern Swedish Theology* (1969).

Biography by E. Montan (1943).

NOEL S. POLLARD

Bingham, Rowland Victor (1872–1942)

Pioneer missionary and founder of Sudan Interior Mission. Born in East Grinstead, England, he embarked as a youth on a spiritual search that culminated when he came to Christ through the ministry of the Salvation Army. In 1889, shortly after his conversion, he moved to Canada. There he first heard of Sudan from a woman who had invited him to lunch. That night God gave him a vision to reach Sudan, which became his lifelong passion. He traveled to Nigeria in 1893 with two other missionaries, the group calling themselves the Sudan Interior Mission (SIM) by 1894. The first to contract malaria, Bingham remained on the coast to coordinate supplies while the others traveled to the interior. At the end of one year

57

both of the others had died of malaria. Bingham, in need of logistical reinforcements, was forced to return to Canada. In 1898 he formally organized SIM as an interdenominational mission council to help recruit missionaries for the African interior. The next year he returned to Africa, and was again sent home to recover from malaria. Because of his health problems, he was never able to remain in the continent of his calling. In Canada, however, he was able to work as the driving force behind the development of SIM International. He also founded Evangelical Publishers (1912) and *Evangelical Christian* magazine, and established the Canadian Keswick Conference, a summer resort and spiritual retreat center.

Biography by J. H. Hunter (1961).

A. SCOTT MOREAU

Blackstone, William Eugene (1841–1935)

Author, lecturer, and missionary. Reared in a Christian family in Adams, New York, he was early converted at a Methodist revival. During the Civil War he engaged in Christian relief work, and afterwards he managed real estate in Oak Park, Illinois—so successfully that he entered full-time ministry as a Methodist layman. He is best known for *Jesus Is Coming* (1878), which defends Jesus' personal, premillennial, and imminent return, a work widely distributed before Scofield's Bible (1911). Blackstone was prominent on the Prophecy Conference circuit. There he reiterated two themes: the need for foreign missions, and Jewish aspects of prophecy, especially Palestine's restoration to the Jews. He helped establish Moody Bible Institute, the Bible Institute of Los Angeles, the Chicago Hebraic Mission, and educational institutions overseas. He organized a Christian-Jewish conference in Chicago in 1890. He drafted the Blackstone Memorial, calling for an international conference to consider the Jewish problem and the restoration of Palestine to the Jews. Signed by prominent religious, political, and business leaders, it recirculated in 1916, was endorsed by most major Protestant denominations, and may have influenced President Wilson. His close friendships with Jews brought him the title "Father of Zionism."

TIMOTHY R. PHILLIPS

Blackwood, Andrew Watterson (1882–1966)

American Presbyterian pastor, teacher, and author. Born in Clay City, Kansas, he graduated from Harvard in 1905, and studied theology at Princeton and Xenia (1905–1908). Following ordination in 1908 he was engaged in home mission work until 1911, and was then pastor of churches in Pittsburgh, Pennsylvania; Columbia, South Carolina; and Columbus, Ohio. In 1925 he became professor of English Bible at the Presbyterian Theological Seminary in Louisville, Kentucky, and in 1930 professor of homiletics at Princeton Theological Seminary, remaining there until retirement in 1950. For the next eight years he was professor of homiletics at Temple University School of Theology. Blackwood was one of the most prominent American Protestant homileticians of his era. Among his twenty-two books were *The Fine Art of Preaching* (1937), *Pastoral Work: A Source Book for Ministers* (1945), *The Preparation of Sermons* (1948), and *The Growing Minister, His Opportunities and Obstacles* (1960).

JACK MITCHELL

Blaiklock, Edward Musgrave (1903–1983)

Classical scholar and communicator. Born in Birmingham, England, he was educated in New Zealand where he trained as a high school teacher and graduated with double first-class honors at Auckland University. He taught there for all his professional career, retiring as professor of Greek in 1968. A superb lecturer, he was much in demand as a preacher and convention speaker. He was elected president of the Baptist Union of New Zealand in 1971. Gifted with the pen of a ready writer, he wrote for both the secular and the religious press. He was a writer for the New Zealand *Herald*, and for forty-one years wrote a weekly newspaper article under the pen name of Grammaticus. He was one of the Scripture Union's most successful commentators, writing the *Daily Notes* on many books of the Bible. For several years he led tours to archaeological sites in the Middle East, the Aegean, Greece, and Italy. When his city celebrated its centennial he was named as one of the "Hundred Makers of Auckland, 1871–1971." Three years later he was made an Officer of the Order of the British Empire (OBE) for "services to scholarship and the community." A prolific writer, he produced works on classical themes in addition to popular works such as *The Acts of the Apostles* (1959), *The Archaeology of the New Testament* (1970), and *The Pastoral Epistles* (1972). He also edited *The Zondervan Pictorial Bible Atlas* (1969).

S. BARTON BABBAGE

Blake, Eugene Carson (1906–1985)

Ecumenical leader. Born in St. Louis, Missouri, into a devout, middle-class home, he attended a prep school in New York and then Princeton University, where he was deeply involved in student religious activities, and had a "conversion experience." He graduated in 1928, spent a year teaching at Forman Christian College in India, and obtained his theological education at New College, Edinburgh, and Princeton Seminary. Ordained in 1932, he served the Collegiate Church of St. Nicholas in New York City, and Presbyterian congregations in Albany, New York, and Pasadena, California, where he became known for his preaching on social issues and involvement in denominational activities. In 1951 he was elected stated clerk of the (United) Presbyterian Church in the USA, and for the next fifteen years he labored to make it a truly national denomination and to promote ecumenical involvement. Controversy swirled about him as he denounced the anticommunism of the McCarthy era, supported women's ordination, broadened the creedal basis of the church, and fervently worked for racial justice. In 1963 he was arrested for trying to integrate an amusement park in Maryland and stood alongside Martin Luther King, Jr., in the march on Washington.

Ecumenism was the hallmark of Blake's ministry, beginning with local-level cooperation and culminating in a term as president of the National Council of Churches (1954–1957) and launching the movement in 1960 to merge the mainline U.S. denominations (Consultations on Church Union). In 1966–1972 he served as general secretary of the World Council of Churches, where he was a strong supporter of East–West dialogue, did much to involve the Orthodox churches in its work, promoted social justice and peace concerns, and looked toward eventual reunions with the Catholic Church.

Biography by R. Douglas Brackenridge (1978).

RICHARD V. PIERARD

Blanchard, Charles Albert (1848–1925)

Educator, pastor, and Bible conference speaker. Born in Galesburg, Illinois, to devoutly evangelical parents, he graduated in 1870 from Wheaton College where his father, Jonathan, was president. By that time he had already preached and spoken out against secret societies (e.g., Freemasonry), and upon graduation began to lecture as general secretary of the National Christian Association, which was opposed to such groups. Ordained in 1878, he pastored in Wheaton (1878–1883) and later for two years at Chicago Avenue church (now Moody Memorial Church). It was, however, as his father's successor (1882–1925) that he found a full range for his energies and gifts. In addition to administrative duties, he taught a full schedule of classes. Through the force of his own character and commitment he maintained the college on its conservative evangelical course and gave it stature as an educational institution. All the while he constantly toured, generating funds for the school and speaking at Bible conferences across the country. He was also a strong advocate of foreign missions.

Biography by F. C. Blanchard (1932).

JACK MITCHELL

Blanke, Fritz (1900–1967)

Swiss-German church historian. Born in Kreuzlingen, he moved with his parents to Emmishofen, Switzerland, where his father established one of the first Protestant bookshops in the Pietist tradition. He attended the universities of Tübingen, Heidelberg, and Berlin, and on completion of his doctorate in 1925, accepted a position as privatdozent at Königsberg. In 1929 he was appointed full professor at the University of Zurich, where he remained until his death. Most of his energies were devoted to the study and teaching of the history and theology of the Reformation, but he never lost sight of the larger historical framework and of congregational life and work in the Reformed tradition. From 1926, journals, newspapers, festschriften, and pamphlets carried his essays. Blanke was respected for his insightful, painstaking transmission and analysis of archival sources as coeditor of several volumes in the modern critical edition of Zwingli's works. In his teaching he combined attention to historical detail with a vision of the broader historical issues. As a pastor of the Reformed Church of Zurich he supported the Pietist "ecclesiola in ecclesia" tradition, and actively worked for the Blue Cross movement against alcohol abuse. His scholarly writing was aimed at informing educated laypersons as much as speaking to historians and academics. Works such as his studies on J. G. Hamann, essays on sectarianism and on other relevant issues, and his careful editorial work are part of Blanke's lasting literary legacy.

EDWARD J. FURCHA

Bloom, Anthony (Andre Borisovich) (1914–)

Russian Orthodox archbishop of Sourozh, with jurisdiction over the Russian congregations in the British Isles. Born in Lausanne, Switzerland, son of an Imperial Russian diplomat who made his home in Paris after 1917, he obtained his degree in medicine at the Sorbonne in 1943. He was also active in the wartime resistance movement. After the war he practiced medicine for a time, but his religious vocation was already assured. He had taken monastic vows in 1943, and was ordained to the priesthood in 1948. In 1949 he moved to London, where he has remained ever since. In 1957 he was made titular bishop of Sergievo. On becoming archbishop in 1960 he took the title of Sourozh, the name of an ancient Crimean bishopric. He had been widely admired for his many books on prayer, and has been greatly sought after as a spiritual director. As a result of his ministry there has been a steady stream of English converts to the Orthodox Church, though his impact has extended to all denominations. His main writings are *Living Prayer* (1965), *School for Prayer* (1970), *God and Man* (1971), *Meditations on a Theme* (1972), and *Courage to Pray* (1973).

GERALD BRAY

Blyden, Edward Wilmot (1832–1912)

Theologian, churchman, and statesman. He was born on the Danish West Indian island of St. Thomas, and though a capable student was refused acceptance by U.S. theological colleges because of his race. As a result, he journeyed to Liberia, and spent the greater part of the rest of his life in the West African context. A passionate and gifted visionary, he had difficulty staying in one place and working as part of a team, resulting in a widely varying career of manifold accomplishments. An ordained Presbyterian minister who received two honorary doctorates, he was president of Liberia College. He founded an Institute of Higher Education in Nigeria, edited newspapers, and served as ambassador and secretary of state. Influenced by his perceptions of Islam as a religion that tolerated racial differences, he promoted Islamic concepts while maintaining that only Christianity, if stripped of its cultural bondage, held the ultimate solution to the need of Africans to gain independence and autonomy in their own continent. Blyden is recognized as a leader who championed the cause of those of African descent through his writings and lectures. He was a spiritual forefather not only of Pan-Africanism, but also of modern African theology. His best-known books include *Christianity, Islam and the Negro Race, African Life and Customs, Vindication of the Negro Race*, and *The Significance of Liberia.*

Biography by H. R. Lynch.

A. SCOTT MOREAU

Bodelschwingh, Friedrich, I (1831–1910)

German Lutheran pastor. Born in Westphalia, son of a prominent Prussian statesman, he worked in the areas of mining and agriculture, then from 1854 studied theology at Basel, Erlangen, and Berlin. After serving pastorates in Paris and Westphalia, and two periods as army chaplain during his country's wars, he gave himself from 1872 to the work at Bielefeld of the Innere Mission: "an organized effort to promote the spiritual and bodily welfare of the destitute and indifferent who are, at least nominally, within the Church." Under his direction the work grew in many directions: a home for some 1,800 epileptics (it came to be known as "Bethel"), a headquarters for nearly one thousand deaconesses serving at home and abroad, a "workingmen's colony" (an imaginative pioneer project seeking to care for hoboes), a missionary seminary for theological students, and much more. Even the most severely handicapped were given work to do—work that was regarded as a preparation for the second coming of Christ. Bodelschwingh was both a far-seeing visionary and a superb administrator in the practical outworking of his ministry. From 1903 he was a member of the Prussian diet.

Bodelschwingh's son Friedrich II (1877–1946) succeeded his father as head of the Bethel institutions. Regarded highly by the German Evangelical Church, it elected him Reichsbishop, but the Nazi authorities intervened and replaced him by someone more sympathetic to their cause.

Bodelschwingh stoutly and successfully refused to give up the sick of Bethel in accordance with Nazi "euthanasia" policies.

J. D. DOUGLAS

Boff, Leonardo (1938–)

Prominent Roman Catholic liberation theologian. Of modest background, he was born into a large family of Italian descent in southern Brazil. A man of impressive intellectual capacity, he earned a Ph.D. at Munich, and on returning to Brazil in 1970 became editor and theological teacher. Works such as *Jesus Christ Liberator* (ET, 1978), *Liberating Grace* (ET, 1979), and *Passion of Christ, Passion of the World* (ET, 1987) quickly gained him a hearing as an articulate spokesman for progressive thought in Latin America. If his writings in the 1970s reflected the theologies of Bultmann, Rahner, and Teilhard de Chardin, in the 1980s Boff became increasingly speculative with works on Mary as the hypostatic incarnation of the Holy Spirit (*The Maternal Face of God* [ET, 1987]), social trinitarianism as a model for liberation, and the suggestion that the Roman Catholic hierarchy might better be inverted with the church of the poor as the real voice of God (*Church: Charism and Power* [ET, 1985]). From the late 1970s Boff increasingly became a focal point in the clash between liberation theology and Rome, such that he twice suffered Vatican interdicts of silence. He finally abandoned his Franciscan priesthood and married in 1992. Immensely popular in Brazil and among liberationists worldwide, Boff has published over fifty books, many translated into multiple languages.

J. SCOTT HORRELL

Bonhoeffer, Dietrich (1906–1945)

German pastor and theologian. Born the son of a Breslau psychiatrist who moved the family to Berlin in 1912, Dietrich was educated at Tübingen and Berlin. After Lutheran ordination he was briefly pastor in Barcelona and student at Union Theological Seminary, New York, before returning to lecture in systematic theology at Berlin University (1931–1933). When the Nazis came to power and demanded for Hitler an obedience due to God alone, Bonhoeffer left his post in protest and went to minister in London (1933–1935). Thereafter he went back to Germany and, known to the authorities as a leader of the Confessing Church, was forbidden to enter Berlin or to speak in public. He directed an "underground" seminary for his church, but with World War II imminent, friends persuaded him to leave for America. Soon he was back, explaining, "I shall have no right to participate in the reconstruction of Christian life in Germany after the war if I do not share the trials of this time with my people."

Deeply involved in the German resistance movement, which to him was more important than his natural pacifism, he was arrested by the

Gestapo in 1943. He commanded the respect of guards and fellow prisoners alike by his fearless testimony. For his participation in the plot against Hitler, he was (by the personal order of Heinrich Himmler) hanged at Flossenburg concentration camp, within a month of the end of the war in Europe.

Bonhoeffer made a notable contribution to the whole discussion about how Christians should behave under state tyranny. Among his writings were *Sanctorum Communio* (1927), *Act and Being* (1931), *Ethics* (1949), *The Cost of Discipleship* (1948), *Letters and Papers from Prison* (1953), and *Life Together* (1954).

Biographies by E. H. Robertson (1966), M. Bosanquet (1968), E. Bethge (1977), and A. Dumas (1971).

J. D. DOUGLAS

Boonstra, Juan S. (1926–)

Argentine evangelical radio speaker and writer. Known throughout Latin America for the rolling cadences and superb phrasing of his radio voice, Boonstra was born in Tres Arroyos, Argentina, and graduated from Calvin College and Calvin Seminary. Associated with the Christian Reformed Church, he was involved with the mass media as an announcer, speaker, and director of Spanish broadcasting for his denomination from 1965 until his 1993 retirement. He produced programs such as "Alfa y Omega," "Reflexion," and "La hora de la Reforma" ("Reformation Hour"), heard on over five hundred stations throughout Central and South America, the Caribbean, Spain, and the United States. It has been estimated that these programs reach over 50 million people. In recent years Boonstra produced a number of television specials and videos for Reforma-TV, some of them joint productions with HCJB-TV, such as a contextualized version of Dickens' *A Christmas Carol*, filmed in Ecuador. A prolific author, he has written numerous booklets and articles and several books on the family, basic Christian doctrines, and the Bible and current events. In demand as a speaker, especially to educated audiences, he has also preached throughout the continent.

STEPHEN R. SYWULKA

Booth, Ballington (1857–1940)

Salvation Army evangelist and founder of the Volunteers of America. Born in Brighouse, England, the second son of William and Catherine Booth, he rose rapidly through the ranks of the Salvation Army. An officer when only seventeen, he attained the rank of colonel within six years, and commanded the first Salvation Army training home for male officers. Trained as an evangelist and a gifted orator and musician, Booth went to Australia in 1883, with the rank of marshal; his two-year stint there proved highly successful. In 1887 he and his wife Maud went to America to take over the newly started—and somewhat floundering—work there, energetically consolidating the work coast-to-coast. He and Maud became U.S. citizens in 1895.

In 1896 disagreements over William Booth's autocratic leadership and organizational policies led to the Booths' resignation from the Army. Two months later Ballington founded the Volunteers of America. In its evangelistic mission and military style, the Volunteers closely resembled the Salvation Army, but with a more democratic structure. Booth was careful not to infringe on the work of the Salvation Army. As general he led the organization for the remaining forty-four years of his life. Maud and he developed a variety of effective humanitarian and social services blended with evangelism and Christian teaching. He wrote *The Faith That Prevails* (1920).

H. Douglas Buckwalter

Booth, Evangeline Cory (1865–1950)

Fourth general of the Salvation Army. The seventh child of General William and Catherine Booth, she was born and trained in London where she soon rose to key positions in the Army. She commanded the work in Canada (1896–1904) and in the United States (1904–1934), where she extended the range and efficiency of the outreach, not least during World War I (President Woodrow Wilson gave her a Distinguished Service Medal) and in the Depression years. She was recalled to London headquarters as General (1934–1939), but after retirement returned to the United States, of which she had earlier become a citizen. A forceful and enterprising leader of independent mind, Evangeline Booth said once, "What matters in Christianity is not the immovability of our faith, but where we have fixed it." To her the Salvation Army owes many of its best-known songs. She wrote *Love Is All* (1925), *Songs of the Evangel* (1927), *Toward a Better World* (1928), *Woman* (1930), and (with Grace Livingston Hill) *The War Romance of the Salvation Army* (1919).

Biographies by P. W. Wilson (1948) and M. Trout (1980).

J. D. Douglas

Booth, William (1829–1912)

Founder of the Salvation Army. Born in Nottingham and successively pawnbroker's assistant and Methodist pastor, Booth in 1865 began a rescue operation in London's East End for "these vast, unmanageable masses of sunken people." He waged war on a dual front: against the pinch of poverty and the power of sin. The establishment shunned his Salvation Army (so called from 1878). Police offered little protection against threatening mobs. By 1884 some six hundred Salvationists had gone to prison in defense of open-air preaching. Booth's financial affairs were investigated in a public inquiry (he was exonerated). Bishops criticized him in the House of Lords; the dean of St. Paul's refused permission for a service in the cathedral. Nonetheless, the Army spread throughout the world. A writer sent to interview Booth said he expected to meet a visionary, but found instead the most astute businessman in the city. Booth finally overcame the opposition, ending as honorary doctor of Oxford, guest of King Edward VII and the U.S. Senate, and Freeman of the City of London. When the general "laid down his sword" in 1912 thousands of mourners gathered for a tearful but joyful farewell. His Army's 1965 centenary celebrations drew distinguished guests to London's Albert Hall, including the queen, the archbishop of Canterbury, and the cardinal archbishop of Westminster. Booth's *In Darkest England and the Way Out* (1890) tells of his motivation and philosophy.

Biographies by G. S. Railton (1912), H. Begbie (2 vols., 1920), S. J. Ervine (1934), R. Collier (1965), and C. Barnes (1977).

J. D. DOUGLAS

Boreham, Francis William (1871–1956)

Baptist preacher and writer. Born in Tunbridge Wells, England, he became a clerk. An accident led to the loss of a foot and a permanently weakened leg. On New Year's Day 1886 he had a profound religious experience that led to his being rebaptized and studying for the ministry at Spurgeon's College, London, from 1892. Before his studies were completed he was called to Mosgiel, New Zealand, and ministered there from 1895. His first book of sermons was published in 1903, but he wrote also for local papers, edited *The New Zealand Baptist,* and was president of the national Baptist Union in 1901. Called to Hobart and then to Melbourne, he ministered until 1928, after which he devoted himself to writing and itinerant preaching. His fame grew steadily in Australasia, Britain, and North America, for he had a rare capacity for communicating the faith. In addition to preaching on Sundays, he began Wednesday lunchtime services in Scots Church, Melbourne (1937–1956). He wrote regularly for the Hobart *Mercury* and *The Age* in Melbourne. Thousands of copies of his forty-six books were sold every year, and he was well known also on radio. His attractive style was built on self-criticism and wide reading. Christ was always central to his ministry. Few of his generation shared the gospel so creatively with the whole community. Boreham was also an authority on cricket. Among his writings were *A Bunch of Everlastings* (1920) and *My Pilgrimage* (1940).

Biography by T. H. Crago (1961).

IAN BREWARD

Bosch, David Jacobus (1929–1992)

South African missiologist. Born in South Africa of Afrikaner parents, he undertook doctoral studies in Basel, then returned to southern Africa to work as a missionary and educator in the Transkei until 1971, when he became professor of missiology at the University of South Africa (UNISA). From 1982 until his death he was dean of the university's faculty of theology. Apart from his work at UNISA he was involved in many other activities that gave him his international reputation. He was editor of the well-known journal *Missionalia*, which he helped establish in 1973, and was general secretary of the Southern African Missiological Society. Bosch was a unique theologian and missiologist. He made people think through issues without necessarily compromising their own position. He has been described as an ecumenical Christian par excellence. He was deeply committed to the gospel of Jesus Christ, and saw that as the only answer to man's problems. This conviction caused him to refuse several high-profile international positions in order to better communicate the gospel in his own country. His most influential writings include *Witness to the World* (1980) and *Transforming Mission* (1991), the latter destined to be a major missiological textbook.

ROGER KEMP

Bounds, Edward M. (1835–1913)

Methodist minister and devotional writer. Born in Shelby County, Missouri, he practiced law there for five years. At age twenty-four he sensed God's call on his life and began proclaiming the gospel in a small church in Monticello, Missouri. He was licensed to preach in 1860 in the Methodist Episcopal Church, South, and went to pastor in Brunswick, Missouri. During the Civil War he served as chaplain in the Confederate army. He then pastored in Tennessee, Alabama, and Missouri. In 1883 he began work as associate editor of the *St. Louis Christian Advocate*. In 1888 he was called as the associate editor of the *Nashville Christian Advocate*, the official paper of the Methodist Episcopal Church, South. He wrote to promote revival and stem the growing tide of liberalism within his beloved denomination. Bounds spent the last seventeen years of his life in Washington, Georgia, writing devotional works such as the classic *Power Through Prayer* (1907). He practiced what he preached, rising at 4:00 A. M. each day to pray for three hours.

Biography by L. Dorsett (1991).

TIMOTHY K. BEOUGHER

Bourdeaux, Michael Alan (1934–)

Champion of religious freedom in the countries of the former Soviet Union, and founder and director of Keston College, Kent, England. An Oxford graduate in Russian and French (1957) and theology (1959), he became an Anglican priest while developing an expert knowledge of the plight of believers in the Soviet Union and other communist regimes in Eastern Europe. He first visited Moscow as an exchange student in 1959–1960. Responding to a call to "Be our voice," he founded Keston College in 1969 to research and publicize the fortunes of religious communities under communism. It became the leading center in this field in the English-speaking world, despite limited resources. (Church bodies gave little support.) It published a journal, *Religion in Communist Lands* (now retitled *Religion, State and Society*), and *The Right to Believe* (a more popular bulletin, with a title that was almost Keston's motto), and issued the Keston News Service on which the media heavily depended. Bourdeaux has lectured widely, advised church and government officials, and taken part in the Helsinki human rights process. Following communism's collapse in 1989, he spearheaded Keston's move to Oxford as Keston Research, and its new commitment to East-West exchange. He was awarded the Templeton Prize for Progress in Religion in 1984. Bourdeaux's books include *Opium of the People* (1965), *Patriarchs and Prophets* (1970), *Land of Crosses* (1979, on Catholics in Lithuania), and *Gorbachev, Glasnost and the Gospel* (1989).

DAVID F. WRIGHT

Bousset, Johann Franz Wilhelm (1865–1920)

German New Testament and Patristic scholar. Born in Lubeck and educated at Erlangen, Leipzig, and Göttingen; he began to teach in Göttingen and in 1916 was appointed professor of New Testament at Giessen where he remained for the rest of his life. He was one of the founders of the history of religions school. He was concerned to illustrate the New Testament from a detailed study of contemporary Judaism and the Hellenistic religions. He was an editor of the *Theologische Rundschau* from 1897 to 1917, and of the *Forschungen zur Religion u. Geschichte des A.T. u. N.T.* from 1903. He assumed a mediating position in the controversy over eschatology. He insisted on its importance in understanding pre-Christian Judaism, though Jewish scholars doubted his interpretations of the Talmud. His most famous book was *Kyrios Christos: Geschichte des Christenglaubens . . .* (1913; ET 1970). In it he used his vast learning and imagination to suggest that the title *Kyrios* was of Hellenistic origin. He opined that this Christology arising in Antioch was a mediating position between that of the primitive church and Paul.

NOEL S. POLLARD

Boyd, Robert Lewis Fullarton (1922–)

British scientist. After graduating in engineering at Imperial College, London, he worked for the Admiralty (1943–1946), then earned a Ph.D. at University College, London (1949). There he advanced from research assistant to professor of physics (1946–1983), serving also as professor of astronomy at the Royal Institution (1961–1967) and founding director of the Mullard Space Science Laboratory. He has been the recipient of many honors, among them a fellowship of the Royal Society (1965–1976), and a knighthood conferred by Queen Elizabeth (1983).

A committed Christian, he has been a longtime supporter of many evangelical causes, notably InterVarsity, and has served as president of the Victoria Institute (1965–1976) and chairman of London Bible College (1983–1990). He has been heard on the British Broadcasting Corporation on matters concerning science and faith, and written several booklets with such titles as "Faith in This Space Age," "A Physicist Thinks It Through," and "Creation of the Cosmos." He is also author of a volume, *Can God Be Known?* (1967), which has been published also in Japanese. "Speculation and philosophy cannot search out God," he declares, "but if my experience may be a guide for others, that which can be known of Him will be found in Christ."

J. D. Douglas

Brent, Charles Henry (1862–1929)

Episcopal bishop and ecumenical pioneer. Born in eastern Ontario and educated at Trinity College, Toronto, he served as an Episcopal priest in Buffalo and then Boston, mainly in mission work. Shortly after the American takeover of the Philippines he became the first Episcopal missionary bishop to that country (1901). There his Anglo-Catholic views caused him to skirt the majority Roman Catholic population in his social and missionary endeavors. He energetically combated the opium traffic, and presided at a number of international conferences on the problem. For health reasons he returned to the diocese of western New York in 1917, and in 1926 was given the added responsibility of oversight of American Episcopal congregations in Europe. He participated actively in the Edinburgh Missionary Conference of 1910. From its beginnings he also figured prominently in the ensuing Faith and Order movement, and in 1927 was elected president of its first world conference in Lausanne. He was passionately committed to bridge-building among Christians, and was regarded as a prayerful man unusually gifted in the art of friendship.

Biography by A. C. Zabriskie (1948).

Glen G. Scorgie

Bridges, Robert Seymour (1844–1930)

British poet. Born into a wealthy family in Walmer, on England's southeast coast, he was educated at Oxford and at London, where he graduated in medicine (1874) and set up practice. Financial circumstances allowed him to retire in 1882, to devote himself to literature. In 1899 he was largely responsible for publication of *The Yattendon Hymnal,* to which were indebted the *English Hymnal* of 1906 and the *Oxford Hymn Book* of 1908. Bridges is credited with having raised the standard of music in Anglican churches. He also introduced hymns he had translated from German. Nonetheless his own religious beliefs were elusive, and his work reveals little more than one for whom Christianity had a strong attraction. He published two volumes of shorter poems (1873, 1890). His eminence was recognized in 1913 when King George V appointed him poet laureate. Bridges rendered signal service to literature by editing and sponsoring the work of his friend and fellow poet Gerard Manley Hopkins. Among his other publications were *The Spirit of Man* (1915) and *The Testament of Beauty* (1929), a four thousand-word poetic attempt to reconcile Christianity and science. A cofounder of the Society for Pure English, Bridges was further honored by admission to the prestigious Order of Merit (OM) in 1929.

Biographies by E. Thompson (1944) and J. Sparrow (1962).

J. D. Douglas

Briggs, Charles Augustus (1841–1913)

American biblical and theological scholar. Born into a wealthy New York City family, he studied at Union Theological Seminary (1861–1863) and completed his training in Berlin (1866–1869). There he abandoned a conservative view of Scripture and accepted the historical-critical approach. Ordained in the Presbyterian Church, he joined the Union Seminary faculty in 1874, teaching Hebrew. In 1880 he became a founding coeditor of the *Presbyterian Review,* and was a participant in its landmark series on biblical criticism. Over against B. B. Warfield and A. A. Hodge he rejected propositional revelation. He held that Scripture must be critically examined by contemporary scientific methods, free from dogmatic interference, in order to identify the essential revelation amid foreign influences. Tensions with the conservatives escalated with Briggs' inaugural address (1891), "The Authority of Scripture," on induction to Union's chair of biblical theology. His belligerent attack on the Princetonian view of Scripture led to one of the most famous heresy trials in America. Briggs was suspended from ministry in 1893, and Union Seminary terminated its formal ties with the Presbyterian Church. In 1898 Briggs was ordained in the Episcopal priesthood, and remained at Union. He promoted an organic ecumenism wherein a higher unity subsumed difference among Christians. His *Biblical Study* (1883) introduced criticism to a generation of students, and he was coeditor of the *International Theolog-*

ical Library, the *International Critical Commentary*, and *Hebrew and English Lexicon of the Old Testament.*

Timothy R. Phillips

Bright, William Rohl ("Bill") (1921–)

Evangelist and founder of Campus Crusade for Christ. Born in Coweta, Oklahoma, he received his B.A. from Northeastern State College, Oklahoma, in 1943, then launched Bright's California Confections. The venture was successful, but along the way Bright became involved with Hollywood Presbyterian Church. There, under the influence of Henrietta C. Mears, he committed himself in 1945 to Christ. One year later, he entered Princeton Seminary. His continuing business venture prompted his return to California, where he entered Fuller Theological Seminary in 1947. There, while studying for a Greek exam during his final year (1951), Bright experienced a powerful call from God to enter full-time evangelistic work. He left school, sold his business, and began evangelistic work at the campus of UCLA. He founded Campus Crusade for Christ, which has since grown into one of the largest faith mission organizations in the world. At least part of his success can be attributed to his condensation of the gospel message into four simple points, now known as the *Four Spiritual Laws,* one of the most widely used evangelistic tracts in the world. More recently, Campus Crusade's use of the film *Jesus* has gained worldwide attention. More than three hundred organizations are now using the film, and an estimated 10 percent of the world has seen the film since its release in 1979. Additionally, Bright has produced a continuous stream of books, tracts, and other training/evangelistic materials. His published works include *Revolution Now* (1969), *Come Help Change Our World* (1979), *The Holy Spirit: Key to Supernatural Living* (1980), *Witnessing Without Fear* (1985), *The Secret: How to Live with Power and Purpose* (1989), and *Managing Stress in Marriage: Help for Couples on the Fast Track* (1990).

A. Scott Moreau

Brilioth, Yngve Torgny (1891–1959)

Swedish bishop and church historian. Born in Vastra, Sweden, he was educated in philology, history, and theology. He served for four years as secretary to Archbishop Nathan Soderblom, with whom he continued to work in the Life and Work movement until Soderblom's death in 1931. Brilioth's main interests remained "Life and Work" and "Faith and Order," both of which he supported as a skilled presiding officer and negotiator between the divergent Christian traditions within the two movements. He earned a D.Phil. in 1916, and in 1919 became lecturer in church history at Uppsala. In 1925 he was promoted to the chair of church history at Aabo (Turku), Finland. He returned to Sweden in 1929 as professor of church history and provost of the cathedral in Lund. As bishop of Vaxjo from 1937 and as archbishop of Uppsala from 1950 until his death, Brilioth sought to turn the attention of his church to the "broken culture" of the times while promoting the ecumenical movement through his extensive academic work and his ability to work outside the boundaries of the Swedish church. Among his publications are *The Anglican Revival* (1925), *Eucharistic Faith and Practice* (1933), and *A History of Preaching* (1945).

EDWARD J. FURCHA

Brown, William Adams (1865–1943)

American educator and liberal theologian. Born into a privileged Presbyterian family in New York City, he studied at Yale, Union Seminary in New York, and in Berlin under Adolf Harnack. He joined the Union Seminary faculty in 1892, teaching systematics, and received a Yale Ph.D. degree in 1901. Throughout his four decades at Union, Brown was a renowned champion of theological liberalism and its causes. Influenced by Harnack and Albrecht Ritschl, Brown accepted the cultural relativity of religious concepts and a progressive view of history. He concluded that each generation must work out its own understanding of Christianity in the light of its new knowledge. Brown stressed the church's responsibility to reform society in accordance with Christ's sacrificial love. His ideas are expressed in the widely read *Christian Theology* (1906). As a social activist Brown helped combat New York City slums, prostitution, and Tammany Hall corruption. He assumed leadership roles in ecumenical ventures such as the Federal Council of Churches, the Interchurch World movement, and the Faith and Order movement. Commissioned to direct a study of seminary education, Brown and Mark Mays authored *The Education of American Ministers* (1935). Their suggested reforms generated the Association of Theological Schools. In 1939 Oxford made Brown a D.D. His other publications include *A Teacher and His Times* (1940).

TIMOTHY R. PHILLIPS

Bruce, F(rederick) F(yvie) (1910–1990)

Scottish theologian and writer. Born in Elgin, son of a Christian Brethren evangelist ("I never had to unlearn anything I learned from him"), he graduated in Classics at both Aberdeen and Cambridge. Further study in Vienna made him fluent in German. He lectured in Greek at Edinburgh (1935–1938) and at Leeds (1938–1947) where he began to extend his research and teaching into the Greek New Testament and the study of Hebrew, with more and more of his extramural work on biblical studies. As a result he was appointed to the new chair of biblical studies at Sheffield University (1947–1959) and later to that of biblical criticism and exegesis at Manchester (1959–1978).

His output as a scholar was prodigious and wide-ranging (he was president of both the Society for Old Testament Study and for New Testament Study). He edited *The Evangelical Quarterly* (1949–1980) and *Palestine Exploration Quarterly* (1957–1971). He remained an active member of the Christian Brethren all his life, and adorned it with a wonderfully generous and truly catholic spirit. Students came from many countries to study under a scholar who not only took a personal interest in each of them, but showed that the holding of an evangelical faith is not incompatible with rigorous intellectual investigation.

Among his many publications, apart from commentaries on most of the New Testament books, were *Second Thoughts on the Dead Sea Scrolls* (1956), *The Spreading Flame* (1958), *Israel and the Nations* (1963), *Paul and Jesus* (1974), *The Pauline Circle* (1985), and the autobiographical *In Retrospect* (1980).

PETER S. DAWES

Brunner, Heinrich Emil (1889–1966)

Swiss Reformed theologian who along with Karl Barth pioneered the new theological movement known as neo-orthodoxy in the 1920s. Born near Zurich, he studied at the universities of Zurich and Berlin (Th.D., 1913). After serving as a pastor in the canton of Glarus (1916–1924), he became professor of systematic and practical theology at the University of Zurich where he remained until 1955. In these years, his theological perspective was widely dispersed through his many books (most of which were translated into English) and his frequent lecture tours in Europe, Britain, and America. The climax of his teaching career was spent as visiting professor of Christian philosophy at the International Christian University of Tokyo (1953–1955). During forty-nine years of active writing, Brunner published nearly four hundred books, articles, and sermons.

Brunner has often been characterized as an exponent of Barthian theology. Although he hailed Barth's commentary as signaling a new theological direction, Brunner seems to have arrived independently at similar theological conclusions, namely, that the prevailing Protestant liberalism of Schleiermacher and Ritschl was untenable. Early influences on Brunner included the Christian socialism of H. Kutter and L. Ragaz. The most notable later influences were Søren Kierkegaard's dialectic and Martin Buber's "I-Thou" concept.

Differences emerged between Barth and Brunner in the 1930s. Brunner took a positive view of natural theology, arguing that there was a "point of contact" for the gospel in the consciousness of the natural man. Barth defiantly replied with an article entitled "No!" The breach between them was not healed until near the end of their lives. Brunner's most distinctive contribution to theological thinking in the twentieth century was his concept of truth as encounter: God is not discovered by theorizing, but by divine self-revelation in Christ. Having rejected theological liberalism with its humanistic picture of Jesus, Brunner stressed that God takes the initiative in revealing himself and encountering man.

Brunner's impact on American theology is likely to continue for some time. Concepts such as the personal nature of faith and revelation, truth as encounter, and the christocentric understanding of the church and ethics have lodged themselves in the American theological consciousness. It was Brunner who first introduced neo-orthodoxy to America, yet whether he will be remembered merely as a representative of neo-orthodoxy or as an independent theologian in his own right remains uncertain. Brunner's contributions to twentieth-century theology have the misfortune of being overshadowed by the eminence of Karl Barth.

Among his major publications are *The Mediator* (1926), *The Divine Imperative* (1932), *The Divine-Human Encounter* (1937), *Revelation and Reason* (1942), and *Dogmatics* (3 vols., 1946–1960).

Biography by J. E. Humphrey (1976). Useful biography data are in C. W. Kegley, *The Theology of Emil Brunner* (1962).

FRANK A. JAMES III

Bryan, William Jennings (1860–1925)

Democratic and Populist leader, lawyer, and writer. Born and educated in Illinois, he was admitted to the bar in 1883. He practiced law in Illinois and Nebraska until 1891 when he won a Democratic seat in the U.S. Congress. Coming into the public eye further by his famous "Cross of Gold" speech in 1896, he was for the next thirty years a major force in national politics as leader of the Free Silver Movement, as a three-time unsuccessful candidate for the U.S. presidency, and as Secretary of State under Woodrow Wilson. He labored hard for progressive measures such as the direct election of U.S. senators, the graduated income tax, and women's suffrage. A magnetic orator and folk hero who embodied the agrarian unrest of the Midwest, he was "The Great Commoner" who sought to champion the fundamentalist ideals that he identified with the Populist program and the constitutional declaration of equality. His life concluded in Dayton, Tennessee, at the famous "Monkey Trial." Ostensibly concerned with the right of J. T. Scopes to teach Darwinian evolution in the public high school, the ensuing debate between Clarence Darrow and Bryan crystallized the brewing fundamentalist-modernist controversy in America. Bryan was broken by the debate and died five days after the trial concluded.

Biographies by P. W. Glad (1960), P. E. Coletta (1964), and L. W. Levine (1965).

JACK MITCHELL

Buchman, Frank Nathan Daniel (1876–1961)

Founder of Moral Re-Armament. Born in Pennsburg, Pennsylvania, he graduated from Muhlenberg College, trained as a Lutheran pastor, ministered in his home state (1902–1915), and taught personal evangelism at Hartford Seminary (1916–1921). When in 1921 he founded the body that later became known as the Oxford Group movement and then Moral Re-Armament, he ran it on faith-mission lines. After divine guidance had been given, commitments were often made in the absence of resources—and always, it was claimed, the funds arrived on time. Yet Buchman dealt in theological generalities, and the name change to MRA in 1938 was intended to further the appeal to people of all faiths, and to bring each one "the next stage" nearer God. As his reputation grew Buchman evoked strong reactions. Those commending him included President Truman, the Burmese and Japanese prime ministers, the king of Morocco, leading cardinals and archbishops, and even the atheist George Bernard Shaw. "Leave that fellow Buchman in a forest," marveled Henry Ford, "and he'll change the trees." He had as many critics, however; the historian H. A. L. Fisher referred to "this Salvation Army of snobs." Yet Buchman never confined his outreach to the "up-and-outs." He took time and trouble to comfort, confront, help, and pray with ordinary folk. He contributed substantially to Franco-German reconciliation after World War II, and was decorated by both nations. He welcomed Japanese and Germans to his Swiss center when feelings were running high against them, and he served widely as a peacemaker, notably on the African continent. There was always something disarming about a leader who explained success in terms of having been "wonderfully led to those who were ready." His thinking was reflected in *Remaking the World* (1947).

Biographies by his successor Peter Howard (1947) and Garth Lean (1985).

J. D. DOUGLAS

Bulgakov, Sergei Nikolaevich (1871–1944)

Russian philosopher and theologian. Born in Livny, son of an Eastern Orthodox priest, he graduated from the University of Moscow in 1894, and studied further at Berlin, Paris, and London. He became professor of national economy, first at Kiev Polytechnical Institute (1901–1906), then at the Moscow Institute of Commercial Science before his appointment to a similar position at Moscow University (1917–1918). He was also active politically, but the Marxism for which he had abandoned the church soon failed to satisfy him, and he returned to faith and was ordained as a priest in 1918. After teaching in the Crimea area, he was considered an undesirable by the government in 1923 and compelled to leave the Soviet Union. He taught political economy in Prague, then in 1925 became divinity professor (and later dean) of the Orthodox Theological Institute in Paris, where he remained until his death. His orthodoxy was often called into question. Influenced by Soloviev and Florensky, he was a strong advocate of sophiology, which "centered on problems of the creation of the world and which stressed the unity of all things." The topic is developed in his *The Wisdom of God* (1937). Bulgakov's many other religious works included *The Undying Light* (1917, an account of his conversion), *The Unburning Bush* (1927), *The Lamb of God* (1933), *The Orthodox Church* (1935), and *The Comforter* (1936).

J. D. DOUGLAS

Bultmann, Rudolph Karl (1884–1976)

Protestant theologian and New Testament scholar. Born in Oldenburg, Germany, he was educated at the universities of Marburg, Tübingen, and Berlin, and held academic appointments at Breslau (1916–1920), Giessen (1920–1921), and Marburg (1921–1951). Along with Martin Dibelius and Karl Schmidt, he pioneered the development of form criticism, a method of examining the Gospels in order to discover the oral tradition on which the text was based.

Influenced by Martin Heidegger, he developed an existential understanding, or as he called it, a "demythologization" of the New Testament. As he explained, the primitive gospel was presented in a mythological form and the only way to make it relevant to modern times was through radical reinterpretation. Thus, beliefs such as the end of the age and the last judgment, like those of a three-storied universe, are meaningless in a scientific age. Once the New Testament is reinterpreted in a proper way, it will add power to the gospel because people will be forced to find existential reality in their lives. They will abandon the pursuit of manmade security and selfishness and recognize the transient nature of life. The mystery of God and the threat of death lead them to make this existential commitment.

Bultmann has been criticized for giving faith decisions absolute authority. It is possible to believe in evil things as well as desirable ones. The test of faith should be more than mere conviction. It must also have some external corroboration subject to rational scrutiny.

Bultmann's major publications include *Jesus and the World* (1935), *Jesus Christ and Mythology* (1946), *Gnosis* (1952), *Theology of the New Testament* (2 vols., 1951, 1955), *Primitive Christianity in Its Contemporary Setting* (1956), *History and Eschatology* (1957), *Existence and Faith* (1961), *The History of the Synoptic Gospels* (1963), *The Gospel of John: A Commentary* (1971), and *The Second Letter to the Corinthians* (1985).

ROBERT G. CLOUSE

Burkitt, Denis Parsons (1911–1993)

Irish surgeon and epidemiologist. Born in Enniskillen, Northern Ireland, he lost an eye in an accident as a child. He was converted as a student at Trinity College, Dublin, where he qualified in medicine in 1935. After further training he became a Fellow of the Royal College of Surgeons (FRCS). In World War II he served as an army doctor in East Africa, and, with a sense of divine calling, returned there to work in Uganda in the Colonial Medical Service (1964–1966). There his researches into facial tumors in children identified what came to be known as Burkitt's lymphoma. His African experiences proved useful also when, back in England and working for the Medical Research Council (1966–1976), he ran counter to establishment opinion by suggesting a link between the low fiber content of Western diet and the incidence of coronary heart disease, colon cancer, gall stones, and other ailments. His view prevailed, and *The British Medical Journal* in 1993 acknowledged Burkitt had "changed the breakfast tables of the Western world, and he was nicknamed 'the bran man.' "

An effective communicator of the gospel and a president of the Christian Medical Fellowship, Burkitt displayed also a touching humility, presenting himself as "just a catalyst," and frequently quoting 1 Corinthians 4:7. His published works included *Don't Forget to Put Fibre in Your Diet* (1979) and *Western Diseases: Their Emergence and Prevention* (1981).

J. D. DOUGLAS

Burkitt, Francis Crawford (1864–1935)

English biblical scholar. Educated at Cambridge, he became a first-class Syriac scholar who made significant contributions to New Testament textual criticism. He was the first to recognize the importance of the Old Syriac version of the Gospels discovered at St. Catherine's Monastery on Mount Sinai. He transcribed the manuscript *Evangelion da-Mepharreshe: The Curetonian Version of the Four Gospels* (1904). Burkitt made other important contributions to New Testament textual criticism, especially in the Gospels. He analyzed the Gospel citations made by the Fathers, such as Ephraem and Clement of Alexandria, and classified their text type. He also provided many valuable books on the origins of the Gospels. His most effective work was *The Gospel History and Its Transmission* (1906). Burkitt was also one of the pioneers of form criticism. For example, he thought the Book of Mark has essentially the same form it had when Matthew and Mark used it in writing their Gospels. He was convinced that this criticism applied to the Gospels would reveal Jesus was a historical person, and that behind the Gospels was Jesus' actual teachings and actions.

PHILIP W. COMFORT

Burrows, Eva Evelyn (1929–)

General of the Salvation Army. Born in Tighes Hill, New South Wales, Australia, she graduated from the University of Queensland in 1950. Thereafter she studied at the Salvation Army's International Training College in London and at the University of London's Institute of Education. She served in Zimbabwe (1958–1969) before returning to London as vice principal of the International College for Officers (1969–1975), after which she was head of Women's Social Services. Her ability as an educator and administrator led to periods as territorial commander in Sri Lanka, Scotland, and Australia. She showed a capacity for innovation, dealing with crises and conservative senior officers very effectively. In 1986 she was elected (the youngest-ever) general. Her stress on evangelism and church growth and her high profile on public issues went with a fundamental reform of administration that separated the United Kingdom and International offices. She recommenced the Army's work in Eastern Europe, the Soviet Union, and China, and retired to Australia in 1993.

Biography by H. Gariepy (1993).

IAN BREWARD

Burton, Ernest Dewitt (1856–1925)

Baptist New Testament scholar. Born in Granville, Ohio, he graduated from Denison University and taught in Michigan and Ohio before going to Rochester Theological Seminary (B.D., 1882). He also pursued further studies at the universities of Leipzig and Berlin. In 1883 he became professor of New Testament at Newton Theological Institute. His major contributions, however, were at the University of Chicago where he began teaching in 1892, and where for the final two years of his life he was president. Burton was one of the early developers of biblical theology as a historical discipline. In addition to his many books, he edited the journals *Biblical World* and *American Journal of Theology.* His own books include *Syntax of the Moods and Tenses in NT Greek* (1893), *Records and Letters of the Apostolic Age* (1895), *Handbook of the Life of Paul* (1899), *Studies in the Gospel of Mark* (1904), and *Commentary on Paul's Epistle to the Galatians* (1920), which is still viewed as one of the most significant works on that epistle. He also edited with E. J. Goodspeed *Harmony of the Synoptic Gospels* (1920) and organized *A Sourcebook for the Study of the Teaching of Jesus in Its Historical Relationships* (1923).

Biography by T. W. Goodspeed (1926).

A. SCOTT MOREAU

Bush, Luis (1946–)

Missions leader and motivator. Born in Argentina to an English mother and Argentine father, and raised in Uruguay, Brazil, Argentina, and England, Bush studied economics at the University of North Carolina. Converted while in Argentina to fulfill his military obligation, he began a career in business, but left it to enter Dallas Theological Seminary, graduating in 1978 with a Th.M. degree in New Testament. During his seven years as pastor of the Iglesia Nazareth in San Salvador, Bush guided the church to send its own missionaries to Spain, and organized a ground-breaking Central America-wide missions conference at the church. He then served as president of the Ibero-American Missions Congress (COMIBAM) held in São Paulo, Brazil, in 1987, with three thousand participants from fifty-five countries—a key event in stimulating Third World missions in Latin America. In 1985 Bush joined Christian Nationals Evangelism Commission (now Partners International) as Latin American coordinator, and became international president in 1987, directing seventy indigenous partner ministries in over forty countries. In 1992 he became international director of the A.D. 2000 and Beyond movement. As a plenary speaker at the Lausanne II Congress in Manila in 1989, Bush coined the phrase "10–40 Window" to describe the least-evangelized region of the world, from western Africa to eastern Asia. His published works include *Partnering in Ministry* (1990), *Funding Two-Thirds World Ministries* (1990), and (as editor) *The A.D. 2000 and Beyond Handbook* (1992).

STEPHEN R. SYWULKA

Busia, Kofi Abefa (1913–1978)

African sociologist, statesman, and churchman. Born in Wenchi of the Brong-Ahafo Region in Ghana, he received his education from Wesley College, University of London, and Oxford, from which he received a doctorate in social anthropology. After returning to Ghana he held several administrative positions in the government. In 1947 he became a research lecturer at the University College of the Gold Coast (now the University of Ghana). The first major step in his political career came when he was elected to Accra's Legislative Council in 1951. By 1957 he was leader of the party opposing Nkrumah's political machine, which resulted in his forced exile in 1959. Until 1966 he taught in the Netherlands, Mexico, the United States, and England, after which a successful coup brought Nkrumah's downfall. Busia returned to Ghana and resumed an active role in politics, culminating in his election as prime minister of Ghana in 1969. However, an uncooperative civil service and army resulted in insurmountable problems. While in England for medical treatment in 1972, Busia was again in exile when the army staged a coup. He returned to lecture at Oxford until his death. His significant writings include *The Challenge of Africa* (1962), *Africa in Search of Democracy* (1967), *Purposeful Education for Africa* (1969), and *Apartheid and Its Elimination* (1971).

A. SCOTT MOREAU

Buswell, James Oliver, Jr.   (1895–1975)

American Presbyterian pastor, theologian, and educator. Born in Wisconsin, he graduated from the University of Minnesota, the University of Chicago, McCormick Theological Seminary, and New York University where he earned his Ph.D. After courageous service as an army chaplain in World War I (he received the Silver Star and the Purple Heart), he was ordained in 1918 and ministered to congregations in Minnesota, Wisconsin, and Brooklyn. Thereafter he was president of Wheaton College (1926–1940), which he led through a difficult transition period, and taught theology at what was to become Shelton College (1941–1955) and at Covenant Theological Seminary in St. Louis, Missouri (1956–1969). A strong theological conservative, he helped found the American Council of Christian Churches, the International Council of Christian Churches, and the Bible Presbyterian Church. He wrote *A Systematic Theology of the Christian Religion* (2 vols., 1962–1963).

JACK MITCHELL

Buttrick, George Arthur   (1892–1980)

Presbyterian minister and educator. Born in Seaham Harbour, England, he graduated from the Victoria University, Manchester, studied at Lancaster Independent College in Lancashire, and in 1915 was ordained a Congregational minister. He was pastor of the First Congregational Church in Quincy, Illinois (1915–1918); there followed further ministries in Rutland, Vermont (1918–1921), and Buffalo, New York (1921–1927), before he succeeded H. S. Coffin at Madison Avenue Presbyterian Church in New York City (1927–1954). He became widely known as a preacher and writer of liberal Protestant Christianity. During this period he served also as president of the Federal Council of Churches (1939–1941), twice delivered the Lyman Beecher Lectures on Preaching at Yale, and taught homiletics at Union Theological Seminary. On leaving New York he was campus preacher and professor of Christian morals at Harvard University (1954–1960). Among his writings were *Jesus Came Preaching* (1931), *Christ and History* (1963), and *God, Pain and Evil* (1966). He was also general editor of *The Interpreter's Bible* (12 vols., 1952–1957), and *The Interpreter's Dictionary of the Bible* (4 vols., 1962).

H. DOUGLAS BUCKWALTER

C

Cable, Mildred (1877–1952)

Missionary to China. Born in Surrey, England, she gave up a career in pharmacy and went to China under the China Inland Mission in 1901. In Hochow with Evangeline and Francesca French she established a school, but the three women (their names always linked together) had a vision of outreach to the regions beyond. So they went, despite the civil war raging at the time. Sometimes they were captured by brigands, sometimes by communist bands. The great Gobi desert, inner Mongolia, and the far western outposts of Kansu, Sinkiang, and Chinese Turkestan were the fields of the intrepid trio. Living in tents, eating poor food, and traveling by mule cart or camel, they took the gospel to remote places. In 1936 deteriorating political conditions forced the three women to leave the Gobi desert, which they had traversed five times. Cable later worked for the British and Foreign Bible Society. Her published works include *Through Jade Gate and Central Asia* (1927), *Something Happened* (with Francesca French, 1935), *The Gobi Desert* (1944), and biographies of Percy Mather (1935) and George Hunter (1948).

Biography by Phyllis Thompson (1957).

EILEEN J. KUHN

Cabrini, Frances Xavier (1850–1917)

Founder of the Missionary Sisters of the Sacred Heart, and first American canonized by the Roman Catholic Church. Born in Sant' Angelo Lodigiano, Italy, she completed training as a school teacher in 1870. Because of her lingering frailty from contracting smallpox in 1872, she was denied entrance to the Daughters of the Sacred Heart and was refused permission to go to China as a missionary. In 1874 she took over the direction of an orphanage in Codogno until its closure in 1880. Taking formal vows in 1877, she and seven orphan girls founded the Institute of Missionary Sisters of the Sacred Heart in 1880. Upon the success of this venture, Pope Leo XIII sent Cabrini and six sisters to New York City in 1889 to minister to the many Italian immigrants there. Despite continuing poor health, Cabrini was intrepid in spirit. Showing a keen sense for business, she soon founded orphanages, schools, training centers, hospitals, and prison work in New York City, other major cities across the country, and eventually Latin America. She became a U.S. citizen in 1909. Canonized as the first

American saint in 1946, she was designated by Pope Pius XII in 1950 as the patroness of immigrants.

Biographies by T. Maynard (1945), J. Mary (1955), and P. D. Donato (1960).

H. DOUGLAS BUCKWALTER

Cadbury, Henry Joel (1883–1974)

Quaker biblical scholar, historian, and peace activist. Graduate of Haverford College (1903) and Harvard University (1904; Ph.D., 1914), he was professor of biblical languages at Haverford (1910–1919). He became involved in the peace movement and organized a conference at Winona Lake (1915) that later developed into the American Friends Service Committee, whose chairman he was for twenty years. His peace activities during World War I led to his resignation from Haverford. He then taught at Andover Seminary (1919–1926) and Bryn Mawr College (1926–1934) before appointment as professor of divinity at Haverford (1934–1954).

Cadbury introduced German form criticism to American audiences. Works such as his *The Making of Luke–Acts* demonstrated that various forms such as parables, miracles, stories, and paradox must be studied to understand the New Testament. Later he contributed to the debate on the historical Jesus in *The Perils of Modernizing Jesus* (1937) and *Jesus, What Manner of Man* (1947). He was also a key member of the translation committee for the Revised Standard Version of the New Testament (1946).

After his retirement he lectured at Haverford and Pendle Hill and published books on Quaker history, including *John Woolman in England* (1971), *Friendly Heritage* (1972), and *The Narrative Papers of George Fox* (1972). In 1947 he received the Nobel Peace Prize on behalf of the American Friends Service Committee. Asked how he related scholarly and humanitarian activities he said they were both attempts to translate the New Testament.

Biography by M. H. Bacon (1987).

ROBERT G. CLOUSE

Caesar, Shirley (1938–)

Black gospel singer and evangelist. Born in Durham, North Carolina, she was singing from the age of twelve. Her career began as she sang with an evangelist at obscure meetings throughout the southern United States. She has continued to grow in recognition and prominence to the point where she is heralded as the First Lady of Gospel. While singing with the renowned Caravans, she developed a style of singing similar to that utilized by many African-American preachers. When singing a song, she would act out the story. For example, when singing "Sweeping Through the City," she would act out sweeping the floor. She has become known for her "mama" songs, in which she appeals to children to obey their mothers and not to disappoint them. Characteristic of this focus are the songs "No Charge" and "Don't Drive Your Mama Away." This song and sermonette singing style, coupled with the emotional content of her songs and her fiery delivery, have sustained her appeal through the years.

Caesar has served as a member of the county council in her hometown of Durham and as copastor with her husband of Mount Calvary Holy Church. Much of her effort and resources goes toward helping those in need through the Shirley Caesar Outreach Ministries, Inc.

In 1971 Caesar received a Grammy award for her "Put Your Hand in the Hand of the Man." She has been nominated eleven times and received a total of five Grammy awards. Other professional recognition includes six Dove Awards for Gospel Music, five Stellar Gospel Music Awards, and two NAACP Image Awards. She has been inducted into the Gospel Music Hall of Fame.

ROBERT C. SUGGS

Cairns, David Smith (1862–1946)

Scottish theologian and ecumenist. Educated at the universities of Edinburgh and Marburg, punctuated by two profound religious crises and a breakdown in health, he was ordained in 1895 at Ayton, Berwickshire. He served three churches following Presbyterian reunions: the United Presbyterian Church, the United Free Church, and the Church of Scotland. He was professor of systematic theology at Aberdeen U.F. (now Christ's) College (1907–1937; principal from 1923). Deeply interested in the relationship of social and economic conditions with the spiritual life of a community, he saw this as part of the understanding of the meaning of the kingdom of God, a theme that remained central to his theology. At the Edinburgh 1910 World Missionary Conference he chaired the Commission on the Missionary Message. Service with the YMCA in France in World War I led to the publication of *The Reasonableness of the Christian Faith* (1918) and the report on *The Army and Religion*. His own struggle against ill health was reflected in *The Faith That Rebels* (1928). True faith for Cairns was the faith that rebels with the power of God against all evils. *The Riddle of the World* (1937) shows him as a great Christian apologist. His autobiography was published in 1950.

HENRY R. SEFTON

Camara, Helder Pessoa (1909–)

Brazilian theologian and former archbishop of Olinda and Recife. Though not an articulator of liberation theology, without his charismatic defense of the poor this theology would have had great difficulty obtaining the backing of the Brazilian Roman Catholic hierarchy. Camara founded the

National Conference of Brazilian Bishops in 1952 and served as its secretary for twelve years. He was made auxiliary bishop (1952) and then auxiliary archbishop of Rio de Janeiro (1955) at which time he cooperated in the formation of the Council of Latin American Bishops (CELAM) in which he served as vice president (1959–1965). In 1964 he was made archbishop of Olinda and Recife, where he served until retirement in the late 1980s. In 1961 he initiated the Movement for Basic Education. Classes given by radio were to cover the whole of lesser-developed Brazil. However, the primer, *The Struggle to Live*, was suppressed following the 1964 military coup. Preaching pacifism as early as 1965, Camara took decisive action in 1968 to overthrow social structures by nonviolent methods. As a result, he was banned from public speaking in Brazil from 1968 to 1977. Though trained entirely in Brazil, Camara has been awarded more than fifteen honorary doctorates, including those of the universities of Harvard, Louvain, and Fribourg. He was awarded the Martin Luther King Memorial Award in 1970 and has been a Nobel Peace Prize nominee. Camara's writings, while not many, express his profound concern for the poor. *Revolution through Peace* (1971) is an example of his sermons, and *The Desert Is Fertile* (1974) of his poetry.

RICHARD J. STURZ
ESTEVAN F. KRISCHNER

Campbell, Reginald John (1867–1956)

English theologian. Born a pastor's son in London, he was reared in Northern Ireland, studied at Nottingham and Oxford, and was ordained as Congregational minister. He served Union Chapel, Brighton (1895–1903), before succeeding the famous Joseph Parker at London's City Temple (1903–1915). In an attempt to counter what he saw as the irrelevance of the contemporary church, he published *The New Theology* (1907), which stressed divine immanence, rejected original sin, and saw Christian revival as obtainable through social reform and moral action. This volume's liberalism stirred up a nationwide controversy—so much so that Campbell withdrew the book from circulation. He turned to Anglo-Catholicism, and in 1916 was ordained in the Church of England. He served parishes in Westminster and Brighton before becoming canon (1930) and chancellor (1936–1946) of Chichester. Among his publications were *The Restored Innocence* (1898), *Christian Faith in Modern Light* (1932), *The Life of the World to Come* (1948), and biography of David Livingstone (1929).

J. D. DOUGLAS

Canclini, Arnoldo (1926–)

Latin American writer and pastor. Born in Argentina, grandson of the famous evangelist Juan C. Varetto, he earned a doctorate in philosophy and literature from the University of Buenos Aires. A well-known preacher and teacher on biblical subjects and literary theory, he has lectured throughout Latin America. He has served as president of the National Bible Society and the Argentine Baptist Convention, as well as other denominational posts, and has directed several Christian periodicals, including the Spanish edition of *Decision*. In 1992 Canclini became the first evangelical to be admitted as a member of the National Academy of History in his country, and was honored for the various historical volumes he has written, four of which were presented in a special ceremony. Three other books published that year brought his total production to sixty-six on biblical topics, literature, history, missionary biographies, and the Argentine Patagonia, on which he is recognized as an outstanding authority. He has written also children's books and novels, and has contributed numerous articles to the leading newspapers in Argentina.

MARTHA SAINT BERBERIAN

Carey, George Leonard (1935–)

Archbishop of Canterbury. Born in Dagenham, Essex, he left school at age fifteen and became an office boy, and then carried out national service as a radio operator in the Royal Air Force. He studied at the London College of Divinity and gained a B.D. at London University. He was ordained to a curacy at St. Mary's, Islington, in 1962. After further study he lectured at Oak Hill Theological College from 1966 and at St. John's College, Nottingham, from 1970, in which year he earned a Ph.D. from London University. In 1975 he returned to parish work as vicar of St. Nicholas, Durham, a church with a student ministry, which he radically reconstructed as he recorded in *The Church in the Market Place* (1982). He was principal of Trinity College, Bristol, from 1982, but such was his stature as an evangelical and charismatic leader that in 1987 he was consecrated bishop of Bath and Wells. His appointment to Canterbury in 1991 took the country by surprise. Among his other works are *I Believe in Man* (1975), *The Meeting of the Waters* (1985), and *The Gate of Glory* (1986).

NOEL S. POLLARD

Carlile, Wilson (1847–1942)

Founder of the Church Army. Born in London and converted after a severe illness, he left his business career and in 1878 entered the London College of Divinity to study for the Anglican ministry. Soon after his ordination he left his Kennington curacy in order to work in a slum mission, and from 1882 united local evangelical Anglican parish "armies" into a national Church Army, on the model of the interdenominational Salvation Army founded in 1865. A training college for men (1884) was followed by one for women (1887); graduates (men, 1897; women, 1921) were admitted to the office of evangelist in the Church of England. The Church Army's evangelistic and social activities were supplemented from 1889 by social and moral welfare schemes in London and provincial cities. Work among the armed forces during World War I (1914–1918) led to the foundation of independent sister organizations in Australia, New Zealand, Canada, the United States, the Caribbean, and East Africa. Carlile combined parish appointments with the post of honorary chief secretary of the Church Army. He was appointed prebendary of St. Paul's Cathedral (1906) and on his retirement (1926) was made a Companion of Honour by King George V. His books include *The Church and Conversion* (1882), *Spiritual Difficulties* (1885), *Continental Outcast* (1906), and *Baptism of Fire* (1907).

Biography by S. Dark (1945).

PHILIP HILLYER

Carmichael, Amy Wilson (1867–1951)

Missionary to India. Born in Northern Ireland, she was converted in her teens, and in 1893 went as a missionary to Japan. Ill health forced her to return to Ireland in 1894. Undaunted, she set out again the following year. This time her destination was Tinnevelly, South India, sponsored by the Church of England Zenana Missionary Society. Her heart was touched by the temple slavery of little girls—prostitution perpetrated in the name of religion. She rescued her first child in 1901, her seventeenth in 1904. Her Dohnavur Fellowship became an independent society of almost nine hundred endangered boys and girls. The work involved long, weary, sometimes fruitless trips to all corners of India. Those children who arrived at Dohnavur were cared for, educated, and trained for lives of service. Carmichael set high spiritual standards for them and for herself, aided by a growing body of fellow workers. The world learned about her work in numerous books, sentences, and poetry that have found their way into magazines, hearts, and homes all over Christendom. Among her publications are *Things as They Are* (1903), *Walker of Tinnevelly* (1916), *If* (1938), *Rose from Brier* (1950), and *Gold Cord* (1952).

Biographies by Frank Houghton (1953) and Elisabeth Elliot (1987).

EILEEN J. KUHN

Carnell, Edward John (1919–1967)

Evangelical scholar and theologian. Born in Antigo, Wisconsin, he grew up in a Baptist parsonage. After attending Wheaton College (1937–1941), where he was strongly influenced by Gordon H. Clark, he went to Westminster Seminary (1941–1944), where he received his Th.B. and Th.M. degrees. Cornelius Van Til's approach to theology had a lasting influence on him. At Harvard (Th.D., 1948) his dissertation was on *The Theology of Reinhold Neibuhr* (published in 1950). A Ph.D. followed from Boston University (1949); Carnell's dissertation appeared in 1965 as *The Burden of Søren Kierkegaard.* Carnell taught apologetics and philosophy of religion at Gordon College (1945–1948), and philosophical apologetics and systematic theology at Fuller Seminary (1948–1954), where he served as president from 1954 to 1959, returning to teach at Fuller as professor of ethics and philosophy of religion until his death.

No issue was more important to Carnell both academically and personally than that of establishing the truth of Christianity's claims. Truth and faith go together, and "The Spirit's work is to ensure proper response to evidence, not to create evidence." This synthesis is seen successively in *Introduction to Christian Apologetics* (1948), *A Philosophy of the Christian Religion* (1952), *Christian Commitment* (1957), *The Case for Orthodox Theology* (1959), and *The Kingdom of Love and the Pride of Life* (1960). Carnell's openness to new ideas was sometimes misunderstood as wavering in respect to fundamentals, but he remained orthodox to the end. Biblical revelation is the ultimate criterion by which we explain and understand everything; it is never subject to correction by secular knowledge. Carnell insisted that "evangelical Christianity should not jettison the doctrine of inerrancy" no matter how troublesome the historical details of Scripture might be.

Biography by J. A. Sims (1979).

WALTER A. ELWELL

Carr, Burgess (1935–)

African churchman, teacher, and Christian activist. Born in Crozierville, Liberia, he graduated in science from Cuttington College, and in theology from Cuttington Divinity School and Harvard Divinity School (Th.M., 1966). His pastoral experience ranges from canon-in-residence of Trinity Cathedral, Monrovia, to associate rector, St. Cyprian's Episcopal Church of Massachusetts. In addition to direct pastoral responsibilities, Carr has served extensively in ecumenical circles and has held several key positions, notably that of secretary-general of the All-Africa Conference of Churches (1971–1979). In the latter position he was known as a dynamic leader who changed the organization from a weak collective to an actual functioning ecumenical body. He was moderator of the 1972 negotiations in Addis Ababa that ended one phase of Sudan's civil war. His teaching experience includes visiting professor at Union Theological Seminary (1971), visiting lecturer at Harvard Divinity School (1978–1981), and an associate professorship at Yale Divinity School (1982–).

A. SCOTT MOREAU

Carter, Charles W. (1905–)

Wesleyan theologian. After his conversion in 1923 and some training at God's Bible School and Training Home, Carter and his wife served a three-year missionary term in Sierra Leone. Further training followed at Marion College in arts and theology at Winona Lake School of Theology (Th.M.). Carter then returned to Sierra Leone (1934–1945). He taught at Taylor University (1959–1971), in Taiwan (1972–1974), and went back to teach at Marion College (now Indiana Wesleyan University) where he is currently scholar-in-residence. Building upon a high view of Scripture and the limitations of human reason, Carter emphasizes the practical nature of theology, which requires fulfillment of the Great Commission, a task that should combine evangelization with social and political liberation. The motivating and energizing power that accomplishes this is the Holy Spirit. The final goal of the believer is heaven, where the love of God will be fully experienced throughout all eternity. Carter has written or edited some twenty volumes, including *Wesleyan Bible Commentary* (6 vols., 1964–1969), *The Person and Ministry of the Holy Spirit* (1974), *Missionaries Extraordinary: The Life and Labors of Charles and Elizabeth Carter* (1982), *A Contemporary Wesleyan Theology* (2 vols., 1983), and *Life's Lordship over Death* (1988).

WALTER A. ELWELL

Carter, James Earl, Jr. (1924–)

Thirty-ninth president of the United States and Baptist lay leader. Born in Plains, Georgia, he graduated from the Naval Academy, and served mostly in the submarine service (1946–1953). He resigned his commission when his father died, and returned to Plains to devote himself to farming, the family business, and civic activities. He became a deacon and Sunday school teacher in Plains Baptist Church, served Georgia as state senator (1963–1967) and governor (1971–1975), and was U.S. president (1977–1981). His political career reflected a faith that was an integral part of his identity. His understanding of Christianity convinced him that Jesus called his followers to be servant-oriented, and that this included politics. His personal style—marked by self-discipline, a commitment to hard work, orderliness, and fiscal responsibility—displayed his evangelical worldview. While his administration, like his earlier legislative and gubernatorial career, received mixed reviews, he engineered a peace accord between Egypt and Israel at Camp David in 1979, and established human rights as a basic tenet of American foreign policy. After leaving office in 1981, Carter became the most energetic ex-president in recent American history. Nearly all his activities have centered around his church and his passion for social justice. He is the author of numerous books, among them *Why Not the Best?* (1975), *Keeping Faith: Memoirs of a President* (1983), *The Blood of Abraham* (1985), and *Turning Point: A Candidate, a State, and a Nation Come of Age* (1992).

ROBERT D. LINDER

Case, Shirley Jackson (1872–1947)

Church historian and theologian. Born in New Brunswick, Canada, he graduated from Acadia University and from Yale University where he later also gained a Ph.D. degree in 1907. In 1908 he began a distinguished career at the University of Chicago Divinity School, teaching New Testament and later entering the church history department. His analyses of Christianity's relationship to its successive cultural contexts were pioneering demonstrations of the sociohistorical method in religion. Case viewed Christianity as a function of its historical and social milieu. Christian revelation, beliefs, practices, and institutions are human products developed in view of contemporary religious and social needs. *Jesus Through the Centuries* (1932), for instance, explains the differing Christologies in the church's history from the interaction between these respective Christian communities and their environment. Case concludes that nothing historical is normative. The endurance of any Christian product is determined by its functional significance for contemporary believers.

Case was a central figure in the "Chicago School of Theology" and its battles with fundamentalism at the beginning of the twentieth century. Case recruited a prestigious faculty in his school's church history department and revitalized the institutions undergirding this academic discipline, including the American Society of Church History. By the time he was dean (1933–1938), Chicago rivaled Harvard as the leading center of the academic study of religion.

TIMOTHY R. PHILLIPS

Cassels, William Wharton (1858–1925)

Missionary bishop. Born in Portugal and educated in England, he prepared for the ministry by reading theology at St. John's College, Cambridge. He was ordained in 1882, served a curacy in the slum parish of South Lambeth, London, then became one of the famous Cambridge Seven, offering himself to the China Inland Mission in 1884. After language studies in 1885 he was posted to Paoning in Szechwan, which from that time became the center of his ministry. While on furlough in England in 1894–1895 he was chosen and consecrated as the first bishop of West China. For the next thirty years he pastored and evangelized his vast diocese, successfully holding together the Church Missionary Society and the China Inland Mission areas of that diocese. He himself spent at least a quarter of each year traveling in often difficult and dangerous times. His goal was to let the Chinese take control in the long run, but he and his wife died of a fever while still working in China.

NOEL S. POLLARD

Cassidy, (Charles) Michael (Ardagh) (1936–)

South African evangelist and founder of African Enterprise whose mission is "to evangelise the cities of Africa through word and deed in partnership with the Church." Born and educated in Johannesburg, he graduated also from Cambridge University in 1958. He discarded his love of teaching and interest in politics for theological studies at Fuller Theological Seminary, where he gained a B.D. degree in 1963. As an evangelical leader, Cassidy has toiled to guide church and political leaders in South Africa toward a policy of reconciliation. He is at once a Christian leader and a patriot. Primarily an evangelist, he has the heart, will, and skill of a teacher, and the drive of a politician. In response to a call to evangelize, and his dedication to the continent of Africa, Cassidy founded African Enterprise in 1962 and linked up with Ugandan fellow-Anglican, Bishop Festo Kivengere. As a black and white team they labored to win Africa for Christ. African Enterprise continues as an interdenominational, interracial, and international evangelistic mission team that operates as a service agency and auxiliary to the churches around Africa. As well as being in demand internationally as a speaker, he has initiated efforts in South Africa to build up the church and heal the nation, the most recent of these in 1993 when he chaired a consultation on Human Rights and Religious Freedom. Among his numerous publications are *Bursting the Wineskins* (1983), *The Passing Summer* (1989), and *The Politics of Love* (1991).

W. H. OLSON

Castro, Emilio (1927–)

General secretary of the World Council of Churches (WCC). Born in Montevideo, Uruguay, he studied at Union Theological Seminary in Buenos Aires (1944–1950), and with a WCC scholarship pursued graduate work in Basel (1953–1954) under Karl Barth. In 1984 he completed a doctoral degree at the University of Lausanne. Ordained by the Evangelical Methodist Church of Uruguay in 1948, Castro held pastorates in La Paz, Bolivia, and in Montevideo where he also taught in the Mennonite Seminary, and served as president of the Uruguayan Methodist Church (1970–1972). He has been vice president of the Christian Peace Conference, coordinator for the Commission for Evangelical Unity in Latin America (UNELAM) (1965–1972), and executive secretary of the South American Association of Theological Schools (1966–1969). He was director of the WCC Commission on World Mission and Evangelism (1973–1983), and since 1985 has served as the WCC's general secretary and has edited several of its publications. His own published works include *Amidst Revolution* (1975), *Freedom in Mission* (1975), and *When We Pray Together* (1989).

STEPHEN R. SYWULKA

Castro, George F. (1936–)

Bishop and general superintendent of the Evangelical Methodist Church in the Philippines. Born in Tondo, Manila, he graduated from the University of the East with a degree in business administration (1956). Although not specifically trained for the ministry, he has had a significant influence in mainline churches in the Philippines. He was general secretary for the Metro Manila Billy Graham Crusade in 1977, and from 1978 he has been chairman of the consultative committee of the National Council of Churches and the Philippines Council of Evangelical Churches. He is well known for hosting an ecumenical prayer breakfast in his restaurant in Manila, and has provided Christian leadership both in his own denomination and in the Christian community in general.

FRANK ALLEN

Catherwood, (Henry) Frederick (Ross) (1925–)

Irish churchman. Born into a Christian home in Ireland, he came to faith in Belfast as a boy, but his faith matured during student years at Cambridge. He qualified as a chartered accountant in 1951, rose rapidly in the world of commerce, and served the government as director of the National Economic Development Council and as director of the Board of Overseas Trade. In 1979 he was elected to the European Parliament, later becoming one of its vice presidents and the recipient of a knighthood from Queen Elizabeth II. Throughout his career he has maintained the evangelical faith sharpened through active membership of Westminster Chapel, London, under the ministry of Martyn Lloyd-Jones (whose daughter Elizabeth he married). An active supporter and encourager of student work, he is currently (1995) president of the British Evangelical Alliance. Catherwood's first important book was *A Christian in Industrial Society* (published in America as *Nine to Five, USA,* 1983), a landmark in showing how Christian principles could be applied in industry. Other books include *God's Time, God's Money* (1987) and *David: Poet, Soldier, King* (1992).

JOHN MARSH

Cauthen, Baker James (1909–1985)

Minister and missionary administrator. Born in Huntsville, Texas, he was converted and baptized at the First Baptist Church, Lufkin. He began to preach at age sixteen. He graduated from Stephen F. Austin College (now University) (1929), Baylor University (1930), and Southwestern Baptist Theological Seminary (Th.D., 1936). Even before finishing graduate studies he began to teach missions at Southwestern. By 1939 the call of God to serve as a missionary to China had become inescapable, and on the eve of the Japanese invasion he and his wife Eloise (daughter of missionaries to China) found themselves in language school in Peking. Forced by the war to leave Shantung Province in North China, the Cauthens by sheer determination continued their ministry at Kweilin in Free China. Between bombing raids, Cauthen continued his evangelistic ministry until he and his family were forced to flee before the advancing Japanese. In 1945, while on furlough, he was elected area secretary for the Orient. After the war he established his office in Shanghai, but was forced out of China once again in 1951. Upon the death of Theron Rankin (1953), Cauthen succeeded him as executive secretary, and under his leadership the missionary force grew from 908 in 33 countries to 2,981 in 94 countries. A most forceful preacher, Cauthen had so effectively preached missions that Southern Baptists had truly became a "Missions People."

W. R. ESTEP

Ch'eng, Ching-yi (1881–1939)

Chinese Congregationalist pastor and indigenous church leader. Born in Peking, Ch'eng was son of a pastor. He studied in England and contributed to the Union Version translation of the Chinese New Testament. He attended the World Missionary Conference in Edinburgh (1910), in which he told the churches of the West that "Your denominationalism does not interest Chinese Christians." He called for an indigenous, interdenominational Church of Christ in China. After Edinburgh he accompanied and interpreted for John R. Mott while Mott lectured and convened meetings for the WMC's Continuation Committee (1912–1913). From 1913 to 1922 he was secretary of the China Continuation Committee, which sought ways to implement comity and cooperation among mission agencies and churches in China. From 1924 to 1934 he was secretary of the National Christian Conference, hailed as the birthday of the indigenous church in China. Ch'eng served from 1934 on as the secretary of the Church of Christ in China. The CCC was organized in 1927, made up of Presbyterian, Congregational, and a few Methodist congregations. Ch'eng was also a vice president of the International Missionary Council (1928–1938).

SAMUEL LING

Ch'eng, Marcus (Ch'en Chung-kuei) (1883–1963)

Chinese evangelist and church leader. Born in Mucheng, Hupeh province, China, he began teaching in 1909 at Kingchow Theological Seminary, operated by the Evangelical Covenant Church of both Sweden and America. Ch'eng became fluent in English and Swedish and traveled to the West in 1920, 1928, and 1948. He was the first Chinese graduate of Wheaton College (1923). In 1925 he began work as chaplain for the "Christian General," Feng Yu Hsiang. Ch'eng soon became one of China's greatest evangelists and conservative Protestant leaders. His first two books were *Echoes from China* (1921) and *Marshal Feng: The Man and His Work* (1926). *Escape from Singapore* (1944) tells of Ch'eng's internment by the Japanese. In 1945 he worked with the China Inland Mission to found Chungking Theological Seminary. Ch'eng wrote *After Forty Years* in 1947.

On his final trip to the United States in 1948, Ch'eng publicly sympathized with Chinese communist forces. He was appointed one of four vice-chairmen of the Three-Self movement in 1951. This organization worked to unite all Chinese Protestant churches under one polity. Ch'eng lost this position after a 1957 speech in which he criticized the government. His autobiography was destroyed during the Cultural Revolution.

O. THEODORE ROBERG

Chafer, Lewis Sperry (1871–1952)

Dispensationalist theologian. Born in Rock Creek, Ohio, he attended Oberlin College but withdrew in 1891 to become an itinerant revivalist and singer. He worked for some years with D. L. Moody, Ira Sankey, and C. I. Scofield at the Northfield Conferences. His contact with Scofield ("a real Bible teacher") transformed his life, and he helped Scofield found the Philadelphia College of the Bible in 1915 where he served on the faculty. In 1924 he founded the Evangelical Theological College in Dallas (in 1936, Dallas Theological Seminary), where from 1924 to 1952 he was president and professor of systematic theology. Chafer had been writing extensively all this time, producing *The Kingdom in History and Prophecy* (1915), *Salvation* (1917), *He That Is Spiritual* (1918), and *Grace* (1922). His magnum opus, *Systematic Theology,* in eight volumes, was completed in 1948—the first comprehensive dispensationalist theology ever written. In it he tried to correct seven areas of deficiency he detected in other systematic theologies. Chafer's distinctive views embroiled him in controversy over the years, but to the end he defended the proposition that only by properly distinguishing the dispensations could biblical truth be known. In the broader theological arena Chafer was a committed evangelical and staunchly defended such fundamental Christian doctrines as the deity of Christ, the bodily resurrection, and the infallibility of Scripture.

WALTER A. ELWELL

Chambers, Oswald (1874–1917)

Baptist evangelist. Born in Aberdeen, Scotland, where his father was a Baptist pastor, Oswald was converted after hearing C. H. Spurgeon preach. Having a marked aptitude for fine art, which he studied in London and Edinburgh, he forsook a promising career in that field and went in 1897 to train for the ministry at Dunoon College in western Scotland. He began tutoring there the following year, remaining until 1906. He became known widely as a preacher, and subsequently served with the Pentecostal League of Prayer; his work involved extensive travel and included conferences in the United States and Japan (1909–1911). In 1911 he became principal of the Bible Training College, Clapham Common, London, where his holiness and versatility enhanced his reputation. In 1915, during World War

93

I, he went to Egypt to minister to British troops under YMCA auspices, and proved able to get through to soldiers with the gospel as few chaplains did. Pressing into service his gifts as an artist, he pinned up notices the men found irresistible. Military personnel and missionaries alike felt a profound loss when he died suddenly in Egypt.

Chambers had a winsome and sometimes provocative way with words. "Be godly in the grubby details," he would urge, or "Beware of men, especially good men," or "God won't do for you what you can do for yourself." He loathed hypocrisy, but refused to criticize or worry. He was a prolific and appealing writer, but none of his works is better known than *My Utmost for His Highest.* This book of daily devotional readings, compiled from lectures and talks given in London and Egypt, was first published in 1927 and went through twelve editions in as many years.

Written contributions by numerous friends were brought together as *Oswald Chambers: His Life and Work* (rev. ed., 1959). Biography by David McCasland (1993).

J. D. DOUGLAS

Chao, Jonathan T'ien-en (1938–)

China watcher and indigenous theological educator. Born in Liaoning, China, he grew up in Kobe, Japan. He graduated from Geneva College in 1962, and Westminster Theological Seminary. He turned to Oriental studies at the University of Pennsylvania, receiving the Ph.D. in 1986. He was ordained into the Baptist General Conference in 1977. Chao was deeply affected by the "ministerial crisis" in the church in Taiwan during 1964–1965, and in 1967 organized the Seminary Preparation Committee in Philadelphia, which founded the China Graduate School of Theology in Hong Kong in 1975, a post-baccalaureate seminary run by the Chinese. During this period Chao was critical of theological education in Asia because of its Western orientation and leadership. He called for an indigenous theology and indigenous theological training by and for the Chinese church. He also wrote on the state of Christianity in China, and in 1980 left the China Graduate School of Theology to found the Chinese Church Research Center, which published *Zhongguo Yu Jiaohui* (China and the Church), and the *China News and Church Report.* In 1987 he founded the Chinese Mission Seminary in Hong Kong, and in the same year his various ministries were brought under China Ministries International. Chao has lectured widely around the world, and has written *Chinese Communist Religious Policy towards Christianity* (Chinese, 1983) and *China Mission Handbook* (1989). His Ph.D. dissertation was on the "Chinese Indigenous Church Movement, 1919–1927: Protestant Response to Anti-Christian Movement in Modern China."

SAMUEL LING

Chao, Tzu-ch'en (Zhao, Zi-chen) (1888–1979)

China's most prolific indigenous theologian in the twentieth century. Born in Soochow, T. C. Chao graduated from Soochow University in 1910, and Vanderbilt University (M.A. sociology, 1916; B.D., 1917). He taught at Soochow University (1917–1926). He participated in the National Christian Council, Shanghai (1922) and several international ecumenical conferences. From 1926 he taught at Yenching University in Peking (Beijing), and from 1928 he was the dean of its School of Religion until the early 1950s. The Anglican Church ordained Chao in 1941. He was imprisoned by the Japanese during World War II (during which period he wrote hundreds of poems). He was one of the six presidents of the World Council of Churches in 1948. Under the Chinese communists he was stripped of all his posts, and died a private citizen in Peking in 1979. Chao was a strong proponent of an indigenous theology for the Chinese church, and wrote *The Philosophy of Christianity* (1926), *A Life of Jesus* (1935), *An Interpretation of Christianity* (1943), and numerous other articles, prayers, poems, and liturgies. His earlier liberal theology was influenced by personalism (1920s); he portrayed Jesus as having a high God-consciousness. He became more Barthian by the time of the Madras Conference (1938). Toward the end of his life he was convinced that Christianity was irrelevant for the new China.

SAMUEL LING

Chapman, John Wilbur (1859–1918)

Presbyterian minister and evangelist. Born in Richmond, Indiana, he graduated from Lake Forest College and Lane Seminary, Cincinnati, and was ordained as a Presbyterian minister in 1882. He served five charges in seventeen years, but even during that time he felt a wider calling to evangelism, in which area he was to serve his denomination as representative-at-large for the last seventeen years of his life. Associated for a time with D. L. Moody, he later joined with Charles M. Alexander in conducting evangelistic campaigns on four continents. Chapman is remembered also as the first director of the Winona Lake Bible Conference and compiler of (and contributor to) a number of hymnbooks. His church's general assembly elected him as its moderator in 1917. Among Chapman's other books were *Ivory Palaces of the King* (1893), *Revivals and Missions* (1900), *Present-Day Evangelism* (1903), *Another Mile* (1908), and *When Home Is Heaven* (1917).

Biography by J. C. Ramsey (1962).

J. D. DOUGLAS

Charles, Robert Henry (1855–1931)

Biblical scholar and Anglican archdeacon. Born in Cookstown, County Tyrone, Ireland, he was educated at Queen's University, Belfast, and Trinity College, Dublin. He was ordained in 1883 and until 1889 served several London curacies. Ill health restricted his ministry thereafter; while recovering in Oxford he began to study intertestamental Judaism. In 1898 he was appointed professor of biblical Greek at Trinity College, Dublin. As his health improved he became a residentiary canonry of Westminster Abbey in 1913, and in 1919 archdeacon of Westminster. He began producing critical editions of the apocryphal books in 1893. He edited *The Apocrypha and Pseudepigrapha of the Old Testament* in 1913. This volume is still in print and is supreme in its field. Such was the diversity of his skills that he could produce commentaries on *The Book of Revelation* (1920) and *The Book of Daniel* (1929). While his scholarship and linguistic ability were outstanding, his sympathy for the language of apocalyptic was limited.

NOEL S. POLLARD

Cheney, Charles Edward (1836–1916)

First bishop of the Reformed Episcopal Church. Born in Canandaigua, New York, he graduated from Hobart College and the Protestant Episcopal Seminary, Alexandria, Virginia. Ordained priest in 1858, he became rector of Christ Church, Chicago, in 1860, a post he held until his death. He was evangelical, equally opposed to the Roman Catholic Church and to radicalism (especially relating to Scripture). Although the civil courts thwarted a "High Church" bishop's attempt to depose Cheney, the growing ritualism and sacerdotalism in the Protestant Episcopal Church led in 1873 to the formation of the Reformed Episcopal Church, in which action Cheney collaborated with G. D. Cummins, assistant bishop of Kentucky, who became presiding bishop of the new body. Cheney believed in collaborating with all evangelical Christians who held to "the great fundamental principles" of Christianity. Among his published works were *A Word to Old-Fashioned Episcopalians* (1884), *What Do Reformed Episcopalians Believe?* (1888), and *The Enlistment of the Christian Soldier* (1893).

J. D. DOUGLAS

Chesterton, G(ilbert) K(eith) (1874–1936)

English writer and Christian apologist. Son of a Kensington realtor, he studied art and literature in London, and soon established a foothold in the field of reviewing, publishing, and journalism. Chesterton early discovered the value of paradox as "truth standing on its head to gain attention." Soon the young man with strong views on social criticism and a whimsical way with words was making an impact on Edwardian society. He produced over one hundred books on a vast range of subjects, notably biographical, then turned to theology after conversion to Roman Catholicism in 1922. He was a master of the metaphorical Mickey Finn which (perhaps because paradox was involved) had the opposite effect: it galvanized people into thought.

He complained that "the act of defending any of the cardinal virtues has today all the exhilaration of a vice," and he set out to debunk decadence. He held that the acid test of all religions was, What does it deny? Anyone, he felt, could fall into the many fads from gnosticism to Christian Science, "but to have avoided them all has been one whirling adventure . . . [with] the wild truth reeling but erect." Americans loved him, not least for his comment on the dazzling lights of Broadway: "What a glorious garden of wonders this would be to anyone lucky enough not to be able to read!" Among his later works were *The Everlasting Man* (1925), *Saint Thomas Aquinas* (1933), *Avowals and Denials* (1934), and his *Autobiography* (1936).

Biographies by Maisie Ward (1947) and Dudley Barker (1973).

J. D. DOUGLAS

Chew, Benjamin (1907–1994)

Chinese physician and evangelical leader. Born in Malacca, into a Christian family that moved from Malaya to Singapore in 1910, he was converted at thirteen, trained at the King Edward VII College of Medicine, Singapore, and graduated as a doctor in 1929. He served in Singapore during the harrowing years of Japanese occupation (1942–1945). He had been the first to set up a clinical laboratory in British-governed Singapore in 1931, and the first to use penicillin there in World War II days. He later resigned a lucrative post in government service so that he could devote himself to battling the rampant scourge of tuberculosis. Chew evinced a marked social concern in confronting Singapore's problems of drug addiction, gangsterism, and secret societies, and involved himself in prison visitation work. Always a warm supporter of evangelical enterprises, notably the Overseas Missionary Fellowship, his wide acceptance among English- and Chinese-speaking Christians played a large part in 237 of the 265 Protestant congregations joining in support of the 1978 Billy Graham crusade. Chew has always played a full part as elder in his local Brethren congregation. The Anglican bishop of Singapore, Moses Tay (himself a former physician), says of him, "He well deserves the unofficial but affectionate designation—'Patriarch and Archbishop'!"

Biography by Sayyiddah Talib (1991).

J. D. DOUGLAS

Chikane, Frank (1951–)

South African church leader and theologian. Called into ministry at an early age, Chikane recalls preaching his first sermon at age eight. Caught up in the social injustice of South African society under apartheid, he has worked to bring the Christian faith to those who found themselves oppressed by whites who also professed to be Christian. Prevented from completing his university degree because of his leadership of a Christian student group, he was arrested and detained in prison under the antiterrorism laws of South Africa. While in detention, he was tortured. In spite of this treatment, he has not responded with hatred to his persecutors. Ordained as a minister in the Apostolic Faith Mission, he is also a theologian and one of the architects of the Karios Document. This declaration advocated "prophetic theology," taking the Bible's admonitions against injustice as a hermeneutical key to the South African situation. He was also one of the founders of the Institute for Contextual Theology. Having succeeded Desmond Tutu as general secretary of the South African Council of Churches, Chikane is the youngest person to hold that position. He wrote the autobiographical *No Life of My Own.*

JAMES J. STAMOOLIS

Chitambar, Jashwaut Rao (1879–1940)

Indian Methodist bishop. He was born in Allahabad, Uttar Pradesh, to parents, who had been high-caste Hindus before coming to Christ, and who had to flee their home to escape persecution. His father worked as a Methodist school teacher and minister. At age seventeen, Chitambar sensed God's call to serve full-time in Christian ministry, and responded. He earned a B.A. from Allahabad University, followed by a course at Bareilly Theological Seminary. He served variously as preacher, pastor, missionary, superintendent, educator, and churchman. He pastored congregations in Naini Tal and Lucknow, and served as secretary of the Board of Home and Foreign Missions of the Methodist Church in Southern Asia. He was the first Indian principal of Lucknow Christian College, and the first Indian bishop of his denomination. Presenting himself as the Indian ambassador of the gospel, he preached in many countries. He wrote biographies of John Wesley (1914) and Mahatma Gandhi (1933), translated several English hymns into Hindustani, and was on the committee that revised *The Standard Hindustani Dictionary.*

A. SCOTT MOREAU

Cho, David (formerly Paul) Yonggi (1936–)

Korean evangelist and church planter. Born near Pusan, he was reared in a traditionally Buddhist family. At age eighteen he contracted tuberculosis. The doctor predicted he would die in three months, but through the witness of a Christian high school girl who gave him a New Testament he cried out to Jesus for help and recovered. His father drove him out of the home for forsaking the family religion. In Pusan an American ex-Marine Christian introduced him to Pentecostal missionary Lou Richards, whose World Mission Church he joined. In 1956 Richards sent him to Seoul to study at the Full Gospel Bible Institute sponsored by the Assemblies of God. On graduation (1958) a fellow student, a Presbyterian nurse who had escaped from communist North Korea, enlisted Cho's help in starting a Pentecostal tent church in the Seoul slums, volunteering to visit and recruit the poor and the refugees if he would do the preaching. By 1961 the tiny congregation had outgrown the tent and moved to a large new church in downtown west Seoul, naming it the Revival Center (later the Full Gospel Central Church). By 1973 membership had reached 18,000, and the church built a new sanctuary, seating 10,000, on Yoido Island in central Seoul. By the early 1990s it was the largest single Protestant congregation in the world, numbering more than half a million. Cho credits the growth to the power of the Holy Sprit, committed lay evangelism, and home cell groups (17,381 by 1982) through which the enormous membership keeps its integrity of faith, prayer-fellowship, and Bible study.

SAMUEL H. MOFFETT

Choi, Philemon Yuen-wan (1945–)

Chinese youth ministry leader, counselor, speaker, and author. Born in China, he graduated from the University of Manitoba in 1971 in medicine. He served part-time in Evangel Hospital in Hong Kong as well as with the Fellowship of Evangelical Students in Hong Kong (1971–1976). He graduated from Trinity Evangelical Divinity School in 1977, and has served as FES general secretary (1977–1980). From 1981 he served as general secretary of Breakthrough Ltd., a multi-faceted ministry that publishes two monthly magazines for Hong Kong's youth, radio programs on commercial radio, a counseling ministry, a camp, a publishing arm, an audiovisual division, and many other ministries reaching over half a million people in Hong Kong. Choi has served on numerous boards and committees, including several government committees on youth, sexuality, social welfare, and television broadcasting. He was a member of the central coordinating committee for International Youth Year (1985). He was an outspoken voice against the legalization of homosexuality in Hong Kong, and led Hong Kong's Christians both before and after the 1989 Tiananmen Square incident to renew their vision for Hong Kong and China. He has provided leadership on the boards of China Graduate School of Theology and the Chinese Coordination Centre of World Evangelism. Choi has published numerous books and articles, including, "You Can Also Plan for Your Life," and the groundbreaking paperback, *A Father Whom You Have Never Encountered.*

SAMUEL LING

Chow, Wilson Wing-Kin (1943–)

Chinese Old Testament scholar and theological educator. Born in Hong Kong, Wilson Chow graduated from the University of Hong Kong in 1965, and received the B.D. degree from Westminster Theological Seminary in

1969, and the M.A. (1971) and Ph.D. (1973) from Brandeis University in Mediterranean studies. He did research on the Nuzi texts under Cyrus Gordon. He has been a lecturer member of the China Graduate School of Theology since its founding in 1975, and in 1989 was appointed its president. Chow has lectured widely both in Asia and the West. He has contributed to numerous Chinese and English volumes, including the *New Dictionary of Theology* (1988) and *The Bible and Theology in Asian Contexts* (1984). In addition to writing and teaching in Old Testament, Chow appealed to Christian youth of the Chinese diaspora to enter full-time Christian service, and challenged the Hong Kong church to renew her mission in light of China's takeover in 1997. Chow is a leading voice in advocating indigenous theology and indigenous theological training for the church in Asia.

SAMUEL LING

Christoffel, Ernst Jakob (1876–1955)

German missionary. Born in Rheydt (Rhineland), he was reared in a devout family, worked briefly as a teacher, and then attended the mission seminary at Basel. After graduating in 1904, Ernst and his sister, Hedwig, served for three years as missionaries in an orphanage in Sivas, Turkish Armenia. Here they became aware of the needs of blind people and decided to form a special mission to minister to them. After he raised some support in Europe, they returned to Turkey and in early 1909 opened a home in Malatya called Bethesda. Four missionaries soon labored there, and they welcomed the blind and people with other infirmities regardless of their religious faith, witnessed to the love of Christ in "sermons without words," and ministered to both physical and spiritual needs. World War I brought the work to an end, and in 1919 Christoffel was expelled from Turkey. Negotiations with the Turkish government to revive the work of his mission came to naught, but in 1925 he was able to open a home for the blind and infirm in Tabriz in northwestern Iran. In 1928 a second and much larger work was begun in Isfahan. He taught the blind to read and even produced a braille bible, fostered handicrafts so they could be more self-supporting, and trained teachers and evangelists. In World War II Allied troops occupied Iran and the mission staff was interned, but the British Church Missionary Society took charge of the Isfahan and American Presbyterians took over the Tabriz works. Christoffel eventually returned to Germany, but in 1951 he was allowed to come back to Iran and died in Isfahan four years later. Meanwhile the Mission to the Blind extended its work throughout the world; within twenty-five years after his death it was ministering in eighty countries.

Biography by F. Schmidt-König (1980).

RICHARD V. PIERARD

Clark, Francis Edward (1851–1927)

Founder of the United Society of Christian Endeavor. He was born Francis Edward Symmes in Aylmer, Quebec, but was soon orphaned and legally adopted by his uncle, E. W. Clark, a Congregational minister in Auburndale, Massachusetts. Francis assumed his uncle's (and his mother's maiden) surname. He graduated from Dartmouth College (1873) and Andover Seminary (1876), and during his first pastorate at Williston Congregational Church, Portland, Maine, he made young people an important part of his ministry. In 1881 he organized the Williston Young People's Society of Christian Endeavor, a fellowship designed to encourage youth to commit themselves to a life of responsible Christian discipleship. Members pledged to "endeavor" to live a Christian life, to pray and read the Bible daily, and to participate in meetings of the local congregation. Young people responded enthusiastically, and soon Clark was fielding requests for information from other pastors. He published *The Children and the Church* (1882), and moved in 1883 to pastor the Phillips Congregational Church in South Boston. A growing Christian Endeavor movement soon demanded more and more of his time. In 1885 the United Society of Christian Endeavor was incorporated. Clark resigned the pastorate in 1887 to give himself full-time to the society; he was president for thirty-eight years. In 1888 he visited England by invitation to initiate the society's work there, and later traveled much to promote the society, writing *Our Journey around the World* (1894) and *Worldwide Endeavor* (1895). In 1895 he helped organize the World's Christian Endeavor Union and served as its president until 1925. By 1921 over eighty thousand chapters had been formed, consisting of millions of members in forty countries. He edited the movement's magazine, and wrote many other books, including an autobiography.

Biographies by W. K. Chaplin (1902) and E. F. Clark (1930).

TIMOTHY K. BEOUGHER

Clark, Gordon Haddon (1902–1986)

American evangelical philosopher. Born in Philadelphia, son of a Presbyterian minister, he was educated at the University of Pennsylvania and obtained a Ph.D. there before going for further study to the Sorbonne (Paris). He taught philosophy at the University of Pennsylvania (1924–1936) and at Reformed Episcopal Seminary (1932–1936) before transferring to Wheaton College (1936–1943), where philosophy soon became his favorite major. His intellectually demanding courses challenged modern speculation and fundamentalist emotion; this, along with his rigorous Calvinism, precipitated his dismissal. In 1945 he joined the faculty at Butler University where for twenty-eight years he chaired the philosophy department. Clark championed biblical theism as intellectually tenable, and wrote important works on the history of Western thought and on the Christian alternative to contemporary thought. His insistence that public reason (that is, logic) is a test of truth clashed with the more fideistic stance of Cornelius Van Til, who emphasized the incomprehensibility of God. The conflict led to Clark's departure from the Orthodox Presbyterian Church in which he was ordained, and his affiliation with the Reformed Presbyterian Church. A skillful theologian and apologist for evangelical Christianity, he resisted both modernism and neo-orthodoxy. He wrote more than thirty books, among them *A Christian Philosophy of Education* (1946), *A Christian View of Men and Things* (1951), *Biblical Predestination* (1969), and *Language and Theology* (1980).

See R. H. Nash (ed.), *The Philosophy of Gordon Clark* (1968).

CARL F. H. HENRY

Clarke, William Newton (1841–1912)

Baptist clergyman and theologian. Born in Cazenovia, New York, the son of a Baptist clergyman, he graduated from Madison (now Colgate) University (1861) and Colgate Theological Seminary (1863). He was ordained in 1863 and pastored Baptist churches in Keene, New Hampshire (1863–1869), Newton Center, Massachusetts (1869–1880), and Montreal, Quebec (1880–1883). It was during his Newton years that Clarke's theology shifted from traditional theological positions to more liberal viewpoints. Stimulated by interaction with faculty and students at the nearby Newton Theological Institution, his sermons increasingly reflected a reinterpretation of Christian faith in light of higher critical views. Opposition from some of his church members caused him to leave the church. In 1883 he was invited to serve as professor of New Testament interpretation at Toronto Baptist College. In 1887 he returned to the pastorate in Hamilton, New York. This brought him into close contact with the life and students of Colgate Theological Seminary, where he served as professor of Christian theology (1890–1908). After retirement he lectured there in Christian ethics until his death. Through his teaching and writings, he helped promote modernism in American theological seminaries. He held a very optimistic view of humankind, believing that people were still developing as part of the evolutionary process. He published *An Outline of Christian Theology* in 1898, a work that is widely viewed as America's first systematic theology from a liberal perspective. Following Schleiermacher (1768–1834), he argued that the starting point for theology was "religious sentiment," not an authoritative Bible. Since all theology is a product of religious experience, all religions contain a measure of truth. Clarke rejected traditional views of biblical inspiration and argued that the Scriptures should inspire theology, not be its authoritative source.

Other books he authored include *What Shall We Think of Christianity?* (1899), *The Use of the Scriptures in Theology* (1905), and *The Christian Doc-*

trine of God (1909). His work, *A Study of Christian Missions* (1900), rejected traditional motives for missionary work, arguing instead that missionaries should call persons to Christ and Christian civilization because of their superiority over other alternatives.

Bibliography by E. S. Clarke (1916).

TIMOTHY K. BEOUGHER

Cleveland, James (1932–1991)

Pastor, singer, and composer. Born on Chicago's south side, James Cleveland was introduced to gospel music at Pilgrim Baptist Church, where Thomas A. Dorsey, the father of gospel music, was his mentor. His career, which started at an early age, included singing with many musical groups. He formed the Cleveland Singers and led Detroit's one hundred-voice Prayer Tabernacle Choir. Pastor and founder of Cornerstone Institutional Baptist Church in Los Angeles, he said of himself, "Singing is my inspiration, but preaching is my call."

Cleveland's achievements include six gold albums, three Grammy awards, and more than four hundred songs. He has been called the "King of the Gospel" and is the first gospel singer to be immortalized with a gold star on Hollywood's Walk of Fame. *Billboard* magazine selected Cleveland as the best male singer in Soul Gospel with the best album, "Live at Carnegie." Some of his most successful albums are "Peace Be Still," "I'll Do His Will," "Lord, Do It," "I Stood on the Banks," "Lord Help Me," "Jesus Is the Best Thing," and "Amazing Grace," which he recorded with Aretha Franklin. In an effort to support and train those working with choirs, he formed the Gospel Music Workshop of America in 1968.

ROBERT C. SUGGS

Clough, John Everett (1836–1910)

American Baptist missionary in South India. Born in Frewsbury, New York, he began work as a surveyor at age seventeen, eventually becoming licensed by the U.S. government. He went to Burlington College, Iowa, to study law and become a wealthy attorney. There, through the influence of a devout Christian roommate, he became a committed Christian. When a missionary from Burma came to Burlington to appeal for workers, Clough sensed God's call on his life. He transferred to Upper Iowa University, and just after graduation in 1864 the foreign missions board assigned him to serve in Ongole, India. There he and his new wife ministered among the Telugus, a tribe of low-caste people. They started the Ongole Baptist Church with eight members in 1867.

During the terrible famine of 1876–1878 Clough organized relief work that benefited tens of thousands. To provide food for the starving, he took a contract from the Indian government to dig four miles of the one hundred-mile extension of the Buckingham Canal. He organized camps and relief stations that gave work, shelter, and food to many. His staff of thirty preachers oversaw the work and provided spiritual guidance and encouragement for the masses of people. Clough refused to baptize those who asked to join the church during this period, wanting to avoid "rice Christians." After the famine was over, converts were accepted—over two thousand on one day, nearly nine thousand in a six-month period. The Ongole Baptist Church totaled over 21,000 members before it was divided into smaller congregations. Among those who worked under Clough in India was Walter Rauschenbusch. Clough often traveled to America for fund-raising purposes. In 1873 he returned with an endowment of $50,000 to establish a theological seminary among the Telugus. When failing health forced Clough to leave India in 1910 he left behind nearly sixty thousand church members in a mission field that had been almost abandoned in discouragement before his coming.

TIMOTHY K. BEOUGHER

Clouse, Robert Gordon (1931–)

American historian. Born in Mansfield, Ohio, the son of a schoolteacher, he attended Bryan College and Grace Theological Seminary and then took graduate training in history at the University of Iowa. He was then appointed to the faculty of Indiana State University, Terre Haute, and spent his professional career there. He also pastored churches in the Grace Brethren denomination in Cedar Rapids, Iowa, and Clay City, Indiana. His achievements in the fields of Renaissance and Reformation history, seventeenth- and eighteenth-century European Protestantism, and war and peace studies were numerous, but he is best known for his scholarship in eschatological and millennial thought. His *The Meaning of the Millennium* (1977) was a best-seller, while he contributed many articles on the topic to journals and symposia. The recipient of a heart transplant in 1985, his experiences were widely publicized both in church and medical circles. He also was active in the work of the American Heart Association and lectured widely on the ethics of organ donation.

His most important work as a historian of Christianity was the coauthored *Two Kingdoms: The Church and Culture Through the Ages* (1993). Among the other books he authored or coauthored are *Puritans, The Millennium, and the Future of Israel* (1970), *The Cross and the Flag* (1972), *The Church in an Age of Orthodoxy and Enlightenment* (1980), *War, Four Christian Views* (1981), and *Women in Ministry, Four Views* (1989). Clouse was a founder of the Conference on Faith and History, member of the editorial board of the *Brethren Encyclopedia*, contributing editor of the *New Twentieth Century Encyclopedia of Religious Knowledge*, and twice president of the Central Renaissance Conference.

RICHARD V. PIERARD

Coffin, Henry Sloane (1877–1954)

American Presbyterian pastor and educator. Born in New York City, he was educated at Yale, Edinburgh, and Union Theological Seminary, New York. He was ordained in 1900, and by establishing a Presbyterian mission congregation in the Bronx, he gave an early indication of the passion for social activism that was to characterize his life. During his pastorate at Madison Avenue Presbyterian Church (1905–1926) he became one of America's most eloquent preachers. Over that period he also taught practical theology at Union Theological Seminary, and became its president in 1926, serving until 1945. Under his visionary leadership a remarkable faculty was assembled, including Paul Tillich and Reinhold Niebuhr, making the school a potent influence in the religion and politics of midcentury America.

Coffin himself led this influence as preacher, educator, author, hymnologist, proponent of the social gospel, and leader in the ecumenical movement. As a thinker committed to evangelical liberalism and theological inclusivism, he sought to broaden the theological base of the Presbyterian Church, USA, reunite the northern and southern branches of the Presbyterian Church, and moderate the antagonism between conservatism and liberalism. His influence extended into national and international politics where he was a key figure in America's entrance into World War II and in the formation of the United Nations. His many published works include *Social Aspects of the Cross* (1911), *What Men Are Asking* (1933), *Religion Yesterday and Today* (1940), and *Communion Through Preaching* (1952).

Biography by M. P. Noyes (1964).

JACK MITCHELL

Coggan, (Frederick) Donald (1909–)

Archbishop of Canterbury. Born in London, he found Christian nurture in the evangelical parish of St. Peter, Upper Holloway. When he went to Cambridge he found a natural home in the Cambridge Inter-Collegiate Christian Union (CICCU). He read Oriental languages, including Hebrew, with considerable distinction, and the rigorous spiritual and academic disciplines he developed there stood him in good stead for the punishing workloads he bore in future years. He was in theological education for twenty-two years, at Wycliffe College, Toronto, and later as principal of the London College of Divinity (now St. John's, Nottingham). His sympathies were not always those expected of a 1920s CICCU-trained evangelical: his ecumenical vision, distrust of fundamentalism, and openness to other Christian traditions—all commonplace among evangelical Anglicans today—caused some to doubt his evangelical credentials. But his love of the Bible never diminished, evidenced in his strongly biblical preaching and in his lifelong work for the Bible Societies. He was bishop of Bradford (1956–1961), and as archbishop of York (1961–1974) issued a

"Call to the North," a fruitful program of ecumenical cooperation and evangelism. Coggan traveled widely and exhaustively, making historic visits in Eastern Europe and throughout the Anglican Communion. Among his writings are *The Prayers of the New Testament* (1967), *On Preaching* (1978), *Mission to the World* (1982), and *Paul: Portrait of a Revolutionary* (1984). He retired from Canterbury in 1980.

Biography by Margaret Pawley (1987).

JOHN B. TAYLOR

Coleman, Alice Blanchard Merriam (1858–1936)

Baptist home missions leader. Her rise to national leadership began in Boston where she was born to a missionary-minded family, and where her father served with the Boston City Missionary Society. After graduating from Bradford Academy in 1878 she became involved in the Women's Home Missionary Association of the Congregational Church. Her intense interest in home missions was given sharper focus under the influence of A. J. Gordon, and she joined his Clarendon Street Baptist Church in 1886. Her commitment to the Baptist denomination was cemented by marriage to G. W. Coleman, a deacon and Sunday school superintendent of the church. She became president of the Women's American Baptist Home Mission Society (1890–1909). When in 1910 the society merged with the Women's Baptist Home Mission Society of Chicago, she assumed the presidency of the national organization until 1928. She thus led a movement that served in the United States, Mexico, and the Caribbean, and was involved in orphanages, the education of girls, general evangelistic work, and the support of missionary families. She was also the founder and first president of the ecumenical Council of Women for Home Missions (1908–1916) and a trustee of Gordon and Spelman colleges.

JACK MITCHELL

Colom Maldonado, Alfredo (1904–1971)

Latin American hymnologist and evangelist. Born in El Palmar, Quezaltenango, Guatemala, as Alfredo Colombo Meldonado, "don Alfredo" was converted to Christ in 1924. For years as a municipal employee he wandered from the Lord and suffered several trials, including the death of three children. While praying with a fellow believer in his humble abode, Colom dedicated his life to Christ. There, while kneeling, he saw a vision of Jesus with bleeding hands. This provided the inspiration for many of the hymns he would write until his death, such as "Manos Carinosas" (Bleeding Hands of Jesus) and "Ven a los Pies de Jesus" (Come to the Feet of Jesus). In 1949, after serving as a teacher in Guatemala's capital, he moved to Colombia to preach the gospel. Later he ministered throughout Latin America with Robert Savage. He was called "la fabrica de himnos y coritos" (the factory of hymns and choruses). *Hymnos de Fe y Albanza* (1966) contains thirty-three of his hymns, including "Por la mañana," which sparkles with spiritual warmth, and "America sera para Cristo" (America Will Be Christ's), which features bright, martial music wedded to lyrics that list all the nations of the Americas.

PHILIP BLYCKER

Colson, Charles W. (1931–)

Founder of Prison Fellowship Ministries. Born in Boston, he graduated "with distinction" from Brown University (1953), to which was added a J.D. degree from George Washington University (1959) a year after he had passed the Virginia State Bar. In 1968 he left a lucrative law practice and was a key figure in the 1968 and 1972 Nixon presidential campaigns. Converted in 1973, he confessed to an obstruction of justice charge in connection with the Watergate affair and was imprisoned for seven months. Moved by compassion for prisoners, he promoted reform of prison conditions in the cause of justice and spiritual evangelism. What began as discipleship seminars for small clusters of furloughed inmates soon expanded into prison ministries and an extensive "Angel Tree" program for the families of offenders. In North Carolina in 1992 some 75 percent of the prison population voluntarily attended evangelistic events at which thousands of prisoners made spiritual commitments. The work has become international: in 1992 participants from eighty-four countries shared in the fourth triennial convocation in Seoul, Korea. PFM has given rise to Justice Fellowship (concerned for prisoners' rights), the publication *Inside Rights* (for prisoners, with a spiritual and moral orientation), and "Neighbors Who Care" (a ministry to victims of crime). Awarded the 1993 Templeton Prize for Progress in Religion, Colson designated the $940,000 award for evangelical ministry. His written works include *Born Again* (1976), *Life Sentence* (1979), *Kingdoms in Conflict* (1987), and (with E. S. Vaughn) *The Body* (1992).

CARL F. H. HENRY

Cone, James H. (1938–)

Systematic theologian and author. James Cone is an energetic thinker and controversial theorist whose formal education took place at Philander Smith College, Little Rock, Arkansas, and Garrett Theological Seminary in Illinois. In 1965 he received a Ph.D. degree in systematic theology from Northwestern University. He has championed the view that Christian theology is a theology of liberation. For him, the general focus of Christian theology must be the underclass and the oppressed. His interpretation of the African-American experience and his understanding of Scripture have led him to develop what has been called black theology. He holds that Christ is the norm for this theology. Through teaching and example, Jesus calls for the liberation of the black community.

Cone became the first to employ the term and the foremost spokesperson on black theology. He used his revolutionary work, *Black Theology and Black Power*, to demonstrate what he believed to be the common message of Jesus Christ and the black power movement. He contends that Jesus would be an active participant in the black power struggle. His second book, *A Theology of Liberation*, served to more fully develop the concepts contained in his first book. *God of Oppression* continued the systematic treatment of the material presented in his first two works.

Currently Cone serves as professor of systematic theology at Union Theological Seminary. His books include *Black Theology and Black Power* (1969), *A Theology of Liberation* (1970), *God of Oppression* (1984), and *Martin and Malcolm and America* (1991).

ROBERT C. SUGGS

Conner, Walter Thomas (1877–1952)

Southern Baptist theologian. Born in Cleveland County, Arkansas, amid the poverty of the Reconstruction era, Conner moved at age five with his family to a farm near Abilene, Texas. Converted in a Methodist revival and baptized into and ordained by Baptist churches, he struggled for his education. He graduated from Baylor University, Southwestern Baptist Seminary, Rochester Theological Seminary, and Southern Baptist Theological Seminary (Th.D., 1916; Ph.D., 1931). He served as professor of systematic theology at Southwestern Baptist Theological Seminary (1910–1949). Conner combined in his theology certain aspects of three of his teachers: B. H. Carroll, A. H. Strong, and E. Y. Mullins. Influenced by personalism, he held to general revelation, emphasized the moral self-consistency of the divine attributes, tended toward a kenotic Christology, and shifted from a modified penal theory of Christ's saving work to the concept of *Christus victor*. He espoused a moderate Calvinism (election, perseverance), argued that justification is "vital" and not "declarative," explicated the doctrine of the Holy Spirit, and abandoned postmillennialism in favor of amillennialism.

Conner was preeminently the classroom teacher, and for a substantial period the most influential systematic theologian in the Southern Baptist Convention. His fifteen books include *Revelation and God* (1937), *The Faith of the New Testament* (1940), *The Gospel of Redemption* (1945), and *The Cross in the New Testament* (1954).

Biography by S. A. Newman (1964); theology the subject of unpublished dissertation by J. L. Garrett, Jr. (1954).

J. LEO GARRETT, JR.

Conwell, Russell Herman (1843–1925)

American preacher, lecturer, and philanthropist. He was born in Worthington, Massachusetts, into a poor Christian family whose farm was a station on the Underground Railroad. At Yale he was an avowed atheist. The Civil War interrupted his studies; he achieved the rank of lieutenant-colonel, but a serious wound ended his military career and caused his conversion. He graduated and pursued a career in law, then in 1879 was ordained to the Baptist pastorate in Lexington, Massachusetts. In 1882 he transferred to a church in Philadelphia that became the city's largest Protestant congregation. The church was the center of community life, providing concerts, clubs, classes, and even health care. It established three hospitals, and its night courses, which helped working people to better themselves, developed into Temple University.

Conwell is best known for his inspirational lectures, especially the famous "Acres of Diamonds." Lecturing at least ten thousand times nationwide, he raised over $11 million, which was donated to Temple students. Conwell held that "to make money honestly is to preach the gospel." Money is the power by which one can help the community and "poorer brethren." He denounced both the "lazy poor" and the wealthy who accumulated riches for their own enjoyment only. The best-known Baptist minister of his day, Conwell consistently embodied and practiced what he preached.

Biography by A. R. Burr (1926).

TIMOTHY R. PHILLIPS

Cook, David Caleb (1850–1927)

Methodist author and publisher of Sunday school materials. He was born in East Worcester, New York, but moved when a boy with his family to northern Illinois. Forced to discontinue study at Wheaton College because of health problems, he started a successful sewing machine business in downtown Chicago. His love for teaching the Bible to children, however, soon consumed all his time and interests. At seventeen he became actively involved in teaching Sunday school, often doing as many as three separate classes on Sundays and holding open-air meetings for children on weekday evenings. In 1872 he founded Everybody's Mission for children on Chicago's North Side.

Distressed at the lack of inexpensive teaching materials, in the early 1870s he first produced and published with his wife *Our Sunday School Quarterly*. It was an instant success with a circulation of forty thousand copies, doubling the next year. The ever-growing demand for Sunday school curricula soon led to his founding in Lake View, Illinois, the David C. Cook Publishing Company, which he permanently established in Elgin, Illinois, in 1901. With an eventual worldwide circulation reaching into the hundreds of thousands, Cook published Sunday school materials for all age groups, along with story papers, teachers' manuals, hymnals, and other related literature. He also founded the IAH (I Am His) Circle, a series of lessons aimed at teaching children and adults about the "Charmed Life" of companionship with Jesus. Its members wore a silver ring, inscribed with the initials, reminding them to remain faithful to Jesus. This work also received national and international recognition. Cook's pioneer endeavors in religious education and Sunday school work are recounted in *Memoirs: David C. Cook, The Friend of the Sunday School* (1928).

H. Douglas Buckwalter

Costas, Orlando Enrique (1942–1987)

Missiologist, educator, and writer. Born in Ponce, Puerto Rico, he moved to the United States with his family in 1954. He graduated from the Inter-American University of Puerto Rico (1966), Winona Lake School of Theology (1967), Garrett Theological Seminary (1969), and the Free University of Amsterdam, where he earned a doctorate in theology in 1975. After several pastorates the Latin American Mission sent him in 1970 to Costa Rica. He taught there at the Latin American Biblical Seminary, worked with Evangelism in Depth, and directed the Latin American Evangelical Center for Pastoral Studies. From 1980 to 1984 he was professor of missiology and director of Hispanic studies at Eastern Baptist Theological Seminary, and then served as professor of missiology and dean at Andover-Newton Theological School until his premature death. He wrote fifteen books in Spanish and English on missiology, theology, and communications, and contributed to many others. Truly multifaceted, he was strongly committed to evangelicalism, evangelism, and missions, but was also involved in ecumenical dialogue, human rights, and political causes such as independence for Puerto Rico.

Stephen R. Sywulka

Coucouzis, Iakovos (1911–)

Greek Orthodox archbishop of North and South America. Born Demetrios Coucouzis on the Turkish island of Imbros, he graduated from the Patriarchal Theological Academy of Halki in 1934. Upon ordination the same year he took the ecclesiastical name Iakovos. In 1939 he was transferred to the United States and served as archdeacon in the Greek Orthodox Archdiocese, and later on the faculty and administration of Holy Cross Greek Orthodox School of Theology, Brookline, Massachusetts. After several pastoral assignments he became dean of the Cathedral of the Annunciation in Boston, where he developed an impressive and influential youth ministry (1942–1954). During this period he earned the S.T.M. degree at Harvard University. He was elected bishop of Melita in 1954 and appointed representative of the Ecumenica Patriarchate at the World Council of Churches in Geneva. In 1956 he was promoted to metropolitan of Melita. In Geneva he became well known as an effective ecumenist with an international reputation. He served as a president of the WCC. In 1959 he was elected archbishop of North and South America of the Greek Orthodox Archdiocese, which position he still holds (1993).

STANLEY S. HARAKAS

Cox, Harvey Gallagher, Jr. (1929–)

Baptist theologian, author, and educator. Graduate of the University of Pennsylvania (1951), Yale Divinity School (1955), and Harvard University (Ph.D., 1963), he was ordained in the American Baptist Church in 1956. He served as director of religious activities at Oberlin College (1955–1958), program associate with the American Baptist Missionary Society (1958–1963), and fraternal worker with the Gossner Mission in Berlin (1962–1963). He then taught at Andover-Newton Theological Seminary (1963–1965) before returning to Harvard as assistant professor of church and society (1965–1970) and professor of divinity (1970–). In 1964 Cox prepared a study guide on the issues of secularization and urbanization for use by the National Student Christian Federation. *The Secular City* (1965), with its positive assessment of these phenomena, brought him instant fame. It caused a debate that led to the publication of a second edition as well as a volume of responses, *The Secular City Debate* (ed., D. Callahan, 1966). The success of this early book makes it difficult to assess Cox's life work, but he seems to have made his most significant contribution in commenting on changes in world society from his liberal Protestant perspective. His other works include *The Feast of Fools* (1969), *God's Revolution and Man's Responsibility* (1965), and *Turning East* (1977).

ROBERT G. CLOUSE

Cragg, Albert Kenneth (1913–)

Anglican bishop and Islamics scholar. Born in Blackpool, England, he was educated at Oxford and at Tyndale Hall, Bristol. After a brief curacy he became chaplain in Beirut, Lebanon, in 1939, and during World War II also taught at the American University there. In 1947 he returned to serve an Oxfordshire parish, went to the United States in 1951 as professor of Arabic and Islamics at Hartford Seminary, and returned to the Middle East in 1956 to be canon of St. George's Collegiate Church, Jerusalem. From 1961 he took on the challenge of reviving the Anglican missionary training college, St. Augustine's, Canterbury. By this time his writings on Islam and Christianity were making him a worldwide authority. In 1970 he was consecrated as assistant to the (Anglican) archbishop in Jerusalem. On his return to England he held various academic and parochial posts. Even after official retirement in 1981 he became an assistant bishop in the diocese of Oxford. His publications include *The Call of the Minaret* (1958), *Sandals at the Mosque* (1959), *Alive to God* (1970), *Islam from Within* (1974), *Jesus and the Muslim* (1985), and *The Arab Christian* (1991).

NOEL S. POLLARD

Craig, Archibald Campbell (1888–1985)

Scottish minister and ecumenist. Born in the border town of Kelso and educated at Edinburgh, he won the military cross for valor in World War I, ministered in Galston (1921–1926) and Glasgow (1926–1930), and then became the first chaplain to Glasgow University (1930–1939). He was an early supporter of the Iona Community whose leader, George MacLeod, had like Craig been decorated in World War I and thereafter strongly espoused pacifism. In 1939 Craig turned to full-time ecumenical activity; when the British Council of Churches was formed in 1942 he was its first secretary. In 1947 he returned to Glasgow University as lecturer in biblical studies until 1957, in which year he fought strenuously (and eventually in vain) for a proposal to unite the national churches in England and Scotland. As moderator of the Kirk's general assembly in 1961 he made history and sparked controversy by visiting Pope John XXIII at the Vatican. A courteous and unassuming man who also became known as a broadcaster, Craig published a number of books, among them *God Comes Four Times* (1956), *The Church in the World* (1961), and *Jesus* (1968).

J. D. DOUGLAS

Crawford, Daniel (1870–1926)

Plymouth Brethren missionary to Central Africa. Born in Gourock, Scotland, he was converted at seventeen, and in 1889 was included in the party taken by fellow countryman F. S. Arnot to Central Africa. Like his mentor, Arnot, and their great predecessor David Livingstone, Crawford was a strong individualist. His emphasis was always on teaching and preaching the Bible, calling for individual conversions, and setting up churches. By 1904 he had translated the New Testament into Luba; the Old Testament was published in 1926. In a book that came to be regarded as a missionary classic, *Thinking Black* (1912), he showed that he understood the African mind as few did. He held that the missionary must identify with the people and encourage them as co-workers in ministry.

JAMES TAYLOR

Crawford, Florence Louise (1872–1936)

Founder of the Pentecostal Apostolic Faith movement. Born in Coos County, Oregon, to atheist parents, she was converted after her marriage to F. M. Crawford, and rapidly became involved in championing Christian social reform. In 1906, during meetings in the Azusa Street Mission, Los Angeles, she experienced sanctification, baptism in the Spirit (speaking in tongues), and healing of her spinal meningitis. She immediately immersed herself in the mission's work, and on its behalf made several evangelistic trips to the Northwest and Canada. In 1907 she accepted a call to lead a small mission church in Portland, Oregon. She named the ministry the Apostolic Faith Church, from which the broader movement evolved. She adopted for her members a strict set of holiness codes governing doctrine and lifestyle. Footwashing was considered an ordinance alongside baptism and the Lord's Supper. The soliciting of funds and regular taking of offerings were abolished; the ministry depended solely on free-will offerings deposited in a box at the church's entrance. The divorced were not permitted to remarry. Complete separation from other religions and worldly influences was mandatory.

Crawford was a strong individualist. She highly criticized Pentecostalism, disliking its centralized organization and perceiving other Pentecostal denominations as inadequately separated from worldliness. She kept her movement detached from other Pentecostal and evangelical groups. This exclusivism brought the movement relatively little growth; it numbered only about three thousand members at the time of her death.

H. DOUGLAS BUCKWALTER

Criswell, W(allie) A(mos) (1909–)

Baptist preacher and author. Born in Eldorado, Oklahoma, he graduated from Baylor University (1931, 1934) and Southern Baptist Theological Seminary (Ph.D., 1937). He was pastor of Baptist churches in Chickasha, Oklahoma (1937–1941), Muskogee, Oklahoma (1941–1944), and First Baptist Church of Dallas, Texas (1944–1991), of which he is still senior pastor. Described as one of the greatest preachers of the twentieth century, he is known for dynamic expository preaching without notes. He delivers the gospel with an optimistic emphasis, and affirms the inerrancy of Scripture and the saving work of God through Jesus Christ. His ministry has been extended throughout America and (in 1950) Japan. He has written many books, including *The Gospel According to Moses* (1950), *Five Great Affirmations of the Bible* (1959), *Why I Preach the Bible as Literally True* (1969), and *With a Bible in My Hand* (1978).

NORMAN R. ERICSON

Crosby, Fanny (Frances Mary Van Alstyne) (1820–1915)

Hymnwriter. Born in Southeast, New York, and blinded at six weeks of age through a medical mishap, she was educated and later taught at the Institute

113

for the Blind in New York City. Reflecting her gift for handling words she wrote hymns that won immediate popularity. Within twenty years "Safe in the Arms of Jesus" was known in more than two hundred languages; it was played at President Grant's funeral. "Pass Me Not, O Gentle Saviour," reportedly a favorite of Queen Victoria, was said to have brought more people to Christ than any other hymn. Crosby's aim was maximum singability, the facilitating of worship by "a song of the heart addressed to God," usually written in the first person so that people could readily identify with the words and thoughts.

Her total output of hymns ran into the thousands, often written to order and sometimes in great haste to meet a publisher's deadline. The quality was understandably uneven, but many are still sung, such as "Blessed Assurance," "Jesus Keep Me Near the Cross," and "Tell Me the Story of Jesus." Her remuneration was small, but she would say that her recompense was in the number of souls who had found salvation through her writing. Ira D. Sankey declared that the success of his campaigns with D. L. Moody was due, more than any other human factor, to Crosby's hymns.

At age sixty she embarked on mission work in The Bowery, where she told needy people that there was pardon and love waiting for them. She deplored "prayerless Presidents" and the growing materialism in American society. She traveled widely as an effective evangelist. In her nineties she was carried cheerfully to and from trains and cars ("I'm safe in the arms of the chauffeur"), and was always convinced that blindness had been a positive help to her ministry.

Autobiographies appeared in 1903 and 1906; further memoirs in collaboration with S. Trevena Jackson in 1915.

Biography by Ethel Barrett (1984).

J. D. DOUGLAS

Crouch, Andrae E. (1943–)

Gospel song writer and singer. A native of Los Angeles and lifelong resident of California, Andrae and his twin sister Sandra grew up in a conservative, "old-time" holiness home. Direction for his life was provided by loving parents, who looked to the church for the standard by which to rear their children. In the early years of Andrae's life, the family worshiped at the Emmanuel Church of God in Christ where Crouch's great-uncle, Bishop Samuel Crouch, was the pastor. Saturday afternoons were spent in the church basement where children of the fellowship engaged in what was called the Sonshine Band. The time was divided among Bible study, refreshments, and singing. While Andrae eagerly anticipated these special weekly meetings, it also was a time at which he experienced the frustration of stammering. His stammering continued until he began to play the piano and sing.

Following a streetcar accident in which Andrae's father sustained broken legs and other injuries, he fulfilled his promise to become a preacher. As a pastor, the elder Crouch provided many opportunities for Andrae and his siblings to sing as a group. Andrae started a choir of young people at his father's church, calling it the Church Of God In Christ Singers (COGICS). Later the singing group changed its name to the Disciples. It was with the Disciples that Crouch began to be recognized for his singing and songwriting. The Disciples under the leadership of Crouch successfully combined jazz, rhythm and blues, and pop with a traditional message of the gospel. Crouch has received six Grammys. The Disciples' first album was "Take the Message Everywhere" and was issued by Light Records. Crouch has written many well-known contemporary Christian songs and has performed his songs at many concerts and rallies as well as on television. Two of the most notable of his songs are "My Tribute" and "Through It All," which are often included in church hymnals. In 1975 and 1977 he was named the soul gospel artist of the year.

ROBERT C. SUGGS

Cruz, Nicky (1938–)

Pentecostal evangelist and crusader to inner-city youth. Born in Puerto Rico to parents who were spiritualists, he was sent to New York City when he was fifteen to live with his brother. In a matter of months, however, he left his brother's family, was expelled from school, and became heavily involved with the violent Mau Maus street gang. Three years later, now a principal figure among the New York City gangs, he was dramatically converted through the ministry of the Rev. David Wilkerson.

Shortly after his conversion, he spent three years preparing for the ministry at the Latin American Bible Institute in La Puente, California (1958–1961). Since then, he has pursued an outreach ministry to troubled inner-city youth and young adults caught up in gang activity through Teen Challenge and the Nicky Cruz Outreach program, and has become an effective internationally known evangelist and crusader against drugs and violence. His life and conversion are recounted in his well-known autobiography, *Run, Baby, Run* (1968, rev. 1992), which has been translated into seventy-two languages and read by millions worldwide, and has become required reading in the schools of several European countries. His story has been supplemented in the sequel *Devil on the Run* (1991) and in David Wilkerson's *The Cross and the Switchblade* (1963), which has been put to film in twenty-four languages. Cruz's numerous books include *Satan on the Loose* (1973), *Where Were You When I Was Hurting?* (1986), *How to Fight Back* (1991), and *Armageddon by Morning* (1992).

H. DOUGLAS BUCKWALTER

Cullmann, Oscar (1902–)

German biblical scholar and theologian. Born in Strasbourg, he studied there, added a doctorate in theology in 1930, and pursued further studies at the Sorbonne in Paris. He taught at Strasbourg (1927–1938) and Basel (1938–1972), combining the latter post with teaching at the Sorbonne (1951–1972). Holding that God shows himself in historical events, Cullmann was the most prominent modern advocate of the Heilsgeschichte (salvation-history) School, his views reflected notably in *Christ and Time* (1951) and *Salvation in History* (1967). "We stand in a section of time," he declared in the former work, "in which we are already redeemed through Christ . . . but in which also the sin characteristic of the entire period before the Parousia is not done away." In *The Christology of the New Testament* (1959) he seeks to show what each of the New Testament titles of Christ meant to the world to which Jesus came, and what we know of Jesus' own attitude toward each title.

In an earlier work (*The Earliest Christian Confessions,* 1949) he declared that the oldest Christian formulas did not know the trinitarian division of the latter confessions, and that the work of Christ is related not only to salvation but to creation also (here he cites several texts, including 1 Cor. 8:6 and Heb. 1:10). A meticulous scholar, Cullmann would willingly discard a long-entrenched idea if listening to the text threw up a more compelling position. He was active in ecumenical affairs, especially in Protestant-Roman Catholic dialogue, and was an observer at Vatican II.

His other works include *Baptism in the New Testament* (1950), *Early Christian Worship* (1953), *Peter: Disciple, Apostle, Martyr* (1953), and *The State in the New Testament* (1956).

J. D. DOUGLAS

D

Daimoi, Joshua Kurung (1942–)

International missionary and educator. Born in Sosirih in Irian Jaya, he received his early education at a Dutch Reformed mission school, and in 1958 was sent by the Dutch government to Port Moresby to study medicine at the Papuan Medical College. In 1962, toward the end of his medical studies, he came to faith in Christ, beginning a pilgrimage that progressively led to recognized national and international leadership status. He studied at Sydney Baptist Theological College (1963–1967) and upon ordination joined the faculty at the interdenominational Christian Leaders' Training College (CLTC) in Papua New Guinea (1968–1971). He pastored the Tokarara Christian Fellowship in Port Moresby (1971–1974) while completing a B.A. degree at the University of Papua New Guinea and holding the position of president of the Evangelical Alliance. He then served as executive secretary of the PNG Bible Society (1974–1979), and was among the first Irian Jayans to receive PNG citizenship. He studied at the Fuller School of World Mission before appointment as CLTC principal in 1983. He has represented PNG at several international missiological conventions. As the first chairman of PNG Missionary Association (the first PNG indigenous missionary sending society), he continues to make a significant contribution to missiology and theological education in the developing world.

R. D. FERGIE

Daniel-Rops, Henri (1901–1965)

Pen name of Henri Petiot, known in France as "le bestseller" for his novels, and as "God's historian" for his scholarly works. Graduate of the University of Grenoble (1922), he expressed the intellectual and emotional turmoil of the post-World War I generation in *Notre Inquietude* (1926). He revealed his personal angst in *L'âme obscure* (1929) and *Deux hommes en moi* (1930), the latter revealing his lifelong fascination with the phenomenon of "split personality." He turned to Roman Catholicism to address the spiritual crisis of modern humanity in several following works, and in others, such as *Death, Where Is Thy Victory?* (1934) maintained that suffering only made sense in the light of Christianity. Other volumes argued that the Christian faith safeguards Western civilization. Appalled by the Nazi persecution of Jews, he wrote *Israel and the Ancient World* (1943),

117

which started his career in religious history. Translated into seventeen languages *Jesus and His Times* (1945) epitomized Daniel-Rops' readable historiography, which he elaborated in *History of the Church of Christ* (1943–1956). In addition to some books of literary criticism he published his poetry in *Orphiques* (1947), founded the periodical *Ecclesia* (1948), and edited the *Twentieth Century Encyclopedia of Catholicism* (1956–).

NORMAN F. CORNETT

Davidson, Randall Thomas (1848–1930)

Archbishop of Canterbury. Born in Scotland and educated at Oxford, he was destined for high office, following in the footsteps of his father-in-law, Archbishop Tait. As dean of Windsor (1883–1891) he was a key adviser to Queen Victoria, and enjoyed good relationships with Edward VII and George V. He moved effortlessly among the ruling elite, and was perhaps the last archbishop to enjoy such a close relationship with prime ministers (he saw eight of them come and go). He was a pillar of the establishment, believed in a comprehensive Church of England, and abhorred anything verging on enthusiasm. Liberal Protestant in temperament, he recognized, and to some extent encouraged, the growing Anglo-Catholic movement. His time at Canterbury (1903–1928) was a period of immense social change that included the General Strike, World War I, the Russian Revolution, the collapse of many of the monarchies, and the first Labour government in the United Kingdom. The Church of Wales was disestablished, and parochial church councils were introduced in the Church of England. Anglo-Catholic pressure led to a revision of the 1662 Book of Common Prayer that twice failed to receive parliamentary approval. Davidson argued strongly for it, seeing it as a way of avoiding secession and liturgical anarchy. Ecumenically, his high watermark was the 1920 Lambeth Conference declaration, "An Appeal to all Christian People." It ushered in new hope for church unity, but issues such as episcopacy proved intractable. He coauthored (with W. Benham) A. C. Tait's biography (1891).

Biography by G. K. A. Bell (2 vols., 1935).

JOHN B. TAYLOR

Dawson, Christopher (1889–1970)

English Roman Catholic historian of ideas. Born in Hay Castle, Wales, he was educated at Trinity College, Oxford. He lectured at Exeter (1930–1936) and Harvard (1958–1962). A convert to Catholicism in 1914, he wrote and lectured widely on religion as the dynamic basis of culture, and on the origins and consequences of alternative worldviews such as belief in progress, fascism, and communism. Views expressed in his famous early books, *The Age of the Gods* (1928) and *Progress and Religion* (1929), were developed in the 1947–1948 Edinburgh Gifford lectures published as *Religion and*

Culture (1948) and *Religion and the Rise of Western Culture* (1950), and repeated in his lectures at Harvard. Standing in the intellectual tradition of Newman, von Hügel, and Lord Acton, Dawson held that Western civilization was losing touch with its own spiritual roots and in its ignorance was in danger of being overrun by the forces of materialism, secularism, and evil. Hence *The Crisis of Western Education* (1961). His views, published in *The Formation of Christendom* (1967) and *The Dividing of Christendom* (1965, 1971), were well received in the United States where he was granted the attention and academic honor that appeared to be denied him as a Catholic in England.

Biography by C. Scott (1984).

PHILIP HILLYER

De Lubac, Henri (1896 –)

Jesuit theologian. Born in Cambrai, France, he became a member of the Society of Jesus (Jesuits) and in 1929 was appointed professor of fundamental theology and the history of religions at the Institut Catholique in Lyons. The inaugural address of his teaching career was later republished in *Zeitschrift für Katholische Theologie* in 1976 on the occasion of his eightieth birthday. His first major work, *Catholicisme*, was published in 1938, with an English translation appearing in 1950. In this work de Lubac seeks to reformulate and represent Catholic tradition in a manner that is not only faithful to the past but also meaningful to a contemporary world. However, after publication of his book *Le Surnaturel* in 1946, he was placed under official censure by Church authorities in Rome. As a religious thinker he was ahead of his time, but his reputation was eventually vindicated when he was invited to Rome as one of the outstanding theologians of the Second Vatican Council. In 1983 he was made a cardinal by Pope John Paul II. He has published over forty books on a wide variety of theological topics. His major works in English translation include *Catholicism* (1950), *Splendour of the Church* (1956), *Further Paradoxes* (1958), *Discovery of God* (1960), *Drama of Atheist Humanism* (1963), *Teilhard de Chardin: The Man and His Meaning* (1965), *Mystery of the Supernatural* (1967), *Religion of Teilhard de Chardin* (1967), *Sources of Revelation* (1968), and *Belorussia Under Soviet Rule* (1972).

L. K. GRIMLEY

Deiros, Pablo A. (1945–)

Argentinian Baptist pastor and Latin American church historian. Born in Argentina, he graduated from the Seminario Internacional Teologico Bautista (Baptist International Theological Seminary) in Buenos Aires where he received a Ph.D. degree from the Instituto Superior de Estudios Teologicos (ISEDET). He has served as a pastor in several Baptist churches

119

in his country, and is currently professor of church history at the Baptist International Theological Seminary. In the 1970s he was executive secretary of the Association of Seminaries and Theological Institutions (ASIT) for southern South America. As a member of the Latin American Theological Fraternity (FTL) he has contributed by editing several books, especially on social and political themes. He has written a number of books, all in Spanish, on the history of the Christian Church in Latin America as well as on youth, marriage, and ethics from a pastoral perspective. He is a prominent figure within the evangelical tradition in Latin America because of his ability to combine a pastoral viewpoint with social and political concerns.

DAVID J. SUAZO

Deissmann, Adolf (1866–1937)

German New Testament scholar. Born in Langenscheid an-der-Lahn, he studied at Tübingen (1885–1888) and other German institutions, and taught New Testament, notably at Heidelberg (1897–1908) and Berlin (1908–1934). His *Bible Studies* (1901), brought together chiefly from papyri and inscriptions, was widely acclaimed for its contributions to the history of the language, literature, and religion of Hellenistic Judaism and primitive Christianity. Deissmann is, however, best known for his monumental *Light from the Ancient East* (1910) with its striking reminder in the opening words: "It was beneath an Eastern sky that the gospel was first preached and Jesus Christ was first adored by worshippers as 'the Lord.'" This work (thoroughly revised and updated by the author in 1922) greatly benefited from Deissmann's journeyings in Asia Minor, Syria, Palestine, and Greece. He was also a prominent ecumenist who, during the dark days of World War I, circulated a "Protestant Weekly Letter" to foster fellowship among believers at home and abroad.

His many other works included *New Light on the Old Testament* (1908) and *The Religion of Jesus and the Faith of Paul* (1923). Deissmann suggested that the Pauline letters were not literary epistles written for publication and posterity, but simply familiar letters intended for the addressees. Deissmann could be an idiosyncratic, but highly entertaining, writer; even his prefaces and footnotes convey an infectious enthusiasm.

J. D. DOUGLAS

Denney, James (1856–1917)

Scottish theologian and New Testament scholar. Born in Paisley, he graduated in arts with great distinction at Glasgow University, studied theology at the city's Free Church College, did mission work in Glasgow's east end, and in 1886 was ordained at Broughty Ferry. He was appointed professor of systematic theology at his old college in 1897, transferring to the New Testament chair in 1900. He became college principal in 1915. As a theologian he moved from a liberal to an evangelical position. He held to the traditional doctrines of Christology, and asserted the substitutionary character of the atonement. He took an active part in church affairs; a memorial tablet describes him as "supreme alike as scholar, teacher, administrator and man of God, to whom many owed their souls." Denney is famous for his commentary on *Romans* (1900) and *The Death of Christ* (1902). His other volumes include *Jesus and the Gospel* (1908), *The Way Everlasting* (1911), and *The Christian Doctrine of Reconciliation* (1917).

J. R. Taylor has written *God Loves Like That: The Theology of James Denney* (1962).

HENRY R. SEFTON

Devanadan, Paul David (1901–1962)

Indian churchman and scholar. Born of Christian parents in Madras, he received a bachelor's degree from Madras University in 1924, a B.D. from Pacific School of Religion, and a Ph.D. in Christian theology from Yale. His ministry responsibilities included pastoral work, teaching, writing, and administrating. He was ordained by the Church of South India, and taught at United Theological College (Bangalore, India), Selly Oaks College (Birmingham, England), and Union Theological Seminary (New York). He was active in the World Council of Churches, and served as literature secretary for the YMCA in India for fifteen years, and as director of the Christian Institute for the Study of Religion and Society. He is recognized as a pioneer in interfaith dialogue: throughout his writings he expresses the concern that Christians must come to understand non-Christian faiths through dialogue, and be able to recognize God's hand as present in peoples of all faiths, since all of creation is already redeemed by the work of Christ. He wrote several books, including *The Concept of Maya* (1950), *The Gospel and Renascent Hinduism* (1959), *Christian Concern in Humanism* (1961), and *Christian Issues in Southern Asia* (1963). He was also a co-editor of the journal *Religion and Society*.

A. SCOTT MOREAU

Dibelius, (Frederick Karl) Otto (1880–1967)

German Lutheran bishop and ecumenist. Son of a Berlin civil servant, he trained in theology, and after ordination served what he referred to as "quite unpretentious congregations." Returning to Berlin, he became general superintendent there in 1925. When the National Socialists came to power in 1933, he was at once targeted as an enemy of the regime, having told its leaders that "the dictatorship of a totalitarian state is irreconcilable with God's will." He was ousted from his post, his public activities and speaking opportunities were

121

severely restricted, and he was arrested three times, but released presumably for lack of evidence. Nonetheless he was one of the leaders of the Confessional Church who stood out against state interference in religious matters.

With the defeat of Germany in 1945 he was elected bishop of the Berlin-Brandenburg Church, and subsequently was president of the Council of the Evangelical Church in Germany from 1949. Part of his diocese was now under Russian control, bur Dibelius was as courageous in confronting communism as he had been under the earlier tyranny. The bishop came to further international attention through his ecumenical involvement, which had earlier been stimulated by attendance at the Edinburgh (1910), Stockholm (1925), and Lausanne (1927) conferences. He strongly supported the founding of the World Council of Churches in 1948, and was to serve as one of its presidents (1954–1961). He participated also in the Berlin World Congress on Evangelism in 1966.

His autobiography, *In the Service of the Lord,* was published in English in 1965.

J. D. DOUGLAS

Dibelius, Martin Franz (1883–1947)

German scholar and pioneer of the form criticism *(formgeschichtliche)* method of treating Gospel accounts. A cousin of Otto Dibelius, he studied at various German universities, including Tübingen (Ph.D., 1905). He taught at Berlin (1908–1915), then until his death was professor of New Testament at Heidelberg. Early influenced by the work of Adolf Harnack, he forsook his original interests in philology and comparative religion, and, with his contemporaries K. L. Schmidt and Rudolph Bultmann, developed an approach to the Synoptic Gospels that sees them as a collection of many separate units. There was a need to classify the "forms" underlying written documents, and to trace the process that determined their present shape. He was also an advocate of the ecumenical movement, more particularly in its theological aspects. His major works translated into English include *From Tradition to Gospel* (1934) and *Studies in the Acts of the Apostles* (1951).

J. D. DOUGLAS

Dickie, Edgar Primrose (1897–1991)

Scottish theologian. Born in the Scottish border country, son of a newspaper editor, he enlisted at 17 and won a Military Cross in World War I. He graduated from Edinburgh and Oxford, was ordained, and served parishes in Lockerbie (1927–1933) and Edinburgh (1933–1935). His brilliant academic record was recognized by appointment as professor of divinity at St. Andrews University (1935–1967). A gentle man of great good humor and friendliness, he was beloved by students in all faculties, and much in demand as speaker at their society meetings. Active also in the larger work of the Church of Scotland, he served as its director of "Huts and Canteens" in France in World War II, and thereafter served as a chaplain to Queen Elizabeth. His humor was reflected in contributions to *Punch,* and in a series of three books for children. He maintained his serenity to the end of his life, and characteristically bequeathed his body to medical research. During a busy life he produced also a steady stream of books, including *Spirit and Truth* (1935), *Revelation and Response* (1938), *God Is Light* (1953), *The Unchanging Gospel* (1960), and *The Father Everlasting* (1965).

J. D. DOUGLAS

Dickinson, Clarence (1873–1969)

American organist, music director, composer, and educator. Born in Lafayette, Indiana, he attended Miami University (Ohio) and Northwestern University, where he obtained a doctorate in music. In Chicago he held three positions as music director: Church of the Messiah (1892–1898), St. James Episcopal Church (1902–1909), and the Sunday Evening Club at Orchestra Hall (1906–1909). In 1909 he accepted a similar post at Brick Presbyterian Church in New York City. With his wife Helena he organized a popular series of concerts (1920–1937). In 1912 Dickinson began teaching composition and musicology at Union Theological Seminary, and in 1928 the couple helped launch the seminary's School of Sacred Music. Dickinson also received much acclaim as a concert performer. He published more than five hundred compositions and arrangements. Among his collections are *The Coming of the Prince of Peace* (1919), *A Treasury of Worship* (1927), *Sacred Solos for Voices* (1930), and *Choir Loft and Pulpit* (1943).

ROBERT L. MORRISON

Dickinson, Helena (1875–1957)

Musicologist and writer. Reared in Port Elmsley, Ontario, she graduated from Queens University and was later the first woman to receive a Ph.D. degree at the University of Heidelberg, Germany. In 1904 she married Clarence Dickinson who was at that time organist and director of music at St. James Episcopal Church, Chicago. In 1909 he began his long connection with Brick Presbyterian Church in New York City, where the couple organized a popular concert series (1920–1937) and founded the School of Sacred Music at Union Theological Seminary (1928). Among the hymn collections and books she produced (some of them in collaboration with her husband) were *German Masters of Art* (1914), *Excursions in Musical History* (1917), *The Technique and Art of Organ Playing* (1921), and *A Treasury of Worship* (1927).

ROBERT L. MORRISON

Distler, Hugo August (1908–1942)

German composer and organist. Born in Nuremberg, he studied music with Grabner and Ramin, whose lifelong friend he remained, and with Hogner. In 1931 he was appointed organist at the Jakobikirche, Lubeck. Two years later he became organist at Stuttgart, where in 1937 he taught organ and composition and worked as a choir director. He moved to Berlin in 1940 as professor of composition and organ, and as conductor of the State and Cathedral Choir. Distler's unique style, based on the music of the seventeenth century, found expression in liturgical settings, choral motets, and Passion music, and made him a pioneer and most prominent exponent of twentieth-century Protestant church music. He has been honored in articles and books for his creative musical genius. A profound spiritual depression led to his death. Among his most significant works are *German Choral Mass, The Christmas Story,* the *Morike Chorliederbuch,* which premiered in Graz in 1937, and numerous spiritual concerts for voice and organ. He also wrote articles on organ and Protestant church music.

EDWARD J. FURCHA

Dixon, A(mzi) C(larence) (1854–1925)

Baptist minister and evangelist. Born in Shelby, North Carolina, he graduated from Wake Forest College in 1875 and after briefly studying theology under Southern Baptist theologian J. A. Broadus he began a series of pastorates that spanned nearly fifty years. His best-known pulpits were Moody's Chicago Avenue Church in Chicago (1906–1911) and Spurgeon's Tabernacle in London (1911–1919). During his ministry at Immanuel Baptist Church in Baltimore (1882–1890) he became popular as a Bible conference speaker in the United States and England. This led to years of itinerant evangelism and Bible teaching across the United States, and even to mission stations in Japan and China. Dixon was a staunch fundamentalist and premillennialist, and an opponent of Darwinism and biblical criticism. In 1909 he joined R. A. Torrey in publishing *The Fundamentals,* a twelve-volume defense of the basic doctrines of conservative orthodoxy. As executive secretary and editor he oversaw publication of the first five volumes. His own works included *Evangelism Old and New* (1905), *Destructive Criticism vs. Christianity* (1912), and *Higher Critic Myths and Moths* (1921).

Biography by H. C. A. Dixon (1931).

JACK MITCHELL

Dobson, James (1936–)

Founder and president of Focus on the Family. Born in Shreveport, Louisiana, he graduated from Pasadena College (1958) and the University of Southern California (1962; Ph.D., 1967). He was teacher and counselor in California public schools (1960–1964), remaining in the school system as psychologist before becoming assistant (1966) and subsequently associate professor in the School of Medicine at the University of Southern California until his resignation in 1983. He held also special appointments by presidents Carter and Reagan relating to family and children. He was brought into public attention in 1970 with the publication of his first book, *Dare to Discipline*. The public response led to a series of workshops attended by thousands of people, followed by a series of videos based on these presentations and the radio program "Focus on the Family." In 1977 he became the founder and president of Focus on the Family (then in Pomona, California, but now relocated in Colorado Springs). Dobson has sought to demonstrate that scholarly research enriches the lives of Christians when presented lucidly and in accord with biblical teachings. His other books include *The Strong-Willed Child* (1978), *Straight Talk to Men and Their Wives* (1980), *Children at Risk* (1990), and *The New Dare to Discipline* (1992).

NORMAN R. ERICSON

Dodd, Charles Harold (1884–1973)

New Testament scholar and theologian. Born the son of a schoolmaster in Wrexham, Wales, he studied at Oxford and at the University of Berlin where he came into contact with Alexander Souter, A. M. Fairbairn, and Adolf Harnack. Ordained in the Congregational ministry (1912), he served in Warwick and lectured at Mansfield College, Oxford, where he became professor of New Testament. He was then professor of biblical criticism at Manchester (1930–1935) before going to Cambridge as Norris-Hulse professor of divinity (1935–1949). Not for almost three centuries had a non-Anglican filled a chair in that ancient institution. Dodd was committed to Jesus Christ as Savior in a profoundly spiritual way. One student recalls, "We realized that we were sitting at the feet of a man who was not only a first-class scholar, but who owned a . . . deeply simple allegiance to God through Jesus Christ."

Author of numerous books and articles, Dodd was untiring in his defense of the importance of history in the Christian faith and of the historical Jesus. *The Bible and Its Background* (1931), *The Gospels as History* (1938), *Historical Tradition in the Fourth Gospel* (1963), and *The Founder of Christianity* (1970) were all written to that end. The classic statement of this is found in Dodd's reconstruction of the early Christian message, the kerygma, as containing irreducible historical elements, in *The Apostolic Preaching and Its Developments* (1936). Dodd also championed an idea called "realized eschatology" developed to counter the liberal German ideal of "consistent eschatology," that held that the kingdom of God was wholly future (*The Parables of the Kingdom*, 1935).

R. W. Graham produced *Charles Harold Dodd . . . A Bibliography of His Published Writings* (1974). Biography by F. W. Dillistone (1977).

WALTER A. ELWELL

Doke, Clement (1893–1985)

South African Baptist minister. He was a member of an outstanding family that made a significant impact on life in southern Africa and beyond. His father was a Baptist minister and church leader, and Clement followed in his footsteps, ordained by the Baptist Union of South Africa. He spent eight years (1914–1921) with the South African Baptist Missionary Society in Zambia (then Northern Rhodesia), after having first trekked there with his father in 1913 (on that trip Clement walked over 480 kilometers). His most outstanding contribution was in the area of linguistics. In his early years he translated the Bible and several hymnbooks into the logical language, Lamba. After returning to South Africa due to ill health, he was appointed senior lecturer in the newly established department of Bantu studies at the University of the Witwatersrand in 1923. He gained a doctorate there in 1924. He became an expert on Bantu languages and wrote many papers and books, including *Zulu-English Dictionary* and the *English-Lamba Dictionary*. Both these works are used as reference material today. Many missionaries have been made more effective in their ministry as a result of Doke's work. Doctorates were conferred on him at Rhodes University (1971) and Witwatersrand (1972). During the latter ceremony it was claimed that "no one south of the Zambesi has given the African language such service over so many fruitful years."

ROGER KEMP

Dooyeweerd, Herman (1894–1977)

Dutch Reformed scholar. Born in Amsterdam and educated at the Free University, he became professor of law there (1929–1965). Dooyeweerd continued in the Neo-Calvinist tradition of the Dutch theologian and politician, Abraham Kuyper (1837–1920). Agreeing with his mentor that the roots of culture are always religious, he developed a "transcendental critique" that exposed the religious presuppositions of allegedly neutral theoretical thought. Every culture, Dooyeweerd insisted, is driven by either a God-affirming or a God-denying ground motive. The Christian ground motive is that of creation–fall–redemption. Non-Christian religious ground motives that developed throughout the history of Western civilization include form and matter of Greek philosophy, the medieval ground motive of nature and grace, and the Kantian dualism of nature and freedom. Dooyeweerd also expanded Kuyper's sphere-sovereignty into a more complex "modal theory" in order to account for both the unity and diversity of created reality. Creation, Dooyeweerd argued, is governed by distinct modal structures, each with a unique nucleus of meaning and subject to its own laws, and none reducible to any other. These include the numerical, spatial, kinematic, physical, biotic, psychic, logical, historical, symbolic, social, economic, aesthetic, juridical, moral, and pistic. Together with his colleague and brother-in-law, D. H. Th. Vollenhoven, Dooyeweerd founded the Association for Calvinistic Philosophy (later changed to Christian Philosophy). For forty years he edited its journal, *Philosophia Reformata*. His influence has spread to North America in Dutch Reformed contexts through students who have gone on to teach at institutions such as Calvin College and the Institute for Christian Studies in Toronto. Altogether, Dooyeweerd published over two hundred books and articles on law, political science, and philosophy. His major works include *Philosophy of the Law-Idea* (1935–1936) and *A New Critique of Theoretical Thought* (1953–1958).

JOHN R. MUETHER

Dorsey, Thomas A. (1900–1993)

Song writer and publisher. As a young man, Thomas A. Dorsey was known professionally as "Georgia Tom." He played piano for Ma Rainey and others. He had been a blues singer known for his off-color lyrics until he "got religion." Then he turned his attention to expressing his new beliefs in music. He believed the power of the gospel ought to be available on records, so he wrote songs that couched the gospel message in the sound of the popular music of his day. He has been credited with coining the term "gospel music" and became known as the Father of Gospel Music, even though songs of this genre were first known by his name, "Dorseys." As a result of Dorsey's efforts, gospel music became so favored that it required large venues for performance. It was often performed in concert halls and theaters. Radio stations were also eager to air this music. Dorsey was a significant influence in Mahalia Jackson's life. He was her mentor, writer, and publisher. While some have criticized gospel music for being too emotional, the music has continued to be used to minister to many. Some of Dorsey's better known compositions are "Peace in the Valley," "Precious Lord, Take My Hand," and "When I've Done My Best." Dorsey left a rich legacy of more than one thousand gospel songs and many arrangements.

ROBERT C. SUGGS

Driver, Godfrey Rolles (1892–1975)

British Old Testament scholar. Born in Oxford, he graduated and taught classics at the university, where later he was professor of Semitic philology (1938–1962; in 1962 he was knighted). Driver used Semitic languages to explain one another, such as in uncovering the hitherto unknown lexical meaning of words or explaining grammatical features. In a single year (1925) he published three books: on Syriac, Accadian, and colloquial Arabic, to which were subsequently added works on Aramaic and Ugaritic. A scholar who read widely, he was in 1965 appointed joint director (with

C. H. Dodd) of the New English Bible project. He headed the group of Old Testament scholars, and translated several of the biblical books.

WONG CHAN KOK

Du Plessis, David (1905–1987)

Ecumenist and leader in the charismatic movement. Born near Cape Town, South Africa, he was converted in his teens, studied at colleges in Ladybrand and Johannesburg, was ordained by the Apostolic Faith Mission (AFM) in 1930, and became its general secretary (1936–1947). He resigned when AFM did not share his vision of global Pentecostalism, and from 1949 served as organizing secretary of the Pentecostal World Conference, and also taught at Lee [Church of God] College, Cleveland, Tennessee (1950–1952), and was on the staff of the Far East Broadcasting Company (1952–1954). His ecumenical concern impressed John A. Mackay and W. A. Visser 't Hooft, and he addressed the World Council of Churches assembly at Evanston in 1954, lectured at leading American and Swiss theological centers, was received by three successive popes, and was the sole representative of Pentecostalism at Vatican II.

His endorsement of the modern charismatic movement upset traditional Pentecostalism, and the Assemblies of God (which had accepted his AFM credentials) withdrew his ministerial status (1962–1980). The National Association of Evangelicals, on the other hand, was suspicious of his WCC involvement. Du Plessis was a key figure in initiating Catholic Pentecostal dialogue, and was latterly resident consultant for ecumenical affairs at Fuller Theological Seminary (1985–1987).

A naturalized American with a simple lifestyle, du Plessis produced *The Spirit Bade Me Go* (rev. 1976), *Simple and Profound* (1986), and the autobiographical *A Man Called Mr. Pentecost* (1977).

J. D. DOUGLAS

Dussel, Enrique (1934–)

Roman Catholic liberation theologian and historian. Born in Argentina, he did extensive graduate work in Europe, earning a doctorate in philosophy from the Universidad Central de Madrid (1959), the licentiate in theology from the Institut Catholique de Paris (1965), and a doctorate in history from the Sorbonne (1967). Returning to Argentina, he taught at the Universidad Nacional de Resistencia del Cuyo from 1968 to 1975, when he was forced by political conditions to leave his homeland. Since 1976 he has lived in Mexico City and taught at the Universidad Nacional Autónoma de Mexico. At present he also heads the Commission on the Study of the History of Latin America, which is preparing a multivolume history of the Christian church in the region. The major effort of his work has been to approach history and philosophy in ways he feels are appropriate to the struggle for liberation. Dussel holds, for example, that the past of Latin America and its current sociocultural realities cannot be understood apart from the center-periphery paradigm. He has argued that capitalism is inherently oppressive, as well as destructive of community. Dussel is a prolific writer with over thirty books to his credit. Works in English include *Ethics and the Theology of Liberation* (1978), *A History of the Church in Latin America; Colonialism to Liberation, 1492–1979* (1981), *Philosophy of Liberation* (1985), and *Ethics and Community* (1988).

DANIEL R. CARROLL

Easton, Burton Scott (1877–1950)

New Testament scholar. Born in Hartford, Connecticut, he studied at the universities of Göttingen and Pennsylvania (Ph.D., 1901) and Philadelphia Divinity School, and was ordained in the Protestant Episcopal Church in 1905. He taught New Testament at Natoshah House, Wisconsin (1905–1911), Western Theological Seminary, Chicago (1911–1919), and General Theological Seminary, New York (1919–1948), where he served also as librarian. Easton was a founder (and an editor) of the *Anglican Theological Review* (1918) and was elected president of the Society for Biblical Literature (1931). A systematic and precise scholar (his doctorate was in mathematics), he wrote *The Gospel According to St. Luke* (1926), *The Gospel before the Gospels* (1927), *The Apostolic Tradition of Hippolytus* (1934), and a commentary on the Pastoral Epistles (1947).

J. D. DOUGLAS

Eddy, Sherwood (1871–1963)

YMCA secretary for Asia and author. Born into a Congregational family in Leavenworth, Kansas, he graduated from Yale in 1891. After being inspired by the teaching of D. L. Moody at a Student Volunteer movement summer meeting, he attended Union and Princeton theological seminaries. His long career with the YMCA started with a one-year assignment in New York City. Subsequently he was persuaded by John R. Mott to pursue student work in India, and in 1896 he began his fifteen-year term as national secretary of the YMCA in India. In 1911 he became the secretary for all of Asia, and held that post until 1926. At the outbreak of World War I he ministered to both British and American troops. Between 1907 and 1948 he led evangelistic campaigns in Japan, Korea, China, India, Russia, Turkey, and Egypt. From 1911 he labored without salary, relying on his own family fortune. During Eddy's lifetime the focus of his evangelism and theology shifted from personal salvation to social religion. He was greatly influenced by the writings of Walter Rauschenbusch and Reinhold Niebuhr. This change is reflected in his more than thirty books, among which were *The New Era in Asia* (1913), *The New World of Labor* (1923), *Religion and Social Justice* (1928), *Revolutionary Christianity* (1939), *Pathfinders of the World Missionary Crusade* (1945), and the autobiographical *Eighty Adventurous Years* (1955).

JACK MITCHELL

Edman, Victor Raymond (1900–1967)

Missionary and educator. Born of Swedish immigrant parents in Chicago Heights, Illinois, he studied at the University of Illinois (1919–1921), Nyack Missionary Training Institute (1921–1922), and Boston University (1922–1923). He worked in Ecuador as a missionary to the Quechua Indians (1923–1928), but poor health forced his return to America and he became pastor of the Christian and Missionary Alliance Tabernacle in Worcester, Massachusetts (1929–1935), and pursued graduate studies at Clark University (Ph.D., 1933).

Edman began his academic career teaching history and missions at Nyack Missionary Training Institute (1935–1936), then became professor of history and political science (1936–1940), president (1940–1965), and chancellor (1965–1967) of Wheaton College. Under his leadership the college experienced dramatic growth, and gained North Central Association accreditation. Billy Graham, a student under his presidency, called Edman "the most unforgettable Christian I ever met." Prexy (as he was fondly known to students) was a popular teacher and speaker, and traveled the globe on behalf of missions. A prolific author, Edman wrote a personal advice column for *Christian Life* (1951–1966), and served latterly as editor of the *Alliance Weekly* (1965–1967). Most important among his many books were *Light in the Dark Age* (1949), *Finney Lives On* (1950), and the autobiographical *Out of My Life* (1961).

ROBERT D. LINDER

Eliot, T(homas) S(tearns) (1888–1965)

Poet, playwright, literary critic, and editor. Born in St. Louis, he was educated at Harvard, the Sorbonne, and Oxford, from which the influence of Santayana and Babbit, Bergson and Fournier, found expression in his work. He met Ezra Pound, another major influence in his life, in 1914. In 1927 Eliot was baptized and confirmed in the Anglican Church and became a British citizen. He described himself as classical in literature, royalist in politics, and Anglo-Catholic in religion. He founded a literary periodical, *The Criterion,* in 1922, in which year he produced *The Waste Land,* a scintillating combination of literary techniques that won him an international reputation. His influence grew during the ensuing years, finding its culmination in the publication of *Four Quartets,* leading to the award of the Order of Merit by King George VI and the Nobel Prize for Literature in 1948. Eliot's faith permeates *The Idea of a Christian Society,* in which he advocates a genuinely Christian society as the only hopeful alternative for the world. He affirms the value and ultimate triumph of the church in *The Rock* (1934) and *Murder in the Cathedral* (1935).

LUDER G. WHITLOCK, JR.

Elliot, Elisabeth (1927–)

Missionary, writer, and radio show host. Born in Brussels, Belgium, to missionary parents, she graduated from Wheaton College in 1948, and studied further at the University of Oklahoma and at Prairie Bible Institute, Alberta. She spent eleven years as a missionary in Ecuador, working with three Indian tribes. In 1956 her husband, Jim Elliot, and four other missionaries were killed by Auca (Waorani) Indians. Two years later, Elliot and her daughter continued their missionary work by living among the Aucas. In 1963 Elliot returned to the United States, where she continued writing and speaking. Her second husband, Addison Leitch, died in 1973. Elliot taught at Gordon-Conwell Seminary, and was writer-in-residence at Gordon College, in Massachusetts. She currently (1995) hosts a radio program, Gateway to Joy. Together with her third husband, Lars Gren, she also runs a mail-order, tape, pamphlet, and book service. Elliot's writings cover a wide variety of topics, and include *Through Gates of Splendor* (1957), *Shadow of the Almighty* (1958), *The Making of a Man* (1981), and *Loneliness* (1983).

ROBERT L. MORRISON

Ellis, Edward Earle (1926–)

New Testament scholar. Born in Fort Lauderdale, Florida, he graduated from the University of Virginia (1950), Wheaton College (1953), and the University of Edinburgh (Ph.D., 1955), and studied further at Tübingen, Göttingen, Marburg, and Basel. He taught at Aurora College, Illinois (1955–1958); Southern Baptist Theological Seminary, Louisville (1958–1960); Bethel Theological Seminary, St. Paul, Minnesota (1960–1961); and New Brunswick Theological Seminary, New Jersey (1962–1985), before becoming research professor of theology at Southwestern Baptist Theological Seminary, Fort Worth, Texas.

Ellis pioneered in the study of "Old Testament in New Testament" research as the basis for New Testament theology, including midrashic methods, reassessed the role of ministry in the Pauline churches, especially concerning gifts, co-workers, and praxis, and gave attention to the eschatologies of Luke (present and future) and Paul (corporate). He has fostered international dialogue among New Testament scholars through more than eighty-five lectureships on four continents, his writings, and exemplary "believing criticism" (Bruce Corley, Alan Brehm). He was founder and chairman (1970–1981) of the Institute for Biblical Research, established for "the study of the Scriptures within an evangelical context." His publications include *The Gospel of Luke* (1966), *Prophecy and Hermeneutic* (1978), *Pauline Theology* (1989), and *The Old Testament in Early Christianity* (1991).

J. LEO GARRETT, JR.

Ellul, Jacques (1912–1994)

French Reformed sociologist, historian, ethicist, and lay theologian who was educated at the University of Bordeaux (Doctor of Law, 1936) where he served as professor of the history and sociology of institutions in the faculty of law and economic sciences from 1946 to 1980. Converted to the Christian faith while a young man, he always maintained a Christian witness through a combination of activism and thought. He was dismissed from his university position for protesting the Nazi occupation and worked in the French Resistance aiding Jews to escape from the Germans.

His prolific writings include over six hundred published articles and fifty books dealing with history, sociology, social criticism, biblical studies, and ethics. Among these the most widely read deal with a critical analysis of the impact of technology on contemporary life. Ellul believed that such an approach included not just the use of machines but also a change in thinking and values. Technology fosters rationality, quantification, and measurable standardization that replaces God, goodness, and individualism at great human cost. This social analysis was developed in numerous volumes, including *The Technological Society* (1964), *The Meaning of the City* (1970), *The Politics of God and the Politics of Man* (1972), and *The Ethics of Freedom* (1976).

A profound student of Scripture, he was also influenced by the work of Karl Marx, Max Weber, Søren Kierkegaard, and Karl Barth. He challenged believers to be less conformed to the modern world, at times offending both conservatives and liberals. He condemned many statist panaceas but also believed in occasional anarchism and theological universalism.

For further information about him, see J. Ellul, *In Season, Out of Season* (1982) and J. M. Hanks, assisted by R. Asal, *Jacques Ellul: A Comprehensive Bibliography* (1984).

ROBERT G. CLOUSE

Engstrom, Theodore Wilhelm (Ted) (1916–)

Parachurch agency executive and management specialist. Born in Cleveland, Ohio, he graduated from Taylor University in 1938, then became the school's director of promotion. He worked then as editorial director for Zondervan Publishing House (1940–1951), during which time he organized the Billy Graham Grand Rapids Crusade (1947). He became president of Youth for Christ International, overseeing a fourfold expansion of budget and staff, then served World Vision International as executive vice president (1963–1980), president and chief executive officer (1980–1987), and president emeritus. He served also as board member for numerous evangelical agencies and several colleges. Beginning in 1971, he conducted "Managing Your Time" seminars with Ed Dayton, coauthoring a best-selling book with that title. Building on his experience of working among young people, coordinating relief efforts around the world, and managing large organizations, Engstrom authored forty books and many articles on subjects ranging from time management to leadership development to evangelism. He was named evangelical layman of the year in 1970 by the National Association of Evangelicals.

PAUL A. ERICKSEN

Epp, Theodore Herman (1907–1985)

Mennonite minister and pioneer religious broadcaster. Born in Oraibi, Arizona, into a missionary family working among the local Hopis, he became a Christian as a teenager and soon felt the call to the ministry. He graduated from Southwestern Baptist Theological Seminary and served as pastor of the Zoar Mennonite Church, Goltry, Oklahoma (1932–1936). Epp's first broadcasting experience came when he served as a substitute speaker for radio broadcaster T. Myron Webb in Oklahoma in 1934. He later left the pastorate to become an evangelist and part-time assistant to Webb. In 1939 Epp launched the first Back to the Bible Broadcast over a 250-watt station in Lincoln, Nebraska, and eventually became director (1939–1984) of a worldwide radio ministry. He became the familiar "voice" of the BBB network, and in the early years also sang in the mixed and male quartets featured on its broadcasts.

By 1985, supported by voluntary contributions, the BBB was carried six days a week on five hundred selected radio stations worldwide, with staff on five continents. The ministry now includes not only daily inspirational talks and Bible teaching, but also children's programs, literature distribution, a correspondence school, and missionary information and support.

Among Epp's numerous books are *Faith in Action* (1958), *David* (1965), *Practical Studies in Revelation* (1969), *The Believer's Spiritual Warfare* (1973), and the autobiographical *Forty-Five Years of Adventuring by Faith* (1984).

ROBERT D. LINDER

Erdman, Charles Rosenbury (1866–1960)

Presbyterian minister and educator. Born in Fayetteville, New York, son of a preacher, he earned degrees at Princeton College (1886) and Princeton Theological Seminary (1891). He was ordained in 1891 and pastored churches in Pennsylvania (1890–1906) before appointment as professor of practical theology at Princeton Theological Seminary where his sermons and lectures were remembered for their careful, articulate exposition and practical theological concern. He was moderator of his church's general assembly (1925), and served as president of the Board of Foreign Missions (1928–1940).

Conservative in theology, he contributed numerous articles to *The Fundamentals* (1910–1915) and was an adviser for the dispensationalist *Scofield Reference Bible* (1909). During the heated fundamentalist-modernist controversy of the 1920s he felt that at church and seminary level, disunity between liberal and orthodoxy Christianity represented a greater threat than theological pluralism. His hope was that the seminary (and denomination) could accommodate both views. The incompatibility of the two positions, however, led to the eventual withdrawal of numerous conservatives from Princeton in 1929 to form Westminster Theological Seminary in Philadelphia. Erdman, who also pastored First Church, Princeton (1924–1934), wrote numerous books, some of which appeared in other languages, and which included a biography of D. L. Moody.

Brief biographical details of his life by C. T. Fritsch and others appeared in *The Princeton Seminary Bulletin* (1960–1961).

H. DOUGLAS BUCKWALTER

Escobar, Samuel (1934–)

Latin American theologian, missiologist, and writer. An ordained Baptist minister, he was born in Arequipa, Peru. He received his B.A. and M.A. from Universidad Nacional Mayor de San Marcos, Lima, and his Ph.D. from Universidad Complutense of Madrid, Spain. He has had vast experience in the areas of education and missions. Escobar worked as a teacher at elementary and high school levels (1955–1958), served as a traveling associate general secretary with the International Fellowship of Evangelical Students (1959–1972), traveled widely in Latin America, Europe, Asia, and Africa in evangelistic and discipling ministries (1968–1972), served as general director of InterVarsity Christian Fellowship of Canada (1972–1975), and was a professor of missiology from 1981 to 1985 at the Evangelical Seminary of Lima, Peru. He has also been a speaker since 1966 on numerous occasions and in different parts of Europe, Latin America, Canada, and the United States. Escobar is president emeritus and founder of the Latin American Theological Fraternity (1970–1983), member of the American Society of Missiology, member of the Board of Latin American Mission, and presently a professor of missiology at Eastern Baptist Theological Seminary. He has published many works in Spanish, the latest of which is a biography of Pavlo Freire (1993).

JAVIER VELÁSQUEZ

Evans, Anthony T. (1949–)

Pastor, theologian, writer, and lecturer. Born in Baltimore, Maryland, Tony Evans was educated at the black Carver Bible Institute in Atlanta, Georgia, and later at Dallas Seminary, where he was the first African American to receive a Th.D. Evans is the senior pastor of Oak Cliff Bible Fellowship in South Dallas. This three thousand-member church, which began with ten members, ministers to a predominately African-American congregation. Oak Cliff has a multidimensional ministry, which includes social services, counseling, and family-life teaching. Evans has developed a church ministry that can serve as a model to the entire nation. He and the Oak Cliff Bible Fellowship are giving reality to Evans' dream of Dallas becoming a prototype that will draw those who want to learn how to reach the black community for Christ.

Evans is a dynamic biblical expositor who retains the distinctive style of traditional black preachers. The content of his message is clearly seasoned with his theological preparation. He speaks not only of the need for salvation but also of the need for the black church to become a life-changing force within its own community. Evans is careful to minister not only to individuals but also to families, and these families are being strengthened and restored.

Urban Alternative, of which Evans is the founder and president, is a national organization designed to bring about spiritual renewal and community development in urban America through the church. A popular speaker and preacher, Evans has had speaking engagements that have taken him to many cities, states, and countries. He has also preached evangelistic crusades in India, China, and other continents. He has written *Are Blacks Spiritually Inferior to Whites?* (1992).

ROBERT C. SUGGS

Evans, Robert P. (1918–)

Mission founder and executive. Born in Baltimore, Maryland, he grew up in Cameroon where his missionary parents worked, and was educated at and graduated from Wheaton College, Eastern Baptist Theological Seminary, and Manchester University. Serving in the U. S. Navy (1943–1946), he was the first chaplain to go ashore with troops in southern France in 1944. He was Youth for Christ International's executive secretary and vice president (1946–1948), during which time he was European coordinator for the 1948 World Congress on Evangelism in Beatenburg, Switzerland. In 1949 he cofounded Greater Europe Mission (GEM) and established the European Bible Institute, where he also taught and was the school's director until 1953. The school exemplified what became GEM's emphasis on "training Europeans to evangelize greater Europe." He was also part-time European director of the Billy Graham Evangelistic Association (BGEA). From 1952 until retirement in 1986, Evans as GEM's European director oversaw the development of Bible institutes and seminaries in over ten countries on the European Continent. From his broad familiarity with the European context, he wrote several books and various articles about the spiritual environment and needs of the area. After retirement Evans worked with the BGEA on special projects and writing.

PAUL A. ERICKSEN

F

Fabio D'Araujo Filho, Caio (1955–)

Brazilian evangelist and evangelical leader. Born into a wealthy family in Manaus whose fortunes changed for the worse with a military takeover in the mid-1960s, he came to faith shortly after the conversion of his father. A Christian for less than a year, eighteen-year-old Caio was given a program on local television (1974) that launched his dual ministry as charismatic Presbyterian pastor and conference evangelist. Moving to Rio de Janeiro, he founded National Vision for Evangelization and soon appeared weekly on television throughout Brazil. The influence of his evangelistic crusades and interdenominational conventions, coupled with satellite and video communications, made Caio Fabio—with his personal dynamism and comfortable, eloquent style—the leading spokesman for Brazilian evangelicalism by the mid-1980s. Self-taught and influenced by diverse elements (Pentecostalism, Billy Graham, Francis Schaeffer, liberation theology, Jacques Ellul), he has been a reference point for many seeking to integrate spirituality and social involvement. With the formation of the Brazilian Evangelical Association in 1990, Caio Fabio was selected to be its first president, a position he still holds. Along with active roles in various other Christian organizations and representation of Brazilian evangelicalism around the world, Caio Fabio has enjoyed an increasing influence among Brazilian political leaders. His more than forty-five books and booklets have sold over 1.5 million copies (1993).

J. Scott Horrell

Fairbairn, Andrew Martin (1838–1912)

Congregationalist scholar and preacher. Born in Fife, Scotland, his early education was limited, but he worked and read hard, and finally graduated from Edinburgh University. He went on to theological studies, ministered to Evangelical Union congregations in Bathgate and Aberdeen, then moved to England as principal of Airedale (Congregational) Theological College (1877–1886). When his denomination founded Mansfield College, Oxford, he was its first principal (1886–1909). While in theology he was said to have reflected the views of modern German thinkers, his preaching had all the fervency of one to whom Christ was all. Said one listener, "He himself . . . was sufficient proof of the existence of the God whose being he was there that night to demonstrate. That man has seen God face to face." Acknowledged as a profound scholar, he was active also in the fields of religious and secular education. Much in demand as a lecturer, he paid several visits to America. Among his published works were *Studies in the Philosophy of Religion and History* (1876), *Studies in the Life of Christ* (1880), and *The Philosophy of the Christian Religion* (1902).

J. D. DOUGLAS

Falwell, Jerry (1933–)

Baptist pastor and founder of Moral Majority, Inc. Born in Lynchburg, Virginia, he was converted in 1952, and graduated from Baptist Bible College, Springfield, Missouri, in 1956. That same year he became founding pastor of Thomas Road Baptist Church, Lynchburg, whose tiny congregation in three decades rose to some 18,000. He began a radio and television ministry, leading to the popular "Old-Time Gospel Hour." Falwell founded also in 1971 what became known as Liberty University, and was active in the area of children's education. He became even more widely known from 1979 when he started the Moral Majority to provide a rallying-point for conservative opinion, and to encourage the election to office of candidates pledged to oppose secular humanism and liberal views on such topics as abortion, homosexuality, capital punishment, and pornography. The movement was active in 1980 and 1984 presidential campaigns. A mass-circulation magazine in 1982 called him one of the twenty most prominent people in the United States. His movement, which found room for non-Fundamentalists, was declared dissolved by him in 1989, and the ongoing Lynchburg work again took up most of his time and energies. His written works include *Listen, America!* (1980), *The Fundamentalist Phenomenon* (1981), *Wisdom for Living* (1984), and *Strength for the Journey* (1987).

J. D. DOUGLAS

Fanini, Nilson Do Amaral (1932–)

Brazilian Baptist pastor and international evangelist. After earning a degree in law at the Universidade Federal Fluminense, Fanini studied at the Seminário Batista do Sul in Rio de Janeiro. Later he earned a Th.M. from Southwestern Baptist Theological Seminary in Fort Worth, Texas. Combining evangelism, pastoral skills, and social outreach, Fanini has served for many years as pastor of the six thousand-member First Baptist Church of Niteroi. Along with his preaching in countries around the world, his evangelistic program *Reencontro* (Reencounter) is transmitted by more than one hundred Brazilian television stations in Brazil. In greater Rio de Janeiro, Fanini has developed a social and educational ministry that seeks to help the destitute and marginalized of society. He has served as president of the Brazilian Baptist Convention, vice president of the World Baptist Alliance, and president of the Brazilian organization of the World Bible League. In the 1960s and 1970s Fanini's evangelistic crusades, television programs, and several popular books were the first mass evangelistic effort to penetrate largely Roman Catholic Brazil.

CURTIS ALAN KREGNESS

Farrell, Monica (1899–1982)

Irish evangelist. Born into a Roman Catholic home in Dublin, she was cast out from her family as a teenager when she began attending a Protestant church. She was converted (and wrote about it in *From Rome to Christ)* and trained as a teacher of underprivileged children under Irish Church Missions to Roman Catholics. Invited to Sydney, Australia, in 1937 by "The Builders," an Anglican committee whose aim was evangelism, she later became independent and founded "The Light and Truth Crusade." This was an interdenominational movement that sought "to lead Roman Catholics as well as Protestants to Christ, and to witness from God's Word against idolatry, modernism, and materialism." She responded to calls to conduct thousands of evangelistic meetings in many lands, including Britain, New Zealand, North America, France, Spain, Holland, and all the states of Australia. Farrell was a gifted expositor of Scripture for all ages and circumstances. She ardently prayed for her family all her life, and in her latter days could rejoice that all of them, including two sisters who were nuns, had come to believe in Christ. Among her written works were *The Evil of Mixed Marriages, Laughing with God* (escapes from dangerous situations as evangelist), and *Why Am I a Protestant, Daddy?*

C. K. HAMMOND

Faunce, William H. P. (1859–1930)

Baptist pastor, ecumenist, and university president. Born in Worcester, Massachusetts, he graduated from Brown University (1880) and Newton Theological Institute (1884). Upon his ordination he accepted a call to the State Street Baptist Church in Springfield, Massachusetts. In 1889 he became pastor of the Fifth Avenue Baptist Church in New York City. During his tenure there he took leaves of absence to study at the University of Jena and to lecture at the University of Chicago Divinity School and at Harvard. In 1899 he was appointed president of Brown University, a post he held until his retirement in 1929. During his presidency Brown grew and increased its endowment dramatically. Amid many of the disagreements between fundamentalists and modernists Faunce maintained a moderate position. Among his books are *The Educational Ideal in the Ministry* (1908), *What Does Christianity Mean?* (1912), *Social Aspects of Foreign Missions* (1914), and *Religion and War* (1918).

ROBERT L. MORRISON

Fee, Gordon Donald (1934–)

New Testament scholar. Born in Ashland, Oregon, he graduated from Seattle Pacific College and the University of Southern California (Ph.D., 1966). After a pastorate with the Des Moines Assembly of God Church (1958–1962), he taught at Southern California College (1966–1969) and Wheaton College (1969–1974) before appointment to the chair of New Testament studies at Gordon-Conwell College (1974–1988). He is currently at Regent College, Vancouver. His publications include textual criticism, commentaries on the Pastoral Epistles, and *New Dimensions in New Testament Studies.*

EDWARD J. FURCHA

Fernando, Ajith Rammohan (1948–)

Asian evangelist. Born in Ceylon (now Sri Lanka), he graduated in biology from Vidyalankara University there, and later studied at Asbury Theological Seminary (M.Div., 1974) and Fuller Theological Seminary (Th.M., 1976). Converted from Buddhism as a teenager, Fernando has been national leader of Youth for Christ since 1976. His ministry, largely focused on the economically poor, has seen many Buddhist and Hindu young people converted to Christ. In 1980 he and his wife Nelun started a Methodist church comprised mainly of such converts. His ministry has been so successful that in 1993 Buddhist monks in northern Sri Lanka called for YFC to cease further evangelism. When Fernando refused, they proceeded with threats and an effort to persuade the largely Buddhist government to pass legislation forbidding "unethical conversions" in Sri Lanka. Such legislation is "in process" at the time of writing. Fernando has written several books in English and Sinhala, has been the featured Bible expositor at three InterVarsity Missions conferences, and has led two similar conferences in Sri Lanka in 1988 and 1992.

ARTHUR W. DEYO

Fernando, Benjamin E. (1918–)

Sri Lankan lay leader. He came to vital faith in a university mission conducted in Colombo, Sri Lanka, by E. Stanley Jones. On completing degrees in physics and mathematics he served the Sri Lankan government for thirty-two years, retiring as national Commissioner of Inland Revenue. Then he served World Vision International for twelve years as field director in Bangladesh and Sri Lanka. A Methodist local preacher, he was for many years superintendent of a large Sunday school in Colombo, and held numerous national positions in the denomination. He has been national president of the YMCA, the Bible Society, and the Evangelical Alliance, and has served on the executive committees of the World Evangelical Fellowship, the World Methodist Council, and the World Alliance of YMCAs. As a respected layman he helped initiate and encourage many Christian evangelistic and other ventures, and helped give the church credibility in the difficult decades following independence from the "Christian" British. Perhaps his most enduring contribution has been in pioneering community-based Christian development projects through his work with World Vision.

AJITH FERNANDO

Ferrer, Felipe S. (1943–)

President of the Church of the Foursquare Gospel in the Philippines. Born in Odiongan, Romblon, he graduated from the Foursquare Bible Institute in 1966, received a B.A. in journalism from the Manuel L. Quezon Institute in Manila (1970), and a B.Th. from the Foursquare Bible College (1972). He was director, Halls of Life Bible College (1971–1978), lecturer and dean (1966–1971), and director (1978–1985), Foursquare Bible College, pastor of Capitol City Foursquare Church (from 1978), president of the Foursquare Gospel Churches (from 1984), and chairman of the Philippine Council of Evangelical Churches (from 1989). He has made a major contribution to the field of education, and thus the advance of the Church of the Foursquare Gospel in the Philippines.

FRANK ALLEN

Figgis, John Neville (1866–1919)

Anglican historian. Born in Sussex, England, he graduated brilliantly at Cambridge. He regarded himself as an agnostic, which for him meant "a distrust of the intellect as an instrument for grasping the final meaning of life and of purely logical approaches to religion." The death of a close friend, however, led him to respond to the claims of Christ. He was ordained and was a curate (1895–1898) in Cambridge and also lecturer in political science (1895–1901). Health problems forced his removal to a rural Dorset parish (1902–1907), which suited his contemplative disposition; further withdrawal from the world came in 1909 when he joined the (Anglican) Community of the Resurrection based in northern England.

His reputation as a scholar had grown with publication of his *Divine Right of Kings* (1896), *Christianity and History* (1904), and *From Gerson to Grotius* (1907), but that these were also the work of a truly spiritual man was seen in his Hulsean Lectures at Cambridge, published as *The Gospel and Human Need* (1909). This showed his true humility, but showed too his opposition to the "New Theology" of his time of which he said, "It is Christianity without penitence that is the supreme evil of our day and the source of our thin and flabby regionalism." His lectures at Harvard were published as *Christianity at the Crossroads* (1912), and those at New York

141

as *The Fellowship of the Mystery* (1914). Never physically strong, Figgis died two years after publishing his final work, *The Will to Freedom* (1917). Biography by M. G. Tucker (1950).

J. D. Douglas

Finkenbinder, Paul Edwin (1921–)

Evangelist and Christian communicator. Born in San Turce, Puerto Rico, he studied at Zion Bible Institute in East Providence, Rhode Island, and at Central Bible College, Springfield, Missouri. He was ordained to the ministry with the Assemblies of God in 1945, and served as a missionary in El Salvador (1943–1964). In 1955 he founded Hermano Pablo Ministries, Inc. in San Salvador, the current headquarters of which are in Costa Mesa, California. He has produced several films, including the award-winning biblical dramatization, "Elijah and Baal." His evangelistic program "Un Mensaje a la conciencia" ("A Message to the Conscience"), is carried on over 1,500 radio stations and almost 300 television channels in 24 countries, while a column with the same name is published in some 140 newspapers. Among other honors, he received a Milestone award from National Religious Broadcasters for fifty years of service, and was given a D.D. degree by Southern California College.

Stephen R. Sywulka

Fisher, Geoffrey Francis (1887–1972)

Archbishop of Canterbury. Born in a Leicestershire rectory, he earned a "Triple First" at Oxford. After ordination he fulfilled an ambition to become a schoolmaster, and was subsequently appointed headmaster of the prestigious Repton School (1914–1932). He thereafter became bishop of Chester (1932–1939) and of London (1939–1945) during the momentous World War II years. On the sudden death of William Temple he was appointed archbishop of Canterbury, a post he held until his retirement in 1961.

Despite his immense learning, Fisher had no great desire for an academic life, being much more interested in people and practical affairs. Against the background of regular work and ministry of a bishop, he showed throughout his life his great gifts of administration, which he regarded as a pastoral task. The headmaster in him never quite disappeared even when he became a bishop, and he characteristically insisted the postwar years in the Church of England should be spent revising Canon Law. His sermon in 1946, addressed to the Free Churches, was something of a landmark; another was his personal visit to the pope in 1960. Many regretted that in his years of retirement he still continued to interfere, particularly in national ecumenical matters, in opposition to his successor. Biography by Edward Carpenter (1992).

Peter S. Dawes

Florovsky, Georges V. (1893–1979)

Greek Orthodox clergyman, educator, and author. Born in Odessa, Russia, he graduated from the universities of Odessa and Prague. He was lecturer in philosophy, Odessa University (1919–1920), taught philosophy of law at the Russian Graduate School of Law, Prague (1922–1926), was professor of patristics and systematic theology at the Orthodox Theological Institute, Paris (1926–1948), professor of divinity (1948–1955) and dean (1950–1955) at St. Vladimir's Theological Seminary, adjunct professor of Eastern church history at Harvard Divinity School (1956–1964), associate professor of dogmatic theology at Holy Cross Greek Orthodox Theological School (1955–1959), and visiting professor at Princeton Theological Seminary from 1972 until his death. He was very active in the rapprochement between the Orthodox and Anglican churches, and was the foremost member of the Orthodox constituency to the World Council of Churches. His *Collected Works of Georges Florovsky* are in four volumes.

JACK MITCHELL

Flynn, John (1880–1951)

Presbyterian pioneer in the Australian outback. Born in Moliagul, Victoria, he was educated at University High School and subsequently served as a teacher (1898–1902). He joined the home mission of the Presbyterian Church of Victoria and studied at the Theological Hall, Ormond College, Melbourne. His pastoral concern for people in the outback led to his being commissioned in 1912 to report on the spiritual needs of people in remote Australia. The result was the Australian Inland Mission, in which Flynn as superintendent pioneered new forms of ministry. Patrol padres and simple hospitals were part of the mantle of safety, completed by the commencement of flying doctor services in 1928 and the development of pedal radio by Alfred Traeger. Flynn had a genius for enlisting the support of people with special gifts and experience, and was revered for his pastoral care. His work was officially recognized by his appointment as an Officer of the Order of the British Empire (OBE). He traveled constantly. His final years were difficult, marked by financial strains and disagreement with the AIM board over decentralization. His proposals were rejected, and he died in Sydney deeply disappointed, but he was a striking exemplar of serving the community without strings or sectarian considerations. He wrote *The Bushman's Companion* (1910).

Biography by W. S. McPheat (1963).

IAN BREWARD

Ford, Leighton Frederick Sandys (1931–)

International evangelist. Born in Toronto, adopted as a child, and reared in Chatham, Ontario, Ford was educated at Wheaton College and Columbia Theological Seminary, Decatur, Georgia, and ordained to the Presbyterian

(Southern U.S.A.) ministry in 1955. He married Jean Coffey Graham, sister of Billy Graham, in 1953 and two years later began a lengthy career with the Billy Graham Evangelistic Association (BGEA), serving for most of this time as vice president (1958–1986) and contributing prominently to the BGEA's Hour of Decision radio programs and television ministries. In 1986 he left the BGEA to become founder and president of Leighton Ford Ministries, an evangelistic organization with special interest in the development of emerging evangelists worldwide. Ford has also given leadership to international cooperation in evangelistic efforts. He chaired the program committee for the (Lausanne) International Congress on World Evangelization (1974) and its Continuation Committee (1976–1992), of which he is now honorary life chair. He also chaired the Lausanne II Congress in Manila (1989), and the program committees for International Conferences for Itinerant Evangelists in Amsterdam in 1983 and 1986. He has endeavored to model evangelism with the social conscience. His books include *Sandy: A Heart for God* (1985), *Meeting Jesus* (1988), and *Transforming Leadership* (1991).

Biography by Norman Rohner (1981).

GLEN G. SCORGIE

Forsyth, Peter Taylor (1848–1921)

British theologian. Born and reared in a Congregationalist home in Aberdeen, he graduated from the university there, then spent a term of study at Göttingen under Albrecht Ritschl. The latter brief period proved vital in Forsyth's theological development; his writings reflect how closely he kept abreast of German theological thought.

It was toward the beginning (1876) of his service in various English Congregationalist pastorates that Forsyth had a deep evangelical experience of the "Grace" of God's "Holy Love"—the theme most dominant in his preaching and writing. During his time as principal of Hackney College, London, he produced such works as *Positive Preaching and the Modern Mind* (1907), *The Person and Place of Jesus Christ* (1909), *The Principle of Authority* (1913), and *The Church and the Sacraments* (1917). Involved as he was in a wide range of contemporary issues, his approach throughout was unashamedly theological. Prophetically stressing God's grace in the cross of Christ, he sought to convey a sure sense of authority and of the corporate-spiritual personality of the church and humanity. He fought against the prevalent liberalism, notably against the "New Theology" of R. J. Campbell, and urged a revision of Protestant orthodoxy, with its claim of verbal biblical inspiration buttressed by out-of-date rationalistic arguments.

Biographies by G. O. Griffith (1948), R. M. Brown (1952), A. M. Hunter (1974), and D. G. Miller et al. (1981).

J. NELSON JENNINGS

Fosdick, Harry Emerson (1878–1969)

American pastor and writer. Born in Buffalo, New York, he was educated at Colgate University and Union Theological Seminary, received Baptist ordination, and ministered in Montclair, New Jersey (1904–1915). He then began a longtime teaching association with Union Theological Seminary (1908–1946). After service with the YMCA in France he became, by an unusual arrangement, "associate or preaching minister" of the First Presbyterian Church, New York City. It was there in 1922 that Fosdick preached a sermon on "Shall the Fundamentalists Win?" and found himself the central figure on the modernist side of a bitter controversy. The presbytery gave him an ultimatum: indicate adherence to the Westminster Confession or resign. Fosdick resigned (1925). Still teaching at Union, he had wealthy sympathizers who shared his professed outrage that fundamentalists would "drive out from the Christian churches all the consecrated souls who do not agree with their theory of inspiration." Fosdick was called to the city's Park Avenue Baptist Church, which under the patronage of John D. Rockefeller, Jr., developed into the interdenominational Riverside Church. Fosdick remained there until retirement in 1946. A former jingoist turned pacifist, Fosdick urged that in the war against fundamentalism there should be no studious neutrality, and that intolerance must not be tolerated. He had a twenty-year radio ministry. Among his many books were *The Manhood of the Master* (1913), *The Modern Use of the Bible* (1924), and his autobiography *The Living of These Days* (1956).

Biography by R. M. Miller (1985).

J. D. DOUGLAS

Fowler, James W., III (1940–)

American theologian. Born in Reidsville, North Carolina, he graduated in history from Duke University (1962) and in theology and ethics from Drew University (1965). In 1968–1969 he served as associate director of Interpreters' House, an ecumenical center for clergy and laity, and there he began the pioneering research that would lead to his theory of stages of faith development. He was director of continuing education and lecturer in applied theology at Harvard Divinity School (1969–1971) and received a Ph.D. degree in religion and society at Harvard University (1971). From 1973 to 1977 Fowler and his associates, supported by a grant from the Joseph P. Kennedy Foundation, conducted extensive interview research on moral and faith development. In 1977 Fowler went to Emory University where he founded the Center for Research in Faith and Moral Development. He has written or edited nine books and some forty-five articles or chapters for collections. Among his best-known volumes are *Life Maps* (with Sam Keen, 1978), *Stages of Faith* (1981), *Becoming Adult, Becoming Christian* (1984), and *Faith Development and Pastoral Care* (1987). His most recent work is *Weaving the New Creation: Stages of Faith and the Public Church* (1991).

L. K. GRIMLEY

Freire, Paulo (1921–)

Innovative Brazilian Roman Catholic educator. After studying law, he changed to the field of education, earning his Ph.D. at the University of Pernambuco (Recife) in 1959. Explicit in his Roman Catholic faith, he gained worldwide recognition for his adult literacy program, which began with an experiment that taught three hundred illiterate farm workers to read and write in only forty-five days. By 1964 some twenty thousand "alphabetization" groups were being organized to reach two million illiterate adults. However, Freire's identification with the liberationist wing of the Brazilian church, together with his work among the poor through class-structured educational methods, led to his exile from Brazil following the military coup of 1964. Exiled in Chile from 1964 to 1970, he wrote books including one translated into English as *Pedagogy of the Oppressed* (1972). His main contribution to education is the insistence that no true education occurs in a vacuum. Rather, especially among an oppressed people, the development of a sociopolitical consciousness must be an intrinsic part of the learning process. Viewing education as the practice of individual liberation and social revolution, Freire coined such terms as "conscientization," "banking education" (i.e., simply a deposit of knowledge), "problem-posing education," and "liberating education." Freire has received numerous doctorates from around the world. Among other works of his to appear in English is *Literacy: Reading the Word and the World* (1987).

DANIEL FERNANDES LIMA

Fuller, Charles E. (1887–1968)

Radio evangelist and cofounder of Fuller Theological Seminary. Born in Los Angeles, he earned a degree in chemistry at Pomona College in 1910. He was converted at a Paul Radar evangelistic meeting in 1916 and subsequently studied at the Bible Institute of Los Angeles (now Biola). He adopted the dispensational fundamentalism of R. A. Torrey. In 1920 he began teaching an adult Sunday school class at the Placentia Presbyterian Church. His class grew rapidly, but his dispensationalist theology differed from the church's position. In 1925 he left the church with his class and founded the independent Calvary Church of Placentia. Through the Baptist Bible Union he was ordained that year, and served as the church's pastor until 1932.

Fuller had a passion for missions and evangelism. In the early 1930s he began an evangelistic radio ministry with "The Pilgrim Hour" and "The

Old-Fashioned Revival Hour." Through the Mutual Broadcasting System his programs in 1937 were aired nationwide; 1942–1943 saw them peak—456 stations carried them to over twenty million regular listeners worldwide. He was a resourceful and rugged individualist. After Mutual greatly reduced his air time in 1944, he quickly developed a network of independent stations to carry his programs. With a popular down-home style, his broadcasts (done with his wife Grace) were upbeat and evangelistic. In 1947 with H. J. Ockenga he founded Fuller Theological Seminary to give graduate students a quality conservative Christian education in theology and to promote evangelism and world missions.

Biographies by W. M. Smith (1959) and D. P. Fuller (1972).

H. Douglas Buckwalter

G

Gaebelein, Arno Clemens (1861–1945)

Fundamentalist Bible teacher and writer. Born in Thuringia, Germany, he immigrated to America in 1879 and worked in a textile mill. He was converted in a German Methodist Episcopal church, studied privately for the ministry, was ordained in 1885, and held pastorates in Baltimore and Hoboken, New Jersey. Assigned in 1891 to work among Jews at the Methodist City Mission Society in New York City, he was such a devoted Bible student and gifted linguist that he quickly learned Hebrew and Yiddish and became convinced of the prophetic future of the Jewish people. In 1894 he founded a separate Hope of Israel Mission, which engaged in social work and proclaimed a gospel message based on the return of Christ. He also began to publish *Our Hope* (1894–1958) to focus on prophecy and Jewish evangelism. In 1899 he left the mission and devoted his entire time to writing and Bible conference speaking. He had also become disillusioned with the spread of liberalism within Methodism, and in 1899 he left the church. He was a strong critic of anti-Semitism and believed Jews would have a key role in events surrounding Christ's return. He believed too that the Jewish return to Palestine had to precede the second coming. He published nearly fifty books and pamphlets on Bible study, prophecy, and the Jews, and the autobiographical *Half a Century* (1929).

Biography by D. A. Rausch (1983).

RICHARD V. PIERARD

Gaebelein, Frank Ely (1899–1983)

Educator, author, theologian, and musician. A graduate of New York University (1920) and Harvard University (1921), he was also an ordained minister of the Reformed Episcopal Church and recipient of honorary doctorates from Wheaton College, the Reformed Episcopal Theological Seminary, and Houghton College. As founding headmaster of the Stony Brook School (1922–1963), he developed a highly respected model for Christian secondary education, and was active in both the Council for Religion in Independent Schools and the Headmasters Association. Following his years as coeditor of *Christianity Today* (1963–1966), his many magazine articles and preaching missions focused increasingly on the need to articulate a Christian perspective on issues of human life and dignity. He was a signatory of the landmark 1973 Chicago Declaration of Evangelical Social Concern. He was also particularly influential in strengthening the Scripture outreach of the American Tract Society. Affectionately termed a "renaissance man" by his colleagues, his last book, *The Christian, The Arts, and Truth* (published posthumously), drew on his literary background and experiences as a skilled mountaineer and accomplished pianist to urge a renewed appreciation of the goodness of God's creation and God-given creative gifts. His breadth of interests enabled him to communicate effectively as a distinguished lecturer on Christian campuses in the United States, Canada, and Europe, and contributed to his reputation as an elder statesman of twentieth-century American evangelicalism. He was author of sixteen books, among which *The Pattern of God's Truth* (1954) reflected his deep concern with integrating Christian faith and academic excellence, while *Christian Education in a Democracy* (1951) continues to influence the debate about the importance of Christian teaching in a pluralistic society. He was also general editor of *The Expositor's Bible Commentary.*

GRETCHEN GAEBELEIN HULL

Gairdner, William Henry Temple (1873–1928)

Anglican missionary and Arabic scholar. Born the son of a distinguished physician in Ardrossan, Scotland, he graduated from Oxford and was then associated with J. R. Mott in work with British students. He went to Cairo in 1899 in the service of the Church Missionary Society with a "special view to work among students and others of the educated classes of Moslems." He was ordained priest in 1901 and became canon-missioner of the pro-cathedral in Cairo. A gifted linguist, he became an authority on Islam and Arabic language and literature. He encouraged missionaries in acquiring a knowledge of colloquial Arabic and published textbooks on Arabic phonetics, grammar, and syntax. His translation of *The Niche for Lights,* a classic commentary on a passage of the Koran by the Sufi philosopher Ghazzali, was published in 1923 and reissued in 1980. Several missionary societies published his *The Reproach of Islam* (1909), and he was requested to write the official account of the Edinburgh 1910 World Missionary Conference.

Biography by C. E. Padwick (1929).

HENRY R. SEFTON

Gatu, John (1925–)

Presbyterian minister and ecumenist. Born into a Christian family in Kenya, he began his education at Kambui Mission School, but was drafted into the army in 1940. As a soldier he abandoned the faith of his parents and grew bitter toward the British and the apparent indifference of the missionaries to the plight of the Africans. He left the army in 1948 and actively participated in the Mau Mau Liberation movement against British rule. In 1951 he was converted in the East African Revival, studied at St.

Paul's United Theological College (1951–1955), and in 1956 was ordained in the Presbyterian Church of East Africa (PCEA). He served his church in administrative posts, studied further in Scotland and the United States (he was later to take a M.Th. degree at Princeton), and was appointed the first African secretary general of the PCEA (1964–1979). He was then moderator of the PCEA's general assembly (1979–1985) and senior pastor of St. Andrew's Church, Nairobi (1985–1990). Gatu also held key posts in the World Alliance of Reformed Churches, the All Africa Conference of Churches, and the WCC's Faith and Order Commission. He has insisted that the best way to promote African initiative and participation in the growth of the church in Africa is through limiting its dependence on Western personnel and funds.

BENJAMIIN MUSYOKA

Geisler, Norman L. (1932–)

American theologian and philosopher. Educated at William Tyndale College and Wheaton College, he taught at Detroit Bible College (1963–1966) before joining the faculty at Trinity Evangelical Divinity School in 1969. He chaired the department of philosophy of religion (1970–1979), moved to Dallas Theological Seminary as professor of systematic theology (1979–1988), then became dean of Liberty Center for Research, Liberty University, Lynchburg, Virginia. He is currently dean of Southern Evangelical Seminary. A Ph.D. of Loyola University, Chicago (1970) who has lectured widely at home and abroad and does not shrink from public controversy, Geisler became more widely known as a defense champion in the "Scopes II" creation/evolution trial in Arkansas in 1981, and wrote of it in *The Creator in the Courtroom* (1982). Among his numerous other works are *Is Man the Measure?* (1983), *Origin Science* (1987), *Christian Ethics* (1989), and *Miracles and the Modern Mind* (1992).

J. D. DOUGLAS

Gibbons, James (1834–1921)

First American-born Roman Catholic cardinal. Born in Baltimore, eldest son of Irish immigrants, he moved back to Ireland with his family in 1837, but returned with his widowed mother and siblings in 1853, and settled in New Orleans. After theological training at St. Mary's Seminary, Baltimore, he was ordained in 1861. He served two congregations in Baltimore and as a chaplain to Union troops during the Civil War. In 1868 he became bishop of the newly formed vicariate of North Carolina in time to attend the First Vatican Council (1869). From 1872 to 1877 he carried out additional duties as administrator of the diocese of Richmond, Virginia. In 1879 he was named ninth archbishop of Baltimore, the nation's premier Catholic see. He subsequently became chancellor of the Catholic University of

America, presided over the Third Plenary Council of Baltimore (1884), and was made cardinal by Pope Leo XIII (1886).

Gibbons did much to promote the acceptance of Roman Catholicism in America. He was a friend and adviser to several presidents, and his reputation and writings helped soften the criticisms of many who opposed the Catholic Church. He contributed substantially to the acceptance of American culture by the Vatican, and strengthened and consolidated the American Catholic Church by alleviating ethnic tensions among various immigrant groups.

Among his writings were *The Faith of Our Fathers* (1871), *The Ambassador of Christ* (1896), and *A Retrospect of Fifty Years* (1917).

Biographies by A. S. Will (2 vols., 1922) and J. T. Ellis (2 vols., 1952).

ROBERT L. MORRISON

Gilson, Etienne (1884–1978)

French Roman Catholic philosopher. Son of a Paris merchant and educated at the Sorbonne and the College de France, he dealt in two published doctoral dissertations with the influence of scholasticism on Descartes. Further works countered Cartesian doubt and Kantian critique with Thomist epistemology. He rejected Descartes' dichotomy between philosophy and theology, and sought to integrate them in *The Unity of Philosophical Experience* (1937), *Christianity and Philosophy* (1939), and *The Philosopher and Theology* (1962). He defined Christian philosophy as "revelation begetting reason." He traced this concept through *Bonaventure* (1924), *Augustine* (1929), *Bernard* (1934), and *Duns Scotus* (1952). In *Aquinas* (1956) and *The Spirit of Thomism* (1964), Gilson presented Aquinas as the paramount Schoolman who had perfected the synthesis of reason and revelation. Gilson's theologization of medievalism constituted a watershed in medieval studies. In *Painting and Reality* (1955) he imputed the disintegration of Western culture to its polarization of reason and revelation after the Middle Ages.

C. J. O'Neil edited *An Etienne Gilson Tribute* (1959). Biography by L. K. Shook (1984).

NORMAN F. CORNETT

Gladden, (Solomon) Washington (1836–1918)

Congregationalist pastor, writer, and pioneer of the social gospel movement. Born in Pottsgrove, Pennsylvania, he graduated from Williams College and entered the ministry in 1860. He served pastorates in New York and Massachusetts before accepting a call to Columbus, Ohio (1882–1914). Gladden sought to apply Christian principles to many social and economic problems. Among the targets of his criticisms were abusive employment policies, predatory capitalism, racism, political corruption, regressive taxation, and religious intolerance. Gladden received some notoriety for his unsuccessful effort to persuade his denomination to decline a $100,000 gift from Standard Oil Company, which he regarded as an unjust employer. He encouraged greater cooperation between labor and management as well as between different religious groups. He was an editor of *The Independent,* and his *Plain Thoughts on the Art of Living* (1868) was the first of over thirty-five books. He also wrote many hymns, the most famous of which is "O Master, Let Me Walk with Thee."

The Systematic Theology of Washington Gladden has been discussed by R. D. Knudten (1968). Biography by J. H. Dorn (1886). Gladden's own *Recollections* appeared in 1909.

ROBERT L. MORRISON

Glegg, A(lexander) Lindsay (1882–1975)

British lay evangelist. The son of Scottish parents who had settled in London, he trained as an electrical engineer. His business connections prospered and provided an income that he used to carry on his main life's work after conversion at Keswick in 1905—preaching the gospel. For more than fifty years he worked among the poor in the London borough of Wandsworth, usually attired splendidly in top hat, frock coat, and white waistcoat. He also had a wider ministry, preaching in prisons, ballrooms, universities, army camps, and in the presence of prime ministers and archbishops. At a service in Westminster Abbey he surprised everyone by making an appeal, to which fifty responded. Like his friend F. B. Meyer he was welcomed by the queen of Sweden as an old friend because of his best-selling books, notably *Life with a Capital 'L'.* For sixteen nights during World War II he packed the Royal Albert Hall, though German bombers came over on four of the nights. In postwar years he was an early encourager of Billy Graham. Glegg loved golf, and encouraged (and financed) young evangelists to play for their soul's good. When he died the *Catholic Herald* gave the news three times as much space as a deceased cardinal got in the same issue.

Biography by J. D. Douglas (1975).

J. D. DOUGLAS

Glover, Terrot Reaveley (1869–1943)

Lay Baptist scholar and writer. Born in Bristol, the son of a Baptist minister, Glover was educated at St. John's College, Cambridge. He commenced a career in teaching the Classics as a fellow of his college in Cambridge. His appointment as professor of Latin in Canada began his passion for travel, and he crossed the Atlantic forty times to lecture in North America. In 1901 he returned to become Classical lecturer in his old college in Cambridge. In 1811 he became university lecturer in ancient history. His involvement with the Baptist Church led to his becoming president of the Baptist Union in 1924.

As a classical scholar he refused to be bound by the strict canons of classical scholarship. He was equally at home writing for a more popular audience. His life centered around his teaching at Cambridge. He held various offices in the university such as that of Public Orator where he revelled in the duty of presenting six prime ministers, two kings, and the Crown Prince of Japan for honorary degrees in elegant Latin. His studies were naturally given over to Classical subjects, but he had strong interests in identifying the New Testament against its Classical background. Out of the latter came books such as *The Jesus of History* (1917) and *Paul of Tarsus* (1925). These were published by the Student Christian Movement Press and were some of its early best-sellers.

NOEL S. POLLARD

Gnanakan, Ken R. (1940–)

Indian evangelist and theologian. He was converted as a youth and served Youth for Christ, showing talent as a musician and singer. He went to England for doctoral studies, and on his return to India founded ACTS Institute. In addition to his work as general director of ACTS ministries he became general secretary of the Asia Theological Association and editor of its journal. Well-known as a Bible teacher and conference speaker, Gnanakan has written various books, including *Pluralistic Predicament, Growing, Still Learning*, and *Managing Yourself.*

FRANCIS SUNDERARAJ

Goforth, Jonathan (1859–1936)

Canadian Presbyterian missionary to China. Reared in western Ontario, he was inspired by George Mackay from Formosa (Taiwan) to dedicate himself to evangelistic missionary service. Following studies at Toronto's Knox College and evangelistic work in that city, he embarked in 1888 for China's Honan province, where he engaged in years of daunting itinerant evangelism, attracting significant numbers of Chinese scholars and training many for church leadership roles. He and his family dramatically survived the Boxer Rebellion, and after visiting the widespread revivals in Korea in 1906 he gave leadership to subsequent revivals in Manchuria and Honan (1907). Devout, resilient, and compelling, Goforth was welcomed home on furloughs as a missionary statesman, and his *By My Spirit* (1912), which recounted the Chinese revivals, helped promote the cause of missions in China. An admirer of Hudson Taylor and a staunch (premillennial) theological conservative, he declined to join the United Church of Canada in 1925, a decision that obliged him to relinquish the Honan field. He turned in his old age to pioneer Presbyterian work in Manchuria. Blinded in 1933, he carried on for another year before returning to Canada to advocate the missionary cause until his death.

His wife Rosalind wrote *Goforth of China* (1937).

GLEN G. SCORGIE

Gogarten, Friedrich (1887–1967)

German theologian. Born in Dortmund, he studied at Munich before going on to pursue theology at Jena, Berlin, and Heidelberg. Harnack and Troeltsch were among his influential teachers. He served as vicar and assistant pastor in Stolberg, Rhineland, Bremen, and Stelzendorf, and was then parish minister in Dorndorf near Jena (1925–1931), where he also lectured in systematic theology. He was professor in Breslau (1931–1935) and Göttingen (1935–1955). Although perceived by some as a "German-Christian," Gogarten held to a theology largely determined by the tension of law and gospel in the experience of the believer who comes to terms with the Word of God. In the tradition of Martin Luther, he sought to define the Christian religion as having ethical relevance in its endeavor to order all dimensions of life by relating the human person to God the creator and sustainer. Tradition, the mystical experience of the individual, and the historical reality of living and acting responsibly in a secularized world were prominent foci in Gogarten's major writings, which spanned the two World Wars and extended to his death.

EDWARD J. FURCHA

Gonzalez, Justo L. (1947–)

Church historian and writer. Born in Cuba, he was the son of Justo and Luisa Gonzalez, founders of an organization dedicated to teaching illiterate adults to read and write. An ordained minister in the United Methodist Church, he has been a professor at several theological institutions in the United States, and is the author of the widely used *History of Christian Thought* (3 vols., 1970–1975), which has been translated into English, Chinese, and Korean. Besides serving as an international lecturer and visiting professor (he received a Ph.D. from Yale University), his main occupation is writing and editing books and periodicals in English and Spanish. His works on church history are used as textbooks in many theological institutions in the United States, Latin America, and Korea. He can write in a popular style for the lay reader as well as produce technical treatises for the academic world. Theologically he is known for his emphasis on the incarnation as the focal point of theology and history. His other books include *Liberation Preaching* (1980, with his wife Catherine) and *The Story of Christianity* (3 vols., 1984).

DAVID J. SUAZO

Goodspeed, Edgar Johnson (1871–1962)

New Testament scholar and linguist. Son of the founder of the new University of Chicago, he was born in Quincy, Illinois. By his mid-teens he was adept in Latin and Greek, and went on to graduate in Classics at Denison University in 1890. To this was added in 1898 a Ph.D. in New Testament studies from the University of Chicago. There followed two years of study in Europe and visits to the Holy Land and Egypt. Goodspeed taught at Chicago (1902–1937), served as president of the Society of Biblical Literature and Exegesis (1919), and was on the committee preparing the Revised Standard Version of the Bible. He also produced in American vernacular his own translation of the New Testament (1923), which was well received by the public, and the Apocrypha (1938). A prolific author right up to the time of his death (over sixty books and two hundred articles) in areas of paleography, papyrology, patristics, and New Testament studies, his well-known works include an *Introduction to the New Testament* (1937), *A History of Early Christian Literature* (1942), *How to Read the Bible* (1946), *Paul* (1947), and *A Life of Jesus* (1950).

His autobiography was published in 1953. Biographies by J. H. Cobb and L. B. Jennings (1948) and J. I. Cook (1981).

H. DOUGLAS BUCKWALTER

Gordon, Charles William (Ralph Connor) (1860–1937)

Canadian Presbyterian novelist and churchman. Born to Scottish Highlander stock in what is now Ontario, and educated in Toronto and Edinburgh, Gordon was ordained in 1890 by the Presbyterian Church in Canada (PCIC). After serving as a missionary near Banff, Alberta, he was called in 1894 to Winnipeg's St. Stephen's Presbyterian Church, which grew greatly under his inspirational, anecdotal oratory and where he remained for the rest of his life. Doubtful of the defensibility and relevance of strict evangelical orthodoxy, he sought with Celtic passion to root Christian faith in an admiration of the great, good, and noble. He was deeply involved in such issues as temperance, immigration, moral reform, and industrial relations, and was a leader in the formative years of the interdenominational Social Service Council of Canada. He viewed Canada's World War I effort as a sacred cause, forcefully promoted enlistment and conscription, was appointed senior Protestant chaplain to the Canadian forces, and personally pleaded with President Woodrow Wilson to end American neutrality. Gordon called for "a rebirth of moral passion" while preaching to the League of Nations in Geneva at its founding in 1932. An advocate of larger church union with Canadian Methodists and Congregationalists, he was elected moderator of the general assembly of the PCIC in 1921. Under the pseudonym of Ralph Connor, he was the most popular Canadian writer of his generation. In an era when novel reading was still suspect in many religious quarters, he wrote some twenty-six moralistic novels, including *The Sky Pilot* (1899), *The Man from Glengarry* (1901), *Glengarry School Days* (1902), and an autobiography (1938).

GLEN G. SCORGIE

Gordon, George Angier (1853–1929)

Congregationalist pastor and writer. Born in Aberdeenshire, Scotland, he immigrated to the United States in 1871, settled in Boston, and became active in a Presbyterian church. Through the encouragement of his minister, Luther H. Angier, he entered Bangor Seminary and graduated in 1877. He then enrolled at Harvard College, and after graduating in 1881 served as pastor of Second Congregational Church, Greenwich, Connecticut. In 1884 he accepted a call to the Old South Church in Boston. Gordon became a well-known representative of the theological liberalism of his time, known as the New Theology. He strongly criticized the Calvinist doctrines of total depravity, limited atonement, and election. His sermons emphasized the fatherhood of God, the moral influence of Jesus, the importance of Christology, the priority of experience over doctrine, and the moral progress that could be made through human effort. One sermon, "The Gospel for Humanity," proved extremely influential. Delivered in 1895 before the American Board of Commissioners for Foreign Missions, the sermon urged missionaries to purify their message of cultural elements that were alien to primitive Christianity. He wrote several books, including *The Christ of Today* (1895), *The New Epoch for Faith* (1901), *Through Man to God* (1906), *Aspects of Infinite Mystery* (1916), and *My Education and Religion* (1925).

ROBERT L. MORRISON

Gordon, Samuel Dickey (1859–1936)

Devotional writer and lecturer. Born in Philadelphia, he became assistant secretary of the YMCA there in 1884. Two years later he was appointed state secretary of the Ohio YMCA, a position he held for ten years. During this time Gordon lectured frequently, developing a popular speaking style. In 1896 he embarked on a four-year lecture tour of Europe and Asia. During his travels he spoke at many Bible and missionary conferences. In 1901 he published his first book, *Quiet Talks on Power.* He followed this with several similarly titled volumes such as *Quiet Talks on Prayer* (1904) and *Quiet Talks on Jesus* (1906). Over a million copies of books from the series have been sold.

ROBERT L. MORRISON

Gore, Charles (1853–1932)

Anglican bishop. Born in Wimbledon, he performed brilliantly at Oxford where in 1875 he was elected a fellow of Trinity College. He was vice principal of Cuddesdon Theological College (1880–1883), and when Pusey Hall was founded he became its first principal (1884–1901). During his time there his lifelong social concern was seen when he began the Christian Social Union in 1889. Three years later he founded the Community of the Resurrection, and remained its head until 1901. After holding a canonry at Westminster Abbey (1896–1902), Gore was successively bishop of Worcester (1902–1905), Birmingham (of which he was the first incumbent, 1905–1911), and Oxford (1911–1919). Although a High Churchman and fervent supporter of the Episcopal system, he reflected the more liberal wing of the Oxford Movement, bringing him the criticism of fellow Anglo-Catholics. He was nonetheless one of the most influential figures in the Church of England. His numerous books included *The Ministry of the Christian Church* (1880), *The Sermon on the Mount* (1896), *Body of Christ* (1901), and *Christ and Society* (1928). He edited and contributed to the widely circulated volume of essays, *Lux Mundi* (1889).

Biographies by G. Crosse (1932) and G. L. Prestige (1935).

J. D. DOUGLAS

Graham, William Franklin (Billy) (1918–)

Evangelist, author, and religious leader. He was born on a dairy farm outside Charlotte, North Carolina, and while in high school committed his life to Christ. After one semester at Bob Jones College, he enrolled at Florida Bible College, graduating in 1940. After a period of inner struggle he was ordained by the Southern Baptist Convention. He continued his education at Wheaton College, married Ruth, daughter of missionaries Nelson and Virginia Bell, and on graduation became pastor of Western Springs Baptist Church, Illinois. The experience gave him valuable insights into local church conditions, but also convinced him his lifetime calling was evangelism. In 1944 he became the first evangelist for the newly formed Youth for Christ, speaking at rallies throughout America and Britain. This travel continued after he reluctantly accepted the presidency in 1947 of the Northwestern Schools, Minneapolis, at the urging of that institution's founder.

Graham did not gain national attention until 1949, when an extended city-wide crusade in Los Angeles unexpectedly attracted widespread media attention. Campaigns in other major cities followed. The sixteen-week London crusade in 1954 brought him international prominence; tours on every continent followed. Graham has preached in person to more people than anyone else in Christian history—over 110 million by the early 1990s. He became known as "the evangelist to the world" through his growing ability to penetrate cultural and political barriers, including the communist nations of Eastern Europe and Asia. He was the first evangelist to utilize radio and television extensively, and later pioneered the use of intercontinental satellite technology in evangelism. He has authored over a dozen books that have been widely translated.

Graham's sponsorship of several major international conferences on evangelism and evangelical theology (Berlin, 1966; Lausanne, 1974; Amsterdam, 1983, 1986), and his role in founding *Christianity Today* magazine and Gordon-Conwell Theological Seminary, have made him a catalyst for evangelical Christianity's resurgence in the late twentieth century.

Authorized biography by J. C. Pollock (2 vols., 1966, 1979).

JOHN N. AKERS

157

Gray, James Martin (1851–1935)

Reformed Episcopal minister and president of Moody Bible Institute. He was born in New York City, but little else is known of his early life. In 1877 he was ordained in the Reformed Episcopal Church. He pastored the Church of Redemption in Greenpoint, New York, Church of the Cornerstone in Newburgh, New York, and for twelve years from 1880 the First Reformed Episcopal Church in Boston, where he also taught at what was later to become Gordon College. He moved to Philadelphia in 1892 to teach English Bible at Reformed Episcopal Seminary.

Beginning in 1893, he spent his summers preaching at Moody's Northfield Conference in Massachusetts and lecturing at Moody Bible Institute in Chicago. This led to his appointment as dean of Moody in 1904 and president in 1925 (to 1934). Under his administrative guidance the institute moved to the fore as a conservative institution in its school, radio, and publishing ministries during the tumultuous fundamentalist-modernist controversies of the 1920s.

Committed to dispensational fundamentalism, Gray was an editor of the *Scofield Reference Bible* (1909) and contributed to *The Fundamentals* (1910–1915). His synthetic method of Bible study, aimed at examining the Bible and its books as an organic whole, became standard curriculum for many Bible colleges. Some of his writings are *How to Master the English Bible* (1909), *Christian Workers' Commentary on the Old and New Testaments* (1915), and *Prophecy and the Lord's Return* (1917). He also wrote numerous hymns and gospel songs.

Gray's work at Moody is recounted in W. Runyan's biography (1935), supplemented by G. A. Getz's history of MBI (1969).

H. DOUGLAS BUCKWALTER

Greely, Andrew Moran (1928–)

Roman Catholic sociologist and novelist. Born in Oak Park, Illinois, he studied for the priesthood at St. Mary of the Lake Seminary, and was ordained in 1959. He ministered in Chicago, wrote *The Church and the Suburbs* (1959), and studied sociology at the University of Chicago (Ph.D., 1962). He then joined the staff of the National Opinion Research Center at the university; he also taught there and at the University of Illinois. In 1978 he was named professor of sociology at the University of Arizona. An expert in Catholic education, he did not consider it necessary to the survival or vitality of American Catholicism. Greely wrote numerous books, produced a syndicated newspaper column, and lectured widely. His works examined the role of the church in American society, criticized the church's leadership and called for far-reaching reforms, and sought to make spiritual teachings of Catholicism relevant to the everyday needs of contemporary Americans. In 1979 he began writing novels with religious themes and sexual overtones, and some, like *The Cardinal Sins* (1981), became best-sellers.

RICHARD V. PIERARD

Grenfell, Wilfred Thomason (1865–1940)

Missionary to Labrador. Born near Chester, England, he graduated in medicine after study at Oxford and London. Converted as a student at a D. L. Moody mission service in London, he joined the Royal National Mission to Deep Sea Fishermen in 1889. He fitted out the first hospital ship for North Sea fishermen, and established homes for their use. In 1892 Grenfell began his four decades of service to the scattered communities of Labrador, himself raising most of the funds, which from 1912 were channeled through the International Grenfell Association. He operated medical ships, and had hospitals and nursing stations located at strategic points along the coast of Labrador and Newfoundland. He also set up orphanages, cooperative stores, and other institutions designed to help the fisherfolk and their families. Among his many honors were fellowships of both the Royal (British) and the American College of Surgeons, a knighthood from King George V (1927), and the rectorship of St. Andrews University—a student appointment (1929). He retired in 1935 and died in Charlotte, Vermont. Grenfell was author of some two dozen books, among them the autobiographical *A Labrador Doctor* (1922) and *Forty Years for Labrador* (1932).

Biography by J. L. Kerr (1959).

JAMES TAYLOR

Griffith Thomas, William Henry (1861–1924)

Anglican theologian. Born in Oswestry, Shropshire, England, he grew up in difficult circumstances with his grandfather. While working with an uncle in Clerkenwell, he attended King's College, London, and was ordained deacon in the Church of England in 1885. In 1889 he became senior curate at St. Aldate's Church, Oxford, and during his seven years there finished his academic training (apart from a D.D. earned at Oxford in 1905). While rector of St. Paul's, Portman Square, London (1896–1905), he published *Methods of Bible Study* (1902) and *The Catholic Faith* (1904). In 1910 he became professor of Old Testament (and later also of systematic theology) at Wycliffe College, Toronto, where he ministered until his death. In 1924 he, with L. S. Chafer and A. B. Winchester, founded the Evangelical Theological College (later, Dallas Theological Seminary), but he died before he could assume the chair of theology there. Griffith Thomas wrote extensively in journals, magazines, and books; his concern was to create "a deeper love and desire for God as revealed in His Word" in his readers. To achieve this end he wrote scholarly works in simple, understandable terms. His books are singularly lacking in heavy academic jargon. Thirteen of his major works are still in print, but the most significant is *The Principles of Theology: An Introduction to the Thirty-nine Articles* (1930).

Biography by M. G. Clark (1949).

WALTER A. ELWELL

Grubb, Kenneth (1900–1980)

English missionary and ecclesiastical statesman. Born into a Nottinghamshire clerical family and educated at Marlborough School, he became a lay missionary with the Worldwide Evangelization Crusade, working initially in the Amazon region. He became an excellent linguist, concentrating on native dialects prior to Bible translations, and his subsequent researches for the World Dominion Press produced books on several South and Central American republics, and one on Spain.

In 1939 he was recruited for the wartime British government's Ministry of Information, first for his knowledge of South America and then in a more extended capacity. His excellent record here brought him into prominence in public life. After the war he became president of the Church Missionary Society, a leading figure in the World Council of Churches, and chairman of the church assembly of the Church of England (1959–1970). He was knighted by Queen Elizabeth in 1953. His autobiography, *Crypts of Power* (1971), is a lively and self-revealing account of an unusual life.

PETER S. DAWES

Grubb, Wilfrid Barbrooke (1865–1930)

Lay missionary to Latin America. Brought up in Scotland and converted at a D. L. Moody mission at age nineteen, he offered to go to South America in 1884. After brief preparation with an English vicar he was accepted by the (Anglican) South American Missionary Society, and sent to Keppel Island in the West Falklands in 1886. In 1889 he was posted to the Gran Chaco in Paraguay among the Lenguas people, and began his pioneering work there in 1890. A man of great energy and strong constitution, he entered the area of the wild and warlike tribes, befriended them, and initiated a policy of attracting them to central mission stations. Here they were encouraged to create their own villages and to run their own cattle stations.

Biblical translation and evangelization work was slow but firm. Despite tough conditions and many setbacks, Grubb's work spread to many parts of the Chaco in Paraguay, Bolivia, and Argentina. His efforts between 1890 and 1921 made a firm foundation for the basic missionary work of the society among the Indian tribes in central South America. He retired to his native Scotland because of ill health in 1921, but continued to advise the society until his death. He was the author of *A Church in the Wilds* (1914).

NOEL S. POLLARD

Guinness, Henry Grattan (1835–1910)

Evangelist, writer, and missionary strategist. Born in Ireland of the religious branch of the well-known brewing family, he was educated in England. After his conversion he began training at New College, London, but as his talent for evangelism, which rivaled that of Spurgeon and Moody, grew, he became an undenominational roving evangelist. When his reputation diminished in the early 1870s, he was associated with Hudson Taylor in the founding of the East London Institute for training missionaries in 1873, a work that flourished and was eventually located at Cliff College, Derbyshire. Over one hundred men and women were regularly in training. In 1878 Guinness began the Livingstone Inland Mission to the Congo. This work spread to South America and India, and in 1899 was renamed the Regions Beyond Missionary Union. While he remained the inspiration behind all this work, Guinness left much of the day-to-day running of it to members of his large family, while he gave himself increasingly to his interests in prophecy, astronomy, and Zionism. His later reputation as a popular writer and lecturer in Europe, North America, and beyond was enormous. His astronomical calculations won him a Fellowship of the Royal Astronomical Society, but in his eyes these were purely a tool for his prophetical studies. His lasting reputation lay in his books on prophecy, which went through many editions and included *Approaching End of the Ages* (1878), *Light for the Last Days* (1896), and *Creation Centered in Christ* (1886).

NOEL S. POLLARD

Guinness, Howard Wyndham (1903–1979)

Anglican minister and evangelist. Born into a junior branch of the well-known Irish family of that name, he became a dedicated Christian at age fourteen, and helped launch a Christian Union at The Leys School, Cambridge, in 1919. After training at St. Bartholomew's Hospital, London, he qualified as a medical practitioner in 1928. He never practiced as a doctor, however; his life was caught up in a whirl of evangelistic work among students. He became traveling representative for the InterVarsity Fellowship, which took him to Canada (1928) and Australia (1930). He returned to Australia in 1933, and saw the formation of Evangelical Unions in each university, as well as the foundation of the Crusaders' Union. This experience was to develop into a permanent commitment to Christian ministry. He was ordained in 1939, served as an Air Force chaplain until 1946, and then joined the Oxford Pastorate for three years, after which he went

161

back to Sydney as rector of Broadway, then of Vancluse, until his retirement in 1971. Guinness had great charm with Irish nonchalance, was a compelling preacher and student evangelist, had enormous influence in the lives of hundreds of undergraduates, and left a mark for God that will never be forgotten by that generation.

MARCUS L. LOANE

Gutiérrez Merino, Gustavo (1928–)

Latin American theologian, writer, and ordained Roman Catholic priest. Born in Lima, he graduated from the University of Louvain and from the Institut Catholique de Lyon; he was also awarded the D.Th. from University of Nymegen. Gutiérrez is probably best known as the first major author on liberation theology. He has worked as a professor of theology at Universidad Católica de Lima, Peru; director of Instituto Bartolomé de las Casas, Lima; member of the Pastoral Theological team at the Latin American Conference of Catholic Bishops (CELAM); visiting professor of and lecturer at many universities, colleges, and seminaries in the United States, and a writer. His works include *Praxis of Liberation and Christian Faith* (1974) and *Theology of Liberation: History, Politics, and Salvation* (1973). Gutiérrez discusses in many of his books Latin American social issues, and attempts to define theologically the role of the Catholic Church in resisting oppression.

JAVIER VELÁSQUEZ

Gutiérrez-Cortes, Rolando (1934–)

Pastor and theologian. Born in Managua, Nicaragua, he graduated from the Spanish-American Baptist Seminary in Los Angeles (1958), the Faculty of Protestant Theology in Strasbourg, France (1962), and the National University of Mexico (1971). He has taught theology and philosophy in several seminaries and universities, and served as dean of the Nicaraguan Baptist Seminary. Ordained in 1959, he served in California and Nicaragua, and has from 1968 been pastor of the Horeb Baptist Church in Mexico City. Under his leadership the congregation developed a strong missions program and has established nine daughter churches. Gutiérrez-Cortes has also held several denominational posts, including four years as president of the Mexican National Baptist Convention, and is currently (1994) vice president of the Baptist World Alliance. He has written nine books, has twice been president of the Latin American Theological Fraternity, and has been a board member of the Latin American Mission.

STEPHEN R. SYWULKA

Gutmann, Bruno Albrecht (1876–1966)

Missionary to Tanzania. Born in Dresden, Germany, he served as a Lutheran missionary to the Chagga people of the Kilimanjaro area of Tanzania from 1902 to 1938. He is known as a pioneer in the field of ethnology and missiology. The primary principle that guided his ethnographic work, his doctrinal approach, and his missionary practice was that man is not to be considered as merely an individual, but to be seen as a member of an organic communal relational system. He theorized that God had created three primeval forms of human organization (clan, neighborhood, and age-group) and that they were being destroyed by traditional missionary methods that separated people from their culture by focusing on individual conversion. He proposed that missions strategy work within a culture to revive the remnants of these God-given social structures. The result was a theoretical foundation for the concept of mass conversion and a mission methodology of perfecting existing social structures (Christianizing). His publications include some twenty-five books and a large number of articles, most of which resulted from his lifelong study of the Chagga people. Major works are *Das Recht der Chagga* (*Chagga Law*) and *Stammeslehren der Chagga* (*Chagga Tribal Concepts*).

Biography by Ernst Jaeschke (1985).

A. Scott Moreau

H

- -

Habgood, John Stapylton (1927–)

Archbishop of York and scientist. After graduating at Cambridge where he later earned also a Ph.D. (1952), he took theological training at Cuddesdon College, but also spent three further years at Cambridge as demonstrator in pharmacology. After a two-year curacy in Kensington (1954–1956) he returned to Cambridge as vice principal of Westcott House. He was thereafter rector of St. John's Church, Jedburgh, Scotland (1962–1967), principal of Queen's College, Birmingham (1967–1973), and bishop of Durham (1973–1983) before transferral to York.

Habgood cites as his chief interests the study of philosophy and the social implications of science. He has been active in the ecumenical movement, and was moderator of the World Council of Churches' Hearing on Nuclear Weapons and Disarmament, held in Amsterdam in 1966. While the imprecision of some of his theological views has found criticism in evangelical circles, the archbishop has exhibited an extraordinary tolerance of radical views which, perpetuated by a senior bishop within his archdiocese, outraged more conservative believers throughout Britain.

Habgood's books include *Religion and Science* (1964), *A Working Faith* (1980), *Church and Nation in a Secular Age* (1983), and *Confessions of a Conservative Liberal* (1988).

Biography by J. S. Peart-Binns (1983).

J. D. DOUGLAS

Haile Selassie (1892–1975)

Emperor of Ethiopia. Born Tafari Makonnen into a noble family near Harar, Ethiopia's only walled city, he was educated there by teachers of the French mission. At age fourteen he succeeded his father as governor of Harar; at twenty-four he became regent and heir to the throne; at thirty-eight he was crowned emperor and took the name Haile Selassie ("Might of the Trinity"). His rule over an empire that traces its dynasty from Solomon and that accepted Christianity in the fourth century was interrupted when Mussolini's Italian troops invaded the country, forcing the emperor into exile (1936–1941). The appearance of this small, dignified figure pleading vainly for help before the League of Nations in 1936 is one of the twentieth century's most poignant and discomforting scenes.

Only slowly in the postwar years did he open his country to foreign missionaries, but under great restrictions—his Coptic Church regarded change as interference with divine order. Haile Selassie belatedly espoused reform, especially in education, but in 1973 the government-suppressed news of a terrible famine was publicized worldwide by students. Haile Selassie ("The Lion of Judah," regarded as the one true God by Rastafarians) was deposed and ignominiously treated by the army in 1974.

Addressing the World Congress on Evangelism in Berlin in 1966, he declared that "this age above all ages is a period in history when it should be our prime duty to preach the Gospel of Grace to mankind." He was host to the 1971 central committee meeting of the World Council of Churches in Addis Ababa.

J. D. DOUGLAS

Hallesby, Ole Kristian (1879–1961)

Norwegian theologian and writer. Born in Aremark, into a home where Lutheran piety was strong, he studied theology at Oslo University (1898–1903). There he was introduced to theological liberalism, but a deep-rooted conversion experience in 1902 turned him back to the biblical faith and piety of his home. His work as an itinerant evangelist thereafter saw the outbreak of many revivals. Soon after the Free Faculty of Theology was founded, Hallesby returned from Berlin with a doctorate and became professor of dogmatics (1909–1952). Hallesby had a profound influence on a whole generation of students and pastors. He was longtime chairman of the Lutheran Home Mission, and the first president of the International Fellowship of Evangelical Students (1947). He was prominent in putting an end to cooperation with liberal theologians (1920). During World War II he was one of the most outspoken church leaders against the Nazi occupation, and was put under arrest (1943–1945). Hallesby's theology was determined by Lutheran piety of the "Haugean" tradition, mixed with strong impulses from various revival movements on the periphery of the Lutheran state church tradition. This combined to form the background for his understanding of conversion as an experiential reality. Hallesby wrote sixty-seven books, of which his works on dogmatics and ethics, and his devotional works, are the best known. Among those appearing in the English language are *Prayer* (1948), *Why I Am a Christian* (1950), and *Conscience* (1951).

OLA TULLUAN

Halverson, Richard Christian (1916–)

Presbyterian minister and chaplain of the U.S. Senate. Born in Pingree, North Dakota, he graduated from Wheaton College (1939) and Princeton Theological Seminary (1942). After ordination he served congregations in

Missouri and California before beginning a notable ministry in Bethesda, Maryland (1958–1981). Thereafter as chaplain to the U.S. Senate he became pastor-counselor to the senators, their families, and staff members. He is an evangelical influence in the national arena, a leader in global Christian ministries, and a frequent participant in worldwide pastors' and leaders' conferences. He has been active in the International Prayer Breakfast Movement since 1956, and a board member of numerous evangelical and missionary agencies, notably as U.S. chairman of World Vision, Inc. (1966–1983), for which he traveled widely. His many books emphasizing dynamic faith in Christ in all of life include *Be Yourself . . . and God's* (1956), *The Quiet Man* (1963), *A Day at a Time* (1974), *No Greater Power* (1986), and *We the People* (1987).

ALBERT H. FREUNDT, JR.

Ham, Mordecai F. (1877–1961)

Baptist evangelist. Born and reared in Kentucky, he attended Ogden College in Bowling Green, then embarked on a business career in Chicago. In 1901 he began his traveling evangelistic ministry in the South. He broadcast many sermons over radio, often as an advertisement for his itinerant meetings. At one time more than thirty radio stations carried his sermons. He served as pastor of the First Baptist Church of Oklahoma City (1927–1929), and as president of the Interdenominational Association of Christian Evangelists (1936). An ardent fundamentalist, Ham opposed communism, the teaching of evolution, and alcohol consumption. His sermons were often caustic in tone, and he was frequently accused of anti-Semitism, in part because of his fears of Jewish banking conspiracies. He claimed to have converted over a million people, including Billy Graham, who in 1934 responded to Ham's altar call in Charlotte, North Carolina.

Biography by E. E. Ham (1950).

ROBERT L. MORRISON

Hammond, Thomas Chatterton (1877–1961)

Anglican preacher, writer, and college principal. Born in Cork, Ireland, he graduated from Trinity College, Dublin, and after ordination served St. Kevin's Church, Dublin (1903–1919), before becoming superintendent of Irish Church Missions (1919–1936). In his sixtieth year he went to Australia as principal of Moore Theological College, Sydney (1936–1954), during which time he was made archdeacon (1949). A leading and good-humored controversialist against the doctrinal errors of the Roman Catholic Church, he engaged also in parish work. Of dominant influence in the diocesan synod, he helped frame the new constitution of the Anglican Church of Australia, which came into force in 1962. He was known also for his weekly broadcasts of "The Protestant Faith" and for his strong support of the InterVarsity Fellowship. A tireless worker of impressive scholarship and unwavering adherence to evangelical truth, Hammond was also a prolific writer. Among his books were *Perfect Freedom* (1938), *The 100 Texts* (1939), *Reasoning Faith* (1943), and *In Understanding Be Men* (1954).

BERNARD G. JUDD

Han, Chul-Ha (1924–)

Korean educator, theologian, and missionary strategist. Born into a Christian family, he graduated from Seoul National University, and studied in America at Westminster Theological Seminary and Union Theological Seminary, Virginia (Th.D., 1960). Later he pursued research in Geneva, Erlangen, and Cambridge. After lecturing in philosophy at Yonsei University in Seoul, he became associate professor, professor, and dean of the Graduate School at the Presbyterian Theological Seminary (*Tonghap*) (1952–1973), serving also as part-time lecturer at the Graduate School of Seoul National University. He has also lectured in numerous schools worldwide. Han is best known as an indefatigable advocate of the Christian evangelization of Asia by Asians. He was the principal Korean founder in 1974 of the interdenominational Asian Center for Theological Studies and Mission in Seoul, serving there as associate director and professor (1974–1981) and as president (1981–). He is an ordained minister of the Presbyterian Church of Korea (*Tonghap*). He was president of the Korea Evangelical Theological Society (1981–1986) and chairman of the Asia Theological Association (1982–1988). Since 1982 he has been the first president of the Asia United Theological College in Seoul. He has published extensively in both English and Korean, most notably *Asian Christian Thought* (1990), which is already in its fifteenth edition.

SAMUEL H. MOFFETT

Han, Kyung-Chik (1902–)

Korean evangelist, college president, and founder of the world's largest Presbyterian church. Born into a Christian family in Chachak (now in North Korea), he was sent to a Christian high school by his parents who sold their only cow to make this possible. Intending to study Western science, he entered Soongsil College in Pyongyang, founded by Presbyterian missionaries as the first Western-style college in Korea, but there he felt called by God to Christian ministry. He studied at Emporia College, Kansas, and finished his theological training at Princeton Seminary in 1929.

Returning to Korea, he ministered to a church in Sineuiju, on the Yalu River. When World War II ended Japanese colonial rule in Korea, the city elected Han as their first mayor, but Russian communist occupation forces quickly removed the Christian from office. In 1945 he escaped south and gathered a group of twenty-seven fellow refugees to form a church, Young Nak, the Church of Everlasting Joy. In little more than a decade, despite the communist invasion and destruction of Seoul, the congregation had grown to 12,000. Han's emphasis, however, was on growth in outreach and Christian missions. He led his people also in providing employment for refugees, education for the illiterate, shelter for the homeless, and relief for the poor and orphaned. In the next thirty years they started more than 350 churches in Korea and all over the world, with Young Nak's missionaries serving in 21 countries. This outflow of membership increased instead of depleting the growth of the core congregation. By 1991 they numbered 60,000 believers.

Han was elected moderator of the Presbyterian Church of Korea in 1955. He refounded Soongsil College in Seoul, and served as its first postwar president (1967). In 1971 he was decorated with the Rose of Sharon medal, the government's highest honor to civilians. He retired as senior pastor, but still preached regularly. The Templeton Prize for Progress in Religion awarded annually to a living person who had advanced humankind's understanding of God, was given to Han at Buckingham Palace in 1992.

SAMUEL H. MOFFETT

Hardie, James Keir (1856–1915)

First leader of the British parliamentary Labour party (1906). Born in Lanark, he was a journalist and a battling trade unionist who sought to build his political principles on a Christian basis. He was intolerant of lay churchmen whose outward piety was coupled with exploitation of their employees, as though religion and business were unconnected, and he saw Christ's image "crucified in every hungry child." Sometimes after the House of Commons recessed at midnight he would spend two hours working in a Salvation Army shelter. Hardie was incorruptible, did nothing to court popularity, and did not live long enough to see many of the causes he espoused become accepted parts of the national life. Nonetheless the enormous debt owed to him by the British Labour movement was acknowledged thus by the party's first prime minister, J. Ramsay MacDonald: "He will stand out for ever as the Moses who led the children of labour in this country out of bondage."

Biographies by Emrys Hughes (1956) and Ian McLean (1975).

J. D. DOUGLAS

Harkness, Georgia Elma (1891–1974)

Methodist theologian and educator. Born in Harkness, New York, she experienced what she considered a definitive conversion to Christ at age fourteen. Her spiritual pilgrimage took her from an orthodox evangelical upbringing to theological liberalism and, finally, in later life, to a self-styled evangelical liberalism in which she insisted that "only in Christ is revelation ultimate and unequivocal." She graduated from Cornell University and from Boston University, where she later also took a Ph.D. (1923). She was ordained as a Methodist local deacon (1926) and elder (1938), but declined ordination when it became available to women in 1956. She taught at Elmira College for Women (1923–1937), Mt. Holyoke College (1937–1939), Garrett Biblical Institute (1939–1950), and the Pacific School of Religion (1950–1961).

After a tour of war-ravaged Europe in 1924, Harkness became a committed Christian pacifist and ecumenist. She often represented her church at international conferences, and engaged in theological discussion with America's most prominent theologians. She became a steady advocate of women's rights within Christianity, and perhaps the most visible woman theologian of the mid-twentieth century.

Her numerous works, intended mainly for a popular audience, included *John Calvin* (1931), *Women in Church and Society* (1972), and the autobiographical volumes *The Dark Night of the Soul* (1945), *A Special Way to Victory* (1964), and *Grace Abounding* (1969).

ROBERT D. LINDER

Harnack, (Karl Gustav) Adolf (1851–1930)

German theologian and church historian. Born the son of a theological professor in Dorpat, Livonia, he was educated there and at Leipzig (Ph.D., 1873). He taught successively at Leipzig (1874), Giessen (1879), Marburg (1886), and Berlin (1888), retiring in 1921, but continuing as active emeritus until 1929. He was also founder and president of the Evangelical Social Congress (1903–1911) and director general of the Royal Library in Berlin (1905–1921). Influenced particularly by Albrecht Ritschl, Harnack was prominent in the critical school of theology. He never shunned controversy. He viewed Christian dogma as "a work of the Greek spirit on the soil of the gospel," and he wanted the Apostle's Creed superseded by a shorter confession of faith that took account of Reformation principles and the findings of more recent research.

Harnack was acclaimed as the foremost church historian of his age, most notably in the area of patristics, as seen in his *History of Early Christian Literature to Eusebius* (3 vols., 1893–1904) and in *The Mission and Expansion of Christianity in the First Three Centuries* (1902). He sought to get back to the original message of Christianity, freed from the accretions of centuries, and this quest was the subject of his monumental *What Is Christianity?* (1901). Less controversial were his later studies on *Luke the Physician* (1907), *The Sayings of Jesus* (1908), and *The Acts of the Apostles*

(1909), but these were to be followed by *Essays on the Social Gospel* (1917). Harnack was also one of the editors of, and a contributor to, the prestigious series *Theologische Literaturzeitung* and *Texte und Untersuchungen zur Geschichte der altchristlichen Literatur.*

An assessment of Harnack as church historian and theologian is offered by G. W. Glick in *The Reality of Christianity* (1967).

J. D. DOUGLAS

Harper, William Rainey (1856–1906)

Baptist scholar and educator. Born in New Concord, Ohio, he entered Muskingum College at age ten, and received his Ph.D. from Yale eight years later. He taught at various institutions, including Muskingum College, Denison University, Baptist Union Theological Seminary, and Yale. He developed at Yale a national reputation as a teacher, author, organizer, and editor. When John D. Rockefeller established the new University of Chicago he invited Harper to become its first president. Harper led the university for fourteen years until his early death. Under his tenure it was established as one of the leading universities in the United States. An able administrator, in addition to his academic responsibilities, his service ranged from founding the American Institute of Hebrew to directing the Haskell Oriental Museum at the University of Chicago. A prolific scholar, he authored many books, including *Elements of Hebrew Syntax by an Inductive Method* (1883), *Constructive Studies in the Priestly Element in the OT* (1902), and *A Critical and Exegetical Commentary on Amos and Hosea* (1905). He was an editor of *The Biblical World*, the *American Journal of Theology*, and the *American Journal of Semitic Languages and Literatures.*

Biography by T. W. Goodspeed (1928).

A. SCOTT MOREAU

Harris, James Rendel (1852–1941)

Biblical scholar and Orientalist. Born in Plymouth and educated at Clare College, Cambridge, he was originally a Congregationalist, but moved into the Society of Friends after 1880. He began teaching New Testament Greek at the Johns Hopkins University, Baltimore, Maryland (1882–1885), but left because of difficulties created by his denunciation of vivisection. He moved to Haverford College, Pennsylvania (1886–1892), a Quaker school, as professor of biblical languages and literature, before becoming university lecturer in paleography at Cambridge (1893–1903). He then became director of studies at the Friends' Settlement for Social and Religious Study, Woodbrooke, near Birmingham, England (1904–1918). In 1916 during World War I he set out by sea to join in India the Greek papyrological scholar James Hope Moulton (1863–1917), but their ship was torpedoed in the Mediterranean; he experienced a similar disaster the next year in the company of Moulton, who died following their four-day exposure at sea. Thereafter he was a curator of manuscripts, the John Rylands Library, Manchester, England, until retirement (1918–1925). He was elected Fellow of the British Academy (1927).

Harris traveled widely in the Near East, where he discovered many important manuscripts related to a broader study of the Bible and its related literatures. Retirement, though marred by approaching blindness and lameness, saw his attention turned to the spread of Egyptian culture in the millennium before Christ. Yet he is also remembered as "a mighty believer" for his devotional addresses. His works include *Letters from Armenia* (1897), *Biblical Garments from Mount Sinai* (1890), and *Popular Account of the Newly Recovered Gospel of St. Peter* (1892). W. G. Hanson compiled *The Life Indeed: Thoughts from the Devotional Writings of Dr. J. Rendel Harris* (1942).

CLYDE CURRY SMITH

Harris, William Wade (ca. 1865–1929)

West African self-styled prophet. He was born in Liberia, a member of the Grebo, a subdivision of the Kra peoples. Although brought up a Methodist, he was influenced by the American Protestant Episcopalians. He was a teacher and a catechist for their mission. In 1909 he became involved in a premature rebellion, and was accused of raising the British flag as a signal for revolt. In prison he had a vision that God wanted him to be a prophet to convert West Africa. On his release in 1912 he dressed himself in white, and preached throughout Liberia, the Ivory Coast, and the Gold Coast (now Ghana). Such was the impact on the Ivory Coast that 120,000 were baptized. When World War I began in 1914 French officials became hostile, and Harris was expelled in 1915. Native Methodist preachers, however, continued to guide his converts. When the first expatriate missionaries came in 1924 there were over 25,000 catechumens. After 1915 Harris never had similar successes. Some of his followers who were not absorbed into Methodist churches called themselves "Harrisites."

NOEL S. POLLARD

Harrison, Everett Falconer (1902–)

New Testament scholar. Born a pastor's son in Skagway, Alaska, he was educated at the University of Washington, Princeton Theological Seminary, Dallas Theological Seminary (Th.D., 1938), and the University of Pennsylvania (Ph.D., 1950). He was ordained in the Presbyterian Church in 1927, served as pastor of the Third Presbyterian Church, Chester, Pennsylvania (1940–1944), and taught in Dallas Theological Seminary various periods between 1928 and 1947. He then joined the faculty of Fuller Theological Seminary, where he served until retirement in 1980. Among his publications are *John, The Gospel of Faith* (1962), *Introduction to the New Testament* (1964), *A Shorter Life of Christ* (1968), and *Jesus and His Contemporaries* (1970). He also revised Alford's Greek New Testament, was editor (with C. F. Pfeiffer) of *The Wycliffe Bible Commentary,* and New Testament editor of the revised *International Standard Bible Encyclopedia.*

NORMAN R. ERICSON

Harrison, Roland Keith (1920–1993)

Old Testament scholar and theologian. Born in Lancashire, England, he received his B.D. (1943) and M.Th. (1947) from the University of London. He was ordained a priest in the Church of England (1943) and served as chaplain at Clifton Theological College, Bristol, from 1947 to 1949. From 1949 to 1952 Harrison was instructor of New Testament and Greek at Huron College, an Anglican school affiliated with the University of Western Ontario in London, Ontario, Canada. In 1952 he was awarded a Ph.D. from the University of London (England); he was also appointed Hellmuth Professor of Old Testament Studies at Huron College and head of the department of Hebrew at Western Ontario University. From 1960 until his retirement in 1990 Harrison was chair of Old Testament at Wycliffe College, an Anglican school connected with the University of Toronto, Canada. Harrison was a renowned scholar in the conservative tradition and was honored by his students with the festschrift, *Israel's Apostasy and Restoration* (1988). No bibliography of his numerous writings exists, but they number in the hundreds. He is best remembered for his commentaries, extensive editorial work, which includes the revised *International Standard Bible Encyclopedia, Baker Encyclopedia of the Bible,* and the *New International Commentary on the Old Testament,* and his monumental *Introduction to the Old Testament* (1969), which is the standard conservative Old Testament introduction even today. In it he deals forthrightly with current liberal theories and finds them wanting. "In the end," he says, "it is a matter of method, and in the view of the present writer it is only when criticism is properly established upon an assured basis of ancient Near Eastern life rather than upon occidental philosophical or methodological speculations that Old Testament scholarship can expect to reflect something of the vitality, dignity, and spiritual richness of the law, prophecy and the sacred writings."

WALTER A. ELWELL

Hastings, James (1852–1922)

Scottish pastor and encyclopedist. Born in Huntly and educated at Aberdeen University, he was ordained and ministered to Free Church (1884–1901) and United Free Church congregations (1901–1911). He founded and edited *The Expository Times,* (1889–1922) a monthly periodical (still published) to keep pastors and others abreast of recent theological and biblical literature, and offering sermons and children's addresses. Hastings' most famous compilation, the massive and magisterial *Encyclopedia of Religion and Ethics* (12 vols., 1908–1921) is still in print. He was also responsible for several large dictionaries of the Bible (1898–1904), *Christ and the Gospels* (1906–1907), and the *Apostolic Church* (1915, 1918). His series on "Great Texts of the Bible" and expository commentaries have helped many preachers. A series on "Great Christian Doctrines" was cut short by his death after volumes on *Prayer* (1915), *Faith* (1919), and *Peace* (1922). Much of this work was done during pastorates in Dundee and Kincardineshire, but in 1911 he resigned to devote himself to his editorial work. He edited a series of volumes, *The Scholar as Preacher,* and was himself an excellent evangelical preacher.

HENRY R. SEFTON

Hatfield, Mark Odom (1922–)

Christian educator and politician. Born in Dallas, Oregon, he graduated from Willamette University and Stanford University, both degrees in political science. Hatfield served in the United States Navy from 1943 to 1946, and was a combat veteran of the Pacific Theater of Operations. He returned to Willamette University to teach political science (1949–1956), and later became dean of students. His early political career was coterminous with his academic life, when as a Republican, he was elected to serve first in the Oregon House of Representatives (1951–1955) and then in the Oregon State Senate (1955–1957). He resigned his university post to serve first as Oregon secretary of state (1957–1959) and then as governor (1959–1967). In 1966 Oregonians voted to send him to the U.S. Senate for the first of five terms (1967–).

An admirer of the compassionate politics of Abraham Lincoln and Herbert Hoover, Hatfield made a decision while in the state legislature to serve Christ through the political process. This commitment was tested in 1958, when the handsome, personable, and energetic young Hatfield came to national attention when first elected governor as a Republican during a national Democratic landslide. He became the focus of even more intense press notice when, in 1965, he became one of the few national politicians of either party publicly to oppose the Vietnam War. In the years that followed, Hatfield became an outspoken Christian in the political arena as he attempted to bridge the gap between his evangelical Christian faith and the world of politics by stressing compassion in government policy. This led him to become one of America's foremost peace advocates, a champion of the poor and oppressed, and a consistent opponent of abortion on demand.

Hatfield is the author of numerous articles and several books, the most important of which are *Not Quite So Simple* (1968), *Conflict and Conscience* (1971), and *Between a Rock and a Hard Place* (1976).

ROBERT D. LINDER

Heidegger, Martin (1889–1976)

German theologian. Born in Messkirch (Baden), he studied Catholic theology and philosophy and wrote in 1914 a doctoral dissertation on *Die Lehre vom Urteil im Psychologismus,* a critical analysis of logic. In close proximity to Husserl, he concerned himself with the question of being, in a Neo-Kantian mode. In 1923 he was appointed professor at Marburg, and by 1928 had succeeded Husserl at the University of Freiburg in Breisgau. His importance lies in seeking to relate philosophy and theology. Although the French occupation forces suspended Heidegger from teaching between 1945 and 1951, his thought gained prominence. After becoming professor emeritus in 1952 he continued through dialogue and seminars to disseminate his ideas.

EDWARD J. FURCHA

Heim, Karl (1874–1958)

German theologian. Born into a Pietist home in Frauenzimmern, near Brackenheim, he experienced a religious conversion, studied theology at Tübingen, and served for several years as parish minister and educator in the public school system. From 1899 to 1907 he was secretary of the German Christian Student Association, and became in 1907 privatodozent at Halle. After the publication of several major works he was promoted in 1914 to professor of dogmatics in the Protestant Theological Faculty at Münster. During World War I he served briefly as a military chaplain. A professorship of systematic theology at Tübingen from 1920 saw Heim at the height of his academic career. In 1928 he participated in the Second Conference on World Mission in Jerusalem; he lectured at Princeton in 1936, but declined a professorship there. After retirement in 1939 he returned to two years of active teaching (1946–1948) at the Evangelical Academy, Bad Boll.

Heim's theological orientation has been described as christocentrism. As a Lutheran theologian he has been influential, both through his numerous publications and because of his personal piety that earned him the respect of many who recalled him as one of the last "Swabian Pietists." His magnum opus (*Der evangelische Glaube und das Denken der Gegenwart*) had two of its sections translated into English as *God Transcendent* (1935) and *Christian Faith and Natural Science* (1953).

EDWARD J. FURCHA

Henderson, Ian (1910–1969)

Scottish theologian. Born in Edinburgh, he graduated in arts and divinity there, and studied further at Zurich and at Basel under Karl Barth. Ordained in the Church of Scotland, he ministered in Fraserburgh (1938–1942) and Kilmany (1942–1948) before appointment to the chair of systematic theology at Glasgow (1948–1969). Doctrinally radical, he produced *Myth in the New Testament* (1952) and a separate study on *Rudolf Bultmann* (1965). He is more widely known, however, for *Power Without Glory: A Study in Ecumenical Politics* (1967) in which he set out to expose the tricks of the ecumenical trade. Here he detected a cosmic swindle—a world of studied ambiguity and hidden motives, of ecclesiastical takeover bids and failure to recognize institutional churches as power structures, of the tendency to disinherit critics as enemies of God. "The heathen who marveled at the way Christians loved one another," he suggested, "didn't known them very well." Henderson's well-written and highly entertaining satire was directed also at his church's dialogue with the Church of England, a subject he pursued in *Scotland: Kirk and People* (1969).

J. D. DOUGLAS

Henry, Carl Ferdinand Howard (1913–)

American Baptist theologian, evangelical leader, and editor. Henry, born in New York City, worked as a journalist. After his conversion he graduated from Wheaton College, Northern Baptist Theological Seminary (Th.D., 1942), and Boston University (Ph.D., 1949). He was professor of theology and philosophy of religion at Northern Baptist Theological Seminary (1942–1947), and founding professor of theology and Christian philosophy at Fuller Theological Seminary (1947–1956). He was chosen first editor (1956–1968) of *Christianity Today*, which became a leading voice for evangelicalism and soon earned the respect of many outside the evangelical tradition. Thereafter he was professor, Eastern Baptist Theological Seminary (1969–1974), and visiting professor, Trinity Evangelical Divinity School (1974–). He has lectured at institutions around the world, has received six honorary doctorates, and has produced a great number of profound theological works. He was president, Evangelical Theological Society (1968–1969); chairman, World Congress on Evangelism (1966); lecturer-at-large, World Vision International (1974–1987) and Prison Fellowship Ministries (1990–); and president, American Theological Society (1979–1980). His theology stresses biblical theism, objective revelation in propositional form, the authority and inerrancy of Scripture, and the logical defense of Christianity against its rivals. Henry is an advocate of evangelical unity, and has criticized evangelicals for failure to apply their theology to the frontiers of discussions in contemporary theology and to modern social dilemmas. *Time* magazine recognized him as "the leading theologian of the nation's growing evangelical flank." His writings include *The Uneasy Conscience of Modern Fundamentalism* (1947), *Fifty Years of Protestant Theology* (1950), *The Drift of Western Thought* (1951), *Christian Personal Ethics* (1957), *Aspects of Christian Social Ethics* (1964), *Frontiers in Modern Theology* (1966), *Evangelicals in Search of Identity* (1976), *The Christian Mindset in a Secular Society* (1984), the autobiographical *Confessions of a Theologian* (1986), *Toward a Recovery of Christian Belief* (1990), and his six-volume magnum opus, *God, Revelation, and Authority* (1976–1983).

Biography by B. E. Patterson (1983).

ALBERT H. FREUNDT, JR.

Henry, Paul Brentwood (1942–1993)

United States Congressman. Born in Philadelphia, he graduated from Wheaton College and received his Ph.D. in political science from Duke University. In 1963 he entered the Peace Corps, and served in Liberia and Ethiopia for two years. In 1965 he married Karen Borthiste, and they had three children—Kara, Jordan, and Megan. After teaching political science at Duke University (1969–1970) and Calvin College (1970–1978), Henry entered political life full-time with his election to the Michigan House of Representatives in 1978. He was elected a Michigan state senator in 1982 and a United States representative in 1984. His political career was marked by intelligence, credibility, and integrity and was shaped by his Christian faith. Among his achievements in Congress were the "College Savings Bond Program," enabling Americans to save for their children's college education, and legislation requiring colleges and universities to disclose athletics department revenues and expenditures. Henry had a deep commitment to solving environmental problems, and was the author of legislation that sought to establish a nationwide refund on beverage containers. He also authored legislation that led to reforms of the National Endowment for the Arts, and he initiated a law that created a Hostage Awareness Day at a time when hostages were being held in Beirut, Lebanon. He was recognized as "Friend of the Taxpayer" by the National Taxpayers Union and was the recipient of the "Bulldog of the Treasury Award" for fighting wasteful government spending. In 1990 the *National Journal* recognized Henry as a "rising star" of Congress. He was best known, however, for his Christian character and exemplary life. He touched many with his testimony to God's goodness as he suffered from the brain tumor that took his life. Henry was the author of numerous articles and of the book, *Politics for Evangelicals*. In 1994 Calvin College established the Paul B. Henry Chair in

Christianity and Politics and the Paul B. Henry Archives for the Study of Faith and Politics.

JOHN P. STEIGENGA

Higginbottom, Sam (1874–1958)

Agricultural missionary. Born in Manchester, England, he is remembered as the first Christian missionary to see the importance of scientific agricultural training and the reconstruction of the rural areas in India. After he completed his schooling, Higginbottom worked on his father's farm until age nineteen, when he crossed the Atlantic to further his education, which was climaxed by a B.A. from Princeton in 1903. He left immediately for India as a Presbyterian missionary, and spent the rest of his life until retirement working with indigent peoples. He taught economics, biology, English, and Bible at Allahabad Christian College (1903–1909), but became convinced that the best way to train Christians in India was by improvement of their agricultural skills. Returning to the United States he completed a degree in agriculture at Ohio State University in 1911. Back in India he founded and became principal of the successful Allahabad Agricultural Institute, thanks to funding by the Ford Foundation. Gwalior State made him director of agriculture (1916–1919), and he performed many services for the Indian government in rural affairs. He and his wife Jane were also in charge of the Naini Leper Asylum (1903–1934). He received many honors from India and other nations. When he retired in 1944 he became president of the Christian Service Training Center in Frostproof, Florida, and was moderator of the Presbyterian Church USA's general assembly. He wrote *The Gospel and the Plow* (1921) and *Sam Higginbottom, Farmer* (1949)

LESLIE R. KEYLOCK

Hill, Edward V. (1935–)

Preacher and lecturer. Born in a log cabin in Texas, he was reared in poverty and considers his first success as when he won a state fair competition. It was the first time an African-American had ever won. For more than thirty years, Hill has been the pastor of the Mount Zion Missionary Baptist Church of Los Angeles. In 1961 he responded to the call to Mount Zion where his ministry has included the feeding of the hungry, community development, and a fiery brand of preaching to his congregation. Because of his vibrant preaching style, he has become a much sought-after speaker at conferences, on television, and in other settings. His theology is a conservative evangelical approach to traditional African-American gospel. This interesting blend of theology within a traditional black setting has produced a reputation that highlights what would appear to be a conflict of conviction. Characteristic of this apparent conflict is the fact that he is an unabashed Republican, who has been critically involved in the campaigns of Ronald Reagan and George Bush. He has twice served as the head of the Clergy for Reagan Committee and gave the prayer at Richard Nixon's inaugural. But he has also assisted Jesse Jackson in fund-raising during his campaigns for president. Hill speaks his mind and beliefs without concern for whether others agree or whether they fit into neat definitions. He refers to himself as a "Negro" and has never found it necessary for all people of color to be in the same camp. While these divergent beliefs have resulted in criticism, he was one of few community leaders who were called on by the mayor of Los Angeles to help calm the city following the 1993 disturbances. President Bush visited Hill's church after the 1992 riots. Rev. E. V. Hill continues to be one of the more recognizable and most often heard African-American preachers today.

ROBERT C. SUGGS

Hillis, Newell Dwight (1858–1929)

Congregational pastor and social activist. Born in Magnolia, Iowa, he earned degrees from Lake Forest University (1884) and McCormick Theological Seminary (1887). He pastored several churches in Illinois before accepting a call to Plymouth Congregational Church, Brooklyn (1899–1924), served previously by H. W. Beecher and Lyman Abbott. He became an outstanding and widely read preacher. In addition, he averaged about one hundred lectures a year. He also pursued social development, seen in his series of lectures on urban planning that influenced U.S. government thinking during and following World War I. Less positively, from 1914 to 1917 he inflamed American passion against Germans by preaching in some 250 cities across the United States on alleged German atrocities committed during the war, even favoring a plan to exterminate the German people. He also promoted investments in Canadian timber lands that resulted in financial embarrassments for many. Of lasting legacy are his books, which include *A Man's Value to Society* (1896), *Right Living as a Fine Art* (1899), *Building a Working Faith* (1903), *Rebuilding the Ruined Lands of Europe* (1919), and *The Better American Lectures* (1922).

A. SCOTT MOREAU

Hocking, William Ernest (1873–1966)

American philosopher of religion. Born in Cleveland and reared in Illinois, he studied civil engineering at Iowa State College of Agriculture and the Mechanical Arts. He then took up philosophy at Harvard (Ph.D., 1904), taught at Andover Theological Seminary, University of California, and Yale, then in 1914 returned to Harvard where he remained until his retirement in 1943. His philosophical method combined absolute idealism's comprehensiveness and rational speculation with pragmatism's focus on experience. Hocking appealed to religious experience to demonstrate and shape his concept of God. His understanding of the Absolute differed significantly from those of other idealists, because it was strongly qualified by the notion of personhood. In response to those who claimed that Christianity was totally unique among world religions, Hocking emphasized the relative merits of non-Christian religions and the similarities among mystics of various traditions. He devoted himself to many nonacademic tasks and causes. He served as a military engineer during World War I; published a report of morale for the U. S. armed forces; encouraged the establishment of the League of Nations; chaired the Commission of Appraisal for Laymen's Foreign Missions Inquiry; and served on the Commission on the Freedom of the Press. His published works include *The Meaning of God in Human Experience* (1912), *Human Nature and Its Remaking* (1918), *Re-Thinking Missions* (1932), *Living Religions and a World Faith* (1940), and *The Coming World Civilization* (1956).

ROBERT L. MORRISON

Hoekema, Anthony Andrew (1913–1988)

Reformed theologian. Born in Drachten, Holland, he moved with his parents to the United States in 1923. He graduated from Calvin College (1936) and Seminary (1942), the University of Michigan (1937), and Princeton Theological Seminary (Th.D., 1953). Ordained in the Christian Reformed Church in 1944, he served several pastorates until appointed lecturer in dogmatics at Calvin Theological Seminary in 1955. He was professor of Bible at Calvin College (1956–1958), then until retirement, professor of systematic theology at Calvin Seminary (1958–1978). His lifelong concern was with the truth of the gospel as it applied to the human heart. His first major work, *The Four Major Cults* (1963), named Christian Science, Jehovah's Witnesses, Mormonism, and Seventh-day Adventism as distortions of the gospel. *What about Tongue-Speaking?* (1966) criticized Pentecostalism's doctrine of the baptism of the Holy Spirit, but acknowledged its many praiseworthy features. *Created in God's Image* (1986) and *Saved by Grace* (1989) deal with the nature of the human person and the nature of salvation. Hoekema was critical of some orthodox theologies because of their denigration of humanity, but he emphasized that we are saved only by God's gracious action in Christ. In *The Bible and the Future* (1979) Hoekema emphasized the importance of seeing eschatology as a combination of the already and the not-yet, and defended a traditional amillennial position that sees Revelation 20:4–6 as a present reality and the second coming as terminating this age and inaugurating the final state.

WALTER A. ELWELL

Holl, Karl (1866–1926)

German church historian. Born in Tübingen, he was a seminarian at Maulbronn and Blaubeuren followed by military service before pursuing theology and philosophy at the University of Tübingen. He was ordained in 1888 and subsequently came under the influence of Harnack and Julicher. On Harnack's invitation Holl worked on patristics for the Prussian Academy of Sciences. He was lecturer at the University of Tübingen (1900–1906) and thereafter full professor of church history at the University of Berlin. Although recognized as a universal church historian, with interests ranging from historical studies of the New Testament, through English and Russian church history, to contemporary religious movements, his main academic interest was Calvin and Luther. Intensive textual studies of the writings of the Reformers led Holl to an important reappraisal of Luther's significance to modern Protestantism in its struggle with nineteenth-century liberalism. Blanke, Bornkamm, Hirsch, and Pauck were some of the prominent students of Holl's approach to the past. Although Holl's Luther interpretation is significant, he should not be considered as the instigator of a "Luther Renaissance." His extensive literary work is contained in three volumes of collected works and in edited volumes of some of his correspondence.

Erich Seeberg and Robert Stupperich are among the scholars who have written assessments of Holl's seminal work.

EDWARD J. FURCHA

Hollenweger, Walter Jacob (1927–)

Scholar of Pentecostalism. Born of Swiss parents in Antwerp, Belgium, he left school at age sixteen, worked in a bank in Switzerland, then after an intense spiritual struggle decided to enter the ministry. He studied at an English Bible college (1948–1949), then served as youth leader and pastor in the Swiss Pentecostal Mission. Since his critical, open-minded attitude led to difficulties within the group, he resigned in 1958, began graduate studies in theology, and was ordained in the Swiss Reformed Church. In 1966 he completed his dissertation at Zurich: a ten-volume study of the global Pentecostal movement, the core of which was published in 1969 as *Enthusiastisches Christentum.* Appointed the World Council of Churches' secretary for evangelism in 1965, he promoted cross-cultural theology and fostered ecumenism among Pentecostal groups around the world. In 1971 he became professor of mission studies at the University of Birmingham (England) and Selly Oak Colleges. After retiring in 1989 he produced dramas and musical plays conveying his ideas about narrative theology and communication of the gospel. Hollenweger authored over thirty books, tracts, and plays, and numerous articles and sermons. In his magnum opus, *Interkulturelle Theologie* (3 vols., 1979–1988), he stressed the intercultural dimensions of the Christian faith and the need to build the sort of bridges between Western and non-Western peoples that made understanding possible. He felt that the charismatic movement and indigenous Pentecostalism offered the church a "new chance" to recover its reason for existence.

RICHARD V. PIERARD

Hoover, Willis Collins (1856–1936)

Father of Pentecostalism in Chile. Born in Freeport, Illinois, he studied architecture and medicine (M.D., University of Chicago, 1884), but felt called to South America. He taught at the English school in northern Chile from 1889, and in 1893 began working with the Methodist Episcopal Church, becoming a district superintendent in 1897 and pastor of the large Valparaiso church in 1902. In 1907, through a book on a Pentecostal revival at the Pandita Ramabai school in India, he sought this new experience, including tongues, and encouraged others to do so. Opposition from Methodist leaders led Hoover and the Valparaiso elders to split off in 1910 and form a new body, the National Methodist Church, which grew phenomenally. Internal divisions and accusations of immorality against Hoover led to another division in 1932, in which he established the Evangelical Pentecostal Church of Chile, which he headed until his death. Today the denominations founded by Hoover, which retain some of their Methodist heritage, are the largest churches in the country, with almost one million members.

STEPHEN R. SYWULKA

Horner, Ralph Cecil (1854–1921)

Canadian Holiness evangelist. Born in Canada East (later Quebec), he claimed entire sanctification at a Methodist camp meeting in 1872 and soon began popular revivalist-style preaching. He attended the Methodists' Victoria College in Cobourg (1883–1885), studied rhetoric in Philadelphia (1885–1886), and was ordained by the Methodists' Montreal Conference in 1887. He spurned a standard circuit to continue evangelistic campaigns marked by audience agonies of conviction, physical collapses, and dramatic vocal outbursts. Having earlier embarrassed some Victoria College faculty by alleging that their Methodist experience was deficient, Horner encountered mounting criticism of his doctrine, ministry style, and disregard for Conference authority. Such criticism led to his removal from the Methodist ministry in 1895. He responded by organizing his followers into the Holiness Movement Church (HMC) and becoming its first bishop. The HMC eventually had its own Bible school and publishing house in Ottawa, and a support base of about six thousand adherents in the Ottawa Valley and on the western Canadian prairies. When his leadership of this group was challenged in 1916, he formed the Standard Church in America (SCA). The small (1,600-member) HMC joined the Free Methodists in 1958, while the slightly larger SCA still exists as a small body. As a transitional figure Horner had affinities to both a disappearing older Methodism and an emerging new Pentecostalism.

He wrote *Ralph C. Horner, Evangelist: Reminiscences from His Own Pen* (n.d.).

GLEN G. SCORGIE

Horton, Douglas (1891–1968)

American Congregational and ecumenical leader. Born in Brooklyn, New York, he graduated from Princeton University in 1912 and studied in Europe. He prepared for the congregational ministry at Hartford Seminary, Connecticut, graduating in 1915. His first pastorate was in Connecticut, during which he was also a chaplain to the navy during World War I. During his second pastorate at Brookline, Massachusetts, recognizing the importance of Karl Barth's work, he produced the first English translation of Barth's sermons, published as *The Word of God and the Word of Man* (1928). In 1931 he became minister of the United Church in Chicago, Illinois, and lectured on pastoralia at Chicago Theological Seminary. From 1938 to 1955 his leadership was recognized by his appointment as secretary to the Congregational Christian churches. He also lectured on Congregational polity at Union Theological Seminary. His growing academic status led to his appointment as dean of Harvard Divinity School in 1955. During the 1950s and 1960s he was a leader of the ecumenical movement: influential in the creation of the United Church of Christ in 1957 and involved in the World Council of Churches as chairman of its Faith and Order Commission (1957–1963) and observer at the Second Vatican Council. His publications include *Congregationalism, a Study in Church Polity* (1952), *The Meaning of Worship* (1959), and *Toward an Undivided Church* (1967).

NOEL S. POLLARD

Houghton, William Henry (1887–1947)

Baptist pastor and president of Moody Bible Institute. Born in Massachusetts, he was converted in 1901. He became an entertainer and performed on the vaudeville circuit. In 1909 while attending a Nazarene church he experienced a spiritual renewal that led him to leave the stage and enroll in Eastern Nazarene College. He soon left college and entered evangelistic work in 1910. He became song leader for R. A. Torrey, was ordained to the Baptist ministry in 1915, and served several churches in Pennsylvania (1915–1924). During these years he became widely known as a fundamentalist through a series of tracts he wrote and a periodical he edited.

After a pastorate in Atlanta, Georgia (1925–1930), he was pastor of Calvary Baptist Church in New York City (1930–1934), and president of Moody Bible Institute (1934–1947), where he also edited (and doubled the circulation) of *Moody Monthly* (1934–1936). Perhaps his most innovative achievement was supporting the evangelistic ministry of Irwin A. Moon who gave a series of "Sermons from Science." This eventually led to the founding of the American Scientific Affiliation. Some of Houghton's radio messages are published in *Let's Go Back to the Bible* (1939).

Biography by W. M. Smith (1951).

ROBERT G. CLOUSE

Howard, David Morris (1928–)

Missionary and mission executive. Born in Philadelphia to a devoutly Christian family, he attended Wheaton College, from which he received an A.B. in 1949. During his college years he established close friendships with future missionary martyrs Jim Elliot and Ed McCully. After completing an M.A. in theology at Wheaton College, Howard served for fifteen years as a missionary in Costa Rica and Colombia with the Latin American Mission. In 1969 he became the missions director for InterVarsity Christian Fellowship and served as the director of the Urbana Missions conferences in 1973 and 1976. During this volatile period on U.S. campuses, Howard published several books, including *Student Power in World Evangelism* (1979), and spoke on hundreds of campuses. He helped stimulate a dramatic shift in student perception of missionary work from the hostility of the late 1960s to a more positive assessment by the mid-1970s. An able executive and spokesman for world evangelization, Howard served as director of the Consultation on World Evangelization in Pattaya, Thailand, in 1980 and as the general director of the World Evangelical Fellowship for the decade following 1982. He has authored numerous articles and books, and is respected for his work as a bridge-builder among evangelicals and missionaries from diverse cultural and theological backgrounds. His other works include *Words of Fire, River of Tears* (1976), and *What Makes a Missionary* (1987).

ALAN SEAMAN

Hromadka, Josef Luki (1889–1969)

Czech Reformed theologian. Born in Hodslavice, Moravia, he studied at Basel, Heidelberg, Vienna, Aberdeen, and Prague (Ph.D., 1920), where he became theological professor (1920–1939). He held a similar post at Princeton Theological Seminary (1939–1947), returned to teach in Prague, and was appointed dean of the Comenius faculty in 1950. At the first World Council of Churches assembly in Amsterdam in 1948, Hromadka was already recognized as spokesman of the Eastern Europeans at a time when

183

the communist takeover of his homeland was barely six months old. He denied that communism was either totalitarian or atheistic, and suggested that it was in many ways "secularized Christian theology, often furiously anti-Church." Hromadka was active in the founding of the Christian Peace Conference (1958), which sought to bring together Christian churches in Eastern Europe in their search for peace. He was the CPC's first president, and the recipient of the Lenin Peace Prize (1958). He was disillusioned, however, when in 1968 the Russians invaded his homeland, and he resigned from the CPC in protest. His published writings in English included biographies of Jan Masaryk (1930), Luther (1935), and Calvin (1936), and *Doom and Resurrection* (1945), *The Gospel for Atheists* (1958), and *My Life between East and West* (1969).

J. D. DOUGLAS

Hulme-Moir, Francis Oag (1910–1979)

Australian bishop and chaplain-general. Born in Sydney, his boyhood and early manhood affected by family problems and the Great Depression, he was converted and trained for the Anglican ministry at Moore College, Sydney. He was ordained in 1936, and three years later, on the outbreak of World War II, he became the first Australian army chaplain (1939–1945), serving continuously in the Middle East and the Pacific area. After two parish appointments in postwar years he was consecrated as bishop of Nelson, New Zealand (1954–1965). He returned to Sydney as dean of the cathedral in 1965, and became senior assistant bishop of the diocese in 1966 and chaplain-general of the Australian army in 1974. When he retired from Episcopal duties in 1975, the government appointed him to the Parole Board and made him an officer in the Order of Australia. Hulme-Moir was a big man in every way, a born leader with a remarkable gift for friendship with people from all walks of life.

MARCUS L. LOANE

Hunter, Archibald Macbride (1906–1991)

Scottish New Testament scholar. Born in Kilwinning, Ayrshire, a son of the manse, he was educated at Glasgow and Marburg universities. From 1931 he lectured at Glasgow University. In 1934 he was called to the parish of Comrie, Perthshire. In 1937 he was appointed professor of New Testament at Mansfield College, Oxford, and gained a D.Phil. degree at Oxford University. During World War II, he returned to Scotland to be minister of Kinnoul, Perthshire. In 1945 he was appointed professor of New Testament exegesis at Aberdeen University. From 1957 he was also master of Christ's College. In addition to being a skillful teacher, he had the knack of writing books on New Testament subjects for which generations of students and laypeople blessed him. Starting with books such as *Paul and His Prede-*

cessors (1940), *The Words and Works of Jesus* (1950), and *Interpreting the New Testament* (1951), he kept up a steady flow of studies and commentaries even after his retirement in 1971. While his writings were clearly in the mainstream of British critical scholarship, he was conservative about the reliability of the Gospel tradition.

NOEL S. POLLARD

1

●●●

Idowu, E. Bolaji (1913–)

African theologian and churchman. Born in Nigeria, he is recognized as one of the pioneers in the development of modern African theology. His call for the sensitive handling of traditional religions and his cry for African scholarship continue to echo modern African theology. Building on a broad view of revelation, Idowu explores the imprint of God's self-disclosure within traditional religious settings. He maintains that these traditions should be recognized as having merit in their own light, and that they should not be simply rejected without being understood. The broadness of revelation was also a philosophical cornerstone used by Idowu in his instrumental role in the development of *Orita*, a journal devoted to the exploration of areas of convergence among Christianity, Islam, and African traditional religions. In addition to his theological work, he was vitally active in the Methodist Church of Nigeria, in which he was inaugurated as the "life patriarch" in 1975 when the church added bishops to its ecclesiastical hierarchy, taking the title of "His Pre-Eminence." His significant works include *African Traditional Religions: A Definition, Towards an Indigenous Church,* and *Olodumare: God in Yoruba Belief.*

A. SCOTT MOREAU

Inge, William Ralph (1860–1954)

Dean of St. Paul's, London, and writer. Born in Yorkshire, he was educated at Eton and King's College, Cambridge, and after ordination was made fellow of Hertford College, Oxford. Out of his classical and mystical studies came his Bampton Lectures, *Christian Mysticism* (1899). He pioneered the revival of interest in Christian mysticism in the early part of the twentieth century. After short spells as a vicar in London and a professor at Cambridge, he was made dean of St. Paul's Cathedral, London, in 1911. He remained there until his retirement in 1934.

Brought up in the Tractarian mold he became a moderate liberal and for a time president of the Modern Churchmen's Union. His liberalism was best expressed in his popular writing for newspapers, some of which were gathered in his *Outspoken Essays* (2 vols., 1919, 1922) and *Lay Thoughts of a Dean* (1926). From an early age he suffered from depression and was plagued with deafness. These problems spilled over into his preaching and writings, so that he was often called the "gloomy Dean." His classical and mystical studies were fully revealed in his magnum opus, *The Philosophy of Plotinus* (Gifford Lectures, 1918). He continued to lecture, preach, and write until he was ninety years old.

NOEL S. POLLARD

Ironside, Henry Allen (Harry) (1876–1951)

Evangelist and Bible teacher. Born in Toronto to a godly Plymouth Brethren couple, he had read the Bible through fourteen times by his fourteenth birthday. Initially with the Salvation Army, he then joined the Plymouth Brethren, and gradually became known as an itinerant speaker and writer on biblical themes. He became pastor of the Moody Memorial Church, Chicago (1929–1948), during which time he still traveled much, had an extensive writing and radio ministry, and taught at Moody Bible Institute. He preached over five hundred sermons a year. His theology was dispensationalist, but never of a sensationalistic sort. At heart he remained a pastor and soul-winner, not a theologian, and is best remembered for his ability to communicate the gospel simply and with deep conviction. Because of this he was respected and his counsel valued, even in the academic world where he served as board member of at least fifteen organizations, ranging from Wheaton College, Dallas Theological Seminary, and Moody Bible Institute to the Overseas Missionary Fellowship and the American Association for Jewish Evangelism. Ironside died while on a preaching tour in New Zealand. His numerous published works include a series of *Notes* on various biblical books, *The Unchanging Christ* (1938), and *The Great Parenthesis* (1943).

Biographies by E. S. English (1976) and E. Reese (1976).

WALTER A. ELWELL

Isáis, Juan M. (1926–)

Leader in cooperative evangelism in Latin America. Born in Zacatecas, Mexico, Isáis first dreamed of an acting career. Then, hearing an artist proclaim on stage, "What shall it profit a man, if he shall gain the whole world, and lose his own soul?" the stage-struck teenager came under conviction and that day gave his life to Christ. From conversion, Isáis made evangelism his life's passion. After attending Bible institute in Guatemala, Isáis went to Costa Rica to cooperate in the radio and evangelistic work of Latin America Mission (LAM). There he became a close colleague of LAM general director, Kenneth Strachan, who was just developing the principles of Evangelism-in-Depth (EID), an innovative program encouraging the mobilization of every believer in continuous witness. Isáis helped lead the first EID effort in Nicaragua in 1960, plus subsequent projects in other Latin nations. EID brought together evangelical Christians of every stripe for a year of intense, united witness. The united campaigns in the 1960s and early 1970s gave Latin America's still small and embattled evangelical church a new sense of identity and confidence. Isáis has since continued to promote EID efforts in his native Mexico as founder and director of the Latin America Mission of Mexico (MILAMEX). He is a supreme motivator in getting Christians to witness to their faith. Isáis also became an accomplished poet, writer, and composer. His chorus "Te Vengo a Decir" ("I've Come to Tell You") is sung in churches across Latin America. But cooperative evangelism is what he lives and breathes. He has written *The Other Side of the Coin* (1996), *The Other Revolution* (1970), and *The Other Evangelism* (1988).

JOHN MAUST

J

Jackson, Mahalia (1911–1972)

Gospel singer. A native of New Orleans, Mahalia Jackson sang with the children's choir at her home church, Mount Moriah Baptist Church. Her understanding and appreciation of music were influenced by the jazz that was so prevalent in the city, as well as by the "sanctified" church near her home. It is reported that she was reduced to tears by the powerful beat and rhythms at the sanctified church, beats and rhythms that she believed had been retained from the antebellum era of slavery. Although both the sanctified church and jazz had a powerful influence on her personal style of singing, Jackson's primary motivation was obedience to the Bible's teachings to "make a joyful noise unto the Lord" and to "praise the Lord with the instruments."

In 1927 Mahalia moved to Chicago to live with an aunt. It was in this mecca of gospel music that she met and began to work with Professor Thomas A. Dorsey. Dorsey wrote songs for her as well as becoming her mentor and publisher. Within a relatively short period of time she went from touring the storefront churches of Chicago to being offered many lucrative singing engagements. Some jazz recording labels sought to woo her away from gospel to blues and jazz. She rejected these offers and continued to establish herself as a distinctive personality in black gospel music. London's *New Statesman* acknowledged Jackson as "the most majestic voice of faith" of her generation. From her first recording, "God Shall Wipe Away All Tears" in 1937 through some of her most popular recordings, "Upper Room," "Didn't It Rain," "Even Me," and "Silent Night," the sales of her recordings continue to bear testimony to her broad acceptance.

Jackson was active in the civil rights movement in the United States, singing at many rallies, including the March on Washington in 1963. She established the Mahalia Jackson Scholarship Fund to assist poor young people in attending college. She has been honored by the Grammy committee with a Lifetime Achievement Award, having more than thirty recordings to her credit.

ROBERT C. SUGGS

Jacobs, Henry Eyster (1844–1932)

Lutheran theologian. Born in Gettysburg, Pennsylvania, he earned degrees from Pennsylvania College, Gettysburg (1862), and Gettysburg Theological Seminary (1865). He began his teaching career at Thiel Hall, Phillipsburg, Pennsylvania, where he was pastor and principal, then moved to Pennsylvania College, Gettysburg, to teach Classics. In 1883 he accepted a post in systematic theology at Lutheran Theological Seminary, Mount Airy, serving there as dean from 1885 until he became president (1920–1928). He played a significant role in the confessional and liturgical renewal of Lutherans. He is recognized as one of the major Lutheran Confessional figures between the Civil War and the Great Depression, and as one who enabled American Lutherans to be more in touch with their German heritage through his translation of significant German Lutheran works. His books include *A History of the Evangelical Lutheran Church in the United States* (1893), *The Elements of Religion* (1896), *Martin Luther* (1898; repr. 1973), and *A Summary of the Christian Faith* (1905). He also edited or translated thirteen additional volumes, including the *Works of Martin Luther* (1915–1943) and *The Lutheran Encyclopedia* (1899) with J. A. W. Haas.

A. Scott Moreau

Jaffray, Robert A. (1873–1945)

Canadian missionary. Born in Toronto, son of a newspaper owner, he was converted at sixteen. He later forsook insurance sales for missions under the Christian and Missionary Alliance (C&MA). Serving in Wuchow, South China (1886–1920), he was Bible school principal, editor, pastor, field chairman, and (from 1916) superintendent of the Indochina area. From 1928 he concentrated on the East Indies (now Indonesia), founding the Chinese Foreign Missionary Union and initially recruiting Chinese missionaries. By 1941 the C&MA had 190 workers there. Jaffray founded *The Borneo Pioneer,* the Malay *Bible Magazine,* and a Bible school that attracted students from sixteen language groups. He initiated ministry in Ringlet, Malaya, constructing a Bible school and mission station until the Japanese invasion in World War II. Refusing retirement, he suffered internment (1942–1945) and died of starvation two weeks before Japan surrendered.

Jaffray the pioneer opened country after country. With tireless zeal he studied maps, traveled extensively, and dispatched his troops to evangelize untouched sections of China, Vietnam, Cambodia, and Indonesia. Though dogged by diabetes and heart disease from childhood, he never stopped. He created a desk that hung over his bed so that he could work while resting. When conservative boards obstructed his bolder ventures, a persistence inherited from his Scottish ancestors led him to press on—and most of his dreams materialized. Beyond evangelism, he envisioned a strong church. He established Bible schools and three presses.

See A. W. Tozer, *Let My People Go!* (1947).

Gerald E. McGraw

James, Gnanamuthu Dixon (1920–)

Evangelist. He was born into a staunch Hindu family in Salem, South India, and, despite his father's dislike for Christianity, was sent to a Christian mission school noted for its academic excellence. In 1937, while studying the Bible as part of his curriculum, he was gripped by a vision of the Christ dying for him: "For the first time in my life I realized Jesus Christ loved me, that he sacrificed his life for me. . . . I knelt down and surrendered myself to Jesus." Persecution followed. He was thrown out of his home, but his began a wonderful adventure with the living God. James relinquished his ambition to become a medical doctor when God called him to Christian service. This "compelling call" took him all over India as an evangelist. In 1941 he went to Malaysia to evangelize the Indians working in the rubber plantations. In 1960 this ministry extended to other people groups, which brought to birth a local mission organization, the Malaysia Evangelistic Fellowship, later renamed the Asia Evangelistic Fellowship. The seeds planted in the Tamil ministry resulted in the Tamil Bible Institute in 1977, a training center for mission among the Hindu-Indians. In 1977 James moved to Sydney, Australia, to minister among the Indo-Chinese refugees, Asian students, and the Brethren assemblies. For the past fifty years James has faithfully served as a missionary-evangelist in Southeast Asia and Australia. Through numerous city-wide crusades thousands have been converted. He has published Christian tracts in English and Tamil, and several books, among which are *Words of Comfort* (1974) and *Amazed by Love* (1977).

B. VIOLET JAMES

Jaramillo, Luciano (1934–)

Latin American editor and Bible scholar. Born in Colombia's staunchly traditional Antioquia region, Jaramillo was ordained to the Roman Catholic priesthood at age twenty-five. He served as parish priest and secretary to the archbishop of Cartagena for three years. Then in 1962, through the witness of a Protestant evangelical friend and after his own soul searching, Jaramillo had what he called his "conversion experience as an evangelical new-born Christian." Leaving the Roman Catholic Church—no small step given his background and country's conservative Catholic culture—Jaramillo went on to become a leading Presbyterian educator and pastor in his own country. He served two terms as president of Colombia's national Confederation of Evangelical Churches. In 1979 Jaramillo moved to Miami, Florida, and worked at the Americas Regional Center of the United Bible Societies (UBS). There he launched the Bible Societies' radio program, which would be heard daily on three hundred stations in the Americas and Spain. Also, he created a continent-wide music contest, "The Bible Sings," which encouraged people to put music to the Scripture text.

191

Some two hundred new hymns emerged as a result. Known across Latin America as a gifted journalist and Bible scholar, Jaramillo also served eight years as editor of the Bible Societies' one hundred thousand-circulation *La Biblia en las Américas* magazine. In 1990 he began work with the International Bible Society as executive secretary of its translation project to do the popular New International Version of the Bible in Spanish.

JOHN MAUST

Jaspers, Karl Theodor (1883–1969)

German philosopher. Born in Oldenburg, he studied law, pursued medical studies to their completion, then shifted to the study of psychiatry. Various changes in academic orientation seem to have been connected with his indifferent health as a youth. By 1916 he qualified for the teaching of philosophy, and in 1922 he accepted a full professorship in that subject at the University of Heidelberg. Because of his liberal views and his marriage to a Jewess, Jaspers was forced to retire in 1937 and was prohibited from publishing a year later. Greatly disappointed in the political direction of postwar Germany, he accepted a call to Basel in 1948, and remained there until retirement in 1961. Jaspers' philosophical orientation was rooted in the thought of the world of classical Greece and shaped by Renaissance ideals. Although he was highly critical of Christianity as the dominant religion of Europe, he also recognized its positive impact in preventing people from falling to a level of unreflective existence. His numerous publications had a far-reaching impact on twentieth-century intellectuals.

Robert Carr has written on *Jaspers as an Intellectual Critic* (1983).

EDWARD J. FURCHA

Javalera, Elizabeth ("Betty") (1934–)

Christian educator. Born in Manila she graduated with a teacher's certificate from the Philippine Normal College in 1953. To this she added in 1968 a B.S. degree in psychology from Far Eastern University, in 1973 an M.A. degree in Christian education from Trinity Evangelical Divinity School, Deerfield, Illinois, and in 1984 a Ph.D. in education from Michigan State University. Javalera is known as one of the leading Christian educators in the Philippines and in Asia generally. She has taught at Far Eastern Bible Institute, Philippine Missionary Institute, Haggai Institute's Women's Training Session in Singapore, and Asian Theological Seminary. She has been involved also in editing work, and was national missionary with Philippine Crusades (1969–1975). She currently serves as general secretary of the Philippine Association of Christian Education, and as founder/director of the PACE Graduate School of Christian Education in Quezon City, the Philippines.

FRANK ALLEN

Jefferson, Charles Edward (1860–1937)

Congregational minister and writer. Born in Cambridge, Ohio, he earned degrees at Ohio Wesleyan University and Boston University. He ministered at Central Congregational Church in Chelsea, Massachusetts, for twelve years before accepting the pulpit of Broadway Tabernacle in New York City, where he served from 1898 until retirement in 1930. Jefferson was regarded as a clear-thinking speaker, able to express himself passionately yet conversationally, and became known as one of the great preachers of his day. He was also a strong advocate of social justice, seen in his *Christianity and International Peace* (1915) and his involvement in the Church Peace Union. Though a leader in the liberal movement of the early 1900s, he maintained an orthodox stance on issues such as the deity of Christ (*The Character of Jesus,* 1908), while still accepting the modern critical approach to the Scriptures (*Cardinal Ideas of Isaiah,* 1925). Other works included *Things Fundamental* (1903), *The Minister as Shepherd* (1912), and *Christianizing a Nation* (1929).

A. SCOTT MOREAU

John Paul I (1912–1978)

Pope from August 26 to September 28, 1978. Born Albino Luciani at Forno di Canale, Italy, he grew up in a poor but devout Christian home. He studied at the Gregorian University in Rome (where he later completed a doctorate in theology), and was ordained priest in 1935. He was deputy director of the Belluno Seminary (1937–1947), vicar-general of his diocese (1947–1958), bishop of Vittorio-Veneto (1958–1969), and archbishop of Venice (1969–1978). He had earlier participated in Vatican II and expressed his support of its spirit of renewal. Made cardinal in 1973, he was the first pope since Pius X (1903–1914) to stress a pastoral ministry. His sudden death from a heart attack, under somewhat mysterious circumstances, created a lingering controversy in church circles. His "September Papacy," lasting only thirty-four days, was the shortest in modern times.

ROBERT D. LINDER

John Paul II (1920–)

Pope from 1978. Born in Wadowice, Poland, Karol Wojtyla grew up in an impoverished but devoted Catholic home. He was a student at the Jagiellonian University at Krakow (1937–1939). During the Nazi occupation of Poland he worked in a quarry and later in a chemical plant before joining an underground seminary in 1942 to study for the priesthood. Ordained in 1946, he traveled to Rome to earn a doctorate at Angelicum University in 1948, to which was added a Th.D. from the Jagiellonian University in 1949. He held chaplaincy and university teaching posts before becoming bishop of Ombi (Egypt) and auxiliary bishop of Krakow (1958–1964), archbishop of Krakow (1964), and cardinal (1967). In 1978 he became the first non-Italian pope in 456 years and the first Polish pope. He took seriously his duties as bishop of Rome by frequently visiting its parishes and institutions. He also traveled extensively to every continent.

In his encyclicals he has firmly endorsed traditional church views on such matters as abortion, contraceptives, homosexuality, divorce, political officeholding by priests and nuns, clerical celibacy, and the ordination of women to the priesthood. He has also, however, advocated human rights and stressed the need for economic justice while denouncing abuses of power in both capitalistic and socialistic systems. The most important of his books are *Love and Responsibility* (1960) and *Foundations of Renewal* (1972).

Biographies in English, all published in 1982, by P. Hebblethwaite, P. Johnson, and Lord Longford.

ROBERT D. LINDER

John XXIII (1881–1963)

Pope from 1958. Born Angelo Guiseppe Roncalli near Bergamo, northern Italy, he studied in Rome and was ordained and served as secretary (1904–1914) to a social-minded bishop (1904–1914). He participated in Catholic action among the working class, taught at the diocesan seminary, and published the first of many scholarly works. He went to Rome, reorganized the papal funding agency for missions (1921), and taught patristics at the Lateran University. Joining the papal diplomatic corps in 1925, he was the papal representative in Bulgaria, Greece, and Turkey. He promoted the use of their respective national languages in Catholic schools, publications, and the liturgy. Based in Istanbul he sent back intelligence obtained as a confidant of diplomats. He helped Jewish refugees from eastern Europe. Appointed nuncio to France (1944) he supported its worker-priest experiment. In 1953 he became patriarch of Venice. As pope from 1958 he was nicknamed "John-outside-the-Walls" because he broke with precedent by often leaving Vatican City to visit parishioners. He convened Vatican II to update (*aggiornamento*) the church, which motif epitomized his pontificate. He suppressed the invective against Jews in the Good Friday liturgy. His socially progressive encyclical *Mater et Magistra* (1961) troubled conservative Catholics. *Pacem in terris* (1963) endorsed the United Nations, which used this document as the basis of a symposium on world peace. The advent of television effectively communicated John XXIII's charisma to millions. *Journal of a Soul* (1965) and *Letters* (1970) constitute his memoirs.

Biographies by G. DeRosa (1967), G. Zizola (1978), and P. Hebblethwaite (1985).

NORMAN F. CORNETT

Johnson, Douglas (1904–1990)

First secretary of the (British) InterVarsity Fellowship. He studied English, theology, and medicine at King's College, London, and was a leader in starting small evangelical Christian unions in London colleges and in other parts of Britain, and in establishing a doctrinal basis for them. When in 1928 these formed the IVF he was appointed secretary, a post he held until 1964, retiring then to become secretary of the Christian Medical Fellowship until 1974. Though little known outside IVF circles he was one of the outstanding evangelical leaders in Britain. His method of leadership was as far as possible to keep in the background himself and push others to the front as speakers, writers, and committee chairpersons. He developed an enormous correspondence of mainly handwritten and often witty letters, and his friendship, enthusiasm, and encouragement had a major impact on the Christian scene.

At that time the very large and prestigious Student Christian Movement (SCM) was increasingly liberal. Evangelicals by reaction were often anti-intellectual and therefore antitheological. "DJ," as he was always known, taught generations of students to love biblical doctrine and to find there the foundations for evangelism and spiritual life. He worked hard to bring into the student work speakers such as D. Martyn Lloyd-Jones and Daniel Lamont, who exemplified these virtues. He helped the small Christian unions and many individual ministers and lay leaders to contend for the faith, including the infallibility of Scripture and substitutionary atonement, and yet never to become doctrinaire, but to make these the basis for evangelism and spiritual life. Johnson was a major force in the development of IVF literature and of the International Fellowship of Evangelical Students (IFES). He was a key figure also in setting up Tyndale House, Cambridge, for biblical research.

OLIVER R. BARCLAY

Johnson, Hewlett (1874–1966)

Dean of Canterbury and social activist. Born into a prosperous Cheshire family, he was educated at the universities of Manchester and Oxford, and was an engineering apprentice and welfare worker in the slums of Manchester before ordination in 1905. Parish work was followed by promotion to the deanery of Manchester (1924–1931), thence to Canterbury (1931–1963) at the instigation of Labour Prime Minister Ramsay MacDonald. There Johnson caused uproar after uproar by tireless championship of communist states and Marxist causes. After a visit to the Soviet Union in 1938 he published *The Socialist Sixth of the World* (22 editions, 25 languages). Though never a member of the Communist party, he journeyed far to world peace rallies, was awarded the Stalin Peace Prize in 1951, charged the Americans with germ warfare in Korea, and played down the 1956 Russian suppression of revolution in Hungary. To four successive archbishops, four monarchs, and eleven British governments the distinguished-looking Johnson ("you can call me red") was a thorn in the flesh that could not legally be removed. His voluntary retirement from the historic post in 1963 was hailed with profound relief by the English political and ecclesiastical establishments. His other published works included *Christians and Communism* (1956) and the autobiographical *Searching for Light* (1968).

J. D. DOUGLAS

Johnson, Torrey Maynard (1909–)

American evangelist, pastor, teacher, and director of Youth for Christ International. Born in Chicago, he was educated at Northwestern University, Wheaton College, and Northern Baptist Theological Seminary, had a conversion experience at the age of eighteen, and was ordained to the ministry of the Baptist Church in 1930. He traveled the upper Midwest as a youth evangelist, and in 1933 became pastor of the fledgling Midwest Bible Church in Chicago. In response to a growing nationwide Youth for Christ movement that was interdenominational and evangelistic, Johnson organized and directed Chicagoland Youth for Christ in 1944. In January 1945 Youth for Christ International was organized in Chicago to centralize a movement that would eventually spread to every continent. At the first Youth for Christ Conference held at Winona Lake, Indiana, delegates elected Johnson director of Youth for Christ International and drew up a seven-point doctrinal platform. Billy Graham was appointed the first field evangelist for Youth for Christ International, and, in 1946, *Youth for Christ* magazine was established. Johnson exhibited the rare ability to combine the talents of an accomplished organizer/administrator with the zeal and personality of an effective pastor/evangelist. His primary work is *Reaching Youth for Christ.*

MAXIE BURCH

Jones, Bob, Sr. (1883–1968)

American revivalist and educator. Reared in a pious Methodist home in Alabama, Jones began preaching at age thirteen and leading revival services at fifteen. During studies at Southern (now Birmingham Southern) University, Jones commenced work as an itinerant evangelist, mostly in the southern states. Sensing that many educational institutions were abandoning their Christian heritage in the years following World War I, he opened Bob Jones College in northern Florida in 1926. He moved it first to Cleveland, Tennessee, in 1933, and then to its present location in Greenville, South Carolina, in 1947. A staunch fundamentalist, he sparred in public with evangelist Billy Graham over the latter's acceptance of modernists in his crusades. Jones firmly opposed moves to integrate the races toward the end of his life. His educational work created a unique institution, now called Bob Jones University, with an international reputation, work carried on after his death by his son, Bob Jones, Jr., and his grandson, Bob Jones III.

Biography by R. K. Johnson (1982).

THOMAS G. REID, JR.

Jones, Eli Stanley (1884–1973)

American missionary to India. Born in Baltimore, he went to India as a missionary of the Methodist Episcopal Church in 1907, later became an itinerant evangelist, and declined a bishopric in 1928. Concerned equally for social justice and spirituality, he supported Indian aspirations for independence—to the extent of being banned for a time by the British authorities—and was sensitive to Indian religious traditions. He founded two Christian ashrams, one at Sat Tal in 1930 and the other in Lucknow, where he also founded a psychiatric center. He set up similar centers in the United States and Europe, and was well known outside India for his many books, although none became more famous than *The Christ of the Indian Road* (1925). *Christ at the Round Table* (1928) and *Mahatma Gandhi: An Interpretation* (1948) were also significant attempts to influence the Indian intelligentsia for Christ. Retiring in 1954, Jones continued to spend part of each year in the Far East, visiting India in alternate years. He received the Gandhi Peace Prize in 1961. His spiritual autobiography was called *A Song of Ascents* (1968).

R. W. Taylor wrote *The Contribution of E. Stanley Jones* (1973).

PHILIP HILLYER

Jones, Rufus Matthew (1863–1948)

American scholar, mystic, and activist. Born in South China, Maine, he studied at Haverford College, the University of Pennsylvania, and Harvard University. After teaching at Quaker preparatory schools he became professor of philosophy at Haverford College, where he served for over forty years. Active among Quakers, he edited the *American Friend* (1894–1912) and encouraged the formation of the Friends United Meeting. He served as chairman or honorary chairman of the American Friends Service Committee from its founding in 1917 until his death. His academic work consisted of interpreting Quaker and European mystics to a large audience of English-speaking people. He was editor and coauthor of the Rowntree Quaker history series, which included *Studies in Mystical Religion* (1909) and *The Quaker in the American Colonies* (1911). Many who were not interested in his historical work read his books on mysticism, prayer, and the spiritual life, especially *Pathways to the Reality of God* (1931), *New Eyes for*

Invisibles (1943), *The Luminous Trail* (1947), and *A Call to What Is Vital* (1949).

Biographies by D. Hinshaw (1951) and E. G. Vining (1958).

ROBERT G. CLOUSE

Jowett, John Henry (1864–1923)

English Congregational preacher and writer. Born near Halifax, Yorkshire, he was educated at Airedale College, Bradford, and at Edinburgh University. In 1889 he became minister of the Congregational Church in Newcastle-upon-Tyne, and gained such a reputation for preaching that in 1895 he was called to the prestigious Carr's Lane Chapel in Birmingham. He was chairman of the Congregational Union in 1906 and president of the Free Church Council in 1910. After speaking at the Northfield Conference in 1909 he was called to Fifth Avenue Presbyterian Church, New York City (1911–1918). During World War I he became a widely known figure in the United States, and many of his sermons were published. In 1918 he returned to England to minister in Westminster Chapel, London, but his health was poor and he retired in 1922. Jowett's powerful and attractive preaching avoided theological controversy. Only in his final years at Westminster did he begin to preach on social and political issues. His Lyman Beecher Lectures at Yale (1911–1912) were published as *The Preacher: His Life and Work* (1912). His other writings include *Thirsting for Souls* (1902), *The Epistles of Peter* (1905), and *The High Calling* (1909).

Biography by A. Porritt (1925).

NOEL S. POLLARD

K

Kagawa, Toyohiko (1888–1960)

Japanese evangelist, author, and social activist. Born in Kobe, an illegitimate son of a wealthy Buddhist shipping magnate, he lost both parents at age four, and lived as an outcast with his father's legal wife. Kagawa had, however, a rich uncle who later agreed to house him and pay his school fees. He began to study English under Harry Myers, an American missionary who led the boy to Christ and baptized him in 1903. His uncle disinherited Kagawa when he announced his intention to enter the ministry rather than attend university. In 1907 he began roadside preaching in Toyohashi. He contracted tuberculosis and was forced to leave the slums to recover. Convinced that Christian witness must be expressed in social service, he moved to the Shinkawa slums in 1909 and lived in a six-foot cell. Graduating from Kobe Theological School in 1911, he went on to study at Princeton (1914–1917). On his return to Japan he moved back to the slums; his experiences moved him to write *Beyond the Line of Death* (1920), which became a best-seller and financed his work. He organized the first labor union in Japan (1921), founded the National Anti-War League (1928), led strikes, and served in public office. A major triumph was a new law designed to rehouse slum-dwellers. But Kagawa always kept priorities, founding the Kingdom of God movement (1928) that sought to win a million people to Christ. He was arrested twice (1940, 1943). He served postwar in the Upper House of Diet, and helped found the Japan Socialist party. His books include *The Religion of Jesus* (1931), *Christ and Japan* (1934), and *Meditations on the Cross* (1936).

A. Scott Moreau

Kalu, Ogbu Uke (1944–)

Nigerian historian and theologian. He was born in Anambra State, Nigeria, and after receiving his early education locally he went abroad. He graduated from the University of Toronto (1967, 1970), and earned his Ph.D. degree at London University in 1972. Further study at Princeton Theological Seminary led to a master's degree in divinity in 1974. Kalu then returned to Nigeria and from 1974 served at the University of Nigeria where he currently holds the position of professor of church history. He is affiliated with the Presbyterian Church of Nigeria. Kalu's most significant contribution to Christian scholarship in Africa has been in the area of historiography. He has been a pioneer in raising awareness about the study of the African Christian past, and the impact that one's concept of the church has on writing church history. Kalu has drawn particular attention to the conflicting perspectives of overly Western-oriented missionary historiography and the reactionary nationalist perspective. He has called for a new ecumenical perspective to break the impasse and move beyond merely institutional or patriotic historiography. Kalu's publications include *The History of Christianity in West Africa* (1970), *Divided People of God: Church Union Movement in Nigeria 1875–1966* (1978), and, as editor, *African Church Historiography* (1988).

MARK R. SHAW

Kantzer, Kenneth Sealer (1917–)

American theologian. Born in Detroit, he graduated from Ashland College, Ohio State University, Faith Theological Seminary, and Harvard University (Ph.D., 1950), followed by studies at Göttingen and at Basel under Karl Barth. Kantzer is an ordained minister in the Evangelical Free Church of America, has taught at King's College, Gordon College, Gordon-Conwell Theological Seminary, Wheaton College, and Trinity Evangelical Divinity School of which he was dean and president, and is now chancellor. He served as editor of *Christianity Today* (1978–1982), and is now a consulting editor and dean of its research institute. Kantzer has contributed to many other publications, and is regarded as a leader in modern American evangelicalism.

SAM HAMSTRA, JR.

Kato, Byang Henry (1936–1975)

African theologian and church leader. Born the son of a fetish priest in Sabzuro, Nigeria, he committed his life to Christ at the age of twelve, and attended Igbaja Bible College in preparation for ministry. After teaching at a Bible school, he attended London Bible College, receiving a University of London B.D. in 1966. As a leading evangelical theologian, Kato initiated the call for an African theology that was truly African and truly biblical. His focus in his most significant work, *Theological Pitfalls in Africa* (based on his Dallas Theological Seminary Th.D. dissertation), was on the biblical element. As a churchman, he served as general secretary of the Evangelical Churches of West Africa (ECWA), was the first African general secretary of the Association of Evangelicals of Africa and Madagascar (AEAM), and a vice president of the World Evangelical Fellowship. As a visionary, he called for the formation of stronger theological education on the African continent, a vision now fulfilled in two graduate-level seminaries. His works include *African Faith and the Cultural Revolution, Biblical Christianity in Africa* (a collection of articles), and *The Spirits* (a pamphlet discussing the biblical teaching on spirits). He died while on vacation, in a swimming accident off the coast of Kenya.

A. SCOTT MOREAU

Khair-Ullah, Frank Safi-Ullah (1914–)

Educationalist and writer. Born in Nowshera, Pakistan, son of an Afghan convert, he was educated at Forman Christian College, Lahore, and later at Edinburgh University where he earned a Ph.D. degree. In World War II he served as a YMCA secretary with the Indian Army in the Middle East. In 1942 he was lecturer and then head of the English department at Murray College, Sialkot, where he served also as principal from 1964 to 1972. His great integrity and spirituality led to his appointment to many boards and committees in Pakistan, especially in education and church work. He read papers at international conferences, notably at the 1974 Lausanne Congress. His published works include an Urdu Bible dictionary containing more than five thousand articles, many of them written by him; a Hebrew-Urdu primer; and a three-volume Urdu Bible commentary. He was appointed director of a creative writing project by the Christian Publishing House, Lahore, and is also a presbyter in the Church of Pakistan and vicar of St. Andrew's Church, Lahore.

PATRICK SOOKHDEO

Kil, Son-Chu (1869–1935)

Korean evangelist, pioneer pastor, and patriot. Born in Anju, in what is now North Korea, he studied in a Confucian school, tried his hand as a merchant, but returned to Taoist and Buddhist philosophical meditation in the early 1890s. For a while he practiced Oriental medicine, but in Pyengyang in 1895 he was converted and baptized. Ordained elder in the Pyengyang Central Presbyterian Church (Changtaehyun) in 1901, he itinerated widely as a lay evangelist, and entered the newly established Presbyterian Seminary in Pyengyang in 1903, graduating in its first class in 1907. He was ordained at the first presbytery meeting of the new self-governing and self-supporting Presbyterian Church of Korea. A month later he replaced the missionary founder of Pyengyang Central Church, S. A. Moffett, as the first installed Korean pastor of a Korean church. He was also head of the Korean Presbyterian Board of Missions (1907–1913) and became known nationally as the primary figure in "the great Korean revival" of 1906–1908, which increased church membership fourfold in five years. The Korean independence movement of 1919 again vaulted Pastor Kil into national prominence as leader of the Christian wing of demonstrations protesting Japanese colonial cruelty in Korea. Fifteen of the thirty-three signatories of Korea's Declaration of Independence were Christians, and Kil was imprisoned for three years. He retired in 1927, but died still evangelizing.

SAMUEL H. MOFFETT

Kim, Helen (1899–1968)

Korean advocate for women's rights, university president, and evangelist. Born near Seoul into a wealthy Confucian merchant's family that had recently become Christian, she was educated at a Methodist school. Converted in 1913, she determined to seek higher Christian education at the newly formed Ewha College, graduating in 1918 and being made dean in 1928. In America, at Columbia University, she was the first Korean woman to earn a Ph.D. degree (1931). Returning to Korea, she continued to devote herself to the cause for women's education at Ewha, whose president she became (1939–1961), and which grew to be the largest women's university in the world. Helen Kim jealously guarded its Christian character, promoting annual evangelistic meetings and resisting calls for religious pluralism.

The Korean war brought both danger and new responsibilities. Fleeing the communist invasion, the school set up a tent refugee college in the Pusan perimeter. The government, also fleeing south, appointed Helen Kim as director of the Korean Red Cross administration, and then as director of the Office of Public Administration. In that capacity she founded in 1950 Korea's influential English language newspaper, *The Korea Times*. She served as a member of the Korean delegation to the United Nations (1956–1959), and was a delegate to the International Missionary Council conferences at Jerusalem (1928) and New Delhi (1961). When she retired from Ewha University and was asked what she wanted to do, she replied, "Now I want to be an evangelist." Her autobiography was published in 1964.

SAMUEL H. MOFFETT

Kim, Joon-Gon (1925–)

Korean evangelist. Born in Chi-do Island he came to Christ in 1942, and graduated from Korean Presbyterian Theological Seminary in 1948. His plans for ministry, however, were cut short in 1950 when North Korea invaded South Korea. Fearing for their lives, the Kim family fled to Chi-do Island, but this was taken by the North Korean forces who honored the zeal of those willing to kill non-Communists. The Kim family was rounded up with some sixty of the island's inhabitants. Kim witnessed the brutal murder of his father and wife, and was himself beaten and left for dead. He regained consciousness, but was beaten twice more, after which he was able to escape. Twice more his life was miraculously spared. At the end of that time God touched Kim in a way that enabled him to forgive his enemies and pray for their salvation. He was revived in his faith, and he no longer feared those who could destroy him physically. He led one Communist to Christ, and this man became a faithful witness among his fellows. Kim realized that he had been called to preach the gospel to the Communists. At war's end he remarried and came to the United States to study at Fuller Theological Seminary. There he encountered Campus Crusade for Christ. Its founder, Bill Bright, persuaded Kim to join CCC and begin a ministry in Korea, and this Kim did in 1958. Kim was the organizer of EXPLO '74, a conference that attracted over 300,000 delegates with nightly meeting audiences estimated at 1 to 1.5 million. In 1980 he organized Here's Life Korea, which drew about 10 million. His vision extended: 3,000 Koreans under his direction participated in an outreach to Manila in 1990.

SAMUEL H. MOFFETT

Kimbangu, Simon (1889–1951)

Founder of The Church of Jesus Christ on Earth Through the Prophet Simon Kimbangu (EJCSK), the largest independent denomination in Africa. Born in Nkamba, Zaire (formerly Belgian Congo), he was educated at a Baptist Missionary Society school, became a catechist, taught briefly at a mission school, and served as an evangelist. In 1921 he healed a sick woman. Within two months, thousands had left their jobs and were flocking to him, many considering him an African messiah. He denied this and exhorted his followers to stay in the mission churches, which were soon filled. The Belgian authorities, alarmed at the explosive growth of his popularity and fearing insurrection, arrested Kimbangu. He was tried in a military tribunal and sentenced to death, but the Belgian procurator, together with some of the missionaries, protested the injustice of the sentence and King Albert commuted it to life imprisonment. He died in prison after thirty years there for six months of ministry.

The EJCSK, organized underground by Kimbangu's children and other followers, was outlawed until Zaire's independence in 1960. It was the first African-initiated church to be accepted into the World Council of Churches (1969); by 1984 its membership had been estimated at 5 million. Though official church doctrine has an evangelical appearance, one scholar's analysis indicates that many Kimbanguists elevate their founder's role to that of the Holy Spirit (e.g., his name replaces the Spirit in Trinitarian formulas found in several Kimbanguist hymns). Kimbangu himself denied any such status, however, and deserves recognition as a humble Christian who in a few months left a greater spiritual impact on Zaire than the Belgians did in fifty-two years of colonial rule

A. SCOTT MOREAU

King, Martin Luther, Jr. (1929–1968)

Baptist minister, civil rights advocate, and winner of the Nobel Peace Prize. Born in Atlanta, he was educated at Morehouse College, Crozer Theological Seminary, and Boston University (Ph.D., 1955). He became pastor of the Dexter Avenue Baptist Church, Montgomery (1954–1959), and was elected president of the Improvement Association, which supervised the successful boycott of the local bus system. After a year of struggle the U.S. Supreme Court ruled that bus segregation was unconstitutional and King became a national hero. In 1957 he and other African-American leaders formed the Southern Christian Leadership Conference (SCLC) to coordinate civil rights activity.

So that he could have more time to work with this movement, he became in 1960 copastor with his father of the Ebenezer Baptist Church in Atlanta. Thereafter he provided major leadership in the changes that led to an expansion of rights for minorities in the United States. Influenced by neo-orthodoxy and the teaching of Jesus and Gandhi, he stressed a non-violent approach. He was often arrested, received many death threats, and came to personify the struggle of powerless people for justice. He led the "March on Washington" (1963) when 250,000 people demonstrated support for the civil rights bill. His "I Have a Dream" speech delivered at the Lincoln Memorial moved the nation. After 1965 he expanded his work less successfully in the north, and he denounced the Vietnam war. He was assassinated in Memphis, Tennessee. Among his writings were *Stride Toward Freedom* (1958) and *Strength to Love* (1963).

Major biography by S. B. Oates (1982).

ROBERT G. CLOUSE

Kirkby, Sydney James (1879–1935)

Australian bishop. Born in Bendigo and trained for the Anglican ministry at Moore Theological College, Sydney, he taught there and ministered in the diocese until 1919. That year saw the establishment of the Bush Church Aid Society, to expand evangelical influence in the Australian outback. Kirkby became its founding director, and worked tirelessly for bush people over twelve years. He traveled throughout the outback, recruited evangelicals to staff the hostels, hospitals, and ministry centers established in eastern Australia, cared for his workers, and raised money to support them. This enormous effort destroyed his health. In 1932 he became assistant bishop of Sydney, and in 1933 bishop administrator until the appointment of Archbishop Mowll. Kirkby was Mowll's assistant until his premature death. His commitment to the spiritual and physical needs of others marked him as an outstanding Australian and Christian leader. Kirkby told something of his work in *These Ten Years* (1930).

DONALD G. ANDERSON

Kittel, Gerhard (1888–1948)

German New Testament scholar. Son of Rudolf Kittel, he was born in Breslau and embarked on academic life with lectureships at Kiel and Leipzig. In 1921 he was appointed professor of New Testament at Greifswald, and moved to Tübingen in 1926. During 1939–1943 he taught in Vienna. Kittel was discredited by his ties with the Nazis, as reflected in his anti-Semitic tract *Die Judenfrage* (1934). Arrested by French occupation forces in 1945 and imprisoned for seventeen months, he was not allowed to return to his university post or to receive a pension.

Although he published several books about the Jewish world at the time of early Christianity, he is best-known as general editor of the *Theologisches Worterbuch zum Neuen Testament*. He began work on this in 1928; the first volume appeared in 1933. The lexicon's operating principle was that of tracing out the history of each word, and this included both its secular usage in classical and *koine* Greek and religious connotations derived from its use in the Septuagint and rabbinical literature. Strong emphasis was placed on the interaction between Hellenism and Judaism in the New Testament's composition. Four volumes had appeared by 1942 when World War II halted the project. Gerhard Friedrech completed it after Kittel's death, and the ten volumes were translated into English by Geoffrey Bromiley as the *Theological Dictionary of the New Testament* (1964–1976).

RICHARD V. PIERARD

Kittel, Rudolf (1853–1929)

German Old Testament scholar. Born in Eningen, Württemberg, he studied theology at Tübingen (Ph.D., 1879). He worked for two years as a tutor at Tübingen, then taught in a Stuttgart high school. Because he rejected much of the Wellhausen view about the evolution of the Old Testament and argued for an earlier dating of the historical material in Scripture, he had difficulty in securing an academic post. Finally in 1888 he was named professor of Old Testament exegesis at the University of Breslau, and in 1898 moved to Leipzig where he remained until retirement in 1924. He used the archaeological discoveries of the time to develop a new understanding of the prehistory of Israel and to combat "Panbabylonianism," the idea that the teachings of the Old Testament derived from Babylonian religions.

His major work, a three-volume history of the people of Israel (1888–1909), underwent numerous revisions as new information became available. He tended, however, to overestimate the role of individual personalities in the history of Israel, as seen in *Great Men and Movements in Israel* (1929). A prolific scholar, he published numerous essays on historical themes and translations of ancient writings. He is best-known for his two-volume critical text of the Old Testament, *Biblica Hebraica* (1906), which did not restrict itself to the old Textus Receptus and for three decades was the authoritative work in the field.

RICHARD V. PIERARD

Kivengere, Festo (1919–1988)

Ugandan bishop and evangelist. Born of royal blood in North Kigezi, Western Uganda, he was converted at sixteen through the Rwanda Mission, and at their prompting trained as primary school teacher at Bishop Tucker College. In 1945 he and his wife Merabu responded to a call to go as missionaries to Tanzania where he served as teacher and evangelist for thirteen years. Returning to Uganda, he was a supervisor for church schools in Kigezi District, but resigned in 1962 to concentrate on preaching. Multilinguist and gifted evangelist and communicator, he cooperated with Michael Cassidy in founding Africa Evangelistic Enterprise ministry in East Africa, and was its leader. He preached the gospel on every continent and not least at international conferences.

In 1972 Kivengere was nominated bishop of Kigezi; he accepted on condition that he would still carry on his worldwide preaching ministry. He challenged Uganda's presidents about government injustices and atrocities. He was the bishops' spokesman during the Idi Amin regime, which took the life of Archbishop Luwum and finally drove Kivengere into exile until the tyrant was overthrown (1979). Thereafter he participated in reconciliation talks between the various political factions and helped in the formation of a new government. He was also in the forefront of social action, believing strongly that faith in Christ called for this.

His published works include *When God Moves, I Love Idi Amin, Hope for Uganda*, and *Christ Our Reality*.

Biography by Anne Coomes (1990).

LAZARUS SERUYANGE

Kline, Meredith G. (1922–)

Professor of Old Testament at Gordon-Conwell Seminary, Massachusetts, and Westminster Seminary, Escondido. He was educated at Westminster Seminary, Philadelphia, and the Dropsie College of Hebrew and Cognate Learning, Philadelphia (Ph.D.). Operating from a Reformed theological perspective, Kline's work provides a defense of classical Reformed systematics and a framework for cultural analysis, with fresh exegetical insights that stress covenant and eschatology. Canonicity, the integrity of the Genesis creation account, and the Mosaic authorship of the Pentateuch are all built on the covenantal structure of divine revelation. Employing the biblical-theological method in the tradition of Geerhardus Vos, Kline focuses on the eschatological character of biblical covenants: both in the covenant of creation with Adam and in redemptive covenants that follow, the Sabbath is a sign of God's consummation rest that is promised to the faithful covenant-keeper. Against dispensational interpretations, Kline has emphasized covenantal continuities; against the recent challenges of Christian reconstruction, Kline has affirmed certain discontinuities, especially the uniqueness of Old Testament theocratic Israel as a type of the eternal kingdom of God. Kline's writings include *Treaty of the Great King* (1963), *By Oath Consigned* (1968), *The Structure of Biblical Authority* (1972), and *Images of the Spirit* (1980) and numerous journal articles and reviews.

JOHN R. MUETHER

Knox, David Broughton (1916–1993)

Theologian, historian, and educator. Born in South Australia, he graduated from Sydney University in 1938, but service with the Royal Navy during World War II interrupted his studies at Cambridge. He later graduated from London (M.Th., 1947) and Oxford (D.Phil., 1953). As principal of Moore College, Sydney, Australia (1959–1985), he was an outstanding teacher, shaping students in classroom and chapel with a theology that was both evangelical and Reformed. He constantly returned to the first principles of the knowledge of God in the Scriptures. Under him the college became an important national center for the study of theology and training for the ministry. Its library, one of the finest theological collections in Australia, is a tribute to his energy and foresight. Knox also involved himself with controversial issues within the Australian Anglican Church. He became the founding principal of Whitefield College, South Africa (1988–1992), and in England contributed to the renaissance of evangelical theology through the Tyndale Fellowship. Among his major publications were *The Doctrine of Faith in the Reign of Henry VIII* (1961), *Thirty-Nine Articles* (1967), *The Everlasting God* (1982), and *The Lord's Supper from Wycliffe to Cranmer* (1983).

See also P. T. O'Brien and D. G. Peterson, *God Who Is Rich in Mercy* (essays presented to D. B. Knox, 1986).

PETER F. JENSEN

Knox, Edmund Arbuthnott (1847–1937)

Church of England bishop. Born in Bangalore, India, where his father was a chaplain of the East India Company, he graduated from Oxford where he became fellow and dean of Merton College. He ministered near Leicester (1884–1891) and in Birmingham (1891–1894), was consecrated suffragan bishop of Coventry (1894–1902), and finished his career as bishop of Manchester (1903–1921). He took a keen interest in educational reform in church and state, and rallied public support for religious education in elementary schools. He was concerned also with social and moral issues in commerce and industry. One of the most prominent evangelical preachers of his generation, he was famous for founding the Blackpool beach mission. He also promoted overseas missions. Behind the scenes he was an innovator in diocesan administration and clergy support and training. In a long and active retirement he campaigned vigorously against the Revised Prayer Book, and wrote several books, including studies of Bunyan (1928), Robert Leighton (1930), the Tractarians (1933), and his autobiographical *Reminiscences of an Octogenarian, 1847–1934* (1935).

PHILIP HILLYER

Knox, John (1900–1991)

New Testament theologian and educator. Born in Frankfort, Kentucky, he graduated from Emory University (1925) and the University of Chicago (Ph.D., 1935). He was a minister in the Methodist Church, South, serving pastorates in West Virginia and Baltimore (1919–1924), taught Bible at Emory University (1924–1927), ministered at Fisk University (1929–1936), and held chairs at the University of Chicago (1939–1943), Union Theological Seminary (1943–1968), and the Episcopal Seminary of the Southwest in Austin, Texas (1966–1972). While at Union he was ordained in the Protestant Episcopal Church (1962).

His scholarship involved two major areas, one dealing with questions of faith and history that focused on Jesus, the other with the interpretation of Pauline thought. The major stimuli for most of his books were invitations to lecture at other institutions. These works tended to be shorter and clearer in style without the technical apparatus that often limits scholarly books to specialists. His works include *He Whom a Dream Hath Possessed* (1932), *Christ the Lord* (1945), *Chapters in the Life of Paul* (1950), *The Early Church and the Coming Great Church* (1955), *The Death of Christ* (1958), and *The Humanity and Divinity of Christ* (1967).

ROBERT G. CLOUSE

Knox, Ronald Arbuthnott (1888–1957)

English scholar, Bible translator, preacher, and writer of detective stories. Born in Leicestershire, son of an Anglican evangelical, later bishop of Manchester, he had a brilliant career at Oxford where he resigned a fellowship on his conversion to Roman Catholicism. He served as RC chaplain at Oxford University (1926–1939). He published his translation of the New Testament in 1945, the Old Testament in 1949. Many of his sermons were published, including *The Mass in Slow Motion* (1948) and *The Creed in Slow Motion* (1949). His commentary on the New Testament in three volumes was published during 1953–1956. Knox described his *Enthusiasm*

(1950) as "the unique child" of his thought which had taken him more than thirty years to write. It had begun as a warning of what happens to those who stray from the Catholic Church, "but somehow in the writing my whole treatment of the subject became different; the more you got to know the men the more human did they become, for better or worse; you were more concerned to find out why they thought as they did than to prove it was wrong."

Biography by Evelyn Waugh (1959).

HENRY R. SEFTON

Kolbe, Maximilian (1894–1941)

Polish priest and martyr. Born into a pious Catholic family near Lodz, Russian-occupied Poland, and baptized as Raymund, he went at age thirteen to the Franciscan seminary at Lwow. At sixteen he was admitted as a novice, given the name Maximilian, and showed such promise that he went on to study at Cracow and Rome. Despite a body wracked by tuberculosis, he and six other young men launched in the name of the Virgin Mary a crusade to spread love and counter evildoers, especially the anti-Catholic Freemasons of Italy. Ordained in 1918, he returned to teach in the Cracow seminary, and threw himself into a breathless ministry of literature to confront the contemporary secularization of society. Despite all odds and prophecies and parlous health he established an extensive community that by 1937 had grown to number 762 friars involved in publishing, farming, medicine, education, and various industrial pursuits. Kolbe never, however, lost sight of spiritual priorities. In 1930 he and four companions went to Japan where, despite daunting linguistic and financial difficulties, they established a friary and a magazine. By 1936 Kolbe's health had so deteriorated that his superiors ordered him back to Poland. With the German invasion in World War II the friars were initially imprisoned but were unexpectedly released. They then continued work among refugees and casualties of war. Kolbe's Polish patriotism and steady proclamation of truth and the need for victory "in our innermost personal selves" could lead only to one end. He was herded with others into a cattle truck consigned to Auschwitz concentration camp where despite hard labor and barbaric treatment his indomitable spirit comforted fellow prisoners and infuriated the guards. He volunteered to die in place of another prisoner, and during the short time left led those condemned in worship. He died on the day he himself might have chosen—August 14, when Poland celebrates the Assumption of the Virgin Mary. He was beatified in 1971, and canonized in 1982 by his fellow Pole, Pope John Paul II, on which occasion in St. Peter's, Rome, Poles and Germans exchanged the kiss of peace.

J. D. DOUGLAS

Koop, C(harles) Everett (1916–)

U.S. surgeon general and writer. Born in Brooklyn, New York, he graduated from Dartmouth College (B.A., 1937), Cornell Medical College (M.D., 1941), and the University of Pennsylvania (Sc.D., 1947). After holding various posts at the University of Pennsylvania (1949–1971) he became professor of pediatrics (1971–1981) before joining government service in 1981 and being appointed the following year as surgeon general of the United States. Honored by medical associations in Britain, America, and mainland Europe, and known for his conservative stance in current ethical issues, he has written several books, including *The Right to Live, The Right to Die* (1976), *Pornography: A Human Tragedy* (1987), and *Ethical Imperatives and the New Physician* (1988).

NORMAN R. ERICSON

Kraemer, Hendrik (1888–1965)

Dutch lay missionary, theologian, and ecumenist. A Bible Society missionary to Indonesia (1922–1937) before being appointed professor of religions at Leiden, he came to prominence in 1938 for *The Christian Message in a Non-Christian World,* commissioned as preparatory reading for the Tambaram World Missionary Conference on evangelism. The book was a response to the liberal report *Re-thinking Missions* (1932), and supported the dialectical theology or neo-orthodoxy associated with Karl Barth, stressing the discontinuity between Christianity and other religions. It was to influence missionary thinking for twenty years or more.

As well as being committed to Christianity, Kraemer was deeply committed to the church: to indigenous rather than missionary-led churches abroad, to renewal of the Netherlands church at home after World War II through the mobilization of the laity, and to ecumenical cooperation. He was first director of the WCC Ecumenical Institute at Bossey (1948–1955). His later books included *The Communication of the Christian Faith* (1957), and *A Theology of the Laity* (1958). *Why Christianity of All Religions* (1962) continued to champion Christianity, if not in such absolute terms as in 1938.

C. F. Halleucreutz wrote *Kraemer towards Tambaram* (1966).

PHILIP HILLYER

Krishna, Purushotnam (ca. 1930–)

Christian apologist. Born into a traditional Hindu family in South Africa, he drifted from Hinduism until he had finished his university studies and begun practicing law. With a renewed interest in his ancestral faith he pursued further studies at Benares Hindu University in India. Eventually he earned a master's degree from Durham University and a Ph.D. from the New School for Social Research in New York. He became a skilled apologist for Hinduism, publishing several books on the subject. Initiated into the esoteric teaching of philosophical Hinduism, he regarded the ritualistic practices of folk Hinduism as primitive. A providential encounter with some Christians left a New Testament in his possession. The witness of an ordinary Indian Christian laborer led him to discover the Christ who breaks the cycle of reincarnation. Resigning his post as head of the department of Oriental studies at the University of Durban–Westville, he studied and later taught at Trinity Evangelical Divinity School, Illinois. Returning to South Africa, he rejoined his university as a professor of Christianity. His ability to understand Hinduism and to present the Christian message makes him a powerful evangelist. He called his autobiography *Journey from the East.*

JAMES J. STAMOOLIS

Kuhlman, Kathryn (1907–1976)

American evangelist. Born in Concordia, Missouri, she was baptized in a Baptist church at fourteen, left high school at age sixteen, and began an itinerant ministry after ordination by what was later the Evangelical Church Alliance. In 1933 she established herself in Denver, and within two years was ministering in a two thousand-seat Revival Tabernacle and also reaching a radio audience. That ministry was inhibited by her 1938 marriage to a divorced evangelist, but by the mid-1940s she had left him and moved east. She developed a healing and a daily radio ministry, first in Franklin, Pennsylvania (1946–1948), then in Pittsburgh where her services in Carnegie Hall impressed local clergy and the press.

From 1965 she operated also in Los Angeles where her seven thousand-capacity Shrine Auditorium was usually full. By this time she was a national celebrity, commuting between California and Pittsburgh, and televised widely on CBS network, her programs prefixed by her typically dramatic declaration, "I believe in miracles!" Kuhlman did not like to be called a faith healer, stressing that it was the Spirit's working, and was candidly antagonistic when asked why some were healed while others were not. She became identified also with the charismatic movement, while not herself speaking in tongues, nor encouraging the phenomenon in her healing services. Striking in appearance, she aroused hostility and skepticism, but also fierce loyalty that did not lack supporting medical testimony. She wrote the best-sellers *I Believe in Miracles* (1968) and *God Can Do It Again* (1969).

Biographies by Jamie Buckingham (1966) and H. K. Hosier (1976).

J. D. DOUGLAS

Küng, Hans (1928–)

Swiss theologian. Born in Sursee, Switzerland, he studied at the German College, Rome, the Gregorian University and at L'Institut Catholique, Sorbonne, as well as in Amsterdam, Berlin, London, and Madrid. After ordination to the priesthood in 1954 he served in a parish in Lucerne before being appointed scientific assistant for dogmatics at the Catholic Theological Faculty, Münster. He became professor at the Catholic Theological Faculty, Tübingen, in 1960, and has been professor of dogmatics and director of the Ecumenical Institute of the University of Tübingen since 1963. In 1962 he was adviser to Pope John XXIII. Although critical of the hierarchy of the Church, Küng has remained a faithful Roman Catholic. In his numerous books, articles, and public lectures he promotes a deeper understanding of the essentials of the faith and openness to contemporary issues. He works long days with a large team of helpers to stay abreast of developments and to maintain his vast literary output. In a 1993 interview on German television he seriously questioned the wisdom of the New Creed. He travels and lectures extensively. Significant works are *The Council and Reunion* (1961), *The Living Church* (1963), *Apostolic Succession* (1968), *Infallible?* (1972), *On Being a Christian* (1974), *The Church* (1976), *Does God Exist?* (1980), and *The Küng Dialogue* (1980). His books have been translated into all major languages.

EDWARD J. FURCHA

Kuyper, Abraham (1837–1920)

Dutch theologian and statesman. Son of a Dutch Reformed Church clergyman, he studied at the University of Leiden and received a doctorate in theology in 1862. In his first parish in Beesd he was converted from the theological liberalism of his university training to a living faith in Christ. He moved to Utrecht in 1867, and to Amsterdam in 1870. During this time he met Groen van Prinsterer, a fellow Calvinist who led a small political group known as the Anti-Revolutionaries. In 1870 Kuyper became editor of the weekly *De Heraut,* and in 1872 he founded a daily, *De Standard,* which served as the group's organ. In 1874 he was elected to parliament and gave up his pastorate. In 1878 he converted Groen's movement into a full-fledged political organization, the Anti-Revolutionary party. In 1880 Kuyper created the Free University of Amsterdam, which he envisioned as a genuine Christian and Calvinistic institution. He served as its first rector and taught there for many years. In 1886 Kuyper led a breakaway reform movement in the state church. His political party grew steadily, and during 1901–1905 he served as prime minister. He retired from the university in 1908 and from active politics in 1913, but continued writing until his death. He is best known for his idea that divine sovereignty must be exercised over three "spheres"—the state, society, and the church. These realms are separate from one another, and society itself is divided into various individual spheres. Upon these the state may not intrude and in them justice must prevail (see his *Lectures on Calvinism,* 1898).

Biography by F. V. Berg (1960).

RICHARD V. PIERARD

Kyle, Melvin Grove (1858–1933)

Archaeologist and educator. Born in Cadiz, Ohio, he earned degrees from Muskingum College (1881) and Allegheny Theological Seminary (1885). After serving as a Presbyterian minister he taught biblical theology and archaeology at Xenia Theological Seminary until 1922, when he became president. He edited *Bibliotheca Sacra* before its move to Dallas Theological Seminary, and participated in establishing the Bible League of North America and the League of Evangelical Students. As an archaeologist he took part in digs at Sodom and Gomorrah (1924) and Kirjath-sepher (1926–1928). Throughout his career Kyle insisted that archaeology is "exactly in harmony" with the biblical teachings, and that eventually archaeological discoveries would undermine the foundation of the Documentary Hypothesis and higher criticism. For *The Fundamentals* (1910) he wrote on "The Recent Testimony of Archaeology to the Scriptures." His books include *The Deciding Voice of the Monuments of Biblical Criticism* (1912), *Moses and the Monuments* (1920), and *The Problem of the Pentateuch* (1933).

A. SCOTT MOREAU

L

Ladd, George Eldon (1911–1982)

Biblical scholar. Born in Alberta, Canada, he was converted in 1929, and graduated from Gordon College of Theology and Missions in 1933. After serving in the Baptist pastorate he completed a Ph.D. in Classics at Harvard University under H. J. Cadbury in 1949. Ladd began teaching at Fuller Theological Seminary in 1950, where he became a major leader among evangelical biblical scholars. He sought to create a body of scholarship that was both fully critical in the sense of repudiating biblical inerrancy and fully orthodox in the sense of holding to the basics of historic Christianity. In *Jesus and the Kingdom* (1964) Ladd defended premillennialism while attacking both Bultmannian and dispensationalist understandings of the kingdom of God. Though this book was savaged by some liberals it established Ladd's reputation in conservative circles. He went on to write *The New Testament and Criticism* (1967), which tried to show how one could be both thoroughly orthodox and thoroughly committed to historical-critical methodology. He also wrote *Theology of the New Testament* (1974), a conservative alternative to Bultmann. After Ladd's death a survey of scholars in the Institute for Biblical Research rated him as the "most influential" scholar.

BRUCE GRIFFIN

LaHaye, Beverly (ca. 1930–)

Lecturer, author, and political activist. Reared in Michigan, she graduated from Bob Jones University and married Pastor Tim LaHaye. She founded and is president of Concerned Women for America, which grew from a group of about 1,200 women who first rallied against the Equal Rights Amendment in 1978 to a membership today of reportedly six hundred thousand. Based in Washington, D.C., the movement promotes its values most noticeably through battling the gay rights agenda while supporting anti-abortion legislation and the parents' right to direct the upbringing of their children in matters of education and religion. LaHaye conducts radio broadcasts and appears on television periodically in support of her views. While many mainstream evangelicals have worked closely with CWA, many are hesitant to embrace the group fully, primarily because of concern over the blending of religion and conservative politics. Among her books are *The Spirit-Controlled Woman* (1976) and *How to Develop Your*

Child's Temperament (1977). The two books she coauthored with her husband, *The Act of Marriage* (1976) and *Spirit-Controlled Family Living* (1978), summarize their popular and influential convictions about Christian marriage.

NANCY CALVERT

Laidlaw, Robert A. (1885–1971)

New Zealand businessman and author of "The Reason Why." Born in Dalry, Scotland, he was one year old when the family emigrated to the New Zealand town of Dunedin, which had been founded by Scottish settlers. Laidlaw left school at age sixteen and joined the successful hardware business of his father who was a Brethren evangelist. The son was converted when the Torrey Alexander Mission visited Dunedin. In 1908 he began a mail-order business in Auckland that grew and prospered spectacularly. Just as spectacular was the reception given to "The Reason Why," a sixty-four page booklet written in 1913, originally intended for his staff as a testimony to his Christian faith. By 1969 some 16 million copies in over thirty languages had been published; thousands of lives have been influenced by its message. In *The Story of "The Reason Why"* (1969) Laidlaw told part of his life story, and the impact of his booklet on the lives of some of those who read it. An inspiring speaker and leader, Laidlaw was described by Billy Graham as "one of the world's great Christian laymen." King George V made him a Companion of the Order of the British Empire (CBE).

J. D. DOUGLAS

Lake, Kirsopp (1872–1946)

Church historian born in Southampton, England, he was educated at Oxford, and was ordained in the church of England (1895). He served curacies in Durham (1895–1897) and Oxford (1897–1904) before assuming an academic career. He was professor of theology at the University of Leiden (1904–1913) before moving to Harvard University, where he was successively professor of early Christian literature (1914–1919), ecclesiastical history (1919–1932), and history (1932–1938). Like James Rendel Harris before him, Lake was interested in the family groups of manuscripts of the New Testament, and he traveled extensively in Greece searching for items that were published in facsimile and edited. With F. J. Foakes-Jackson he compiled in five volumes a massive study of the Acts of the Apostles under the title, *The Beginnings of Christianity* (1919–1932). For the Loeb Classical Library, he prepared editions and translations of the Apostolic Fathers (1912) and of Eusebius's *Ecclesiastical History* (1927). In the Middle East for Harvard University he directed various archaeological expeditions. With his second wife, Silva Tipple New, he edited a series of *Studies and*

Documents (16 vols., 1934–1946), containing editions of biblical and patristic texts, or studies of historical and archaeological problems; and they jointly wrote *An Introduction to the New Testament* (1937).

A festschrift, *Quantulacumque,* was published in 1937.

CLYDE CURRY SMITH

Lang, Cosmo Gordon (1864–1945)

Archbishop of Canterbury. Like Randall Davidson, his predecessor at Canterbury, he was a Scotsman and a patrician. He is, however, usually credited with a deeper spirituality, though sometimes depicted as over prelatical. He was firmly in the Anglo-Catholic tradition of the Church of England: at York he was the first archbishop since the Reformation to wear a mitre, and under his careful influence many of the "trappings" of Catholic worship—vestments, candles, wafers, water mixed with the communion wine, incense—found their way into the heart of the Church of England. He worked assiduously for the promotion of Christian unity and enjoyed particularly good relations with the Eastern Orthodox Church. In his relationship with the royal family he played a key role in the Edward VIII abdication crisis (1936). Close to George V, he had regarded with some dismay the prospect of crowning Edward VIII, a man he believed to have fallen into bad company. His radio address to the nation after the abdication was considered by many to have been too harsh. But he was a great admirer of George VI, and viewed the conduct of the coronation ceremony as the climax of his public ministry. He hoped that it would lead to an evangelistic "Recall to Religion," but the buildup to World War II took over. He fully backed Prime Minister Chamberlain's policy of appeasement, but was loyal and patriotic when war came. Lang, who was at Canterbury from 1928 to1942, wrote *The Parables of Jesus* (1906) and *The Miracles of Jesus* (1907).

Biography by J. G. Lockhart (1949).

JOHN B. TAYLOR

Latourette, Kenneth Scott (1884–1968)

Historian of the expansion of Christianity. Born into a Baptist home in Oregon, he graduated from Linfield College (1904) and Yale University (1906; Ph.D., 1909) where he joined the Student Volunteer movement. He taught in China (1910–1912), but illness forced his return home. He taught at Reid College (1914–1916) and Denison University (1916–1921) until he went back to begin his long tenure at Yale, retiring in 1953 as professor of missions and Oriental history. Latourette, who had been ordained as a Baptist minister in 1918, also maintained active support of missions and student work. He attended the meeting at Utrecht (1938) that led to the postwar formation of the World Council of Churches at whose first assembly in Amsterdam (1948) he was a speaker. Latourette's publication and teaching interests were in East Asian history and the missionary expansion of the church. He adopted a global view based on his conviction that the world was moving inexorably toward a better society led by Christianity. During the closing years of his career he was honored as both a historian and a churchman. His more significant works include *History of Christian Missions in China* (1929), *The History of the Expansion of Christianity* (7 vols., 1937–1948), *Christianity in a Revolutionary Age* (5 vols., 1958–1962), and the autobiographical *Beyond the Ranges* (1967).

ROBERT G. CLOUSE

Laubach, Frank Charles (1884–1970)

Congregational missionary and educator. Born in Pennsylvania and educated at Princeton, Columbia (Ph.D., 1915), and Union Theological Seminary, he began his career as a missionary to the Philippines in 1915. Initially on the southern island of Mindanao, he eventually moved to Manila where he held a number of academic positions, including the deanship of Union College. By the late 1920s he had developed two emphases that would shape his long life's work: experiment in prayer, which he viewed as the practice of the presence of God, and literacy work among underprivileged people using his own highly innovative system of phonetic symbols and pictures. His numerous and extended "literacy tours," beginning in the 1930s, took him to most corners of the earth. In addition, his "Each One Teach One" approach to adult literacy instruction, which he developed on Mindanao, was imitated internationally and became known as the Laubach Method. Aided latterly by the Laubach Literacy organization, which he founded in 1955, he became responsible for the creation of literacy primers for approximately three hundred languages and dialects in more than one hundred countries. His diversified literary output of more than thirty other books reflected and clarified his unusual balance of spirituality and practical social engagement. These include *The Silent Billion Speak* (1943), *Prayer, The Mightiest Force in the World* (1951), and *Toward World Literacy* (1960).

Biography by D. E. Mason (1967).

GLEN G. SCORGIE

Laws, Robert (1851–1934)

Scottish medical missionary and educationist. Born in Aberdeen, he was apprenticed as a cabinet-maker on leaving primary school, but continued his education by taking evening classes. By 1875 he had graduated in both arts and medicine at Aberdeen University, and had also completed at the United Presbyterian Church College in Edinburgh a theological course leading to ordination. He was seconded to the new Free Church mission in Nyasaland (now Malawi), which had been named Livingstonia in honor of David Livingstone. In accordance with the latter's thinking it was assumed that the mission would promote honest trading and would work against the slave trade and war. Laws was appointed leader after only three years in the field, and in 1880 moved his base to Bandawe on the west side of Lake Malawi. This enabled more effective work among the Tonga and Ngoni peoples. In 1894 he established at Khondowe an "Institution" for training teachers, pastors, health workers, and craftsmen. One result was the setting up of community churches over wide areas of Malawi, and the provision of trained leaders for the autonomous Church of Central Africa Presbyterian, which Laws helped to bring into being in 1926. The most famous of the African ministers trained by Laws was David Kaunda, father of the first president of Zambia. Laws wrote *Reminiscenses of Livingstonia* (1934).

Biographies by W. P Livingstone (1922) and Hamish McIntosh (1993).

HENRY R. SEFTON

Lecerf, Auguste (1872–1943)

French Calvinist theologian. Born into a secularized Jewish family, he was converted to Christianity as a young man by reading Romans 9–11. Early contact with Calvin's *Institutes* helped settle his theological direction. A graduate of the liberal Protestant Faculty of Theology in Paris (1895), Lecerf pastored Reformed churches in northern France for twenty years, then served as a military chaplain during World War I. He then worked for the French Bible Society in Paris, and taught New Testament Greek and English courses at the Protestant Faculty of Theology, as well as "free" classes in Reformed theology. He was named professor of dogmatics in 1935, but World War II hastened his death. Lecerf founded the French Calvinistic Society in 1926 and edited its *Bulletin;* after his death his disciple Pierre Marcel expanded it into *La revue reformee,* in which many of Lecerf's writings appeared. He spoke at the Calvinistic conferences held throughout Europe during the 1930s, and wrote many Calvin studies for French religious periodicals. Within the French Reformed Church he led in the development of a group of Calvinistic pastors and laypeople that has continued to have a significant impact within the French-speaking world and beyond. Two of his works appeared in English translation as *Introduction to Reformed Dogmatics* (1949). A number of his Calvin studies were assembled by Andre Schlemmer as *Etudes Calvinistes* (1949).

This "First of the Modern French Calvinists" was the subject of *Auguste Lecerf: An Historical Study* by Thomas Reid (Th.M. thesis, Reformed Theological Faculty, Aix-en-Provence, France, 1979).

THOMAS G. REID, JR.

Lefebvre, Marcel [François] (1905–1991)

Born in Tourcoing, France, he completed his basic education at the College du Sacre Coeur, studied at the French Seminary, Rome, and was ordained in 1929. Through his work at Lomme, a suburb of Lille, he came to be known as "a young priest of shining faith." His later work took Lefebvre to the Holy Ghost Seminary, Gabon, and as Vicar Apostolic, to Senegal. In 1947 he was consecrated bishop by Cardinal Lienert and in 1948 he became archbishop of Dakar. While he identified in his youth with ultraright monarchist views, his anti-ecumenical position developed only during his work as apostolic delegate for French West Africa, an office he carried out until 1959. In 1962 he was named titular archbishop of the defunct See of Synnada/Phrygia. Lefebvre objected strenuously to the modernizing trends of Vatican II, stating in 1974, "we refuse to follow Rome in the neo-modernist, neo-Protestant tendencies . . . which continue to contribute to the destruction of the Church . . . , the priesthood, the sacrifice and the sacraments." Lefebvre's break with Rome began in 1976 during the pontificate of Paul VI when he celebrated a Tridentine Mass in Besançon and set up his own seminary for the training of priests. His followers number about sixty thousand worldwide. The Society founded by him published the periodical *Econe*. His literary legacy is *I Accuse the Council* (1976), *A Bishop Speaks* (1974), and collections of sermons and addresses published between 1963 and 1974.

EDWARD J. FURCHA

Lehmann, Theo (1934–)

German evangelist and musicologist. Son of a missionary to India, he was born in Dresden and educated at the famous Francke school in Halle. He studied theology at both the mission seminary and university in Leipzig, and then earned a doctorate in religion at the University of Halle. His studies focused on Negro spirituals and other forms of African-American music. His books on this topic included *Blues and Trouble* (1966) and a biography of Mahalia Jackson, *Gospel Music Is My Life* (1973). In 1964 he was ordained in the Lutheran Church of Saxony and took a parish in Chemnitz, which at the time the communist regime had renamed Karl-Marx-Stadt. In 1971 he began holding youth services at the church that drew such crowds that the East German authorities tried in vain to force him and his family to leave the country. By the early 1980s he had become East Germany's most prominent youth evangelist, and he and Baptist pastor Jörg Swoboda conducted enormously successful meetings all over the country, much to the dismay of the government. The two composed many songs for young people that are popular in Germany today, and Lehmann himself published many books of sermons and meditations. His work became so widely known that he was appointed to the Lausanne Committee for World Evangelization and the International Task Force for Hymnology. Since reunification in 1990 his ministry has been extended to all parts of Germany.

RICHARD V. PIERARD

LeTourneau, Robert Gilmour (1888–1969)

Industrialist, inventor, lay evangelist, and philanthropist. Born in Richford, Vermont, he was converted at sixteen, two years after he forsook school for labor. Industry remembers his mechanical genius. His numerous patents included the electric drive wheel and offshore drilling rig. Developer of the world's largest earthmoving machinery, he supplied 70 percent of America's earthmoving equipment for World War II. He revolutionized road building and jungle clearing. Christians esteem him as cofounder and president, Christian Business Men's Committee, International; president, International Gideon Society; and founder of LeTourneau Foundation (1935) and College (1946). Honorary vice president of the Christian and Missionary Alliance (1943–1969), LeTourneau traveled two hundred thousand miles annually for ministry, and contributed 90 percent of his income to Christian work. His autobiographical *Mover of Men and Mountains* was published in 1972.

Biographies by A. W. Lorimer (1941) and D. F. Ackland (1949).

GERALD E. McGRAW

Lewis, Clive Staples (1898–1963)

British writer. Born in Belfast, Northern Ireland, he was educated first at schools in England and, after a brief period of service in World War I during which he was wounded, at Oxford. Having obtained a first-class degree in Classics and philosophy and English, he was a fellow at Magdalen College, Oxford (1925–1954), until appointment as professor of medieval and renaissance English at Cambridge.

Lewis is best known as a popular lay Christian apologist. Although an Anglican he hardly ever shows signs of denominational bias in his work. He was a prolific writer, both in his own field of English literature and in the realms of Christian truth. He became more widely known through highly successful radio broadcasts during World War II; these talks formed the basis of *Mere Christianity* (1952). *Screwtape Letters* (1942) gave him an enormous vogue before he reached a totally new readership with his space fiction novels and the Narnia series of children's books. He wrote an account of his conversion in *Surprised by Joy* (1955). In 1956 he married Joy Davidson, who died of cancer four years later. His account of the bereavement, *A Grief Observed* (1961), has remained another of his best-known books. Since his death, voluminous literature has sprung up concerning Lewis and his work.

Biographies by Roger Green and Walter Hooper (1974), William Griffin (1986), and A. N. Wilson (1990).

PETER S. DAWES

Libert, Samuel Osvaldo (1927–)

Evangelical pastor and church leader. Born in Rosario, Argentina, to a family with a long line of pastors, Libert has dedicated his life to pastoral and evangelistic activities, in which he is a recognized voice in national and international circles. He has pastored several churches, including the Arroyito Baptist Church in his native city, where he has had remarkable success. During several years he worked full-time in evangelism, and he continues this ministry in many countries. He has had an important leadership role in Baptist circles. In Argentina he has served in various top denominational posts, and has been coordinator of international evangelistic efforts such as the "Crusade of the Americas" and the World Reconciliation Mission of the Baptist World Alliance. He has also shared in and helped coordinate many international congresses, especially on evangelism, and was a speaker at the second Conference for Itinerant Evangelists in Amsterdam (1986). Currently he is president of the Theological Commission of the Latin American Evangelical Confraternity (CONELA). He has written several books as well as numerous articles and columns for secular and religious journals. He has edited Baptist magazines, written for radio and television, and produced poetry, including several well-known hymns.

ARNOLDO CANCLINI

Liddell, Eric Henry (1902–1945)

Scottish athlete and missionary. Born of missionary parents in Tianjin, China, he excelled in sports at Edinburgh University where he graduated in science in 1924. That year, at the Paris Olympic Games, his Christian convictions led him to turn down the prospect of a virtually assured gold medal in the 100 meters, because the heats were held on a Sunday. He then caused a sensation by winning gold in record-breaking time in the 400 meters, a distance in which he was comparatively inexperienced. In 1925 he went to China under the London Missionary Society, first as science teacher, then as itinerant evangelist.

Liddell was widely admired for his combination of athletic prowess and firm but unassuming Christian virtue. People loved him for his benign and Christ-centered personality. When he died from a brain tumor in a Japanese internment camp where his strength of character and daily kindnesses had become legendary, tributes ascribed his influence to a "complete surrender" to God's will—words that were on his lips as he died.

After his death he became a comic-book hero and subject of popular sermons. The film *Chariots of Fire* (1981), which celebrated his Olympic feats, spread his fame further. His reputation rests on the way he stood for Christian principles without being dogmatic or sanctimonious. He was feted for personifying the faith he preached and for making goodness interesting. He offered successive generations what they have always craved—a hero. Liddell wrote *The Disciplines of the Christian Life* (1985).

See biographies by D. P. Thomson (1971) and Sally Magnusson (1981), and memorial booklet by David Michell (1992).

SALLY MAGNUSSON

Lightfoot, Robert Henry (1883–1953)

New Testament scholar. Born in Northamptonshire, he was educated at Eton and Worcester College, Oxford. He was ordained in 1910. After a curacy he taught at Wells Theological College for seven years. He was appointed a fellow of Lincoln College, Oxford, in 1919, but moved to New College, Oxford, in 1921. There he was fellow and dean of divinity until his retirement in 1950. His stature as a New Testament scholar was recognized by his appointment as Ireland professor in biblical studies in 1934.

His development as a New Testament scholar took a new direction when he visited Germany in 1931. As a result of the contacts he made, he became a spokesman in England for form criticism. This was first expressed in his Bampton Lectures of 1934, published as *History and Interpretation in the Gospels* (1935). His accuracy and careful scholarship found an outlet in his editorship of the *Journal of Theological Studies* from 1941 to 1953. At the end of his life he was working on the Fourth Gospel. This resulted in the posthumous publication of *St. John's Gospel* (ed. C. F. Evans, 1956). He gave himself unstintingly to college and university concerns. His main influence can be detected in the next generation of Oxford New Testament scholars.

NOEL S. POLLARD

Lilje, Hanns (Johannes Ernst Richard) (1899–1977)

German bishop and ecumenist. Born in Hanover, he did military service, cut short by his being wounded. He studied theology and art history at Göttingen and Leipzig, was ordained in 1924, and later became student chaplain in Hanover. As general secretary of the German Student Christian Association he participated in the World Student Christian Federation's assembly in Mysore, India. He earned the degree of Dr.Theol. at Zurich, and worked from 1935 to 1945 as general secretary of the Lutheran World Congress. In cooperation with Martin Niemoller and others he participated in the Christian youth movement within the Protestant Church of Germany that opposed National Socialism. After a brief imprisonment by the Gestapo he was liberated by the American occupation forces. He cosigned the Admission of Guilt by the German people, an ecumenical document prepared at Stuttgart. In 1949 he became bishop of the Evangelical Lutheran Church of Hanover and presiding bishop of the United

Evangelical Lutheran Church of Germany (1955–1969). He was prominent in the leadership of the World Council of Churches and the Lutheran World Federation, and was recognized worldwide for his significant contribution to the life and work of the modern Protestant church in Germany and abroad. Among his publications were *The Last Book of the Bible* (1940), *Atheism, Humanism and Christianity* (1965), and *Martin Luther* (1972).

EDWARD J. FURCHA

Linder, Robert Dean (1934–)

American historian. Born in Salina, Kansas, he attended schools in his native state and became an active member and lay worker in a Baptist church. Although he had a promising career in professional baseball, he decided instead to enter academic life. He received a Ph.D. degree from the University of Iowa in 1963 and joined the history faculty of Kansas State University in Manhattan in 1965, rising to the rank of professor. He was also involved in local political life, and served two terms as mayor of Manhattan between 1969 and 1979. His major contributions are in the relationship between religion and politics, Reformation history, civil religion in the United States, and religious history in Northern Ireland. A prolific author, he has authored or edited numerous books and dozens of articles. Among his most noteworthy books are *Calvin and Calvinism* (1970), *Twilight of the Saints* (1978), and *Civil Religion and the Presidency* (1988). He was coeditor of the *Lion Handbook to the History of Christianity* (1977) and the *Dictionary of Christianity in America* (1990). Linder was the founding editor of the journal *Fides et Historia* in 1968 and held this position for a decade. While serving as a Fulbright professor at the University of Wollongong in Australia in 1987 he developed a strong interest in the history of Australian religion, and has published several works on evangelicalism in the Antipodes.

RICHARD V. PIERARD

Lindsey, Hal (1930–)

Author, lecturer, and minister. Born in Houston, Texas, he was educated at the University of Texas, after which he served in the Coast Guard during the Korean War and as a tugboat captain on the Mississippi River. He attended Dallas Theological Seminary and later ministered with Campus Crusade for Christ for eight years. In recent decades Lindsey has supported the spread of popular millennialism, particularly through his best-selling book, *The Late Great Planet Earth* (1970), which was written in collaboration with Carol C. Carlson. His reading of contemporary history through prophetic lenses attracted millions of readers. Lindsey's approach was especially popular with members of the new religious right, such as Jerry Falwell and Jim Bakker. Other books by Lindsey are *Satan Is Alive and Well on Planet Earth* (1972), *There's A New World Coming* (1973), and *The Liberation of Planet Earth* (1974). He is senior pastor of the Telestai Christian Center in California, and has both a radio and a television show.

NANCY CALVERT

Liu, Tingfang (T. T. Lew) (1890–1947)

Chinese leader in higher education, Christian education, and the indigenous church movement. Born in 1890 in Chekiang (Zhejiang) province, he attended the Anglican-operated St. John's University, Shanghai, and transferred to the University of Georgia in 1913. He received his M.A. in 1915, and Ph.D. in education and psychology in 1920 from Columbia University, New York. In 1920 he was appointed to teach simultaneously at Yenching University's School of Religion, Peking Normal University, and Peking National University. He lectured in religious education at Union Theological Seminary (1927–1928)—the first Chinese to teach a non-Chinese subject in an American seminary. Lew was instrumental in introducing Western educational testing techniques to China. He edited the *Life Journal*, an indigenous Chinese hymnal, the revised version of which is still in use today. Lew's favorite slogan was "Catholic Appreciation." He had a wide circle of friends. In 1936 Lew became a member of the Legislative Yuan of the Nationalist government in Nanking.

SAMUEL LING

Livingston Hill, Grace (1865–1947)

Described as the "Queen of the Christian Novel." Born the only child of a Presbyterian minister, she was influenced toward writing by listening to her parents read to her. Her first novel, *A Chautauqua Idyl* (1887), was but the start of a long career that blossomed out of necessity on the sudden death of her husband. Averaging two novels a year, she wrote to convey the solid fundamentals of Christian living and commitment. One novel, *The Witness* (1939), caught the attention of the *Sunday School Herald,* and became its focus for a time. The book turned many to Christ and renewed commitment to Christian living. Writing simply and with purposeful conviction, she produced works that sold nearly 4 million copies and were translated into other languages. She also wrote a religious column, "The Christian Endeavor Hour," and collaborated with Evangeline Booth to write *The War Romance of the Salvation Army* (1918).

WENDY S. LARSON

Lloyd-Jones, David Martyn (1899–1981)

Welsh preacher and writer. Born in South Wales, he studied medicine in London and became a distinguished physician there. In 1926 he forsook medicine to minister in a small Presbyterian church in Aberavon, Wales. Here his evangelical convictions and preaching developed, and many were converted under his ministry. In 1939 he was called to be copastor with Campbell Morgan at Westminster Chapel in central London; he became sole pastor in 1943. He preached there almost every Sunday (apart from a regular summer break) until 1968 when ill health forced him to retire. Lloyd-Jones had no formal theological training, but he taught many to think theologically. He read widely, especially on the Puritans, and was up to date on current affairs. He was above all an expository preacher with a rich knowledge of the Bible. He constantly exposed the doctrinal issues that lay behind his passage before making an application—a matter of diagnosis before cure. A very skillful pastor, he was widely consulted by other church leaders as well as ordinary church members. He led discussions in a masterful fashion. He taught many to love doctrine, and to use it to solve practical problems. He became probably the most influential evangelical leader in Britain, but his impact was worldwide, especially through his part in the growth of evangelical student work in post–World War II years.

Lloyd-Jones met regularly with ecumenical leaders to discuss differences until the issues became so clear that nonevangelicals ceased to attend. His own position on cooperation gradually hardened, and he played a big part in helping the growth of independent evangelical churches. He helped evangelicals to a new confidence that biblical truth can stand up to any attack and is the power of God. Among his publications are *Studies in the Sermon on the Mount* (2 vols., 1959, 1960) and *Spiritual Depression* (1965).

Official biography by I. H. Murray (2 vols., 1982, 1990).

OLIVER R. BARCLAY

Loane, Marcus Lawrence (1911–)

Australian archbishop and scholar. Born in Tasmania, he graduated from the University of Sydney and Moore Theological College, and was ordained in 1935. He joined the staff of Moore Theological College (1935–1958), serving his last five years there as principal. During World War II he was an army chaplain in New Guinea. He was consecrated bishop in 1958, and in 1966 was elected archbishop of the Anglican diocese of Sydney (1966–1982), latterly serving additionally as Anglican primate of Australia. In that post he did much to foster tolerance and cooperation between the various dioceses regardless of churchmanship, with a steady program of pastoral and teaching visits throughout the country. He also traveled extensively overseas and became known as an international church leader. His leadership of the Anglican Church in Sydney and his writings demonstrate his determination to encourage and maintain the distinctive character of evangelical testimony. Queen Elizabeth II conferred a knighthood on Marcus Loane in 1976.

Writing with enviable skill over many decades, he has addressed theological, doctrinal, and biographical themes. Among his books are *Oxford and the Evangelical Succession* (1950), *Makers of Religious Freedom in the Seventeenth Century* (1961), *They Were Pilgrims* (1970), and *John Charles Ryle* (1983). His devotional books "are all based on the lifelong belief that we take the Bible in our hands, knowing that it is the Word of God. God has spoken; this is His Word written; and not one word of His shall fall to the ground" (thus the preface of Loane's *Thy Kingdom Come*, 1989).

W. H. OLSON

Lockward Perez, Jorge Alfonso (1937–)

Writer, educator, and political leader. One of the few evangelicals in Latin America involved in high-level politics, he was born into an evangelical family in Puerto Plata, Dominican Republic. He studied philosophy and education at the National University of Santo Domingo and held several government posts, including a presidential secretariat. He was president of the national Evangelism in Depth campaign in 1965–1966. He served as president and then general secretary of the Partido Revolucionario Social Cristiano (Revolutionary Social Christian Party) and ran unsuccessfully for the presidency of the country as his party's candidate in 1978. He also served as president of CETEC University in the Dominican Republic. He has published eight books of poetry and six on history, including one on Columbus and his religious beliefs (all in Spanish), and writes a weekly column for one of Santo Domingo's leading newspapers. He has also written and lectured on the social and political responsibility of the Christian.

STEPHEN R. SYWULKA

Loisy, Alfred Firman (1857–1940)

French Catholic modernist. Born in Ambrières, Champagne, to a peasant family, he attended various schools and entered the seminary at Châlons-sur-Marne in 1874. Ordained in 1879, he served two years as a parish priest and then became a teacher of Hebrew and biblical exegesis at the Catholic Institute of Paris. In 1889 he was named professor of Holy Scripture. Strongly influenced by J. E. Renan and Louis Duchesne, he adopted the tenets of modern biblical criticism and in 1893 was dismissed for having moved too far from orthodoxy. Reassigned to a

Dominican convent in Neuilly-sur-Seine as a chaplain, Loisy continued his research in the development of the Bible and history of doctrine. His publications alarmed the hierarchy all the way to Rome, although he claimed (in *The Gospel and the Church* [ET, 1903]) he was really refuting the radicalism of Adolf Harnack and defending the true faith. In 1900 he began lecturing at the École des Hautes Études of the Sorbonne, but his superiors forced him out in 1904. Five of his works were placed on the Index in 1903 for their "very grave errors," and in 1908 he was excommunicated for refusing to accept the papal decrees condemning Catholic modernism. In 1909 Loisy was appointed professor of the history of religions at the Collège de France, where he remained until retiring in 1930. During his career he published over thirty books, among the most important being *The Religion of Israel* (1910), *The Birth of the Christian Religion* (1933), and *The Origins of the New Testament* (1936). He came to see all religions as alike in their quest for justice, and a moral religion of humanity as the ultimate end of the religious and moral evolution of the ages. The story of his struggles is contained in his three-volume *Memoires* (1930–1931) and an English autobiography, *My Duel with the Vatican* (1924).

RICHARD V. PIERARD

Lonergan, Bernard J(oseph) F(rancis) (1904–1984)

Roman Catholic theologian. Born in Buckingham, Quebec, Canada, he studied at Loyola High School and College in Montreal, then he entered the Society of Jesus. He studied philosophy at the Jesuit Heythrop College in Chipping Norton, England (1926–1929) and received a B.A. from the University of London in 1930. After teaching for three years in Montreal, he went to the Gregorian University in Rome, where he took a licentiate in theology in 1937, and finished his doctoral work three years later, receiving the S.T.D. in 1945. He was ordained a Roman Catholic priest in 1936. Beginning in 1940 Lonergan taught theology for thirteen years in Jesuit seminaries in Montreal, then returned to teach at the Gregorian University until 1965. From 1965 to 1975 he taught at Regis College, Willowdale, Ontario, and from 1975 at Boston College, Chestnut Hill, Massachusetts. Considered one of the foremost Catholic scholars of the century, Lonergan was a leading transcendental Thomist who sought through his writings and teaching to reinterpret the medieval synthesis of St. Thomas Aquinas in the light of Kantian philosophy, later phenomenology and existentialism. His epistemological masterpiece, *Insight: A Study of Human Understanding* (1957), sought for the unity of scientific, artistic, and commonsense cognition in preconceptual intellect. It was followed by many other writings, among them *Method in Theology* and *Philosophy of God and Theology: the Relationship Between Philosophy of God and the Functional Specialty, Systematics.*

JOHN FAWCETT

Luccock, Halford Edward (1885–1960)

American educator and writer. Born in Pittsburgh, he was educated at Northwestern University, Union Theological Seminary, and Columbia University. After ordination to the Methodist ministry in 1910 he held pastorates at Windsor, Connecticut, and at New Haven. He was editorial secretary of the Methodist Board of Foreign Missions (1918–1924), and an editor of the *Christian Advocate* (1924–1928). His most lasting contribution came during his years as professor of homiletics at Yale Divinity School (1923–1953). His literary legacy consists of twenty-seven books, six hundred letters, and more than one thousand sermons, and spans the years 1916–1960. Most noteworthy among his works are *Christianity and the Individual in a World of Crowds* (1937), *The Acts of the Apostles in Present-Day Preaching* (1938), *American Mirror: Ethical and Religious Aspects of American Literature, 1930–1940* (1941), and *In the Minister's Workshop* (1944).

EDWARD J. FURCHA

Luwum, Janani (1922–1977)

Ugandan archbishop and martyr. Born the son of poor Christian parents in East Acholi, he trained at Boroboro Teachers' Training College, but some time after his conversion in 1948 studied for the ministry at the new Buwalasi Theological College, where he was ordained in 1955. He was a parish priest for three years, studied further in England, and was principal at Buwalasi for two years; he later became bishop of northern Uganda (1969–1974). In 1971 an army general overthrew the government, and posters in Kampala proclaimed "Amin—Our Christ." Tribal warfare and a reign of terror ensued as Idi Amin sought to convert to Islam a land 70 percent Christian. Archbishop from 1974, Luwum several times boldly confronted Idi Amin about the injustices of the government, thereby putting his life in danger. In 1977 Luwum and his bishops wrote a strongly worded memorandum, protesting against the government's atrocities, especially against Christians. The half-crazed dictator chose to interpret this as a threat against the state, and the archbishop was thereafter a marked man, especially after he and his colleagues prepared a catalogue of the regime's crimes. In February 1977 Amin staged a public mock trial, after which Luwum and two others were condemned to die. It is said that Amin himself shot Luwum that evening. The government reported that he had died in a car accident, but refused to release his body to the church, and had taken it north for secret burial. No memorial service for him was permitted. Though his death was a profound shock, God used it to strengthen the church in Uganda.

Biography by Margaret Ford (1978).

LAZARUS SERUYANGE
J.D. DOUGLAS

M

Maak, Hay Chun (1930–)

Evangelist, pastor, and educator. Born in Canton, China, he graduated in Hong Kong from Bethel Bible Seminary, from the Baptist College, and from Asia Baptist Graduate Seminary. He later resumed studies in the United States at Southwestern Baptist Seminary (D.Min., 1974). He was missionary pastor to Singapore (1953–1961), lecturer in Malaysia Baptist Theological Seminary (1965–1969), chaplain and lecturer in Hong Kong Baptist College (1969–1973), and vice principal (1975–1977) and principal (1978–1992) of Singapore Bible College (SBC). As pastor and teacher in Singapore and Malaysia he planted four churches. As evangelist he preached in many Asian churches. His "Tapevangelism," a forty-message tool for personal evangelism, has been released in Mandarin and in five other dialects.

As principal of SBC he displayed an enterprise that saw the growth of the school in many areas. Student numbers increased from 118 to 275, from 17 countries. Accreditation was obtained from the regional association for bachelor (1978) and master (1985) programs, the School of Church Music was inaugurated (1983), and a diploma course was offered in theological education for grassroot ministries (1987). Maak is now engaged in writing work, and is consulting pastor, Richmond Hill Chinese Christian Community Church, Toronto, Canada.

MICHAEL SHEN

Macartney, Clarence Edward Noble (1879–1957)

Presbyterian scholar and lecturer. Born in Northwood, Ohio, he graduated from the University of Wisconsin, Princeton University, and Princeton Theological Seminary. He was ordained to the Christian ministry in the Presbyterian Church, and served as pastor of the First Church, Paterson, New Jersey (1905–1914), Arch Street Church, Philadelphia (1914–1927), and First Church, Pittsburgh (1927–1953). In 1924 he was moderator of the general assembly of the Presbyterian Church, USA. Two years earlier he had been prominent in opposing H. E. Fosdick's well-publicized sermon, "Shall the Fundamentalists Win?" While he supported the founding of Westminster Theological Seminary he, unlike some other conservatives, remained within his mainline denomination. Macartney distinguished himself as lecturer at conferences, colleges, and seminaries. His numerous publications include historical studies, sermons, and biblical exegesis, among them *Prayer at the Golden Altar* (1944), *You Can Conquer* (1945), and his *Autobiography* (ed. J. C. Henry, 1961).

EDWARD J. FURCHA

MacDonald, George (1824–1905)

Scottish writer and Congregationalist pastor. Born in Huntley, Aberdeenshire, and reared in a strong Calvinist environment, he graduated from King's College, Aberdeen, in 1845. After studies at Highbury Theological College, London, he was ordained at Trinity Congregational Chapel, Arundel, in 1851. Two years later he was forced to resign because he espoused several Arminian doctrines. He gave up the pastoral ministry, but not preaching. He supported his large family by writing over fifty books of fiction, poetry, sermons, and Christian commentaries, as well as numerous essays on sundry topics. His writing profoundly influenced such important authors as G. K. Chesterton and C. S. Lewis. Lewis called him his "master," and admitted that "I have never written a book in which I did not quote from him." Lewis edited an anthology of MacDonald's works. Many of MacDonald's books are still in print. His best-known works are *Phantastes* (1857), *The Miracles of Our Lord* (1870), *At the Back of the North Wind* (1871), *Diary of an Old Soul* (1880), and *Lilith* (1895).

Biographies by Greville MacDonald (1924) and Michael Phillips (1987).

LYLE W. DORSETT

Machen, John Gresham (1881–1937)

New Testament scholar and churchman. Born into a prominent Baltimore family, he graduated from Johns Hopkins University (1901) and Princeton Seminary (1905). He then spent a year in Germany, studying leading liberal scholars whose radical views convinced him that liberalism and orthodoxy were essentially two different religions. The rest of his life was spent defending orthodox Christianity against liberal detractors.

His first major work was *The Origin of Paul's Religion* (1921). Liberal theology had called Paul a perverter of Jesus' religion and the second founder of Christianity, turning it into a mystery religion based on the death of a savior-god. Machen argued that Paul built his theology on the teachings of Jesus whose vicarious death was the very essence of Christianity. To reject that was to destroy the gospel. In 1923, at the height of the fundamentalist-modernist controversy, Machen published *Christianity and Liberalism*. In it he carefully outlined the fundamental doctrines of the church, putting his heaviest emphasis on the propitiatory nature of the death of Jesus. It was liberalism's failure to understand this that made it a different religion. *What Is Faith?* (1925) and *The Christian Faith in the Modern World* (1936) spoke to the same issues. In *The Virgin*

Birth of Christ (1930) Machen refuted liberalism's assertion that the story of Jesus was just another ancient myth. The truth of Christianity depends on the historical nature of the virginal conception of Jesus and the incarnation of the second person of the Trinity.

As a churchman, Machen was embroiled in the ecclesiastical controversies of the Presbyterian Church, USA. In 1929, with O. T. Allis, R. D. Wilson, and others, he resigned from Princeton Seminary because of the political maneuvers of the liberals, and founded Westminster Theological Seminary. In 1933 he established the Independent Board for Presbyterian Missions. In 1936 he was forced out of the PCUSA, and with others founded the Presbyterian Church of America. Machen was eulogized by Princeton Seminary's C. W. Hodge as evangelical Christianity's "greatest leader."

Biographies by W. Masselink (1938) and N. B. Stonehouse (1954).

WALTER A. ELWELL

MacKay, Donald MacCrimmon (1922–1987)

Scientist, philosopher, and Christian apologist. Born in Lybster, Caithness, Scotland of a general practitioner father who was also a minister of the Free Church of Scotland, firm foundation knowledge of the Bible, which remained with him throughout his life, was laid in his childhood. He graduated in natural philosophy (physics) at St. Andrews University in 1943 and worked during World War I on radar research at the Admiralty Signals Establishment. Thereafter he taught physics at King's College, London University. His work in 1946 on high-speed analogue computers and on information theory had a lasting influence on his late thinking. He saw the language of information science as the lingua franca of an interdisciplinary group of physiologists, physicists, psychologists, and engineers showing a common interest in investigating the sensory communication systems of the brain and their malfunctioning in blindness and deafness. In 1960 he was appointed professor of communication at the University College of North Staffordshire (now the University of Keele). He held many distinguished lectureships and in 1985 received the prestigious Hermann von Helmholtz Prize for Distinguished Research in the Cognitive Neurosciences, in New York.

He was a prolific writer, not only on science, but also on philosophical studies, on artificial intelligence and cybernetics, on the mindbrain problem, and on the interface between science and Christian faith. He made good use of his expertise in information theory and physics to produce refreshing new insights into problems such as the freedom of the will and the sovereignty of God in a mechanistic universe. He embodied and exemplified the openness of the mind of a good scientist. He consistently advocated and emphasized the responsibility of the scientist to faithfully map out the territory he investigated. An active churchman, founding member of the Research Scientists Christian Fellowship (now Christians in Science), he was widely known as a speaker, debater, broadcaster, and television personality. His writings, talks, and personal friendships, especially in the United Kingdom and the United States, continue to have an enduring major influence on those concerned with issues at the interface of science and Christian faith. His many publications, culminating in his 1986 Gifford Lectures at the University of Glasgow published under the title *Behind the Eye* (1991), included *Brains, Machines and Persons* (1980), *Human Science and Human Dignity* (1979), *Science, Chance and Providence* (1978), *The Clockwork Image* (1974), and his Eddington Memorial Lecture *The Freedom of Action in a Mechanistic Universe* (1967).

MALCOLM A. JEEVES

Mackay, John Alexander (1889–1983)

Presbyterian missionary and educator. Born in Inverness, Scotland, he received an M.A. in 1912 from the University of Aberdeen, then studied in the United States at Princeton Theological Seminary (B.D., 1915). He spent a year studying at the University of Madrid, then returned to Scotland in 1915, where he was ordained in the Free Church of Scotland and married Jane Logan Wells. They were appointed by the church as missionaries to Lima, Peru, where he founded and served as principal of the Anglo-Peruvian College until 1925. From 1925 until 1932 Mackay worked with the YMCA as a writer, lecturer, and evangelist, living for a while in Montevideo, Uruguay, and Mexico City. From 1932 until 1936 he served in the United States as secretary for the Latin America Division of the Board of Foreign Missions of the Presbyterian Church, USA. In 1936 he became president of Princeton Theological Seminary, arriving shortly after the turmoil caused by the departure of several conservative faculty to establish Westminster Theological Seminary, and remaining until 1959. While there, Mackay founded *Theology Today* (1944), which he also edited until 1951. A leader in the ecumenical movement, he played a central role in the founding of the World Council of Churches and served as the chairman of its Joint Committee and of the International Missionary Council from 1948 to 1954. He was also the moderator of the general assembly of the Presbyterian Church USA (1953) and president of the World Presbyterian Alliance from 1954 to 1959. A prolific writer, Mackay constructed an ecumenical theology, particularly in *Christianity at the Frontier* (1948), *God's Orders* (1953), and *Ecumenics: the Science of the Church Universal* (1964). After retiring from Princeton, he lectured widely and taught Hispanic thought at the American University in Washington, D.C., from 1961 to 1964.

JOHN FAWCETT

233

Mackintosh, Hugh Ross (1870–1936)

Scottish theologian. Born in Paisley, where his father was minister of the Gaelic Free Church of Scotland, he studied in Edinburgh and Germany before serving charges in Tayport (1897–1901) and Aberdeen (1901–1904). Thereafter until his death he was professor of divinity in New College, Edinburgh. In 1900, with the bulk of the Free Church, he had moved into the United Free Church. With the further church union that took him into the Church of Scotland in 1929 he served latterly in the Edinburgh University divinity faculty. He was moderator of the Church of Scotland general assembly in 1932. Mackintosh was a theologian who remained a preacher committed to evangelism and missions. "To study with H. R. Mackintosh was a spiritual and theological benediction, for he was above all a man of God, full of the Holy Spirit and of faith" (T. F. Torrance). He viewed a theologian's attitude to "petitionary prayer" as an unfailing touchstone. His books on *The Doctrine of the Person of Christ* (1912) and *The Christian Experience of Forgiveness* (1927) remain of solid value today. They reflect a broad evangelicalism that welcomed, though not uncritically, Barth's earlier works. His *Types of Modern Theology* (1937) ranged from Schleiermacher (whose *The Christian Faith* he had translated with J. S. Stewart) to Barth.

A memoir by A. B. Macaulay appears in Mackintosh's *Sermons* (1938).

DAVID F. WRIGHT

MacLeod, George Fielden (1895–1991)

Presbyterian minister and founder of the Iona Community. Born the son of a Glasgow member of Parliament, he was educated at Oxford and Edinburgh, won two World War I medals for bravery, and in 1924 was ordained in the Church of Scotland. He ministered at St. Cuthbert's in central Edinburgh (1926–1930) and at Govan in industrial Glasgow (1930–1938). Convinced that the Christian message was not getting through to ordinary people, he forsook the parish ministry, and with a small group of clergy and craftsmen settled on the island of Iona made famous by the sixth-century Columba. Their aim was "to find a new community for men in the world today." They began to rebuild the ruined Benedictine abbey, and to share the fellowship of work and worship. MacLeod and his Iona Community were for many years regarded with misgiving by the Kirk establishment, not least because the erstwhile war hero had become a militant pacifist. His dynamism and charisma, however, plus the impact made on the church's parishes by Iona Community members, won the day, and in 1957 MacLeod was elected moderator of the Kirk's general assembly. He remained to the end a strong individualist, fond of suggesting that Christ's greatest contribution to religion was to do away with it, and that "God has run down the Church in order to build it up." He was awarded a life peerage in 1967, the Union Medal by Union Theological Seminary, New York, in 1986, and the Templeton Prize in 1989. His major publications are *We Shall Rebuild* (1944) and *Only One Way Left* (1956).

Biography by Ron Ferguson (1990).

J. D. DOUGLAS

Magalit, Isabelo F. (1940–)

Educator and evangelist. Born in Capiz, Panay, the Philippines, he graduated from the University of the Philippines School of Medicine in 1964 (voted one of the ten outstanding interns that year). Relinquishing what could have been a brilliant career in medicine, Magalit accepted the position of general secretary of the InterVarsity Christian Fellowship in the Philippines until 1973, when he started his nine-year post as associate general secretary in East Asia of the International Fellowship of Evangelical Students. In 1982 he accepted a call to the pastorate of the Diliman Bible Church, comprised largely of students from the University of the Philippines. This work he combined with service to various key Christian agencies. In 1989 he became the first Filipino president of the Asian Theological Seminary. In this position he has distinguished himself as much as he did in pastoral work and in student evangelism.

FRANK ALLEN

Magbanua, Federico M., Jr. (1932–)

Gospel broadcaster. Born in Isio, Cauayan, Negros Occidental, the Philippines, he eventually migrated to Manila, where he graduated from the Mapua Institute of Technology. He also attended FEBIAS College of the Bible and Criswell College, Dallas, Texas. He served with the Conservative Baptist Association of the Philippines in Laguna province prior to becoming pastor of the Capitol City Baptist Church (1964–1969). Magbanua's greatest contribution was made as managing director of the Far East Broadcasting Company (FEBC) from 1971 to 1992. During these years he also served as president of the Far East Development Services (1973–1992); administrative director of FEBC, Indonesia (1970–1971); board chair of World Vision, Philippines (1976–1984), Philippines Bible Broadcaster, Inc. (1973–1979), FEBIAS College of the Bible (1975–1978), and Philippine Bible Society (1974, 1979, 1982); and board member, Wycliffe Bible Translators (1985–1989). He has also served as a delegate to the World Congress on Evangelism (1966), the Congress on the Worldwide Mission of the Church (1966), the Asia South Pacific Congress on Evangelism (1968), the International Congress on World Evangelization (1974), and the Lausanne Congress on World Evangclization (1989). He retired in 1992, and now serves FEBC as minister-at-large.

FRANK ALLEN

Maier, Walter Arthur (1893–1950)

Old Testament scholar and radio preacher. Born in Boston to German immigrant parents, he was educated at Boston University, Concordia Seminary, St. Louis, Missouri, and Harvard University (A.M., 1920; Ph.D., 1929). His doctoral dissertation in Assyriology was entitled "Slavery in the Time of the Hammurabi Dynasty."

After two years as executive secretary to the International Walther League (1920–1922), the youth organization of the Lutheran Church, Missouri Synod, he began teaching at Concordia Seminary as professor of Semitic languages and Old Testament interpretation, where he remained until his death. He continued to edit the Walther League *Messenger* (1920–1945). He served as assistant pastor of St. Stephen's Lutheran Church, St. Louis (1930–1950), of which he was founder.

He became much better known as a major radio preacher for the weekly "Lutheran Hour." Begun in 1930 as a local broadcast on the thirty-six-station Columbia Broadcasting network, suspended during the Depression, but reestablished in 1935 over a larger national network, the Mutual Broadcasting System, it became international in 1943, reaching fifty-five countries in thirty-six languages and an estimated 20 million listeners. Twenty books were generated out of these radio talks, beginning with *The Lutheran Hour* (1931). Maier became identified as "the greatest radio preacher of all time" and his wartime sermons took on a patriotically religious flavor, though also calling America back to Christ.

Biography by P. L. Maier (1963), who also edited *The Best of Walter A. Maier* (1980).

CLYDE CURRY SMITH

Makarios III (1913–1977)

Orthodox archbishop and first president of the Republic of Cyprus. Born Mihail Christodoulou Mouskos near Paphos, he graduated from the University of Athens in 1942 and was ordained in 1946. Postgraduate studies at Boston University were interrupted by election as bishop of Kition in 1948. In 1951 he became archbishop of the autonomous Church of Cyprus. Suspected of collaborating with anti-British elements during preindependence years, he was exiled, but returned after a 1959 agreement that gave Cyprus independence and made Makarios head of state. He needed all his native shrewdness to cope with the island's 18 percent Turkish Muslim minority, extremists who sought union with Greece, and criticism from within the church of his dual role. Makarios reacted ruthlessly against each group of enemies, but a short-lived pro-Greece coup removed him briefly from leadership in 1974 and precipitated an invasion of the island by Turkish forces that annexed (and still retains) some 37 percent of the national territory. Makarios was never thereafter able to regain control. After his death a chapter of Byzantine history closed: God and Caesar now have separate representatives.

Biographies by Stanley Mayer (1971) and P. N. Vanezis (1974).

J. D. Douglas

Malik, Alexander John (1944–)

Anglican bishop and Islamics scholar. Born in the Punjab, Pakistan, he graduated from the University of Punjab; Bishop's College, Calcutta; Serampore University; and McGill University, Montreal. After holding various church posts in Pakistan he was elected bishop of Lahore (Church of Pakistan) in 1980. He is a recognized scholar in Islamic theology as it applies to Christian theology and mission in Islamic cultures, a leader in a movement addressing the needs of the Christian community, and an outspoken defender of and advocate for the rights of Christian Pakistani believers. Under his leadership the Lahore district has become involved in education, health care, and women's ministries, while maintaining his priority of evangelism.

Myrna R. Grant

Malik, Charles Habib (1906–1987)

Lebanese statesman and educator. Born in Bterram, Al-Koura, Lebanon, he was to leave an indelible stamp in the arena of world politics and education. He served for almost fourteen years in the United Nations. He was the only person to have presided over the five major organs of the UN, including the Security Council (1953–1954) and the General Assembly (1958–1959), giving him an instrumental role in developing the Universal Declaration of Human Rights. He was decorated by more than a dozen nations, and was his own country's foreign minister (1956–1957) and a member of its parliament. His educational background, including a Ph.D. from Harvard, led to professorships at American University, Harvard, Dartmouth, and the Catholic University of America.

Malik showed a rare blend of outstanding academic qualities and humble Christian piety. His goal was to win souls and minds, noting, "If you win the whole world and lose the mind of the world, you will soon discover that you have not won the world. Indeed it may turn out that you have actually lost the world." He served the Holy Orthodox Church faithfully throughout his career and was named its Grand First Magistrate. Three times he accompanied his Ecumenical Patriarch to visit Pope Paul VI in the mid-1960s. He was vice president of the United Bible Societies (1966–1972) and president of the World Council of Christian Education (1967–1971).

His numerous publications include *War and Peace* (1950), *The Problem of Asia* (1951), *Christ and Crisis* (1962), *Wonder of Being* (1974), and *A Christian Critique of the University* (1982).

A. Scott Moreau

Manning, Ernest Charles (1908–)

Canadian politician and Christian layman. Born in Carnduff, Saskatchewan he was drawn to William Aberhart's religious radio broadcasts and studied at his Prophetic Bible Institute in Calgary. He became the institute's executive secretary, and served in Aberhart's political cabinet. Upon Aberhart's death, he became leader of the Social Credit party and premier of Alberta. He was reelected seven times as premier, serving until 1968 as one of Canada's most effective politicians. His government was free of corruption, and marked by conservative financial policies. He published *Political Realignment: A Challenge to Thoughtful Canadians* in 1967 as an appeal to the nation to reorder Canadian politics, without much success.

Upon his resignation in 1968, Manning served in the Canadian Senate for one year (1970) and was made a companion of the Order of Canada. He continues his weekly religious radio broadcasts in Canada and the United States. His son Preston now leads the Reform Party of Canada.

JOHN FAWCETT

Manson, Thomas Walter (1893–1958)

English biblical scholar. Born in Tynenouth, he was educated at Glasgow University and Westminster (Presbyterian) College, Cambridge. He taught at the latter institution, but was soon called to serve a number of Presbyterian congregations in northern England. During this time he produced his best-known book, *The Teachings of Jesus* (1931). In 1932 he was appointed to the chair of New Testament Greek at Mansfield (Congregational) College, Oxford. In 1936 Manson became professor of biblical criticism at Manchester University. He remained there until his death, devoting much of his time to both the university and the church. His other major book was *The Sayings of Jesus* (1949). He was well equipped to write on both the Old and New Testaments. Besides his important work on the Gospels, he wrote on the New Testament epistles as well as the ministry and priesthood of the church. He was a brilliant teacher and gave himself unstintingly to his students, but was good also at communicating with ordinary people in the congregations of his church.

NOEL S. POLLARD

Maritain, Jacques (1882–1973)

French Roman Catholic philosopher. Born in Paris, reared in a liberal Protestant environment, and educated at the Sorbonne in natural sciences, he grew disillusioned with positivism and scientism. When he studied Thomas Aquinas it resulted in his (and his wife's) conversion to Catholicism. He taught at the College Stanislas (1911–1914), the Catholic Institute of Paris (1914–1933), and the Institute of Medieval Studies in Toronto (1933–1939). He served as French ambassador to the Vatican

238

(1945–1948) and was professor of philosophy at Princeton University (1948–1956). As a Thomist, Maritain insisted that existence precedes essence, and Thomism was the original existentialism. He proved the existence of God by arguing that the realization of our personal finitude leads us to seek the ground of our own existence in God's eternal being. He held democracy to be the ideal form of government, and contributed much in the area of aesthetics. Maritain published many books applying Thomistic concepts to contemporary issues, and produced also the autobiographical *The Peasant of the Garonne* (1968).

Analyses of his work include J. W. Evans, *Jacques Maritain: The Man and His Achievement* (1963); C. A. Fecher, *The Philosophy of Jacques Maritain* (1979); and D. W. Hudson and M. J. Mancini, *Understanding Maritain* (1987).

RICHARD V. PIERARD

Marshall, Catherine Wood (1914–1983)

American religious writer. While a student at Agnes Scott College, Catherine Wood fell in love with Peter Marshall (1902–1949), pastor of the Westminster Presbyterian Church in Atlanta, Georgia. Shortly after their marriage, he became pastor of the New York Avenue Presbyterian Church in Washington, D.C., and later, a celebrated chaplain to the U.S. Senate. Following her husband's untimely death, Marshall turned to writing to support herself and their son Peter John. Her first book, a collection of her husband's sermons entitled *Mr. Jones, Meet the Master* (1950), was immensely popular, so she recounted his story in *A Man Called Peter* (1951), which was soon turned into a Hollywood movie. Other books of Marshall's writings, guides to the Christian life (such as *To Live Again*, 1957), and a novel, *Christy* (1967), more than fifteen in all, have established her as one of the most popular Christian writers of our time. In 1959 she married Leonard LeSourd, executive editor of *Guideposts* magazine and a widower with three small children. Her writing eventually took on a more subjective, even charismatic, tone.

Autobiography published in 1980.

THOMAS G. REID, JR.

Marshall, Peter (1902–1949)

Presbyterian minister and chaplain of the U.S. Senate. Born in Coatbridge, Scotland, he studied at the Coatbridge Technical School and Mining College, came to the United States in 1927, and worked with the *Birmingham News* in Alabama. He received a B.D. degree from Columbia Theological Seminary, Decatur, Georgia, and was ordained to the ministry in 1931. He pastored churches in Georgia (1931–1937) before being called to New York Avenue Presbyterian Church, Washington, D.C. (1937–1949). Having become a U.S. citizen in 1938, he was chaplain of the U.S. Senate (1947–1949). A man of dynamic faith, he was a popular and straightforward preacher, who emphasized the reality of God and prayer in human experience, commitment to Jesus Christ, the relevance of Christian faith for everyday life, and personal and national righteousness. He was called "the conscience of the Senate." He wrote *The Exile Heart* (1949).

His wife, the former Sarah Catherine Wood, edited a volume of his sermons that sold over a million copies (*Mr. Jones, Meet the Master,* 1949), and *The Prayers of Peter Marshall* (1954). She wrote his best-selling biography, *A Man Called Peter* (1951), which became even more successful after it was turned into a movie.

ALBERT H. FREUNDT, JR.

Martin, T(homas) T(heodore) (1862–1939)

Southern Baptist evangelist. Born the son of a celebrated preacher in Smith County, Mississippi, he graduated from Mississippi College (1886) and Southern Baptist Theological Seminary (Th.M., 1896). After teaching at Baylor Female College in Belton, Texas, he was ordained and became a pastor in Glenview, Kentucky, and in Colorado where he preached to miners in the open air. In 1900 he began full-time evangelistic work, mostly in circus tents that seated six to eight hundred people. Martin disapproved of emotional displays, stressing instead the free offer of salvation, God's sovereignty, and the authority of God's Word. By recruiting and training the Blue Mountain Evangelists, gospel singing and preaching teams, he booked revivals throughout the country, and in 1930 founded the American School of Evangelism. A prohibitionist and an opponent of the "dirty theory" of evolution, he attended the 1925 Scopes trial as a friend of W. J. Bryan. Though he attacked Southern Baptists who departed from fundamentalism, he did not leave his denomination, and criticized J. F. Norris for doing so.

Biography by A. D. Muse (n.d.).

LESLIE R. KEYLOCK

Marty, Martin Emil (1928–)

American church historian. Born in West Point, Nebraska, he was reared and educated in a Lutheran Church–Missouri Synod environment, and in 1956 earned a Ph.D. degree from the University of Chicago, on whose faculty he has subsequently served from 1963. Marty has become a bridge person between the more theologically conservative traditions and the liberal Protestant tradition represented by *The Christian Century,* with which he has been editorially associated since 1956. He has also been president of the American Catholic History Society. His interest in American religious phenomena has made him the unofficial dean of the commentators on religion as is evidenced in the frequency that his opinions are cited in the secular media. A prolific writer and editor, Marty claims he has always held at least two careers at once: that of pastor and editor or of professor and editor. He has authored over fifty books and coauthored or edited a further thirty. Among his writings are *The New Shape of American Religion* (1959), *Righteous Empire: The Protestant Experience in America* (1986), and *Pilgrims in Their Own Land: Five Hundred Years of Religion in America* (1984). An example of his ability to write on pastoral themes is *A Cry of Absence: Reflections for the Winter of the Heart* (1983).

JAMES J. STAMOOLIS

Mason, Charles Harrison (1866–1961)

Cofounder of the Church of God in Christ. Born near Memphis, Tennessee, to tenant farmers who had become members of a Missionary Baptist Church, he was converted at the age of twelve, became involved in spiritual healing, and soon after experiencing sanctification in 1882 preached his first sermon at Preston, Arkansas. He was first licensed by the Mount Gale Missionary Baptist Church, had a brief stint at Arkansas Baptist College, and left in 1894 for an evangelistic ministry that stressed spiritual healing. Because he emphasized Holiness teaching of entire sanctification he was excluded from the Baptist denomination, and as Elder Mason he and others began in 1897 the Church of God in Christ. In 1907 he shifted the basis of his organization to incorporate Pentecostal elements under the influence of the Azusa Street revival. He experienced baptism in the Holy Spirit and assumed full leadership of the church as its senior bishop, a post he held until his death. In 1970 the Mason Theological Seminary was inaugurated, making it the first Pentecostal seminary. Today the Church of God in Christ is said to be the second largest black denomination in the world.

Biographies by E. Lee (ed.) (1967), and M. E. Mason (1979).

EDWARD J. FURCHA

Matheson, George (1842–1906)

Presbyterian preacher and hymnwriter. Born into a wealthy Christian family in Glasgow, Scotland, he suffered from a progressive eye ailment that made him blind by age eighteen. An early Christian commitment, funds to employ male secretarial help, and assistance from fellow students all helped toward the completion of an Arts degree at Glasgow University followed by divinity studies. He was ordained in 1868, and served Church of Scotland parishes in Innellan (1868–1886) and St. Bernard's, Edinburgh (1886–1899), where the freshness and originality of his sermons and prayers electrified large congregations. When he preached once in the presence of Queen Victoria on the Book of Job the widowed monarch was so impressed that she requested the address be printed.

241

Matheson's books had a huge circulation. Although some of them reflected the radical views of German theologians, he was best known for his devotional works, notably *Studies of the Portrait of Christ* (2 vols., 1899, 1900) and other volumes written after he retired from pastoral work. It is, however, as a hymnwriter that he won the hearts of many by a hymn now known worldwide: "O Love That Wilt Not Let Me Go," written, he said, within a few minutes in his Innellan Manse.

J. D. DOUGLAS

Mathews, Shailer (1863–1941)

Early exponent of the social gospel and modernism in the United States. Born in Portland, Maine, he studied at Newton Theological Institution; he received a license to preach, but never sought ordination. After graduate studies at the University of Berlin, he taught at his alma mater, Colby College (1887–1894), and at the divinity school of the University of Chicago (1894–1933). There he was successively professor of New Testament history and interpretation; systematic, historical, and comparative theology; and dean. In *The Social Teachings of Jesus* (1897) he articulated a hermeneutic for making Christianity relevant to contemporary society. In *The Faith of Modernism* (1924), he argued that new insights from science, history, and other disciplines must inform Christian beliefs. These books became standard texts for the social gospel and modernist movements. Through *The Growth of the Idea of God* (1931) and *Christianity of the Social Process* (1934) he elaborated theological liberalism in the face of "fundamentalism." He coauthored *Principles and Ideas for the Sunday School* (1903) and directed the religious department of the Chautauqua Institute (1912–1934). He helped found the Northern Baptist Convention (1907) and wrote *Scientific Management in the Churches* (1911). In accord with his "functional" philosophy of religion, he promoted practical, not doctrinal, ecumenicity. He was president of the Federal Council of Churches (1912–1916). His autobiographical *New Faith for Old* was published in 1936.

NORMAN F. CORNETT

Matthews, Mark Allison (1867–1940)

Presbyterian pastor. Born in Calhoun, Georgia, he was converted at age thirteen, began preaching at nineteen, and was ordained the following year. In 1888 he graduated from Gordon County University, and after pastoring churches (1888–1902) in Georgia and Tennessee, he went to Seattle's First Presbyterian Church and stayed there until his death. Matthew's ministry was "a strange mixture of biblical fundamentalism and social reform," according to C. Allyn Russell. He was opposed to professional evangelists, insisting instead on doing the evangelizing himself. As part of his ministry he organized the first church-owned and -operated radio station in the country, KTW, and helped found a major hospital that is now part of the University of Washington Medical School. Though he insisted that at least a third of the faculty of coeducational institutions be women, supported socialized medicine, and wrote to Hitler asking him to abdicate, he opposed female suffrage. A bronze bust in Seattle honors him for his civic and political work.

Biography by E. P. Gibney and A. M. Potter (1948).

LESLIE R. KEYLOCK

Mauriac, François (1885–1970)

French Roman Catholic novelist. Born in Bordeaux, he was educated at a rigorous school operated by the Marist Fathers and at the universities of Bordeaux and Paris. In 1909 he published a small book of verse, and spent the rest of his life as a writer. He had his mark with *A Kiss for the Leper* (1922), and thereafter produced a steady stream of novels, essays, plays, and biographies. In 1937 his *Life of Jesus* appeared. He supported the Republican cause during the Spanish Civil War, wrote anti-Nazi pieces as part of the French resistance during World War II, and in the 1950s condemned French colonialism in Algeria. In 1952 he was awarded the Nobel Prize for Literature. Religious themes and concepts were essential elements of his novels, all of which in some way dealt with evil, human sin and failure, and salvation. Although his characters sought fulfillment in human loves, they fell short of genuine fulfillment until they encountered the love of God. *The Viper's Tangle* (1932) had an especially strong religious twist, but more orthodox Catholics were unhappy about his unusual expressions of piety. Some criticized him for an apparent obsession with evil, but he replied that his characters actually had a soul. He once stated, "Any writer who has maintained in the center of his work the human creature made in the image of the Father, redeemed by the Son, illumined by the Spirit, I cannot see in him a master of despair, however somber his painting may be."

Biographies by J. E. Fowler (1969) and R. Speaight (1976).

RICHARD V. PIERARD

Maxwell, Leslie Earl (1895–1984)

Educator and writer. Born in Kansas and converted during high school while living at the home of a Presbyterian aunt, he served in the U.S. Army in World War I, and after the war, studied at the Midland Bible Institute in Kansas City. After graduating in 1922, Maxwell moved to Three Hills, Alberta, in response to a request from some farmers who desired Bible instruction. He founded Prairie Bible Institute there and remained until his death in 1984. He served as president until 1977, and continued teaching until 1980. Under his aegis, the school became one of the most influ-

243

ential of its kind in the world. Attendance at the institute and its Christian high school peaked at nine hundred in the post-World War II years, and nearly two thousand men and women entered missionary service as a result of their training there. Maxwell edited the *Prairie Overcomer*, begun in the 1920s, and published several popular devotional works, most notably *Born Crucified* (1945). Despite dispensational leanings and strict behavioral standards, Maxwell emphasized evangelism, Bible training, and missions more than cultural separatism, as evident through the curriculum of the institute and the content of the *Overcomer*. Upon his death in 1984, Maxwell was honored by friends and alumni of Prairie Bible Institute for his widespread influence and evangelistic zeal.

JOHN FAWCETT

Mbiti, John Samuel (1931–)

African theologian and churchman. Born in Kenya, he came to faith in a conservative mission, but chose ordination in the Anglican Communion as a more appropriate expression of the universal nature of the church, and a church in which he was free to explore his theological agenda. Woven throughout his works is the theme of integrating the cultural questions of Africa with the Christian faith. In this regard he has consistently criticized the theological reflection of those who focus on the discontinuities between the Christian faith and African traditional religions (e.g., Byang Kato), insisting instead on the need to focus on exploring the continuities. Of particular importance to Mbiti is the consideration that the gospel came to Africa as a fulfillment of ATRs, which served as a *praeparatio evangelica*. This outlook is combined with his call for the freedom of the African church to be able to formulate its own particular creative African approach to making the universal gospel relevant to its peoples. In addition to his writing, he has a long-standing international reputation as an ecumenical churchman, having directed the World Council of Churches Ecumenical Institute in Celigny, Switzerland, where he has resided since 1972. Perhaps the most prolific of modern African theologians, his numerous books and articles range from poetry to African traditional religions (ATR). His significant works include *African Religions and Philosophy, Concepts of God in Africa,* and *New Testament Theology in an African Background* (his Cambridge Ph.D. dissertation).

A. SCOTT MOREAU

McClain, Alva J. (1888–1968)

Brethren educator and theologian. Born in Aurelia, Iowa, he was converted under the ministry of L. S. Bauman in 1911 at a prophecy conference. He attended the University of Washington, Seattle, and Antioch College before receiving a diploma in theology from Xenia Theological

Seminary in 1917. He was ordained that same year and served as pastor of the First Brethren Church of Philadelphia (1918–1924). In 1925 he received the Th.M degree from Xenia and the A.B. from Occidental College and began his teaching career at Ashland College in Ohio as a professor of Old Testament theology. From 1927 to 1929, he taught at the Bible Institute of Los Angeles, then returned to the newly established Ashland Theological Seminary to teach theology and apologetics and serve as an administrator (1930–1937). As a result of doctrinal conflicts with Ashland, McClain was dismissed in 1937 and along with others, founded Grace Theological Seminary, eventually located in Winona Lake, Indiana, where he served as president until 1962.

McClain was a founding member of the Evangelical Theological Society and a board member of the Foreign Missionary Society of the Brethren Church from its inception in 1917 until 1962. He was a respected teacher and a frequent lecturer at conservative seminaries throughout the country. A leading dispensationalist, his systematic approach to theology was opposed by Brethren advocates of noncreedalism, but his theological expertise proved formative in the development of the Fellowship of Grace Brethren Churches.

He was the author of *Bible Truths* (1919), *Outline and Argument of Romans* (1927), *Daniel's Prophecy of the Seventy Weeks* (1940), *Law and the Christian Believer in Relation to the Doctrine of Grace* (1954), and *The Greatness of the Kingdom* (1959).

JOHN FAWCETT

McClure, Robert (1900–1991)

Canadian missionary doctor. Born in the United States, he studied medicine at the University of Toronto, graduating in 1922. He worked as missionary doctor in China and Taiwan, for a time as field director of the International Red Cross in Central and North China, as well as in West and Southwest China. In 1941 he became commandant of the Friends Ambulance Unit's China Convoy, and remained in China until 1948. After a brief stint at a private clinic in Toronto, McClure became chief surgeon at an Anglican hospital in Gaza City (1951). From 1954 to 1967 he worked at Ratlam, Central India. The 1968 general council of the United Church of Canada elected him its first lay moderator. After formal retirement McClure continued medical services in Malaysia, Peru, St. Vincent, and Zaire, and in native peoples' communities in British Columbia. He was made a Companion of the Order of Canada in 1971. McClure's remarkable career in the service of God and humanity will be recalled for his unorthodox approach to healing, his sense of humor, and his unstinting labors in medicine for over fifty years.

Biographies by Munroe Scott (1977, 1979).

EDWARD J. FURCHA

245

McGavran, Donald A. (1897–1990)

Missionary to India, father of the Church Growth movement, and founding dean of the School of Mission at Fuller Theological Seminary. Born in India, he graduated from Butler College and Yale Divinity School, and later earned a Ph.D. degree at Columbia University. During his thirty-year career as a third-generation missionary he became concerned about the lack of conversions and membership growth experienced by his mission during a fifty-year period, in spite of a substantial commitment of money and personnel. So he resigned his position in the United Christian Missionary Society and spent the next seventeen years as a church planter analyzing missionary practice so that he could determine the causes as well as the obstacles to growth. This research became his great purpose in life. He became convinced that church growth was directly related to evangelistic activity in dependence on the Holy Spirit, and that in most instances in India evangelism was neglected in favor of social action, renewal, or nurture. His objective was to promote the effective propagation of the gospel and the multiplication of churches. He utilized the social sciences in order to gain greater understanding, to eliminate incorrect perceptions, and to press for the application of new insights. He defined church growth as all that is involved in bringing people into fellowship. He established the Institute of Church Growth in Portland in 1961 to train missionaries on furlough. In 1965 he moved the institute to Fuller Theological Seminary. He wrote *Bridges of God* (1955), *How Churches Grow* (1959), and (more comprehensively) *Understanding Church Growth* (1970). In 1964 he started and became editor of the *Church Growth Bulletin*.

LUDER G. WHITLOCK, JR.

McGiffert, Arthur Cushman (1861–1933)

Historical theologian. Born in Sauquoit, New York, he studied under Philip Schaff at Union Theological Seminary, and pursued further studies in Berlin, Rome, and Paris. Harnack became his mentor and friend at Marburg. He immersed McGiffert in Ritschlian theology, and encouraged him to translate and edit ancient Christian documents. *Dialogue Between a Christian and a Jew* (1888) was his published doctoral dissertation. He taught at Lane Theological Seminary (1888–1893). His critical translation of *Eusebius' Church History* (1890), a definitive text for forty years, helped establish McGiffert's reputation. While professor of church history at Union (1893–1926) he authored *The Gospel of Peter* (1894) and *A History of Christianity in the Apostolic Age* (1897). The latter was a landmark in American scholarship. He maintained that no doctrine can exist forever since time and circumstances inevitably alter religious "truth." He developed this rationale in *The Problem of Christian Creeds as Affected by Modern Thought* (1901). He advocated the anti-Marcionite origin of *The Apostles' Creed*

(1902), a theory generally held until 1919. McGiffert's *History of Christian Thought* (1933) became a standard textbook in seminaries. *Christianity as History and Faith* (1934) showed his espousal of the social gospel and modernism. As president of Union (1917–1926) he revamped its curriculum and introduced major educational innovations.

NORMAN F. CORNETT

McIntire, Carl (1906–)

American fundamentalist Presbyterian leader. Following graduation from Westminster Theological Seminary in 1931, McIntire had a successful pastorate in Atlantic City, New Jersey, before accepting the call of the large Collingswood Presbyterian Church in Collingswood, New Jersey, in 1933. For more than sixty years, Collingswood has served as the base for a large number of ministries that McIntire has developed. A pioneer of Christian radio broadcasting in the 1930s, McIntire has broadcast the "Twentieth Century Reformation Hour" since 1955. He also founded Faith Theological Seminary, *Christian Beacon* magazine, a retirement home, a summer camp, and Shelton College, and he took control of the Independent Board for Presbyterian Foreign Missions in the late 1930s. McIntire militantly advocates a nationalist, capitalist, and anticommunist form of Christianity. Defrocked by the Presbyterian Church in the USA along with J. Gresham Machen in 1936, McIntire soon fell out with his mentor over Machen's acceptance of nonpremillennial viewpoints and drinking and smoking within the emerging Orthodox Presbyterian Church. McIntire's Bible Presbyterian Church has suffered several subsequent splits, usually attributed to his domineering style of leadership. He helped form the American Council of Christian Churches in 1941 and the International Council of Christian Churches in 1948, both designed to counteract the major liberal ecumenical organizations. McIntire has had numerous conflicts with government agencies over his activities, and his influence has waxed and waned.

THOMAS G. REID, JR.

McKay, James Frederick (1907–)

Superintendent of the Australian Inland Mission. Born in Crabhollow, Queensland, he nearly died at the age of six; his mother dedicated him to God when he recovered. He was educated at Thornburgh College and Emmanuel College, University of Queensland, and by 1932 had graduated in arts and divinity. In 1941 McKay was recruited by John Flynn for work with the AIM at Cloncurry, instead of traveling to Edinburgh for postgraduate theological study. From 1940 to 1946 he served as an Air Force chaplain, gaining a reputation for unconventionality and sacrificial pastoral work. In 1951 he succeeded Flynn as superintendent of the AIM, expanding its work in a number of new directions, such as the care of the aged, education, and hostels. He worked closely with mining companies and governments in the provision of services to the new mining communities of the 1960s and 1970s, dealing with the frontier as effectively as Flynn had done earlier. McKay was a hands-on leader with great people skills. He worked at a hectic pace and was moderator of the Presbyterian Church in New South Wales, as well as (national) moderator-general (1970–1973). Retiring in 1980, he undertook ministry at St. Stephen's, Sydney, for six years, was twice honored by awards from Queen Elizabeth II, and was further distinguished by having the Art Gallery at Cloncurry named after him in 1988.

Biography by M. McKenzie (1990).

IAN BREWARD

McLaurin, John Bates (1884–1952)

Canadian Baptist missionary. Born in India of missionary parents, he was educated in the United States and Canada, and in 1905 graduated in engineering from McMaster University before studying further at McMaster Divinity School. In 1909 he was accepted by the Canadian Baptists as a missionary to South India. His ministry there among the Telegu-speaking peoples was, according to one source, "remarkably effective." For a time he taught at Ramapatnam Theological Seminary, but he then established the Jeevamruta Seminary in Kakinada. McLaurin strongly advocated turning missionary activities over to nationals at the earliest possible opportunity. He especially felt that Indian nationals should be doing the church's evangelism, not foreigners. He was also critical of the longstanding custom of missionaries living separate from their Indian colleagues, arguing that it created a physical and a social distance between the two groups. Though McLaurin does not appear in most of the biographical sources, he was one of Canada's most important and well-known missionaries between 1900 and 1950. On his return to Canada in 1939 he served as general secretary of the Canadian Baptist Foreign Missions Association until his death. A number of Canadian churches are named in his memory.

Biography by E. C. Merrick (1955).

LESLIE R. KEYLOCK

McNeill, John Thomas (1885–1975)

Church historian. Born on Prince Edward Island, Canada, he was educated at Prince of Wales College, McGill University, Presbyterian College, Montreal, and Westminster Hall (now part of the Vancouver School of Theology), New College, Edinburgh, Halle, Germany, and the Divinity School, University of Chicago. After ordination to the Presbyterian ministry in 1914, he served a pastorate at Chipman, New Brunswick, before becoming lecturer at Westminster Hall, Vancouver (1915–1920). From 1920 to 1922 he lectured at Queen's University, Kingston, and between 1922 and 1927 he was professor at Knox College, Toronto. He was professor of European Christianity at the University of Chicago (1927–1944) and Auburn Professor of Church History at Union Theological Seminary (1944–1953) before retirement in 1953. McNeill was a highly respected lecturer and scholar. Among his many notable achievements is the Library of Christian Classics series and a number of publications, ranging from a history of Celtic churches to studies on Calvinism and a history of Canadian Presbyterianism. Among his primary works are *The Presbyterian Church in Canada, 1875–1925* (1925), *Christian Hope for a World Society* (1937), *Books of Faith and Power* (1947), *History of the Cure of Souls* (1951), *History and Character of Calvinism* (1954), *Modern Christian Movements* (1954), and *Unitive Protestantism* (1964).

In 1960 H. M. Shepherd produced *A Bio-Bibliography of John T. McNeill*.

EDWARD J. FURCHA

McPherson, Aimee Semple (1890–1944)

Founder of the International Church of the Foursquare Gospel. Born in Ingersoll, Ontario, she became a Pentecostalist in 1907 under the preaching of Robert J. Semple, whom she married in 1908 before joining him to do missionary work in China. After his death she returned to North America to work as a preacher of the Full Gospel Assembly. Twice more she entered marriage, on both occasions unhappily. Despite a certain notoriety, she successfully crossed the North American continent nine times before 1923, preaching a mixture of pietism and faith healing. She established in 1927 the International Church of the Foursquare Gospel, which grew into a major Pentecostalist denomination. She founded a Bible college in 1926, set up welfare organizations, and saw her denomination expand to four hundred congregations, despite several lawsuits over her leadership between 1926 and 1936. She suffered a nervous breakdown in 1930, and was later to die reportedly of an overdose. The four pillars of her denomination were: Jesus-Savior, Baptizer by the Holy Sprit, healer of human infirmities, and returning King of kings. In her flamboyant, dramatic preaching style she focused on the love and forgiveness of Christ, and advanced some millenarian notions. In 1920 she was the first woman to preach over the radio, and her organization was the first to purchase an entire radio station (1924). The Foursquare Church has now more than nine thousand congregations in forty-eight countries. Collection 103 at Wheaton College, Illinois, contains important primary sources on her life and work. She published an autobiography in 1927.

Biographies by N. B. Mavity (1931) and Robert Bahr (1979).

EDWARD J. FURCHA

McQuilkin, J. Robertson (1927–)

Missionary, theologian, and college president. Born into a prominent evangelical family with strong mission ties, McQuilkin graduated from Columbia Bible College (B.A., 1947), which his father had founded, and Fuller Theological Seminary (M.Div, 1950). From 1956 to 1968 he was a church-planting missionary in Japan. There he argued for greater sensitivity in relating the gospel to Japanese cultural values. He assumed the presidency of Columbia Bible College and Seminary in 1968. His leadership significantly strengthened Columbia academically, while retaining its traditional interdenominational evangelicalism and vital Christian piety. Among evangelicals Columbia is regarded as a leading missionary training center.

An important evangelical spokesperson and academic, McQuilkin concentrated on the core of the Bible college cirriculum: world evangelization, biblical authority, and the Christian life. Among his works, *Understanding and Applying the Bible* (1983, rev. 1992) and *An Introduction to Biblical Ethics* (1989) are standard college texts. An objectivist in biblical interpretation, he also argues that no biblical teaching may be set aside merely by appeal to cultural conditioning. In recent years, McQuilkin has been widely respected for the consistency of his Christian life. He resigned as president in 1990 to care for his wife, who has Alzheimer's disease. In "Living by Vows," McQuilkin poignantly retells his decision to live by his promise, "till death do us part," and affirms that even these trials have enabled him to "know God and to make Him known."

TIMOTHY R. PHILLIPS

McQuilkin, Robert Crawford, Jr. (1886–1952)

Founder and president of Columbia Bible College and Seminary. Born in Philadelphia, he worked as a clerk and estimator (1903–1911) before studying at the University of Pennsylvania. Meanwhile, under the influence of Charles G. Trumbull, he became associate editor of the *Sunday School Times* (1912–1917). Though he wanted to be a missionary to Africa, World War I prevented his aspirations from being fulfilled. Already in 1913 he had begun a series of victorious life conferences, so he poured himself into them and gave them their strong missions emphasis. By 1923 he and several supporters turned the conference ministry into Columbia Bible College, and he became its president until his death at the Ben Lippen Conference Center and Ben Lippen Boys School, near Asheville, North Carolina, which he had also founded.

Biography by Marguerite McQuilkin (1955).

LESLIE R. KEYLOCK

Mears, Henrietta Cornelia (1890–1963)

Christian educator and publisher. Born in Fargo, North Dakota, Mears grew up in Minneapolis, Minnesota, where she began teaching Sunday school at age twelve. She overcame severe nearsightedness to complete a degree in education at the University of Minnesota and worked for several years as a high school teacher. In 1928 Mears accepted a position as director of Christian education at the First Presbyterian Church of Hollywood, California. During her first two and one-half years of leadership, the Sunday school enrollment increased dramatically from 450 to over 2,400 and eventually averaged over 6,000. Mears was, however, disturbed by the dearth of quality material available for Christian education. In 1933 this concern led her to found Gospel Light Publications, which eventually became one of the largest publishers of biblically-based literature for Sunday schools. Mears also established the Forest Home Camp Grounds as a youth center in the late 1930s and was a cofounder of the National Sunday School Association in 1946. A gifted speaker and Bible teacher, she is particularly remembered for her influence on the thousands of young people who attended her programs, including many who became missionaries and others, such as Bill Bright and Richard Halverson, who became influential Christian leaders.

Biography by E. M. Baldwin and David Benson (1966).

ALAN SEAMAN

Men', Aleksandr Vladimirovich (1935–1990)

Russian Orthodox priest. Born in Moscow, he was brought up in a Christian family. As a young man he decided to enter the Orthodox priesthood, and was ordained in 1963. From that time until his death, he ministered in the Moscow diocese. Men' was a man of wide interests and deep culture, at a time when such people were very rare in the Russian Orthodox priesthood. He developed a significant ministry among students and intellectuals, to whom he constantly emphasized the deeply Christian roots of Russian culture. This made him highly unpopular with many Communist party officials, as well as with their collaborators inside the church hierarchy. There is a lingering suspicion that some of these elements may have had a hand in his murder, on the way to a church service, on September 9, 1990. Men' combined a conservative, orthodox theology with a contemporary and ecumenical approach in the spirit of Vladimir Solov'yov (1853–1900), a great Russian thinker who provided him with a model and inspiration for his own work.

Men' lectured and wrote extensively, but most of his works were either published abroad or remained in manuscript form. Only since his death and the change of political regime in Russia has it been possible to edit and publish his writings freely. His most important work is a six-volume history of human spirituality.

GERALD BRAY

Mendoza, Vicente (1875–1955)

Mexican pastor, educator, editor, and hymnwriter. Born in Guadalajara, Jalisco, Mexico, Vicente Mendoza Polanco attended a Congregational church as a boy. His father, a linotypist, taught him that trade after the family moved to Mexico City. There he studied in the Seminario Presbiteriano and later in the Instituto Metodista of Puebla. His pastorates included the prestigious "Holy Trinity" on Gante Street in the Federal District where he also served as editor of *El Mundo Cristiano, El Abogado Cristiano,* and *El Evangelista Mexicano.* In his final years he taught in the Centro Evangelico Unido seminary where his preaching and his classes in theology, Romanism, and hymnology made a great impression on his students.

While still a student, he published *Himnos Selectos* for the Sunday school in Emanual Methodist Church of Puebla, a collection of hymns that went through ten editions. Author or translator of many hymns in current usage, Mendoza is both author and composer of the crown jewel in Mexican hymnody, *Jesus es mi Rey soberano* ("Jesus is my sovereign King"), written in 1920 while Mendoza was ministering in California. It appears in both *The United Methodist Hymnal* (1989) and *The Presbyterian Hymnal* (1990) in bilingual versions.

PHILIP BLYCKER

Merton, Thomas (1915–1968)

Monk, mystic, writer, and prophet of nonviolence. Born in France, the son of a New Zealand artist and an American mother, he was educated in the United States, Bermuda, France, and England. At age six he lost his mother, at fifteen his father, and during his teens and early twenties led a sensual but searching life. In 1941 he entered the Cistercian abbey at Gethsemani, Kentucky, was fully professed in 1947, and ordained as priest in 1949.

His spiritual autobiography, *The Seven Storey Mountain* (1948), has been described as the first significant statement by an American writer about monastic spirituality. It became a world best-seller. Merton wrote some sixty books, eight volumes of poetry, and about six hundred articles. His literary productivity was not entirely welcome in an order that emphasized intellectual humility, but Columbia University awarded him its Medal for Excellence in 1963 and Kentucky University gave him the honorary L.D. in 1964. In his latter years Merton became increasingly attracted by Buddhist and Hindu spiritual wisdom, which he felt stressed experience rather than doctrine, but his own faith remained grounded in the personal experience of God in Christ. He vehemently opposed the Vietnam war, the nuclear arms race, and the violation of the rights of African-Americans. He was also critical of some of the effects of modern technology. He became a hermit in 1965 and was accidentally electrocuted on a visit to Bangkok, Thailand.

Biographies by D. Q. McInerny (1974) and Anthony Padovano (1982).

HENRY R. SEFTON

Metaxakis, Meletius E. (1871–1935)

Greek Orthodox leader. Born in Parsa, Greece, he was reared on the island of Crete. He was theologically educated in the School of the Holy Cross in Jerusalem. After various ministries, he was appointed metropolitan of Kitos (Cyprus) in 1910. In 1917 he was elected the new metropolitan of Athens and All-Greece. During this time the church's synod approved the establishment of the church in the United States. After being removed from office in elections during 1920, he maintained claims to his position and took over the work in America. In September 1921 the American archdiocese was formed under his leadership. Saint Athanasious Greek Orthodox Seminary for educating priests was founded by him shortly after this. In November 1921 he was elected ecumenical patriarch and served as the unofficial head of all of the Eastern Orthodox Church. Finally in 1922 the Greek Orthodox archdiocese was officially recognized under his leadership. The remaining decade was one of intense strife as he fought with the royalist bishop, Germanos Troianos, who was sent to organize a rival diocesan structure. In 1930 an agreement was approved at the Lambeth Conference for the reunification of the Greek and Anglican churches. Metaxakis was a man of intense influence and took initiatives to spread the church during his time of leadership. He was viewed as bringing liberal trends into the Greek church as he expanded the church to the West.

FRED R. WILSON

Metzger, Bruce Manning (1914–)

New Testament scholar and Bible translator. Born in Middletown, Pennsylvania, he graduated from Lebanon Valley College, Princeton Theological Seminary, and Princeton University (Ph.D., 1942). He was ordained by the Presbyterian Church USA in 1939. He taught New Testament at Princeton Theological Seminary from 1938 until 1985. Metzger's specialization is New Testament textual criticism, but he has also made numerous contributions in the areas of philology, paleography, and translation. During his distinguished career he has had key roles in many learned bodies, including the presidency of both the Society of Biblical Literature and the *Studiorum Novi Testamenti Societas,* and the chairmanship of the Revised Standard Version and the New Revised Standard Version Bible committees. His numerous works include *An Introduction to the Apocrypha* (1957), *The Text of the New Testament* (1964), *The New Testament: Its Background, Growth, and Content* (1965), *Manuscripts of the Greek Bible* (1981), and *The Canon of the New Testament* (1987).

ROBERT L. MORRISON

Meyendorff, John (1926–1992)

Eastern Orthodox theologian. Born in Neuilly-sur-Seine, France, he was a leading interpreter of Eastern Orthodox Christianity to the English-speaking world. A priest and historical theologian by training, he wrote in the scholarly areas of history and systematic theology, as well as about ecumenical relations and popular church education. His parents left Russia after the 1917 Revolution. He earned a theological degree from the Orthodox Theological Academy of St. Sergius in Paris (1949) and a doctorate from the Sorbonne (1958). In 1959 he was appointed to the faculty of St. Vladimir's Theological Seminary in Crestwood, New York, where he also served as dean from 1984 until shortly before he died. As a churchman, Meyendorff served for more than twenty years as editor of the American newspaper, *The Orthodox Church,* and was the first general secretary of "Syndesmos," the international Orthodox Youth Association. An active ecumenist, he sat on the central committee of the World Council of Churches. He is best known as a scholar of international repute, writing in English, Russian, and French, and lecturing at numerous universities. His publications include *St. Gregory Palamas and Orthodox Spirituality* (1974), *Christ in Eastern Christian Thought* (1975), and *Byzantine Theology: Historical Trends and Doctrinal Themes* (rev. 1987).

STANLEY S. HARAKAS

Meyer, F(rederick) B(rotherton) (1847–1929)

English preacher and writer. A London merchant's son, he graduated from London University in 1869 and became a Baptist pastor. In Leicester he kept a predawn vigil to welcome released prisoners, and established small businesses for unemployed men and boys. In London, prostitutes were converted because "he cares for the likes of us." He organized a campaign that compelled Britain's Home Secretary to ban a boxing contest featuring Jack Johnson and Bombardier Wells. A gripping speaker, he lectured for years under YMCA auspices to hundreds of budding Sunday school teachers. As president of the World's Sunday School Association he once insisted Mrs. Taft join her husband on the platform, and introduced her as the real president of the United States. British statesmen and Anglican bishops regarded him highly and listened to him. In Stockholm the Swedish queen greeted him warmly as an old acquaintance whose books she had read. (More than 5 million copies of his devotional works were published.) Moody and Sankey, stranded in England without sponsors in 1873, were "adopted" by Meyer and a colleague. Meyer spoke regularly at Northfield and Keswick, and traveled widely on all continents, his appeal enhanced by the startling openness with which he shared his inner experiences to help others.

Biographies by A. C. Mann (1929), and by W. Y. Fullerton (1929) who called him "a Christian cosmopolitan, an evangelical opportunist; the world was his parish, and Christ was his life."

J. D. DOUGLAS

Meyer, Lucy Jane Rider (1849–1922)

Methodist deaconess and social worker. Born in New Haven, Vermont, she attended several colleges, including Oberlin (A.B., 1872), Philadelphia Medical School, and Massachusetts Institute of Technology. She was soon writing Sunday school literature. In 1879 she became chemistry professor at McKendree College, Lebanon, Illinois. In 1880 she was awarded the M.A. degree from Oberlin and attended the World Sunday School Convention in London. She was field secretary for the Illinois Sunday School Association (1880–1884). In 1885 she married Dr. Josiah S. Meyer, and started the Chicago Training School for City, Home and Foreign Missions (now part of Garrett-Evangelical Theological Seminary), which prepared students for missions and social work. In 1887 she received her M.D. degree from the Women's Medical College at Northwestern University and helped found a deaconess home for Chicago's poor. Her proposal for the creation of the deaconess order based on the German model was approved by the Methodist Conference in 1888. She became a leader in the movement, edited *The Deaconess Advocate,* and was responsible for founding over forty humanitarian organizations, including a hospital, a children's home, a retirement home, and several boarding schools. She successfully defended herself and the movement against attempts of the Methodist Church to take over her work. In 1904 she was among the first women to be seated at a Methodist general conference. Her writings include *Deaconesses: Biblical, Early Church, European, American* (1889), *Deaconess Stories* (1900), and a novel, *Mary North* (1903).

ALBERT H. FREUNDT, JR.

Miguez Bonino, Jose (1924–)

Protestant liberation theologian. Born in Santa Fe, Argentina, he graduated from the Facultad Evangelica de Teologia in Buenos Aires (1948), Emory University (1952), and Union Theological Seminary (Th.D., 1960). He was ordained as a Methodist minister in 1948, and has pastored churches in the Buenos Aires area. He combines a strong piety with a concern for the poor and oppressed. Despite the fall of the Berlin Wall, Miguez believes there can be a Latin American socialism, and uses some of the Marxist categories for social analysis, though he rejects Marxism as a holistic Weltanschauung. His now classic work, *Doing Theology in a Revolutionary Situation,* served as a starting point for an international dialogue on liberation theology. His dozen other books and many articles, some translated from Spanish into other languages, reflect his social commitment, call for an orthopraxis of love and justice, and demand that the denunciation of socioeconomic injustices be amply voiced and heard. Miguez has been active with human rights groups in Argentina and in theological consultations, and in 1974 was elected as a president of the World Council of Churches. He was the only Latin American Protestant observer at Vatican II. He has spent much of his life teaching theology at the Protestant Institute for Higher Theological Education in Buenos Aires, along with visiting professorships in Europe and the Americas.

ARNOLDO CANCLINI
GUILLERMO MENDEZ

Milingo, Emmanuel (1930–)

Roman Catholic archbishop and spiritual healer. Born in eastern Zambia, he was ordained to the priesthood in 1958. Three or four years after his appointment as archbishop of Lusaka in 1969, Milingo discovered that he had a gift of healing. It quickly became obvious as he exercised the gift that he was touching an area of great need in his native country; his healing services were received "as if they were the one thing the people had been waiting for." His increasing popularity among some was matched by mounting and sustained opposition from others, especially those within the Catholic hierarchy. He was reported to Rome through the Apostolic Delegate in Lusaka and in 1974 received a message instructing him to cease the healing meetings. He sought to obey the injunction but the people could not be kept away. In 1982 Milingo was summoned to Rome where initially he was kept more or less isolated. However, with papal approval, regular healing services continued to be held there, attended by people from all over Italy. His healing ministry has spread internationally, mainly through charismatic channels. Although no longer resident in Zambia, Milingo's ministry continues to have widespread appeal there and elsewhere on the African continent because he addresses the traditionally recognized categories of spirit and demonic forces that cause alienation and sociospiritual disruption (exorcism has characterized much of his healing ministry). He advocates an integrated, all-embracing spirituality. Compelled to relocate in Italy, his ministry has received widespread recognition and impetus from the international charismatic community who share many of Milingo's own emphases. He has written *The World in Between: Christian Healing and the Struggle for Spiritual Survival* (edited with introduction, commentary, and epilogue, by Mona Macmillan, 1984). Milingo has also authored many pamphlets, some in English, the majority in Italian.

GORDON MOLYNEUX

Mills, Benjamin Fay (1857–1916)

Prominent advocate of the social gospel. Born in Rahway, New Jersey, he graduated from Lake Forest University and served as minister of Congregational churches in Minnesota, New York, and Vermont. From 1886 to

1897 he was an evangelist before joining the Unitarians. After four years, however, he returned to work with the Los Angeles Fellowship (1904–1911) and the Chicago Fellowship (1911–1916) under Presbyterian auspices. The earlier denominational shift marked a change in theological emphasis away from his Presbyterian roots to a universalized religion in which the Bible was not seen by him as the sole authority in matters of faith. Disillusionment with universal principles of religion and with the effectiveness of socially oriented organizations led Mills back to the moderate position of Presbyterians. He based his independent fellowship groups on "absolute trust as the fixed attitude of the mind and perfect love as the unvarying practice of life." His major publications were *Powers from on High* (1890), *Twentieth Century Religion* (1898), and *The Divine Adventure* (1905).

EDWARD J. FURCHA

Mindszenty, Jozsef (1892–1975)

Hungarian cardinal implacably opposed to communism. Born in Csehimindszent into a family of farmers and wine growers, he became active in the Catholic youth movement, was ordained to the priesthood in 1915, and served as vicar at Felsopaty. Although theologically conservative, he was politically radical, and this led to his imprisonment by the Communists in 1919. In subsequent years he worked diligently against the incarceration of Jews by the Nazis, suffering hardship and imprisonment during the military rule of Horthy as a result. He was made cardinal, prince bishop of Hungary, and archbishop of Esztergom by Pius XII, and in 1947 attended the Marian Congress in Ottawa, Canada. After years of house arrest and embassy exile in Budapest, during which time he became a symbol of corporate suffering for the people of Hungary, Mindszenty went into permanent exile in 1971. His removal from the office of archbishop of Esztergom was made public in 1974 against his express wish. His autobiographical *Recollections* (1974) tries to set the record straight about conditions in communist prisons.

EDWARD J. FURCHA

Moffatt, James (1870–1944)

Scottish Bible translator. Born in Glasgow and educated there at the university and the Free Church College, he ministered at Dundonald (1896–1907) and Broughty Ferry (1907–1911). He was professor of Greek and New Testament exegesis at Mansfield College, Oxford (1911–1915), and of church history at the United Free Church College, Glasgow (1915–1927), before taking a chair of church history at Union Theological Seminary, New York (1927–1940). While conceding that it is not lost what a friend gets, a prominent fellow minister "could not but grieve at this kind of transatlantic rapacity." Moffatt was involved in the preparation of the Revised Standard Version of the Bible, and wrote extensively, mainly on aspects of biblical crit-

257

icism. Among his works were *The Historical New Testament* (1901), *Presbyterianism* (1928), and *Grace in the New Testament* (1931). He also edited a series of New Testament commentaries. He is, however, best known for his single-handed translation of the Bible (New Testament in 1913, Old Testament in 1924). Though well received, it was based on critical theories that aroused the suspicion of evangelicals and were later virtually abandoned by scholars.

JAMES TAYLOR

Moltmann, Jurgen (1926–)

German theologian. Born in Hamburg, he finished high school, then served in the German army, spending time in England as a prisoner of war. He returned to the study of theology at Göttingen in 1948, and served as vicar and student chaplain in Bremen before becoming lecturer in theology at Göttingen and Wuppertal. He earned a Dr. Theol. degree, taught at the University of Bonn from 1958, and became full professor of systematic theology at Tübingen in 1963. He has lectured widely in Europe and North America, and is the author of numerous books and articles. Among them are *Theology of Hope* (1964), *The Crucified God* (1972), *On Human Dignity* (1984), and *On Creation* (1985).

EDWARD J. FURCHA

Montgomery, Carrie Judd (1858–1946)

Pentecostal writer, social worker, and teacher. Born in Buffalo, New York, she grew up in a pious Episcopal home. As a schoolgirl she suffered a fall that left her an invalid, but she was healed through the ministry of Mrs. Edward Mix, an event that changed the course of her life. Soon afterwards she wrote a book, *The Prayer of Peace* (1880), which both recounted her experience and advocated prayers for physical healing. This was followed by the initial issue of her periodical, *Triumphs of Faith*, which provided a forum for teaching and discussion of common themes of concern to the Pentecostal and Holiness movements, particularly focused on issues of healing, social work, and missions. Judd married a wealthy businessman, George C. Montgomery, who became her partner in a number of Christian social work and missionary enterprises, including the founding of an orphanage and a missionary training school in Oakland, California. She conducted these ministries in close affiliation with the Christian and Missionary Alliance and the Salvation Army. She maintained her connection with these groups, valuing unity and love, even after she prayed for and received the baptism of the Holy Spirit in 1908. She became active in the emerging Pentecostal movement, and became a charter member of the Assemblies of God. She wrote *Under His Wings* (1936).

Biography by C. J. Montgomery (1985).

CARLA C. WATERMAN

Montgomery, Helen Barrett (1861–1934)

Baptist leader and Bible translator. Born in Kingsville, Ohio, Helen Barrett was brought up in a Baptist family in Rochester, New York. She attended Wellesley College (1880–1884) and taught at the Rochester Free Academy and Wellesley Preparatory School. Her marriage to a successful businessman, William A. Montgomery, in 1887 provided her with opportunities to meet leaders in the struggle for women's rights. She organized and taught a women's Bible class in her father's church for many years, and in 1892 was licensed to preach by the congregation. She became the first president of the Women's Educational and Industrial Union, which campaigned for the reform of government, education, and social conditions. When the school board was reorganized, she became its first woman member. She became a leader in the cause of overseas missions, and toured the Far East to see the state of mission there. She became president of the Women's American Baptist Foreign Mission Society (1914), president of the National Federation of Women's Boards of Foreign Missions (1917–1918), and president of the Northern Baptist Convention (today's American Baptist Churches in the USA), thus becoming the first American woman to lead a major denomination. In 1924 her *The Centenary Translation of the New Testament,* one of the first modern translations, was published. She wrote two study books, *Christus Redemptor* (1906) and *Western Woman in Eastern Lands* (1919). Other publications include *Following the Sunrise* (1913), *The Bible and Missions* (1920), *The Story of Jesus* (1927), and *The Preaching Value of Missions* (1931).

ALBERT H. FREUNDT, JR.

Moon, Charlotte (Lottie) Diggs (1840–1912)

Missionary to China. She was born in Albemarle County, Virginia, and taught school in Danville, Kentucky, and Cartersville, Georgia. In 1872 her sister, Edmonia, went to China as one of the first two single women Southern Baptist missionaries; the next year Lottie followed her on the same mission. After some years of depression and loneliness as a teacher to a few girls, she complained to the home board that women should have the same rights as men in mission meetings and in the conduct of evangelistic work. In 1885 she moved to P'ing-tu to begin a difficult work in pioneer evangelism. Her first opportunity to reach Chinese men came in 1887. She established a church, and the first baptisms were administered by an ordained minister in 1887. Within two decades more than a thousand converts had been baptized, and P'ing-tu had become the greatest Southern Baptist evangelistic center in all of China. Moon's time was spent partly in villages doing evangelistic work, partly in Tengchow training missionaries and counseling women. She wrote books that stirred interest in foreign missions among Southern Baptist women, and, on furloughs, spoke to large audiences. She urged women to take the leadership in sponsoring mission work. She started the Women's Christmas Offering, which since 1918 has been named for her, and lived to see many single women missionaries appointed. During the troubled times after the Boxer uprising, followed by epidemics and famine, she organized a relief service. Using the last of her savings and starving herself, she was sent home but died aboard ship at port in Kobe, Japan. In the years that followed, the "Lottie Moon Christmas Offerings" increased into the millions. Her impact on missions was enormous, and today she is known as the "patron saint of Southern Baptist missions."

ALBERT H. FREUNDT, JR.

Moore, George Foot (1851–1931)

American Old Testament scholar. Born in West Chester, Pennsylvania, of Scotch-Irish ancestry, he was educated at Yale, Union Theological Seminary, and Tübingen, and in 1878 was ordained to the Presbyterian ministry at Zanesville, Ohio. He then taught, mainly in the areas of Old Testament and the history of religions, at Andover Theological Seminary (1883–1902), serving also as president (1899–1928), until appointment as professor at Harvard (1902–1928). Moore's erudition was seen in two monumental works. His *History of Religions* (2 vols., 1913–1919) looked at religion as a part of human activity and helped shape the study of religion as a part of "humanities." He focused on "civilized" religion, subscribing to the prevailing assumption of its evolutionary development. His *Judaism in the First Centuries of the Christian Era* (1927–1930) looked at Judaism for its own sake rather than as an antithesis to Christianity—and was criticized for equating rabbinic Judaism with "normative" Judaism, but it is still definitive to a large extent. Moore had earlier established himself as an Old Testament scholar with *A Critical and Exegetical Commentary on Judges* (1895). Through his books, articles, and editorship of the *Harvard Theological Review* he did much to introduce German "scientific" scholarship into the United States.

WONG CHAN KOK

Morgan, George Campbell (1863–1945)

British Bible expositor. Born into a Baptist parsonage in Gloucestershire, he became a teacher though he had no academic training. His great desire was, however, to be a preacher, but he was rejected first by the Salvation Army and then by the Methodists who faulted his trial sermon. He had a crisis of faith after reading works by Huxley and Darwin, but after regaining his spiritual balance he was ordained as a Congregational minister in 1889. He served pastorates in Staffordshire, Birmingham, and London, and was awarded a D.D. degree by Chicago Theological Seminary before he was called to Westminster Chapel (1904–1917). There his lucid and gripping Bible expositions attracted huge crowds to what had been an almost moribund church. "The preacher is not merely asking a congregation to discuss a situation, and consider a proposition, or give attention to a theory," he once declared. "We are out to storm the citadel of the will, and capture it for Jesus Christ." Morgan was also president of Cheshunt College, Cambridge (1911–1917), prominent in the promotion of missions, and a regular speaker at the Northfield Conferences. After some years of itinerant ministry, notably in North America, culminating in a pastorate at Tabernacle Presbyterian Church, Philadelphia (1929–1932), he returned to Westminster Chapel for a second pastoral term (1933–1945), where he was joined in 1938 by D. M. Lloyd-Jones, who was to succeed him. Morgan was credited with over sixty books, including *Discipleship* (1898), *The Crisis of the Christ* (1903), and *Preaching* (1937).

Biography by J. Morgan (1951).

J. D. DOUGLAS

Morling, G(eorge) H(enry) (1891–1974)

Australian Baptist college principal. Born in Sydney he graduated from the university there, trained for the ministry, and taught church history in New South Wales Baptist College where later he became principal (1923–1961). Under him hundreds of men were prepared for the ministry, and in his honor the college was subsequently renamed after him. His balanced, noncontroversial approach was largely responsible for overcoming tensions inherited on assuming office. Influenced by such men as Hudson Taylor and Bishop H. C. G. Moule, Morling sought immediacy in his experience of God, and holiness of life made possible through the work of Christ and applied by the Holy Spirit. He shared his spiritual pilgrimage in a little book, *The Quest for Serenity*. Insisting that theology had to be lived, not merely thought, he emphasized the doctrine and experience of the Holy Spirit and the soul's union with Christ. He was a frequent speaker at Keswick-type conventions. He served terms in the highest offices of Inter-Varsity and the Baptist Union of Australia, and for his "services to religion" he was made an officer of the Order of the British Empire (OBE) by Queen Elizabeth in 1963.

E. R. ROGERS

Morris, George Frederick Bingley (1884–1965)

Bishop of the Church of England in South Africa (CESA). Born in Edinburgh he graduated from Cambridge and joined the Africa Inland Mission, of which he later became field director in the Congo and West Nile Uganda. He was then missionary in Morocco and rector of a parish in southwestern England before consecration by Archbishop William Temple as bishop in North Africa. In 1954 he resigned to become bishop of the CESA which, according to Archbishop of Canterbury Geoffery Fisher, put him "outside the fellowship of the Anglican Communion" that in South Africa recognized only the Church of the Province (CPSA). A godly man who never lost his strong evangelicalism, Morris carried on his ministry despite CPSA hostility and the sometimes unguarded utterances of Dr. Fisher whose successor, A. M. Ramsey, insisted on "reordaining" a CESA clergyman. To ensure the continuance of episcopal ministrations in the CESA, Morris in 1959, acting alone, consecrated the Australian Stephen Bradley who carried on the work after Morris died. Australian bishops in 1984 took the imaginative step of consecrating Dudley Foord for service in the CESA, thus taking a step toward healing a division that had lasted since the latter nineteenth century.

J. D. DOUGLAS

Morris, Lelia Naylor (1862–1929)

American hymnwriter and composer. She was born in Pennsville, Ohio. Christian conversion in her early youth resulted in deep convictions by which she sought to live. After marriage to Charles H. Morris in 1881 she became an active worker with her husband in the Methodist Episcopal Church. A decade into her marriage, she became interested in using her literary and musical gifts to write gospel songs, especially as she and her husband visited and assisted in Holiness camp meetings throughout the East. A quiet and reserved housewife, her hymn writing often took place as she went about her daily housework with writing materials handy in her kitchen for moments of inspiration. Her attitudes toward writing and life were closely associated. For her, a noble life was a prerequisite for writing noble poetry.

In 1913, in the prime of her life, Morris became blind. Yet she continued her ministry of hymn writing with the help of family and friends. She wrote more than one thousand hymn texts, as well as numerous tunes. Many of her hymns rank with the compositions of Fanny Crosby and Frances Ridley Havergal. Some of her more well-known compositions include "Nearer, Still Nearer," "Sweeter as the Years Go By," "What If It Were Today?" and "Stranger of Galilee."

FLORENCE SCOTT

Morris, Leon Lamb (1914–)

Australian Anglican biblical scholar. Born in Lithgow, New South Wales, he was educated at Sydney University and Sydney Teachers' Training College, and later earned degrees at London and Cambridge (Ph.D.) universities. After three years of teaching, he was made deacon in 1938 and ordained priest in 1939, serving in the diocese of Sydney and then as a

Bush Church Aid missioner at Minnipa, South Australia. He was vice principal of Ridley College, Melbourne (1945–1960), warden of Tyndale House, Cambridge (1961–1963), and thereafter principal of Ridley College until retirement in 1979. During those years as principal and in retirement he often lectured abroad, chiefly in the United States, but also in Latin America, South Africa, and a number of Asian countries. Much of his writing and preaching has focused attention on the atonement. Preaching has always been of paramount importance to Morris, and in theological training for the ministry he has laid particular emphasis on this and on the importance of the minister's pastoral care of his people. His own deep concern for the needy is evidenced in his being largely instrumental in setting up the Evangelical Alliance Relief Fund (TEAR) in Australia. A prolific author, perhaps his most significant publications have been *The Apostolic Preaching of the Cross* (1955), *Commentary on the Gospel of John* (1971), *Theology of the New Testament* (1986), *The Epistle to the Romans* (1988), and *Commentary on the Gospel of Matthew* (1993).

DAVID J. WILLIAMS

Morrison, Charles Clayton (1874–1966)

Minister, editor, author, and lecturer. Born in Harrison, Ohio, he was the son of Hugh Morrison, an ordained minister of the Disciples of Christ Church. He graduated from Drake University in 1898, and the University of Chicago, where he was a fellow in philosophy from 1902 to 1905. In 1892 Morrison was ordained in the ministry of the Disciples of Christ Church, after which he held pastorates in both Iowa and Illinois. As editor of *The Christian Century*, Morrison addressed many of the controversial issues of his day. He advocated isolationism and pacifism in World War II, and continually addressed the social agenda of the ecumenical movement, trying to resolve theological and ecclesiastical issues within the universal church. *The Christian Century* is considered by some to be the leading nondenominational journal of Protestant opinion in this century. Morrison aggressively took up the ecumenical banner of his denomination in 1949, when he and thirty-five other Protestant officials drafted the "Greenwich" or "Morrison" plan, proposing to create a unified Protestant church. Earlier, Morrison had denounced the revival meetings led by William "Billy" Sunday because, according to him, they lacked any lasting impact on personal piety. Morrison also attacked those who were preoccupied with social reforms alone because he believed such action lacked true theological content. Morrison wrote several books including *The Meaning of Baptism* (1914), *The Daily Altar* (with Herbert L. Willett, 1918), *The Outlawry of War* (1927), *What Is Christianity* (1940), and *Can Protestantism Win America?* (1942).

DAVID P. CAMERA

Morrison, Henry Clay (1857–1942)

Methodist evangelist and educator. Born in Bedford, Kentucky, he was orphaned at an early age. After graduating from Vanderbilt University he was ordained to the ministry of the Methodist Episcopal Church, South, in 1885. After 1897 he functioned as a general evangelist holding camp meetings. In 1910, after a preaching trip around the world, he was named president of Asbury College, Wilmore, Kentucky, which he served until 1925, and from 1933 to 1940. In 1923 he was instrumental in the foundation of Asbury Theological Seminary, and served as its president until his death. He was a representative of optimistic premillennialism and an ardent supporter of the doctrine of entire sanctification. He was the very embodiment of a nineteenth-century frontier revivalist or politician, like the Kentuckian for whom he was named. From 1889 he founded and edited *The Kentucky Methodist,* which was renamed *Pentecostal Herald* and which he continued to edit from 1895.

CLYDE CURRY SMITH

Morton, John (1839–1912)

Canadian Presbyterian missionary. Born in Pictou county, Nova Scotia, to Scottish immigrant parents, Morton was educated at the Presbyterian Free Church College in Halifax and ordained as pastor of a parish in Bridgewater, Nova Scotia, in 1861. On a visit to the West Indies for his health he became concerned for the plight of thousands of East Indian indentured laborers who were brought to work on sugar plantations after the abolition of slavery. He volunteered to the Synod of the Maritimes for a mission among this people. With his arrival in 1868, the Canadian Presbyterian Mission to the East Indians in Trinidad was founded, and he led it until his death. Ninety percent of the East Indians were illiterate and could not speak English; Morton and his wife thus had to learn Hindi and Urdu. With the arrival of other missionaries the work expanded to Guyana, St. Lucia, Grenada, and Jamaica; by 1873 there were twelve schools in operation. The first native ordination took place in 1882, and many of those trained in the schools became civic leaders. Morton's approach to mission effectively combined evangelism and education; he started day schools and training leadership in a teachers' college and a theological college, both of which he established. The result of his ministry was a continuing viable mission and small but self-supporting churches. By 1925 in Trinidad alone there were 101 places of worship and almost 12,000 members.

ALBERT H. FREUNDT, JR.

Mott, John R. (1865–1955)

"Father of the modern ecumenical movement." Born in Sullivan County, New York, and brought up in Iowa, Mott was converted while a student at

Cornell, and in 1888 began a forty-three-year association with the YMCA. One of the founders of the World Student Christian Federation (1895), Mott was to travel 2 million miles enthusiastically, and always knew what he was about. His motto: "With God anywhere, without Him, not over the threshold." On every continent he established an extraordinary rapport with students and church leaders, and was often honored and consulted by heads of state. At thirty-two he was hailed as "Protestantism's leading statesman." At thirty-five he was accused of setting a timetable for God in his best-known book, *The Evangelization of the World in This Generation.* At forty-five he was chairman of the 1910 Edinburgh Assembly (he requested members to *"applaud concisely"*). At fifty-eight he was hailed as "father of the young people of the world" by a Japanese Christian leader.

When Mott declined high academic office, Woodrow Wilson declared, "Mr. Mott occupies a certain spiritual presidency in the spiritual university of the world." Wilson nonetheless tried unsuccessfully to persuade Mott to become ambassador to China, but Mott agreed to join his government's (Root) Mission to Russia in immediate post-revolutionary days. In 1946 Mott shared the Nobel Peace Prize; in 1948 he was the first speaker at the Amsterdam Assembly where he was made honorary president of the newly formed World Council of Churches. Despite Methodist antecedents, Mott always hung loosely to denominational loyalties. C. H. Hopkins places him on "the evangelical side of the social gospel."

John R. Mott (the middle name "Raleigh" was the fiction of an eleven-year-old) wrote many books, including, *The Decisive Hour of Christian Missions* (1910), *The World's Student Christian Federation* (1920), *Liberating the Lay Forces of Christianity* (1932), and *The Larger Evangelism* (1944).

See *Addresses and Papers* (6 vols., 1946–1947). Biographies by Basil Matthews (1934) and C. H. Hopkins (1979).

J. D. DOUGLAS

Mottesi, Alberto H. (1942–)

Latin American evangelist. Born in Buenos Aires, he studied there both at the university and at the Baptist International Theological Seminary. He was ordained to the ministry at the age of nineteen, and founded a church that he pastored for eleven years. After serving with Evangelism in Depth in Chile, and as associate evangelist with Paul Finkenbinder (Hermano Pablo), in 1977 he established the Alberto Mottesi Evangelistic Association, based in southern California, and began a ministry to the entire Hispanic world. He has held campaigns in most of the Spanish-speaking countries. His daily radio program, "Usted y Alberto Mottesi" ("You and Alberto Mottesi") is carried on seven hundred stations, and earned him the "Golden Mike" award from the NRB. He also holds leadership seminars that annually attract over ten thousand pastors and lay leaders. Mottesi was president of "Los Angeles '88," a continent-wide Hispanic church congress, and currently heads Partnership 2000, the Latin American arm of the A.D. 2000 movement.

During 1992 he held a series of 29 "presidential breakfasts" and similar meetings throughout Latin America, attended by key political and civic leaders, including in most cases the president and cabinet members, in connection with the five-hundredth anniversary of Columbus's arrival in the New World. Mottesi wrote a book on "America 500 years later" that was distributed by two governments to all their public school teachers. He has also written eight other books, all in Spanish.

STEPHEN R. SYWULKA

Moule, Hendley Carr Glyn (1841–1920)

Anglican bishop, academic, and writer. Born in Dorset, son of an evangelical vicar, he was educated at Trinity College, Cambridge, of which he was elected a fellow, and taught school for a short time before ordination in 1867. He then returned to the duties of his fellowship and assisted his aging father in his parish. After his father's death he was appointed first principal of Ridley Hall, Cambridge, in 1881. He pioneered the shape of evangelical ordination training for Cambridge graduates until his election as Norrisian professor of divinity at Cambridge in 1899. In 1901 he became bishop of Durham in succession to J. B. Lightfoot and B. F. Westcott.

Moule's influence on evangelicalism in the Church of England came not only from his teaching but also through his writings. Moule's influence was considerable. It was shaped by his acceptance of the Keswick Convention and its spirituality from 1884 onwards. Moule's works were mainly popular New Testament commentaries and studies of Pauline epistles. His other works were spiritual writings such as *Secret Prayer* (1889) and *The School of Suffering* (1905) or studies of Anglican evangelicalism such as *Charles Simeon* (1892) and *The Evangelical School in the Church of England* (1901).

NOEL S. POLLARD

Mowinckel, Sigmund Olaf Plytt (1884–1965)

Old Testament theologian. Born in Kjerringy, Norway, he studied at the universities of Oslo, Copenhagen, Marburg, and Giessen, and completed his D.Th. at Oslo (1916), where he became professor of Old Testament studies. Several times he was also dean of the theological faculty there. His view of the Old Testament was shaped by considerations for the significance of the cult to Israel's religion. His studies on the psalms and the prophets were particularly significant. He contributed also to the translation of the Bible into Norwegian, and advanced biblical criticism far beyond the boundaries of Norway. Included among his publications are *The Deca-*

logue (1927), *Prophecy and Tradition* (1946), and *The Old Testament as Word of God* (1959, 1960).

EDWARD J. FURCHA

Mowll, Howard West Kilvinton (1890–1958)

Anglican missionary and archbishop. Born in Dover, England, he graduated from Cambridge where he was president of the Inter-Collegiate Christian Union at the time it disaffiliated from the Student Christian movement. Ordained in 1912, he taught at Wycliffe College, Toronto, until his consecration as an assistant bishop (1922) in the diocese of West China where in 1926 he succeeded W. W. Cassels as diocesan. Mowll saw his role as a bridge from old-style missionary administration to Chinese leadership. He was elected archbishop of Sydney in 1933 and primate of the Church of England in Australia, retaining these offices until his death.

Mowll was described as "a vigorous personality, exceptionally tall, a man of iron will and marked administrative ability, with depth of spiritual understanding." Always a decided evangelical leader, inside and outside his own church, he gave impetus to causes such as Scripture Union, Inter-Varsity Fellowship, and China Inland Mission. His twenty-five-year episcopate in Sydney stamped that diocese with an evangelical character similar to that given by his nineteenth-century predecessor Frederic Barker, and reinvigorated every aspect of diocesan life, including Moore College. Conscious of his position as head of a diocese distinctive in the Anglican world, he consistently maintained a dignified traditional churchmanship.

He traveled widely and maintained widespread contacts, and attended the inaugural assembly of the World Council of Churches whose cause he supported in Australia as president of its Australian council. His concern for Asia (he led a delegation to China in 1956 to reestablish links with the church there) had a marked influence on the attitude of Australia to its near neighbors. His personal piety, generous friendship, and large-hearted leadership inspired many. He wrote *Seeing All the World* (1947).

DONALD W. B. ROBINSON

Mulago, Gwa Cikala (Vincent) (1924–)

African theologian and educator. Born near Bukavu in Eastern Zaire, he received his advanced education in Rwanda and in Rome. While in Rome he contributed to the seminal work published in French, *Des Pretres Noirs s'Interrogent*, an early milestone in emerging black African consciousness and theological reflection. He returned to his native Zaire in 1956 and held a succession of appointments in and around Bukavu before becoming in 1962 the first African teacher of the Catholic Faculty of Theology in Kinshasa. He supported Tshibangu in the watershed debate on African theology held at the Faculty in 1968.

Since 1966 Mulago has been director of the Centre d'Etudes des Religions Africaines, a research and documentation center on the campus of the Catholic Faculty in Kinshasa. Its stated task is "the scientific understanding of African religions, beliefs, and customs, both traditional and modern," and seeks to answer Mulago's own rhetorical question, "Can we really hope for the blooming of an African theology as long as we lack an explicit and scientifically organized system of noting and interpreting the African reality?" The importance of CERA is enhanced by its scholarly periodical *Cahiers des religions Africaines*, of which Mulago is editor. Mulago's books and scholarly articles have appeared mostly in the French language, and he has been a frequent speaker at conferences.

GORDON MOLYNEUX

Mullins, Edgar Young (1860–1928)

Baptist educator and theologian. Born in Franklin County, Mississippi, he graduated from Texas A & M (1879), Southern Baptist Theological Seminary (1885), and did further graduate work at Johns Hopkins University (1891–1892). During this time Mullins served in various pastorates and for a short time with the Southern Baptist Foreign Mission Board. Southern Baptist Theological Seminary had been embroiled in controversy for several years when Mullins was elected to be the president in 1899; he remained until his death. Mullins was active in Baptist church life, serving as president of the Southern Baptist Convention and the Baptist World Alliance (1923) and was instrumental in the denomination's adoption of its first-ever creedal statement, a revision of *The New Hampshire Confession* in 1925. He strove for moderation in theological matters, especially as they related to higher critical matters and the relation of science and theology. His moderation has been criticized by some for ultimately allowing liberalism to creep into Southern Baptist circles. He himself was decidedly on the conservative side of the spectrum, a position that only deepened during the fundamentalist-modernist controversy, as is evidenced by his *Christianity at the Crossroads* (1924). A competent scholar, he authored several volumes dealing with then current theological problems, including *Why Is Christianity True?* (1905), *The Axioms of Religion* (1908), *Freedom and Authority in Religion* (1913), *The Christian Religion in Its Doctrinal Expression* (1917), and *Baptist Beliefs* (1912).

Biographies by I. M. Mullins (1929) and W. E. Ellis (1985).

WALTER A. ELWELL

Mundelein, George William (1872–1939)

American cardinal and archbishop of Chicago. Born in New York City, the grandson on both sides of German immigrants, he needed financial assistance to attend Manhattan College. He studied at seminaries in Pennsylvania and Italy and was ordained a priest in Rome in 1895. After serving mainly in administrative posts in Brooklyn, he was appointed archbishop of Chicago in 1915. Mundelein became one of the most influential Catholic leaders of the century. He streamlined the administration of the church (including finances, charities, and construction) and created what was in effect the first diocesan central bank in the United States. His sound management not only supported many building projects, but allowed Chicago to be a major donor to the Vatican, increasing American influence there. Mundelein was a major Chicago civic leader, with close ties to the city's business, political, and social elite. He was a believer in Americanization of immigrants and permitted (except for special cases) only English instruction in Catholic schools. Very early in his administration (1920) he announced the construction of a new institution for the training of priests, St. Mary of the Lake Seminary (popularly called Mundelein Seminary). Rome recognized Mundelein's leadership by elevating him to cardinal in 1924. In 1926 he was the host of the 28th International Eucharistic Congress, the first ever held in the United States and attended by an estimated million people. In the 1930s he was one of the few supporters in the Catholic hierarchy of Franklin Roosevelt's New Deal. He condemned the anti-Semitic broadcasts of Roosevelt critic Father Charles E. Coughlin, and was also outspoken in his attacks on Adolf Hitler. Mundelein was one of several twentieth-century archbishops who gave American Catholics new confidence by expanding the church's power and influence while underlining its support of American institutions.

ROBERT SCHUSTER

Murray, John (1898–1975)

Presbyterian theologian. Born in Sutherland, Scotland, his early loyalties were with the Free Presbyterian Church. While its attitudes were in some ways too rigid for him, Princeton and mainline American Presbyterianism proved too lax when he crossed the Atlantic. Murray joined Gresham Machen in the Orthodox Presbyterian Church in 1930, and taught for thirty-six years at its new Westminster Theological Seminary. A considerable scholar, he never took refuge in that obscurity of language by which some theologians safeguard themselves against challenge. The best Christian teaching, he asserted, advocates piety as much as learning. He was a faithful Sabbath-keeper, a meticulous if not brilliant lecturer, a taker of the gospel to New England townships during vacations, and a champion of the decent and orderly in chairing meetings or in dealing with youthful high spirits. The man who lost an eye in World War II could see right to the heart of an issue; his sermons were models of lucidity and, for a Scottish Calvinist, show a remarkable economy of words. So, too, with his book reviews that pronounced on prominent scholars of his time. His *Principles of Conduct* (1957) and *Commentary on the Epistle to the Romans* (2 vols., 1959, 1965) are still widely used.

Murray's *Collected Writings* (4 vols., 1976–1982) include a 155-page biography by Iain Murray.

J. D. DOUGLAS

Mutchmor, James Ralph (1892–1980)

Canadian pastor and social activist. Born at Providence Bay, Manitoulin Island, Canada, he was educated at the University of Toronto, Columbia University, and Union Theological Seminary, New York. He was ordained in 1920, and served in Winnipeg until 1936. During the Great Depression he took up the plight of the workers, one of the numerous social issues he was to champion as secretary of the Board of Evangelism and Social Services, the United Church of Canada (1938–1963). He was moderator of the United Church from 1962 until 1964, when he retired from active ministry. In combining the mandate of the gospel for holy living with genuine social concern, Mutchmor became a religious and political force to be reckoned with, and was often referred to as "the last of the ranting old Methodists," though he was Presbyterian in background. "Jim" Mutchmor challenged provincial premiers and prime ministers when he felt that injustice was being perpetrated and he advocated strong measures against the sale of alcohol and other forms of substance abuse. He was one of the first to involve the United Church of Canada in the building and maintaining of senior citizens' homes. For a generation of churchgoers Mutchmor was the voice of the United Church of Canada.

EDWARD J. FURCHA

Muzorewa, Abel Tendekayi (1925–)

Zimbabwean pastor and politician. Born in Umtali (now Mutare), Zimbabwe, he worked as a teacher in Mrewa district (1943–1947), but soon moved into pastoral work (1947–1958; ordained 1953). In 1958 he began studies at the United Methodist College in Fayette, Missouri, where he received his B.A. and then pursued further training at Scarritt Theological College in Nashville, Tennessee (M.A., 1963). Muzorewa returned to his native country (then Rhodesia and still officially a British colony) in 1963, just as it was undergoing a period of dramatic political struggle against the white minority government. After Muzorewa's appointment as bishop in 1968 he joined the political struggle for black majority rule with his election to the African National Council, which opposed the government of prime minister Ian Smith. Muzorewa's political involvement reached its climax in 1978–1979 when he was appointed prime minister of what was then called Zimbabwe-Rhodesia. Though vocal in his call for full political liberation and equally outspoken against the spread of violence, more radical political factions soon toppled his transitional government. In 1983 Bishop Muzorewa was arrested and detained. After his release in 1984 he moved to the United States where he has lectured at Scarritt Theological College. His published works include *Manifesto for African National Council* (1972) and *Rise Up and Walk* (1977).

MARK R. SHAW

N

Nacpil, Emerito P. (1932–)

Methodist bishop and ecumenist. Born in Tarlac, the Philippines, he was admitted to the Methodist ministry in 1951. His career has included pastoral work (1951–1958), various administrative posts within the Philippines, and key positions within the World Council of Churches, of which he has been a strong advocate. He graduated from Union Theological Seminary, Manila, the Philippine Christian University, and Drew University (Ph.D., 1962). He has served as academic dean and president of Union Theological Seminary (Manila) as well as executive director of the Association of Theological Schools in Southeast Asia. He has also been dean of the Southeast Asia Graduate School of Theology (1974–1980). Elected to the episcopate in 1980, 1984, and 1988, he was assigned by the central conference as presiding bishop of the Manila Episcopal Area.

FRANK ALLEN

Nazir-Ali, Michael (1949–)

General secretary to the Church Missionary Society. He was educated in Pakistan. He read economics and sociology at the University of Karachi, and theology at Fitzwilliam College and Ridley Hall, Cambridge. He has carried out research in many areas, including comparative literature and comparative philosophy of religion and theology. He has taught at universities in the United Kingdom and Pakistan. In Pakistan, he taught at Karachi Theological College, was parish priest in a poor urban area, became provost of Lahore Cathedral, and was the first bishop of Raiwind. In 1986 he was appointed to assist with the planning and preparation for the 1988 Lambeth Conference and joined the staff of the archbishop of Canterbury in the United Kingdom. He was editor of the Report and Pastoral Letters of the 1988 Lambeth Conference. He serves as secretary to the Archbishop's Commission on Communion and Women in the Episcopate, as a member of the Anglican and Roman Catholic International Commission, and as chair of the Mission Theological Advisory Group. He was general secretary to the Church Missionary Society, the first person from outside the United Kingdom to be appointed to this position (held since 1989). In 1994 he was consecrated bishop of Rochester, the first Asian to head a diocese in England. His works include *Islam—A Christian Per-*

spective (1983), *Frontiers in Christian-Muslim Encounter* (1987), and *From Everywhere to Everywhere—A World View of Christian Mission* (1991).

PATRICK SOOKHEDO

Nee, Watchman (Nee Shu-Tsu) (1903–1972)

Leader of the "Little Flock." Born in Guangdong, China, he was trained in Chinese classics and Christian studies. His dislike for Christianity caused him to cheat in a Bible examination, for which he was barred entrance into the university. This was the greatest humbling factor for him. At age seventeen he was converted: "I realized the magnitude of my sins and the reality and efficacy of Jesus as the Saviour." As his mission in life became clearer, his name was changed to To-Sheng ("God's watchman"). He was influenced by the writings of renowned Brethren such as J. N. Darby and also by the Holiness and Keswick movements. He published a magazine, *The Christian,* and a three-volume work on sanctification, *The Spiritual Man* (1968). As most of the mainline Protestant churches had not heard of holiness or sanctification in the Christian's life, many Chinese believers were challenged by these publications. Nee also began to establish local centers of worship based on his belief in "one church for one locality." Headquartered in Shanghai, these groups came to be known as "Little Flock."

The political, economic, and spiritual uncertainties in China caused many Christians to leave their own denominations to join these indigenous assemblies. During 1923–1949 there were more than seven hundred assemblies with a membership of seventy thousand. These became the nucleus of the "house-churches" during the communist regime. In 1952 Nee was arrested. After a series of false allegations he was imprisoned. He died in 1972 in prison. His other books include *Sit, Walk, Stand* (1961) and *The Normal Christian Church Life* (1969).

Biography by Angus Kinnear (1973).

B. VIOLET JAMES

Neill, Stephan Charles (1900–1984)

Anglican bishop and missiologist. Born in Edinburgh, he had a brilliant career at Cambridge, culminating in a fellowship at Trinity College. In 1924, however, he turned his back on academic life and went to India as a lay missionary. Although his desire was to communicate the gospel directly in village India, he found himself put in charge of theological training. He was ordained in India, was closely associated with the plans for a united church in South India, and in 1939 became bishop of Tinnevelly. In 1944 he left India, partly because of ill health, and he never thereafter occupied a post that fully matched his abilities. His interest in ecumenism led to a post with the World Council of Churches. In 1960 he went to Germany as professor of mission at Hamburg; in 1965 he was appointed professor of religion at University College, Nairobi. He retired in 1973 and lived his last years in Oxford, where he continued to lecture, write, and serve as an assistant bishop. Among the thirty-one books he wrote were *Anglicanism* (1958), *Christian Mission: A History* (1964), *The Interpretation of the New Testament 1861–1961* (1966), and *The Supremacy of Jesus* (1984).

In the autobiographical *God's Apprentice,* Neill makes no secret of his quick temper, and his problems with insomnia and recurrent depression. Against these handicaps he still became a significant figure in the Christian world, particularly in regard to mission and ecumenism.

PETER S. DAWES

Newbigin, James Edward Lesslie (1909–)

Missionary bishop and theologian. Born in Newcastle upon Tyne and educated at Queens' College, Cambridge, he prepared for ordination at Westminster College, Cambridge. After a short period as a Student Movement secretary he was ordained and in 1936 went as a missionary of the Church of Scotland to India. When the Church of South India was formed he became one of its first bishops. In 1959 he left India to become secretary of the International Missionary Council. He was recalled to India to become bishop of Madras in 1965. On his return he lectured at Selly Oak Colleges in Birmingham. In 1978–1979 he was Moderator of the United Reformed Church. In 1980 he became a minister of the URC in Birmingham, England.

Newbigin's writings cover many subjects, reflecting his interest in mission, ecclesiology, and apologetics. His earlier writings include *The Household of God* (1953) and *Honest Religion for Secular Man* (1966). More recently he has written *Foolishness to the Greeks* (1986) and *The Gospel in a Pluralist Society* (1989). His thinking and his books are a prime source of the movement in Britain called "The Gospel and Our Culture," which is designed to promote a missionary encounter with contemporary culture.

NOEL S. POLLARD

Newman, Albert Henry (1852–1933)

Church historian, author, and teacher. Born in Edgefield County, South Carolina, he early proved proficient in Latin and Greek, entered Mercer University as a junior, and graduated first in his class in 1871. He entered Rochester Theological Seminary in 1872, majoring in Hebrew and the Old Testament, and graduated in 1875. He spent a further year at Southern Baptist Theological Seminary, studying with C. H. Troy, Abraham Yeager, and J. A. Broadus. Newman's excellent linguistic preparation proved invaluable when he succeeded his church history professor at Rochester. Although church history was not his "first love, it became his true love." It was not, however, the only subject he taught in a career of more than fifty years in eight institutions in the United States and Canada. He was largely responsible for designing the curricula of both McMaster University and Southwestern Baptist Theological Seminary.

International acclaim came to Newman from the quality of his writings. Among his major books were *A History of the Baptist Churches in the United States* (1894, rev. 1915), *A Manual of Church History* (2 vols., 1899, 1902, which went through twenty-four printings), and (editor and author) *A Century of Baptist Achievement* (1901). He contributed to numerous encyclopedias in both English and German, and his work generally established him as the foremost Baptist church historian of his generation.

Biographies by Frederick Eby (1958) and W. G. J. Jonas, Jr. (1992).

W. R. Estep

Nicholson, William Pattesson (1876–1959)

Irish evangelist. Born near Bangor, Northern Ireland, son of a Merchant Navy captain, he left his Belfast school early, and at age fifteen went to sea as an apprentice. It was a rough life that he exchanged for one just as rough: as a member of a South African railway construction gang. Back in his mother's strongly Presbyterian home in Belfast in 1899, he was suddenly convicted of sin and made his decision for Christ. After studying at the Bible Training Institute in Glasgow (1901–1903), he was appointed as an evangelist by the Lanarkshire Christian Union (1903–1908), and joined Chapman and Alexander in their missions in Australia and North America (1908–1910). Later returning to America, he settled with his family in Pennsylvania, was ordained as an evangelist in the Presbyterian Church in the USA (1914), and soon afterwards joined the extension staff of the Bible Institute of Los Angeles.

He returned to Ireland in 1920, and became known for a series of missions that brought thousands into the kingdom—and this at a time when intercommunal strife in Ulster had reached a serious stage. The press described how one Saturday afternoon seven thousand converts marched through the streets of Belfast, while a friendly source called him "the best loved and most hated man in Ulster." In 1926 he seemed an incongruous last-minute substitute at Cambridge University for a missioner who had been taken ill, but about a hundred students professed conversion. In his latter years he preached on four continents, and died just before he settled for retirement in his native Bangor.

J. D. Douglas

Nicoll, William Robertson (1851–1923)

Scottish minister, journalist, and editor. Born in Aberdeenshire, son of a Free Church of Scotland minister, he graduated from the University of Aberdeen, and after theological studies was ordained in 1874. He served Free Church congregations in Dufftown (1874–1877) and Kelso

(1877–1885), but ill health led to his resignation from the ministry. In London he became editor of *The Expositor* (1885) and *The British Weekly* (1886), holding both posts until his death. The latter paper under his leadership became a journal of national influence, especially during World War I. He was a strong critic of modern literature, and took a prominent part in social reform and politics. Knighted by King Edward VII (1909), he was made a Companion of Honour by King George V (1921). Nicoll also edited *The Bookman, The Expositor's Bible, The Expositor's Greek Testament,* and the complete works of Emily Bronte. Among his own religious volumes were *The Lamb of God* (1883), *The Return to the Cross* (1897), *Reunion in Eternity* (1918), and *Princes of the Church* (1921).

Nicoll's *Life and Letters* was edited by T. H. Darlow (1925).

JAMES TAYLOR

Nida, Eugene Albert (1914–)

Linguist and Bible translation scholar. Born in Oklahoma, Nida studied classical languages and linguistics in California and received the Ph.D. from the University of Michigan in 1943. He was ordained as a Baptist minister in 1943, but has spent his whole life in the service of Bible translation. He taught at the Summer Institute of Linguistics (1937–1953), and from 1943 to 1980 was executive secretary for translations with the American Bible Society, spending long periods in overseas travel connected with Bible translation. Since 1981 he has been a consultant for the United Bible Societies. As a linguist, his most important contribution has probably been making N. Chomsky's "generative-transformational grammar" accessible to national Bible translators (in *Towards a Science of Translating*). This has enabled the production of modern "dynamic equivalence translations" of the Bible. He has also made considerable contributions to the componential analysis of meaning. His books and articles on these topics together with a number of commentaries on Old Testament and New Testament books designed for translators, are in constant use around the world. His works include *Towards a Science of Translating* (1964), and (with C. R. Taber) *The Theory and Practice of Translation* (1974), *Meaning across Cultures* (1981), and (with Jan de Waard) *From One Language to Another* (1986).

JOCELYN MURRAY

Niebuhr, (Helmut) Richard (1894–1962)

Neo-orthodox theologian and minister in the Evangelical and Reformed Church. After studies at Elmhurst College, Eden Theological Seminary, and Yale University (Ph.D., 1924), he served as pastor, president of Elmhurst (1924–1927), and professor of Christian ethics at Yale Divinity School (1931–1962). With his more activist elder brother, Niebuhr is credited with the development of an American neo-orthodoxy that was more socially oriented than its European counterpart. Niebuhr stressed the transcendence of God over all other being or value. Sin results from the denial of God's sovereignty and the substitution of another at the center of value. Niebuhr emphasized the communal dimension of the Christian life: revelation has meaning only in a community of memory and interpretation. Faith was also relative, a relativism of personal context; thus Niebuhr resisted the formulating of universal categories in theological method. Niebuhr's published work concentrated mainly on the relationship of Christians to their society. *The Social Sources of Denominationalism* (1929) applied sociological categories of Weber and Troeltsch to American Protestantism, and attacked the complacency of denominations in embracing bourgeois values. It was balanced by a more appreciative study, *The Kingdom of God in America* (1937), which called for the restoration of Reformation roots in America and a recovery of the Puritan prophetic voice that set the church against the world. His best-known book, *Christ and Culture* (1951), explored five Christian approaches to culture, sympathizing most with the model of "Christ the Transformer of Culture." His final book, *Radical Monotheism and Western Culture* (1960), was in many respects a modern appropriation of Jonathan Edwards, arguing that true virtue was not in bettering oneself but in the love of Being generally considered.

JOHN R. MUETHER

Niebuhr, (Karl Paul) Reinhold (1892–1971)

Pastor, educator, and author. Born in Wright City, Missouri, he was the son of an immigrant pastor of the Evangelical and Reformed Church (now United Churches of Christ). He graduated from Elmhurst College, Eden Theological Seminary, Yale Divinity School, and Yale University. After ordination he was pastor of the Bethel Evangelical Church in Detroit (1915–1928), which greatly shaped his future thought, causing him to become a critic of capitalism and an advocate of socialism. He became convinced that business always tends to defraud the worker. He promoted the unions as a means to justice for the worker. In 1928 he joined the faculty of Union Theological Seminary in New York, and remained there until retirement in 1960. During this time he became a powerful intellectual, Christian, and social influence. He ran for political office several times on the socialist ticket, wrote about democracy, and helped shape a public philosophy. He became a founding member of Americans for Democratic Action. In the 1930s he abandoned pacifism to oppose Hitler, trying to persuade the Protestant church that military intervention was necessary. After World War II he supported the Cold War containment policy of resistance to Soviet expansion.

A neo-orthodox theologian, he advocated "Christian Realism." He noted the persistent roots of sin and evil in all people at every level, so he emphasized justice rather than love as the goal of Christianity in society. He was convinced that liberal churchmen in their effort to bring biblical values to bear on society were not tough enough to confront and contend with evil in the real world. The state could balance matters by serving as the ultimate power broker and the actual or potential moral guarantor, responsible to reform society. Yet a balance of power between contending classes or factions would be essential for the effective operation of democratic government, resulting in a rough or imperfect justice.

His books included *Does Civilization Need Religion?* (1927), *Moral Man and Immoral Society* (1932), and *The Nature and Destiny of Man* (2 vols., 1941, 1943). He also founded and edited *Christianity and Crisis* (1941–1966).

Biographies by R. H. Stone (1972), R. Harries (1986), and R. W. Fox (1986).

LUDER G. WHITLOCK, JR.

Niemoeller, Martin (1892–1984)

German Lutheran pastor and political activist. Born into a Westphalian pastor's family, he was sensitized to the needs of the victims of the industrial age by his father's involvement in social issues. After cadet training he was commissioned as a navy officer and commanded a submarine in World War I. He then studied for the ministry and after ordination in 1924 worked for the Inner Mission, a social service agency. In 1931 he became pastor in Berlin-Dahlem, where after Hitler's rise to power he was embroiled in conflict with the pro-Nazi "German Christians" who tried to seize control of the Protestant church. In 1933 he formed the Pastors' Emergency League to resist anti-Jewish laws in the church. He had part also in the formation of the "Confessing Church," which upheld traditional beliefs and rejected doctrinal innovations. His attacks on the nazification of the church and "Aryan" racial doctrines led to his arrest in 1937. A Berlin court acquitted him, but Hitler ordered him confined in Sachsenhausen concentration camp as his "personal prisoner." His international reputation persuaded the Nazis that it was more expedient to keep him alive. He was moved to Dachau (1941– 1945), whence he was rescued by American soldiers. After World War II controversy swirled around him for his advocacy of disarmament and nuclear pacifism, and for his insistence that German Protestants should accept some responsibility for Nazi evils. He served as leader of the Hesse-Nassau church (1947–1964) and as a presidium member of the World Council of Churches (1961–1968). His best-known book was *From U-Boat to Pulpit* (1936).

Biography by James Bentley (1984).

RICHARD V. PIERARD

Nikodim, (Boris Georgyevich Rotov) (1929–1978)

Metropolitan of Leningrad. Born near Ryazan in Soviet Russia, son of an atheist father and an apparently believing mother, he was secretly baptized as a teenager, served as an altar boy, and was debarred from further secular education when his Christian beliefs became known. He became a monk in 1947, but after ordination in 1949 he engaged in parish work and in further studies. He rose swiftly in the ranks of the Orthodox Church, and by 1957 was heading its mission in Jerusalem. At a time of fierce religious persecution he took over the key post of chairman of the Department of Foreign Relations in the patriarchate of Moscow. Questions were asked about his true relationship with the communist government when he denied that the church was not free. During his chairmanship (1960–1972) he became bishop at thirty-one, metropolitan at thirty-three. Nikodim led the Russian Orthodox Church into the World Council of Churches in 1961, and served a term as one of the latter's six presidents. His ecumenicity extended also to the Roman Catholic Church; he originated an encyclical in 1969 that permitted Roman Catholics to participate in confession and communion at the hands of Orthodox priests, leading Rome to participate in kind. Nikodim collapsed and died during a Vatican audience with Pope John Paul I.

J. D. DOUGLAS

Niles, Daniel Thambirajah (1908–1970)

Sri Lankan Methodist minister and ecumenical leader. Born near Jaffna, northern Sri Lanka, he was active in the Student Christian Movement (SCM) and later became chairman of its international body, the World Student Christian Federation. He preached at the first assembly of the World Council of Churches in Amsterdam (1948) and at the fourth assembly in Uppsala (1968) where he was elected one of the WCC's presidents. A founder of the East Asia Christian Council, he edited its *Hymnal* to which he contributed forty-five hymns. A brilliant thinker and author of over twenty books, his writings express his attempts to be biblical and his commitment to a warm, experiential faith and to Christian mission. His emphasis on the universality of grace caused him to speak of the "previousness" of Christ's activity in people before they heard the gospel, and made him refuse to answer the question of whether all humanity will be saved. His writings may have paved the way for more radical departures by other Asians from the traditional views regarding the uniqueness of Christianity. Niles played a major role in shaping the direction of the church in Sri Lanka, especially the Methodist Church of which he was president at the time of his death. Prominent among his writings was *Upon the Earth* (1962).

AJITH FERNANDO

279

Nisiotis, Nicholas (Nikos) A. (1924–1986)

Greek Orthodox ecumenist and systematic theologian. Born the son of a University of Athens professor, he graduated in 1947 from the University of Athens School of Theology. He then studied in Zurich, Basel, and Louvain in the field of systematic theology, establishing lifelong ecumenical contacts and earning a doctorate from the University of Athens (1965). In 1948 he was elected as the first vice president of the World Council of Churches Christian Youth movement. In 1958 he was appointed codirector of the Ecumenical Institute at Bossey, Switzerland. He was made the permanent representative-observer of the WCC at Vatican II, and at the Pan-Orthodox Consultation in Rhodes in 1961 and 1962. In addition to teaching regularly at Bossey, he served on the faculties of the universities of Geneva and Athens. A prolific author, he wrote in the fields of philosophical theology, systematic theology (especially with reference to ecumenical thought), and missiology, as well as on general theological issues. His most important contribution was the long-term development of the Faith and Order studies in baptism, Eucharist, and ministry, through which many historical Christian traditions were reintroduced into ecumenical theological discussions.

STANLEY S. HARAKAS

Nommensen, Ludwig Ingwer (1834–1918)

Missionary to Sumatra. Born on the (then Danish) island of Nordstrand, he enrolled in the Barmen Mission School in 1857, and in 1861 went to Sumatra (in modern Indonesia) where he directed the recently reestablished Batak mission for over fifty years. His work there was enhanced by his determination to live simply, some medical skills, and his acquisition of the Batak language. He translated Luther's Catechism, the New Testament, and selected portions of the Old Testament into Batak, and wrote numerous hymns. He initiated native teachers' training in 1875, and the first theological school in Sumatra (1883) was named after him. In 1861 he helped create a church order by which congregations were joined in an association under his general supervision. Since 1940 the mission has become an independent denomination.

EDWARD J. FURCHA

Nunez, Emilio Antonio (1923–)

Latin American theologian, writer, and educator. Born in El Salvador of proletarian parents, he became a school teacher. In 1944, shortly after his conversion, he moved to Guatemala for his initial theological studies. By 1947 he had begun teaching in his alma mater, the Central American Bible Institute, Guatemala. He pioneered evangelical radio ministries, and launched a Christian school to assist children of poor evangelical pastors.

Nunez graduated from Southern Methodist University (1964) and Dallas Theological Seminary (1964; Th.D., 1969) and resumed teaching in Guatemala where he was elected dean and later rector (president). He resigned those tasks in 1979 in order to dedicate himself to teach, write, and mentor scores of younger Latin Christian leaders. In addition to other leadership contributions he wrote six books in Spanish, and in English *Liberation Theology* (1985) and (with W. D. Taylor) *Crisis in Latin America: An Evangelical Perspective* (1989).

WILLIAM D. TAYLOR

Nygren, Anders Theodor Samuel (1890–1978)

Swedish theologian and philosopher. Born in Göteborg and reared in a Christian environment, he was sent to the Cathedral School at Lund. After theological studies there he engaged in parish work while continuing studies toward his doctorate. He was made lecturer in the philosophy of religion at the University of Lund in 1921, and full professor in 1924, a position he held until 1948. In 1947 he was elected president of the Lutheran World Federation for a five-year period, and in 1948 was appointed bishop of Lund. He was widely respected beyond the boundaries of Sweden for his work in the Faith and Order and Life and Work movements, and in the formation of the World Council of Churches, as well as for his numerous publications. These include *Commentary on Romans* (1949), *The Gospel of God* (1951), *Agape and Eros* (1953), and *Christ and His Church* (1957). The bulk of Nygren's literary legacy has not yet been translated into English.

I. Kegley edited *The Philosophy and Theology of Anders Nygren* (1970).

EDWARD J. FURCHA

O

....

Ockenga, Harold John (1905–1985)

American pastor and educator. Born in Chicago, he was converted at age eleven, and was educated at Taylor University, at Princeton and Westminster Theological seminaries, and at the University of Pittsburgh (Ph.D., 1939). He warmly approved the formation of Westminster Theological Seminary, was ordained in the Presbyterian Church, and ministered in Breeze Point Church, Pittsburgh (1931–1936), and Park Street Church, Boston (1936–1969). He conducted outdoor services on Boston Common next to the church, spoke on the radio, and emphasized missionary giving until his missionary budget equaled the local church budget. He served also as president of Fuller Seminary, dividing his time with his Park Street pulpit. He founded the New England Youth for Christ, which joined with Youth for Christ International. Ockenga was the first president of the National Association of Evangelicals.

One of the outstanding revivals under Billy Graham's ministry took place at Park Street Church and the Boston Garden in 1950. It closed with a rally on Boston Common attended by fifty thousand people. Graham toured all of New England with Ockenga's support, with astonishing responses, and returned to Boston Garden at Ockenga's invitation in 1964 for a highly successful mission.

His publications include *Our Protestant Heritage* (1938), *Power Through Pentecost* (1959), and *Faith in a Troubled World* (1972).

Biography by Harold Lindsell (1951).

SHERWOOD E. WIRT

Oldham, Joseph Houldsworth (1874–1969)

Lay ecumenist. Born in Bombay, India, he was educated at Trinity College, Oxford. Converted under D. L. Moody, he abandoned his plan to enter the Indian Civil Service. Instead, after three years' work among students with the Scottish YMCA in Lahore and theological study in Edinburgh and Halle, Germany, he devoted his life to the ecumenical movement, working closely with J. R. Mott. Oldham was secretary of the Edinburgh Missionary Conference (1910), its continuation committee, and the International Missionary Council (1921). He organized the Church, Community, and State Conference at Oxford (1937), and helped form the World Council of Churches. He was founder and first editor of the *International Review of*

Missions (1912–1927), and edited the *Christian News Letter* (1939–1945). Besides promoting ecumenical study, especially among the laity, he was a focus of missionary concerns about education in India and Africa, and about race relations. His books include *The World and the Gospel* (1916), *Christianity and the Race Problem* (1924), and, with B. D. Gibson, *The Remaking of Man in Africa* (1931).

PHILIP HILLYER

Oman, John Wood (1860–1939)

Scottish Presbyterian theologian. Born in Orkney, he went to Edinburgh University, graduating in 1882. He studied in Germany in 1885 at Erlangen and Heidelberg. His first publication was a translation of Schleiermacher's *Speeches on Religion* (1893). The controversy over the Robertson Smith heresy trial led to his call to the ministry. He trained at the United Presbyterian College. He received a call in 1889 to the English Presbyterian church at Alnwick, Northumberland. During his ministry there he wrote *Vision and Authority* (1902). His growing scholarly reputation led to his appointment as professor of theology at Westminster College, Cambridge, in 1907. The rest of his working life was spent there; he was appointed principal in 1922. He worked closely with the Cambridge divinity faculty and lectured in the philosophy of religion. There is continuing discussion about the obscurity of his writing and lecturing, but there is no doubt that his major work, *The Natural and the Supernatural* (1931), was a powerful philosophical justification of religious experience.

Studies on his theology were produced by F. G. Healey (1965) and S. B. Bevans (1992).

NOEL S. POLLARD

Orr, James (1844–1913)

Scottish theologian and philosopher. Born in Glasgow, he graduated from the university there in 1870, went on to study divinity, and ministered in Hawick (1873–1890). In 1891 his *The Christian View of God and the World* sought to show three things: the ultimate rationality of Christianity; the absolute and non-negotiable importance of the incarnation; and the need for Christianity to enter into combat with the growing naturalism of the day. Orr was professor of church history at the United Presbyterian Divinity Hall (1891–1900) and then held the chair of systematic theology at the United Free Church College in Glasgow (1900–1913). In 1897 his *The Ritschlian Theology and the Evangelical Faith* reportedly did "more than any other critic to discredit Ritschl in the estimation of the English public." In *God's Image in Man* (1905) Orr was concerned to defend the biblical view of humanity against Darwinism. Although not rejecting all forms of evolution, Orr insisted humanity was "the produc-

283

tion of something perfectly new by the direct act of God." *The Problem of the Old Testament* (1906) was a profoundly learned broadside at the Graf-Wellhausen theory of Old Testament origins, in an attempt to defend the supernatural origins of Scripture, a point to which Orr returned in 1910 with *Revelation and Inspiration.* While not defending traditional plenary verbal inspiration, Orr did staunchly defend what he called supernatural historical revelation and the trustworthiness of Scripture as a testimony to that. *The Virgin Birth of Christ* (1907) argued that "a supernatural act in the production of Christ's bodily nature" was demanded by Christianity. In *The Resurrection of Jesus* (1908) Orr said, "The resurrection is a retrospective attestation that Jesus was indeed the exalted and divinely-sent Person he claimed to be." Editor of the *International Standard Bible Encyclopedia* (1915), Orr's legacy is his steadfast defense of orthodoxy. He asserted that he would not part with a single article of the evangelical faith in the interests of modern thought and of a reconstructed theology.

Biographical studies of Orr and his work by A. P. Neely (1960) and G. G. Scorgie (1988).

WALTER A. ELWELL

Orr, James Edwin (1912–1987)

Evangelist, author, and educator. Born in Belfast, Northern Ireland, he was converted at age nine, and after high school worked as a clerk to help support the family. By 1930 he was holding open air meetings on the streets of Belfast, and by 1933 had the conviction that God wanted him to be an evangelist. He began a lifetime of independent evangelistic travel, first through the British Isles, then to various European countries, and then worldwide, especially to Canada and the United States. He also began writing about his experiences, and produced popular books on faith, scholarly histories of revivals, and autobiographical descriptions of his travels. After an interruption in the 1940s when he served as a chaplain in the United States Army in the Pacific, he earned his first doctorate at Oxford University and continued his preaching tours, often with special meetings for university students. He became a professor at Fuller Seminary's School of World Mission (1966–1981), and stimulated the study of revivals and evangelism through the founding in 1974 of the Oxford Reading and Research Conference on Evangelical Awakenings. Orr had a great influence on the growing Protestant evangelical movement in many countries, was closely linked with Billy Graham and Abraham Vereide, and participated in Andrew Gih's Evangelize China Fellowship. Among his books were *A Call for the Restudy of Revival and Revivalism, The Second Great Awakening,* and *Can God—?*

ROBERT SCHUSTER

Ortiz Hurtado, Jaime (1933–)

Colombian evangelical pastor, theologian, and national leader. Born in Girardot, Colombia, and reared in Medellín, Ortiz was converted at age seventeen during the persecution of evangelicals. Despite strong opposition, he became active in the local Presbyterian church and studied for a year at the Latin American Biblical Seminary in Costa Rica. In 1959 he was selected by the Colombian church to receive a scholarship to the Presbyterian Theological Seminary in Campinas, Brazil. He returned to Colombia in 1963 with more conservative convictions than the incipient liberation theology to which he had been exposed. After a pastorate in Armero, he moved in 1967 to the Presbyterian church in Medellín, where he also began teaching at the United Biblical Seminary. He served as academic dean of the seminary, and in 1975 became the president, expanding dramatically the number of students and programs. In 1977 Ortiz received a doctorate in law and political science from the Universidad Pontificia Bolivariana in Colombia. He has served as moderator of the national Synod, president of the Evangelical Confederation of Colombia (CEDECOL), and president of the Latin American Association of Theological Schools. In 1990 he was asked by CEDECOL to run for the national Constituent Assembly and was one of two evangelicals elected. His doctoral thesis on "The State as Minister of God" proved valuable as he played a key role in the rewriting of Colombia's constitution. In 1992 he retired from the seminary but continues to be active in ministry and politics.

STEPHEN R. SYWULKA

Osei-Mensah, Gottfried (1934–)

African evangelical leader. Born in Berekem, Ghana, he attended Prempeh College in Kumasi, then went to England to study chemical engineering at Birmingham University. He accepted Christ while at Prempeh, and got a decisive call to Christian service in his second year at Birmingham. He joined the Ghana Mobil Oil Corporation as sales engineer, then served the Pan-African Fellowship of Evangelical Students for five years before becoming senior pastor of Nairobi Baptist Church, Kenya, in 1971. In 1974 he was appointed the first executive director of the Lausanne Committee for World Evangelization, a post he held for nine years. He is now associated with the Billy Graham Evangelistic Association with special responsibility for conferences worldwide; he is also a life member of the Lausanne Committee, and president of the International Fellowship of Evangelical Students.

Osei-Mensah's identifying tag is his challenge for the African church to go for leadership that serves. His acumen in Christian leadership in the context of the continent, coupled with his familiarity with African Chris-

285

tianity, are invaluable assets. His book, *Wanted: Servant Leaders* (1990), is a classic in this area.

JAMES KOMBO

Otto, Rudolph (1869–1937)

German theologian. Born in Peine, Hanover, son of a fur manufacturer, he was educated at the universities of Göttingen and Erlangen, and later taught theology at Göttingen (1897), Breslau (1914), and Marburg (1917). From a strict Lutheran family that bordered on the legalistic, Otto moved to openness toward other religions and became an advocate of religious peace conferences and of a worldwide association of world religions. Despite indifferent health he traveled widely, being one of the first international travelers among German theologians. Diaries of these journeys and letters offer insights into his thoughts. In his later years he helped set up a museum for the comparative study of religions in Marburg, which was to focus on world religions as living faiths. He retired in 1929. A committed Lutheran, Otto explored the experiences that led to religious belief. Under the influence of the philosophy of Kant he sought to transcend the limits of the thing itself and to express the nature and the truth of religion scientifically. He enhanced his own theological understanding through travels in Asia (1910) and by a marked interest in the sciences. Although he was fully aware of the rational dimension in the religious experience, he stressed in his major work, *The Idea of the Holy* (ET, 1923), the hidden, nonrational element. The book went through fourteen German editions and was translated into several languages. His other writings include *India's Religion of Grace and Christianity* (1930), *Mysticism* (1932), *Naturalism and Religion* (1907), *The Philosophy of Religion* (1931), and *The Kingdom of God and the Son of Man* (1938). His private papers are housed at the University of Marburg.

EDWARD J. FURCHA

Oxnam, Garfield Bromley (1891–1963)

Methodist bishop, ecumenical leader, and social reformer. Born in Sonora, California, he was ordained a Methodist minister in 1915, and pastored two churches in California (1916–1926). While in Los Angeles, he supported the labor movement and other social causes, and taught social ethics at the University of Southern California, from which he had graduated. He taught one year at Boston School of Theology before he accepted the presidency of DePauw University (1928–1936). He lectured extensively and wrote over twenty books, many on faith and social issues. His influence within the Methodist Church grew by serving as bishop of Omaha, Boston, New York, and Washington, D.C. (1936–1960), and as secretary of the Council of Bishops (1939–1956). He traveled widely in support of missions and advocated that Methodist bishops should visit at least one foreign field to be exposed to world conditions. He provided leadership in ecumenical circles as president of the Federal Council of Churches (1944–1946), a founding officer of the National Council of Churches (1950), and a president of the World Council of Churches (1948–1954). In 1953 he appeared before the House Committee on Un-American Activities, which had released documents alleging that he was a communist; his testimony did not earn an apology or retraction from the committee, but the church supported his innocence. He wrote *Preaching in a Revolutionary Age.*

PAUL A. ERICKSEN

P

Packer, James Innell (1926–)

Anglican evangelical theologian. Born in Gloucestershire, England, he was educated at Oxford University where he later earned a D.Phil. degree (1954). Ordained in the Church of England (1952), he served as curate, St. John Church, Harborne, Birmingham (1953–1955); senior tutor, Tyndale Hall, Bristol (1955–1961); librarian (1961–1962) and warden (1962–1969), Latimer House, Oxford; principal, Tyndale Hall, Bristol (1969–1971); associate principal, Trinity College, Bristol (1972–1979); and professor of historical and systematic theology, Regent College, Vancouver, Canada (1979–). Packer is one of the most influential thinkers and apologists for Christianity in the twentieth century. His work has inspired younger scholars and ministers with a sense of confidence by its intellectual integrity and coherence. He has been greatly influenced by Puritan thought. Internationally recognized as a perceptive and profound theologian in the evangelical Reformed and Puritan tradition, his work has popular appeal because of its clarity, vigor, insight, and practicality. An advocate of biblical inerrancy, he provided leadership at meetings of the International Council on Biblical Inerrancy (1978–1987). He has an ironic attitude toward Anglican comprehensiveness and has participated in interfaith dialogues. He also has an appreciative but not uncritical stance toward charismatic life and practice. He is persuaded that Christianity is on the verge of a great reawakening. He is currently working on a comprehensive systematic theology and is in great demand as lecturer, conference speaker, and visiting professor. His books include *"Fundamentalism" and the Word of God* (1958), *Evangelism and the Sovereignty of God* (1961), *Knowing God* (1973), *I Want to Be a Christian* (1977), *Knowing Man* (1979), *Hot Tub Religion* (1987), *Rediscovering Holiness* (1992), and *Concise Theology: A Guide to Historic Christian Beliefs* (1993). He has contributed to and edited many other volumes.

ALBERT H. FREUNDT, JR.

Padilla, Carlos René (1932–)

Latin American theologian and writer. Born in Ecuador and reared in Colombia, René Padilla showed writing prowess from an early age. In high school he started his first magazine, *The Evangelical Clarion*. After graduation from Wheaton College and Wheaton Graduate School, Padilla began a lengthy student ministry in Latin America with the International Fellowship of Evangelical Students (IFES), during which time he also earned a Ph.D. in New Testament from the University of Manchester (England). A voracious reader and prolific writer with an agile, critical mind, Padilla quickly emerged as one of Latin America's leading theologians. At a time when many Latin evangelicals still leaned heavily on U.S. and European thinking, Padilla expounded a distinctly Latin American view of ministry and theology. He also advocated social, not just evangelistic, ministry in a continent plagued by poverty. Padilla's theological expertise is recognized not just in Latin America, but worldwide. He is active in the Lausanne movement and other international forums. He was a leading force in the creation of the Latin American Theological Fraternity, a kind of evangelical "think tank," and was its general secretary from 1984 to 1992. He also founded and still edits *Misión* magazine, a thought journal distributed throughout Latin America, and has written *Mission Between the Times* (1985). A Baptist pastor and member of Latin America Mission, Padilla in 1990 fulfilled a longtime dream of establishing a Christian conference center, the Kairos Center for Discipleship and Mission, just outside Buenos Aires, Argentina.

JOHN MAUST

Padilla, Washington (1927–1990)

Ecuadorian educator and theologian. He was born in Quito, Ecuador, and spent most of his life in that city. After obtaining a B.A. degree from Rockmont College, Denver, and an M.Div. from Fuller Seminary, he returned to Quito where he served as director of Spanish programming for Radio Station HCJB, as chaplain and professor of philosophy, ethics, and Bible at the Teodoro W. Anderson School, president of the Christian Center for Educational Resources, and professor of English at the Central University of Ecuador. He also pastored, and was a founding member of the Association of Evangelical Ministers of Ecuador. He worked with the national Bible Society in various capacities, including that of executive secretary, and for six years was president of the Ecumenical Commission on Human Rights. He helped coordinate the Commission on Studies of the History of the Church in Latin America, and was active in the Latin American Theological Fraternity. His books (all in Spanish) include a commentary on Amos and Obadiah, and a history of Protestantism in Ecuador.

EMILIO NUNEZ

Page, Kirby (1898–1957)

Pacifist, social reformer, and minister. Born in Tyler County, Texas, educated at Drake University, University of Chicago, Columbia University, and Union Theological Seminary, he was student pastor at Moneith, Iowa, from

1912 to 1915. In 1915 he was ordained in the Disciples of Christ Church and became pastor of the Morgan Park Church in Chicago. Page's indefatigable passion for pacifism arose from his experience working for the YMCA in France during World War I. Between the two wars he traveled with YMCA leader Sherwood Eddy (1871–1963) in evangelistic campaigns in America, China, Japan, and Korea. After 1921 he also lectured extensively in promotion of pacifism for the American Friends Service Commission and the Fellowship of Reconciliation. He wrote widely on social issues, authoring nearly a dozen books on pacifism and social reform. These include *The Sword or the Cross* (1921), *Industrialism and Socialism* (1933), and *How to Keep America out of War* (1939). Page has been called by some "itinerant evangelist for peace."

DAVID P. CAMERA

Pagura, Federico J. (1923–)

Methodist bishop and ecumenical leader. He was born in Arroyo Seco, Argentina, in the home of a Methodist pastor. His grandparents, Italian immigrants, were converted through reading the Bible. Pagura graduated from the Evangelical School of Theology in Buenos Aires and did postgraduate studies at Union Theological Seminary, New York, and at Claremont School of Theology. He was ordained in the Methodist Church in 1950 and was a pastor in Argentina and chaplain of the School of Theology. He served as bishop in Costa Rica and Panama (1969–1973) and Argentina (1977–1989). He describes himself as having a "deep pastoral and teaching vocation." Since his youth he has been in ecumenical circles and in the struggle for human rights, and in those areas has held key positions in religious and secular organizations, including his current presidency of the Latin American Council of Churches. He is known also as a poet who has written or translated a number of hymns, including the first tango with Christian words (the popular "We Have Faith"), and Christian folk songs.

ARNOLDO CANCLINI

Paik, L. George (1895–1985)

Korean Christian, scholar, and statesman. Born in a poor farm home in northeastern Korea, Paek Nak-Chun attended a Confucian elementary school, then in 1905 entered a Presbyterian school. Its missionary principal, G. S. McCune, virtually adopted him after the death of his parents, and sent him to China in 1915 to escape Japanese persecution. After study at the Anglo-Chinese College in Shanghai, he went in 1916 to America, graduating from Park College (1922), Princeton Theological Seminary (1925), and Yale University (Ph.D., 1927). Returning to Korea, he became in 1928 chairman of the department of literature at what is now Yonsei University in Seoul. In 1936 his opposition to Japanese-enforced Shinto shrine ceremonies led him to leave Korea for England as the only Korean delegate to the ecumenical conferences at Edinburgh and Oxford. He briefly taught in America, courageously returned to Korea in 1939, but resigned from Yonsei to avoid the Shinto ceremonies. Declining the presidency of what is now Seoul National University, he returned to Yonsei as its first freely elected president (1946–1957). In 1950 he served the newly formed republic as minister of education, and in 1960 became president of the senate. He was chief of the Korean delegation to many international conferences. His *History of Protestant Missions in Korea (1832–1910)* (rev. 1971) is still the definitive work on that period.

SAMUEL H. MOFFETT

Paisley, Ian Richard Kyle (1926–)

British parliamentarian and founder of the Free Presbyterian Church of Ulster. Born in Northern Ireland, he studied at the Reformed Presbyterian College in Belfast, and was ordained by his Baptist-minister father in 1946. He later ministered to a group that had broken from the Presbyterian Church in Ireland, and there emerged a body known as the Free Presbyterian Church with Paisley as its moderator (a position he still holds) in affiliation with the International Council of Christian Churches. Public demonstrations have led to imprisonment, a bar on entering Italy, and ejection from the European Parliament for loud protest against the pope as guest speaker in 1988. Paisley has been a member of the British Parliament since 1970 and of the European Parliament since 1979, and pastors the large Martyrs' Memorial Church in Belfast. Strongly pro-British and violently opposed to Rome, the World Council of Churches, and the unification of Ireland, Paisley is a rousing orator who inspires both fanatical devotion and deep distrust. Recipient of an honorary doctorate from Bob Jones University, he has written *Exposition of the Epistle to the Romans* (1968), *Billy Graham and the Church of Rome* (1970), and *Mr. Protestant* (1985).

J. D. DOUGLAS

Palau, Luis (1934–)

Evangelist. Born in Buenos Aires, Argentina, he was converted at age twelve and discipled by British missionaries. He studied at St. Albans College in Argentina, and after completing the graduate program at Multnomah School of the Bible in Portland, Oregon, in 1961, he served in Colombia with Overseas Crusades before founding the Luis Palau Evangelistic Team and beginning a campaign ministry that has taken him throughout Latin America as well as to much of the world. As Eastern Europe began opening, he held crusades in Poland, Hungary, Romania, and the Soviet Union. He has preached to over 8 million people in some fifty countries. His two

291

daily radio programs, "Cruzada" (Crusade) and "Luis Palau Responds," and newspaper column are widely syndicated, and he has held several large-scale radio satellite campaigns. "Continente '75" and "Continente '85" covered most of Latin America, and "Commonwealth '84" was broadcast to fifty English-speaking nations. Palau has written some thirty books in Spanish and English, and publishes a magazine for Christian leaders in Latin America, *Continente Nuevo.* He contributed a two-volume commentary on John to the *Continente Nuevo* Bible commentary series, which is in process.

Autobiography (with Jerry Jenkins) (1983).

STEPHEN R. SYWULKA

Pannell, William (1929–)

Writer, lecturer, and educator. He was educated at Wayne State University, majoring in black history, and received his master of arts degree in social ethics at the University of Southern California. He has served as assistant pastor, youth director, and pastor of various fellowships. His heart for evangelism can be seen in his service as vice president of the Tom Skinner Evangelistic Association; consultant on the Gospel and Culture at the Lausanne Conference on Evangelism in 1977; board member of Youth for Christ, U.S.A.; and president of the Academy for Evangelism. Pannell has long been a member of the evangelical Christian community and has often served as the forerunner and mentor for other people of color in many educational and church settings. He has written many articles in Christian periodicals dealing with the state of racial relations in the church, and has developed the reputation of telling it as he sees it regarding race relations within the church. Two of his books, *My Friend, the Enemy* and *The Coming Race Wars?*, have added to this perception. He is the director of black ministries and associate professor of evangelism in the School of Theology at Fuller Seminary. Among his publications are *My Friend, the Enemy* (1968), *Evangelism from the Bottom Up* (1992), and *The Coming Race Wars?* (1993).

ROBERT C. SUGGS

Pannenberg, Wolfhart (1928–)

German theologian. Born in Stetin, son of a civil servant, he was reared outside the church, but had a meaningful religious experience as a teenager. He studied philosophy at Göttingen, but then spent a year under theologians Barth and Jaspers at Basel. He completed his doctorate at Heidelberg in 1953, and was successively professor of systematic theology at Wuppertal (from 1958) and at Mainz (1961) before joining the Protestant faculty at Munich in 1968. His theology stresses the unity of the church and its place in a secularized world. For him the church's task is to witness to the coming kingdom of God, where fellowship among humans, and between them and God, will find fulfillment. He held Christian faith to be validated not by experience but by rational critical inquiry. Ultimate truth, however, will be found in the future, and finally the deity of God will be open to all. He placed hope in God's eventual rule over all creation. Jesus makes possible our reconciliation with the Divine. *Introduction to Systematic Theology* (1991) offers the mature statement of his system.

RICHARD V. PIERARD

Papasarantopoulos, Chrysostom (1903–1972)

First twentieth-century Greek Orthodox missionary to Africa. Papasarantopoulos was born in Vasilitsion, Greece, with the baptismal name of Christos. At age fifteen, Papasarantopoulos left home to become a disciple of a holy ascetic monk, who taught him the disciplines of prayer, fasting, and study of Scripture. He was called to serve in the Greek army in 1923, but following this service he entered the Marthakion Monastery. On August 4, 1925, he was tonsured a monk and given the new name Chrysostom. A year later he was ordained a deacon, and then priest; shortly thereafter he became abbot of Gardikiou Monastery. Over the next twenty years, he became abbot of two other monasteries on the recommendation of the archbishop of Athens. It was only in 1953 that he finally received grammar and high school degrees. Then, in 1958, he earned the Licentiate in Theology from the University of Athens. Upon his graduation from the university, Papasarantopoulos responded to an inner call to missions in Africa. He became the first twentieth-century missionary from Greece, and spent the following thirteen years working in Uganda, Zaire, Tanzania, and Kenya. During that period he helped establish the Orthodox Church in these regions. He learned Swahili, translated liturgical books, built churches and schools, baptized the faithful, and prepared indigenous candidates for the priesthood. Through his voluminous correspondence with Greek Orthodox individuals and organizations, he inaugurated a new period of missions with the Greek Orthodox Church. He died in Zaire in 1972, and is buried at the Church of St. Andrew in Kananga.

LUKE VERONIS

Paredes, Rubén Elias (1949–)

Latin American missiologist and anthropologist. Born in the heart of the Peruvian Andes, "Tito" Paredes developed a love for the Quechua people, descendants of the once-proud Incas. He translated that concern into ministry in behalf of Latin America's indigenous peoples, and he became a leading expert on the fast-growing evangelical church among them. Uniquely qualified, Paredes earned both a Ph.D. in anthropology from the University of California at Los Angeles and an M.Div. degree from Fuller Theological Seminary. He moves equally well among world-class anthropologists and unlettered Indian pastors. In 1977 Paredes spearheaded the founding of the Evangelical Center for Andean/Amazonian Missiology (CEMAA) in Lima, Peru. Early missionaries sometimes taught Quechua converts to reject certain aspects of their culture, such as their typical music, but Paredes and CEMAA encouraged indigenous believers to value their own culture—developing worship styles and ministries that were biblical, but that also utilized the native language and respected the culture. CEMAA organized music festivals among Andean Christians, who put Christian lyrics to native melodies. In 1992 Paredes was elected general secretary of the influential Latin American Theological Fraternity, a forum for theological reflection with about 160 members in a dozen Latin countries. A member of Latin America Mission, he also is founding director of Peru's first graduate school of missiology.

JOHN MAUST

Parham, Charles Fox (1873–1929)

Founder of modern Pentecostalism and the Apostolic Faith Movement. Born in Muscatine, Iowa, he studied at Southwest Kansas College from 1890 to 1893. After he survived a severe bout of rheumatic fever in 1891, his belief in divine healing grew. In 1898 he founded the Bethel Healing Home in Topeka, Kansas, and began publication of *Apostolic Faith*, a Holiness journal. Strongly attracted to Holiness theology, he founded Bethel Bible School (College) in Topeka in 1890 to train students as missionary evangelists. Parham modeled the school after Frank W. Sandford's Holiness center near Durham, Maine. He was intensely interested in reception of the Holy Spirit and xenolalia (tongues as known foreign languages) of the early New Testament church (Acts 2). In 1901 one of his students, Agnes N. Ozman, spoke in tongues, as did Parham and a number of other students a few days later. At the time little came of it.

But with the 1903 revivals in Galena, Kansas, which spread to Missouri and Oklahoma, and his founding of numerous Apostolic Faith churches and a Bible School in Houston, Texas, in 1905, Parham's Pentecostalism attracted a growing number of followers and had a broadening range of influence. It led to the 1906 Azusa Street revival in Los Angeles under the black Holiness evangelist, William J. Seymour, who had attended Parham's Bible School in Houston.

The remaining years of Parham's life were marked by controversy and waning influence. During his ministry he authored a couple of books and intermittently edited *Apostolic Faith*. He is best remembered for furnishing Pentecostalism with its distinct teaching on speaking in tongues as signaling Spirit baptism.

Biography by S. A. Parham (1930).

H. DOUGLAS BUCKWALTER

Parzany, Ulrich (1941–)

German evangelist. Born in Essen, he was converted as a teenager through the ministry of the Weigle House, a Protestant youth center in his hometown. During 1960–1964 he studied theology at Wuppertal, Göttingen, Tübingen, and Bonn, followed by a year as student pastor with the German Lutheran church in Jerusalem. He completed his studies at the seminary of the Protestant Church in the Rhineland, and was ordained in 1967. He then became head of the Weigle House and worked in youth evangelism throughout Germany. He organized large youth missionary conventions in Essen (1976) and Nuremberg (1988), and from 1978 served as chair of the Gerhard Tersteegen Konferenz (a conservative Bible conference) and editor of the Christian magazine *Schritte*. In 1984 he was appointed general secretary of the YMCA, the largest Christian youth organization in Germany, and under his leadership it focused on evangelism and missionary work. He chaired the committee for the Pro Christ '93 campaign of Billy Graham and its follow-up effort to reach every part of German-speaking Europe by satellite. He has also authored numerous books of sermons for young people.

RICHARD V. PIERARD

Paton, John Gibson (1824–1907)

Pioneer missionary to the New Hebrides (now Vanuatu). Born in Dumfriesshire, Scotland, he worked with the Glasgow City Mission (1847–1856) while preparing himself for overseas service by studies in medicine and divinity. Ordained by the Reformed Presbyterian Church in 1858, he established a station on the New Hebrides island of Tanna, but incredible privations, including native hostility and the loss of his wife and son, forced his removal in 1862 to Australia. He extended the missionary challenge there and in Scotland where his church elected him moderator in 1864. He returned to the New Hebrides and settled on the island of Aniwa (1866–1881). Paton campaigned fearlessly against the white man's trade in arms and alcohol, and against unjust labor practices. From 1881 he made his base in Melbourne. He was instrumental in having vast sums contributed to missionary work in the South Pacific region. Paton was a simple but riveting speaker of whom, on his death in 1907, one obituary said that "earth had lost and heaven gained a soul whose life had been an inspiration, and whose memory will be honored while honor remains among men." His fame was recognized also by Cambridge University, which gave him an honorary D.D. degree. His autobiography was edited by James Paton, his brother (1889).

J. D. DOUGLAS

Paton, William (1886–1943)

Missionary statesman and writer. The son of Scottish parents who had settled in England, he was educated at Oxford and Cambridge, and ordained in the Presbyterian Church of England ("to save him from [World

295

War I] conscription," notes his biographer). He was missionary secretary of the Student Christian movement (1911–1921), combined latterly with work for the YMCA under whose auspices he went to India. He returned there as a general secretary of the newly formed National Christian Council of India, Burma, and Ceylon (1921–1928) before appointment as joint secretary (with J. H. Oldham) of the London-based International Missionary Council. Paton was an ecumenical pioneer, a champion of war-orphaned missions, an ardent pacifist, an indefatigable writer on a wide range of subjects, and the possessor of wit as seen in the parody (of Mott's famous watchword), "The Moon turned to Blood in our Generation." An ecumenical enthusiast who hung loose when it came to denominational affiliations, Paton made a substantial contribution to the movement that in 1948 became officially the World Council of Churches. His published works included *Jesus Christ and the World's Religions* (1916), *Christianity in the Eastern Conflicts* (1937), and *The Church and the New Order* (1941). For sixteen years he served as editor of the *International Review of Missions.*

Biographies by Margaret Sinclair (1949) and E. M. Jackson (1980).

J. D. Douglas

Paul VI (1897–1978)

Pope from 1963. Born near Brescia, Italy, Giovanni Battista Montini was educated at the Gregorian University and the University of Rome, and was ordained in 1920. He served the Vatican's Secretariat of State (1924–1953), wrote devotional books for students, lectured on papal diplomacy at the Apollinaris, and headed Vatican relief work during World War II. In a palace coup in 1954 he fell from favor by advocating the papacy's withdrawal from Italian politics. Appointed to the see of Milan, Montini was "moved up in order to be moved out." Calling himself the "archbishop of workers," he offered them free medical and legal services through the Office of Charity he founded. He provided housing for three thousand needy people, and established "domestic" churches in homes, shops, and garages. In 1957 he conducted "Mission of Milan," an evangelistic campaign. In 1958 he became the first cardinal nominated by John XXIII, whom he succeeded (1963) during Vatican II. Overriding the latter, Paul VI proclaimed Mary "Mother of the Church" (1964). He forbade the council to discuss birth control. His encyclical, *Mysterium fidei* (1965), warned clergy and laity not to deviate from the Eucharist doctrines of transubstantiation and the "Real Presence." *Sacerdotalis caelibatus* (1967) insisted on clerical celibacy, which hastened the exodus from religious orders. Paul VI demanded social justice for underdeveloped countries and (rejecting his commission's advice) condemned contraception. This position alienated progressive Catholics and set the papacy, it was said, on a reactionary course.

Biographies by W. J. Wilson (1968) and P. Hebblethwaite (1993).

Norman F. Cornett

Paul, Kanakarayan Tiruselvam (1876–1931)

Indian Christian nationalist. He was a founder (1905) and secretary of the National Missionary Society, then secretary (1913) and general secretary (1916) of the YMCA. Like other Indian Christians of the time, he interpreted the British connection with India and the rise of Indian nationalism positively and theologically. He argued in pamphlets and in his book *The British Connection with India* (1928) that the Christ hidden but undoubtedly present in Western culture was calling to the Christ in Indian culture and preparing India for new life. Paul was a friend of Gandhi and represented the Indian Christian Association at the London Round Table Conference in 1930. His belief that Indian Christians should be at one with Indian political aspirations was matched by a desire to see a fully Indian church. As president of the South India United Church, he supported the development of indigenous forms of worship and the movement toward church unity that was to culminate in the formation of the Church of South India.

Biography by H. A. Popley (1938).

PHILIP HILLYER

Peake, Arthur Samuel (1865–1929)

English biblical scholar. Born in Leek, Staffordshire, into a family actively associated with Primitive Methodism (his father was a minister), he was educated in Classics and theology at Oxford. He taught at Mansfield College (1889–1892) and at Hartley (Primitive Methodist) College (1892–1904) before becoming the first Rylands professor of biblical criticism and exegesis in Manchester University (1904–1929). Peake's literary output was prodigious. One of his concerns was to disseminate to ordinary people the critical methods originating from Germany, that he had encountered at Oxford. One such medium of communication was through the *Primitive Methodist Leader* in which he had a correspondence column. Perhaps the best known was the one-volume *Peake's Commentary of the Bible*, which he edited in 1919, the year in which he became editor of the *Holburn Review.* As a church leader he was active in ecumenical circles, and in 1922 he began attending the conferences in Lambeth following the famous "Appeal to all Christian People."

See J. T. Wilkinson (ed.), *Arthur Samuel Peake, 1865–1929* (1958).

WONG CHAN KOK

Peale, Norman Vincent (1898–1993)

Reformed Church of America minister and advocate of positive thinking. Son of a Methodist preacher, he was born in Bowersville, Ohio. After a brief stint as a journalist, he prepared for the ministry and was ordained in the Methodist Episcopal Church in 1922. He pastored several churches before moving his affiliation to the Reformed Church of America in 1932. He pastored Marble Collegiate Church in New York City, where he remained until his retirement in 1984. Peale was an early proponent of integrating psychiatry with ministry, and wove this conviction into his messages and writing and the program of his church. He was a prolific communicator, using *The Power of Positive Thinking* (1952) and forty other books on motivational themes or the life of Christ to spread his simple message of self-help through optimism and prayer. Added to these were speaking engagements, a newspaper column, a weekly radio program, and *Guideposts* magazine, which featured inspiring stories of people who overcame difficulty. His impact extended beyond his own ventures to influence other motivational speakers and the self-help movement. Peale's critics said his positive thinking message watered down Christian theology, elevated American middle-class values, and ignored social problems.

Biography by C. V. George.

PAUL A. ERICKSEN

Peguy, Charles (1873–1914)

French poet and philosopher. Born in Orleans, he left his training as a philosophy teacher in order to pursue the socialism that he considered the solution to society's problems. He dedicated his play *Jeanne d'Arc* (1897) to "the advancement of a universal socialist republic." He defended Dreyfus through articles (1895–1899) and his book *Notre Jeunesse* (1910). He founded a periodical that became a forum for the French literati and his own polemical writings. Further volumes accused the intelligentsia of spiritual domination for materialistic ends. In keeping with his idealism, Peguy chose a life of poverty. He theologized history in *Clioi* (1909), which manifested his religious renaissance. He articulated his mysticism in works such as *Eve* (1913), which portrayed the human condition in four thousand Alexandrines drawn from the Bible. He was influenced by Bergson, rejected the "triumphalism" of modern science in *M. Descartes* (1924), and earlier contributed to Maritain's conversion to Rome. To keep his patriotic vows he volunteered for the army and died in battle during World War I.

Biographies by Y. Servais (1953), Marjorie Villiers (1965), and G. Hill (1983).

NORMAN F. CORNETT

Peloubet, Francis Nathan (1831–1920)

Congregational pastor, author, and editor. Born in New York City, he graduated from Williams College (1853) and Bangor Theological Seminary (1857). After ordination he served pastorates in Massachusetts (1857–1883). He is chiefly remembered, however, for his pioneering work in the Sunday school movement. His annual *Select Notes on the International Sabbath [Sunday] School Lessons* (1875–1920) early won spectacular success at home and abroad, and over the years reportedly sold over one million copies. His many other works include *Loom of Life* (1900), *The Front Line of the Sunday School Movement* (1904), *Studies in the Book of Job* (1906), *Gates to the Prayer Country* (1907), and several New Testament commentaries of a popular kind. He also edited or revised various other volumes, notably William Smith's renowned and durable Bible dictionary (1912).

SHERWOOD E. WIRT

Perkins, John (1930–)

Lecturer, writer, and community organizer. He was one of eight children born to sharecropping parents in New Hebron, Mississippi. His mother died when he was seven months old, and he and his seven siblings were reared by their paternal grandmother. Perkins dropped out of school in the third grade, but continued to educate himself through personal reading and study. He moved to California at age seventeen to seek opportunities not available to him in his home state. He became a Christian through the study of the Bible in Sunday school. Perkins later founded and directed the Voice of Calvary Ministries, a biblically based community development project in Mendenhall and Jackson, Mississippi. This economic development effort, in a Christian context, stands as a model for programs over the nation and in other countries. Perkins received a coveted Ford Foundation Grant in order to travel to Europe, the Caribbean, and Israel. His travels focused on the methods employed by cooperatives and other community development projects. Perkins is listed as a Distinguished Black American in the 1980 edition of the *International Who's Who of Intellectuals*. Having stepped down from his duties at Voice of Calvary, Perkins returned to California in 1982, where he established the Harambee Christian Family Center in Northwest Pasadena. He is the founder of the Christian Community Development Association and the founder and publisher of *Urban Family* magazine.

He has written *A Quiet Revolution* (1976), *With Justice for All* (1982), and *Beyond Charity* (1993).

ROBERT C. SUGGS

Pew, J. Howard (1882–1971)

American philanthropist. He joined his father's Sun Oil Company in 1901, serving as a development engineer to discover new products, nearly one hundred of which emerged, including the first commercially successful petroleum asphalt. When his father died suddenly in 1912, he was elected president and remained so until 1947. He successfully led the company into new refining, marketing, and distribution techniques. Sun Oil became the first company to use mercury vapor to separate lubricants, and the first to use a catalytic cracking process to make gasoline. He also successfully ventured into shipbuilding. Politically, he opposed the growth of government and considered inflation the greatest economic evil.

He and his family established the Pew Memorial Foundation in 1948, and at the time of his death its assets were some $400 million. He gave about 90 percent of his annual income to charitable causes. He continued the family tradition of support for Grove City College, serving as chairman of the board (1931–1971). He provided the funds to purchase a campus for the newly merged Gordon-Conwell Seminary. He generously supported the Billy Graham Evangelistic Association and various other evangelical organizations. Pew's munificence was displayed also in the founding of three Christian periodicals: *Christianity Today, Christian Economic*, and *The Presbyterian Layman*. He was elected president of the board of trustees of the Presbyterian Church general assembly in 1940. He served also as the chairman of the National Lay Committee of the National Council of Churches (1950–1955).

LUDER G. WHITLOCK, JR.

Phillips, John Bertram (1906–1982)

English Bible translator, writer, and broadcaster. Born in Barnes, Middlesex, he was educated at Emmanuel College, Cambridge, ordained in 1930, and held parish appointments in London, Lee, and Redhill before becoming prebendary of Chichester Cathedral (1957–1960) and canon of Salisbury Cathedral (1964–1969). He was made famous by *Letters to Young Churches* (1947), translations of Paul's epistles begun in 1940 to encourage his church youth club, and in due course by the complete *New Testament in Modern English* (1958). Besides making Scripture readable well in advance of the spate of modern translations of the Bible, he wrote a dozen forthright bestsellers, including *Your God Is Too Small* (1952), the play *A Man Called Jesus* (1959), and *Ring of Truth: A Translator's Testimony* (1967). The royalties from his work supported other Christian communicators. Few were aware, until the posthumous publication of his autobiography, *The Price of Success* (1984), and letters to others in similar situations (*The Wounded Healer*, 1984) of his continuous battle against depression from 1960.

PHILIP HILLYER

Pidgeon, George Campbell (1872–1971)

Canadian Protestant leader. Touched in adolescence by an evangelical revival in his Scottish community on Quebec's Gaspe Peninsula, Pidgeon was later mentored by D. H. MacVicar at Presbyterian College, Montreal, before serving pastorates in Quebec and Ontario. He taught practical theology at Westminster Hall, Vancouver (1909–1915), then accepted the influential pulpit of Toronto's Bloor St. Church, where he earned renown for his powerful preaching (1915–1948). He was the first convener of the Presbyterian Church in Canada's Board of Moral and Social Reform (1907), but remained essentially an evangelist who saw the relevance of a good environment to enhancing religious responsiveness. In 1917 he became convener of his church's Board of Home Missions, which gave special attention to western Canada. The challenge of ministering to the thinly scattered rural population there impressed him with the need for broader church cooperation, and in 1921 he chaired a joint committee finalizing a union of Canadian Presbyterians, Methodists, and Congregationalists. In 1925 he was honored as first moderator of the resultant new United Church of Canada (an unprecedented ecumenical achievement). Gracious and statesmanlike, Pidgeon embodied the best of late nineteenth-century evangelical Presbyterianism, and on the strength of his reputation assured many nervous fellow churchmen that union was both safe and wise. His great unrealized hope was that this union would bring revival to Canada. He also helped draft the constitution of the World Council of Churches.

Biography by J. W. Grant (1962).

GLEN G. SCORGIE

Pierard, Richard Victor (1934–)

American historian. Born in Chicago, he moved in 1944 with his family to Richland, Washington, where his father worked on the atomic bomb project, and as a teenager he became deeply involved in the life of a Baptist church. He was educated at various colleges in California, and received a Ph.D. in modern European history from the University of Iowa in 1964. Military service in Japan (1955–1956) and a Fulbright research appointment in Germany (1962–1963) brought a lifelong interest in world Christianity. In 1964 he joined the history faculty of Indiana State University at Terre Haute, but he often held appointments abroad in European universities.

Pierard is best known for his works in religion and politics, which analyze the questionable ties between conservative or evangelical Protestantism and the modern state, and draw attention to the phenomenon of civil religion, such as *The Unequal Yoke* (1970) and the coauthored books *Protest and Politics* (1968), *The Cross and the Flag* (1973), *Twilight of the Saints* (1978), and *Civil Religion and the Presidency* (1988). An advocate of biblically based Christian social action and an evangelical Christianity that is global rather than American in its orientation, he was a drafter of the 1973 Chicago Declaration, secretary-treasurer of the Conference on Faith and History, and writer of articles on missionary topics. He also coauthored *Two Kingdoms: The Church and Culture Through the Ages* (1993).

ROBERT G. CLOUSE

Pierce, Bob (Robert Willard) (1914–1976)

Evangelist and founder of World Vision. He was born in Fort Dodge, Iowa, the son of a carpenter. The family soon moved to Colorado, then to Redondo Beach, California, when he was aged twelve. There he became involved with a Nazarene church through which he came to Christ. He started an evangelistic ministry when he was thirty-three. His ministry broadened and he was ordained a Baptist minister in 1940, becoming assistant pastor at Los Angeles Evangelistic Center. There he was impressed with the significance of foreign mission work. Thereafter he underwent a series of personal crises in his faith that caused him to drop out of church work altogether for more than two years. Confronted by a man he had led to Christ five years previously, he returned to the faith, and went to work for Youth for Christ, of which he became vice president at large in 1945. In 1947 he made his first evangelistic trip to Asia, and came face to face with the realities of human misery. As a response, he founded World Vision in 1950 as an organization to support existing evangelical relief work in Asia. He was a pioneer in the use of documentary films to raise the evangelical social conscience. Pierce gave himself fully to the work until 1963, when his health began to fail, leading to his retirement in 1967. After a year in the hospital he was given the opportunity to lead Food for the World, which he rebuilt as Samaritan's Purse.

A. Scott Moreau

Pierson, Arthur Tappan (1837–1911)

Minister, writer, and promoter of missions. Born in New York City, he graduated from Union Theological Seminary (1860), and was ordained by the Presbyterian Church. He served congregations in Binghampton and Waterford, New York, Detroit, Indianapolis, Philadelphia, and later at the Metropolitan Tabernacle, a Baptist church in London where he filled in for (and then replaced) Charles H. Spurgeon. Pierson's energy for missions and evangelism expressed itself in various ways, making him the leading American spokesman for foreign missions during the late nineteenth century. He inspired missionary commitment at Bible and missionary conferences, including that of his friend D. L. Moody in Northfield, Massachusetts. He played a key role in the founding of the Student Volunteer Movement for Foreign Missions. He authored over fifty books (e.g., *The Crisis in Missions*), served for over twenty years as editor of the *Missionary Review,* participated in ecumenical conferences (1888 and 1900), and supported missionary efforts. He supported the Keswick movement's emphasis on personal holiness, and as a premillennialist promoted Christ's second coming as a motivation for spreading the gospel. He also contributed to *The Fundamentals* and was the first editor of the Scofield Reference Bible. He wrote the biography of George Müller (1905).

Paul A. Ericksen

Pike, James Albert (1913–1969)

American Protestant Episcopal bishop. Born into a Roman Catholic family in Oklahoma City, he began studies for the priesthood at Santa Clara University, but left when he found himself at odds with his church's teaching. He earned degrees at the University of Southern California and at Yale (J.S.D., 1938). He practiced and taught law in Washington D.C., joined the Protestant Episcopal Church, and was ordained in 1944 after briefly serving in the U.S. Navy. He studied further at Virginia Theological Seminary and Union Theological Seminary, New York. He was a diligent chaplain and head of the department of religion at Columbia University before appointment as dean of St. John's Cathedral, New York. His sermons attracted crowds; his six-year Sunday afternoon TV program made his name known to millions more.

In 1958 he was elected bishop of California where his controversial views led to three arraignments for heresy. Personal tragedy dogged him: his son's suicide, a battle with alcoholism, an extramarital affair with a woman who finally killed herself, and a divorce (his second). In 1966 he resigned his bishopric, became a spiritualist, and died three years later alone in the Judean desert.

His radical views are reflected in *A Time for Christian Candor* (1964), *What Is This Treasure?* (1966), and *If This Be Heresy* (1967).

J. D. DOUGLAS

Piper, Otto Alfred (1891–1981)

Presbyterian New Testament scholar. Born in Lichte, Germany, he attended various universities until military service interrupted his studies. After World War I he completed his doctorate at Göttingen and began lecturing in systematic theology. He became deeply interested in the areas of Christian ethics and Heilgeschichte (salvation history). In 1930 he succeeded Karl Barth at Münster, but was forced into exile after Hitler came to power. In 1934–1937 he taught philosophy of religion in Wales and critiqued the situation in his homeland in *Recent Developments in German Protestantism* (1937). Piper then served as professor of New Testament literature and exegesis at Princeton Theological Seminary for the rest of his career. After World War II he also dedicated himself to relief efforts in war-torn Europe. In his works he interpreted authority, revelation, and inspiration experientially and not as mere subjects of inquiry and argumentation. Among his works are *God in History* (1939), *The Christian Interpretation of Sex* (1941), *Protestantism in an Ecumenical Age* (1965), and *Christian Ethics* (1970).

RICHARD V. PIERARD

Pius X (1835–1914)

Pope from 1903. Born into a poor family in Riese, Italy, Giuseppe Melchior Sarto studied theology at Padua, was ordained in 1858, and ministered in

Venetia until he was made bishop of Mantua in 1884. He advanced to be cardinal and patriarch of Venice in 1893. His motto on election to the papacy, "to restore all things in Christ," was perhaps a tilt at his more politically minded predecessor, Leo XIII. Pius, it was said, remained a country pastor at heart. He encouraged daily communion by the laity, and warmly supported Catholic Action. At the same time he was critical of the wrong sort of Catholic action as found in the Christian Democracy movement. In 1906 he condemned the French separation of church and state, but his pontificate saw improved relations with the Italian government. In 1907 the decree *Lamentabili Sane Exitu* and the encyclical *Pascendi Dominici Gregis* denounced modernism, which Pius called "the summation and essence of every heresy." Among his major achievements were the consolidation of the church's central government and the revision of canon law. He restored the Gregorian chant to the church's worship and effected important liturgical reforms. His canonization was effected in the unusually short period of forty years after his death.

Biographies by F. A. Forbes (1918), B. Pierarmi (1928), and Katherine Burton (1951).

J. D. DOUGLAS

Pius XI (1857–1939)

Pope from 1922. Born in Desio, Italy, Ambrogio Damiano Achille Ratti studied in Milan and Rome and won doctorates in philosophy, theology, and canon law. Ordained in 1879, he was a seminary teacher until 1888, then joined the Ambrosian Library, Milan, of which he became prefect (chief librarian) in 1907. He transferred to the Vatican Library in 1912, went to Poland as apostolic nuncio in 1919, and was made cardinal and archbishop of Milan in 1921. During his pontificate the Lateran Treaty (1929) recognized the Vatican's independence and Catholicism as the state religion of Mussolini's Italy. Pius subsequently had reason to condemn the dictatorships in both Italy (1931) and Germany (1937; despite a 1933 concordat with Hitler). Atheistic communism was similarly denounced (1937), as was persecution of Catholics in Spain and Mexico. Pius encouraged Catholic Action—a youth organization that aimed at "the participation of the laity in the apostolate of the Church's hierarchy"—and insisted that every religious order should engage actively in overseas missions. Pius also consecrated the first Chinese bishops (1926). His scholarly interests were reflected in his making systematic provision for research in archaeology (1925) and science (1926).

Biographies by Philip Hughes (1937), L. Browne-Olf (1938), and Zsolt Aradi (1958).

J. D. DOUGLAS

Pius XII (1876–1958)

Pope from 1939. Eugenio Maria Giovanni Pacelli was born in Rome, studied at the Gregorian University, and was ordained in 1899. He joined the Vatican Secretariat of State in 1901, was made archbishop and nuncio to Bavaria (1917) and Berlin (1925), and later became cardinal (1929) and papal secretary of state (1930). Soon after his election as pope, World War II presented him with new and complex problems. Some remembered that he had been largely responsible for the drafting of the 1933 concordat with Germany, and questioned his neutrality, not least in accusing him of not intervening in Hitler's genocidal onslaught against the Jews. (This inaction was later dramatized in the German Rolf Hochhuth's postwar play, *The Representative*.) It has been suggested that official protest might have provoked Hitler into even more extreme action, and that Pius did use diplomatic immunity to shield many from persecution. Pius permitted Catholic scholars to use scientific methods of biblical criticism (1943), relaxed the rules on fasting before communion (1953), and reminded missionaries to respect whatever was valuable in alien cultures. He found himself, however, once more the center of controversy in non-Catholic circles when in a 1950 encyclical he defined the dogma of the Assumption of the Virgin Mary.

Biographies by J. O. Smit (1949), O. Halecki (1954), N. Padellaro (1956), and Katherine Burton (1958).

J. D. Douglas

Pobee, John S. (1937–)

African scholar and ecumenist. Born in Ghana, his religious background is Anglican. He studied at Oxford University, and later became professor of New Testament and church history at the University of Ghana at Legon. He has also served on secondment to the World Council of Churches as associate director of its Programme on Theological Education. He has given lectures and pursued further studies in the United States and Europe, has written many scholarly articles in English and German, and has been the author of five books, including *Toward an African Theology.*

Michael Kyomya

Polanyi, Michael (1891–1976)

Hungarian physical chemist and philosopher. Born in Budapest, he studied there and at Karlsruhe, and lectured in Berlin and Manchester (1931–1958). He left Germany because of the rise of Hitler, and later published his concern about totalitarianism in *The Contempt of Freedom* (1940). He worked on reaction kinetics and crystal structure, and wrote widely on the philosophy of science. In *Personal Knowledge* (1958) he argued that in their search for objective truth scientists unnecessarily contrast knowledge and objectivity with faith and subjectivity. In fact, all knowledge needs a framework of faith: science can only proceed in the belief that truth exists to be discovered and that scientific methods are fundamentally sound. In *The Tacit Dimension* (1967) he explored a further aspect of knowledge. "We know more than we can tell"; our explicit knowledge is based on an underlying implicit knowledge. These concepts of personal participation in knowledge and "tacit knowing," suggesting strong similarities between scientific and theological ways of knowing, have been explored more recently by Scottish theologian T. F. Torrance. The latter in 1980 edited *Belief in Science and in Christian Life: The Relevance of Michael Polanyi's Thought for Christian Faith and Life.*

PHILIP HILLYER

Poling, Daniel Alfred (1884–1968)

Pastor, writer, broadcaster, and social activist. Born in Oregon, the son of two ministers of the United Evangelical Church, he was licensed to preach in that church in 1904 after graduating from Dalles College in Oregon. Although he pastored churches in three denominations (UEC, Reformed, Baptist) he probably wielded greatest influence through his leadership of nondenominational organizations, publications, and radio work. He ran for governor of Ohio in 1912 on the Prohibition ticket, was prominent in the Christian Endeavor Union, edited *Christian Herald* (1927–1966), and helped found the J. C. Penney Foundation in 1923 and served as its general director until 1936. From 1924 to 1932 he had a national audience for his radio programs. After World War II he was fervently anticommunist and a supporter of conservative political causes, running unsuccessfully for mayor of Philadelphia on the Republican ticket in 1951. He was also a prolific author; his works included *Radio Talks to Young People* (1936), *A Preacher Looks at War* (1943), *Jesus Says to You* (1961), and *He Came from Galilee* (1965).

ROBERT SCHUSTER

Pollard, Samuel (1864–1915)

Missionary to southwest China. Born in Cornwall, the son of a Bible Christian minister, he worked in the civil service for five years until his call to missionary work in China. He was adopted as a missionary by the Bible Christian Church in 1885 and sent out to Yunnan province in 1887. After a period of language study, he began pioneering work among the Chinese at Chaotung and Kunming. Soon he became aware of the various primitive tribes just over the Chinese border in Nosu territory. The work among the Chinese was difficult. During 1895 and 1896 he took his first furlough back in England. After 1897 the work began to make progress, although in 1900 Pollard had to flee to Shanghai because of the Boxer Rebellion.

His mission to the aboriginal tribes, especially the Miao, began at the end of 1903. A mass movement of the Miao began almost immediately. Within ten years around ten thousand tribal people entered the church. Over a third of these were baptized. At the same time Pollard learned their language, created a separate script, and began to translate the New Testament. He completed and published the Gospels for the Miao. At the same time he traveled, preached, and encouraged the infant church. With only a tiny number of missionaries it was an enormous job in primitive and rough mountainous conditions. From the headquarters he created at a place called Stonegateway, he organized and developed an indigenous church until his death from typhoid.

NOEL S. POLLARD

Porras, Aristomeno (1917–)

Author and editor. Known by the pen name Luis D. Salem, which has appeared on most of his thirty books and thousands of articles, he was born in Socota, Boyaca, Colombia. He studied theology in San Jose, Costa Rica, and was ordained as a Presbyterian minister in 1947, serving in several churches in Colombia. In 1949 his church was destroyed in the religious violence, and he and his congregation had to flee. After serving for two years as executive secretary of the Colombian Bible Society, he moved to Mexico in 1962 to work with the American Bible Society. In addition to editing the ABS magazine, *La Biblia en America Latina* (which under his direction saw an increase in circulation from 9,000 to 85,000) Porras has written extensively for the secular press—very unusual for an evangelical in Latin America. He has contributed weekly articles and columns for the Mexican newspaper *Excelsior* for over eighteen years. His literary work, all in Spanish, includes poetry, stories, essays, history, and biblical analysis. He retired from the Bible Society in 1984, but has continued to write.

STEPHEN R. SYWULKA

Purdie, James Eustace (1880–1977)

Canadian Pentecostal educator. A native of Prince Edward Island and a graduate of Wycliffe College, Toronto (1907), Purdie served a number of Anglican parishes across Canada from 1907 to 1922. Having claimed a Pentecostal experience in Saskatoon in 1919, he became founding principal (1925–1950) of the Canadian Pentecostal Bible College in Winnipeg, the first full-time Bible school operated by the Pentecostal Assemblies of Canada (PAOC). Patterning his curriculum after that of the evangelical Anglican Wycliffe College, he devoted his career to laying a foundation of doctrinal stability for the PAOC. His influence was extended nationally through his leadership role in the PAOC's National Committee of Bible Schools (ca. 1941), and through the wide distribution of his lecture notes in doctrine, church history, and biblical and pastoral studies. By the early 1960s most Canadian Pentecostal leaders either had been trained by him personally, or by those who had been trained by Purdie. He continued to minister widely in the PAOC following his retirement, and to maintain his earlier Anglican ties and lifelong involvement in evangelistic endeavors. He wrote *Concerning the Faith* (1951), a widely distributed and substantive Pentecostal catechism.

GLEN G. SCORGIE

Q

Queiroz de Oliveira, Edison (1948–)

Brazilian missionary statesman. Son of a Baptist minister, he sensed a divine calling to Christian service at twenty-five years of age. Trained by Campus Crusade for Christ and Operation Mobilization and a graduate of the Faculdade Teológica Batista, he assumed the pastorate of the First Baptist Church of Santo André in greater São Paulo. Owing to Queiroz's dynamic vision for evangelism, the church grew rapidly in numbers and modeled a missiological strategy for the Third World, sending over fifty workers to foreign fields. Founder of the Brazilian mission Project PAS and himself a missionary-evangelist in some thirty countries, Queiroz has done much to make his country one of the largest missionary-sending forces in the Third World. While continuing as conference speaker and pastor, Queiroz has served as executive director of the Ibero-American Missions Commission (COMIBAM), executive secretary of the Association of Church Missionary Councils (Brazil, ACMI), secretary of the Missions Commission of the Brazilian Evangelical Association, director of World Thrust (Brazil), and member of the Missions Commission of the World Evangelical Fellowship.

J. SCOTT HORRELL

R

Ragaz, Leonhard (1868–1945)

Swiss Reformed pastor and social activist. Born in Tamins, German-speaking Switzerland, he studied at Basel, Jena, and Berlin before ordination as a Reformed pastor in 1890. After serving the cathedral at Basel (1902–1908) he was appointed professor of systematic and practical theology at Zurich University (1908–1921). A strong pacifist, he made the union of religious and social movements "the central search of [his] soul." He gave the impression of regarding religion almost as a cosmic swindle, its great figures often overrated, its revivals godless. What was needed was not religion but the kingdom of God. For Ragaz, clericalism was the worst evil—an alliance between power and religion that downgraded God who is the only power. He upheld the right to strike as an essential element of social improvement, and gave up his theological chair, renouncing a secure income "to represent Christ in poverty." Ragaz was no uncritical socialist; he acknowledged capitalism's worthwhile achievements, but held that it had brought incredible unrest into the world. Neglect by the church had helped drive the workers into materialistic philosophy. Social change and religious reform were interdependent. On an American trip Ragaz found the status of black people "utterly offensive." For him, most believers fell into three errors: apprehending God too theoretically, seeing him as too much a God of the past, and standing helpless before the world's evil.

Ragaz's books and biographies of him are in German, but see Paul Bock (ed.), *Signs of the Kingdom: A Ragaz Reader* (1984).

J. D. DOUGLAS

Rahner, Karl (1904–1984)

German theologian. Born in Freiburg in Briesgau, Germany, he entered the Society of Jesus (Jesuits) in 1922 and was ordained a priest in 1932. While studying philosophy at the University of Freiburg he came under the influence of Martin Heidegger. He later obtained his doctorate in theology at the University of Innsbruck where in 1937 he began to teach dogmatic theology. During World War II he served at the Pastoral Institute in Vienna before moving to Pullach bei Munchen where he was professor of theology from 1945 to 1948. In 1949 he returned to the University of Innsbruck to teach dogmatic theology. In 1964 he became professor of theology at the University of Münster until his retirement in 1971. Rahner is considered to be one of the most influential theologians of his time. He strove to situate traditional dogmatic teaching within the broader framework of the ability inherent in all human beings to respond to God's self-communication in history. His concept of the "anonymous Christian" implied that all human beings can experience the reality of grace through human acts of knowing, willing, and loving. Because Rahner's writings were considered controversial, he was excluded by the Roman Curia from the preliminary proceedings of the Second Vatican Council. Eventually, however, he was to become one of the most influential theologians of Vatican II. In addition to writing over thirty books, he served as editor of Denzinger's *Enchiridion Symbolorum* (1952), of the ten-volume *Lexikon für Theologie and Kirche* (1957–1965), and of the six-volume *Sacramentum Mundi* (1968–1970). Some of his major works in English translation include *The Eternal Yes* (1958), *Encounters with Silence* (1960), *Free Speech in the Church* (1960), *Church and the Sacraments* (1963), *Theology for Renewal* (1963), *Dynamic Element in the Church* (1964), *Nature and Grace* (1964), *Studies in Modern Theology* (1965), *On Prayer* (1968), *The Shape of the Church to Come* (1973), *Encyclopedia of Theology* (1975), *Foundations of Christian Faith* (1978), *Dictionary of Theology* (1981), and *Love of Jesus and Love of Neighbor* (1983).

L. K. GRIMLEY

Ramabai, Pandita (1858–1922)

Indian evangelist and advocate for young women. Born into a Chitpavan Brahmin family in South Kanara, India, Ramabai (unlike other women) was taught Sanskrit by her father, a scholar and teacher among this most respected Hindu caste. Her remarkable knowledge gained recognition in Calcutta where men began to call on her ability to recite Sanskrit. Her talents earned her the title of "Pandita" ("Mistress of Learning"), one never before given to a woman. She married but was left a widow with a child after only nineteen months. This condition and her education impressed upon her the need to promote the education of Hindu women and, more important, the need to improve the conditions for young Hindu widows. Having turned to Christianity after struggling with the inadequacies of Hinduism, she opened a school that later developed into a large institution in Kedgaon. Following its name Mukti ("Deliverance"), she brought in widows, orphans, and other girls of lower caste in need of help. Hundreds of young women became Christians as a result of this work. In addition, she translated the entire Bible into Marathi so that it could be read by educated Hindus.

Biographies by M. L. B. Fuller (1945) and P. Sengupta (1970).

WENDY S. LARSON

311

Ramm, Bernard (1916–1992)

Baptist scholar and theologian. Born in Butte, Montana, he graduated from the University of Washington, Eastern Baptist Theological Seminary, and the University of California (Ph.D., 1950). He taught at a series of theological schools, including the Bible Institute of Los Angeles (1945–1951), California Baptist Theological Seminary (1959–1974), Eastern Baptist Theological Seminary (1974–1977), and the American Baptist Theological Seminary of the West (1978–1986). He worked also with many organizations, including Young Life and World Vision. Influenced by Abraham Kuyper and Karl Barth, Ramm saw his mission to be the steering of a middle way between fundamentalism and modernism, while speaking to twentieth-century concerns. Ramm was a creative and versatile theologian whose works seem to be probings rather than pronouncements. He felt that he was defending "the historic Christian faith as reflected in the great creeds of the ancient Church, and in the spirit and writings of the reformers," which is how he defined evangelicalism. He was the author of numerous volumes, among them *The Christian View of Science and Scripture* (1954), *Special Revelation and the Word of God* (1961), *The Evangelical Heritage* (1973), *After Fundamentalism* (1983), and *An Evangelical Christology* (1985).

WALTER A. ELWELL

Ramsay, William Mitchell (1851–1939)

Scottish Classical and New Testament historian and archaeologist. Born in Glasgow, Scotland, he was educated at the universities of Aberdeen, Oxford, and Göttingen. He was an Oxford traveling scholar (1880–1882) and research fellow (1882–1887), professor of Classical art and archaeology in the University of Oxford (1885–1886), and professor of humanity at the University of Aberdeen (1886–1911). He became noted for his research in early Christian history and archaeology. He lectured and traveled widely and received many honors for his archaeological explorations, especially in Turkey (1880–1890; 1900–1914). He was knighted in 1906. Although he made great contributions in the fields of archaeology and geography, his importance for New Testament studies was to provide background for the life of Paul, support for the historical reliability of Luke's writings, and powerful evidence for the south Galatia destination of Paul's Epistle to the Galatians. Among his more important publications are *Historical Geography of Asia Minor* (1890), *The Church in the Roman Empire before A.D. 170* (1893), *St. Paul the Traveller and Roman Citizen* (1895), *Historical Commentary on St. Paul's Epistle to the Galatians* (1899), *The Letters to the Seven Churches of Asia* (1904), *The Cities of St. Paul* (1907), *Luke the Physician* (1908), and *The Bearing of Recent Research on the Trustworthiness of the New Testament* (1914).

ALBERT H. FREUNDT, JR.

Ramsey, (Arthur) Michael (1904–1988)

The one-hundredth archbishop of Canterbury. Son of the president of Magdalene College, Cambridge, he graduated from the university there and was ordained in 1928. After varied experience in the parish ministry and as theological college tutor, he became successively professor of divinity at Durham (1940) and Cambridge (1950), bishop of Durham (1952), archbishop of York (1956), and archbishop of Canterbury (1961–1974). Primarily a theologian in an Anglo-Catholic tradition, he never forgot his free church roots or his Cambridge training under E. C. Hoskyns. He took a leading part in the passing of the Worship and Doctrine Measure, which gave to the Church of England considerable freedom from Parliament. The Alternative Service Book was also begun in his time. While maintaining contacts with the Roman Catholic Church, and particularly with the Orthodox, with whom he felt a special affinity, he was prominent also in the two abortive attempts for unity with the Methodist Church. Ramsey's time at Canterbury coincided with upheavals in social ethics, particularly in such matters as abortion, capital punishment, homosexuality, and immigration, where his own contribution was valued. He was an extensive traveler. His published works include *The Gospel and the Catholic Church* (1936), *From Gore to Temple* (1960), *Sacred and Secular* (1965), and *God, Christ and the World* (1969).

Biographies by Owen Chadwick (1990) and Michael De-La-Noy (1990).

PETER S. DAWES

Rauschenbusch, Walter (1861–1918)

Scholar and social activist. Born in Rochester, New York, son of an immigrant Baptist minister, he was raised partly in Germany and partly in the United States in a Pietist environment. He studied at Rochester College and Seminary, and at the universities of Berlin and Leipzig. Because of his liberal theological views he was denied an appointment to India by the American Baptist Foreign Mission Board, but he accepted a call to the Second German Church, New York City, in 1886. During his work over eleven years among the poor he developed a program of Christian social action that he found to be sanctioned by the teaching of Jesus, and which later found expression in his major writings. In 1897 he was appointed professor by the German department of Rochester Theological Seminary, becoming in 1902 chairman of the church history department. He remained there until his death. His literary legacy is extensive, and includes several editions of hymn books that he published in conjunction with Ira D. Sankey. His most prominent publications are *Christianizing the Social Order* (1912), *The Social Principles of Jesus* (1916), and *A Theology for the Social Gospel* (1917).

Biographies by D. R. Sharpe (1942), W. S. Hudson (1984), and P. M. Minus (1988).

EDWARD J. FURCHA

Ray, Chandu (1912–1983)

Indian bishop, Bible translator, and evangelist. Born into a well-to-do Hindu Sindhi family, he became a Christian at the age of twenty-seven, and spent much time producing and distributing books, especially the Bible, and proclaiming the gospel. In 1956 he was appointed to work in Sindh. Using his gifts of evangelism and encouragement, he led the work among the Kohlis, a large tribal group. He served as secretary of the Pakistan Bible Society for nine years, and was the chief translator of the Sindhi Old Testament, reviser of the Sindhi New Testament, and publisher of the Punjabi New Testament, and of the Sindhi, Gurmukhi, and Tibetan Bibles. He became archdeacon of Lahore, then bishop in 1951, transferring to the influential diocese of Karachi in 1960. In 1969 he moved to Singapore as executive director of the Co-ordinating Office for Asian Evangelism of the Asia-South Pacific Congress on Evangelism. In 1975 he joined the Haggai Institute, serving in Singapore, and later became their director of Third World Outreach until his retirement in 1982. He was also involved with the International Alliance of YMCAs, and was active at the Evanston and New Delhi meetings of the World Council of Churches. His dynamic personality, love for Christ, concern for evangelism, and infectious enthusiasm inspired many throughout the world to become involved in mission. He dealt sensitively with people of other faiths.

PATRICK SOOKHDEO

Rees, Paul Stromberg (1900–1991)

Evangelical pastor and leader. Born in Providence, Rhode Island, he graduated from the University of Southern California and was ordained to the ministry of the Evangelical Covenant Church of America (1921). He was associate pastor, Pilgrim Tabernacle, Pasadena, California (1920–1923); ministerial superintendent, Detroit Holiness Tabernacle (1928–1932); pastor, First Covenant Church, Minneapolis, Minnesota (1938–1958); vice president, World Vision International (1958–1975); editor, *World Vision* magazine (1964–1972); and director of Pastors Conference (1964–1975). He was moderator, Evangelical Covenant Church of America (1948); president, National Association of Evangelicals (1952–1954); vice president, World Evangelical Fellowship; and adviser at World Council of Churches assemblies (1961, 1968). He received many awards and honorary doctorates, and participated in several Billy Graham crusades. He was an articulate leader and spokesman for the evangelical movement. His entry in *Who's Who in America* (1984–1985) concludes: "I am convinced that the

Christian world-view answers more questions, resolves more doubts, subdues more fears, meets more needs, humbles more pride, preserves more dignity, holds more hope than any other." His writings include *If God Be for Us* (1940), *Stir Up the Gift* (1952), *Christian: Commit Yourself* (1957), *Triumphant in Trouble* (1962), *Proclaiming the New Testament— Philippians, Colossians, Philemon* (1964), and *Nairobi to Berkeley* (1967). He also edited *Don't Sleep Through the Revolution* (1969).

ALBERT H. FREUNDT, JR.

Reid, John (1928–)

Australian bishop and international chairman of the Lausanne Committee on World Evangelization. Graduate of Moore College, Sydney, he was a traveling representative of InterVarsity Fellowship, curate at St. Matthews' Manly, and rector of Christ Church, Gladesville (1956–1969) before his appointment as archdeacon of Cumberland and canon of St. Andrew's Cathedral, Sydney. In 1972 he was consecrated as an assistant bishop of Sydney, and served as administrator of the diocese when Archbishop Robinson retired in 1993. Reid has always seen deep commitment to the parish ministry as fundamental to the church's mission, not least in inner-city work. He has been the moving spirit behind outreach to the Aboriginal, Chinese, Italian, Maori, Turkish, Arabic, Vietnamese, and Iranian communities in Australia's largest city. His involvement in international mission and evangelism began early in his ministry. This took him initially to East Africa, but has since included four continents, including communist-ruled Eastern Europe. His worth was recognized not only by evangelical Anglicans worldwide when they elected him their international chairman, but by an even wider constituency when he accepted a similar post with the Lausanne Committee on World Evangelization. Although now officially retired from local Episcopal responsibilities, Reid in his mid-sixties is reported to swim every day in Sydney harbor.

J. D. DOUGLAS

Reith, John Charles Walsham (Lord Reith) (1889–1971)

Widely regarded as "the creator of the British Broadcasting Corporation" (BBC). Son of a Free Church of Scotland minister in Stonehaven, he was trained as an engineer, and during World War I served in civil and military posts. His service with the BBC (1922–1938) included the inauguration of British television. As one whose roots were deep in Calvinism he was determined to build a worthy institution whose staff would maintain high moral standards both personally and professionally. He limited Sunday broadcasting, brought together a religious advisory committee, and regarded absentees from its meetings as failing in imagination. A man incapable of compromise, he clashed frequently with the BBC's new governors. In 1938

315

Reith was persuaded by Prime Minister Chamberlain to enter political life, and as a member of Parliament he subsequently held ministerial office (1940–1942). He then became a highly efficient director of combined operations at the Admiralty during World War II; he regarded his postwar career in commerce as anticlimactic. Despite his hopes, no key governmental post was offered him, and he came to regret having left the BBC. He was knighted by King George V in 1927. Later honors included a barony, the rectorship of Glasgow University, and two terms as Lord High Commissioner (the queen's representative) to the Church of Scotland general assembly. Reith wrote the autobiographical *Into the Wind* (1949) and *Wearing Spurs* (1966). Charles Stuart edited *The Reith Diaries* (1975).

J. D. DOUGLAS

Rema, Lal C. (1925–)

Indian Baptist leader. Born in Mizoram, India, he served with the government of Assam before joining the staff of the Baptist General Conference Board of World Mission. He was for twenty-two years pastor of the Baptist church in Tezpur, Assam, and had been coordinator of the church-planting ministry for the North Bank Baptist Christian Association. He saw 350 new churches established, 100 of them in Assam, 250 in Arunachal Pradesh. Committed to the authority of the Bible and to the preeminence of Christ, he has participated in many conferences on missions and evangelization, and is involved in relief and development work.

FRANCIS SUNDERARAJ

Rembao, Alberto (1895–1962)

Mexican evangelical intellectual, writer, and educator. Born in Chihuahua, Mexico, he fought in the Revolution, losing a leg in battle. He graduated from Pomona College and from the Pacific School of Religion, after which he studied at the University of California and at Yale Divinity School. Well-known as preacher and lecturer, he taught at the University of Guadalajara, Mexico, and the Theological Seminary of Matanzas, Cuba, and was visiting professor in many other institutions. He served also as director of the International School in Guadalajara. For over thirty years he was editor of *La Nueva Democracia* magazine, published by the Committee on Co-operation in Latin America. He wrote a number of books, in English and Spanish, on theology and culture, and a novel, *Lupita*, set in the Mexican Revolution. Along with a unique style as a writer, he was known for his neologisms, coining words to express new concepts. Rembao was considered an expert on Hispanic-American affairs, and his home in Manhattan became an informal center for visiting intellectuals and exiled politicians from all over Latin America.

STEPHEN R. SYWULKA

Reza, Honorato Tamez (1913–)

Church of the Nazarene theologian and hymn translator. A native of Alahuixtlan, Guerrero, Mexico, he graduated from the Seminario Teologico Nazareno (Bible Training School) in Mexico City in 1935, and also from Pasadena College, California. He pursued graduate studies in the Universidad Nacional de Mexico, pastored Nazarene churches in Mexico, Los Angeles, and Kansas City, and served as executive director of the international publications of the Church of the Nazarene. After teaching for twenty-three years at the Nazarene Theological Seminary in Kansas City, he founded the Seminario Nazareno Mexicano in Mexico City in 1980. Author of seven books, Reza also translated some four hundred hymns and worked closely with Haldor Lillenas, founder of the Lillenas Publishing Company, a division of the Nazarene Publishing House. Reza helped with the compilation and translation of a series of six gospel songbooks entitled *Ioyas Favoritas* (Favorite Jewels), which began in 1949 and enjoyed great popularity throughout Latin America. He was a member of the commissions that produced two major hymnals, *Lluvias de Bendicion* (Showers of Blessing) (1947) and *Gracia y Devocion* (Grace and Devotion) (1968). The latter contains 424 selections with sixty-eight translations by Reza.

PHILIP BLYCKER

Rhee, Jong-Sung (1922–)

Korean theologian and seminary president. Born into a traditionally Buddhist home in southeast Korea, he was sent at age seventeen to Japan, graduating from what is now Tokyo Union Theological Seminary in 1951. He pursued his studies at Fuller Theological Seminary, Louisville Presbyterian Theological Seminary, and San Francisco Theological Seminary (Ph.D., 1963), with advanced research at Princeton, Bonn, and Cambridge. In Korea he served the large Young Nak Presbyterian Church in Seoul as assistant minister (1957–1958), and was called to Yonsei University as professor, dean of students, and dean of chapel (1959–1965). He was then professor, dean, and finally president of the largest Presbyterian seminary in the world, the Presbyterian (*Tonghap*) Theological Seminary and College in Seoul (1966–1988). He has served internationally as director and executive member of the North East Asia Association of Theological Schools (1968–1982), and as editor of the *North East Asia Theological Review.* In 1985 the Korean Presbyterian Church elected him moderator of its general assembly. His twelve-volume *Systematic Theology* (in Korean) has become a standard text.

SAMUEL H. MOFFETT

Rhee, Syngman (1875–1965)

First president of the Republic of Korea. Born of distant royal lineage, he was reared in the strict Confucian tradition. At age nineteen, however, attracted by the reputation for new ways and new learning of a recently formed Methodist high school in Seoul, he entered Paejae Academy, and soon joined the Independence Club, a group of young democratic-minded reformers. His zeal in leading mass protests against the conservative Yi dynasty brought imprisonment in 1897. During his six-year confinement, missionary friends visited him and led him to the Christian faith. On being released he was sent to America to plead the case for Korean independence from encroaching Japan. He was unsuccessful but remained to study at George Washington University, Harvard, and Princeton (Ph.D., 1910). While at George Washington he was baptized at the Presbyterian Church of the Covenant.

In 1911 he returned to Korea, but found Japanese rule intolerable and dangerous, and left in 1912 for Hawaii. As principal of the Methodist Korean Elementary School in Honolulu, he clashed with American Methodist acceptance of Japan's colonization of Korea, and left to organize an independent school for Koreans in Honolulu in 1916, the Korean Christian Institute. He nonetheless remained a Methodist all his life. Becoming more and more involved politically, he was elected president of the Korean government-in-exile in Shanghai (1919–1925). When Korea finally won independence in 1945 and free elections could be held only in the south of the arbitrarily divided country, Syngman Rhee was elected first president of the Republic, and was reelected three times. A student revolution forced him from office in 1960, and he died five years later in Hawaii.

Biographies by R. T. Oliver (1954) and R. C. Allen (1960).

SAMUEL H. MOFFETT

Rice, John R. (1895–1980)

Baptist fundamentalist champion. Born in rural Texas, and reared and educated in Southern Baptist circles, he left the Southern Baptist Convention in the 1920s in protest against apparent denominational tolerance of evolutionary theory. A decade of cooperation with J. Frank Norris ended acrimoniously in 1936. While pastoring the Fundamentalist Baptist Church in Dallas (1932–1940), Rice founded (1934) *The Sword of the Lord,* an independent weekly promoting fundamentalist views and attacking modernism, ecumenism, and moral laxity. The publication proved widely influential, especially among independent Baptists, and after 1940, when he resigned his pastorate and moved to Wheaton, Illinois, Rice devoted a large portion of his lengthy career to editorial work. He became well known for his polemical opposition to theological modernism, Catholicism, communism, and the civil rights movement, as well as to dancing, smoking, movies, and alcohol. In 1957 he condemned Billy Graham for collaborating with modernists. He founded the "Voice of Revival" radio program in 1959, and conducted popular "Sword Conferences" on revival and soul-winning. A flamboyant preacher, he also authored over one hundred books and pamphlets, including an enormously popular sixteen-page evangelistic booklet entitled *What Must I Do to Be Saved?* He was perhaps America's most prominent midcentury fundamentalist.

Biography by R. L. Summer (1960).

GLEN G. SCORGIE

Richard, John (1923–)

Bible expositor and administrator. Born in Rangoon, Burma, he moved to India after World War II, and became well known as an evangelical conference speaker and writer. He served as general secretary of the Evangelical Fellowship of India (1976–1983) and of Asia (1984–1989), and subsequently became associate international director for the Global Consultation on World Evangelization scheduled to be held in Seoul, Korea, in 1995. It is widely acknowledged that under his leadership the Evangelical Fellowship of India developed into one of the most significant national bodies anywhere in the world. Richard was also a member of the Lausanne Committee for World Evangelization.

FRANCIS SUNDERARAJ

Richard, Timothy (1845–1919)

Welsh missionary to China. Born in Carmarthenshire and converted during the 1858 revival in Wales, he entered Haverfordwest Baptist College. While there he felt called to be a missionary in China. In 1869 the Baptist Missionary Society sent him to serve in Chefoot, Shantung. While there he developed theories of evangelism that depended on educational, literary, and cultural approaches to the Chinese rather than direct preaching. He used simple medical knowledge and organized famine relief in the severe conditions in Shansi province after 1876. When there was opposition to his methods in 1891, he took up the position of secretary of the Christian Literature Society, though he remained a Baptist missionary. The breadth and quantity of the output of the society were phenomenal. Such was Richard's influence among the ruling and educated classes that when he advised the creation of the first modern university in Shansi province, funded from the Boxer Rebellion indemnity, he was made its chancellor for the first decade. He became a national figure in China, seeking reform and reconciliation. He has been described as "a seer and a poet with the heart of a little child and with an irresistible charm."

NOEL S. POLLARD

Riley, William Bell (1861–1947)

American fundamentalist leader. Born in Indiana, he graduated from Hanover College, and pastored churches in Kentucky, Indiana, and Illi-

319

nois before accepting the pastorate of First Baptist Church, Minneapolis, in 1897. This remained the base of his activities until his death. Unlike some of his premillennial contemporaries, he was active in civic affairs as a moral reformer, fighting the liquor trade and evolutionary teaching, and (later in life) communism. From an early age Riley campaigned steadfastly against modernism, and eventually was one of the founders of the World's Christian Fundamentals Association in 1919 and the Baptist Bible Union in 1923. A leader in the Bible School movement, he founded the Bible Training School in Minneapolis in 1902, which developed into the Northwestern schools. Riley wrote more than sixty volumes, including the extensive set *The Bible of the Expositor and the Evangelist* (1924–1938).

Biographies by M. A. Riley (1938) and W. V. Trollinger (1990).

THOMAS G. REID, JR.

Rios Montt, Efrain (1926–)

Guatemalan political leader. The first "born-again evangelical" to become president of a Latin American country, he was born in Huehuetenango, Guatemala, and decided as a young boy to pursue a military career. Rejected by the Polytechnic Institute (Guatemala's West Point) because of poor eyesight, he enlisted as a private, but later managed to graduate from the Polytechnic, was commissioned as an officer, and rose to the rank of brigadier general. In 1974 he ran for the presidency as the candidate of the Christian Democrats and lost; there were widespread accusations of fraud. Converted through a Bible study associated with the charismatic Verbo Church, he was serving as administrator of the church's school in 1982 when young officers leading a coup d'etat asked him to head a military junta. Taking over a country on the verge of anarchy, Rios Montt established order, fought corruption, preached morality, and confronted the major leftist guerrilla movement with "beans and bullets," a policy of armed civil patrols combined with rural development. Accused during his controversial seventeen months in office of human rights repression and provoking religious confrontation, he was ousted by another coup in 1983. His attempt to run again for president in 1990 won strong popular support, but was blocked by the courts. He remains a political force as head of his own party; he has also continued to be active in the Verbo Church.

STEPHEN R. SYWULKA

Rios, Asdrubal (1913–)

Venezuelan journalist and church leader. Born in Maracaibo, he was converted at age fourteen, graduated from the Maracaibo Bible Institute (where he later taught) in 1934, and was ordained to the ministry in 1942. Longtime editor of *La Estrella de la Mañana* (Morning Star) magazine, he has written forty-five books, all in Spanish, and over four thousand magazine and newspaper articles. He has held various posts in his church, which relates to The Evangelical Alliance Mission (TEAM), and in interdenominational and international bodies. He served as chairman of the board of the Seminario Evangelico Asociado in Maracay, Venezuela, and was founder of the Latin American Evangelical Confraternity (CONELA). He served also one term as a Congressman in the Venezuelan National Assembly.

STEPHEN R. SYWULKA

Ritschl, Otto Karl Albrecht (1860–1944)

German theologian. Born in Bonn, son of a famous theologian, he attended the universities of Göttingen, Bonn, and Giessen. He obtained his licentiate in theology at Halle in 1885, and became privatdozent in church history. He held teaching positions at Kiel (1889) and Bonn (1894), and became full professor of systematic theology in 1897. Although less widely known than his father Albrecht, whose biography he wrote, he published extensively in historical theology and in the German language, most notably *Dogmengeschichte des Protestantismus* (4 vols., 1908–1927).

EDWARD J. FURCHA

Ro, Bong-Rin (1935–)

Korean theologian and missionary statesman. He became a Christian during the troubled years of the Korean War (1950–1953). After a year at Seoul National University (1955–1956), he graduated from Columbia Bible College (1960), Wheaton College (1962), Covenant Seminary (1961), and Concordia Lutheran Seminary (S.T.M., Ph.D., 1964–1969). He taught at Singapore Bible College (1970–1974), Wheaton College, and Trinity Evangelical Divinity School, and at Tunghai University, Taiwan (1981–1984). As executive secretary of the Asia Theological Association (1974–1991) he visited more than two hundred theological schools in Asia. He has been prominent also in the World Evangelical Fellowship, the Asia Graduate School of Theology, and the Asian Center of Theological Studies and Mission in Seoul.

SAMUEL H. MOFFETT

Roberts, (Granville) Oral (1918–)

American evangelist, author, and university president. Roberts was born near Ada, Oklahoma, the son of a pastor in the Pentecostal Holiness Church. His own religious doubts were answered when he was healed of tuberculosis during services held by evangelist George Moncey in 1935. The following year he was ordained as a minister in the PHC. After several years as a denominational pastor and evangelist, he received the gift of healing in 1947 and decided to start an independent program. Roberts started what became the Oral Roberts Evangelistic Association in 1948. For the next two decades he traveled around the country and the world holding meetings and healing services. He made early use of radio and expanded into television in 1954. By the 1960s he was one of the few evangelists whose name was instantly recognized by the general population. Oral Roberts University was started in 1965 and expanded in the 1970s to include graduate-level programs in medicine and law. Roberts established closer ties with Protestant evangelicals during his attendance in 1966 at the World Congress on Evangelism. In 1968 Roberts joined the United Methodist Church. The same year he stopped holding evangelistic meetings, although his television specials, after a brief hiatus, went on. He continued through most of the rest of the century to become one of the best-known religious leaders in the country, although also one of the most controversial. His fund-raising efforts, such as his description in 1980 of a vision of a nine hundred-foot Jesus who assured him that the City of Faith Medical Center Roberts had started would be completed, caused ridicule in the secular press and criticism from Christian leaders. Besides leading the evangelistic organization (which had a multimillion-dollar budget) and the university, Roberts authored numerous books, including an autobiography.

ROBERT SCHUSTER

Roberts, Evan John (1878–1951)

Welsh revival leader. Born in Glamorgan, the son of a miner, he went down the mine at the age of twelve. In 1904 he believed himself called to the ministry of his Calvinistic Methodist Church. He began training in its college at Newcastle Emlyn. For eleven years he had been praying for revival. Many in Wales believed that a revival like that of 1858 was imminent. He attended a meeting at Blaenannerch and experienced the power of the Holy Spirit. Instead of returning to college he went home to Loughor. He held regular meetings that marked the outbreak of the revival. Numbers attending grew. Emotional experiences were high. Spontaneity was their hallmark. In the year that followed, Roberts and his friends made tours throughout Wales and Merseyside until early 1906. The revival was believed to have gathered one hundred thousand converts. The intensity of the revival broke Roberts. At the end of 1905 he retired to the retreat offered him by Jessie Penn-Lewis in Leicestershire. Although he returned to Wales in 1925 and died in Cardiff, he never recovered the power of his earlier experiences.

NOEL S. POLLARD

Roberts, J. Deotis, Sr. (1927–)

Preacher, writer, and theologian. A native of Spindate, North Carolina, he was educated at Johnson C. Smith University, Shaw University, and Hartford Seminary. He received his Ph.D. from the University of Edinburgh. The focus of his studies was comparative religions, and he traveled in Asia,

Africa, and Europe, where he observed other religions. His goal was to understand religion's particularity and universality. He has spent much of his career as a professor at the Howard University School of Religion in Washington, D. C.

While already a theologian of some note in his own right, Roberts was influenced by the publication of James Cone's work on black theology, and his goal became to develop a black theology from a more inclusive perspective. He has written in partial support and partial opposition to Cone, believing that reconciliation between the races is vital to the freedom of African Americans. Contrary to Cone's approach, Roberts believes it is not necessary for whites to become "black" in order to be reconciled with blacks. He calls for reconciliation as between equals and contends that whites ought to become occupied with the task of preparing their own communities for the acceptance of African Americans. He asserts that God's revelation is personal and social; it is both existential and political.

He has written *Liberation and Reconciliation: A Black Theology* (1971).

ROBERT C. SUGGS

Robertson, Archibald Thomas (1863–1934)

New Testament scholar. Born near Chatham, Virginia, he was licensed to preach by the Southern Baptist Convention when he was sixteen, and went on to earn degrees at Wake Forest College (1885) and Southern Baptist Theological Seminary (1888). He taught New Testament at the seminary from 1888 to 1934, apart from a three-year interlude teaching biblical introduction. His numerous writings included Greek grammars, works on the life and teaching of Jesus and Paul, biographical and historical studies, commentaries, and studies of biblical criticism. *A Harmony of the Gospels* and *An Introduction to the Textual Criticism* were the most widely used, but his crowning achievement was the almost 1,500-page *A Grammar of the Greek New Testament in the Light of Historical Research* (1914), which remains in print. His writing and teaching were characterized by a devotion to academic quality and spiritual passion, appealing to both scholars and the Christian public. His distinguished work in biblical scholarship made him the principal Greek scholar of his day.

PAUL A. ERICKSEN

Robertson, Marion Gordon "Pat" (1930–)

Christian educator and broadcaster. Born in Lexington, Virginia, he received degrees from Washington and Lee University and, after service in the United States Marine Corps (1950–1952), from Yale University (J.D., 1955) and New York Theological Seminary (M.Div., 1959). He was ordained in the Southern Baptist ministry (1961), and has become a modern charismatic leader. He is president of the Christian Broadcasting Network, Inc., Virginia Beach, Virginia (1959–), which broadcasts internationally, and is chancellor of Regent University (1978–), both of which he founded; he is also host of the television talk show, the "700 Club" (1968–), which made him a public evangelical personality. Operation Blessing Relief and Development, which he started in 1978, has become a worldwide humanitarian relief agency. Heads Up, a literacy organization that he founded in 1985, has helped hundreds of thousands of persons of all ages learn to read. He was a member of the Presidential Task Force on Victims of Crime (1982–1983), and he is the recipient of many awards. Robertson, whose father was a U.S. senator, fears that the United States is in danger of giving up its Judeo-Christian heritage for secular humanism. He began to mobilize Christians to influence political life. In 1987 he resigned from the ministry in order to conduct an unsuccessful campaign to become the Republican party's nominee for the office of president. Today he continues efforts to renew Christian witness in public affairs, particularly through the Christian Coalition that he founded (1989). His writings include *Shout It from the Housetops* (1972), *The Secret Kingdom* (1982), *Beyond Reason* (1984), *Answers to 200 of Life's Most Probing Questions* (1984), and *America's Date with Destiny* (1986).

ALBERT H. FREUNDT, JR.

Robinson, Donald William Bradley (1922–)

Australian bishop and New Testament scholar. Son of an Anglican archdeacon, he served in the army during World War II, after which he earned degrees at the universities of Sydney and Cambridge. Ordained in 1950, he gained pastoral experience before joining the staff of Moore Theological College, Sydney, in 1952, serving as vice principal from 1959. In 1973 he was consecrated second bishop in Parramatta; in 1982 he was elected archbishop of Sydney, a post he held until retirement in 1993.

Robinson became well known throughout the church in Australia as a member of the Liturgical Composition, which prepared the revision of *The Book of Common Prayer* and oversaw the composition of *An Australian Prayer Book*. His special interest is in the New Testament; he is a member of the International Societas Novi Testamenti Studiorum. He has also lectured in Sydney University Divinity School, and has represented the Anglican Church of Australia on the Anglican Consultative Council. His evangelical interests are reflected in his strong support of missionary work at home and abroad, and his past presidency of the Australian Fellowship of Evangelical Students.

J. D. DOUGLAS

Robinson, Henry Wheeler (1872–1945)

English Old Testament scholar. Born in Northampton, he was educated at Edinburgh, Oxford, and German universities before ordination as Baptist pastor in 1900. He served congregations in Pitlochry and Coventry, then was tutor at Rawdon College, Leeds (1906–1920) and principal of Regent's Park College, London (1920–1942). In 1927 he oversaw the transfer of the college from the capital to Oxford—Robinson wanted his students to have the advantage of a university environment. He became widely known and respected beyond his own denomination. Oxford University acknowledged his scholarship by making him reader in biblical criticism (1934–1941) and, unusual for a non-Anglican, he served also as chairman of the theological faculty (1937–1939). While he kept abreast of developments in German scholarship, Robinson never lost his evangelical convictions. His published works included *The Christian Doctrine of Man* (1911), *The Religious Ideas of the Old Testament* (1913), *The Christian Experience of the Holy Spirit* (1928), and *Suffering, Human and Divine* (1940).

Biography by E. A. Payne (1946).

J. D. DOUGLAS

Robinson, John Arthur Thomas (1919–1983)

Anglican bishop and theologian. Born in Canterbury, he graduated from Cambridge; Scottish theologian John Baillie described Robinson's Ph.D. thesis as "the best ever to have come my way." He was ordained in 1945, and after parish work in western England (1945–1951) he was dean of Clare College, Cambridge (1951–1958), until consecration as suffragan bishop of Woolwich (1959–1969). In 1960 he hit the headlines by defending D. H. Lawrence's novel *Lady Chatterley's Lover* in court. In 1963 he scandalized the theologically orthodox in his book *Honest to God,* the sales of which that year reportedly exceeded those of *The New English Bible,* then two years old. Robinson's book questioned the biblical view of God, declared that the only intrinsic evil was lack of love, scoffed at the atonement as "frankly incredible to man come of age," and called the incarnation "God dressed up—like Father Christmas." With an odd combination of flashy sensationalism and engaging diffidence, Robinson professed to be "merely thinking aloud" but with "a sense of divine imperative," giving the impression that no thoughtful reader could come to any other conclusions but his. He returned to academic life at Cambridge in 1969, but received no further academic or ecclesiastical preferment. To help others, he spoke out freely about the cancer that ended his life. His later works, some of them displaying a more conservative approach to New Testament history, included *The Human Face of God* (1973), *The Priority of John* (1985), and *Where Three Ways Meet* (1987).

Biography by Eric James (1986).

J. D. DOUGLAS

325

Rodeheaver, Homer Alvan (1880–1955)

Songleader, trombonist, composer, and music publisher. Born in Ohio and reared in Tennessee, Rodeheaver enrolled in Ohio Wesleyan University in 1896. During the Spanish-American War, he served with the Fourth Regiment Band of Tennessee. He then returned to Ohio Wesleyan, which he left in 1904 to work as a music director and song leader for evangelist William E. Biederwolf. In 1910 Rodeheaver began a twenty-year tenure as the songleader for well-known evangelist Billy Sunday. In this capacity, he set the mood for Sunday's sermons by singing and playing solos, telling song stories, leading audience singing, and directing the choir. Rodeheaver won considerable praise from observers, many of whom considered his warm, easy-going manner a key element in Sunday's success. In 1910 he founded Rodeheaver Publishers of Sacred Music, which later became known as Rodeheaver Hall-Mack Company. In 1920 Rodeheaver started the summer School of Sacred Music at Winona Lake, Indiana. In 1950 he founded the Rodeheaver Boys' Ranch in Palatka, Florida. Among the books and song collections Rodeheaver published were *Song Stories of the Sawdust Trail, Hymnal Handbook for Standard Hymns and Gospel Songs, Twenty Years with Billy Sunday,* and *Song Leadership: A Practical Manual for All Who Want to Help Folks Sing.*

ROBERT L. MORRISON

Romero, Oscar Arnulfo (1917–1980)

Martyred Roman Catholic archbishop. Born in Ciudad Barrios, El Salvador, he began studying for the priesthood at age thirteen. A poem praising the pope won him a scholarship from the local bishop to the Pio Latino Americano school in Rome. Although he never finished his degree because of the wartime situation, he was ordained to the priesthood in 1942 and returned the next year to El Salvador, where he served in the diocese of San Miguel, developing a reputation for asceticism, devotion to the Virgin, and capacity for work. In 1967 he was named secretary of the Episcopal conference of El Salvador, in 1970 auxiliary bishop of San Salvador, and in 1974 bishop of Santiago de Maria. Selected as archbishop of San Salvador in 1977, largely due to his conservatism and allegiance to Rome, Romero became increasingly critical of government repression and social injustice as unrest and violence grew in his country, including the murder of several priests and the expulsion of others, primarily Jesuits, seen by the ruling oligarchy as Marxists. His stance earned him a nomination for the Nobel Peace Prize. With his country moving toward civil war and his church badly divided, Romero received death threats from both left- and right-wing extremists. On March 24, 1980, he was killed by an unidentified gunman as he said Mass in a small chapel near his spartan residence in San Salvador.

Biographies by Dermot Kelogh (1981) and J. R. Brockman (1982).

STEPHEN R. SYWULKA

Rookmaaker, Hendrik Roeloff (Hans) (1922–1977)

Dutch art historian. Born in the Hague, son of a Dutch colonial officer in Sumatra, he was studying at a school for marine officers when the Germans occupied the Netherlands (1940). Arrested for underground activities and later held in POW camps, he was introduced by a fellow prisoner to Herman Dooyeweerd's work, and found that his faith in Christ "acquired a firm underpinning of philosophic thought." Encouraged by Francis Schaeffer, in 1946 he decided to be "a Reformed Christian professor of art history." Rookmaaker held that "God's hand in history" had not been comprehensively discerned and understood by Protestants, who had an irrational distrust of beauty. He graduated from the Municipal University of Amsterdam (1952) and later earned a doctorate there (1959). He lectured in the history of art at Leiden University (1958–1965), and was professor of the same subject at the Free University of Amsterdam (1965–1977). A pioneer who is perhaps not yet sufficiently appreciated by religious conservatives, Rookmaaker made little attempt to be all things to all men. He smoked in other people's cars, offered whisky to InterVarsity staffers, charged an evangelical society for first-class travel, as a newlywed squandered a month's meager housekeeping money on jazz records and art books, was irritable before 11 A.M., clicked his fingers at waiters, and reduced girl students to tears by ill-worded comments. Nonetheless, he taught many to bring a Christian mind to many of the outstanding issues of the day. He wrote *Modern Art and the Death of a Culture* (1970).

Biography by Linette Martin (1979).

JAMES TAYLOR
J. D. DOUGLAS

Roseveare, Helen (1925–)

Missionary, physician, and author. Born in Hertfordshire, England, she studied at Cambridge University where she was converted in 1945, and qualified as a medical doctor. She went to Africa in 1953 and established in the Belgian Congo (now Zaire) a medical center under the auspices of the Worldwide Evangelization Crusade (WEC). In 1964 she suffered severely as rebellion and civil war spread throughout Zaire. She was held captive by rebel forces and forced to leave the field. In 1966 she returned and helped establish the Evangelical Medical Center in Nyankunde. She returned to the United Kingdom in 1973 and wrote *He Gave Us a Valley* (1976), based upon her missionary experiences. Roseveare later served on the staff of the WEC's Missionary Training College in Glasgow, Scotland. Known for her great devotion to service to God, she has also been an inspirational speaker internationally. Her other books include *Give Me This Mountain* (1966), *Doctor among Congo Rebels* (1965), and *Doctor Returns to Congo* (1967).

NANCY CALVERT

Rouault, Georges (1871–1958)

French Roman Catholic artist. Born in a cellar during bombardment of Paris, he studied under Elie Delaunay and Gustave Moreau from 1890 to 1898 before retiring to the Benedictine abbey at Liguge. Although Rouault has spiritual affinities with the Romantic tradition of Baudelaire he was not seen as an adherent to any particular school of aesthetics. His aesthetics were expressed in the art that he created from within his spirit and not from nature. Although influenced by several clergy, he worked independently of the church. He was never commissioned by the church to do any work because "he placed material objects in the way of spiritual appreciation," according to Father Couturier in 1938. He tended to have a dark and fierce style that grew out of his experiences with life rather than idyllic, romantic realism. He believed that when one looks at man apart from God there is only evil. This led to his emphasis on man's suffering, judgment, and relative justice as he painted prostitutes, clowns, judges, the poor, and the miserable as penetrating types of this condition. His *Miserere* series of engravings focused on the complacency of the rich and the hopelessness of the poor. The *Passion* was originally published in 1939 in a limited edition. It contained seventeen color etchings and eighty-two wood engravings examining Christ's passion. The work portrays the sufferings of both Christ and man. Grace is seen as the divine meaning that is given to human life by the continuing passion of Jesus Christ as they focus on the cross, Christ's countenance, and his suffering for humankind's salvation. Many consider him the greatest painter of religious themes since Rembrandt.

Biography by W. A. Dyrness (1971).

FRED P. WILSON

Rowley, Harold Henry (1890–1969)

English Old Testament scholar. Born in Leicester and educated at Bristol Baptist College, he served the troops in Egypt through the YMCA in 1916. Poor health brought him home and he became a Baptist minister in Wells, Somerset, in 1917. In 1924 he was appointed associate professor in a Christian university in Shantung, China. On his return to England in 1929 he completed a degree at Mansfield College, Oxford, and was appointed lecturer in Hebrew at University College, Cardiff, in 1930. In 1935 he transferred to University College, Bangor, as professor of Hebrew, moving on to a similar post at Manchester University (1945–1959). In addition to teaching and writing, Rowley was a prominent figure in the Baptist Union, and served as its president in 1957–1958. In the English-speaking world after World War II he was probably the most prominent British Old Testament scholar. His many books displayed his comprehensive knowledge of the literature on the Old Testament. Beginning with his specialist study of the book of Daniel, he wrote numerous essays, many of which were gathered into volumes such as *The Servant of the Lord* (1951) and *Man of God* (1963). He also wrote popular studies of Old Testament themes such as *The Relevance of Apocalyptic* (1944) and *The Faith of Israel* (1956).

NOEL S. POLLARD

Runcie, Robert Alexander Kennedy (1921–)

Archbishop of Canterbury. Born in Crosby, Lancashire, he was awarded the Military Cross during war service, and achieved a first-class degree at Brasenose College, Oxford, before going for ordination training at Westcott House, Cambridge. Following a curacy at Gosforth, Newcastle, he was successively chaplain, then vice principal of Westcott House (1953–1956); fellow and dean of Trinity Hall, Cambridge (1956–1960); principal of Cuddeson Theological College, Oxford (1960–1969); and bishop of St. Albans (1970–1980). His archepiscopate (1980–1991), which included the Falkland's War, Pope John Paul II's visit to Britain, and the 1988 Lambeth Conference, attracted more public attention than that of any of his predecessors. His inclusive role, as focus of unity of the Church of England and of the Anglican Communion, was neither understood by the media nor always appreciated by pressure groups in the church who wanted clear endorsement of their own positions on such matters as bishops as defenders of doctrine, relations with Rome, the ordination of women, the remarriage of divorcees, and the treatment of homosexual clergy. Runcie's own position is expressed in his sermons and addresses, collected as *Windows onto God* and *Sermons of the Spirit* (1983), *Authority in Crisis?* (1988), and *The Unity We Seek* (1989).

Biographies by L. Mantle (1991) and A. Hastings (1991).

PHILIP HILLYER

Rupp, Ernest Gordon (1910–1986)

Church historian. Born in London, he was a Methodist lay preacher before graduating from King's College, London. He studied for the Methodist ministry at Richmond College, and went on for further training to Strasbourg and Basel. He was a minister in Chislehurst, Kent (1938–1946), tutor at Richmond College (1947–1952), lecturer at Cambridge (1952–1956), and professor of ecclesiastical history at Manchester (1956–1967) and Cambridge (1968–1977). He was also principal of Wesley House, Cambridge (1967–1974). He was that rare combination: a gripping orator, a lucid writer who could make even church history come alive, and an engaging personality. He was an invited Protestant observer at Vatican II, and was elected president of the Methodist Conference in 1968. A specialist in the Reformation era, he wrote many books, including *Luther's Progress to the*

Diet of Worms (1951), *The Righteousness of God* (1953), *The Old Reformation and the New* (1967), *Thomas More* (1978), and *Religion in England: 1688–1791* (1986).

J. D. DOUGLAS

Ryang, Ju-Sam (1879–1950)

Missionary, educator, and first Korean Methodist bishop. Yang Chu-Sam was born in northwestern Korea and educated in the Confucian Chinese classics. Dissatisfied with traditional learning, and having read two Christian books in Chinese, he entered the Anglo-Chinese College of the Southern Methodists, and was baptized there in 1902. In 1906 he went to America and started the Korean church in San Francisco, receiving ordination as a Methodist minister in 1912. He graduated from Vanderbilt University's Theological School in 1913, and studied for a further year at Yale Divinity School. Back in Korea by 1915, he was brought by Yun Tchi-Ho to the Methodist Academy in Songdo as teacher, and later vice principal. There he founded an influential Christian journal in 1916. In 1919 he became pastor of the large Chong-kyo Methodist church in downtown Seoul, at the same time promoting a Christian mission to Koreans in Siberia (1920–1930). In 1928 he was a Korean delegate to the Jerusalem conference of the International Missionary Council. When in 1930 the two American Methodist missions united their work in Korea and formed a self-governing Korean Methodist church, Ryang was elected its first bishop (1930–1938). When Seoul fell to the North Korean invaders in 1950, Ryang conscientiously stayed at his government post as head of the Korean Red Cross, was taken by the communists, and disappeared.

SAMUEL H. MOFFETT

Ryrie, Charles C. (1925–)

Pastor, administrator, and scholar. Born in St. Louis, Missouri, he studied at Haverford College, Dallas Theological Seminary, and the University of Edinburgh (Ph.D., 1954). Ordained to the ministry in the Baptist Church in 1947, he has served in professorial and administrative roles at Midwest Bible and Missionary Institute, Westmont College, Dallas Theological Seminary and (as president) Philadelphia College of the Bible. He was among those fundamentalist scholars who condemned neo-orthodox views as inconsistent, illogical, and unbiblical, particularly in his work *New Orthodoxy* (1956). He feared that conservatives would be attracted because such views allowed them to be intellectually respectable within the larger scholarly sphere while sounding like conservative evangelicals. One of the key theologians supporting dispensationalism, he has written numerous books that support his position, including *The Basis of the Premillennial Faith* (1953), *Biblical Theology of the New Testament* (1959), and *A Survey of Bible Doctrine* (1972). He has produced also *Balancing the Christian Life* (1969) and the notes for the *Ryrie Study Bible* (1976).

NANCY CALVERT

S

Sa'eed, Mohammed (1863–1942)

Iranian physician and evangelist. Son of a Muslim mullah, he was born in Sennah, Iran. His mother died when he was ten, his father when he was thirteen. Shortly afterwards, he was formally invested as a mullah by a local sheik. Over the next several years, while teaching in a Koranic school, Sa'eed experienced a growing dissatisfaction with Islam. Then, at the age of seventeen, he agreed to tutor a Syrian missionary whose quiet and gentle witness eventually led him to Christ. He began to share his new faith with friends and family, but such antagonism arose that he fled Sennah, went to live with a missionary doctor in a small clinic and, as a result, resolved to take up medicine himself. At the same time he also itinerated in the local community, beginning the practice of combining medical work with evangelism that was to become his life's work. For almost fifty years this deeply spiritual man traveled throughout the country, attending to both the physical and spiritual needs of the people, developing an international reputation as a skilled and caring physician/evangelist. His outspokenness for Christ in a strong Islamic context resulted in many enemies, but his medical skills were in such demand that he was able to continue his witness unabated until his death.

Biography by J. M. Rasooli and C. H. Allen (1957).

A. SCOTT MOREAU

Sanday, William (1843–1920)

Theologian and New Testament scholar. Born in Nottinghamshire, England, he graduated from Oxford, was ordained an Anglican priest in 1869, and served in academic and pastoral posts before returning as professor to Oxford in 1883. Well-read in German and British biblical studies, Sanday became the foremost interpreter to Englishmen of the hermeneutical theories being applied to the Scriptures at the turn of the century, and was influential in encouraging wide acceptance of modern critical methods. Though not regarded as an original thinker, he was comprehensive and patient in presenting his ideas. His works included an acclaimed commentary on Romans (1895, with A. C. Headlam), *The Life of Christ in Recent Research* (1908), *Christology and Personality* (1911), and *Criticism of the Fourth Gospel* (1905).

PHILIP W. COMFORT

Sanders, J. Oswald (1902–1992)

Missionary statesman and Bible teacher. Born in Invercargill, New Zealand, he trained as a solicitor. He joined the staff of the New Zealand Bible Training Institute as secretary-treasurer in 1926, and became superintendent in 1933. He occupied that position until 1945, when his obvious administrative and executive abilities led to his appointment as home director of the China Inland Mission in Australia (1946–1954), and then general secretary of what was renamed the Overseas Missionary Fellowship (1954–1969). He had the responsibility of reorganizing the OMF work after the final communist takeover of mainland China. New fields of work were pioneered to Chinese-speaking people in Southeast Asia. For the next twenty years Sanders continued to fulfill a demanding schedule of itinerant travel. As a speaker he was equally acceptable to both students and seasoned missionaries. Many of his addresses to them and at conventions were published in book form. Twenty-two of his thirty-two volumes were translated into two or more languages. Among his titles were *The Holy Spirit of Promise* (1954), *Spiritual Maturity* (1962), *Robust in Faith* (1965), and *Paul the Leader* (1983). He was made an Officer of the Order of the British Empire in 1981, and his notable contribution to the churches and mission fields of Southeast Asia was further recognized in 1992 by the Australian College of Theology, which conferred on him an honorary doctorate in theology.

S. BARTON BABBAGE

Sangster, William Edwyn Robert (1900–1960)

English Methodist preacher. Born in London and converted in a Methodist mission, he left school early and became an accountant. After having served briefly in the army he trained for the ministry at Richmond College and served various congregations, chiefly in northern England, until appointment to Westminster Central Hall in 1939. In his thirties he completed an M.A. degree at London University, and followed that with a Ph.D. thesis on Wesley's teaching on sanctification, published as *The Path to Perfection* (1943). Even in war-bombed London his preaching packed the vast Central Hall. He was widely recognized for his saintly leadership in the Methodist Church. Hoping to stem the decline of English Methodism, he accepted the secretaryship of the home mission department in 1955. Before his premature retirement in 1957 his many popular devotional books included *He Is Able* (1936), *The Pure in Heart* (1954), and *The Secret of Radiant Life* (1957).

NOEL S. POLLARD

Sankey, Ira David (1840–1908)

Evangelistic singer, hymn composer, and hymnbook compiler. Born in Edinburgh, Pennsylvania, he was converted at the age of sixteen at revival services near his home. His musical background included leading a church choir and singing at large gatherings. Following high school, he served in the Union Army during the Civil War, worked with his father, and was secretary and president of a local YMCA. Sankey met evangelist D. L. Moody in 1870, and by early 1871 was persuaded to become the songleader and soloist for Moody's revival meetings in Chicago. The collaboration lasted until Moody's death in 1899. It was during their tour of Great Britain (1873–1875) that the two gained an international reputation for their evangelistic techniques. Sankey's simple and expressive baritone singing, usually as he accompanied himself on a small organ, was intended to tell a story (e.g., "The Ninety and Nine" and "Jesus of Nazareth Passeth By") and to reinforce Moody's evangelistic message. His music, characterized by simple lyrics and easily learned melodies, mirrored contemporary dance and march rhythms. Although Sankey wrote few hymns himself, the collections he edited (*Sacred Songs* and *Gospel Hymns*) became best-sellers. He helped establish the role of the gospel hymn in evangelism and contributed to the acceptance of gospel music in England.

PAUL A. ERICKSEN

Sanneh, Lamin Ousman (1942–)

Gambian historian and missiologist. Born in Georgetown, Gambia, he grew up as a follower of Islam, but converted to Christianity out of an intense longing to know God in a more personal way. He pursued higher education in the United States, Lebanon, and England (Ph.D., University of London, 1974). He then returned to Africa, teaching at the Fourah Bay College, Freetown, Sierra Leone (1974–1975), and the University of Ghana (1975–1978) before taking an appointment at the University of Aberdeen, Scotland, as lecturer in Islamic and religious studies (1978–1981). He spent most of the 1980s as assistant professor of the history of religion at Harvard University. By 1989 Sanneh was at Yale Divinity School as professor of missions and world Christianity. His major contribution to Christian scholarship to date has been his investigation of the impact of Bible translation on African church history. His controversial thesis is that vernacular translation by Western missionaries was a powerful force in preserving and renewing African culture and raising African aspirations for national independence, thus directly challenging the traditional interpretation of missions as an agent of colonialism and cultural imperialism. His publications include *West African Christianity* (1983) and *Translating the Message* (1989).

MARK R. SHAW

Sayers, Dorothy Leigh (1893–1957)

Novelist, playwright, academic, and Christian apologist. Born in Oxford, daughter of a country vicar, she was educated at Sommerville College,

Oxford, in modern languages. Although she was for a time a schoolteacher and advertising copywriter, her real interests lay in medieval studies. In 1921 she published the first of sixteen detective novels, which brought her fame and independence by her skill in joining together a popular genre with more serious literary merits. As she was completing the last of these she was beginning her second literary career as a Christian apologist. Her most famous work was *The Man Born to be King*, a series of radio plays first performed on the BBC in 1941–1942. But she had already written a verse play for the Canterbury Cathedral festival called *The Zeal of Thy House* (1937). Works like *The Mind of the Maker* (1941) reveal how skillful an apologist for orthodox Christian teaching she was. Her own academic interests are seen in her excellent translation of Dante's *Divine Comedy*. Sayers was a prominent member of that midcentury group of English Christian writers of whom C. S. Lewis is the best known.

NOEL S. POLLARD

Schaeffer, Francis August (1912–1984)

American scholar, described in one secular publication as "spiritual guru to young students struggling with existential and philosophical problems of the 20th century." Born in Philadelphia, he graduated from Hampden-Sydney College (1935) and Faith Theological Seminary (1938). He was ordained in the Reformed Presbyterian Church in 1938, and served pastorates in Pennsylvania and Missouri before he and his wife Edith were sent as missionaries to Switzerland. There in 1955 they founded L'Abri [Shelter] Fellowship, which was to become ever more popular over the years as a study center and meeting place for thoughtful believers or seekers. Communities developed in four other countries. Schaeffer did much to broaden evangelical perspectives by encouraging interest in the arts, at the same time regarding modern culture as a deviation from biblical Christianity. He spoke out strongly against abortion and communism, and regarded the nuclear deterrent as necessary. Among his two dozen books were *Escape from Reason* (1968), *Pollution and the Death of Man* (1970), *How Should We Then Live?* (1976), and (with C. E. Koop) *Whatever Happened to the Human Race?* (1979; also available as a film).

J. D. DOUGLAS

Scherer, Paul Ehrman (1892–1969)

American Lutheran minister and educator. Born in Mount Holly Springs, Pennsylvania, he was educated at the College of Charleston, South Carolina, and Mount Airy Theological Seminary in Philadelphia. Ordained to the Lutheran ministry in 1916, he was an assistant pastor in Buffalo, New York, before serving as pastor of the Church of the Holy Trinity, New York City (1920–1945). Then he became Brown professor of homiletics at Union

Theological Seminary (1945–1960). After leaving Union he was visiting professor of homiletics at Princeton Theological Seminary and a distinguished lecturer at various educational institutions.

He was recognized as one of America's foremost preachers and delivered sermons for the nationally broadcast *Sunday Vespers* from 1932 to 1945. He contributed articles to such publications as *McCalls, Journal of Religious Education,* and the *Lutheran Quarterly Review.* He was also assistant editor of *Religion in Life* (1944–1969) and one of the editors of the *Interpreter's Bible* (1942–1957). Some of his more popular sermons are collected in *When God Hides* (1934), *Facts That Undergird Life* (1938), *For We Have This Treasure* (1944), *The Plight of Freedom* (1948), and *The Word God Sent* (1965).

ROBERT G. CLOUSE

Schillebeeckx, Edward Cornelius Florentius Alfons (1914–)

Roman Catholic theologian. Born in Antwerp, Belgium, he was educated in Flemish in a strict Catholic family, and sent at age twelve to the Jesuit school at Turnhout. Resenting the rigid discipline there, he joined the Dominicans in 1934, and during his novitiate came under the influence of the great medieval mystics. He studied philosophy at Louvain, performed compulsory military service, and began theological studies in the early 1940s. After World War II he pursued postdoctoral studies at Le Saulchoir and began his teaching career in dogmatic theology at Louvain in 1947. Concurrent pastoral duties and a prison chaplaincy for eight years occupied the young priest/theologian. In 1958 he became professor of dogmatics and the history of theology at Nijmegen, the Netherlands. He played an active role during Vatican II, and was cofounder of the internationally acclaimed journal *Consilium.*

His alienation from the Roman Church set in by 1968, and since 1979 when he was summoned to Rome to give account of his teaching, an official silence has been imposed on his theological work. He retired from his Nijmegen post in 1982. For his important contribution to European culture he was the first theologian to receive the Erasmus Prize in 1982. In 1983 he was made a Commander of the Order of Orange-Nassau, the highest civil honor in the Netherlands.

His numerous books include *Christ the Sacrament* (1963), *Revelation and Theology* (1967), *Jesus* (1979), *Christ: The Christian Experience in the Modern World* (1980), and *Ministry* (1981).

Biography by John Bowden (1983).

EDWARD J. FURCHA

Schlatter, Adolf (1852–1939)

Swiss Reformed theologian. Born in St. Gallen, Switzerland, he studied at the universities of Basel and Tübingen, then worked in Swiss reformed parishes at Neumünster and Kesswil. He began his teaching career at Berne in 1880, and subsequently held professorships at Griefswald (1888), Berlin (1893), and Tübingen (1898). Although he joined no theological school, his theological position tended to be conservative. His extensive works include studies of Judaism and the New Testament in historical theology. He produced a translation of the Bible, authored numerous biblical commentaries and expositions, and edited the theological journal, *Beitrage zur Forderung Christlicher Theologie.* His publications range from studies of Israel (1901) to *The Church in the New Testament Period* (1926). He also wrote important works on ethics, systematic theology, and church history, stressing faith rather than speculative thought, and he maintained a lifelong concern for Christian social action. Schlatter is still widely read in conservative circles in Germany and Switzerland.

EDWARD J. FURCHA

Schmemann, Alexander (1921–1983)

Eastern Orthodox liturgical theologian. Born in Reval, Estonia, he received his theological education at the Theological Academy of St. Sergius in Paris (1945) where he was for the next six years a lecturer in church history. Having been ordained to the priesthood and having graduated from the Sorbonne, he was called in 1951 to serve on the faculty of St. Vladimir's Theological Academy, where he was dean during a period of growth and academic establishment and accreditation. As an ecumenist he was a representative of the Ecumenical Patriarchate in his early years to many World Council of Churches commissions and meetings, and was active in the Anglican-Orthodox organization "The Fellowship of St. Alban and St. Serguis." He was also an official observer at Vatican II. He wrote *The Historical Road of Eastern Orthodoxy* (1966), but is best known for his work in liturgical theology, in which area his volumes included *Introduction to Liturgical Theology* (1966) and *Eucharist* (1988).

STANLEY S. HARAKAS

Schonherr, Albrecht (1911–)

German Protestant church leader. Born in Katscher, Upper Silesia, he studied theology in Tübingen and Berlin. After joining the Confessing Church in 1934 he was excluded from the university, but studied at the illegal Confessing seminary in Finkenwalde directed by Dietrich Bonhoeffer. Ordained in 1936 at Martin Niemoller's church in Berlin-Dahlem, he pastored Confessing churches at Greifswald and Brussow, and was drafted into the army in 1940. He was wounded in Italy and taken prisoner by the British. Returning to his home that now lay in the Soviet occupation zone, he was appointed a superintendent and in 1951 director of the seminary in Brandenburg. In 1958 he took part in founding the Weissensee Study

Group (clerics critical of the national church tradition in Germany) as well as the Christian Peace Conference. In 1963 he became general superintendent of the Berlin-Brandenburg church district in Eberswalde, and in 1967 an administrator in the church's episcopal office. He played a major role in the formation of the Federation of Protestant Churches in the [East] German Democratic Republic in 1969, and was named its chairman. In 1972 he was elected bishop of the Eastern Region of the Church of Berlin-Brandenburg. He promoted a conciliatory attitude toward the communist state, which in 1978 granted the church far-reaching concessions. He retired in 1981.

RICHARD V. PIERARD

Schuller, Robert H. (1926–)

Minister of the Reformed Church in America and popular host of the television program "Hour of Power." Born in Alton, Iowa, he was educated at Hope College (1947) and Western Theological Seminary (1950), RCA schools in Holland, Michigan. In 1955 Schuller set out to plant a church in Orange County, California, where he rented a drive-in theater and launched an innovative and successful drive-in ministry. Today, his ten thousand-member Garden Grove Community Church conducts drive-in and walk-in services in the massive, $20 million Crystal Cathedral, constructed in 1980. Schuller has drawn praise from supporters who feel that he has effectively repackaged Reformed theology and worship to meet the contemporary needs and attract the unchurched, as well as criticism from those who perceive him accommodating Christianity to a narcissistic and therapeutic age. In his more than two dozen books and through his popular "Institute for Successful Church Leadership," Schuller espouses "Possibility Thinking," a variant of the "Positive Thinking" of his mentor, Norman Vincent Peale, which emphasizes the positive and affirming effects of Christianity. In his most substantive book, *Self-Esteem: A New Reformation* (1982), he defines sin as a lack of self-esteem; the work of Jesus Christ restores human dignity and enables Christians to overcome personal trials and pursue their dreams.

JOHN R. MUETHER

Schulz, Charles M. (1922–)

Popular cartoonist and lay preacher. Born in Minneapolis, he took correspondence courses from the Art Instruction School in Minneapolis (1940–1943). He then served for two years in the army, taking part in the liberation of the notorious Dachau. When he returned home he began to publish cartoons while working for his former correspondence school. In 1948 he initiated a weekly cartoon series for the *St. Paul Pioneer Press*. He published also some cartoons in the *Saturday Evening Post*. In 1950 Schulz

338

started the nationally syndicated *Peanuts* cartoon series, which proved highly successful. Much of the cartoon's appeal stems from the way his characters illustrate adult pretensions, obsessions, cruelties, and evasions. A lay preacher in the Church of God (Anderson, Indiana), Schulz weaves Christian themes into some of his cartoons. By 1970 *Peanuts* appeared in over nine hundred newspapers. In addition, Schulz published many collections of cartoons, and created several animated *Peanuts* specials for television, including *A Charlie Brown Christmas.*

Robert L. Morrison

Schürer, Emil Johannes (1844–1910)

German New Testament scholar. Born in Augsburg, he was educated at the universities of Erlangen, Berlin, Heidelberg, and Leipzig, from the latter of which he received his doctorate (1868) for a dissertation on Schleiermacher. He began teaching at the University of Leipzig (1869–1873), became associate professor (1873–1878), and then full professor at Giessen (1878–1890), Kiel (1890–1895), and Göttingen (1895–1910), where he was professor of New Testament exegesis and rector of the university. He founded (1876), and edited from 1881 with Adolf Harnack (1851–1930), the periodical *Theologische Literaturzeitung.*

In 1874 he began the work subsequently translated into English as *A History of the Jewish People in the Time of Jesus Christ* (5 vols., 1890–1891). This was the "first attempt to present a political, religious, and literary history of Judaism in the centuries preceding the rise of Christianity and up to the Bar Kokhba rebellion," thereby initiating a new field of study, that of late Judaism, as well as placing the study of Christianity within a larger and appropriately Jewish context.

A new English edition of his magnum opus, edited by Geza Vermes et al. (3 vols., 1973–1986), is indicative of the stature this innovative work continues to be accorded.

Clyde Curry Smith

Schutz-Marsauche, Roger-Louis (1915–)

Founder and prior of the Taizé Community in France, an international ecumenical monastic community. It was founded to open up ways of healing the divisions between Christians and, through the reconciliation of Christians, to overcome conflicts within humanity.

Born in 1915 in Provence, Switzerland, of a Swiss father and a French mother, he studied theology in Lausanne and Strasbourg. Acquiring a house in 1940 in the village of Taizé, near Cluny in France, he began by sheltering in his home Jews and other refugees fleeing the Nazis. When the war ended, he obtained permission to welcome German prisoners from a nearby camp. In 1944 in Geneva he was joined by his first brothers. In 1949 the first seven brothers committed themselves for life to community of material and spiritual goods, celibacy, and acceptance of the ministry of the prior. They were all from different Protestant backgrounds. Since 1969 the community has included Roman Catholic brothers as well. Today there are some ninety brothers from over twenty countries and every continent. They support themselves by their work alone. Some brothers go to live in small groups on different continents to share the living conditions of the poor. Brother Roger himself has often spent time in places of suffering and division, including poor areas of New York City, Calcutta, as well as in Chile, South Africa, Lebanon, Haiti, sub-Saharan Africa, Ethiopia, the Philippines, and Eastern Europe.

Since 1958, the community has welcomed young adults in increasing numbers. Weekly intercontinental meetings bring together youth from numerous countries, those in the summer drawing up to six thousand participants at a time. The meetings are centered on three times of common prayer each day in the Church of Reconciliation. The themes for reflection are based on "inner life and human solidarity." Songs from Taizé are used in groups and parishes around the world. At the end of every year, Taizé brothers lead a "European meeting" where many tens of thousands of young people from eastern and western Europe are welcomed for several days by the parishes of a major city. Similar meetings have been held in North America and Asia.

Taizé's ecumenical vocation has led it to have constant links with the different churches. Brother Roger was invited to the Second Vatican Council by Pope John XXIII; he has visited Orthodox patriarchs of Constantinople; three archbishops of Canterbury have been to Taizé; and brothers have worked in the World Council of Churches. In 1986 Pope John Paul II came to Taizé as a "pilgrim and friend of the community."

Brother Roger has received the Templeton Prize (1974), the German Peace Prize (1974), honorary doctorates from Warsaw (1986), Louvain (1989), and Glasgow University (1991), the UNESCO Prize for Peace Education (1988) and the *Karlspreis* for the building up of Europe (1989). He has published a number of books that have been translated into many languages, including his personal journal in several volumes.

L. K. GRIMLEY

Schweitzer, Albert (1875–1965)

Missionary, musician, physician, and theologian. Born in Kaysersberg, Upper Alsace, son of a Lutheran pastor, he began organ studies in childhood, and later took up theology and philosophy at the universities of Strasbourg, Paris, and Berlin. While he was supply preacher in Strasbourg and lecturer in New Testament, he studied medicine. He earned several doctorates. In 1913 he founded the Lambarene Hospital in French Congo

(Gabon). After a forced return to Europe (1917–1924) during which time he gave organ recitals, lectured, and published, he returned to Lambarene. In 1952 he received the Nobel Peace Prize, and later was honored by both France and Germany. He developed the notion of "reverence for all life," which he practiced from 1915. Because he did not advocate orthodox Christian views he was at times accused of having left Christianity when, in fact, he advanced Christianity as Jesus' religion of love. His literary legacy includes a significant book on Bach (1908), works on Paul (1930), Goethe (1932), and the famous work translated as *The Quest of the Historical Jesus* (1909). Autobiographical details were provided by him in *Memoirs of Childhood and Youth* (1925), *My Life and Thought* (1933), and *From My African Note-Book* (1938).

Biographies by E. N. Mozley (mainly on Schweitzer's theology) (1950), G. Seaver (1955), N. Cousins (1960), and G. McKnight (1964).

EDWARD J. FURCHA

Scofield, (C)yrus (I)ngersoll (1843–1921)

Champion of dispensationalism. Born in Michigan, Scofield eventually settled in Kansas where, due in part to an alcohol problem, his promising career in law and state politics (elected 1871) became derailed and his marriage failed. In St. Louis (ca. 1879) he experienced an evangelical conversion; he was ordained in 1882 by the Congregationalists, developed one of their mission churches in Dallas into a large congregation (eventually independent Scofield Memorial Church), and served as Congregational superintendent of missions for the south and southwestern United States. Remarried in 1884, he founded the Central American Mission (1890) and with L. S. Chafer the Philadelphia College of the Bible (1914), launched a very successful Bible correspondence program (later sold to Moody Bible Institute), and figured prominently on the Bible conference circuit for years. He was D. L. Moody's pastor at Northfield during the final years of Moody's life. He established himself as a leading defender of dispensational premillennialism with his *Rightly Dividing the Word of Truth* (1888). His seminal defense of this particular eschatology, however, was the enormously influential *Scofield Reference Bible* published by Oxford University Press in 1909 and expanded in 1917. Scofield epitomized the entrepreneurial and independent character of American fundamentalism, and exercised an unusually significant influence on its mind-set.

Biographies by C. G. Trumbull (1920) and J. M. Caufield (1984).

GLEN G. SCORGIE

Scroggie, William Graham (1877–1958)

British Bible expositor and writer. Born in Great Malvern, England, of Scottish parents who were Christian Brethren, he trained for the Baptist ministry at Spurgeon's College, London. His first two pastorates in London and Halifax were brief, largely because his strong conservative evangelicalism would not permit him to compromise in less fervently spiritual surroundings. He found more congenial members in Sunderland (1903–1913) and at Charlotte Chapel, Edinburgh (1913–1933), where the city's university made him a D.D. There followed a period of itinerant ministry in Australia and North America before his final pastorate at the Metropolitan Tabernacle, London (1938–1944). A brilliant expositor who was a regular speaker at the Keswick Convention, Scroggie was welcomed far beyond his own denomination. Though he retired for health reasons in 1944, he continued to preach, and later served on the staff of Spurgeon's College (1948–1952). His writings included *Method in Prayer* (1916), *A Guide to the Gospels* (1948), and *The Unfolding Drama of Redemption* (3 vols., 1954–1957). R. G. Turnbull produced *A Treasury of W. Graham Scroggie* (1974).

J. D. DOUGLAS

Scudder, Ida Sophia (1870–1959)

American medical missionary and founder of Vellore Hospital, South India. Although she had no intention of following the family tradition that stretched back to John Scudder I (1793–1855), the founder of the American Arcot Mission, an incident on a brief visit to India changed her outlook completely. Three times in the same night there were calls to help Hindu and Muslim women in childbirth. In each case the husband refused to let a male doctor see his wife, and the woman died. Back in India in 1900 as a qualified doctor, Scudder began work from a dispensary in her house, moving to her first hospital in 1902 and to new buildings in 1923. As the medical work expanded, so did the training. Courses for nurses (begun 1907) and a medical school for girls (1918), eventually (1942) became an interdenominational Christian medical college affiliated with Madras University. Each stage of the expansion of the hospital and college, including hostel facilities for male postgraduates (admitted from 1945) and undergraduates (1947), was largely achieved through Scudder's vision, persistence, and fund-raising skills.

Biographies by M. P. Jeffery (1939) and D. Clarke Wilson (1959).

PHILIP HILLYER

Segundo, Juan Luis (1925–)

Roman Catholic liberation theologian. Born in Montevideo, Uruguay, he was educated at San Miguel, Argentina, and Louvain, Belgium, where he acquired his doctorate in theology in 1963. He was ordained as a Jesuit priest in 1955. Since the 1960s, the decade of socialism in Latin America and Castro's taking power in Cuba, Segundo has labored with Gustavo

Gutiérrez and others in the forging and evolution of liberation theology. His creative thinking and daring logic are evident in more than a dozen books and many articles. Segundo proposes to keep faith and life, the supernatural and the natural, church and world, united in a single whole. This can be seen in his five-volume course for laypersons, *A Theology for Artisans of a New Humanity* (1968, 1972), and in the five-volume *Jesus of Nazareth, Yesterday and Today* (early 1980s). He attempts to unite the natural and transcendent worlds, combining topics like grace, guilt, faith, ideology, sacraments, and humanity, using secular and religious, modern and classic literature. His main framework of ideas can be traced to his Louvain professor, Leopold Malavez. Besides founding the Peter Faber Center in his native Uruguay, he has specialized in the study of sociology and religion, and has been visiting professor in several U.S. universities. In Uruguay he serves as chaplain to several lay communities.

GUILLERMO MENDEZ

Shahbaz, Imam-U Din (ca. 1844–1924)

Bible translator and poet. Born in Zafarwal, now Pakistan, into a Muslim Punjabi home, he was attracted to Christ by the way His followers did not retaliate when treated contemptuously. He later became a Christian. He was baptized in 1866. He taught in a Christian school in Amritsar. He was an evangelist for some years with the Church Missionary Society, then with the United Presbyterians, after winning a poetry competition for the selection of a translator of the psalms. In 1886 he was ordained and became pastor of the First UP church in Sialkot City for the next twenty years.

He translated the psalms into Urdu. From 1895 to 1916 he worked on his most famous contribution to the church: translating the psalms into Punjabi verses using Eastern tunes. The first edition of two thousand copies sold out completely at the Sialkot Convention. In 1919 the translation of the Punjabi Psalter was completed. In 1921 it was reprinted in Roman Punjabi with indigenous tunes for religious hymns. Later he went blind. Babu Sadiq became his reader. Shahbaz stayed as close as possible to the actual meaning of the texts. He used Urdu, English, and Persian translations. The Punjabi psalms remain the hymnbook of the Punjabi church and have contributed immeasurably to the teaching of what at first was a mainly illiterate gathering of people groups.

PATRICK SOOKHDEO

Shea, George Beverly (1909–)

Often called "America's beloved gospel singer." Born in Winchester, Ontario, son of a Wesleyan Methodist minister, he entered radio broadcasting as an avocation while working as an insurance clerk in New York City. Later he worked on WMBI, Chicago (1938–1944), and on ABC's "Club

Time" (1944–1952), during which time he was also soloist on the Billy Graham Team (from 1947) and on the "Hour of Decision" (from 1950). Since 1951 he has been recording artist with RCA and Word Records, producing nearly seventy albums of sacred music. His bass-baritone voice has been transmitted on weekly shortwave programs around the world. At age twenty-three he composed the music to one of his best-known solos, "I'd Rather Have Jesus," often sung at Billy Graham crusade meetings. Elected in 1978 to the Gospel Music Association Hall of Fame, Shea is noted for the simplicity of his faith and testimony. He published the autobiographical *Then Sings My Soul* in 1968.

J. D. Douglas

Shedd, Russell Philip (1929–)

Missionary, educator, writer, publisher, and conference speaker born in Bolivia to evangelical missionary parents. Shedd has more than thirty-five years of service in Portugal and Brazil. He is founder and director of Edições Vida Nova (New Life Editions), one of the largest evangelical publishing houses in Brazil. After studies in the United States and a Ph.D. at the University of Edinburgh in Scotland (*Man and Community*, 1958), Shedd was appointed for missionary service in Portugal under the Conservative Baptist Foreign Mission Society. His interest in theological education fueled a vision to produce Bible reference works in the Portuguese language. For this purpose he transferred to the much larger context of Brazil in 1962. Shedd continues to teach New Testament and theology at the Faculdade Teológica Batista de São Paulo and is an extremely popular speaker in all of Brazil, with often more than forty conferences a year. He is the author of numerous articles and at least ten books (mostly Bible expositions), including the popular reference work *Biblia Vida Nova* (1976).

Curtis Alan Kregness

Sheen, Fulton John (1895–1979)

Roman Catholic archbishop, author, theologian, and broadcaster. Born in El Paso, Illinois, he graduated from St. Viator's College and Seminary in Bourbonnais, Illinois, and St. Paul's Seminary in Minnesota, and was ordained in 1919. He continued his studies at the Catholic University of America and at Louvain, where in 1923 he received his Ph.D. He then studied briefly at the Sorbonne and the Collegio Angelico in Rome, and taught at St. Edmund College in Ware, England, before returning to the United States to serve as a priest in Peoria, Illinois. In 1926 he began teaching at the Catholic University of America, where he remained until 1950. Partly because of his speaking talents, Sheen advanced rapidly within the church. He became a papal chamberlain (1934), a monsignor (1935), national director of the Society for the Propagation of the Faith (1950), and bishop of Rochester, New York (1966). He was also titular archbishop of Newport, Wales. Sheen's broadcasting success began in the 1930s, when he became well known as a regular speaker on the "Catholic Hour." In 1951 he launched a national television series, *Life Is Worth Living*, which ran for six years and was extremely popular among both Catholics and non-Catholics. During Vatican II he served on the Commission on the Missions. He retired from active church service in 1969, but continued to write. Among his books were *God and Intelligence in Modern Philosophy* (1925), *Peace of Soul* (1949), *Life of Christ* (1958), and *Autobiography* (1980). Many of his books were national best-sellers.

ROBERT L. MORRISON

Sheldon, Charles Monroe (1857–1946)

Congregationalist minister, writer, and leader in the social gospel movement. Born in Wellsville, New York, he graduated from Brown University and Andover Theological Seminary and was ordained in 1886. After a three-year ministry in Waterbury, Vermont, he became in 1889 the first pastor of Central Congregational Church, Topeka, Kansas. Devoted to the social gospel movement, Sheldon developed many outreach programs to benefit the needy. He wrote serialized stories reflecting his concerns; he then read the stories from the pulpit and published them as books. Most of his writings sold well, but *In His Steps* (1897) proved exceptionally popular. The book sold more than 15 million copies and was translated into several languages. *In His Steps* encouraged Christians to plot their course by asking themselves the question, "What would Jesus do?" Sheldon believed the faithful performance of this exercise by Christians would radically improve society. In 1900 the publisher of the *Topeka Daily Capital* invited Sheldon to edit the newspaper—as Jesus would—for a week. During his brief tenure, Sheldon refused to advertise products he considered unacceptable (alcohol or tobacco, for example), or to cover news he considered unedifying. The paper's circulation soared. Sheldon retired as pastor of his Topeka church in 1919. He then served as editor of the *Christian Herald* until 1925. His other books include *Robert Hardy's Seven Days* (1899), *Jesus Is Here!* (1913), *In His Steps Today* (1921), and *Charles M. Sheldon: His Life Story* (1925).

ROBERT L. MORRISON

Shembe, Isaiah (ca. 1870–1935)

African prophet and sect founder. Born into a polygamous family in Natal, South Africa, he had youthful dreams pointing out his sinfulness. Visions and dreams recurred in adult life, leading him to proclaim a message of salvation to the Zulu people in traditional cultural forms. By the time of his baptism in 1906 in the African Baptist Church he was already a well-

345

known preacher and faith healer. After his ordination he began to baptize and have his own following. A strict biblical literalist, he held to a Saturday observance of Sabbath, and broke with the Baptists in 1911 over this issue. His followers, called AmaNazaretha (Nazarites), stress sexual purity and abstinence from unclean practices such as using tobacco and pork; however, polygamy is permitted. The church's center is Ekuphakameni, outside of Durban, where frequent religious celebrations with traditional dancing are held. Shembe does not replace Jesus in the Godhead, but is officially revered as a prophet. The emphasis on God the Father is in keeping with the view of the father in traditional Zulu society. Isaiah Shembe was sequentially succeeded as head of the church by two of his sons, Johannes G. and Amos K.

Biography by Absolom Vilakazi.

JAMES J. STAMOOLIS

Sheppard, David Stuart (1929–)

Anglican bishop. Converted as a student at Cambridge, he switched to theology and prepared for ordination at Ridley Hall, Cambridge. He became curate at St. Mary, Islington, in 1955, and in 1958 warden of the Mayflower Family Centre in Canning Town, in London's East End. During those years he gained an international reputation as a cricketer, even captaining the English team. His experiences were published in *Parson's Pitch* (1964). In 1969 he was consecrated bishop of Woolwich, assistant in a diocese (Southwark) already famous for its radical thinking. He recorded his views on social questions in, *Built as a City* (1974), and, after his appointment in 1975 as a bishop of Liverpool in *Bias to the Poor* (1983). In Liverpool he has developed his social concerns with the leader of the city's Roman Catholics, Archbishop Derek Worlock, and these are recorded in their joint book *Better Together* (1988). Sheppard's leadership of Anglican thinking on social policy was recognized when he became chairman of the Church of England Board of Social responsibility in 1991.

NOEL S. POLLARD

Sheppard, Hugh Richard Lawrie (1880–1937)

Anglican clergyman. Born in Windsor where his father was a minor canon, he graduated from Cambridge, studied theology at Cuddesdon, and was ordained in 1907. He held curacies in London before appointment to the fashionable West End parish of St. Martin-in-the-Fields (1914–1926). As well as attracting the aristocracy there, he opened the premises and his own heart to the capital's poorest, lowliest, and lost. He was one of the first to see the religious potential in radio broadcasts, wrote articles for a Sunday newspaper, and was a tireless champion of pacifism. Ill health forced his resignation both from St. Martin's and from the deanery of Canterbury after a short tenure (1929–1931). He brought fresh air into even the stuffiest institutions, and was given to characteristic utterances such as "I would like to smash Canterbury and then try to rebuild it again." Greatly beloved in the country at large, he was elected rector by Glasgow University students (Winston Churchill was one of the defeated candidates). When Dick Sheppard died, one hundred thousand mourners filed past his coffin. His published works include *The Human Parson* (1924) and *The Impatience of a Parson* (1927).

Biography by Carolyn Scott (1977).

J. D. DOUGLAS

Shields, T(homas) T(odhunter) (1873–1955)

Canadian Baptist pastor. Born in Bristol, England, he immigrated with his family to Ontario in 1888. Lacking a seminary education, he began to preach in 1897. In 1910 he became pastor of Toronto's Jarvis Street Baptist Church, the country's largest Baptist congregation. Shields used his pulpit and the church's publication, *The Gospel Witness,* to voice his fundamentalist disdain for modernism and Roman Catholicism. He also harshly attacked liberalism within his denomination, the Baptist Convention of Ontario and Quebec, and its school, McMaster University. In 1923 Shields founded and became the first president of the Baptist Bible Union, an extreme fundamentalist faction that sought to purge Baptist organizations of modernists. In 1927 the denomination censured Shields for his attacks. In response, Shields and his followers formed the Union of Regular Baptist Churches of Ontario and Quebec. In the same year, Shields served briefly as the president of Des Moines University, which the Baptist Bible Union had purchased. He left the school following student riots and accusations that he was having an affair. Following more denominational schisms, Shields ended up leading the group now called the Association of Regular Baptist Churches. Shields also held leadership roles in the Canadian Protestant League and the International Council of Christian Churches.

Biography by L. K. Tarr (1967).

ROBERT L. MORRISON

Shoemaker, Samuel Moor (1893–1963)

Episcopal priest and writer. Born in Baltimore, he graduated from Princeton University in 1916. He worked with the YMCA in China for two years, and following his return, attended General Theological Seminary and Union Theological Seminary, from which he graduated in 1921. Following his ordination, he served briefly at Grace Episcopal Church in New York City; in 1925 he became rector of the city's Calvary Episcopal Church. Within five years Shoemaker had opened two ministry centers, Calvary

347

Mission and Calvary House, where he practiced personal evangelism and ministered to alcoholics. He also became a leader in the Oxford Group, an international Christian outreach movement that encouraged small group nurture within churches. He helped the founders of Alcoholics Anonymous adapt the small group model for use in their Twelve Step program. In 1941 he severed his ties with the Oxford Group because he believed the movement had become a church rival. In 1946 Shoemaker began a nationally broadcast radio program. Six years later he accepted a call from Calvary Episcopal Church in Pittsburgh. Here he launched a program known as the Pittsburgh Experiment, which trained laypeople in personal evangelism techniques. Besides his parish work, Shoemaker also started the periodical *Faith at Work*. He wrote many books, among them *Realizing Religion* (1921), *Twice-Born Ministers* (1929), *By the Power of God* (1954), and *Beginning Your Ministry* (1963).

Biography by I. D. Harris (1978).

ROBERT L. MORRISON

Sider, Ronald J. (1939–)

North American evangelical theologian and social activist. Son of a Brethren in Christ pastor, he was born and reared on a farm in Ontario, Canada. He graduated from nearby Waterloo Lutheran College where he came under the influence of apologist John Warwick Montgomery. Sider received a Ph.D. from Yale University, publishing in 1974 his thesis on radical Reformer Karl Bodenstein von Karlstadt. He began his teaching career at the Philadelphia branch of Messiah College, but has spent most of his career at Eastern Baptist Seminary. In 1973 he convened a meeting of some fifty evangelical leaders for a two-day workshop that culminated in what became known as the "Chicago Declaration of Evangelical Social Concern," a well-publicized, nonpartisan statement calling for political and social involvement. The following year he founded an organization based upon the declaration's principles, Evangelicals for Social Action, which had 3,200 members in 1993. Sider's most influential work, *Rich Christians in an Age of Hunger* (1977), achieved total sales of more than 250,000 copies. It engendered widespread interest in social justice among evangelicals, as well as intense criticism from some political conservatives.

DAVID A. CURRIE

Simmonds, George P. (1890–1991)

Missionary to Latin America and hymn translator. Born of English parents in San Francisco, he was enthusiastically singing hymns at age four. At ten he felt God's call to foreign missions and studied at Nyack Missionary College in New York. Although he and his New Zealander wife Nessie were Presbyterians, they served under the Christian and Missionary Alliance in

Ecuador, and for a short time with the Methodists in Peru. In 1916 "don Jorge," as he was called in Spanish, made his first hymn translation; he believed that was the best way to communicate the Christian gospel. After serving seven years in Ecuador, Simmonds embarked on a missionary exploration trip in the Amazon basin. Crossing the Andes, he traversed the South American continent to arrive at the Atlantic. Beginning in 1924 he commuted from the Canal Zone to minister in Colombia, Ecuador, and Peru with the American Bible Society. In 1929 he returned to the southwest United States as a Presbyterian missionary, and labored there until retirement in 1956, after which he served as a part-time pastor. He began publishing a series of seventy choral arrangements called *Cantos Corales* in 1935; in 1953 he continued under the name *Canticos Escogidos*. Many of his eight hundred translations have appeared in hymnals, notably *Himnos de la Vida Cristiano* (1939) and *El Himnario* (1964). Through the years he kept singing hymns and never lost his *joie de vivre;* even in his nineties he sang the National Anthem for the Dodgers, Clippers, and Kings.

ROBERT L. MORRISON

Simpson, Albert Benjamin (1844–1919)

Missiologist and founder of the Christian and Missionary Alliance. Born of Scottish ancestry in Prince Edward Island, Canada, he was converted at fourteen, graduated from Knox College, Toronto (1865), and was ordained. He pastored Presbyterian churches in Ontario (1865–1873), Kentucky (1874–1879), and New York City (1879–1881), and was responsible for the continent's first illustrated missionary periodical, *The Gospel in All Lands*. Influences on his ministry included his experience of sanctification after reading W. E. Boardman's *The Higher Christian Life* in 1874, and his healing from heart trouble in 1881 by trusting Christ. Emphasizing foreign missions, cross-cultural evangelization, and "neglected truths," Simpson in 1881 initiated an independent ministry, "Gospel Tabernacle." He edited *The Word, the Work and the World* (now *Alliance Life*) (1882–1919), and by 1883 established Missionary Training College (now Nyack College), North America's earliest surviving Bible college.

In 1887 he founded Christian Alliance, uniting Christians of various denominations around zealous activity and a "Fourfold Gospel" (Christ as Savior, Sanctifier, Healer, Coming King), and the Evangelical (later International) Missionary Alliance, urging foreign missions. These two alliances merged in 1897, forming C&MA.

Another contribution is the Bible college movement. Hundreds of colleges followed Simpson's lead, specializing in ministries. Of evangelical missionaries, 75 percent attended Bible colleges in their first century. Many read Simpson's literature. Besides three hundred hymns and forty years' worth of C&MA periodical articles and editorials, he authored some one hundred books. Among them were *Christ in the Bible* (26 vols., 1888–1929), *The Gospel of Healing* (1885), *The Holy Spirit* (2 vols., 1896), and *The Four-Fold Gospel* (1925).

Biographies by A. E. Thompson (1920) and A. W. Tozer (1943).

GERALD E. MCGRAW

Skinner, Thomas (1942–1994)

Evangelist, lecturer, and writer. He grew up in New York City's Harlem. He joined his local church at the age of seventeen in order to be seen as respectable to his community and his preacher father. The reality was that he was living a double life. This double life manifested itself in Skinner's gaining acceptable grades in school and being president of the Shakespearean Club, as well as serving as a leader of the Harlem Lords, a street gang. He had become bitter toward the organized black church, believing that it was merely a place where pastors who were not called of God sought to repeat weary words to an emotionally oriented congregation. One evening he was confronted by a religious program that had preempted the rock and roll program to which he had been listening on the radio. The apparently uneducated speaker preached on 2 Corinthians 5:17. Even though Skinner had heard the passage many times before, he became a Christian when the truth of the passage penetrated his deep-seated cynicism. His life was radically transformed and he began to exercise his gift of preaching.

While often speaking to predominately white audiences, Skinner became an evangelist to blacks and held large crusades in a number of major American cities. He frequently spoke at Christian colleges and church meetings. He established the Tom Skinner Associates (TSA) in the 1960s, and worked closely with associate evangelist William Pannell. An outgrowth of this ministry was a weekly radio broadcast on black stations across the nation. An important and unique strategy of the TSA was to reach future black leaders while they were enrolled at historically black colleges and universities. Skinner's fiery, candid, and forceful style has resulted in many affiliations such as being the unofficial chaplain of the Washington Red Skins professional football team and being a frequent resource to the U.S. Congress and Senate. His bold and confrontive message for social justice made Skinner an uncomfortable friend to white Christians. Among his writings are *Black and Free* (1968), and *If Christ Is the Answer, What Are the Questions?* (1974).

ROBERT C. SUGGS

Slessor, Mary Mitchell (1848–1915)

Scottish missionary to Nigeria. Born in Aberdeen and brought up in Dundee in a poor home, she received only a basic education and worked in a textile mill. There she acquired a toughness and resilience that would serve her well in later years. She became a Christian in her teens, and devoted her spare time to youth work among the deprived of Dundee. Her interest in the United Presbyterian Church's work in Calabar led eventually to her being sent there in 1876. She worked initially in the Okoyong area, and then at Itu among the Ibo people. She lived close to them, and displayed great qualities of understanding and courage, as well as considerable linguistic skill. She linked her main concern to win Africans for Christ with a deep care for their moral and social welfare. She opposed witchcraft, twin-killing, trial by ordeal, and human sacrifice. She encouraged trade between the coast and inland areas, and was involved in the founding of the Hope Waddell Institute, which trained Africans in trades and medical work. She earned the trust and affection of African leaders, and became an established arbiter in their disputes. "My Life," she said, "is one long, daily, hourly record of answered prayer." She became in 1892 the first woman vice consul (magistrate) in the British Empire.

Biographies by W. P. Livingstone (1916) and Carol Christian and Gladys Plummer (1970).

JAMES TAYLOR

Smith, Alfredo Claudio (1934–)

Latin American church-planter and expository preacher. Born in Buenos Aires, Argentina, to British parents, Smith was converted to Christ during an evangelistic crusade in 1955. Immediately he prepared for the ministry. After fifteen years serving in Argentina with the Christian and Missionary Alliance (C&MA), Smith accepted an invitation to Lima, Peru, to help lead a new church-planting strategy, "Lima to an Encounter with God." In 1973 he became head pastor of the C&MA's only congregation in Lima, a group of about 150 in the city's Lince District. Through intense evangelism and discipleship campaigns, the congregation doubled in membership within eighteen months. Daughter churches were started, and Smith helped launch an evening Bible institute to produce pastors and leaders for the ballooning movement. After twenty years of "Lima to an Encounter with God," the C&MA in Lima had grown from one congregation to more than thirty churches with 15,000 new baptized members. The C&MA has produced similar programs in various Latin countries, and church-growth specialists around Latin America have closely studied the movement. Smith left Peru in 1985 to help lead "Encounter" projects in Quito, Ecuador, and Buenos Aires. Then, in 1993, he spearheaded an urban church-planting project among Hispanics in Miami, Florida, having been sent there as a missionary of the Lince church in gratitude for Smith's pioneer ministry among them. Smith, one of Latin America's most noted expository Bible preachers, is a world-traveled speaker. He has been particularly effective in reaching Latin America's professionals and upper class, who remain largely untouched by the evangelical church.

JOHN MAUST

Smith, George Adam (1856–1942)

Old Testament scholar. Born in Calcutta, India, son of a Scottish editor and journalist, he was educated at Edinburgh, Tübingen, and Leipzig, and after ordination in the Free Church of Scotland was minister of Queen's Cross Free Church, Aberdeen (1882–1892). He was subsequently professor of Old Testament in the Free Church College, Glasgow (1892–1909), and principal of Aberdeen University (1909–1935). He was knighted by King George V (1916). As a scholar his efforts "to make generally acceptable the higher criticism of the Old Testament" nearly led to an arraignment for heresy in his church's general assembly. Smith traveled extensively in the Middle East. His famous *Historical Geography of the Holy Land* (1894) was said to have greatly assisted the British army in that region during World War I. Smith, who became well known in America through lecture tours, published other significant works, including *The Book of Isaiah* (2 vols., 1888–1890), *The Book of the Twelve Prophets* (2 vols., 1896–1898), *Modern Criticism and the Preaching of the Old Testament* (1901), and *Jeremiah* (1923).

Biography by L. A. Smith (1943).

JAMES TAYLOR

Smith, John Coventry (1903–1984)

Presbyterian minister, missionary, and ecumenical statesman. Born in Stamford, Ontario, he grew up in Ohio in the United Presbyterian Church. He was educated at Muskingum College, Pittsburgh Theological Seminary, and the Kennedy School of Missions, Hartford, Connecticut. Soon after ordination he went as a Presbyterian Church USA missionary to Japan (1929–1940), where he served in a variety of ministries. During World War II he was interned for six months, returning to the United States in 1942. He served briefly as assistant pastor of Third Church, Pittsburgh, and then pastor of Mt. Lebanon Church, the largest United Presbyterian congregation. From 1948 he served his denomination in administrative posts, culminating in eleven years as general secretary, Commission on Ecumenical Mission and Relations, before his retirement in 1970. In 1968 he was elected moderator of the Presbyterian General Assembly and a president of the World Council of Churches. Smith believed that ecumenism, justice, and race relations were all involved in faithful proclamation of the gospel, and he traveled widely and campaigned for these causes.

In his autobiography, *From Colonialism to World Community* (1982), he states that when mainline churches become more evangelical and when evangelicals are more concerned with social witness, they might together lead the church in renewal of mission to the whole world.

ALBERT H. FREUNDT, JR.

Smith, John Taylor (1860–1937)

Anglican bishop and British chaplain-general. Born in the English Lake District, he was converted before his twelfth birthday and was active in Christian witnessing during schooldays. He worked for some years as a silversmith and jeweler until called to the ministry. After training at St. John's Hall, Highbury, he was ordained in 1885, and after a five-year curacy in outer London went to West Africa as canon-missioner in the diocese of Sierra Leone, where he ministered also to a strong British expeditionary force. Accompanying the latter was Queen Victoria's son, Prince Henry, who became desperately ill. Smith's ministry to the young man in the days before he died was never forgotten by the queen, who made him honorary chaplain; he thus had a lasting influence on the royal family. Appointed bishop of Sierra Leone in 1897, he was concerned also for the social welfare of the people, and convinced that the evangelization of Africa must eventually be done by Africans themselves. Then in 1914, on the eve of World War I, Smith was asked to be chaplain-general of the British army—according to one general, "the largest missionary society in the world." He accepted this enormous challenge. An uncompromising evangelical, he set about recruiting new chaplains, often asking the searching question, "What would you say to a man who was fatally wounded, but conscious, with only ten minutes to live?" Smith retired in 1925, was knighted by King George V, and died at sea en route home from meetings in Australia.

Biography by Maurice Whitlow (1938).

J. D. DOUGLAS

Smith, Nico (1929–)

South African missiologist and Dutch Reformed pastor. A seventh-generation Afrikaner, he was reared with the traditional view of white supremacy over black Africans. After studying theology, he pastored a church with Beyers Naude, who later staunchly opposed apartheid. Nico and his wife, Ellen, a medical doctor, served as missionaries among the Venda people, building a hospital and church. Nico was invited to join the Broederbond, a secret brotherhood dedicated to the superiority of Afrikaners. His Broederbond connections arranged for him to be offered the prestigious post of professor of missiology at the University of Stellenbosch. While there, Nico began to realize the injustices of the South African situation and resigned from the Broederbond. He edited Storm-Kompass (Storm Compass), a collection of essays by twenty-four leading Afrikaner intellectuals condemning apartheid. Finally, he resigned the chair of missiology to accept the pastorate of a black Dutch Reformed Church in Mamelodi near Pretoria. The Smiths moved into the African township, an unprecedented action in South Africa. In addition to serving his church, Nico founded Koinonia, an organization dedicated to promoting contact between the racial groups in South Africa. Nico Smith is an example of how the power of the gospel can free people from long-held racial prejudice.

Biography by R. de Saintouge.

JAMES J. STAMOOLIS

Smith, Oswald Jeffrey (1889–1986)

Canadian pastor, evangelist, author, hymnwriter, and leader of a conservative Protestant missionary movement. Born in Erneston, Ontario, he underwent a conversion experience in 1906. He then attended Toronto Bible College and McCormick Theological Seminary, from which he graduated in 1915. In 1916 he became pastor of Dale Presbyterian Church in Toronto. In 1920 he started a new church in that city, and soon combined it with a Christian and Missionary Alliance congregation. Smith then launched *The People's Magazine* periodical and the Canadian Bible Institute. In 1928 he started a new Toronto congregation, which later became known as the People's Church. Under Smith's leadership the church promoted missions through fundraising and annual conferences. Smith spent much of his time attending missionary conferences and holding evangelistic crusades around the world. He retired as pastor of the People's Church in 1959, but remained active as a missions advocate for many years. He was named president of the Canadian Evangelical Fellowship in 1965. He wrote more than thirty books and nearly one hundred hymns.

Biography by Lois Neely (1982).

ROBERT L. MORRISON

Smith, Rodney ("Gipsy") (1860–1947)

English evangelist. Born in a tent in Essex, he was converted in 1876 and served as an officer in the Salvation Army (1877–1882), leaving after differing with General William Booth over Booth's interpretation of Army rules. Smith continued in evangelism, and in 1889 made the first of numerous trips to the United States, where he became widely known. He served for some years with the Wesleyan Mission in Manchester, England, during which time he founded the Gipsy Gospel Wagon Mission in Edinburgh (1892). He was missioner with the National Free Church Council (1897–1912), and at a meeting in South Africa refused to have people separated according to race. During World War I he worked with the YMCA, for which King George V made him a Member of the Order of the British Empire (MBE). Smith was also a singer, and made recordings of high-quality gospel songs.

His written works include *Gipsy Smith, His Life and Work* (1901), *A Mission of Peace* (1904), and *The Beauty of Jesus: Memories and Reflections* (1932).

David Lazell, who wrote a biography of Smith, *Out of the Forest I Came* (1970), holds that his "great contribution to the development of inter-church evanglism and to trans-Atlantic goodwill is today under-estimated if not forgotten."

J. D. DOUGLAS

Smith, Wilbur Moorehead (1894–1977)

Presbyterian minister and Bible teacher. Born in Chicago, Illinois, he grew up in the Moody Church and was educated at Moody Bible Institute (1913–1914) and the College of Wooster (1914–1917). Not ordained until 1922, he pastored Presbyterian churches in Maryland, Virginia, and Pennsylvania. He served on the Independent Board of Presbyterian Foreign Missions (1933–1937), but resigned when the board aligned itself with the division in the Presbyterian denomination. He taught English Bible at Moody Bible Institute, Chicago (1938–1947), Fuller Theological Seminary (1947–1963), and Trinity Evangelical Divinity School (1963–1971). His departure from Fuller was due to a difference over the doctrine of biblical inerrancy. He was a popular Bible teacher, a prolific author, and a defender of Christian fundamentals. He loved and collected books, and had an extraordinary knowledge of Christian literature. He had no academic degrees, but his learning inspired a younger generation of evangelical scholars. He edited *Peloubet's Select Notes on the International Sunday School Lessons* (1933–1972), helped to revise the Scofield Reference Bible (1963), and wrote many books, including *A List of Bibliographies of Theological and Biblical Literature Published in Great Britain and America 1595–1931*, *Therefore Stand* (1945), *A Bibliography of Dwight L. Moody* (1946), *World Crises in the Light of the Prophetic Scriptures* (1951), biographies of C. E. Fuller (1949) and W. H. Houghton (1950), and the autobiographical *Before I Forget* (1971).

ALBERT H. FREUNDT, JR.

Smith, William Alexander (1854–1914)

Founder of the Boys' Brigade. Born into a Church of Scotland family in Caithness and educated at the local school, he went to Glasgow in 1868 to join his uncle who had a successful clothing business. His religious beliefs deepened by the campaigns held by Moody and Sankey, he joined the Free Church of Scotland and taught Sunday school. Concerned for the plight of boys just entering their teens, Smith in 1883 began an organization whose object was defined as "The advancement of Christ's Kingdom among boys and the promotion of habits of reverence, discipline, self-respect and all that tends towards a true Christian manliness." The movement quickly spread to England and Ireland. Smith enlisted the support of many eminent people, including George Adam Smith and Henry Drummond. Summer camps started in 1886, and about a decade later the Boys' Brigade had 790 companies and 35,000 boys. Smith would never make boys sing hymns with meaningless words, nor use for proselytizing purposes camps meant for health and enjoyment. He himself left camp on one occasion in 1909 and returned two days later to a tumultuous welcome, having been knighted by King Edward VII. In 1910 the War Office offered special privileges if the BB would consent to become a government-sponsored cadet corps. This was politely declined because, it was stated, the advancement of Christ's kingdom and the provision of qualified cannon fodder did not go together. Yet when World War I came in 1914, some four hundred thousand men with BB connections served, and eleven of them won the Victoria Cross for valor.

J. D. DOUGLAS

Smyth, Walter H. (1912–)

Crusade director. Born in Springfield, Pennsylvania, he studied at Drexel Institute, Philadelphia, and was in the publishing business for six years before entering the ministry as associate pastor, Calvary Memorial Church, Philadelphia, where he was ordained in 1945. He was associated also with Percy Crawford Ministries, Philadelphia, and was vice president of Youth for Christ International. He joined the Billy Graham Evangelistic Association in 1950, and until retirement in 1987 served as international vice president. Possessed of a unique combination of pastoral and administrative abilities, Smyth has prepared crusades in many parts of the world. He chaired two international conferences for itinerant evangelists held in Amsterdam (1983, 1986), where both his logistic and his diplomatic skills were fully reflected. He still serves as a very active consultant with the BGEA.

J. D. DOUGLAS

Söderblom, Nathan (Jonathan) Lars Olof (1866–1931)

Lutheran archbishop, scholar, and pioneer ecumenist. Born in Trönö, Hälsingland, a province of Sweden on the Baltic Sea, Söderblom was the son of a Lutheran pastor and his Danish wife. Brought up in the Pietist tradition, he entered Uppsala University in 1883. He excelled in Classics and languages, and took a degree in 1886, continuing at the university for theological studies. He completed his course with distinction in 1892; his studies were already broadening his religious understandings. In the summer of 1890 he visited the United States under the auspices of the Student Christian Movement, and made his first effective ecumenical contacts. Ordained in 1893, in 1894 he married Anna Forsell and they left for Paris, where he was for seven years chaplain to the Swedish embassy and also studied at the Sorbonne. In 1901 he received his doctorate in theology from the Sorbonne for a thesis on Persian religion. In the same year he was appointed professor of *Religionsgeschichte* at his old university, and returned to Uppsala. From 1912 to 1914 he was also professor of the history of religion at Leipzig. He published several books, traveled widely, and was also a parish priest during this period.

In 1914, at only forty-eight, he was unexpectedly selected to lead the diocese of Uppsala—and so became immediately archbishop of Sweden as well as a bishop. He became known for his liberal and evangelical catholicity, and showed his concern that the church, while not neglecting its spiritual role, also led in matters of social justice. Combined with this was his passion for ecumenical dialogue, which culminated in the Universal Christian Conference on Life and Work, held in Stockholm in August 1925. As early as 1922 he suffered a serious heart attack. This did not prevent him from continuing travel, preaching and lecturing, research, writing, and committee work. His relations with worldwide Lutheranism were important—especially with the Swedish immigrant community in the United States. He also became involved with Christian peace initiatives in Europe, and in 1930 received the Nobel Prize for Peace.

The Nathan Söderblom Archive in the library of Uppsala University contains an extensive collection of letters and papers. Books by him in English are *Christian Fellowship* (ET, 1923) and his 1931 Gifford lectures, published posthumously, *The Living God* (1932).

The life by Bengt Sunkler, *Nathan Söderblom: His Life and Work* (1968), is the best source in English.

JOCELYN MURRAY

Solzhenitsyn, Alexander (1918–)

Leading Russian author and Nobel Prize winner. Born in Kislovodsk in the Caucasus, after his father's death he was reared by his mother in Rostov-on-Don, and graduated from the high school and university there. Trained in mathematics and physics, he served in the Soviet army (1941–1945) and rose to the rank of captain in the artillery. In 1945 he was arrested by the NKVD for critical comments about Stalin. Sentenced to eight years in prison, he was interned in several labor camps, one of which was the setting of his novel *The First Circle* (1968). Although a convinced Marxist, he abandoned that ideology and became an outspoken critic of his superiors. This led to his transfer to a hard labor camp in Kazakhstan, an experience described in *One Day in the Life of Ivan Denisovich* (1962). Released with terminal cancer after Stalin's death in 1953, he made an amazing recovery and later wrote about his illness in *Cancer Ward* (1968). During the de-Stalinization period he was allowed to return from his post imprisonment exile in Siberia to European Russia, where he taught high school physics and mathematics and worked on his writing. During his imprisonment he turned to the Christian faith, and a deep tone of morality entered his work.

Under Krushchev some of his material was published in the Soviet Union an he became and instant celebrity. For several years he struggled against pressure from the KGB. He was dismissed from the Writer's Union and his works were not published in his homeland. Despite such problems he was awarded the Nobel Prize for literature in 1970. However, publication of the first volumes of *August 1914* (1971) and *The Gulag Archipelago* (1973) by foreign presses led the Soviet authorities to exile him to the West (1974). Settling first in Zurich, he later moved to Vermont in the United States.

He continued to write, completing *The Gulag Archipelago,* and *The Calf and the Oak,* the memoir of his last ten years in the Soviet Union. He also worked on a multivolume historical work, *The Red Wheel,* about life in Russia during World War I and the Revolution of 1917. He has received the Nobel Prize for literature (1970) and the Templeton Prize for Progress in Religion. Although his collected works have been published in the United States, France, and Germany, controversy has marked his reception in the West. Many have been offended by his harsh criticism of life in democratic society and his penchant for monarchy and autocratic orthodox faith.

Biographies by E. E. Ericson, Jr. and M. Scammell (1984).

ROBERT G. CLOUSE

Soper, Donald Oliver (1903–)

English Methodist minister. Born in London and educated at Cambridge and the London School of Economics, he was ordained and served his denomination's South London Mission (1926–1929) and Central London Mission (1929–1936) before appointment as superintendent of the West London Mission, Kingsway Hall (1936–1978). An ardent pacifist and open-air speaker, he became a regular institution on Sunday afternoons at Hyde Park Speakers' Corner, where a motley collection of individuals intent on putting the world to rights converged. Soper had a ready wit that could hold its own with the traditional hecklers. Often his socialism was more in evidence than was the Christian message, and evangelicals might echo the wistful comment of one visitor, "I wish he had spoken a good word for Jesus Christ." President of the Methodist Conference in 1953, Soper was made a life peer at the instigation of Britain's Labour government in 1965, giving him a new forum in the House of Lords. His public activity continued even after his ninetieth birthday. One of the most prominent among his many books and pamphlets was *All His Grace* (1957).

J. D. DOUGLAS

Souter, Alexander (1873–1949)

Patristic and New Testament scholar. Born in Aberdeen, where he gained his first degree, he went on to Cambridge to work under the Latinist scholar J. E. B. Mayor. In 1903 he was appointed professor of New Testament Greek at Mansfield College, Oxford. He returned to Aberdeen in 1911 as professor of humanity, and remained there until his retirement in 1937. Souter became an expert in the field of early Christian Latin. He had a special interest in the converted Jew, Ambrosiaster. He identified as Ambrosiaster's some writings originally attributed to Augustine of Hippo. Souter's wider reputation came from his more popular works. His *Oxford Greek New Testament* went through many printings, and appeared in a revised edition in 1947. Also popular were his *Short Manual on the Text and Canon of the New Testament* (1913) and his *Pocket Lexicon to the Greek New Testament* (1916). Even in retirement he made contributions to scholarship as editor-in-chief of the *Oxford Latin Dictionary.*

NOEL S. POLLARD

Sowerby, Leo (1895–1968)

American composer. He made a significant impact on modern church music during his long tenure at St. James Cathedral, Chicago (1927–1962), and at the College of Church Musicians at the National Cathedral in Washington, D.C., which he founded in 1962. In addition he was on the faculty of the American Conservatory in Chicago for more than forty years as head of the composition department. Sowerby exerted a profound influence on his students, many of whom became significant composers themselves. In 1921 he was the first American to win the Prix de Rome and in 1946 he won the Pulitzer Prize for *Canticle of the Sun,* based on the words of St. Francis. Though his compositions number in the hundreds and are in all media except opera, he is best known for his approximately two hundred choral compositions and liturgical settings. *Forsaken of Man* (1939) and *Christ Reborn* (1950) are two strongly dramatic cantatas written with the texts selected by Edward Borgers primarily from the Gospels. *The Throne of God* was commissioned for the fiftieth anniversary of Washington's National Cathedral in 1957. His hymntunes "Rosedale" and "Perry" appear in the Episcopal hymnal of 1982; his most beloved choral anthem is "I Will Lift Up Mine Eyes." His style is modern but always accessible and melodious. "I have been accused by right wingers of being too dissonant and cacophonous and by leftists of being old-fashioned and derivative," he commented.

WILLIAM PHEMISTER

Spartas, Christopher Reuben Mukasa (1890–1982)

Pioneer of the African Greek Orthodox Church of Uganda. Born in Kira, a small village outside of Kampala, Uganda, he was reared within the Anglican

Church of Uganda, but from an early age began questioning the historicity of the Anglican Church. His curiosity of history, combined with his strong individualistic attitude, led him to eventually leave the Anglican Church and unite himself with Marcus Garvey's African Orthodox Church in America. In this church he sought the historicity of the ancient Eastern Orthodox Church. Along with this, the African Orthodox Church in America allowed blacks to rise within the high ecclesiastical ranks of the hierarchy, something that was denied Africans within the Anglican Church. However, Spartas soon realized that the African Orthodox Church in America was unrelated canonically to the worldwide Eastern Orthodox Church. Through contact with numerous Greek Orthodox Christians in Uganda, Spartas came into contact with the patriarch of Alexandria. Through correspondence and interaction, Spartas visited Alexandria in 1946, and eventually received official recognition for himself and the 10,291 members of the African Orthodox Church. In 1959 the patriarch established a diocese of East Africa, with Spartas acting as the patriarchal vicar. Finally, in 1972, Spartas became the first African Orthodox bishop, along with Obadiah Basajjakitalo and Aurther Gathunna. He received the title Bishop Christopher Reuben Spartas of Niloupolis. Through the initiative and vision of Spartas, the Ugandan Orthodox Church grew to more than 30,000 Christians by the time of his death.

LUKE VERONIS

Speer, Robert Elliot (1867–1947)

Presbyterian layman and foreign missions administrator. Born in Huntingdon, Pennsylvania, he was educated at the College of New Jersey (now Princeton University), during which time he worked with the Student Volunteer movement for foreign missions. He studied for one year at Princeton Theological Seminary. At age twenty-four he was appointed secretary of the Foreign Missions Board of the Presbyterian Church, USA, serving from 1891 to 1937. Over that time period the board had oversight of over 1,600 missionaries. Speer was an influential voice for interdenominational cooperation in foreign missions. In 1910 he helped organize the World Missionary Conference in Edinburgh, and he was appointed chairman of the Committee on Cooperation in Latin America, which pioneered Protestant efforts to penetrate Catholic-denominated Central and South America. From 1920 to 1924 he served as president of the Federal Council of Churches. Speer became involved in the fundamentalist-modernist controversy when Presbyterian conservatives, led by J. Gresham Machen, charged the board of Foreign Missions with endorsing modernism on the mission field. Speer tried to steer a middle position, rejecting Machen's complaint yet distancing himself from the modernist manifesto, *Re-Thinking Missions* (1932). His own views were expressed in *The Finality of Jesus Christ* (1933). In addition, he wrote over sixty other books, many on missions.

JOHN R. MUETHER

Spinka, Matthew (1890–1972)

Church historian. Born in Stitary, Czechoslovakia, he came to America as a teenager and soon displayed scholastic skills, culminating in a Ph.D. from the University of Chicago and a Th.D. from the Faculty of Protestant Theology, Prague. He taught church history at Central Theological Seminary, Dayton, Ohio (1920–1926), Chicago Theological Seminary and Divinity School (1926–1943), then at Hartford Theological Seminary (1943–1955) where he had more scope to pursue his writing projects. Spinka's background and interest in Eastern Europe past and present enabled him to make a substantial contribution to the literature and understanding of that region, especially for the post-World War II years. He was a strong critic of communism, and his linguistic expertise was used in propaganda broadcasts to Europe. He retired to California, but remained active by lecturing in various colleges in the Los Angeles area. His meticulous scholarship brought him many honors, including a D.D. from Scotland's oldest university. Among his publications were *Christianity Confronts Communism* (1936), *Advocates of Reform* (1953), and biographies of J. A. Comenius (1943), Nicolas Berdyaev (1950), and John Hus (1968). Spinka also edited *Church History* (1932–1949).

J. D. Douglas

Sproul, Robert Charles (1939–)

Presbyterian pastor, theologian, and writer. Born in Pittsburgh, he graduated from Westminster College, New Wilmington, Pennsylvania (1961), and Pittsburgh Theological Seminary (1964), and went on to earn a doctorate at the Free University of Amsterdam (1969). Formerly in the United Presbyterian Church, he became an ordained minister in the Presbyterian Church, USA in 1976. He taught at Westminster College, Gordon College, and the (then) Conwell School of Theology, was minister of theology at the College Hill United Presbyterian Church, Cincinnati, then in 1971 became president of the Ligonier Ministries in Stahlstown, Pennsylvania. Since 1980 he has served also as professor of systematic theology and apologetics at Reformed Theological Seminary, Jackson, Mississippi. In addition to his teaching ministry, Sproul is well known for his public lectures on Reformation theology, and for some thirty publications, including *God's Inerrant Word* (1975), *Classical Apologetics* (1984), *God's Will and the Christian* (1984), *The Holiness of God* (1985), *Surprised by Suffering* (1989), and *Doubt and Assurance* (1993).

Norman R. Ericson

St. John, Patricia Mary (1919–1993)

Missionary and writer of books for children. Born in England, she began her writing career as a child. As a house-mother in a Christian school in

Wales she was involved with Scripture Union, and under its auspices wrote the best-selling *Tangle-woods' Secret* (1948). Other successful books followed; her mailbag showed how much adults too benefited from her vivid way of presenting Christian truths. In 1948 she joined the North Africa Mission, and served in Morocco for twenty-seven years, founded a training school for nurses, and wrote about her experiences in Tangier and in the more remote areas where she had worked. Her continuing concern for North Africa after her return to England in 1976 was underlined not only by frequent visits back to the field, but by a biography of Lilias Trotter (1853–1928), founder of the Algiers Mission Band. During the final decade of her life she was a tireless president of Global Care, a Christian body that ministered to children in underdeveloped countries.

J. D. DOUGLAS

Stalker, James (1848–1927)

Scottish preacher and writer. Born in Crieff and educated at Edinburgh and at German universities, he was minister in Kirkcaldy and Glasgow before the United Free Church appointed him to the chair of church history in its Aberdeen college (1902–1926). Having benefited from the revival movement that followed the 1873 Moody and Sankey mission in Scotland, he was ever concerned to carry the gospel to the people. He saw the minister as only one of the congregation set apart by his fellows to explore on their behalf a land of peace, light, and joy, and told, "Come, we will elect you, and set you free from toil, and you shall go thither for us, and week by week trade with that land and bring us its treasure and its spoils." Stalker, who was said to have been more widely known in America than any other Scottish preacher of his day, had also a profound social concern, on which he never hesitated to speak his mind frankly and fearlessly. He wrote biographies of Jesus (1879), Paul (1884), and John Knox (1904). His other works included *The Preacher and His Models* (1891), *The Atonement* (1908), and *The Ethic of Jesus* (1909).

J. D. DOUGLAS

Stanford, Sir Charles Villiers (1852–1924)

Irish composer. He was a choral scholar at Queens' College, Cambridge, organist of Trinity College, conductor of the University Music Society and the Bach Choir in London, music director of the Leeds Festival, professor of music at Cambridge (1887–1924), and professor of composition at the Royal College of Music from its inception. Stanford was a gifted composer; he wrote seven symphonies, several operas, and a large number of songs, choral pieces, and chamber works. He was regarded as a superb teacher, being best known as the mentor of such composers as Vaughan Williams, Bliss, Ireland, and Benjamin. Stanford composed for almost every medium but he is chiefly appreciated today for his important and influential choral services for Anglican worship, which serve as classic examples of the English cathedral style. The *Te Deum* from the *Service in B-flat* was sung in Westminster Abbey to celebrate the Armistice on November 11, 1918. His hymn tune "Engelberg," has taken on a new life in recent years with a new text by F. Pratt Green: "When in Our Music God Is Glorified."

Biography by H. P. Greene (1935).

WILLIAM PHEMISTER

Stanway, Alfred (1908–1989)

Australian bishop and missionary leader. As a young man he experienced a call to Africa, which led him to offer to serve with the Anglican Church Missionary Society. He trained for ordination at Ridley College, Melbourne, and began work in Kenya in 1937. In 1951 he was consecrated bishop of Central Tanganyika, at that time a diocese that covered over half the country. Under his dynamic leadership the church continued to grow rapidly. He put strong emphasis on giving responsibility to local Christians. African bishops were consecrated and new dioceses created. He advanced substantially medical and educational work and began to develop a network of Bible schools. His lifelong stress on the value of Christian literature led to the establishment of book shops and the Central Tanganyika Press. When he left Tanzania in 1971 there was an African archbishop, and Stanway himself was succeeded by an African. He was then deputy principal of Ridley College until invited unexpectedly to become president/dean of a new seminary in Pittsburgh, Pennsylvania, to be called Trinity Episcopal School for Ministry. From 1975 to 1978 he worked there to build up its spiritual, physical, and academic foundations. He wrote *Prayer: A Personal Testimony* (1991).

Biography by Marjory Stanway (1991).

JOHN W. WILSON

Stapleton, Ruth Carter (1929–1983)

Baptist evangelist and faith healer. Reared near Plains, Georgia, she attended Georgia State College. At age nineteen she married Robert Stapleton, who qualified as a veterinarian. Following the birth of her four children, she suffered from depression, but was later cured at a Christian camp. After this experience she began to teach techniques of spiritual healing. Among the methods she advocated was that of "faith imagination," where those suffering emotional pain could find relief by picturing themselves telling Jesus of their troubles. Stapleton and her message received widespread attention in 1976, when her brother, Jimmy Carter, was elected president of the United States. Carter attributed much of his spiritual for-

363

mation to his sister's influence. She authored *The Gift of Inner Healing* (1976), *Experiencing Inner Healing* (1977), and *Brother Billy* (1978).

ROBERT L. MORRISON

Stewart, James Stuart (1896–1990)

Scottish pastor, preacher, and scholar. Born in Dundee, he was educated at the universities of St. Andrews, Edinburgh, and Bonn. After ordination in 1924 he ministered in Auchterarder, Aberdeen, and Edinburgh, becoming known as a preacher of outstanding eloquence. He was then appointed professor of New Testament at New College, Edinburgh (1947–1966). He collaborated with H. R. Mackintosh in translating Schleiermacher's *The Christian Faith* (1928) and in 1933 published a much reprinted Bible class handbook, *The Life and Teaching of Jesus Christ.* Among other publications, which included collections of sermons and lectures, were *A Man in Christ* (1935), *Heralds of God* (1946; reissued in 1955 as *Teach Yourself Preaching*), and *Thine Is the Kingdom* (1956). Stewart exemplified the Scottish ideal of the scholarly minister. Although a very shy man, he was an effective pastor in situations of real need. He was elected moderator of the general assembly of the Church of Scotland in 1963.

HENRY R. SEFTON

Stone, John Timothy (1868–1954)

American Presbyterian pastor. Born in Boston, he studied at Amherst College and Auburn Theological Seminary before ordination in the Presbyterian Church. After a chaplaincy in World War I, he served congregations in Utica and Cortland, New York, and Brown Memorial Church, Baltimore. In 1909 he began a twenty-one-year ministry at Fourth Presbyterian Church in Chicago, during which the congregation increased from 638 to 2,650 members, and there was constructed a beautiful gothic building on Chicago's Gold Coast. Stone was also chairman of the committee on evangelism of the Men and Religion Forward movement (1911) and moderator of the general assembly of the Presbyterian Church, USA (1913), president of McCormick Theological Seminary (1928–1940), president of the Chicago Bible Society, and director of the Chicago Sunday Evening Club.

Stone was not a theologian in a strict sense, but a preacher and a pastor with a deep concern for the evangelical witness of the church. His plan for the development of an evangelical emphasis within the local church was considered by many to be his greatest contribution. That plan, developed in Fourth Church, led to the New Life movement.

His many books include *Recruiting for Christ* (1910), *George Whitefield* (1914), and *Winning Men* (1946).

SAM HAMSTRA, JR.

Stonehouse, Ned Bernard (1902–1962)

New Testament scholar. Born in Grand Rapids, Michigan, he graduated from Calvin College, Princeton Theological Seminary, and the Free University of Amsterdam (Th.D., 1929). He was among the first faculty members of the newly founded Westminster Theological Seminary and taught there all his working life (1929–1962), serving also latterly as dean. Ordained in the Presbyterian Church in 1932 he, like many of his colleagues, transferred to the Orthodox Presbyterian Church in 1936. Like them, he also held to and vigorously defended the infallibility of Scripture against the radical tide of higher criticism, notably in connection with the Synoptic Gospels. His breadth of learning, coupled with a gracious personality, won the respect of those who differed from him. Editor of the multivolume *New International Commentary on the New Testament* (1951–) and biographer of J. Gresham Machen (1954), he wrote also *The Witness of Matthew and Mark to Christ* (1944), *The Witness of Luke to Christ* (1951), and *Paul before the Areopagus* (1957).

J. D. DOUGLAS

Stott, John Robert Walmsley (1921–)

Anglican leader and author. He was educated at Trinity College, Cambridge, graduating in 1944. He trained at Ridley Hall, Cambridge, and was ordained as curate of All Souls, Langham Place, London, in 1945. Surprisingly he was made rector of the same church in 1950. It became the most important center of evangelical preaching and influence over the next twenty-five years. In the postwar years he was missioner to the universities of the United Kingdom and the wider English-speaking world. His *Basic Christianity* (1958) contains his message. He revived the Eclectics, a clerical discussion group, which was a force in bringing evangelicals to seek to restore their influence in the mainstream of the Church of England. He was a prominent figure in the Keele (1967) and Nottingham (1977) National Evangelical Anglican conferences. His stature as a preacher and writer is marked by his books such as *I Believe in Preaching* (1982) and his commentaries such as those in *The Bible Speaks Today* series that he is editing. On his retirement in 1975 he set about making All Souls a London center for the Institute of Contemporary Christianity, of which he was the first director and is now the president. His later books mark his wide interests, such as *Issues Facing Christians Today* (1984) and *The Contemporary Christian* (1992). He has been influential in worldwide evangelicalism both through the Evangelical Fellowship of the Anglican Communion and the Lausanne Continuation movement. Despite all efforts to provide him with more exalted rank, he remains firmly married to All Souls Church—and his keen bird watching and photography.

NOEL S. POLLARD

365

Strachan, Robert Kenneth (1910–1965)

Missionary statesman and strategist, as well as architect of the Evangelism-in-Depth movement, and of innovative mission-church relationships. Born in Tamil, Argentina, and reared in Costa Rica, he graduated from Wheaton College, Illinois, in 1935, gaining further degrees at Dallas Theological Seminary (1936) and Princeton Seminary (1943). In 1936 he returned to Costa Rica with the Latin American Mission founded and led by his parents. He served as professor, dean, and director of the Latin American Biblical Seminary, and in 1944 was named deputy director of the mission. He became general director after the death of his mother in 1951. Convinced that the mobilization of every believer was the key to reaching the world, he conceived the Evangelism-in-Depth national campaigns held eventually throughout Latin America and copied on other continents. His pioneering efforts in mission-national church partnerships and "Latinization" led to the formation of the Community of Latin American Ministries (CLAME). He was the author of *The Inescapable Calling* (1968) and numerous articles.

Biographies by Elisabeth Elliot (1968) and W. D. Roberts (1971).

STEPHEN R. SYWULKA

Stravinsky, Igor (1882–1971)

Russian-American composer. Stravinsky is perhaps the greatest twentieth-century composer, largely due to his unique, sharply delineated, often controversial musical vocabulary. His sacred works make up just a small part of his production, yet they are extremely important. In fact, the *Symphony of Psalms* (1930, rev. 1948) and the *Mass* (1948) are two of the most significant pieces of all twentieth-century religious music. A man of great faith who, like Bach, composed "to the glory of God," Stravinsky's religious works have mistakenly found a home more often in the concert hall than in the church. Many of the influences in his music can be traced to the liturgies of the Russian Orthodox Church and to the simple melodies of Russian folk music that achieved a kind of metamorphosis into the special rhythmic and harmonic Stravinsky sound. Other music on biblical or religious subjects includes the cantata *Babel* (1944), *A Sermon, A Narrative and a Prayer* (1960–1961), *Threni; id est, Lamentationes Jeremiae Prophetae* (1958), *Canticum sacrum* (1956), and *The Flood* (1962), and songs such as a *Paternoster* (1926) and an *Ave Maria* (1934).

See Stephen Walsh, *The Music of Stravinsky* (1988) and E. W. White, *Stravinsky: The Composer and His Works* (1979).

WILLIAM PHEMISTER

Streeter, Burnett Hillman (1874–1937)

English New Testament scholar. Born in Croydon, near London, he was educated at Oxford, where he held prominent positions for the rest of his life. Ordained deacon in the Church of England in 1899, Streeter was a scholar of liberal persuasion. His main interest was the philosophy of religion wherein he attempted, as evidenced in his book *Reality* (1926), to correlate science and theology. His most significant contribution, however, was in the field of New Testament study; his most famous work was *The Four Gospels; A Study of Origins* (1924). Other volumes included *Concerning Prayer* (1916), *The Spirit* (1919), and *The Buddha and the Christ* (1926). Streeter died in an accident in Basel, Switzerland.

SAM HAMSTRA, JR.

Stringfellow, Frank William (1928–1985)

American lawyer, Episcopal layman, and social activist. Born in Rhode Island, he was educated at Bates College, London School of Economics, Harvard University, and was admitted to the New York State bar in 1957, the U.S. Supreme Court Bar in 1958, and the Rhode Island State Bar in 1971. He went into private practice in 1961 and served as the special deputy attorney general for New York City. He was a member of the Laymen's Academy for Ecumenical Studies and the Faith and Order Commission of the World Council of Churches. Stringfellow is best remembered for his role as a social and political activist. An advocate of equal rights, he denounced racism, fought for women's ordination in the Episcopal Church, and defended the disenfranchised poor and homeless in East Harlem, New York. His strong opposition to the Vietnam War led him to counsel many who faced criminal charges for opposing the war. Among these was the celebrated Catholic priest, Daniel Berrigan, who was indicted for destroying draft records. In church politics he defended his friend, the controversial Episcopal bishop James Pike, against the charge of heresy. His experiences as an activist provided the material for his best-known works, including *Dissenter in a Great Society* (1966), *The Bishop Pike Affair* (1967), *Suspect Tenderness: The Ethics of Daniel Berrigan* (1971), *An Ethic for Christians and Other Aliens in a Strange Land* (1973), and *Conscience and Obedience* (1977).

MAXIE BURCH

Strong, Augustus Hopkins (1836–1921)

Baptist theologian and educator. Born in Rochester, New York, he was educated at Yale College, Rochester Theological Seminary, and the University of Berlin. He was ordained to a ministry of the Baptist Church in 1861, and after Baptist pastorates in Haverhill, Massachusetts (1861–1865), and Cleveland, Ohio (1865–1872), he was elected president of Rochester Theological Seminary (1872–1912), where he also served as professor of biblical theology. As an active American (Northern) Baptist he was president of the American Baptist Missionary Union (1892–1895), and first president of the Northern Baptist Convention (1905–1910).

His *Systematic Theology* of 1886 went through seven editions before being revised and enlarged to three volumes in 1907–1909. It has been said of this work that it was "characterized by Neoplatonic modes of thought derived from Lutheran sources." Seeking a middle way between Arminianism and Calvinism, Strong accepted a philosophy of evolution focused on the centrality of Christ, and gave up the inerrancy of Scripture. *A Tour of the Missions, Observations and Conclusions* (1918), made worldwide by him and his wife in 1916–1917, reflected another of his concerns.

The *Autobiography of Augustus Hopkins Strong*, edited by Crerar Douglas, was published in 1981. A major study by Grant Wacker, *Augustus H. Strong and the Dilemma of Historical Consciousness*, followed in 1985.

CLYDE CURRY SMITH

Strong, Philip Nigel Warrington (1899–1983)

Missionary bishop and Anglican primate of Australia. Born into a clerical family in Derbyshire, England, he was educated at Cambridge and after ordination in 1922 ministered in poorer areas of northern England before consecration in 1936 as the fourth bishop of New Guinea. Anglican work was concentrated on the north coast of Papua, which experienced bitter fighting in World War II. Strong urged that missionaries not desert the young Papuan church. A number were subsequently executed by the invaders, but the bishop continued to minister within the war zone. During the postwar period of recovery, the Anglican mission was again deeply affected by loss of life and property when Mount Lamington erupted in 1951, killing over three thousand people. Strong built up the indigenous ministry, and in 1960 appointed the first Papuan assistant bishop (George Ambo). He provided forceful leadership, and under him Anglican work in the New Guinea highlands was commenced. He became a member of the legislative council of Papua and New Guinea (1955–1963). In 1963 he was elected archbishop of Brisbane, and from 1966 until his retirement in 1970 he was also Anglican primate of Australia. He is remembered for his missionary vision, enthusiastic preaching, outspokenness on public issues, and simplicity and saintliness of life, combining an evangelical heritage with an Anglo-Catholic churchmanship. He was knighted by Queen Elizabeth II in 1970.

David Wetherall edited *The New Guinea Diaries of Philip Strong 1936–1945* (1981).

JOHN W. WILSON

Studd, C(harles) T(homas) (1862–1931)

English pioneer missionary. Son of a wealthy retired planter, he was educated at Cambridge where he so excelled at cricket that he played for England. He became a Christian in 1878 (his father had been converted under

D. L. Moody the previous year), and soon revealed the dedication that was to characterize his whole life. He was one of the "Cambridge Seven" who sailed for China in 1885 and served there for ten years with the China Inland Mission. While there he gave away all his considerable inheritance to Christian causes, preferring to trust God completely. Ill health brought him home and, following several years working among students in America, he served as pastor of the Union Church at Ootacamund, India (1900–1906). Despite continued ill health he founded the Heart of Africa Mission (later to be the Worldwide Evangelization Crusade), working in Congo, Central Africa, until his death. He gave himself unreservedly to spreading the gospel, reducing local languages to writing, and translating the Scriptures. His motto remains that of WEC: "If Christ be God and died for me, then no sacrifice can be too great for me to make for him."

Biographies by son-in-law Norman Grubb (1933) and daughter Edith Buxton (1968).

JAMES TAYLOR

Suenens, Leon Joseph (1904–)

Roman Catholic cardinal. Born in Brussels, Belgium, he graduated with two doctorates from the Gregorian University in Rome, and was ordained in 1927. He was professor of philosophy at the Malines diocesan seminary in Belgium (1930–1940), vice rector of the Catholic University of Louvain during the difficult war years (1940–1945), auxiliary bishop to Cardinal van Roey (1945–1961), and archbishop of Malines (1961–1979). Cardinal from 1962, Suenens had a key role as one of Vatican II's four moderators, highly regarded by popes John XXIII and Paul VI. A strong advocate of personal renewal and reconciliation, his contribution to progress in religion was recognized by the award in 1976 of the Templeton Prize. In accepting it from Prince Philip in London's Guildhall, he startled a distinguished assembly by twice bursting into songs "from the charismatic movement's repertoire." Of his many publications, those available in English include *The Right View of Moral Rearmament* (1953), *The Nun in the World* (1962), *The Future of the Christian Church* (1971), *A New Pentecost* (1975), *Renewal of the Powers of Darkness* (1982), and *Memories and Hopes* (1992).

Biography by Elizabeth Hamilton (1974).

J. D. DOUGLAS

Sundar Singh (Sadhu) (1889–ca. 1929)

Indian missionary. Born in Patiala State, India, son of a prosperous Sikh landowner, he was converted in 1904 and baptized as an Anglican at Simla the following year. Finding Western ways alien, he became a "sadhu" or solitary holy man, teaching the gospel after the Indian manner, with a special concern to reach Hindus for Christ. He traveled widely in north India and Afghanistan, and was often the victim of persecution and cruelty because of his Christian testimony. In 1908 he made his first journey into Tibet, a "forbidden" land for which he became particularly burdened. His fame spread, and in 1920 and 1922 he visited Europe, America, and Australia. In 1929, despite ill health, he embarked on a further missionary journey to Tibet and disappeared. He wrote *The Search after Reality* (1925) and *With and Without Christ* (1929).

Biographies by Mrs. Arthur Parker (1920) and B. H. Street and A. J. Appasamy (1921).

JAMES TAYLOR

Sunday, William Ashley ("Billy") (1862–1935)

American evangelist. Born the son of a brickmason killed that year in the Union army, he spent four years in an orphanage. From farm life through high school to undertaker's assistant he passed into professional baseball, playing for the Chicago White Stockings (1883–1887), the Pittsburgh Pirates (1888–1890), and the Philadelphia Athletics (1890). He gave up baseball to become a full-time worker for the YMCA (1891–1893), out of which emerged his campaign of religious revivals for American cities that engaged him as an independent (1896–1935). He had begun revivalism as an assistant to J. W. Chapman. His own campaigns employed the help of spectacular song writer and choir leader Homer A. Rodeheaver, who developed group singing techniques.

Ordained in 1903 to the ministry by the Chicago presbytery, Sunday in his theology expressed the emerging "fundamentals" of that era, though he was more prominent as an opponent of alcohol. He began in local churches and tents, and reached a peak of fame in 1917 with the revival in New York City, thereafter to peter out and return to small towns. His wartime preaching was excessively patriotic, and he received contributions from the Ku Klux Klan. He received an honorary D.D. from Westminster College, Fulton, Missouri. Many of his sermons were published. He is said to have "preached to more people than any other man in the history of Christianity," and success was measured by the count of those "hitting the sawdust trail." He could be vulgar and irreverent, yet impressed new converts as "one of the most earnest, serious-minded and deeply spiritual men." He was named one of the twenty-five "most influential preachers of our time" in 1924 by *The Christian Century*.

Biographies by W. G. McLoughlin (1955) and L. W. Dorsett (1991).

CLYDE CURRY SMITH

Sunderaraj, Francis (1937–)

General secretary of the Evangelical Fellowship of India. After two years as associate pastor of Emmanuel Methodist Church, Madras, he went to

Malaysia in 1967 to serve the Methodist Church as pastor and district superintendent. During that ministry he baptized several Hindu converts, and was instrumental in getting a number of young people to enter the pastoral ministry. He began his ministry with EFI in 1976 in the department of Christian education. While serving as its secretary from 1978 to 1991 he consolidated and further developed a strong India-wide Christian education program. In 1984 he became also EFI's general secretary and editor of its magazine, *AIM*. He has taught at Union Biblical Seminary, India, and was for six years chairman of its board. He has organized several national conferences, and in 1991 coordinated the Pan Asia Christian Education Seminar. An elder of the Methodist Church in India, Sunderaraj remains at heart a Bible teacher and pastor.

JOHN A. GRATION

Sundkler, Bengt Gustaf Malcolm (1909–)

Swedish Lutheran missionary and missiologist. Born in rural Sweden, Sundkler was educated locally and then at the University of Uppsala, where he completed his doctoral dissertation in 1937, after graduate study at the University of Strasbourg. Following ordination and marriage he was located to the Zululand, South Africa, mission of the Church of Sweden. During World War II when German Lutheran missionaries in Tanganyika were interned, the Sundklers were relocated (1942–1945) to Bukoba, in western Tanganyika.

After the war Sundkler became a research secretary for the IMO, and for three years lived in Birmingham, England, where he wrote *Bantu Prophets in South Africa* (1948), based on research from his time in Zululand. In that year he returned to Uppsala as professor in ecclesiastical and missionary history, while continuing research and writing.

In 1961 Sundkler was consecrated first bishop of the newly formed Evangelical Lutheran Church of North-Western Tanganyika, the area where he had been sent during the war. He remained in that position until the end of 1964, on leave of absence from his university chair. He was able to facilitate overseas study for several of his diocesan clergy, one of whom, Josiah Kibira, succeeded him as bishop. He then returned to his university post, retiring in 1974. He continues to live in Uppsala, and has worked for a number of years on an important project: a one-volume history of the Christian movement in Africa.

Sundkler has been not only a scholar of Africa and of the history of mission worldwide, but an interpreter and an enabler, both to other scholars and to black and white Christians. In particular, his books and articles on independent churches in southern Africa continue to inform and challenge all who study in this field.

He was active as a teacher and promoter of theses, many published in *Studia Missionalia Upsaliensia*, was editor of *Svensk Missionstidskrift* from

1949 to 1974, and wrote the biography of Nathan Söderblom (1968). Other works in English include *Bantu Prophets in South Africa* (1948), *The Christian Ministry in Africa* (1960), *Bara Bukoba: Church and Community in Tanzania* (1980), and *The Church of South India: the Movement towards Union (1900–1947)* (1954). He has been honored by two festschrifts: Carl F. Halleucreutz, ed., *The Church Crossing Frontiers: Essays on the Nature of Mission in Honour of Bengt Sundkler* (1969), *"Daring to Know": Studies in Bengt Sundkler's Contribution as Africanist and Missionary Scholar* (1974), containing full biographies.

JOCELYN MURRAY

Sung, John (1901–1944)

Chinese church leader. Born near Hinghwa, Fukien, into a Methodist minister's family, even as a youth he showed keen interest in the ministry, assisting his father in preaching and literature work. After earning a Ph.D. degree in chemistry at Ohio Wesleyan University, he continued to study at Union Theological Seminary, New York, where he ran into serious conflict with the school's modernistic theology. He returned to China in 1927, but instead of pursuing a career in science, he shocked everyone by joining the ministry as a member of the Bethel Evangelistic Band, engaging mainly in preaching as a revivalist and evangelist. He left the band in 1934 and became a freelance itinerant preacher. His preaching had a tremendous impact on the Chinese church at home and abroad. Thousands of people were converted, and many nominal Christians were revived. Sung's preaching also overlapped the Five-Year Forward Movement (1930–1935) organized by the National Council of Churches, and so had aroused a major wave of revival in China, building up the faith of many who persisted through the Sino-Japanese war (1937–1945). Sung also successfully channeled the fervor of many revived Christians into further evangelism by organizing them into small evangelistic bands, many of which lasted for years after his death. Sung set a style of preaching for the following generation of Chinese preachers where the main emphasis was always revivalistic. Many of his sermons were published, as was his autobiography written in 1933.

CHRISTOPHER LEE

Swain, Clara A. (1834–1910)

Pioneer woman missionary physician. Generally regarded as the first fully accredited woman physician sent by a mission agency to the non-Christian world, she was born in Elmira, New York. Acknowledging a desire and aptitude for caring for life, she left a teaching profession in the region of her childhood and began medical training in an era when it was difficult for women to practice medicine. She graduated from the Women's Medical

College of Pennsylvania in 1869. Having dedicated her life to a career of Christian service rather than one of personal reward or distinction, Swain sailed for India in early 1870 under the auspices of the Women's Foreign Missionary Service of the Methodist Episcopal Church. Without any precedent for such work, she inaugurated medical instruction for women and for some fourteen years carried on a large practice among women and children in and around the city of Bareilly in northern India. She guided the founding and completion of a dispensary building (1873) and the first women's hospital in India (1874) on land donated by the Nawab of Rampore in appreciation for her tireless medical care among the women of his region.

In 1885, at age fifty, Clara made a journey destined to change her life. Convinced of her calling to an area where no Christian worker had ever lived, she accepted a royal invitation to become medical adviser to the women of the palace of the Rajah of Khetri in Rajputana. During her eleven years in the area she also operated a dispensary for women and children and was instrumental in opening a school for girls. Her last years were spent in her New York home. Her work was highlighted in *A Glimpse of India* (1909).

FLORENCE SCOTT

Sweet, William Warren (1881–1959)

American church historian. Son of an ordained Methodist college president, he was born in Baldwin, Kansas, and educated at Ohio Wesleyan University, Drew Theological Seminary, and Crozer Theological Seminary, New York. Ordained to the ministry of the Methodist Episcopal Church in 1906, Sweet served congregations in Willow Grove (1906–1908) and Langhorne (1908–1911), Pennsylvania, while continuing academic interests, taking degrees at the University of Pennsylvania in Old Testament and Semitic studies (1909), and in American and English history (Ph.D., 1912). His doctoral dissertation, *The Methodist Episcopal Church and the Civil War*, set the tone and initiated the prolific publication that was to make him "the dean of the historians of Christianity in America." Before Sweet such history was denominational at best; after Sweet it became "the story of religion in America."

He taught at Ohio Wesleyan (1911–1913) and DePauw University (1913–1927), during which time he published specific histories of early Methodism in the Ohio Valley and a survey history of Latin America. In 1927 he joined the Divinity School of the University of Chicago, occupying the first chair of American Church History until his retirement in 1946.

He established the categories for that discipline. His fundamental concern was to so give a reputation to church history that its secular counterpart could no longer ignore its role. He influenced both the writing of general American history by reopening its attention to those oft-neglected "civilizing and cultural forces" of religion, and that of denominational histories by broadening individual examples to see their place within the total development of America and its peculiar form of Christianity.

The four-volume compilation of source materials, *Religion in the American Frontier,* serves as his most fitting memorial. *The Story of Religion in America* (2nd rev. ed., 1950) remains his finest work. The archives at DePauw retain some correspondence and minor manuscripts.

J. L. Ash wrote "an intellectual biography" of Sweet (1982).

CLYDE CURRY SMITH

Swete, Henry Barclay (1835–1917)

English New Testament and patristics scholar. Born in Bristol, son of a Church of England priest, he was educated at London and Cambridge universities. After ordination he served as curate to his father at Blagdon, Somerset (1858–1865). The following years saw him engaged in parish work in Essex or lecturing at nearby Cambridge until appointment as professor of pastoral theology at King's College, London (1882–1890). Thereafter he succeeded the famous B. F. Westcott as regius professor of divinity at Cambridge (1890–1915), during which time he founded the *Journal of New Testament Studies* (1899) and was made a royal chaplain (1911). He was no narrow specialist; his scholarship ranged over a wide area of studies, influencing others to do the same. His works included *The Old Testament in Greek* (3 vols., 1887–1891), commentaries on Mark (1898) and Revelation (1906), studies on the doctrine of the Holy Spirit (1909, 1912), *The Forgiveness of Sins* (1916), and *The Parables of the Kingdom* (1920).

J. D. DOUGLAS

Swindoll, Charles R. (1934–)

Pastor and author. Born in El Campo, Texas, he served a tour of duty in the U.S. Marine Corps, after which he attended Dallas Theological Seminary. Ordained in the Evangelical Free Church in 1963, he served initially with J. Dwight Pentecost in Dallas (1963–1965), after which pastorates followed in Massachusetts and Texas. He was senior pastor at the First Evangelical Free Church of Fullerton, California (1971–1994), before becoming president of Dallas Theological Seminary. Swindoll is known for an expository style of preaching with an emphasis on the practical application of the Bible to everyday living. He has written numerous pamphlets, articles, and books, including *Improving Your Serve* (1984) and *Dropping Your Guard* (1985). He has an international ministry through a cassette tape distribution, and a thirty-year minute daily radio broadcast.

NANCY CALVERT

T

Takakura, Tokutaro (1885–1934)

Japanese Christian leader. After the death of Uemura Masahisa in 1925, he became the single most prominent Japanese Reformed spokesman until the early 1930s. While a law student at Tokyo Imperial University, Takakura was converted to Christianity under Uemura's ministry in 1906. He then left law school to enter the Tokyo Theological Seminary, eventually writing his final paper on Schleiermacher. He pastored in Kyoto and Sapporo, then served on the Tokyo Seminary faculty before studying in Britain (1921–1924). While spending a year each in Edinburgh, Oxford, and Cambridge, he became more familiar with Scottish theology, John Oman, and others. His deepest theological longings, however, found a home in the writings of P. T. Forsyth. On returning to Japan, Takakura served as a pastor and seminary president from 1925 until his death. In opposition to "liberal Christianity" and "subjectivism," he consistently stressed the "objective," "evangelical" "Gospel" of God's "Grace," in ways that echoed both the "crisis" theologians in Germany, and Forsyth in Britain. This theme is evident in Takakura's writings (all of which are in Japanese).

J. NELSON JENNINGS

Tamez, Elsa (1950–)

Latin American liberationist, biblical scholar, and feminist theologian. Born in Ciudad Victoria, Mexico, she studied in Costa Rica where she received a master's degree in theology from the Latin American Biblical Seminary (SBL) in 1979 and a master's in literature and linguistics from the National University (1985). She completed a Ph.D. in Lausanne, Switzerland (1990). Presbyterian by background, she is active in the Methodist Church in Costa Rica, where she is professor of biblical studies at the SBL and is on the staff of the department of ecumenical research. Much of her biblical work has concentrated on word studies on the theme of oppression, and her doctoral dissertation offers a new understanding of justification by faith in Romans as the doing of justice on behalf of the oppressed. Tamez is a leading figure among Third World feminists. She has also recently spoken out for the rights of the indigenous peoples of Latin America, and argued for an appreciation of their traditional cultures and religions. Works in English written or edited by her include *Bible of the Oppressed* (1982), *Against Machismo* (1987), *Through Her Eyes: Women's*

Theology from Latin America (1989), and *The Scandalous Message of James* (1990).

DANIEL R. CARROLL

Tanner, Benjamin Tucker (1835–1923)

Bishop of the African Methodist Episcopal Church (AME). Born on Christmas Day as a free African American in Pittsburgh, he attended Avery Institute (1852–1857) and Western Seminary (1857–1860), a Presbyterian agency in Pennsylvania. He was ordained in 1858 as an AME pastor and served several congregations in the Washington, D.C. area. He was editor of *The Christian Recorder* (1868–1884). Under his leadership, America's oldest black weekly gained a reputation for excellence. In 1884 he founded the *AME Church Review*, America's oldest black magazine. This quarterly publication was a leading journal among African Americans. In editorials it advocated economic support of black-owned businesses.

In 1888 Tanner was elected eighteenth bishop of the AME, a position he held until retirement in 1908. As bishop he worked toward the organic union of the three major black Methodist churches. In 1908 he attended the first Tri-Council of Colored Methodist Bishops. Tanner's most popular work was *An Apology for African Methodism* (1867). Other writings include *The Negro's Origin, or Is He Cursed of God?* (1869), *An Outline of Our History and Government for African Methodist Churchmen* (1884), and *Theological Lectures* (1894).

SAM HAMSTRA, JR.

Taylor, (James) Hudson (1832–1905)

Founder of the China Inland Mission (CIM; now the Overseas Missionary Fellowship). Born in Yorkshire, England, he was the answer to his father's prayer for a son who could be a missionary to China. His conversion at age seventeen came after the fervent prayer of his mother. Taylor later reflected, "It would be strange indeed if I were not a believer in the power of prayer." From this confidence came such famous slogans as "Move men, by God, through prayer alone" and "God's work done in God's way will never lack [God's] supply." Taylor showed a relentless determination to evangelize the unreached, whatever the cost and risk.

In 1854 he arrived in China under the auspices of the China Evangelization Society. His frustrations with the CES led to his resignation and a time of independent ministry. After seven years he returned to England due to physical and emotional exhaustion. Distressed by the thought of "a million a month dying without God" he began the CIM in 1865. Its goal was to preach the gospel in the vast inland provinces of China, which had never been evangelized by Protestants. He adopted Chinese dress and customs, and whenever possible, paired foreign missionaries with national Christians. Concluding that the job would never be done if he waited for university-educated and ordained men to volunteer, he recruited primarily from the working class. Since the Chinese would be scandalized if Western men tried to evangelize Chinese women, the CIM accepted women as missionaries, even for work in remote and dangerous areas. Taylor himself lost two wives and four children to famine and disease, and saw fifty-six adults and twenty-three children from the CIM slain in the 1900 Boxer Rebellion.

Taylor was reluctant to draw either personnel or finances from existing works, and avoided any direct solicitation, either publicly or privately; rather, he depended on God alone. For "the speediest possible evangelization of China's millions" he adopted the practice of itinerant ministry, largely leaving it to other organizations to plant and nurture churches. Each of these principles was highly controversial at the time; all but the last two are now axiomatic in missions, and Taylor has been described as "the father of the modern faith-missions movement."

Amazingly he found time to write works including *China: Its Spiritual Need and Claims* (1865), *After Thirty Years* (1895), *A Riband of Blue* (1898), and *Separation and Service* (1898).

Recent biographies by A. J. Broomhall (7 vols., 1981–1989), Daniel Bacon (1984), Roger Steer (1990), and Dr. and Mrs. Howard Taylor (rev. 1990).

CHARLES LOWE

Taylor, Kenneth Nathaniel (1913–)

Bible translator and publisher. Born in Portland, Oregon, he graduated from Wheaton College, Illinois, with a B.S. degree in zoology (1938). After service on the InterVarsity Christian Fellowship staff in Canada, he attended Dallas Theological Seminary (1940–1943) and Northern Baptist Theological Seminary in Chicago (Th.M., 1944), working also as editor of *HIS* magazine. He continued to edit the magazine after his ordination to the pastorate of Central Bible Church in Portland (1944). In 1946 he joined the staff of Good News Publishers, Chicago. From 1947 to 1963 Taylor was director of the Moody Bible Institute's Literature Mission, and during part of this period he was also director of Moody Press. He has served on many other boards, such as InterVarsity Christian Fellowship and Fuller Theological Seminary. Desire to communicate the faith to his own and to other children led to the writing of *The Bible in Pictures for Little Eyes* (1956), to numerous other books, and especially to his paraphrases of the Bible in simple language. Unable to find a publisher for his paraphrases, Taylor and his wife, Margaret, formed a new company, Tyndale House Publishers, for this purpose. The first of the Bible paraphrases to be published was *Living Letters* (1962), which was warmly received and highly endorsed. Other parts of the Bible were put into paraphrase and published until 1971, when the combined portions appeared as *The Living Bible*. Millions of copies of this popular translation have been sold. The proceeds from these sales have gone into Tyndale House Foundation and Living Bibles International, which were founded to support the production of modern language versions of the Bible around the world. Through his efforts many other enterprises have come into existence, such as the Christian Booksellers Association (1950), Evangelical Literature Overseas (1953), and Short Terms Abroad (1965). His achievements have brought him honorary degrees and many other honors and awards. His autobiography is entitled *My Life: A Guided Tour* (1991).

ALBERT H. FREUNDT, JR.

Taylor, Vincent (1887–1968)

New Testament scholar and theologian. Born in Lancashire, he was trained for the ministry at Richmond (Methodist) College and graduated from London University (1911; Ph.D., 1922). The same institution awarded him its D.D. degree for *The Historical Evidences for the Virgin Birth* (1926). Taylor was a circuit minister (1909–1930) before teaching New Testament studies at Headingley College, Leeds, where he became also principal (1936) and served until retirement (1953). He was a staunch defender of the Proto-Luke theory and of Marcan priority, as evidenced in *The First Draft of Luke's Gospel* (1927) and *The Gospels: A Short Introduction* (1930). Both fascinated and alarmed by the radical form criticism of Bultmann, he presented his own view of it in *The Formulation of the Gospel Tradition* (1933). He became disenchanted with the more radical views of form critics, and defended the basic facts of the Gospel story in *The Life and Ministry of Jesus* (1954). His monumental *Gospel According to St. Mark* (1952) attempted to use form criticism in a positive way to understand the early Christian tradition. His books on the person and work of Christ and his attitude toward miracles were in the liberal tradition. Nonetheless, Taylor clearly acknowledged the deity of Christ, the doctrine of the Trinity, and the objective nature of Christ's redemptive work for us.

WALTER A. ELWELL

Teilhard De Chardin, Pierre (1881–1955)

Jesuit priest and paleontologist. Born in Sarcenat, France, he was educated in France and England, was ordained in 1911, was decorated twice for bravery as a stretcher-bearer in World War I, and in 1920 became professor of geology at the Institut Catholic, Paris. Teilhard believed the church should open its vision to a changed and changing world, but this obsession with the here and now saw him cold-shouldered by Rome, debarred from academic advancement, discouraged from lecturing, and savagely criticized by those who simply "did not understand." He argued for evolution, and his Jesuit superiors demanded that he sign a statement of belief in the literal truth of Genesis. He signed, but as a gesture of fidelity rather than as a symbol of intellectual assent. His devotional life was untouched by controversy, the unsought love of women, and a long exile in China. One bitterly cold winter in Peking during World War II, other exiles asked him to come and speak to them of happiness. He did. His story leaves one with the impression of a gifted scientist almost too honest for the priesthood, and of a church stubbornly reactionary while "the ground wheels under our feet."

Biography by Mary and Ellen Lukas (1977).

J. D. Douglas

Temple, William (1881–1944)

Archbishop of Canterbury. Born in Exeter, he gained a "Double First" at Oxford and was awarded a fellowship teaching philosophy. In 1906 he was refused ordination by the bishop of Oxford, who thought Temple was insufficiently certain concerning the doctrines of the virgin birth and the resurrection. After further discussion, he was ordained by Archbishop Davidson in 1908. In 1910 he became headmaster of Repton School, in 1914 rector of St. James, Piccadilly, which post he resigned in order to become the leader of the Life and Liberty movement. This movement resulted in the widening of government within the Church of England.

In 1920 he was appointed bishop of Manchester, in 1929 archbishop of York, and in 1942 archbishop of Canterbury. Temple combined a first-rate philosophical mind with theological acuteness and great social awareness. He was also in the forefront of ecumenical affairs and presided at the meeting that inaugurated the British Council of Churches in 1942. His concern to express the Christian faith was done both in addresses, particularly in university missions, and in his books. Among these were *Mens Creatrix* (1917), *Nature, Man and God* (1934), and *Christianity and Social Order* (1942). Yet his *Readings in St. John's Gospel* (1939) shows that his scholarship was matched by his devotion. It was said of him that he was too much of a philosopher for theologians and too much of a theologian for philosophers. His sudden death was widely felt as a serious loss to the worldwide church.

Biography by F. A. Iremonger (1948).

Peter S. Dawes

Templeton, John Marks (1912–)

American-born investment specialist and philanthropist. Born in Winchester, Tennessee, he displayed entrepreneurial skills as a schoolboy (his mother said he was "born old"). Law graduate *summa cum laude* from Yale and Rhodes scholar at Oxford, he worked briefly with a stock brokerage firm in New York City before accepting in 1937 an administrative post with the National Geophysical Company in Dallas, gaining experience in accounting and tax law. In 1940 he went into business on his own, and prospered through hard work, flair, and well-researched investment strategy. A Presbyterian who sees himself within mainstream Christianity, Templeton seeks to "work in harmony with God's purposes." Investor and stockholder meetings are opened with prayer. Influenced by R. W. Emerson's Transcendentalism and Charles Fillmore's Unity School, Templeton calls himself a panentheist ("All in God"). While denying syncretism, he sees good in all religions, but holds that in a world of spiritual free enterprise Christianity has the most to share. Therein is his rationale for supporting missionaries and evangelists. Templeton, who moved to the Bahamas in the 1960s and later became a British citizen (and holder of a knighthood from Queen Elizabeth), set up in 1972 the annual Templeton Prize for those who through original and pioneering ways have advanced understanding of the knowledge and love of God. Charles W. Colson received the award, worth some $940,000, in 1993. Templeton set out his thinking in *The Humble Approach* (1981).

Biography by William Proctor (1983).

J. D. DOUGLAS

Ten Boom, Corrie (Cornelia) (1892–1983)

Dutch evangelist and author. She was born into a Christian home of Dutch-Calvinist heritage that emphasized family love, reliance upon Scripture and prayer, hard work, and an appreciation of music, art, and language. She took up the occupation of her father and mother, and became the first woman in Holland to qualify as a watchmaker. Using her well-developed abilities as an organizer and Christian worker, Corrie started teenage girls' clubs that multiplied into a worldwide organization.

When the Netherlands was invaded by German forces, the ten Boom family, already actively interested in the Jewish people, began assisting Jews in escaping from the Germans. Betrayed by two fellow Dutchmen, the ten Booms were arrested and imprisoned. Few members of the family survived. The last of Corrie's three imprisonments was in Ravensbruck, known as the concentration camp of no return. By extraordinary circumstances she was released on New Year's Day 1945.

Thereafter she carried out the mission envisioned with her sister Betsie before the latter's death at Ravensbruck. She established a rehabilitation home in Holland for victims of concentration camps, and a home for refugees on the location of a former concentration camp in Darmstadt, Germany. Using her own terrible experiences, she became an ambassador around the world with the message that in all situations Jesus is Victor. With the royalties of her best-seller, *The Hiding Place* (1971), she founded Christians Incorporated to support work of multiracial missionaries. Other works included *Amazing Love* (1959) and *Tramp for the Lord* (1974).

FLORENCE SCOTT

Tendero, Efraim Manguiat (1957–)

General secretary of the Philippine Council of Evangelical Churches (197 member bodies, 43 denominations, 9,000 local churches). Son of a tailor/lay pastor in Calapan, Oriental Mindoro, he was converted and discipled in high school, and turned from political ambitions to follow Christ. He graduated as "Most Outstanding Student" from Febias College of Bible, Metro Manila (1978), and later earned his M.Div. degree at Trinity Evangelical Divinity School, Deerfield, Illinois (1989). While in college he served four years with an evangelistic team in Kamuning, Quezon City, developing skills in evangelism, disciple-making, and church planting. Kamuning Bible Christian Fellowship was born, and Tendero joined the pastoral staff. At age twenty-five he became the youngest president of the Alliance of Bible Christian Churches. KBCF spawned sixteen new churches in fifteen years, and produced ninety-eight members who have gone "full-time" for Christ. In 1993 Tendero was also chairman of the Philippine President's Consultative Committee on national issues. This includes representatives from all major religions and provides conservative Christians with opportunities to positively impact the church and nation for Christ.

CHARLES A. HUFSTETLER

Teng, Philip (1922–)

Chinese pastor, theological educator, and international churchman. Born in Shantung (Shandong) province, Teng attended New College, University of Edinburgh (1947–1950). From 1950 to 1982 he served in numerous capacities in Hong Kong. He pastored the North Point Alliance Church, lectured and served as president of Alliance Bible Seminary, and was president of the China Graduate School of Theology. He was chairman of the board of the Chinese Coordination Centre of World Evangelism and many other boards, and has preached on all six continents. He was the Bible expositor for URBANA '73, InterVarsity Christian Fellowship's student missionary convention in the United States. After his retirement in Hong Kong, he headed the Chinese studies program at Alliance Theological Seminary, Nyack, New York. He is author of numerous books and articles, including *Guideposts* (Chinese, 1971) and *Twelve Crises in the Apostolic Church* (Chinese, 1980). He edited the Chinese version of *Decision* magazine (1973–1977). He was translator of E. M. Bounds' *Power Through Prayer,* and of numerous hymns for the revised edition of *Hymns of Universal Praise.*

SAMUEL LING

Tenney, Merrill Chapin (1904–1985)

New Testament scholar. Born in Boston, Massachusetts, where his father was a theological book dealer, he studied at Nyack Missionary Training Institute, Gordon Theological Seminary, and Boston University, adding in 1944 a Ph.D. from Harvard University. An ordained Baptist minister, Tenney pastored various churches and taught at Gordon during this time. In

1943 he was appointed professor of Bible at Wheaton College Graduate School, where he became dean in 1947, a position he held until his retirement in 1971. Tenney is best remembered for his rigorous scholarship and devotion to Christ in the classroom and in the many books he wrote. In *The Genius of the Gospels* (1956) he led the way in breaking with the two-document hypothesis, a generation before the current disaffection. His other writings include *John: The Gospel of Belief* (1948), *Galatians: The Charter of Christian Liberty* (1951), *The Reality of the Resurrection* (1963), and *The New Testament: An Historical and Analytical Survey* (1955), a book that is available in many languages and is still in use today.

WALTER A. ELWELL

Teresa, Mother (Agnes Gonxha Bojaxhiu) (1910–)

Roman Catholic nun. Born to Albanian parents in Skopje, Yugoslavia, she joined the Congregation of the Loreto Nuns in Bengal at age seventeen, and was sent to Ireland to learn English before going to India. After two years in Darjeeling, she moved to Calcutta, where she taught history and geography for seventeen years. Her room overlooked the slums of Motijeel and in 1946, she received God's call to live there among the poor. She founded a new order, the Missionaries of Charity, which received papal recognition in 1950. The order began its first children's home in 1955 and its first leprosarium in 1957. Since then, the ministry has expanded to include schools, food distribution centers, and AIDS hospices worldwide. The Missionaries of Charity take a unique vow to serve the poorest of the poor. They do all "in the name of Jesus," seeing Jesus in every person and meeting needs as they would meet the needs of Jesus. For her international work of compassion, Mother Teresa received the first John XIII peace prize from Paul VI in 1971, the first Templeton Prize in 1973, and the Nobel Peace Prize in 1979.

Biography by J. L. Gonzalez-Balado and J. N. Playfoot.

JULIE SODERBERG

Thielicke, Helmut (1908–1986)

Lutheran theologian and preacher. Born in Wuppertal-Barmen, Germany, son of the local rector, he studied at Griefswald, Marburg (Ph.D., 1932), and Erlangen (Th.D., 1934), and taught theology at Heidelberg (1936–1940) until removed by the Nazi authorities. He then preached in a small church in Ravensburg, but was forbidden by the Gestapo from traveling or publishing. He was head of the theological office of the Church of Württenberg and was allowed to preach once a week in Stuttgart Cathedral. After World War II Thielicke was professor of systematic theology at Tübingen (1945–1954), and thereafter dean of the faculty of theology at Hamburg. In 1960 he became rector of Hamburg and preacher at the city's St.

Michael's Church. Thielicke was a theologian of the Word, siding with Althaus and Barth on the question of natural revelation. He distrusted human reason or any attempt to reach God from the bottom up. He was suspicious of any doctrinaire view of Scripture, holding that Christ is the Word of God; and he repudiated Bultmann's radical biblical criticism. Thielicke was a man for his times, holding "a basic orthodoxy in lively and thoughtful interaction with contemporary theological discussion." Author of numerous books, most of them in German, Thielicke is best known for his two-volume *Theological Ethics* (1968, 1969), *The Evangelical Faith* (3 vols., 1947–1955), and his many books of sermons, such as *Between Heaven and Earth* (1965), *The Waiting Father* (1959), and *Christ and the Meaning of Life* (1962).

WALTER A. ELWELL

Thiessen, Henry Clarence (1883–1947)

Evangelical educator and theologian. He was born in Henderson, Nebraska, and grew up in a German-speaking, conservative, Mennonite home. He graduated from the Fort Wayne Bible School in 1909, pastored a church in Pandora, Ohio (1909–1916), and was instructor in Bible (1916–1919) and president (1919–1923) at FWBS. He then studied at Northern Baptist Theological Seminary, Northwestern University, and Southern Baptist Theological Seminary (Ph.D., 1929). Later he was appointed to a chair of New Testament at Evangelical Theological College, Dallas (now Dallas Theological Seminary) (1931–1935), and was subeditor of *Bibliotheca Sacra*. Thereafter he was at Wheaton College (1938–1947) where he became director in 1938 (then dean) of what is now Wheaton College Graduate School. Thiessen had no particular interest in the fine points of dispensationalism but was firm on its basics: that Israel and the church are separate, and that the church is not appointed to wrath but to obtain salvation. The strength of Thiessen's position lay in its profoundly biblical orientation, unflinching orthodoxy, and practical value. Thiessen believed that theology is meant to change our lives because it speaks of God, salvation, and the truth. Thiessen wrote several books, but is best remembered for *Introduction to the New Testament* (1943) and *Introductory Lectures in Systematic Theology* (1949).

WALTER A. ELWELL

Thoburn, James Mills (1836–1922)

American Methodist Episcopal missionary bishop. Born in St. Clairsville, Ohio, he attended Allegheny College, Pennsylvania, graduating in 1857. He was the brother of Isabella Thoburn, noted missionary and educator in India. Thoburn was ordained in the Methodist Church in 1858 and left for India as a missionary in 1859. He learned the language with remarkable speed, and in six months was preaching his first sermons. Thoburn's missionary programs focused primarily on the social, medical, and educational needs of the people. He was a man of unusual determination and faith, for in the entire first year of his ministry he saw only one convert, and near the end of his second year of service his infant church had but six standing members and seven probationers. Yet upon his transfer to Calcutta in 1874 Thoburn found himself preaching in a great church costing eighty thousand rupees, seating some 1,600 worshipers who thronged to hear his sermons. He founded Methodism in Burma in 1879, in Malaysia in 1885, and in the Philippines in 1899, just one year after it was included in his bishopric. In 1888 Thoburn was appointed bishop of India and Malaysia, becoming the first resident Methodist bishop in Asia. As bishop he preached extensively throughout India and was largely responsible for developing an organizational structure for Methodism for the entire country of India. He authored numerous books, including an autobiography entitled *My Missionary Apprenticeship* (1884), *The Life of Isabella Thoburn* (1903), *The Christian Conquest of India* (1906), and *Light in the East, India and Malaysia* (1900).

DAVID P. CAMERA

Thomas, Madathilparampil Mammen (1916–)

Indian ecumenical leader and lay theologian. Born in Kerala State, he committed his life to Christ in 1931, and served his own Mar Thoma Syrian Church of Malabar as an active lay leader throughout his life. He directed the Christian Institute for the Study of Religion and Society in Bangalore (1962–1975), was an influential thinker in the ecumenical movement, and moderator of the World Council of Churches central committee (1968–1975). He accepted visiting lectureships at Union Theological Seminary, Princeton, and Perkins School of Theology. In 1990 he became governor of Nagaland in India.

Thomas has written numerous articles and papers. His books include *The Christian Response to the Asian Revolution* (1966), *The Acknowledged Christ of the Indian Renaissance* (1970), *Salvation and Humanism* (1971), and *My Ecumenical Journey* (1990). In his writings he sets forth a theology of continuous dynamic change that posits as a foundation to the development of theological reflection an understanding of our world and the significance of current events, particularly social upheavals. Such events cannot be understood on the basis of a closed theological system, but demand appropriating the multitude of analytical approaches found in our modern pluralist world (including Marxist ideology, Hindu spirituality, process theology, and biblical revelation). Cognitive understanding cannot be separated from action. The goal of contextualized theology (and indeed the mission of the church) is the transformation of society through the church's involvement in political action.

A. SCOTT MOREAU

Thomson, David Patrick (1896–1974)

Church of Scotland evangelist. Brought up in Dundee, he was an apprentice in a jute company before seeing active service in World War I. This experience proved useful later when addressing gatherings of elders or replying to hecklers at open-air meetings. Thomson graduated from Edinburgh and after divinity training was ordained in 1928. He ministered in Dunfermline and Cambuslang, joined the Kirk's home board in 1947, and in 1958 founded St. Ninian's lay training center, Crieff. He gladly cooperated with those of other churches who loved Jesus Christ and meant business in the task of evangelizing Scotland. He had a fertile mind and prodigious energy, and was a great opportunist. During the 1935 Open Championship at Muirfield he organized a special golfers' church service at Gullane. His subject was "The Links of Life," and the subheads were well advertised in advance: "The Course We Play On," "The Clubs We Carry," "The Hazards We Encounter," and "The Card We Return." Many renowned players took the bait and packed the church that day. A man known throughout Scotland by his initials, "D. P." was the first to persuade his friend Eric Liddell to appear on an evangelistic platform. D. P. set the feet of many on the Christian path and encouraged divinity students in public speaking and door-to-door witnessing. He wrote numerous pamphlets on the warriors of the faith who had so enriched Scotland's spiritual heritage. When D. P retired in 1966 the Kirk's general assembly hailed him as "one of the outstanding leaders of the Church in this generation."

J. D. DOUGLAS

Thomson, James S. (1892–1972)

Scottish churchman. Born in Stirling, Scotland, he studied at the University of Glasgow, served with the Queen's Own Cameron Highlanders in France during World War I, and after theological training at Trinity College, Glasgow, was ordained in the Church of Scotland. As secretary of the Committee for Youth and Education he participated in the International Missionary Council, Jerusalem, 1928. In 1930 he became professor of theology, Pine Hill Divinity Hall, Halifax, and in 1937 president of the University of Saskatchewan. In 1949 he accepted the deanship of the Faculty of Divinity, McGill University. On his retirement from McGill he was elected moderator of the General Council of the United Church of Canada. His numerous other roles included presidency of the United Nations Society of Canada and of the Student Christian movement and chairmanship of the Board of World Mission, UCC, and the Canadian Committee on

Nuclear Radiation Hazards. Although a remarkable academic and gifted leader with a broad ecumenical vision, Thomson remained humble and deeply committed to the religious convictions of his Scottish ancestry. Among his published works were *The Hope of the Gospel* (1927), *The Unbinding of Prometheus* (1945), and *Religion and Theology in the Literary History of Canada* (1965).

EDWARD J. FURCHA

Thurman, Howard (1900–)

Minister, theologian, and educator. A native of Daytona Beach, Florida, he began his studies at Atlanta's Morehouse College in 1919. It was generally accepted that he was one of the most brilliant students that had been encountered at that institution. When, because of his race, his application to study at Newton Theological Seminary was rejected, he enrolled at Colgate Rochester Seminary. Following many years of teaching at Howard School of Religion, he accepted the post of dean of Marsh Chapel at Boston University. His messages from the pulpit drew many to Sunday morning worship and touched literally thousands of faculty, students, and others from outside the university. While at the university, he also taught in the School of Theology.

One of Thurman's most significant works is his interpretation of Negro spirituals. His understanding of Christian hope can be seen by his insights into "There Is a Balm in Gilead." He says that the African-American has taken the question mark of Jeremiah and turned it into an exclamation mark. At the end of his service to Boston University, Thurman retired to San Francisco and established the Howard Thurman Educational Trust Foundation, which contains his sermons, lectures, books, and other publications. In 1976 the BBC produced the film *The Life and Thoughts of Howard Thurman* in tribute to his contributions.

His published works include *Deep River* (1945), *Jesus and the Disinherited* (1945), and *The Search for Common Ground* (1971).

ROBERT C. SUGGS

Tienou, Tite (1949–)

African evangelical theologian. A citizen of Burkina Faso, he studied at Nyack, the Faculté Theologies Evangelique, and Fuller Theological Seminary. He was executive secretary of the Association of Evangelicals of Africa and Madagascar (1977–1987). He has been chair emeritus of the International Council of Accrediting Agencies for evangelical theological education since 1989, a member of the governing council (since 1977) and chair (1981–1993) of the Accrediting Council for Theological Education in Africa (ACTEA). He is the current administrator of the ACTEA Consortium of Theological Colleges (ACTC). Tienou founded the Institute Maranatha in

1976 and, while heading this institute, also pastored the central church of the Eglise de l'Alliance Chretienne. His *The Theological Task of the Church in Africa* (1991) is an invaluable contribution to African evangelical development, steering evangelicals back to positive theology and suggesting crucial entry points into this theological strategy.

JAMES KOMBO

Tikhon (Vasili A. Bellavin) (1865–1925)

Patriarch of Russia. A native of Toropetz, Russia, he studied at Pskov Theological Seminary and at the St. Petersburg Theological Academy. He was ordained to the priesthood of the Eastern Orthodox Church in 1891, and consecrated bishop of Ljublin in 1898. He became bishop of Alaska and Aleut Islands in 1899, and was elevated to archbishop in 1905. He was instrumental in having the Eastern Orthodox liturgy translated into English (1906) and set up a theological school in Minneapolis (1903) which became a seminary two years later. He established a monastery at South Canaan, Pennsylvania. After the Russian Revolution he became metropolitan of Moscow, and in the wake of reshaping the Orthodox Church in Russia he was appointed patriarch of Moscow and all Russia. Through very tense relations with the political authorities he maintained a stabilizing influence despite internal conflicts with a breakaway group, the "Living Church."

EDWARD J. FURCHA

Tilak, Narayan Vaman (1862–1919)

Indian Christian poet. Born in Karazgaon of Ratnagiri, he was a Brahmin convert, like Pandita Ramabai, and was baptized in 1895 on his own insistence, by a fellow countryman rather than a foreign missionary. He endured persecution for his new faith. Believing that India should follow Christ rather than the ways of Western Christianity, he left the American Marathi Mission in 1917 to become a *sannyasi* or itinerant holy man in "God's darbar," an organization he founded as "a brotherhood of the baptized and unbaptized disciples of Christ" the supreme guru. Tilak was a leader of the romantic revival in Marathi literature, introducing new meters, styles, and subjects. Many of the three to four hundred lyrics he wrote are still in use. His religious poetry includes songs and hymns (which make up nearly half the Marathi hymnbook); the *Christayan* (an unfinished life of Christ modeled on the *Ramyana*); and the *Abhanganjali* (a collection of devotional songs in the style of the Marathi poet-saint Tukaram, 1607–1649). Some of Tilak's poetry and hymns, translated into English by his biographer J. C. Winslow and the Scottish missionary scholar Nicol Macnicol, have reached a wider audience through their inclusion in the EACC Hymnal (1963).

Biographies by J. C. Winslow (1923) and P. S. Jacob (1979).

PHILIP HILLYER

Tillich, Paul (Johannes Oskar) (1886–1965)

Protestant theologian. Born in Prussia, he studied at various German universities, including Breslau, which awarded him a Ph.D. degree. An ordained Lutheran, he served in World War I as a military chaplain (1914–1918). Thereafter he became a religious socialist and taught in various German universities. Barred for his criticism of the Nazis, he moved to America, where he taught at Union Theological Seminary and at Columbia, Harvard, and Chicago universities.

In his *Systematic Theology* (3 vols., 1951, 1957, 1963) he insisted that theology, drawing on revelation, must answer to the concerns of contemporary culture. Contrary to Barth, he considered philosophy indispensable to theology: not only does philosophy pose questions that theology answers, but it also shapes the form of the reply. Tillich postulated God as "the Ground of all Being," known as life's ultimate concern. His philosophical theology reflected Platonic, mystical, idealist, and existentialist features. Myth or symbol, he averred, is the only way to grasp the ultimate Ground. He interpreted classic Christian doctrine symbolically, thereby aiming to show its supposedly true and deeper meaning.

His view that even secular activity requires a religious basis was rejected by others who disavow that all culture has a religious foundation. Evangelical scholars criticized Tillich for jeopardizing the objective truth and historical factuality of Christian teaching. Some critics commended, others deplored, his system's implicit atheism. Death-of-God proponents thanked him for anticipating their views.

His other works included *Interpretation of History* (1936), *The Courage To Be* (1952), *Theology of Culture* (1959), and *Morality and Beyond* (1963).

CARL F. H. HENRY

Tognini, Enéas (1914–)

Brazilian renewal movement leader. Of Italian-Brazilian heritage, his father an atheist, his mother a Roman Catholic, Tognini was converted into the Baptist faith at eighteen years of age. Graduating from the Seminário Teológico Batista do Sul (Rio de Janeiro) and after evangelistic and pastoral experience, he assumed leadership of the Colégio Batista in São Paulo. Along with pastoring the College church, he founded the Faculdade (Seminary) Teológica Batista de São Paulo (1957). Tognini testifies of a transforming surrender to God in 1958, soon accompanied by speaking in tongues. His vision and fervor led him to eighteen years of itinerant ministry in evangelistic and revival meetings with reports of more than one hundred thousand converts. More than any other person, Tognini was responsible for the charismatic or "spiritual renewal" movement in the mainline denominations of Brazil. Together with others expelled from the Brazilian Baptist Convention (1965), he helped found the charismatic

National Baptist Convention (1967) which today claims over two hundred thousand members, one thousand churches, and twenty-two Bible institutes and seminaries. Together with popular radio programs, Tognini has produced ten LP records, hundred of tracts, and at least thirty books.

J. Scott Horrell

Tolkien, John Ronald Reuel (1892–1973)

English writer. Born in Bloemfontein, South Africa, son of a bank manager, he graduated from Oxford, fought in World War I (1915–1918), and taught English at Leeds University before returning to Oxford as professor of Anglo-Saxon (1925–1945) and of English language and literature (1945–1959). Early influenced by Andrew Lang and George MacDonald, Tolkien was well into middle age and little known outside Oxford when he wrote *The Hobbit* (1937). He held that things deepest felt could be best expressed in tales and myths. *The Lord of the Rings* (3 vols., 1954–1955) reflected its author's restless perfectionism wherein his own invented language and stories (geography, chronology, nomenclature) were meticulously detailed. This hugely popular work was followed by other volumes, notably *The Silmarillion* (edited by his son Christopher, 1977).

An emotional man inclined to pessimism who liked colored waistcoats, plain unrefrigerated food, and did not care for things French, Tolkien never traveled much, reportedly because his imagination did not need the stimulation of unfamiliar landscapes and cultures. He was a Roman Catholic, deeply pained by the substitution of English for Latin in the Mass. His admiration for beautiful Church of England buildings was tempered by sadness that they had been "perverted from their rightful Catholicism." He regretted also the adherence to Anglicanism of his friend C. S. Lewis.

Biography by Humphrey Carpenter (1977).

J. D. Douglas

Tomlinson, Ambrose Jessup (1865–1943)

Early leader of the Church of God and founder of the Church of God of Prophecy. Born in Westfield, Indiana, and reared as a Quaker, he underwent a conversion experience in a Quaker meeting. He then became a traveling salesman for the American Bible Society. In 1903 Tomlinson and his family moved to Camp Creek, North Carolina, to join a Holiness congregation that Tomlinson had discovered during his travels. Soon he was serving as pastor to the Camp Creek church and to a Holiness church in Cleveland, Tennessee. In 1906 a small group of Holiness churches held its first general assembly, and Tomlinson was named moderator. A year later the group became known as the Church of God. In 1908 Tomlinson became the first member of his group to speak in tongues, and soon the denomination embraced Pentecostal beliefs and practices. Tomlinson was named general moderator in 1909 and general overseer in 1910. Four years later he was granted a lifetime appointment as general overseer. For the next eight years he held revival meetings and organized the denomination's ministries and publications. In 1923, following a year of dissension, Tomlinson and two thousand loyal followers (roughly 10 percent of the membership) started a new denomination. Tomlinson held complete authority within the new body. By the time of his death the denomination had more than thirty thousand members. In 1952 the group adopted the name Church of God of Prophecy.

Biographies by D. D. Preston (1962) and Lillie Duggar (1964).

ROBERT L. MORRISON

Torrance, Thomas Forsyth (1913–)

Scottish theologian. Born to missionary parents in China, he was educated at Edinburgh, Basel, and Oxford. He was professor of theology at Auburn Seminary, New York (1938–1939), and of church history (1950–1952) and Christian dogmatics (1952–1979) at New College, Edinburgh. The breadth of his scholarly interaction is due to his keen intellect and sustained preoccupation with Barth's theology. There Torrance found the central vision that animates his work: the incarnate Word of God as the objective scientific basis of dogmatics. This key insight informs his biblical scholarship, energizes his historical studies (particularly in Athanasius, Calvin, and Scottish theology), grounds his ecumenical dialogue (notably with the Orthodox), and demarcates his polemics (against Roman Catholicism, Westminster Calvinism, liberalism, and biblical criticism). He was awarded the Templeton Prize in 1978. Best known for his work in science and theology, he applies in *Theological Science* (1969) his key insight to parallels between theological and scientific method. He posits a thoroughly scientific role for personal faith, classic dogmas, and the Bible, all with the persuasive imprimatur of post-Einsteinian science. His numerous other publications include *Royal Priesthood* (1955), *Space, Time and Resurrection* (1976), *The Trinitarian Faith* (1988), and *The Mediation of Christ* (1992). He was founding editor of *The Scottish Journal of Theology* (1948–1981), and coeditor of Barth's *Church Dogmatics* (1956–1975) and Calvin's *New Testament Commentaries* (1959–1972).

W. DUNCAN RANKIN

Torrey, Charles Cutler (1863–1956)

Liberal biblical scholar. Born in East Hardwick, Vermont, he was educated at Bowdoin College, Andover Seminary, and Strasbourg University (Ph.D., 1892). Torrey went on to become one of the dominant and controversial biblical scholars of the twentieth century. He taught Semitic languages at Andover Seminary (1892–1900) and Yale University (1900–1932) until his retirement. He was one of the founders of the American School of Oriental

Research in Jerusalem, as well as its first president, and in 1915 he became president of the Society of Biblical Literature. He is remembered for his aggressive style and radical views of Old Testament history, none of which is in vogue today. Ezra–Nehemiah he considered as wholly unhistorical, being fictional propaganda invented by the chronicler. The exile, return, and restoration of Israel were imaginary themes used as ammunition against the Samaritans. Jeremiah was a pious fiction created for a "sacred library of the prophets" in the third century B.C. Ezekiel was also third century B.C. and reflects Alexander the Great, not Babylon. Early in his career Torrey was convinced that all four Gospels were written in Aramaic (*Translations Made from the Original Aramaic Gospels* [1912]). He returned to this theme near his retirement with *The Four Gospels: a New Translation* (1933). In *Our Translated Gospels* (1936) he argues strenuously that our present Greek Gospels are translations from written Aramaic originals and, surprisingly, that all four were written before A.D. 50 and in Palestine, while eyewitnesses were still alive. He even goes so far as to say, "Some written accounts of his deeds and words must have circulated in his [Jesus'] lifetime."

WALTER A. ELWELL

Torrey, Reuben Archer, Sr. (1856–1928)

Evangelist, educator, pastor, and author. Born in Hoboken, New Jersey, to moderately wealthy parents, he entered Yale University at age fifteen, and there made his first public profession of Christian faith. In 1878 he graduated from Yale Divinity School, was ordained in the Congregational Church, and accepted his first pastorate in Garretsville, Ohio (1878–1882). After a year's study in Germany and a second pastorate in Minneapolis (1883–1886) he became superintendent of D. L. Moody's Chicago Evangelization Society (now Moody Bible Institute). Torrey remained with the school until 1908, helping shape the emphasis on Bible study and practical programs for training Christian workers. He also pastored the Chicago Avenue Church (later Moody Memorial Church) (1894–1906). In 1901 he began to hold evangelistic meetings outside the United States, often with Charles Alexander as his soloist and song leader. His meetings within the United States between 1906 and 1911 firmly established him as one of the country's leading evangelists. In 1908 he founded the Montrose Bible Conference in Pennsylvania. In 1912 he went to Los Angeles where he served as dean of the Bible Institute of Los Angeles (BIOLA) until 1924, during which period he was also pastor of the Church of the Open Door. A prolific writer, he wrote over forty books, including *How I Bring Men to Christ* (1893), *The Person and Work of the Holy Spirit* (1910), *The Power of Prayer and the Prayer of Power* (1924), and *Lectures on the First Epistle of John* (1929).

Biography by Roger Martin.

ROBERT SCHUSTER

Tournier, Paul (1898–1986)

Swiss physician and writer on the integration of psychology and Christianity. Born in Geneva, son of a pastor, he spent his whole professional life from 1928 (apart from service in the Swiss army in World War II) as a general practitioner in private practice in Geneva. Discovering religious faith through contact with the Oxford Group movement in 1932, he realized the need to treat his patients as whole human beings, as illness could have emotional and spiritual as well as physical origins. In *The Person Reborn* (1967) he declared that "technology and faith work together. Psychoanalysis explores the problems in order to bring them out into the daylight, grace dissolves them"—a view accepted only slowly by his colleagues. *A Doctor's Casebook in the Light of the Bible* (1954) and *The Meaning of Persons* (1957) were followed by other best-selling books, including *Learning to Grow Old* (1972). Many of his personal experiences shine through his works. His more occasional specific autobiographical reflections are collected in *A Listening Ear: Fifty Years as a Doctor of the Whole Person* (1986).

PHILIP HILLYER

Townsend, William Cameron (1896–1982)

Bible translator and missiologist. Born and reared in California, he attended Occidental College in Louisiana, where he joined the Student Volunteer movement. In 1917 he received an appointment to sell Bibles in Central America for the Bible House of Louisiana. Determined to enter foreign mission work, he accepted the post and went to Guatemala, only to find that 60 percent of the people could not read Spanish. This road block led to ten years' work with the Central American Mission among the Cakchiquel people. Without linguistic training, he learned their language, reduced it to writing, and translated the New Testament.

In 1934 he established Camp Wycliffe in Arkansas as a training center for missionaries who wanted to duplicate his translation work among other peoples. Two students came. In 1935, after a second camp with five students, he began work in Mexico. Out of this small beginning emerged the Summer Institute of Linguistics and Wycliffe Bible Translators, destined to become the largest independent Protestant mission agency in the world. Throughout his life Townsend was an innovator. His unique missionary strategies included cooperation with mainline denominations, the promotion of literature in alliance with foreign governments, and the sending of single women to remote tribes.

Biography by J. and M. Hefley (1974).

SAM HAMSTRA, JR.

Tozer, Aiden Wilson (1897–1963)

Pastor, author, and editor. Born in La Jose (now Newburg), Pennsylvania, of English ancestry, he had meager schooling but read avidly. Converted at seventeen, he evangelized in streets, homes, and schoolhouses before undertaking Christian Missionary Alliance pastorates in West Virginia, Ohio, and Indiana. His Southside Chicago ministry (1928–1959) thrust him into prominence. He also held key positions within his denomination, including a thirteen-year editorship of *The Alliance Weekly* (now *Alliance Life)*, during which time circulation doubled.

Penetrating books are Tozer's lasting legacy—some forty in all. About one million English copies of *The Pursuit of God* (1948) sold in four decades, plus sales in fifteen languages. Attacking contemporary Christendom's antinomianism and inconsistencies, Tozer literature urges intimate worship, scrutiny of divine attributes, contemplation of God, prayer, older hymns, practical holiness, discipline, simple lifestyle, Spirit-fullness, missions, zeal, vows, and attention to authors like Fenelon, Faber, Tersteegen, and Guyon. Tozer's preaching was characterized by originality, frankness, intensity, spiritual depth, humor, and good taste. Employing frequent metaphors, he weighed words. He attracted collegians, instructed clergy, preached weekly on Moody radio, and addressed most major U.S. Bible conferences. His other published works include *Wingspread* (1943), *The Divine Conquest* (1950), *The Knowledge of the Holy* (1961), and *The Christian Book of Mystical Verse* (edited, 1963).

Biographies by D. J. Fant (1964) and J. L. Snyder (1991).

GERALD E. MCGRAW

Troeltsch, Ernst (1865–1923)

German theologian, philosopher, and social theorist. Born in Hannstetten, near Augsburg, he studied at Erlangen, Berlin, and Göttingen. He gave up a career as a Lutheran minister to serve as professor of theology at the University of Bonn (1892–1894) and Heidelberg (1894–1915), and of philosophy at the University of Berlin (1915–1923). In addition to his teaching and writing he was active in politics, serving in the parliament of the Grand Duchy of Baden (1909–1914) and as a member of the Prussian Legislature (1919–1921) where he also became minister of education. Although he welcomed World War I and its nationalistic fervor, he changed his opinion and became a liberal, renouncing many of the German war goals. After his nation's defeat and the overthrow of the kaiser's government, he supported the Weimar Republic and its vision of a social democracy.

Strongly influenced by Ritschl, Schleiermacher, and Max Weber, he was the leading theologian of the Religiohistorical School. This approach questioned the uniqueness of Christianity and emphasized the need to gain insights from the comparative study of other religions. While believing that

393

the laws of morality are universal he nevertheless felt that there is a development of moral consciousness over time and across culture. These assumptions seemed accurate due to his belief that absolute morality must be realized through individuals rather than value systems. He presented his ideas in two major studies: *Christian Thought, Its History and Application* (1923) and *The Social Teachings of the Christian Church* (1912, ET, 1923).

Most of his work, including pioneering studies of the family, the guild, and the differing social impact of Lutheranism and Calvinism, is based on extensive analysis of historical and factual data. However, he is most famous for a more general typology dealing with the difference among church, sect, and mysticism. The church he defines as an institution that compromises with the "world," accepts the social order, and dominates the masses. The sect rejects this accommodation and insists on a hostile attitude toward culture. This is done with the expectation that only the kingdom of God will result in a just society. Mysticism emphasizes intense individual experiences of the heart and does not form institutions of any size that can be traced historically.

A recent biography of this influential scholar is Hans-George Drescher, Ernst *Troeltsch, His Life and Work* (1993).

ROBERT G. CLOUSE

Trotman, Dawson (1906–1956)

Evangelist and pastor. Born in Bisbee, Arizona, he was reared in southern California and attended Los Angeles Baptist Theological Seminary and Biola University. He was involved in a discipling ministry by his early twenties. The Navigators ministry that he founded (1943) grew from a Bible study with seamen in his home to an international organization based at Glen Eyrie, Colorado, and ministering on university and college campuses. The identifying characteristics of the organization are Bible memorization, evangelism, and the four-spoked wheel of sources of life and power. The two distinct contributions Trotman made to the church were his emphasis on follow-up for those who were converted and a rediscovery of the evangelistic multiplication principle, summarized by the statement, "each one reach one." Trotman was known for his discipline, love for Christ, generosity, and practical application of Scripture. He authored several pamphlets and was a powerful evangelist and speaker. He drowned while trying to save someone in Schroon Lake, New York.

Biography by B. L. Skinner (1974).

NANCY CALVERT

Trotter, (Isabella) Lilias (1853–1928)

Missionary to Algeria. Born into a genteel family in London, she grew up shielded from the rough reality of the world. Her sensitive nature was to enrich many, both in her presence and in her writings. She also had an exquisite gift of painting that could have made her mark in the secular field. About to put a coin in an offering plate, she noticed that engraved on the bottom of the plate were the pierced hands of Christ. Immediately she emptied her whole purse into it—"there seemed nothing else to do." When that same Hand indicated the barren region of North Africa she emptied her whole life into it. The mission she wanted to join refused her because of poor health, so in 1888 she set off independently with two friends, and for the next forty years persisted in a witness to those to whom her message was strange and unwelcome. Thus was born the Algiers Mission Band (now incorporated into Arab World Ministries). Lilias Trotter's writings were brought together by Constance Padwick under the title *The Master of the Impossible*.

Recent biographies by I. R. G. Stewart (1958) and Patricia St. John (1990).

EILEEN J. KUHN

Trueblood, David Elton (1900–)

Quaker philosopher-theologian. Born in Pleasantville, Iowa, he was educated at William Penn College, Oskaloosa, Iowa (A.B., 1922), Brown University, Providence, Rhode Island (1922–1923), Hartford Theological Seminary, Connecticut (1923–1924), Harvard University, Cambridge, Massachusetts (S.T.B., 1926), and the Johns Hopkins University, Baltimore, Maryland, from which he received his doctorate (1934). He began teaching and served as Dean of Men at Guilford College, North Carolina (1927–1930), and Haverford College, Pennsylvania (1933–1936), before moving on to Stanford University, California, where he was also chaplain (1936–1945). Between 1930 and 1933 he was Executive Secretary of the Baltimore Yearly Meeting of Friends. He came under the impact of the emerging theological literature from the pen of his near contemporary, Clive Staples Lewis (1898–1963), whose Christian writings began to appear in 1933. He finished out his career back within Quaker circles as professor of philosophy at Earlham College, Richmond, Indiana (1946–1970), from whence he also exerted indirect influence upon many students who only knew of him secondhand. He was named Churchman of the Year by American Heritage in 1960. Trueblood was a very popular lecturer and commencement speaker, and was recipient of numerous honorary degrees. He remains involved through his Yokefellow movement, and as Professor-at-Large from Earlham College.

He edited *The Friend* (1935–1947), and in his own writings was an apologist for the Judaeo-Christian spiritual tradition. He was a major force in the church renewal movement as illustrated in *The Company of the Com-*

mitted (1961) and *The Incendiary Fellowship* (1967).*While It Is Day: An Autobiography*, was published in 1974.

CLYDE CURRY SMITH

Trumbull, Charles Gallaudet (1872–1941)

Editor and author. Born in Hartford, Connecticut, he graduated from the Hamilton School in Philadelphia, and received his A.B. from Yale University in 1893 and a Doctor of Letters (Litt.D.) degree from Wheaton College (Ill.). In 1893 Trumbull became associated with his father in the editorial work of the *Sunday School Times,* and by 1903 he was the editor, vice president, secretary, and director of the Sunday School Times Co. He was also a staff writer for the *Toronto Globe,* and each week wrote the Sunday school lessons for the *Philadelphia Evening Public Ledger* as well as for several other daily newspapers. Trumbull was a member of the Victoria Institute, England, the Palestine Exploration Fund, and the Archaeological Institute of America.

Trumbull was a man with a profound personal relationship to the living Christ, which manifested itself in every aspect of his life. He describes it this way: "It is hard to put into words, and yet it is, oh, so new, and real, and wonderful, and miracle-working in both my own life and the lives of others. I [finally] realized that the many references throughout the New Testament to Christ in you, and you in Christ, Christ our life, and abiding in Christ, are literal, actual, blessed fact and not figures of speech." Trumbull was author of several books including, *A Pilgrimage to Jerusalem* (1904), *Taking Men Alive* (1907), *Life Story of C. I. Scofield* (1920), *What Is the Gospel?* (1918), and *Prophecy's Light on Today* (1937).

Biography by P. E. Howard (1944).

DAVID P. CAMERA

Tshibangu, Tshishuku (1933–)

African theologian. Born in the southern Zaire mining town of Kipushi, Tshibangu earned his doctorate in theology at the Catholic University of Louvain in Belgium. In 1960, while still a student at the Catholic Faculty of Kinshasa, he took part in a widely publicized debate arguing (against Alfred Vanneste, then dean of the Faculty) for the legitimacy of African theology. He was named by Pope John XXIII as advisor on African affairs at Vatican II. Tshibangu carried the cause of African theology further at the 4th Theological Week organized by the Catholic Faculty in Kinshasa (1968) where he spelled out the implications of African theology. Always an advocate of a scientifically rigorous methodology, he nevertheless has argued that the academic quest must never become divorced from the perceptions of ordinary church members and must recognize the local church as an important locus of the total theological process. Appointed auxiliary bishop of Kinshasa in 1970, Tshibangu was also rector of the National University of Zaire in Kinshasa from 1971 to 1981, and thereafter chancellor and president of the Administrative Council of Zairian Universities. He is the author of several books and numerous articles in French.

GORDON MOLYNEUX

Tucker, Henry St. George (1874–1959)

Presiding bishop of the Protestant Episcopal Church of America. Son of the bishop of Southern Virginia, he was born and reared in Virginia. In 1902 he was appointed a missionary to Japan, serving as president of St. Paul's College in Tokyo. A decade later he was consecrated as missionary bishop of Kyoto, a post he held until his return to the United States in 1923. After a four-year stint as professor of pastoral theology at the Episcopal Theological Seminary of Virginia, he was made bishop of Virginia and elected to the National Council of his denomination. In 1937 Tucker became the first elected presiding bishop of the Episcopal Church as a result of changes in the bylaws eliminating the old seniority system and giving the presiding bishop real powers. He used his position to speak out on political issues of the day, opposing Japanese expansion into Manchuria and criticizing Western governments for signing the Munich Pact. In 1942 he was elected president of the Federal Council of Churches. He retired in 1946, but continued to address social issues. In addition to his autobiography (1951) he wrote *History of the Episcopal Church in Japan* (1934) and *Providence and Atonement* (1938).

DAVID A. CURRIE

Tutu, Desmond (1931–)

South African archbishop and ecumenist. Born the son of a Methodist schoolteacher in Klerksdorp, Western Transvaal, he was educated at a Swedish Mission boarding school at Roodeport (west of Johannesburg), after which he attended a secondary school for black students. At age fourteen he contracted tuberculosis, and during his convalescence had time to think about the situation in South Africa. He attended a teacher-training college in Pretoria and spent four years teaching in the Johannesburg area. In 1957 he decided to enter the ministry of the Church of England, becoming a deacon in 1960 and a priest in 1961. In 1962 he went to London and studied at King's College. He worked for the World Council of Churches during his five years in England. On returning to South Africa he worked in the diocese of Grahamstown and was lecturer at the University of Botswana, Lesotho, and Swaziland (1970–1974). He was appointed dean of Johannesburg in 1975—the first black person to hold that position. In 1976 he was made bishop of Lesotho and in 1977 became general secretary of the South Africa Council of Churches. He later occupied the see of

Johannesburg before assuming his current position as archbishop of Cape Town and primate of Southern Africa.

Tutu's theology is ecumenical rather than evangelical. He is best known for his public stand for the black people of his country. His publications include *The Divine Intention* (1982), *Crying in the Wilderness: The Struggle for Justice in South Africa* (1982), and *Hope and Suffering: Sermons and Speeches* (1984).

ROGER KEMP

U

Uchimura, Kanzo (1861–1930)

Japanese intellectual and social critic. Born Samurai of a Confucist household, at a time when Japan was opening itself to the outside world, he came to Christ at an American mission school in 1877. He received a B.A. from Amherst College in 1888 and attended Hartford Seminary, after which he returned to Japan. In 1890 he accepted a position as a middle school instructor, but was forced to resign when he caused an uproar by refusing to pay appropriate reverence to the new Imperial Rescript on Education. Over the next decade he taught and edited the English section of a newspaper in which he addressed significant social issues. He founded a number of periodicals, including *Kokyo Kokuritsu Zasshi* (*Tokyo Independent Magazine*, 1898) and *Mukyokai* (*No-church*, 1901), to help Christians outside the institutional church find fellowship and instruction. He was the most influential preacher of his day, and his writings are still popular in Japan. Until his death, he followed the Samurai tradition of choosing the harder but more honorable paths of life, seen in his rejection of both the Japanese imperial orthodoxy and the institutional Christian church. He was a passionate advocate of democracy, pacifism, and personal independence, though he frequently declared that he loved only two J's: Japan and Jesus. His most significant contribution to an indigenous Japanese Christianity was founding of the Mukyokai movement, a Bible study movement not affiliated with an institutional church.

A. Scott Moreau

Uemura, Masahisa (1857–1925)

Japanese pastor, churchman, and intellectual. Born the son of a Samurai in service to a shogun, Uemura came to Christ and was baptized in 1873 while attending an American missionary school. He was ordained to the ministry in the Church of Christ Japan in 1878, and began a church planting ministry at that time. He developed the reputation of a powerful theologian and preacher who engaged the Japanese culture in lively debate while retaining solid evangelical distinctives. This was especially evident in the fight he and Kanzo Uchimura waged against the rise of emperor-centered nationalism in the late 1880s. In 1901 this reputation was further enhanced through his staunch and irenic defense of orthodox Christian theology in a widely read debate with Danjo Ebina, a liberal Unitarian theologian. He is remembered in Japan for three significant legacies that carried on after his death on January 8, 1925. First, after founding two periodicals that folded, in 1892 he successfully launched the widely read *Fukuin Shimpo* (*Evangelical Weekly*). Second, after resigning as professor of systematic theology at Meiji Gakuin Theological Seminary in 1904, he founded the Tokyo Shingakusha (Theological Seminary) in 1905, the first independent theological school in Japan. Finally, in 1906 he established the Fujimicho Nihon Kirisuto Church, for many years the largest church in Japan. Uerema was a man of tremendous vision and courage whose entrepreneurial ventures continue to impact the Japanese church today.

Biography by K. Aoyoshi (1941).

A. SCOTT MOREAU

Underhill, Evelyn (Mrs. Stuart Moore) (1875–1941)

Anglo-Catholic writer on mysticism, religious poet, and spiritual counselor. Born in Wolverhampton, England, she was educated privately and at King's College, London. Converted in 1907, she was concerned to relate personal religious experience to church teaching, and this led to her pioneering study *Mysticism* (1911). There followed many smaller works on the same theme, and introductions to editions of English and continental mystics that laid much of the groundwork for later scholarly study. Under the influence of Friedrich Von Hügel, whom she took as her spiritual director, she moved from a symbolic to a realistic view of Christian doctrine. Her other large book, *Worship* (1936), was an important recognition of the value of corporate liturgical worship. *Practical Mysticism* (1914) is a title that perhaps best shows her overriding interest in promoting the spiritual development of ordinary men and women. She was much in demand for spiritual direction (see the sane advice preserved in her published letters) and as a retreat conductor (from 1924), and tireless as a religious journalist, public speaker, and broadcaster. Toward the end of her life she became a convinced pacifist. Her *Letters* were edited by C. Williams (1943); her *Collected Papers* by L. Menzies (1946).

Biographies by M. Cropper (1958) and C. J. R. Armstrong (1975).

PHILIP HILLYER

Underwood, Horace Grant (1859–1916)

Presbyterian pioneer missionary. Born in London, England, he followed his family to New Durham, New Jersey, in 1872. He studied at New York University and New Brunswick Theological Seminary, was ordained by the Dutch Reformed Church (1884), and went as the first ordained missionary to Korea under the Presbyterian Board of Foreign Missions (1885). In 1886 he started an orphanage-school, and won his first convert—reportedly the first Protestant baptism in Korea. In 1887 he organized the first

Protestant church. As an energetic evangelist, he was soon initiating and holding training sessions for Korean Christian leaders. In 1888 he established the Korean Religious Tract Society, in 1887 founded the first Christian newspaper in Korea, and in 1903 brought the YMCA to Seoul. Underwood was pastor of Sai Munan Church, Seoul (1889–1916), professor of theology at Presbyterian Theological Seminary, Pyongyang (1907–1915), and moderator of the first Presbyterian Church of Korea general assembly (1912). A persistent and courageous missionary, he has been described as "the father of Korean Presbyterianism," adapting the principles of the Nevius self-support method to Korea with great success. He kept free from political turmoil and won a place in the hearts of the Korean people. He was respected and sought out for advice by the Korean and American governments. He saw the completion of the Korean Bible, and wrote *The Call of Korea* (1908) and *Religions of Eastern Asia* (1910).

Biography by his wife Lillias (1918).

ALBERT H. FREUNDT, JR.

Unger, Merrill Frederick (1909–1980)

Old Testament scholar and editor. Born in Baltimore, he was educated at Johns Hopkins University, Southern Baptist Theological Seminary, Nyack Missionary College, and Dallas Theological Seminary (Th.D., 1945). He returned to Johns Hopkins to complete a Ph.D. degree under W. F. Albright (1947). After pastoring churches in New York, Texas, and Maryland, and teaching briefly at Gordon College, he served as professor of Semitics and Old Testament at Dallas Theological Seminary (1948–1967). Among his many publications are *Introductory Guide to the Old Testament* (1951), *Archaeology and the Old Testament* (1954), and *Demons in the World Today* (1971). In addition, his efforts to create useful biblical dictionaries and handbooks, known in successive editions by his name, and expository dictionaries jointly with others, reveal a broad acquaintance with scholarship. He was also a regular contributor to *Bibliotheca Sacra*, and carried on an extensive Bible conference ministry, which was issued posthumously in *Unger's Commentary on the Old Testament* (2 vols., 1981).

CLYDE CURRY SMITH

V

Van Dusen, Henry Pitney (1897–1975)

Presbyterian theologian and educator. Born in Philadelphia, he graduated from Princeton University, Union Theological Seminary, New York, and Edinburgh University (Ph.D., 1932). He was ordained by the presbytery of New York in 1924, though unwilling to affirm or deny the virgin birth of Jesus, and served with YMCA. At Union Theological Seminary he rose from the rank of instructor to professor of theology (1926–1963) and to president (1945–1963). Under his administration the seminary expanded greatly and received international recognition. After 1954 he was president also of Auburn Seminary. He advocated a liberal christocentric theology, the social gospel, and ecumenism; played a leading role in the formation of the World Council of Churches; and coined the term "Third Force" for the charismatic movement and Holiness groups. He was chairman of several influential committees and a prominent participant in international ecumenical conferences. At the World Council of Churches assembly at New Delhi (1961) his plan for the union of the WCC and the International Missionary Council was realized. Van Dusen wrote many books, including *World Christianity* (1947), *One Great Ground of Hope* (1961), *The Vindication of Liberal Theology* (1963), and *Dag Hammarskjöld* (1967), and was on the editorial boards of several religious periodicals.

ALBERT H. FREUNDT, JR.

Van Dyke, Henry (Jackson) (1852–1933)

Pastor, educator, and writer. Born into a Presbyterian manse in Germantown, Pennsylvania, he graduated from Princeton College (1873) and Seminary (1877), followed by a period of study at Berlin University. After pastorates at the United Congregational Church, Newport, Rhode Island (1879–1882) and the Brick Presbyterian Church, New York City (1883–1899), he was appointed professor of English literature at Princeton University (1899–1913, 1919–1923). A friend of President Woodrow Wilson, he served as ambassador to The Netherlands and Luxembourg (1913–1916) just before America entered World War I.

All this time Van Dyke's fame as a preacher and author was growing. Among his wide-ranging writings were *The Reality of Religion* (1844), *The Gospel for an Age of Doubt* (1896), *Spirit of America* (1910), *Chosen Poems* (1927), and *Travel Diary of an Angler* (1929). In terms of popularity, however, nothing surpassed *The Story of the Other Wise Man* (1896), the phenomenal success of which is reflected in its translation into nearly thirty languages. Although himself an unsystematic (and at times a radical) theologian, he was much praised for his chairmanship of the committee that prepared in 1906 *The Book of Common Worship of the Presbyterian Church.*

Biography by T. Van Dyke (1935).

J. D. DOUGLAS

Van Til, Cornelius (1895–1987)

Reformed theologian and philosopher. Born in Grootegast, Holland, he moved with his family to Highland, Indiana, in 1905. He attended Calvin College and Calvin Theological Seminary, transferring thereafter to Princeton Seminary, where he graduated Th.M. in 1925. In 1927 he received a Ph.D. in philosophy from Princeton University. After a brief pastorate and an equally brief lectureship in apologetics at Princeton Seminary, he was prevailed upon to join the faculty of the fledgling Westminster Theological Seminary when it opened in Philadelphia in 1929. He remained there until his retirement in 1972. When the Orthodox Presbyterian Church was founded in 1936, Van Til transferred his membership from the Christian Reformed Church. His theology was a high Dutch Calvinism that is very similar to that of Abraham Kuyper and Herman Dooyeweerd. It is presuppositionalistic; Van Til argues from the theological givens of the ontological Trinity, the doctrine of creation, and the infallibility of Scripture. He rejected the idea that valid knowledge could be had on any other basis, although his followers still debate exactly what that means. Among his best-known works are *The New Modernism* (1946), *Common Grace* (1947), *The Defense of the Faith* (1955), *Christianity and Barthianism* (1964), and *A Christian Theory of Knowledge* (1969).

Biography by William White, Jr. (1979).

WALTER A. ELWELL

Varetto, Juan C. (1879–1953)

Preacher and writer. He was born in Rosario, Argentina, and, left alone in the world, moved to Buenos Aires at age fourteen. With only one year of formal schooling he was self-educated and learned several languages. Converted in 1894 through John Thomson, founder of the Methodist work in Spanish, Varetto went on a colportage trip to the interior of Brazil the following year. He began preaching at age eighteen, and became one of the best-known evangelical orators in Latin America, traveling throughout the continent and in Spain, and speaking in churches of many denominations. His preaching, with a solid biblical base and personal, popular style, influenced a whole generation. In 1909 he was ordained as the first Argentinian Baptist pastor, and served in several churches, especially in La Plata, as well as in a variety of denominational posts. He was a well-known writer whose first book, *Heroes and Martyrs of Missionary Work* (1911), made an impact throughout the continent. He also wrote biographies of pioneer missionaries such as Diego Thomson, Frederick Crowe, and John Thomson, works on church history and apologetics, collections of sermon outlines, and children's books. Several of Varetto's daughters became outstanding leaders among Argentine evangelicals.

ARNOLDO CANCLINI

Vaughan Williams, Ralph (1872–1958)

English composer. Although Vaughan Williams is the completely nationalistic English composer of the twentieth century, his music was influenced by study with Bruch and Ravel, and his admiration of Sibelius. Not only did he collect English folk songs of many eras, but he incorporated them into his compositions, crafting them harmonically in a manner that was based on modal models from the last great period of original English music, that of Byrd and Tallis and other Elizabethans. His original hymn tunes such as "Salve Festa Dies" (1906), "King's Weston" (1925), "Down Ampney" (1906), and "Sine Nomine" (1906) are permanently enshrined in the repertoire. His harmonizations of other composers' hymns, brought about as joint editor of *The English Hymnal Songs of Praise*, and the *Oxford Book of Carols*, are of great interest and in many cases have become the preferred version. The *Mass in G Minor* (1922) is an important musical and liturgical statement merging modern harmonies within a Neo-Tudor a capella style. Other significant large religious works include *Hodie*, a Christmas oratorio, *Dona Nobis Pacem* (1936) with texts from the Agnus Dei, Walt Whitman, and the Bible, a *Magnificat*, the *Festival Te Deum*, and *The Pilgrim's Progress*, an opera based on Bunyan (1951). In addition, there are many anthems, a Morning, Communion, and Evening Service in D minor (1939), and the very lovely *Five Mystical Songs*, based on George Herbert. His most frequently performed anthems include *The Old Hundredth Psalm Tune* and *O Taste and See.*

Biography by Ursula Vaughan Williams (1988).

WILLIAM PHEMISTER

Vencer, Agustin B. (Jun), Jr. (1946–)

Prominent leader in the Evangelical Church in the Philippines. Born in Nueva Sevilla, Iloilo City, the Philippines, he was educated at the Central Philippines University, Southern Island Colleges, and at the University of the East in Manila, earning degrees in science, arts, and law, and passing the bar examinations in 1973. His membership in the Alliance Fellowship Church of Quezon City enabled him to expand his ever-increasing ministry for Christ in various ways. His exceptional ability in teaching the Word of God gave many opportunities for Christian service, including that of conference speaker at home and abroad. In addition to his work at Alliance Fellowship Church, he has been general secretary of both the Philippine Council of the Evangelical Church (1978–1993) and the Philippine Relief and Development Service (1981–1993). His work saw hundreds of churches brought together in the former body. In 1993 he succeeded Dr. David Howard as international director of the World Evangelical Fellowship.

FRANK ALLEN

Vereide, Abraham (1886–1969)

Norwegian immigrant to America. He had a conversion experience in Norway at age eight, traveled to America at age nineteen, and became a Methodist itinerant minister riding the circuit in Montana before pastoring churches in Washington and Oregon. Educated at Northwestern University College of Liberal Arts and Norwegian-Danish Theological Seminary, he became an American citizen in 1910. While pastoring in Seattle he established a branch of Goodwill Industries as a ministry to the social needs of the community and then, in 1931, moved to Boston to become associate general superintendent of Goodwill Industries and executive secretary of Goodwill Industries for New England. In 1934, after serving the needs of the "down and out" through Goodwill Industries, he felt a call to minister to the "up and out." Returning to Seattle in 1935, he started an evangelistic breakfast with executives of Fredrick Nelson, the largest department store in the Pacific Northwest. This breakfast expanded to include civic leaders in the Seattle community, and, in 1940, a similar breakfast was started at the state capitol for the governor and legislature of Washington. In 1941 he took his evangelistic breakfast ministry to Washington, D.C., where he hosted a breakfast for members of Congress. The next year congressional breakfast groups were formed in both the Senate and House, and organized under the title of National Committee for Christian Leadership, with Vereide as executive director. The name was eventually changed in 1945 to International Christian Leadership (ICL) and its headquarters were established on Massachusetts Avenue in Washington, D.C. In 1952 President Eisenhower attended the first Presidential Prayer Breakfast hosted by ICL. Vereide's ministry to the "up and out" made him a diplomat for Christ to the national and international leaders of the world.

MAXIE BURCH

Verghese, T. Paul (Geervarghese Mar Osthathios) (1922–)

Orthodox Syrian churchman. Born of Christian parents in Kerala, India, he taught school in Ethiopia before going to the United States for training at Princeton Theological Seminary. He returned to India where he helped establish a retreat house and organized the Orthodox Student Christian movement. From 1956 to 1959 he served on the personal staff of the Emperor Haile Selassie in Ethiopia, and thereafter was principal of the Orthodox Syrian Seminary in Kottayam, India. Verghese has also been on the staff of the World Council of Churches. Currently (1994) he is metropolitan of the Orthodox Syrian Church. He brings together in his writings the tradition of India combined with both the theological insights of the Western church and the rich tradition of the Eastern Orthodox Church. He has written *The Joy of Freedom: Eastern Worship and Modern Man*, *The Freedom of Man*, *Theology of a Classless Society*, and *The Sin of Being Poor in a Rich World*.

JAMES J. STAMOOLIS

Verwer, George (1938–)

Founder and international director of interdenominational mission, promoter of evangelism. Born in Wyckoff, New Jersey, he was converted in 1955 during a meeting at which Billy Graham spoke. Listening to a tape of Graham's 1957 Urbana message solidified and energized his commitment to follow Christ regardless of the cost. He graduated from Moody Bible Institute (1960). Verwer was arrested and expelled from the Soviet Union in 1961 for distributing literature. His international ministry began in 1957, when he went to Mexico to distribute tracts and sell Christian books door-to-door. In 1958 he founded Send the Light, which was renamed Operation Mobilization (1962) to emphasize "mobilizing" large groups of young people in cross-cultural witness. His passion to reach areas with little exposure to the gospel brought OM workers first to Spain and India, and later European, Muslim, or communist countries. Just as his first exposure to the gospel came through a Christian booklet, Verwer led OM to maximize the impact of evangelism through distributing literature. He also wrote several books, including *Literature Evangelism*, *No Turning Back*, and *The Revolution of Love*, which reflected his determination to preach the gospel and challenge the church to share his single-minded enthusiasm.

PAUL A. ERICKSEN

Vins, Georgi (1928–)

Soviet Baptist leader and editor. Born in Blagoveschensk, Siberia, he was the son of Peter Vins, an American missionary who surrendered his U.S. citizenship to remain in the Soviet Union. The elder Vins was arrested three times, and died in a Siberian labor camp in 1943. His death had a profound and lasting influence on Georgi's life. At sixteen he was baptized in Onsk, Siberia. By eighteen he was actively preaching as well as serving in the choir and his youth group. After graduating from Kiev Polytechnic Institute, he continued his ministry in the church while working as an electrical engineer. He was ordained in 1962 as an evangelist by Alexander Shalashov, a well-known Russian Baptist leader in Kiev. In 1966 Vins was arrested and sentenced to three years' imprisonment, one in Lefortovo Prison and two at camps in the Ural Mountains. He continued ministering until 1974 when he was again arrested and sentenced to ten years for his work as general secretary of the Council of Evangelical Baptist Churches, the governing body of two thousand persecuted churches. *Georgi Vins: Testament from Prison* (translated by Jane Ellis, 1975) is his own story of persecution in the former Soviet Union. Five years into his sentence he was exiled with four other Soviet prisoners to the United States in exchange for two captured Soviet spies. In the United States Vins founded International Representation, Inc. as a ministry to represent, defend, and aid the persecuted church in the Soviet Union. He publishes a quarterly magazine, the *Prisoner Bulletin*, to share the stories of those oppressed. He traveled worldwide to share the plight of his Soviet Christians. He wrote *Konshaubi: A True Story of Persecuted Christians in the Soviet Union* (1988) and *Let the Waters Roar: Evangelists in the Gulag* (1989).

FRED P. WILSON

Visser 't Hooft, Willem Adolf (1900–1985)

Dutch ecumenical statesman. Born in Harlem, he graduated from the University of Leiden, where he wrote a dissertation on the Social Gospel Movement. He served the YMCA (1924–1932) before appointment as general secretary of the World Student Christian Federation (1932–1938). Having early caught the attention of John R. Mott and participated in the international conferences at Stockholm (1925), Oxford (1937), and Edinburgh (1937), he was a natural choice as general secretary in 1938 when the World Council of Churches' provisional committee was formed. World War II curtailed further ecumenical progress, but Visser 't Hooft, from his Geneva base, worked tirelessly on behalf of refugees from Hitler's Germany and sought to maintain links with churches in occupied countries. The first WCC assembly (Amsterdam, 1948) formally confirmed Visser 't Hooft in the post he held until retirement in 1966.

Although an ordained minister in the Reformed tradition, the multilingual Dutchman never regarded himself as a theologian. True unity was his great passion; the Lord's prayer was that all may be one, not "that they may all enter into conversation with each other." In a *Christianity Today* interview in 1966 he held that it was "the duty of every Christian to proclaim the divine Lordship of Jesus Christ"; that this gospel is "to be addressed to every man ... [and] that it is to be given in its purest form ... unmixed with extraneous or cultural elements."

So highly was Visser 't Hooft regarded that five festschrifts were produced in his honor, and he was elected honorary president of the WCC in 1968. Among his numerous publications were *None Other Gods* (1937), *The Struggle of the Dutch Church* (1946), and *No Other Name* (1963). His

Memoirs (1973) and *Genesis and Formation of the WCC* (1982) are invaluable sources of information on the modern ecumenical movement.

J. D. Douglas

Vogel, Heinrich R. G. (1902–1989)

German theologian and writer. Son of a Lutheran pastor, he was born in Pröttlin, Brandenburg, and studied theology at Jena and Berlin. In 1927 he entered the parish ministry at Oderberg, and in 1932 moved to Dobbrikow, near Berlin. After Hitler came to power in 1933 Vogel became involved in the resistance to nazification of the Protestant church as a member first of the Council of Brethren, and then of the Prussian and Reich synods of the Confessing Church. He was constantly harassed by the Gestapo. Banned from public speaking, he was jailed three times for his oppositional activities, including leadership of an "illegal" Confessing seminary in Berlin. After the war Vogel sought to bridge the widening gap between East and West by holding chairs of theology both at Humboldt University in East Berlin and the Kirchliche Hochschule in West Berlin, speaking out against nuclear arms and helping to found the Christian Peace Conference in 1957. In his capacity as a member of the Synod of the Evangelical Church in Germany he was drafter of the synodical statement adopted at Berlin-Weissensee in 1950 that acknowledged the Protestant church's anti-Semitism and guilt for what had happened to the Jews. Vogel wrote many collections of sermons and books in the areas of theology, dogmatics, church music, and aesthetics. His most significant writings were reprinted in the ten-volume *Gesammelte Werke* (1982–1983).

Richard V. Pierard

Von Hügel, Friedrich (1852–1925)

Roman Catholic scholar. Son of an Austrian diplomat whose Scottish Presbyterian wife had converted to Roman Catholicism, Von Hügel was born in Florence, Italy, and from age fifteen lived in England. He inherited a barony, had a comprehensive education at the hands of private tutors, and developed into one of the most influential thinkers and writers of his generation. Here was a Roman Catholic layman who did not believe in purgatory hereafter, a religious man who expressed horror that E. B. Pusey read only religious books, and a mystic who walked the world with open eyes. He became a renowned spiritual counselor, telling Evelyn Underhill that her sophisticated religion needed "de-intellectualizing," and that she should spend two afternoons a week visiting the poor (praying for them was no substitute). The American Quaker scholar Douglas Steere held that Von Hügel had recovered for the Anglo-Saxon world the dimension of transcendence in the Christian faith, thus saving it from a "rebottled import of continental Barthianism." Von Hügel's *Essays and Addresses* (2 vols.,

1921, 1926) and *The Reality of God* (1931) followed Aquinas in interpreting traditional faith according to the best and most durable elements in philosophy, scholarship, and science. Though his modernist views made the Roman Catholic hierarchy uneasy, his deep spirituality as seen in his *Selected Letters* (1928) prevented him from sharing the fate of his friend, the excommunicated George Tyrrell.

The best biography of Von Hügel in English is generally held to be that of Michael de la Bedoyere (1951).

J. D. DOUGLAS

Vos, Geerhardus (1862–1940)

Reformed biblical theologian. Born of German parents in Heerenveen, the Netherlands, he came to the United States in 1881 when his father accepted a pastoral call to Grand Rapids. His theological study began in his hometown at the Theological School of the Christian Reformed Church. He graduated in 1883 and continued his studies at Princeton Seminary, the University of Berlin, and the University of Strasbourg where he received his Ph.D. in Arabic studies in 1888. He also spent time in the Netherlands, where he had contact with Abraham Kuyper and Herman Bavinck, the leading figures in that Reformed community. He began teaching in 1888 at what became Calvin Theological Seminary where he was a popular and highly regarded professor of dogmatics and exegetical theology, known for his deep religious devotion. In 1893 he went to teach biblical theology at Princeton Seminary, remaining there until his retirement in 1932.

Vos is significant as the father of Reformed biblical theology. He was the first to grasp the importance of the progressive character of God's special, redemptive revelation. For Vos, the Bible was a divinely inspired historical drama that gradually unfolds until its focal point—the death and resurrection of Jesus Christ.

Vos made a marked contribution in his *Biblical Theology* (1948), but his most important works are *The Teaching of Jesus Concerning the Kingdom of God and the Church* (1903) and *The Pauline Eschatology* (1930).

SAM HAMSTRA, JR.

W

Wagner, Charles Peter (1930–)

Missiologist and author. Born in New York City, he graduated from Rutgers University and Fuller Theological Seminary. He then served as a missionary to Bolivia (1955–1971), first with the South American Mission and later with the Andes Evangelical Mission. During a second period of study at Fuller Theological Seminary, Wagner met Donald McGavran, who invited him to join the faculty as a specialist in Latin American studies, which post he took up in 1971. He eventually inherited the mantle of McGavran's leadership in the Church Growth movement. Wagner was a charter member of the Lausanne Committee in 1974, and earned a Ph.D. in social ethics from the University of Southern California in 1977.

A turning-point came in the early 1980s when, in association with John Wimber, he taught a highly publicized course at Fuller entitled "Signs, Wonders, and Church Growth," and began to emphasize divine healing, supernatural gifts, and spiritual warfare. Although he claimed to be neither charismatic nor Pentecostal, Wagner viewed these movements in a positive light and coined the term "Third Wave" to describe traditional evangelicals, such as himself, who practice charismatic gifts. Wagner's influence has extended beyond missiologists to the general public through his numerous publications. These include *Frontiers in Missionary Strategy* (1972), *Church Growth and the Whole Gospel* (1981), *How to Have a Healing Ministry Without Making Your Church Sick!* (1988), and *The Third Wave of the Holy Spirit* (1988).

A. Scott Moreau

Waldenström, Paul Peter (1838–1917)

Swedish theologian, educator, and chief founder of the Swedish Mission Covenant Church. Born in Lulea, Sweden, and educated at the University of Uppsala (Ph.D., 1863), he was ordained in the (Lutheran) Church of Sweden in 1864 and taught theology and biblical languages. While influenced by the Pietist tradition of K. O. Rosenius, he was drawn also to the teachings of the German scholar Albrecht Ritschl who had discarded the view of Christ's sacrifice as propitiatory to appease God's just wrath. Waldenstrom's emphasis was not on God's reconciliation to man, but man's to God. The cross was a demonstration of God's love, intended to win man to repentance. This view aroused controversy within the national church whose formalism had in any case depressed "awakened" believers. The latter, led by Waldenström who had organized the Swedish Mission Covenant in 1878, continued (albeit uneasily) within a rigid establishment unwilling to sanction a more relaxed approach to church services. Finally in 1882 Waldenström resigned his Church of Sweden ministry and served the Evangelical National Association, a body concerned with the reform of religion in the country. His devotional writings were popular and widely used. Several visits to the United States led him to organize what became the Evangelical Covenant Church for immigrants there. From 1884 Waldenström served for more than two decades as a member of the Swedish parliament.

J. D. DOUGLAS

Walker, Alan (1911–)

Australian Methodist leader. Descended from convicts transported from Britain, he was born in Sydney and educated at Leigh College and Sydney University. Ordained to the Methodist ministry in 1934, he served in Cessnock, New South Wales, gradually won the confidence of the miners there, and wrote a pioneering sociological study, *Coaltown* (1945). His passion for evangelism and Methodist holiness was combined with strong ecumenism, pacifism, and commitment to social justice. In 1949 he was adviser to the Australian delegation to the United Nations, and then a key figure in the Methodist Mission to the Nation in 1953. In 1958 he was appointed to Sydney's Central Methodist Mission after a notable ministry at Waverley. He gathered a talented team, restored the Mission's finances, and diversified its social witness, while continuing to grow in repute as an evangelist of international standing. Lifeline, established in 1963, has become an outstanding telephone counseling service. His prophetic witness against war, racism, and injustice has often been controversial, but his stature as an evangelist was recognized by appointment as director of evangelism for the World Methodist Council in 1978. In 1988 he founded the Pacific College for Evangelism at North Parramatta, and remains its principal. He continues to remind the Uniting Church (of which Australian Methodism is now a part) of the importance of evangelism and social justice, as well as bearing witness to Christian principles in public forums. Walker, who was knighted in 1981 by Queen Elizabeth II, is a prolific author whose works include *The Whole Gospel for the Whole World* (1957), *God the Disturber* (1973), *Standing up to Preach* (1983), and *Life in the Holy Spirit* (1986).

IAN BREWARD

Walvoord, John Flipse (1910–)

American theologian, pastor, and author. Born in Sheboygan, Wisconsin, he graduated from Wheaton College, Texas Christian University, and Dallas Theological Seminary where he later earned his Th.D. and joined the fac-

411

ulty (1936–1986). He became president in 1953, and chancellor on retirement in 1986. He had also pastored Rosen Heights Presbyterian Church, Fort Worth (1934–1950), and edited *Bibliotheca Sacra*, the seminary's theological journal (1952–1985). One of the most influential dispensational theologians of the twentieth century, Walvoord was prominent in prophetic conferences advocating a pretribulational rapture, a literal thousand-year millennium, and distinction between Israel and the church. Among his thirty books are *The Rapture Question* (1957), *The Millennial Kingdom* (1959), *The Prophecy Knowledge Handbook* (1990), and commentaries on Daniel (1971), Philippians (1971), and the Thessalonian epistles (1976). With R. B. Zuck, he edited the two-volume *Bible Knowledge Commentary* (1983, 1985).

D. K. Campbell edited *Walvoord: A Tribute* (1982).

RICHARD GRIFFITH

Wand, John William Charles (1885–1977)

English bishop and church historian. Born the son of a Lincolnshire butcher, he graduated from Oxford and was ordained a priest in 1909 and had several years in curacies, coupled latterly with a lectureship in Sarum Theological College (1914–1925). He taught theology and church history at Oxford before consecration as archbishop of Brisbane (Australia) (1934–1943) and returned to England as bishop of Bath and Wells (1943), transferring thereafter to the diocese of London (1945–1955). There he took a special interest in education, carried out some sensible and much-needed administrative changes, and supervised a Mission to London that drew 750,000 people and involved 122 centers and 155 special missioners from all over the country. Wand nonetheless affirmed that nothing could replace "the hard, steady, grinding work of the parish priest." As dean of the Chapels Royal he ministered to the royal family, and had a key role in the services marking the death of George VI and the coronation of Elizabeth II, in 1952. He warmly supported episcopal participation in politics—but not party politics.

Knighted in 1955 and made a privy councillor, Wand's retirement at seventy allowed him to continue writing for a further eighteen years. His *History of the Early Church* (1935) was regarded as a classic. Among his numerous other works were *The Life of Jesus Christ* (1955), *Atonement* (1962), the autobiographical *Changeful Page* (1965), and *Letters on Preaching* (1974). Wand also edited the *Church Quarterly Review*.

J. D. DOUGLAS

Wang, Thomas Yung-hsin (1925–)

Chinese evangelist, evangelical churchman, and missions leader. Born in Peking, China, Wang attended the church pastored by Wang Mingdao. In 1961 he started Chinese Christian Mission, an evangelistic agency in Detroit, Michigan. During the 1960s he rallied Chinese Christian students

412

to commitment and service. His favorite term was *kan-ching*, a willing spirit to sacrifice and work hard in the ministry. At the Lausanne Congress of 1974 he laid plans to convene the Chinese Congress on World Evangelism in Hong Kong (1976). At the congress the Chinese Coordination Centre of World Evangelism was organized. Wang left CCM and served as CCCOWE general secretary from 1976 to 1986, visiting Chinese churches around the world to call them to world evangelization. Wang was fond of speaking of the "CCCOWE spirit," a willingness to cross denominational and other barriers for the cause of world evangelization. In 1986 he became the international director for the Lausanne Committee on World Evangelization, directing the Lausanne II Congress in Manila in 1989. In 1989 Wang raised a question in an article: What is God saying to the churches as A.D. 2000 approaches? As a result of the widespread response to the article from Luis Bush and other mission leaders, the A.D. 2000 and Beyond Movement was launched. After Lausanne II Wang started the Great Commission Theological Seminary in Pasadena, California (in cooperation with Gordon-Conwell Theological Seminary), which in 1993 was renamed Great Commission Center. GCC launched evangelistic campaigns and opened mission fields in the former Soviet Union and other countries.

SAMUEL LING

Wangerin, Walter, Jr. (1944–)

Christian creative writer. He was born in Portland, Oregon, son of an educator father. He received a B.S. from Concordia Theological Seminary, an M.A. in English from Miami of Ohio University; and an M.Div. from Christ Seminary, Seminex. He worked at a variety of jobs including migrant pea-picking, ghetto youth work, radio announcer, and instructor in English, and has been an ordained Lutheran minister since 1976. In 1979 his *Book of the Dun Cow* (1978) won the American Book Award. This and several of his other books deal with the ageless struggle between good and evil in the midst of an imaginary kingdom of animals. The book demonstrates through allegorical fantasy the selflessness of the animals as they battle a giant monster, Wyrm, who seeks to escape his God-ordained imprisonment in the earth. It also portrays the desolation and carnage of war through richly drawn characters and gripping excitement. He has been called "exuberantly original" and presents a "frightening representation of modern evil." Eugene Peterson calls him "one of the master story-tellers of our generation," while Calvin Miller states that he may "perhaps be Christianity's most important creative writer." Some of his fiction titles include the *Book of Sorrows* (1985); short essays such as *Ragman and Other Cries of Faith;* and theology in *The Orphan Passages: The Drama of Faith* (1986), and *My Lil and the Chronicles of Grace* (1985) Many of his works have been aimed at children: *My First Book about Jesus* (1983), *In*

413

the Beginning There Was No Sky, Potter (1985), and *The Bible: Its Story for Children* (1986), His work in poetry includes *A Miniature Cathedral* (1987). In 1992 he published *Reliving the Passion: Meditations on Suffering*, which has won critical acclaim for its sensitivity to communicating the death of Christ for the Lenten season.

FRED P. WILSON

Ware, Timothy (Kallistos) (1934–)

Bishop of the Greek Orthodox Church and Oxford University lecturer in Eastern Orthodox Studies. A graduate of Oxford, he became Orthodox in 1958. He initially wanted to join the Russian Church, but political and canonical difficulties made it advisable for him to join instead the Ecumenical Patriarchate of Constantinople. He subsequently spent a number of years in Greece, particularly on the island of Patmos. In 1966 he became a monk under the name of Kallistos, and was ordained priest in the same year. In 1966 he also took up his teaching post at Oxford. He served as the Orthodox secretary of the Joint Anglican-Orthodox Theological Commission (1973–1980). In 1982 he was consecrated as titular bishop of Dioclea, and in this capacity he serves as an assistant to the Greek archbishop of Thyatira and Great Britain. Ware is widely respected as a leading authority on the Eastern Orthodox Church. His book, *The Orthodox Church* (1963), has become a classic and has gone through a number of editions. He has also written *The Orthodox Way* (1979), an introduction to Orthodox spirituality. He is also one of the translators of the *Philokalia*, the standard collection of the sayings of the desert fathers.

GERALD BRAY

Warfield, Benjamin Breckenridge (1851–1921)

Presbyterian scholar and theologian. Born on his family's estate, "Grasmere," near Lexington, Kentucky, on November 5, 1851 into a distinguished family, Warfield entered Princeton University after private schooling at home where he was profoundly influenced by the newly arrived president James McCosh, a strong defender of Scottish common sense philosophy. After European travel Warfield attended Princeton Theological Seminary, where he came under the influence of the aging Charles Hodge. After further studies in Leipzig, Germany, he returned to a brief assistant pastorate in Baltimore, where he was ordained into the Presbyterian ministry. In 1876 he taught New Testament at Western Theological Seminary (Allegheny, Pa.) and upon the death of A. A. Hodge in 1877 he was appointed professor of dialectic and polemic theology at Princeton Seminary, where he taught for thirty-four years until his death on February 16, 1921.

Warfield is remembered in particular for his defense of Calvinistic orthodoxy and the verbal inerrancy of Scripture. "Calvinism is just religion in its purity. We have only therefore to conceive of religion in its purity, and that is Calvinism." Warfield was deeply committed to this as is borne out in his collected essays *Studies in Tertullian and Augustine* (1930), *Calvin and Calvinism* (1931), and *The Westminster Assembly and its Work* (1931). He defined Calvinism as "a profound apprehension of God in His majesty, with the inevitably accompanying poignant realization of the exact nature of the relation sustained to Him by the creatures as such, and particularly by the sinful creature." Regarding the verbal inerrancy of Scripture, Warfield said in his classic essay "Inspiration" (written along with Charles Hodge in 1881) that inspiration was "God's continued work of superintendence, by which, his providential, gracious, and supernatural contributions having been presupposed, he presided over the sacred writers in their entire work of writing, with the design and effect of rendering that writing an errorless record of the matters he designed then to communicate, and hence constituting the entire volume in all its parts the word of God to us." He never wavered from this position throughout his entire career (see *Revelation and Inspiration*, 1927). Warfield was the last and the greatest of all the "Old Princeton" theologians, and his works are still relevant today.

Warfield was a prolific writer who contributed extensively to (and edited) *The Presbyterian Review* (1889), *The Presbyterian and Reformed Review* (1890–1903), and *The Princeton Theological Review* (1903–1921), from which most of his collected works were taken, edited by his brother Ethelbert Dudley Warfield.

WALTER A. ELWELL

Warneck, Johannes (1867–1944)

German missionary leader. Born in Dommitzsch, Saxony, he was educated at various universities. On completing his studies at Halle in 1892, where Martin Kähler had influenced him to become a missionary, he was ordained and appointed by the Rhenish Missionary Society to work among the Batak people in Sumatra. For the next fourteen years he served first as a pioneer missionary, and then as a teacher at the seminary in Si Poholon, where he developed its instructional program and textbooks to provide both academic and practical training for an indigenous ministry. In 1908 he returned home to join the board's staff at Barmen (Wuppertal) and supervised its Indonesian mission. From 1912 Warneck also occupied the first chair of missions at the theological college in nearby Bethel. During this time he produced several scholarly works on the language, literature, and belief system of the Batak, published a history of the Indonesian mission, and served as coeditor of the prestigious *Allgemeine Missions Zeitschrift*. In 1920 he returned to Sumatra to be head (Ephorus) of the burgeoning Batak church. He wrote a new constitution for it, stipulating that two-thirds of the governing board would be Batak Christians; the Dutch colonial authorities gave it legal recognition as an autonomous body in 1930. From 1932 to 1937 Warneck served as the director of the Rhenish Society, a period in which it suffered heavily under Nazi pressures. Through his literary works he fostered a deeper understanding of missions among the general public in Europe and America. Most important was *The Living Force of the Gospel* (ET, 1909, 1954), in which he analyzed the process of conversion among the "animistic" peoples of the East Indies.

His autobiography, *Werfeteure Netze aus*, appeared in 1938.

RICHARD V. PIERARD

Warnhuis, Abbe Livingston (1877–1958)

American missionary and ecumenical leader. Son of an immigrant who was a pastor in the (Dutch) Reformed Church in America, Warnhuis was born in Clymer, New York, and educated at Northwestern Academy (Iowa), Hope College (Michigan), and New Brunswick Theological Seminary (New Jersey). After ordination in 1900 he went to Amoy, China, to serve in his church's mission. For two decades he engaged in itinerant ministry, promoted the education of an indigenous ministry, and was involved in various ecumenical ventures, including laying the groundwork for the formation of the Church of Christ in China. A close friend of John R. Mott, Warnhuis in 1916 was appointed the national evangelistic secretary of the Edinburgh Conference's China Continuation Committee, and then in 1921 a secretary of the International Missionary Council. He played a key role in organizing the IMC's Jerusalem (1928) and Madras (1938) conferences, and prepared significant studies on mission-state relations, slavery, opium usage, and religious liberty. He consistently stressed as fundamental to the Christian mission the saving work of Christ and the need to challenge secularism and the assumptions of a materialistic society. In World War II he developed the IMC's "Orphaned Missions" program, which cared for German missionary efforts. After retiring in 1942 he promoted relief and reconstruction efforts in Europe and Asia, and was primarily responsible for creating Church World Service in 1946, the leading social service agency of the American Protestant churches.

Biography by Norman Goodall (1963).

RICHARD V. PIERARD

Washington, Booker Taliaferro (ca. 1858–1915)

African-American educator and reformer. Born a slave on a Virginia plantation, he gained freedom as a young boy through the Emancipation Proclamation, yet acquired an education solely on his own determination with encouragement from his mother. This led him to seek further education at Hampton Institute and Industrial School (1872–1875) and Virginia and Wayland Seminary, Washington, D.C. (1878–1879). Influenced toward a teaching profession by personal struggles to gain an education, he taught school in his own hometown and later at Hampton Institute. In 1881 he was called to start a normal school for black students in Tuskegee, Alabama. Under his leadership the Tuskegee Normal and Industrial Institute grew from meager beginnings to one of the world's leading centers of black education.

Washington identified himself as a Christian; daily Bible reading was an important part of his life. He held that the best interests of the black race were to be realized through education that involved the mind, hand, and heart. His correlative method, combining academic and trade work, along with his moderate stance toward race relations, was opposed by many intellectuals of his own race who emphasized professional training as well as political and social rights.

Washington established such organizations as the National Negro Business League, and was adviser to several U.S. presidents on racial matters. Harvard University and Dartmouth College gave him honorary degrees.

Biographies by L. R. Harlan (3 vols., 1972) and E. L. Thornbrough, ed. (1969).

FLORENCE SCOTT

Waters, Ethel (1896–1977)

Singer, dancer, and actress. Reared in poverty in the greater Philadelphia area, Ethel Waters began singing in church programs at the age of five. Her maternal grandmother, Sally, had charge of her care from her birth. Because of her need to work as a domestic, her grandmother could not provide a safe and supportive environment in which she could grow, and Ethel quickly saw the negative effects of such activities as drinking and using drugs, which she avoided throughout her life. Attending school for only a few years, she began to clean homes for pay. In her twelfth year, she experienced what she called a spiritual awakening. At age thirteen she was urged by her family to marry, but the marriage lasted for only one year. She continued to enjoy singing to herself and to her co-workers.

Waters' professional singing debut came in a neighborhood saloon in 1917. Her style was sophisticated and dignified, unlike the styles of many of her contemporaries. She performed under the name of Sweet Mama Stringbean, because of her physical appearance. She has the distinction of being the first woman to sing "St. Louis Blues." In 1919 Waters took an engagement in Harlem where she gained popularity. Her refined voice, polished diction, style, and phrasing became her professional trademark. In 1952 she was nominated for an Academy Award for her role in the film version of *The Member of the Wedding*, and 1953 saw her starring in a weekly television series, "Beulah."

In 1957, feeling depressed and empty, she went to Madison Square Garden to hear Billy Graham preach his New York Crusade. She joined the choir and was soon asked by Cliff Barrows to sing "His Eye Is on the Sparrow." She rededicated her life to Christ as a direct result of this experience. From 1957 until her death Ethel Waters was a featured singer with the Billy Graham Crusades. She wrote *His Eye Is on the Sparrow* (1951; reprinted 1978), and *To Me It's Wonderful* (1972).

ROBERT C. SUGGS

Weatherhead, Leslie Dixon (1893–1976)

English Methodist pastor and writer. Born in London, he graduated from London University and trained for the ministry at Cliff and Richmond Methodist colleges in time to be a combatant officer and then chaplain in World War I. He ministered in Madras, India (1919–1922), and in northern England (1922–1936) before going to London's City Temple (1936–1960). He pioneered work in psychological medicine, cured many through hypnosis, espoused pacifism, and would make audible remarks in public about perfect strangers. Theologically he was unpredictable: he supported higher criticism and euthanasia, and rejected hell and the biblical version of miracles. Yet he defended Billy Graham, believed in conversion, denounced the permissive society, and ostentatiously burned the D. H. Lawrence book *Lady Chatterley's Lover.* Introducing him to a religious gathering a Swedish bishop said, "We are very conservative here in Sweden. [Your books] are quite heretical at the beginning, but you always end by being orthodox. Would you please begin near the end when you address our people?" Among Weatherhead's books are *Why Do Men Suffer?* (1936), *The Mastery of Sex* (1939), *Psychology, Religion and Healing* (1951), and *Life Begins at Death* (1969).

Biography by Kingsley Weatherhead (1975).

J. D. DOUGLAS

Weigel, Gustav (1906–1964)

Roman Catholic theologian and ecumenist. Son of Alsatian immigrants, he was born in Buffalo, New York, and joined the Jesuits in 1922. He studied for the priesthood at Woodstock College, Maryland (1926–1934), and worked on a doctorate in theology at the Pontifical Gregorian University in Rome (1935–1937). He then served in the Catholic University of Chile in Santiago (latterly as dean of theology). His independent outlook and openness were too much for the more rigid Chilean Jesuits, and he returned to teach at Woodstock College. Asked to become the specialist in Protestantism for the *Theological Studies* journal, Weigel plunged energetically into this new task, and soon became the most respected Catholic ecumenist in America. He had a deep friendship with many Protestant and Eastern Orthodox scholars, and empathy for their views, but at the same time he held firmly to the traditional understanding of his church as the mystical body of Christ and thus a divinely constituted community. He was actively involved in Vatican II but, discouraged with its progress, returned after the third session to New York, where he died. His many writings include *A Survey of Protestant Theology in Our Day* (1954), *Faith and Understanding in America (1959),* and *The Modern God* (1963).

RICHARD V. PIERARD

Weil, Simone (1909–1943)

French writer and social activist. Born in Paris to Jewish parents, she attended the Lycee Fenelon and was given private lessons because of poor health. She studied with the philosopher Alain, and obtained her aggregation at the Ecole Normal in 1931, assuming her first teaching position at Le Puy (1931–1932). She taught at Roanne (1933–1934) before choosing to work in a factory for one year in solidarity with laborers. She spent the next ten years in writing, extensive travels, and intense involvement in the Spanish Civil War, the Popular Front, and other issues close to her heart. Revolutionary, anti-establishment notions were evident early in Simone's poetry and writings. The note of paradox is dominant in almost all her work; she has been compared to Joan of Arc and Rosa Luxembourg. She moved from agnosticism to faith, identifying most with the spirituality of the Benedictines at Solesmes. As a most controversial twentieth-century thinker she critiqued modern industry as enslaving of persons and as a plunderer of natural resources. Most of her writings and letters were published posthumously. Among her works translated into English are *Waiting for God* (1951) and *The Notebooks of Simone Weil* (1956).

Biography by Simone Petrement (1976).

EDWARD J. FURCHA

Weston, Frank (1871–1924)

Anglican missionary bishop. Born in London, he was educated at Trinity College, Oxford, ordained in 1894, and joined the Universities' Mission to Central Africa (UMCA) in Zanzibar in 1898. He was appointed principal of St. Andrew's Training College, Kiungani, in 1901 and consecrated bishop of Zanzibar in 1908. No stranger to controversy, he opposed a scheme for church reunion in East Africa (the Kikuyu Dispute, 1913), but promoted the 1920 Lambeth Conference "Appeal to all Christian People" for reunion, protested against the appointment of the liberal New Testament scholar B. H. Streeter to a canonry at Hereford (1915), and wrote against forced labor in Africa (*Serfs of Great Britain*, 1920). As chairman of the second Anglo-Catholic Congress (London, 1923), he reminded delegates of the social dimension of their faith: "You cannot claim to worship Jesus in the Tabernacle, if you do not pity Jesus in the slum." His incarnational theology was matched by a concern for an indigenous East African church, with trained African clergy, and church buildings appropriate to local conditions. After his death from blood poisoning on a diocesan tour in Zanzibar, he was mourned as a European who had a unique understanding of the African point of view. His writings include *The One Christ* (1907).

Biography by H. M. Smith (1926).

PHILIP HILLYER

White, Ellen Gould Harmon (1827–1915)

Seventh-day Adventist Church leader. Born into a Methodist family in Gorham, Maine, she was baptized in 1843, but that same year saw the family's expulsion from Methodist membership for having embraced William Miller's premillennial teachings. When Miller's prophecy about Christ's return was not fulfilled, Ellen claimed to have experienced the first of her "two thousand visions and prophetic dreams" associated with Joel 2:28–32. She married James White in 1846, in which year they became "sabbath-keepers." The Adventists had a wider outreach from 1850 when in Rochester, New York, James White began the *Review and Herald.* Five years later they moved to Battle Creek, Michigan, and it was there in 1863 that the Seventh-day Adventist Church had its official origin. Mrs. White was leader, and her writings and counsels were accepted as "the spirit of prophecy" (Rev. 19:10), "one of the identifying marks of the remnant church." Adventists nonetheless hold that acceptance of White's works should not be made a test of orthodoxy. A prolific writer, she brought together many of her views in *Testimonies for the Church* (9 vols., 1855–1909). Like sabbath-keeping, health and education were early emphases in the new church; Andrews University traces its origins back to 1875. In her latter years White took her message to Europe (1885–1887) and Australia (1891–1900) before finally settling in California.

Biographies by D. M. Canright (1919), F. D. Nichol (1951), and A. L. White (1969).

J. D. DOUGLAS

White, Paul Hamilton Hume (1910–1992)

Australian communicator known widely as "the Jungle Doctor." Born in New South Wales, he graduated in medicine from Sydney University (1934) where he distinguished himself also as a long-distance runner. As a Christian his leadership qualities were developed in the Crusaders and the Evangelical Union. Under Church Missionary Society auspices he went to Africa in 1938, and built a hospital in central Tanganyika. His wife's poor health forced them to return to Australia in 1941, and for two years he was CMS's home secretary before entering medical practice. Christian service remained his main concern, however, and he kept his medical commitments to a minimum. He was honorary general secretary of the InterVarsity Fellowship (1943–

1951), and the friend and counselor of hundreds of students. His series of "Jungle Doctor" books made him widely known beyond his own country where he was a familiar figure on radio and television. White's influence as a soul-winner, creative genius, and inspiring leader made him one of the most outstanding Christians in twentieth-century Australia.

MARCUS L. LOANE

Whyte, Alexander (1836–1921)

Scottish preacher and writer. Born into a poor, single-parent home in the little weaving town of Kirriemuir, he was an apprentice shoemaker before his love of reading enabled him to go to Aberdeen University. There followed theological training in Edinburgh and ordination in the Free Church of Scotland. His subsequent ministry at Free St. George's, Edinburgh (1870–1916), was remarkably fruitful. He held that a Christian pastor's duty was humility, prayer, and work—and he was impatient with colleagues who complained of lack of time (he called it lack of motivation). His mornings were spent in the study. He read widely, always with a pencil in hand. He had a unique, dramatic style of preaching that kept his listeners spellbound. A staunch supporter of Christian unity, he kept in touch with believers of other traditions, including Cardinal Newman, and contributed toward a momentous union of Scottish Presbyterian groups in 1900. Whyte's afternoons were spent visiting, but this never degenerated into mere courtesy calls. He combined his latter ministry with the principalship of New College, Edinburgh (1909–1918). His numerous works, mostly of a biographical nature, included *Bible Characters* (6 vols., 1896–1902), *Bunyan Characters* (4 vols., 1893–1908), and *Thomas Shepard, Pilgrim Father and Founder of Harvard* (1909).

Biography by G. F. Barbour (1923).

J. D. DOUGLAS

Wickramaratne, Colton S. (1931–)

Sri Lankan minister. Born in Colombo, he started a life of bold evangelism a few hours after his conversion at age seventeen by speaking about Christ to all who came to his house. From humble beginnings in ministry, involving personal poverty and need, his ministry blossomed until today he is senior pastor of probably the largest Protestant congregation in Sri Lanka, and national chairman of the rapidly expanding Assemblies of God. Endowed with visionary faith, he has led his church to a multifaceted ministry with congregations in three languages, attracting converts from all walks of life. He has also played a major role in the recent movement in Sri Lanka to take the gospel to its many unreached villages. His church has helped spawn numerous congregations in different parts of the nation. Gifted with energy that puts younger workers to shame, he also has an extensive international ministry. He has helped organize Impetus Conferences for motivating Christian leaders in Sri Lanka and other Third World countries. His dynamic messages have helped motivate many to involvement in evangelism.

AJITH FERNANDO

Wigglesworth, Smith (1859–1947)

A pioneer of the British Pentecostal movement. Born into a very poor family in Menston, Yorkshire, he began working at age six and received no formal education. His wife Polly, one of the first officers of the Salvation Army, taught her husband to read and write. They began the Boland Street Mission in Bradford, where she preached and he would sit beside her on the platform. He was nonetheless energetic in personal witness and in the teaching of holiness and healing. He also began a very successful plumbing business in Bradford. A radical change occurred in 1907 when through an Anglican vicar he received the experience of the Pentecostal "baptism." From that moment he was able to preach unaided, somewhat to the consternation of his wife. The healings under his ministry increased, sometimes characterized by unorthodox behavior. Once a woman died while Wigglesworth was praying for her. This so annoyed him that he lifted her from her bed and commanded her to walk, and she was restored to life. In 1922 he founded the Pentecostal movement in New Zealand. In 1936 he visited South Africa and prophesied that David du Plessis would have a prominent part in taking the teaching of the Pentecostal movement to mainline churches throughout the world. Subsequently began du Plessis' unusual ministry that eventually opened doors in the Roman Catholic Church, coinciding with the origins of the modern charismatic movement that eventually took place in the 1960s.

Biographies by S. Frodsham (1948) and Jack Hywel-Davies (1977).

JACK HYWEL-DAVIES

Wilder, Robert Parmelee (1863–1938)

Leader of missionary and student movements. Born in India of American parents, he graduated from Princeton University in 1886. His concern for foreign missions led to the foundation of the Student Volunteer Movement at D. L. Moody's Mount Hermon camp in that year. He went on to study at Union Theological Seminary, graduating in 1891. He was already virtually a traveling secretary for the SVM all over America. That year, on his way to India as a missionary, he helped found the British SVM. In India he worked among students until ill health forced his retirement in 1902. During his convalescence he was active in developing the World Student Christian Federation. When America entered World War I he worked with the YMCA among the troops. After the war he became secretary of the SVM until 1927. Thereafter he was secretary of the Near East Christian Council with a base in Egypt. After he retired in 1933 he found time to write a history of the Student Volunteer Movement.

Biography by R. E. Braisted (1941).

NOEL S. POLLARD

Wiley, Henry Orton (1877–1961)

Church of the Nazarene educator, churchman, and theologian. Born in Marquette, Nebraska, he graduated from the University of California and the Pacific School of Religion, where he later earned his S.T.D. (1933). He was dean and then president of Pasadena College (1910–1916), president of Northwest Nazarene College, Nampa, Idaho (1917–1926), and president again at Pasadena College (1926–1949). His early years at Pasadena College were wracked by controversy over forms of worship in the Nazarene tradition, especially the "freedom of the Spirit," with Wiley taking a more open stance against a more rigid, traditionalist formulation. He was able, in the end, to smooth out many of these difficulties through helping revise the Nazarene denomination's *Manual of Discipline*.

Wiley as theologian is best remembered for his three-volume *Christian Theology* (1941), subsequently abridged in one volume as *Introduction to Christian Theology* (1946). This magnum opus has become a standard for evangelical Wesleyan Arminianism, in the tradition of Richard Watson, John Miley, and William Burt Pope. In it Wiley emphasizes the distinctive Wesleyan doctrine of entire sanctification, yet shows a new and remarkable openness to some of the newer Pentecostal emphases on the one hand, and sensitivity to non-Wesleyan traditions, from Augustine on, in a constructive and irenic way, on the other. He is considered by many as the leading Wesleyan theologian of the twentieth century.

WALTER A. ELWELL

Wilhelmina (1880–1962)

Queen of The Netherlands. Born in The Hague, she was the daughter of King William III and succeeded him in 1890. Initially under her mother's regency, she was inaugurated at the age of eighteen, and at twenty married Duke Henry of Mecklenburg-Schwerin, who was designated prince-consort. In World War I (1914–1918) she successfully maintained her country's neutrality. In World War II, when Hitler's troops took over The Netherlands and much of western Europe, she moved with her ministers to London (1940) and there broadcast to her people encouraging and uplifting messages. In 1948 poor health led to abdication in favor of her daughter Juliana. Her memoirs, published in English as *Lonely, But Not Alone* (1960), reflect the deep religious feeling pervading her whole life.

Her testimony was maintained at her death, which at her request was followed by "a white funeral," and included the hymn "There Is Sunshine in My Soul Today."

J. D. Douglas

Wilkes, A(lphaeus) Paget (1871–1934)

Missionary to Japan. Son of an Anglican clergyman, he was educated at Lincoln College, Oxford. Under the influence of Barclay Buxton he decided to serve the Church Missionary Society in Japan in 1897. Soon he became dissatisfied with what he saw as the lack of evangelism and a growing liberalism, especially after the withdrawal of Buxton. Wilkes then founded a separate interdenominational mission later called the Japan Evangelistic Band. Its hallmarks were aggressive evangelism and the distinctive Holiness doctrines that emanated from the Keswick Conference. In 1903 his mission set up its headquarters in Kobe, at first under the name of the One by One Band. Wilkes gave the whole of his life to mission in Japan as leader of this society. He returned regularly to England and recruited many to serve in Japan, especially from the universities. His influence also spread through his spiritual writings such as *The Dynamics of Service* (1920) and *The Dynamic of Life* (1934).

Noel S. Pollard

Willan, Healey (1880–1968)

Composer, organist, and music educator. He was born in Balham, England, and trained at St. Saviour's Choir School in Eastbourne (1888–1895) and the Royal College of Organists where he studied with Hoyle and was made a fellow in 1899. In 1913 he went to Toronto Conservatory, and in 1914 was appointed a lecturer at the University of Toronto where he became a professor of music in 1937. He was also the university organist (1932–1964) and precentor of St. Mary Magdalene Church in Toronto (1921–1948). In 1956 he was awarded the historic Lambeth doctorate by the archbishop of Canterbury. In 1967 he was the first musician to become a Companion of the Order of Canada. A catalog of Willan's works was published by G. Bryant in 1972. These included A*ndante, Fugue and Chorale* (1965), *Passacaglia and Fugue No. 2* (1959), *A Fugal Trilogy* (1958), and *Passacaglia and Fugue* (1916), his major work for organ.

Biography by F. Clarke (1983).

Sam Hamstra, Jr.

Williams, Charles Walter Stansby (1886–1945)

English writer and lay theologian. Born in London, he spent his professional life at Oxford University Press as reader and literary editor. He produced over thirty volumes of his own: poems, plays, literary criticism, fiction, biography, and theological argument. He is best remembered for his cycle of

Arthurian poems, and for novels such as *War in Heaven* (1930), *The Place of the Lion* (1931), *Descent into Hell* (1937), and *All Hallows' Eve* (1945). The themes in these supernatural thrillers (they made good and evil exciting and momentous) of romantic love, co-inherence and substitution, form a thread that runs through all his later writings, including *The Descent of the Dove* (1939), a brief and idiosyncratic history of the church. His interests were similar to those of C. S. Lewis and J. R. R. Tolkien, whom he joined in the "Inklings" discussion group when Oxford University Press was evacuated from London to Oxford at the outbreak of World War II. His talents as a lecturer and conversationalist were recognized by an honorary Oxford M.A.

Biographies by G. Cavaliero (1983) and A. M. Hadfield (1983).

PHILIP HILLYER

Williams, John Rodman (1918–)

Charismatic theologian. He was born in Clyde, North Carolina, graduated from Davidson College, Union Theological Seminary, Virginia, and Columbia University/Union Theological Seminary, New York (Ph.D., 1954). He taught at Beloit College (1949–1952), Austin Presbyterian Seminary (1959–1972), and Melodyland School of Theology (1972–1985); he is currently professor of theology at Regent University (Virginia). He was also a chaplain in the Marine Corps (1944–1946) and pastor of First Presbyterian Church, Rockford, Illinois (1952–1959). Williams' studies under Paul Tillich at Union (New York) resulted in *Contemporary Existentialism and Christian Faith* (1965), a book that left him dissatisfied and searching for the truth. The answer to his quest occurred in November 1965 with a filling of the Holy Spirit: "It was 'joy unspeakable,' reality amazing, upsurge of 'heavenly language'—glory! I *received* my baptism in the Holy Spirit." This experience so transformed Williams' understanding of theology and the Scripture that his professional career has dealt with little else since.

Williams' theological stance has moved from a Neo-Pentecostal perspective to a more directly Pentecostal one, stressing the necessity for a special experience rather than just the unfolding of a latent presence. He argues for the continuation of the spiritual gifts for today, the reality of their existence throughout the history of the church, and the need for the church to be revitalized by the Holy Spirit for effective witness and service. He wrote *The Era of the Spirit* (1971), *The Pentecostal Reality* (1972), *The Gift of the Holy Spirit Today* (1980), and a three-volume systematic theology, *Renewal Theology* (1988–1992).

WALTER A. ELWELL

Williams, Theodore (1935–)

Bible teacher and missionary statesman. Born into a South Indian Christian family, he came to vital faith at evangelistic meetings in Madras in

425

1954. After completing a master's degree in statistics, he earned also a B.D. degree and taught at South India Biblical Seminary. He launched the Indian Evangelical Mission in 1965, served as its general secretary for twenty-five years, and is now its president. This is one of the largest Third World missions. Williams also served for a time as a Methodist pastor in Bangalore. He has a worldwide ministry and has played a major role in Asia's growing missionary movement. His many books and his teaching ministry through Back to the Bible Broadcast have extended his influence to the growing church in South Asia. His marriage in 1971 to Esther Faulkner, a career American missionary in India, has enhanced his ministry, especially through her abilities as a writer and educator. This is reflected in her *Sacrifice or Investment?* (1990). Williams has, in addition, served for many years as missions secretary of the Evangelical Fellowship of India and as president of the World Evangelical Fellowship. His contribution was recognized by a D.D. degree from Asbury College.

AJITH FERNANDO

Wilson, (Thomas) Woodrow (1856–1924)

Twenty-eighth president of the United States. Born in Staunton, Virginia, he came from a family with deep Presbyterian, Scotch-Irish, and southern roots. Until 1910 his career, although distinguished, was not particularly unusual: Princeton graduate; doctorate in history from Johns Hopkins University; college professor; president of Princeton (1902–1910), where he attempted to improve instruction and undermine what he saw as undemocratic traditions. Opposition led to his resignation and spectacular political rise. In 1910 he was elected governor of New Jersey and received publicity for pushing reforms through the legislature. In 1912 he was elected president. Although intending to concentrate on domestic concerns (and successfully passing many Progressive measures), he is best remembered for his international impact. World War I started in 1914. Wilson tried to keep the United States out and to mediate peace. By 1917 a series of German moves led him to ask Congress to declare war on the Central Powers. Wilson's speeches outlining a just peace helped undermine German morale and win Allied victory. After what he called "the war to end wars" Wilson personally negotiated the peace treaty with other Allied leaders. His idealistic, forceful public persona caused millions worldwide to base unrealistic, indeed messianic, expectations on his efforts. Although he accepted what were later considered harsh and cynical elements in the Versailles Treaty, he pinned hope for the future on the Covenant of the League of Nations, an international authority to preserve peace and the status quo. However, the United States Senate rejected the treaty, including the covenant, in 1920. Wilson was a sick, disappointed man for the remainder of his life. His traditional, deeply held Christian faith is essential to understanding him. It supplied his sense of purpose and morality, as his Calvinist background provided much of the language in which he framed his ideas. Wilson (descendant of many preachers) used the presidency as a pulpit for leading America and the world to the correct moral stands. His admirers and opponents used terms like "church elder" and "prophet" in describing his leadership. The reverse side of his strong faith was a self-righteousness that at times considered as unquestionable not only Christian doctrine, but his own political policies.

Biographies by Link (1947–) and A. Walworth (1958–).

ROBERT SCHUSTER

Wilson, J. Christy, Sr. (1891–1973)

Missionary, pastor, and Near East scholar. Born in Columbus, Nebraska, he graduated from Kansas University, Princeton University, and Princeton Theological Seminary. In 1919, the year after he was ordained to ministry in the Presbyterian Church, he traveled as a missionary under the Presbyterian Board of Foreign Missions to Tabriz, Iran, where he served for twenty years. During his missionary tenure he served as chairman of the Near East Relief Committee for Persia (1921–1922) and the Near East Christian Council (1937–1940). In 1939 he accepted the position of associate professor of ecumenics at Princeton Theological Seminary, where he taught until his retirement in 1962. During his missionary tenure Wilson wrote several books in Persian, including a commentary on Hebrews (1933) and a textbook on the art, archaeology, and architecture of Iran (1938). He also wrote *Introducing Islam* (1950), *The Christian Message to Islam* (1950), and *Apostle to Islam: The Biography of Samuel M. Zwemer* (1952). He contributed articles to *Christian Century, World Dominion, New Collier's Encyclopedia*, and the *Schaff-Herzog Encyclopedia of Religious Knowledge*. After his retirement, he continued ministry by pastoring churches and teaching courses at Fuller Theological Seminary and Mary Stewart International University.

A. SCOTT MOREAU

Wilson, Robert Dick (1856–1930)

Presbyterian minister and Old Testament scholar. Born in Indiana, Pennsylvania, Wilson was educated at the College of New Jersey (now Princeton University), Western Theological Seminary (Pittsburgh), and the University of Berlin. He began his career at Western Seminary in 1880, a colleague of B. B. Warfield. In 1900 he joined Warfield at Princeton Seminary where he was appointed professor of Semitic philology and Old Testament introduction. A supporter of J. Gresham Machen in the battle against modernism in the Presbyterian Church, Wilson joined with him and others to help found Westminster Seminary in 1929. Wilson was a learned linguist, fluent in forty-five languages and dialects. He authored several technical works on the Old Testament and grammars of Semitic languages and a commentary, *Studies in the Book of Daniel* (1917). An influential leader in the early days of the fundamentalist-modernist controversy, he is best known for his defense of the integrity of the Old Testament against the rising higher critical movement of the early twentieth century. Two widely disseminated and translated works of his on this subject are *Is the Higher Criticism Scholarly?*(1992) and *Scientific Old Testament Criticism* (1923).

JOHN R. MUETHER

Wimber, John (1934–)

President of Vineyard Ministries International. Converted in his late twenties he turned from his work in the music field, graduated from Azusa Pacific University, and in 1970 was ordained by the California Yearly Meeting of Friends. After five years of pastoral work he joined with Peter Wagner and helped develop the Charles E. Fuller Institute for Evangelism and Church Growth (1975–1977). He then became the first pastor of Calvary Chapel of Yorba Linda, California. In Wagner's words "This launched Wimber . . . into a renowned national and international 'signs and wonders' ministry that has had a profound effect on tens of thousands of charismatics and noncharismatics alike." It was to lead also to a Wimber-conducted course (1982–1985) that sparked off much controversy at the Fuller School of World Mission. Like Kathryn Kuhlman, he dislikes being called a healer, stressing that it is God who heals. In a lengthy discussion with three prominent Australian evangelicals in 1990, he was ambivalent about his distinction between evangelism and power evangelism (the latter the title of a book published in 1987), agreed that the work displayed an imbalance, lacking (according to the Australians) any real exposition of the gospel of evangelism. The authoritative voice of God for Christian living involves the Scriptures' being complemented by the ministry of gifts. It is perhaps equally significant that fifty-two of the fifty-three songs in the Vineyard song book make no mention of the cross.

J. D. DOUGLAS

Winchester, Alexander Brown (1858–1943)

Canadian Presbyterian pastor. Born in Peterhead, Scotland, he emigrated with his parents to Woodstock, Ontario. There he responded to an appeal by James Robertson, Presbyterian superintendent of missions, for workers in Western Canada. He attended Manitoba College with that end in view, but by the time of graduation in 1887 he felt a call to China. Canadian Presbyterian work had not yet begun there, and Winchester went out under the auspices of the American Presbyterian Board. Health problems having led to his return home, he was asked by his denomination to organize missions to the Chinese in Victoria and Vancouver, British Columbia, and there he remained until called in 1901 to Knox Church, the oldest Presbyterian congregation in Toronto. Under Winchester's leadership it became known for its evangelical witness, strong missionary program, and opposition to the church union scheme that would produce the United Church of Canada in 1925. From 1921 Winchester devoted himself to full-time itinerant Bible teaching and to the World Christian Fundamentals Association. In 1923 he was one of the founders of Dallas Theological Seminary.

SAM HAMSTRA, JR.

Wingren, Gustav (1910–)

Swedish theologian. Born in Tryserum, Sweden, he began teaching at Lund in 1944, was visiting professor at Abo (Turku), Finland, and at Basel in 1947, and from 1951 was professor of systematic theology at Lund. His academic interests range from homiletics and traditional and modern theological issues to studies on Luther's understanding of Christian vocation. Among his numerous publications available in English are *The Christian's Calling* (1957), *Creation and Gospel: The New Situation in European Theology* (1979), *Creation and Law* (1961), *The Living Word* (1960), and *Theologians in Conflict: Nygren, Barth, Bultmann* (1958).

EDWARD J. FURCHA

Wirt, Sherwood Eliot (1911–)

Journalist and author. Born in Oakland, California, he was educated at the University of California, Pacific School of Religion, and Edinburgh University (Ph.D., 1951). After his initial degree he became a professional journalist, serving newspapers in California, Hawaii, and Alaska. Ordained as a Congregational Christian pastor in 1943, he spent two years as an Air Force chaplain and three years ministering to students at the University of Washington. He was received into the ministry of the Presbyterian Church, USA, in 1951 and pastored congregations in Berkeley and Oakland until 1959. In that year he published *Crusade at the Golden Gate* about the Billy Graham campaign in San Francisco, and subsequently became founding editor of *Decision* magazine, a post he held until 1976. During those years the magazine reached a circulation of 5 million and was published in six languages. Since his official retirement Wirt has led writers' workshops around the world, and is known especially for the individual encouragement he gives to young people interested in the ministry of Christian literature. Among his numerous published works are *Not Me, God* (1966), *The Social Conscience of the Evangelical* (1968), *A Thirst for God* (1980), and *The Making of a Writer* (1987).

J. D. DOUGLAS

Wisløff, Carl Fredrik (1908–)

Norwegian theologian and church historian. After graduating from the Free Faculty of Theology (Menighetsfakultetet), Oslo, in 1931 and ordained in

1932, Wisløff became rector of the practical theology department of Menighetsfakultetet in 1947. In 1958 he defended his Dr.Theol. thesis at the University of Oslo, and became professor of church history in 1961, a position he held until 1975. He has made a tremendous impact on evangelical Christianity in Norway. His vigorous defense of the inspiration and authority of all Scripture combined with thorough scholarship have formed a whole generation of pastors, missionaries, and lay preachers. His strong emphasis on the priesthood of all believers and his clear expounding of the Word of God have made him highly respected among lay Christians. Wisløff is a warm spokesman for cooperation between evangelicals from different denominations. He was active in the founding of the International Fellowship of Evangelical Students in 1947, where he served as chairman in the executive committee (1959–1967) and president (1967–1979). For years he collaborated with a team of evangelical theologians on a new translation of the Bible into Norwegian (published 1988). Largely due to his opposition to the World Council of Churches, Norwegian Christians have taken a critical stand toward the WCC. He has authored thirty-three books, of which many have been translated into several languages. The best known are *The Gift of Communion: Luther's Controversy with Rome on Eucharistic Sacrifice* (ET, 1964), *New Catholicism?* (ET, 1966), *I Know in Whom I Believe* (ET, 1983), and *Do the Work of an Evangelist* (1990).

OLA TULLUAN

Wongso, Peter (1931–)

Pastor, educator, translator, and writer. Born in Fujian, China, he was educated at Southeast Asia Bible College, Indonesia, and later earned a master's degree at Fuller Theological Seminary (1976) and a doctorate in theology at Trinity Evangelical Divinity School (1981). From 1953 to the present he pioneered and led the Holy Word Christian Church, which has planted churches and chapels in nineteen cities and thirty villages of Indonesia. Kindergartens and secondary schools have been founded in fourteen cities, with a chaplain placed in each school. Wongso has translated into Chinese many books that have made a significant impact on the Chinese church, notably those by Andrew Murray, O. J. Smith, Herbert Kane, and Mabel Williamson. Principal of Southeast Asia Bible College (1964–1988), Wongso has written in Chinese and Indonesian, some thirty titles in each language, covering Bible commentaries, church history, and theology.

MICHAEL SHEN

Woods, C(harles) Stacey (1909–1983)

University student ministry pioneer. Born in Sydney, Australia, he came to the United States in 1930 and graduated from Wheaton College and Dallas Theological Seminary. He was appointed general secretary of Inter-

Varsity Christian Fellowship–Canada (1934–1952), during which period he accepted also a call to become the first general secretary of IVCF–USA (1941–1960). Woods' goal was to establish campus fellowships of students committed to evangelism and grounded in the Word of God. He coupled this vision with a compassion for students, effective fund-raising skills, and discerning recruitment abilities. Moreover, he provided leadership in establishing the International Fellowship of Evangelical Students (IFES), whose first general secretary he became (1947–1971). Stacey Woods was a highly motivated, dynamic man whose commitment to student ministry shaped the principles, philosophies, and policies that characterized for decades the IVCF movement in North America and around the world. He wrote *Some Ways of God* (1975) and *The Growth of a Work of God* (1978).

J. G. STACKHOUSE

Woolley, Paul (1902–1984)

Presbyterian leader and church historian. Born in Providence, Rhode Island, he was ordained in 1926 in Moody Church, where his father was an associate pastor. He had hoped to become a missionary in China with China Inland Mission, but was prevented by conditions there, and went on to graduate from Princeton Seminary in 1928. He then worked for one year as general secretary of the League of Evangelical Students. Along with other Princeton faculty and graduates opposed to modernist trends at the Seminary, Woolley joined the faculty of Westminster Theological Seminary in 1929 when it opened, teaching church history and serving as registrar. He taught there until his retirement in 1977 and was recognized for his devoted scholarship and capable administrative ability. With J. Gresham Machen he opposed liberalism in the Presbyterian Church, and joined in founding the Independent Board for Presbyterian Foreign Missions (1933) and the Orthodox Presbyterian Church (1936). He served in executive posts for both bodies. His scholarship focused on the history of Calvinism and Presbyterianism, and the Bible's application to individual and civic life. He cofounded *The Presbyterian Guardian* in 1935, and was coeditor (1938–1954) and managing editor (1954–1967) of the *Westminster Theological Journal*.

PAUL A. ERICKSEN

Wright, George Ernest (1909–1974)

Biblical archaeologist. Born in Zanesville, Ohio, he was educated at Wooster College, McCormick Theological Seminary, and Johns Hopkins University (Ph.D., 1937). He was ordained to the ministry in the Presbyterian Church, USA (1934), and served as field secretary for the American Schools of Oriental Research (1938). He founded and edited the innovative periodical *The Biblical Archaeologist* from 1937 to 1962, and remained on its editorial board until his death. He taught from 1939 at McCormick

Theological Seminary and was professor of Old Testament history and theology (1945–1958), before becoming professor of divinity at Harvard University (1958–1974). He was also curator and reorganizer of the Harvard Semitic Museum from 1961, and president of the American Schools of Oriental Research from 1966.

He went to Shechem as archaeological director for the Drew-McCormick ASOR Research Expedition (1956–1964), to Gezer as visiting director of the Hebrew Union College Excavation (1964–1965), and to Idalion, Cyprus, as director of the Joint American Archaeological Expedition (1971–1974).

His publications reveal a dynamic dialogue between his concerns for the distinctiveness of biblical theology and his awareness of the historical results of an archaeological investigation of the biblical environs. Thus his *God Who Acts* (1952) stands beside his *Biblical Archaeology* (1957) to teach the public of the past and to train the scholars for the future, within a conviction that no one has a monopoly on truth. He also wrote *The Old Testament and Theology* (1969).

A fiftieth anniversary salute to him as founder was celebrated and published by *The Biblical Archaeologist* in 1987.

CLYDE CURRY SMITH

Wu, Lei-ch'uan (1870–1944)

Chinese Confucian scholar and indigenous Christian thinker. Born in Hsu-chou (Xuzhou), Wu received a traditional Confucian education, attaining the chin-shih (jinshi) degree in 1898. Wu was named a Hanlin scholar, the highest honor in China, but received no government appointment. He cared for his parents until their respective deaths. Wu served on the Board of Education in China (1912–1925). In 1914 he was converted and baptized an Anglican. Wu taught Chinese at Tenching University, and actively participated in its Christian Fellowship, seeking to find a Chinese form for Christianity. In 1922 the Anti-Christian movement broke out in China, which deeply affected Wu. He was critical of Christianity's Western character, and started an indigenous Christian newspaper, *Truth Weekly*, in 1923. In 1929 Wu was named Yenching's chancellor, a post created to satisfy the Chinese Nationalist government's requirement that every Chinese university have a Chinese president. The university was governed by a New York-based board. Wu, who spoke only Chinese and never traveled outside China, attempted to resign from Yenching twice, and in 1934 left the university. From 1929 on he was critical of the Nationalist government of China. His *Christianity and Chinese Culture* was published in 1936, in which he portrayed Jesus as a political revolutionary. He died a lonely, disappointed figure in 1944.

SAMUEL LING

Y

Yannoulatos, Anastasios (1929–)

Archbishop of the Albanian Orthodox Church. Born in Peraeus, Greece, as a young theologian in the late 1950s he challenged the Orthodox Church of Greece, as well as the Orthodox Church worldwide, to rediscover her rich missionary tradition and to rekindle her zeal for proclaiming the gospel to all nations. More than any other leader, Yannoulatos helped the church realize that to be truly Orthodox, she had to take an active role in missions. In 1960 Yannoulatos founded the Inter-Orthodox Mission Center *Poreuthentes*. In 1968 his staff pioneered the framework of the Bureau of External Missions for the Church of Greece. In 1971 he founded and directed the Center for Missionary Studies at the University of Athens. This center eventually led to the establishment of a chair of missiology in 1976, which Yannoulatos headed. In 1972 the Church of Greece recognized his achievements by making him Bishop of Androussa. In 1981 the Orthodox Church in Africa invited Yannoulatos to become Acting Archbishop of Irinopoulos (East Africa). He served there for ten years, opening the first African Orthodox seminary in Nariobi, Kenya, and ordaining and training sixty-two priests and over forty catechists. In 1991 Yannoulatos became the new archbishop of the church of Albania. Over the past three years, he has worked at resurrecting that church from its atheistic bondage. In ecumenical circles, Yannoulatos has served as the chief missions spokesperson of the Orthodox Church. From the early 1960s he participated in numerous meetings of the Commission on World Mission and Evangelism of the WCC, culminating in his appointment as president of CWME from 1984 to 1991.

To promote the missionary spirit, he published widely. Over the past eighty years, he has written nine scholarly books on missiology and world religions, five catechetical books, over sixty treatises, and some eighty articles. He founded and published two different mission magazines, one in Greek and English, the other in Greek only.

LUKE VERONIS

Yoder, John Howard (1927–)

American theologian, educator, and ethicist. Born in Ohio to Mennonite parents, he was educated at the College of Wooster, Goshen College, University of Akron, and the University of Basel, where his doctoral dissertation examined the relationship between Anabaptists and the Reformers in the early Swiss Reformation. He served the Mennonite denomination in several capacities: as a member of the Mennonite Central Committee directing postwar relief and social work in France (1949–1954); as administrative assistant of overseas work for the Mennonite Board of Missions (1959–1965); and as professor of theology (1965–1984) and president (1970–1973) of Goshen Biblical Seminary. He gave alternative service as a conscientious objector during the Korean War. He is presently a professor of theology at the University of Notre Dame and was the 1987–1988 president of the Society of Christian Ethics. He is best known for his writings in the field of Christian social ethics, especially *The Politics of Jesus* (1972) and *The Priestly Kingdom* (1984).

MAXIE BURCH

Young, Edward Joseph (1907–1968)

Old Testament scholar. Born in San Francisco, he studied at Stanford University, Westminster Theological Seminary, Leipzig University, and Dropsie College (Ph.D., 1943). Ordained in the Presbyterian Church, USA (1935), he transferred to the Orthodox Presbyterian Church (1936), and was instructor (1936–1939), assistant professor (1939–1946), and professor (1946–1968) of Old Testament at Westminster. A modest and approachable man despite his profound scholarship, which included wide-ranging linguistic skills, Young had a deep commitment to the inerrancy of Scripture, as is evidenced by *Thy Word Is Truth: Some Thoughts on the Biblical Doctrine of Inspiration* (1957), and his editorship of the *Westminster Theological Journal*. His other works include *An Introduction to the Old Testament* (1949) (known to generations of theological students), *My Servants the Prophets* (1952), and his magnum opus, *The Book of Isaiah* (3 vols., 1965–1972).

J. D. DOUGLAS

Yun, Tchi-Ho (1865–1945)

Korean reformer, educator, and Christian teacher. Born into a high-ranking family in the late Yi dynasty government, he became the most influential Korean voice in the early introduction of Protestant Christianity to his country. He was the first Korean nobleman to become a Protestant. After training in Japan for government service as a foreign language specialist, he returned in 1883 as interpreter for the first American Minister to Korea, Lucius Foote. Family involvement in the 1884 reform movements in Seoul led Yun to seek safety in Shanghai, where he enrolled in the Anglo-Chinese College. Under the influence of its president, Y. J. Allen, he became a Christian in 1887. He went to America for study at Emory College and graduate work in theology at Vanderbilt. He returned to China (1893) and Korea

(1895), where his connections and linguistic skills won him important civil and government posts (1895–1906). Japanese rule in Korea forced Yun out of government service in 1906 and turned his talents to more direct service to the Methodist Church. He founded the Anglo-Korean School in Songdo and was its first president (1906–1911). He was a delegate to the famous Edinburgh World Missionary Conference (1910) and general secretary of the Korean YMCA (1915–1920). In 1930 he was called out of retirement to help negotiate the union of Methodist missions in Korea, and was the first president of what is now Yonsei University (1939–1941).

SAMUEL H. MOFFETT

Z

Zahn, Theodor (1838–1933)

New Testament scholar. Born in Mörs, Germany, Zahn was educated at the universities of Basel, Erlangen, and Berlin, from the last of which he received his doctorate (1865). He began teaching at the gymnasium in Neustrelitz (1861–1865), then was successively lecturer (1865), privatodozent (1868), and ordinarius (1871) at Göttingen before becoming professor of New Testament successively at Kiel (1877), Erlangen (1878), and Leipzig (1888). He returned to Erlangen to remain until retirement as professor of pedagogics and New Testament exegesis (1892–1909).

Zahn's scholarship was prodigious; it was said of him that he published more in the final decade of his life than most people do in a lifetime. Nevertheless, he was remembered for his preaching as well as his scholarship. He published an extensive study of canon, produced commentaries on Matthew (1903), Galatians (1905), John (1908), Romans (1910), Luke (1913), Acts (2 vols., 1919–1921), and Revelation (2 vols., 1924–1926), and an *Introduction to the New Testament* (ET, 3 vols., 1909), and contributed to the fundamental edition of the works of the Apostolic Fathers (1875–1878). He also prepared an edition of the Acts of John (1880), and attributed the Muratorian canon fragment to Hippolytus.

Zahn was honored with festschrift in 1908 and 1928, and a comprehensive bibliography in 1918.

CLYDE CURRY SMITH

Zapata Arceyuz, Virgilio (1928–)

Guatemalan educator, evangelist, and church leader. Born in Guatemala City, he was an outstanding athlete who set national records in track and basketball. He graduated from Bob Jones University, the University of Southern California, and the Rafael Landivar University in Guatemala (Ph.D.). He has been active in promoting evangelistic efforts, and has preached throughout the Americas; he is also in demand as a speaker on Christian education. He served as president of the Latin American Evangelical Alliance, which represents some 50 million evangelicals (1987–1990), and has held executive posts in other bodies. A man who combines a profound pietistic spirituality with dynamic vision, he is also president of the Latin American Evangelical Institute in Guatemala City, a school he helped found in 1954, which provides primary and secondary education to some five thousand students.

Zapata has written a number of books in Spanish on evangelism and education, as well as a history of the evangelical church in Guatemala, based on his doctoral thesis. His educational philosophy of developing the whole person centered on Christ is coupled with a conviction that the gospel is both the highest call for humankind and the best point of departure for development in the Third World.

GUILLERMO MENDEZ

Zenos, Andreas Constantinides (1855–1942)

New Testament scholar and historical theologian. Born in Constantinople, Turkey, and educated at Robertson College there, he was pastor of the Presbyterian Church at Brandt, Pennsylvania (1881–1883) before becoming professor of Greek at Lake Forest University (1883–1888). He taught New Testament at Hartford Theological Seminary (1888–1891) and church history at McCormick Theological Seminary (1891–1894) before transferring to the chair of historical theology at Presbyterian Theological Seminary, Chicago (1894–1932; dean also from 1920). He was the author and translator of several works, notably in New Testament studies and in the history of the early church. Among them were *The Teaching of Jesus Concerning Christian Conduct* (1905), *The Plastic Age of the Gospel: A Manual of NT Theology* (1927), and *Presbyterianism in America: Past, Present and Prospective* (1937).

EDWARD J. FURCHA

Zimmerman, Thomas Fletcher (1912–1991)

Assemblies of God general superintendent. Born in Indianapolis to a Methodist family, he was aged five when his mother was healed of tuberculosis by the prayers of independent Pentecostal church members, and the Zimmermans joined their church. In 1919 he gave his life to Christ. While in high school he sensed God's call to the ministry, thinking he would go to China as a missionary. In 1928 he began to prepare by serving as a voluntary pastoral assistant, and later gave up his regular job to pastor a small congregation in Harrodsburg, Indiana. Within two years the church had grown to 250 members. He moved to South Bend, where he was ordained in the Assemblies of God in 1936. In 1953 he became assistant general superintendent, and in 1959 general superintendent, a post he held for twenty-six years. He was active not only in Pentecostal circles: he served on the board of the National Association of Evangelicals, and was the only Pentecostalist elected president of the association. He held also important posts with the Lausanne Committee on World Evangelization, the American Bible Society, and the National Religious Broadcasters. He

437

chaired the World Pentecostal Conference six times, and was active in civic affairs, ranging from public television to the United Way.

A. SCOTT MOREAU

Zulu, Alphaeus (1905–1988)

First African diocesan bishop in the (Anglican) Church of the Province of South Africa. Born the son of a policeman in Natal, he worked hard to make up for only a primary school education, and became headmaster of a mission school. Helped by his diocesan bishop, he was able to go to the University of Fort Hare, where he graduated in 1938 before going on to St. Peter's Anglican College in Johannesburg. Ordained in 1940, he ministered in Durban until 1960, was assistant bishop of St. John's (1960–1966), then was elected bishop of Zululand (1966–1975). While his appointment caused some trepidation, he preached peace in all matters concerning racial strife. He was nonetheless barred as a black from occupying the Episcopal residence that was in a white district of Eshowe. His passport was often confiscated by the authorities to prevent his attendance at international church conferences. Once he was arrested on a technicality and drew world attention when he sturdily refused to pay the fine levied. A man of integrity and humility, he was ecumenical in the truest sense, and unlike many Anglican bishops might invite a non-Anglican minister present at a meeting to pronounce the benediction. Zulu was a World Council of Churches president (1969–1975), served on the executive committee of African Enterprise (an evangelical body), and was a member of the Kwa Zulu Legislative Assembly (1975–1987).

J. D. DOUGLAS

Zwemer, Samuel Marinus (1867–1952)

One of the most influential missionary leaders of the twentieth century. Born near Holland, Michigan, he graduated from Hope College and New Brunswick Seminary and in 1890 was ordained as a missionary by the Reformed Church in America. The previous year he and two other seminarians founded the Arabian Mission (later incorporated into the Board of Foreign Missions of the Reformed Church in America). Going to the Middle East with James Cantine, he studied Arabic in Beirut. Stations were opened in Iraq and the Arabian Peninsula. The mission grew; Zwemer's gifts as an organizer, speaker, motivator, and writer led him increasingly into an international and interdenominational ministry. From 1912 he was based in Cairo, the intellectual center of the Islamic world, until his call to Princeton Seminary in 1930 as professor of the history of religion and Christian mission.

In addition to pioneering work with the Arabian Mission, Zwemer made an enormous contribution to the cause of Christian witness to Islam worldwide. Through the years he took a leading role in several international conferences devoted to Muslim evangelization, and traveled to virtually every part of the Muslim world, gathering and disseminating information, motivating missionaries to increased effort, and providing strategic guidance for the task. His visits characteristically brought about spiritual encouragement and greater unity between mission boards, both denominational and independent. A favorite theme was the need to produce and effectively use literature as an evangelistic tool. His evangelistic approach was to directly present the gospel message in a spirit of love. He also spoke widely throughout North America and Europe, where through his influence many felt God's call to missionary service. Zwemer's missionary efforts were enhanced by a prolific output ranging from devotional to evangelistic (written mostly in Arabic) to academic. His works included *Arabia, the Cradle of Islam* (1900) and *The Cross above the Crescent* (1941). He founded and for nearly forty years edited the influential quarterly *The Moslem World*.

Biography by J. C. Wilson (1952).

TIMOTHY WIARDA